Stardom and Celebrity

Stardom and Celebrity

A Reader

Sean Redmond and Su Holmes

SAGE Publications
Los Angeles • London • New Delhi • Singapore

First published 2007

 SAGE Publications Ltd
1 Oliver's Yard
55 City Road
London EC1Y 1SP

SAGE Publications Inc.
2455 Teller Road
Thousand Oaks, California 91320

SAGE Publications India Pvt Ltd
B 1/I 1 Mohan Cooperative Industrial Area
Mathura Road
New Delhi 110 044

SAGE Publications Asia-Pacific Pte Ltd
33 Pekin Street #02-01
Far East Square
Singapore 048763

Library of Congress Control Number: 2006933763

British Library Cataloguing in Publication data

A catalogue record for this book is available from
the British Library

ISBN: 978–1–4129–2320–0 (hbk)
ISBN: 978–1–4129–2321–7 (pbk)

Typeset by Newgen Imaging Systems (P) Ltd, Chennai, India
Printed in India at Replika Press Pvt Ltd
Printed on paper from sustainable resources

Contents

Notes on Contributors

Theodor W. Adorno (1903–1969) was a German sociologist, philosopher, musicologist and composer. He was a member of the Frankfurt School along with Max Horkheimer, Walter Benjamin, Herbert Marcuse and Jürgen Habermas. His publications include *Aesthetic Theory* (University of Minnesota Press, 1998).

Francesco Alberoni is an Italian sociologist, journalist and professor in Sociology. He was a board member and senior board member (chairman) of Rai, the national Italian Television, from 2002 to 2005.

Roland Barthes (1915–1980) was a French literary critic, social theorist and semiotician. His publications include *Mythologies* (Paladin, 1973) and *Camera Lucida* (Hill and Wang, 1982).

Jean Baudrillard is a cultural theorist with a special interest in the postmodern. His publications include *Simulacra and Simulation* (University of Michigan Press, 1995) and *Âmerica* (Verso, 1989).

Mary C. Beltrán is Assistant Professor in Communication Arts and Chicana and Latina Studies at the University of Wisconsin. Her publications include, 'The New Hollywood Racelessness: Only the Fast, Furious (and Multi-Racial) Will Survive' (*Cinema Journal 44:2*, Winter 2005: 50–67).

Walter Benjamin (1892–1940) was a German Jewish Marxist and mystic who was concerned with modernity, industrialization and the role that visual-based technologies, such as photography and film, played in transforming peoples perception of, and access to, art and culture. His publications include *Illuminations* (Shocken, 1969).

Leo Braudy is University Professor and Bing Professor of English at the University of Southern California. His publications include *The Frenzy of the Renown: Fame and its History* (Oxford University Press, 1986), *Native Informant: Essays on Film, Fiction and Popular Culture* (Oxford University Press, 1992) and *From Chivalry to Terrorism: War and the Changing Nature of Masculinity* (Alfred Knopf, 2003).

Nick Couldry is Professor of Media and Communications at Goldsmiths, University of London. He is the author of numerous books, including *The Place of Media Power: Pilgrims and Witnesses of the Media Age* (Routledge, 2000), *Inside Culture* (Sage, 2000) and *Media Rituals: A Critical Approach* (Routledge, 2003).

Richard deCordova (1956–1996) was Lecturer in Film and Television at DePaul University, Chicago. He was the author of the seminal *Picture Personalities: The Emergence of the Star System in America* (University of Illinois Press, 1990).

Philip Drake is Lecturer in Film and Media Studies at the University of Stirling. He has published numerous articles on celebrity and stardom, screen performance, memory and film music, and intellectual property rights. He is currently writing a book on the political economy of stardom in Hollywood cinema and is co-editing a forthcoming edition of the journal *Cultural Politics* on the politics of celebrity.

Richard Dyer is Professor of Film Studies at King's College, London, UK. His publications include *Stars* (BFI, 1978) and *Heavenly Bodies: Film Stars and Society* (Macmillan, 1987).

John Ellis is Professor of Media Arts and Head of Department at Royal Holloway, University of London. He is the author of *Seeing Things* (I.B.Tauris, 2000) and *Visible Fictions* (Routledge, 1982).

Rebecca L. Epstein is a research student at the University of California, Los Angeles.

Mary Flanagan is an artist; inventor-designer-activist, who presently teaches at Hunter College in Manhattan. Her essays on digital art, cyberculture and gaming have appeared in periodicals such as *Art Journal, Wide Angle, Convergence*, and *Culture Machine*, as well as several books. Her co-edited collection, *Reload: Rethinking Women and Cyberculture*, was published by MIT Press in 2002.

Joshua Gamson is Professor in the Department of Sociology at the University of San Francisco. His publications include *Claims to Fame: Celebrity in Contemporary America* (University of California Press, 1994) and *Freaks Talk Back: Tabloid Talk Shows and Sexual Nonconformity* (Chicago University Press, 1998).

Christine Geraghty is Professor of Film and Television Studies and Head of Department at the University of Glasgow. She is the author of *Women and Soap Opera* (Polity, 1991); *British Cinema in the Fifties: Gender, Genre and the 'New Look'* (Routledge, 2000) which takes an historical and cultural approach to textual analysis; and (with David Lusted) *The Television Studies Book* (Arnold, 1998), a collection of varied essays on contemporary television.

Lisa Holderman is an Assistant Professor of Communications in the Department of English, Communications and Theater Arts at Arcadia University. She is currently working upon an edited collection titled *Common Sense: Intelligence as Presented on Popular Television*, Lexington Books, 2008.

Su Holmes is Reader in Television Studies at the University of East Anglia. She is the author of *Coming to a TV Near You!: British TV and Film Culture in the 1950s* (Intellect Books, 2005), and *Entertaining Television: The BBC and Popular Programme Culture in the 1950s* (Manchester University Press, forthcoming 2008). She is the co-editor of *Understanding Reality Television* (Routledge, 2004) and *Framing Celebrity: New Directions in Celebrity Culture* (Routledge, 2004).

Max Horkheimer (February 14, 1895–July 7, 1973) was a Jewish-German philosopher and sociologist, known especially as the founder and guiding thinker of the

Frankfurt School of critical theory. His publications include, *Critical Theory* (Continuum, 1975).

Jo Littler is Senior Lecturer in Media and Cultural Studies at Middlesex University. Her research primarily focuses on the politics of consumer culture, and she edited the 'Celebrity' issue of *Mediactive* (Lawrence & Wishart, 2003).

Catharine Lumby is Associate Professor at the University of Sydney. She is the author of *Bad Girls: The Media, Sex and Feminism in the 90s* (Allen and Unwin, 1997), *Gotcha! Life in a Tabloid World* (Allen and Unwin, 1999) and co-editor of *Remote Control: New Media, New Ethics* (Cambridge University Press, 2003).

Wenche Ommundsen is Associate Dean – Research, Deakin University, Australia. She is the author of *Metafictions* (1993) and the editor/co-editor of *Refractions: Asian/Australian Writing* (1995), *From a Distance: Australian Writers and Cultural Displacement* (1996), *Appreciating Difference: Writing Postcolonial Literary History* (1998) and *Bastard Moon: Essays on Chinese–Australian Writing* (2001).

Sean Redmond is Senior Lecturer in Film Studies at Victoria University, Wellington. He is the co-editor of *Framing Celebrity: New Directions in Celebrity Culture* (Routledge, 2006) and *Hollywood Transgressor: the Cinema of Kathryn Bigelow* (Wallflower Press, 2003). He has research interests in stars and celebrities, whiteness, film authorship, genre, and black and Asian cinema.

Chris Rojek is Professor of Sociology and Culture at Nottingham Trent University. He is the author of numerous books, including *Stuart Hall* (Polity, 2003), *Celebrity* (Reaktion, 2001) and *Frank Sinatra* (Polity, 2004).

Jackie Stacey is Professor in the Department of Sociology at Lancaster University. She is the author of *Stargazing: Hollywood Cinema and Female Spectatorship* (Routledge, 1994), the co-author (with Sarah Franklin and Celia Lury) of *Global Nature, Global Culture: Gender, 'Race' and Life Itself in the Late Twentieth Century* (Sage, 2000) and the co-editor of books such as *Screen Histories: A Screen Reader* (Oxford University Press, 1999).

Graeme Turner is Professor of Cultural Studies at the University of Queensland. His numerous publications include *Understanding Celebrity* (Sage, 2004), *The Film Cultures Reader* (Routledge, 2002) and *Ending the Affair: the decline of television current affairs in Australia* (UNSW Press, 2005).

Yiman Wang is currently Visiting Assistant Professor of East Asian Studies and Comparative Literature at Haverford College. She has published numerous book chapters and articles, invited book reviews, and she has translated books from Chinese into English and from English into Chinese. Wang currently has four papers under review.

Max Weber (1864–1920) was a German political economist and sociologist who is credited with founding the modern study of sociology. Weber's work was concerned with religion and government in terms of an increasing rationalization of everyday social action. Weber thought that individual actors were trapped in an 'iron cage' of rationalized control.

Rebecca Williams is a PhD student in the Cardiff School of Journalism, Media and Cultural Studies at Cardiff University. Her research topic is genre, distinction and fan community/hierarchy. She has published work in *Slayage: The On-Line Journal of Buffy Studies* and *Reading Angel: The TV Spin-off with a Soul* (ed. by Stacey Abbott, I.B. Tauris, 2005), and co-authored work on celebrity for *The European Journal of Cultural Studies*.

Acknowledgements

The editors wish to thank Julia Hall at Sage for her advice and encouragement throughout the development of this book. Southampton Solent University and Victoria University of Wellington provided much needed grant support to help with research and development. As always, immense gratitude goes to our family, friends, students and colleagues for listening to talk about fame.

SR: to Georgie Best – the Belfast Boy – for your marvellous feet and your way with words. And to Dad for letting me be.

SH: to Deborah Jermyn and Nick Rumens for providing (as always) intellectual and personal support, and for always listening.

Permission given by the following copyright holders and authors for the extracts and articles in this collection is gratefully acknowledged.

Extract from Theodor Adorno and Max Horkheimer, 'The Culture Industry: Enlightenment as Mass Deception', Adorno and Horkheimer *Dialectic of Enlightenment*, London: Verso. Reprinted with permission of the publisher © 1972. Extract from Jean Baudrillard, 'The Ecstasy of Communication', Hal Foster (ed) *Postmodern Culture*, London: Pluto (1983). Reprinted with permission from the publisher © 1983. Extract from Roland Barthes, 'Myth Today' and 'Garbo's Face', Barthes, *Mythologies*, London: Paladin (1973). Reprinted with permission of the publisher © and Barthe's Estate. Extract from Roland Barthes 'Part Two', Barthes, *Camera Lucida*, London: Jonathan Cape (1982). Reprinted with permission of the publisher © and Barthe's Estate. Extract from Walter Benjamin, 'The Work of Art in the Age of Mechanical Reproduction', Benjamin, *Illuminations*, London: Fontana (1973). Reprinted with permission of the publisher © The Random House Group. Extract from Leo Braudy, 'The Dream of Acceptability', Braudy. *The Frenzy of the Renown: Fame and its History*, Oxford: Oxford University Press (1986). Reprinted with permission of the author and the Sandra Dijkstra Literary Agency © 1986 by Leo Braudy. Extracts from Nick Couldry, 'Media Power: Some Hidden Dimensions' and 'The Reality of the Fiction', Couldry, *The Place of Media Power: Pilgrims and Witnesses of the Media Age*, London: Routledge (2000). Reprinted with permission of the publisher © 2000 Routledge. Extract from Richard Dyer, 'Stars', Dyer, *Stars*, London: BFI. Reprinted with permission from the publisher © 1979. Extract from Richard Dyer, 'Introduction', Dyer, *Heavenly Bodies*, Basingstoke: Macmillan. Reprinted with permission of the publisher © 1986. Extract from John Ellis, 'Stars as Cinematic Phenomenon', Ellis,

Visible Fictions, London: Routledge. Reprinted with permission of the publisher © Taylor and Francis Ltd. Extract from Rebecca L. Epstein. 'Sharon Stone in a Gap Turtleneck', in David Desser (ed.), *Hollywood Goes Shopping*, Minneapolis: University of Minneapolis Press. Reprinted with permission of the publisher © 2000 University of Minneapolis Press. Extract from Joshua Gamson, 'The Assembly Line of Greatness: Celebrity in Twentieth-Century America', *Critical Studies in Mass Communication*, 9 (1992). Reprinted with permission of the publisher © Taylor and Francis Ltd (1992) (http://www.tandf.co.uk/journals). Christine Geraghty, 'Re-examining Stardom: Questions of Texts, Bodies and Performance', Christine Gledhill and Linda Williams (eds) *Reinventing Film Studies*, London: Arbold. Reprinted with permission from the publisher © 2000. Extract from Chris Rojek, 'Celebrity and Religion', Rojek, *Celebrity*, London: Reaktion Books (2001). Reprinted with permission of the publisher © 2001 Reaktion Books. Extract from Jackie Stacey, 'With Stars in Their Eyes: Female Spectators and the Paradoxes of Consumption', Stacey, *Stargazing: Hollywood Cinema and Female Spectatorship*, London: Routledge (1994). Reprinted with permission from the publisher © 1994 Routledge. Extract from Graeme Turner, 'The Economy of Celebrity', Turner, *Understanding Celebrity*, London: Sage (2004). Reprinted with permission from the publisher © 2004 Sage. Extract from Max Weber, 'The Nature of Charismatic Domination', Weber, *From Max Weber: Essays in Sociology*, Oxford: Oxford University Press (1946). Reprinted with permission of the publisher.

Whilst every effort has been made to contact owners of copyright material reproduced in this book, we have not always been successful. In the event of a copyright query, please contact the publishers.

Introduction: What's in a Reader?

Sean Redmond and Su Holmes

A star confessional: Georgie Best – the Belfast Boy
Sean Redmond

The day that George Best – the internationally revered Irish footballer and 'alcoholic' star – was reported to be close to death, I emailed him at the hospital he was staying in. I was pretty sure that he wouldn't make it through the night to read it given the fact that he was slipping in and out of consciousness, and as he was receiving thousands of these messages each day, I also knew there were too many for him to read in the little time that he had left to live. And yet I felt compelled to write. In fact, although it feels rather embarrassing now, I was tearful – first as I read about his impending death, this time clearly without any possibility of a Lazarus-like recovery (George had 'faced death' at least twice before and had survived 'against the odds'), and then as I composed the email. What was it about George Best, whom I had never met, and whom, as a boy, I had only seen play football on our 19-inch black and white television set, that touched such a deep and emotional chord within me? Surely, as an academic, with an intellectual interest in stars and celebrities, *I should have known better*. George was/is just another media construction, a mythic figure built on gender, class and national signifiers that in many ways could be argued to be politically regressive. The mythic George Best was a playboy, womanizer, the 'fifth Beatle', who came from working-class origins in the roughest quarter of a deeply divided Belfast City. George was stereotypically Irish: he was fun to be with, gregarious, he liked his drink (too much) and he could unite both sides – Catholic and Protestant – of the religious divide. George embodied the success myth (Dyer, 1998) and reinforced notions of aggressive heterosexuality and hard-bodied masculinity, not least with oft-quoted lines such as, 'I spent a lot of money on booze, cars and birds, the rest I just squandered'. How, then, could I get so wrapped up in the fakery and the damaging ideology of the dying Georgie Best?

Of course, in one clear sense, the machinery of myth and personality construction is all to do with creating a space for strong and lasting identifications to emerge. In the end, like everyone else, I am situated or placed in a culture that speaks to me through the confessional language of fame – and I cannot, and maybe I shouldn't – be impervious to its lyrical refrains. I needed to *feel* Georgie's death because of the impact that he had on my young life and no amount of academic self-reflexivity could counteract that need. Whether one argues this to be manipulative, a pseudo or para-social relationship, based on anomic or psycho-social lack (Rojek, 2001), or one that has progressive or liberating potential, as I would like to argue, the mythic story of George Best, and his part in my life, begins to establish the fact that stars and celebrities have a profound and lasting effect on *everyday* life and have done so for most of the 20th century. One only has to recall the adoration from female fans that Rudolph Valentino received in the 1920s (Hansen, 1991); the obsessional fan devotion to Marilyn Monroe and Elvis Presley that emerged in the 1950s and 1960s, and which continues to this present day; the international, cross-gender infatuation with the Beatles in the 1960s; the national mourning that followed Princess Diana's death in 1997; and the similar outpouring of grief, in Northern Ireland in particular, that followed George's death in 2005. Of course, it is the contemporary, ubiquitous, multi-textual, trans-global and 'everywhere' nature of stars and celebrities that cements the sense that their stories, images and representations are at the centre of everyday life and to the identities that circulate there (Couldry, 2000; Redmond, 2006).

My love affair with George Best has its roots in the success myth: being of Irish descent, and growing up in a working-class area in Coventry, England, in the 1970s, he allowed me (and my friends) to dream of unrivalled footballing success. And it was the manner of his success, startling footballing 'genius' conjoined with the trappings of rock star excess, that led us to believe there was – or that we could at least *hope for* – an open doorway to much better things. But George made me feel better about myself in a much more immediate and explicitly political manner. My identification with George Best was at its most acute during the IRA bombings in the mid-1970s, particularly the Birmingham pub bombing in November 1974 that left 21 innocent revellers dead. This produced a media backlash against Irish Catholics and the 'othering' of Irish communities in England. As a 7-year-old boy I felt particularly susceptible to what I perceived to be the stare and the ideological 'fixing' of my English peers. In both symbolic and literal terms, it often felt as if one was being made to feel like a dangerous outsider; the bomb-maker, or the relative or friend of the bomb-maker. In contrast, what George Best provided was a positive, albeit archetypal sense of what it meant to be Irish; he provided the over-determining image of healthy, reproductive masculinity; of sporting success (at least until the mid-1970s), and of gregarious sociability that made him the centre of attention and a figure of desiring identification across class, religious and national lines. The mythic construction of George Best, then, in play before these bombings, stood in triumphant opposition to the (re)emerging discourse of the Irish as uncaring terrorists that left the innocent in corporeal bits and pieces. One could argue that the crooner, Val Doonican, and the comedian, Dave Allen (both prime-time television stars at this time) provided similar, if less kinetic and more sanitized versions of wholesome, healthy Irishness.

In effect, the image of George provided a means of identification that enabled me and my peers to exist outside the negative discourses that were (re)emerging in the press and on the news about the Irish. The star persona of George Best had political consequences that I, and others like me, felt in our everyday lives. Through the mythic figure of George Best we felt good about ourselves, about our Irishness, and we used or appropriated his electric, corporeal, representational energy to resist, at a metaphorical level, the othering that was thrust upon us. George in part saved me from existential annihilation, from a type of nullifying colonial warfare over which I had no control. Although, of course, ironically, in the end George couldn't save himself, he couldn't resist his own wayward-son mythology – killed by the years of alcohol abuse that sustained his fame long after he gave up football for booze, girls and fast cars. His fame saved me but killed him.

The story of George Best has at its centre nearly all the key representational tropes, ideological issues, and production and consumption concerns that drive and shape star and celebrity theory. While this account has been largely a personal one, its reach extends into each and every star and celebrity text. All fans can perhaps recount a similar story about a star or celebrity who changed their lives for the better (this could, of course, be a line from a celebrity magazine: the rhetoric of fame being so extensive that the threads of it run deeply within our culture, seemingly without beginning/cause or end/effect). My email to the dying George Best was an impossible 'thank you' for the pleasure he gave me as a footballer, and for the appropriated power I took from him to be all that I could.

The importance of being famous...
Su Holmes

While on one level this personal narrative plays out a 'traditional' conception of the hierarchal relationship between elevated star and enchanted fan, the self-reflexive and (self) critical nature of the 'confessional' suggests a high degree of active agency. The role of the fan is far from passive: it involves actively negotiating and bringing into being the cultural meanings of the star or celebrity image. In fact, this is one of the reasons why there has been an expansion of writing about fame (of which this book is clearly part); it seems to be a more *pervasive part* of everyday life, flowing over and beyond the borders of rigidly constructed/conceived lines of star/fan identification and emulation.

But the idea of fame as somehow more 'pervasive' should also nod to a note of caution. In the UK documentary series, *The Importance of Being Famous* (Channel 4, 2003), the voice-over, of then newspaper editor Piers Morgan, boldly claims that 'we are living through a sea-change in the nature of what it means to be a celebrity ... how has fame-seeking become a mass-epidemic?' (2 February, 2003). The validity of the question (and the reason for making the documentary series in the first place) is illustrated by showing viewers supposedly 'unmediated' footage of Tara, a student, being introduced as someone who 'just wants to be famous for herself'. Eager, bubbly and initially a little in awe of the experience, Tara is seen talking directly to the camera as she walks across a park in central London:

Tara: I might be someone – am I *someone* yet ... or not yet?
Cameraman [off-screen in a dead-pan voice]: [pause] Not yet.
Tara: But I will be soon [pauses and cocks her head to one side], *won't* I?

As she performs in a self-reflexive documentary mode, passers-by watch Tara being filmed and wonder *who she is?* Simultaneously, Tara momentarily hesitates in a bid to comprehend why they are staring *at her.* Has she made 'it' already? Visibly excited by the experience of commanding the camera's gaze, pulling its focus towards her as she moves around its lens, Tara momentarily plays out the role of being a star or celebrity, re-enacting the experience of being entrapped and adored by the gaze of others. This is certainly one of the many scenarios in the contemporary moment which encapsulate how fame is increasingly seen as promising the ultimate form of social experience and existence. But the description above is not to suggest (as the documentary in fact implies) that Tara is in essence a confused and deluded fame-seeker. Indeed, on the one hand, the scenario epitomizes a shift in which, rather than simply looking on at the famous as they perform on the public stage, the audience is increasingly grabbing the media spotlight – aiming to take charge of 'decisions about their own visibility' (Rein et al., 1997: 150). Yet on the other hand, the mocking presence of Piers Morgan, as indicated by his raised eyebrows and stolen smirks at the camera, suggests otherwise: Tara is also being 'set up', effectively encouraged to perform an increasingly predictable script in which she plays the role of an aspirant fame-seeker.

But within these two scenarios just described – Sean's confessional and Tara's desire for fame – we can see discourses of power at work, particularly, for example, with regard to gender. While the previous discussion venerated a male *star*, famous (at least in the first place) for his meritocratic achievement and talent, this example zooms in on a wannabe female *celebrity*. The cultural hierarchy implicit in the use of these terms (discussed below) is often based on discourses of gender (Geraghty, 2000). Yet this in itself is important here. Circulating through both of these narratives, there are countless examples of how fame is political and why, culturally speaking, thinking about fame is important. Tara might epitomize the contemporary moment of fame, where the feminine self comes into being in and through star or celebrity 'glamour'. The story of George Best might encapsulate fame's heterosexist, predatory present and its past. What both of these examples have at their centre are many of the key issues which drive and shape star and celebrity theory.

Fame matters
Sean Redmond and Su Holmes

Fame matters on one level because of our status as audiences for celebrity (we have all been, or are, a fan of someone). Stars and celebrities are consumed and appropriated by fans in ways which have a profound effect on their identity, self-image and sense of belonging. Celebrity matters to the cultural industries that produce or manufacture the famous for surplus profit. Fame matters to film, television and radio producers, distributors and exhibitors; to the music, sport and print media industries; to the organization and marketing of internet sites and game-playing industries; to the spin-making machinery of the political arena; to the corporate images of businesses, the public status of universities; and to the concerns of cultural commentators, academics and students (to name only a few examples). Celebrity certainly matters in different ways across these spheres, but it begins to capture the extent to which, as Rein, Kotler and Stoller observe, celebrityhood in the Western world has spread into every aspect of everyday life:

> So great is the value of visibility that the manufacturing and marketing of celebrities now reach into business, sports, entertainment, religion, the arts, politics, academics, medicine, and law. Visibility is what every aspiring actor wants and every unknown professional seeks. This is the new world of industrialized celebrity . . . in which individuals . . . can be elevated to a level of visibility unimaginable at any other time – and be compensated with imaginable rewards. (Rein et al., 1997: 1–2)

This forms part of their suggestion that the 'value of visibility' has become a commodity in *its own right*, quite independent from 'accomplishment, sacrifice, heroics' (Ibid: 14). This immediately raises the issue of historical developments in fame, and how these might be valued, but it also suggests the cultural value placed on being famous in itself. As Nick Couldry (2000) has argued, such visibility increasingly functions as a way of ordering the world: to be in the media frame is to be at the 'centre' of things, an idea so heavily naturalized that it often, paradoxically, seems difficult to *see* (through). Of course, this is exactly why star and celebrity matters: we should want to make a critical and questioning sense of this impossible vision of fame, a vision that not everyone has equal access to, or ownership of. While this notion of a hierarchy, or a world increasingly 'divided by those who have access to image-making and the rest' (Biressi and Nunn, 2004: 47), is not the only route into studying celebrity, it does emphasize its relationship with discourses and networks of power and political affect/effect. As the example of Tara above suggests, it allows us to think about how we measure ideas about success, failure and individualism in modern society, and how the phenomenon of fame shapes the understandings of our own identities, achievements and aspirations. This is why celebrity matters, not only to the range of economic, cultural and social structures above, but also *to us*, as students and academics undeniably caught up in the sometimes pleasurable and intimate matter of fame as it enters – perhaps sometimes without us even wishing it to – our everyday lives.

Studying stars and celebrities

As the collection of arguments in this *Reader* suggests, evidence of this interest in celebrity is not difficult to find. The study of celebrity and stardom has expanded considerably in recent years, particularly when we survey the last decade. This was not always the case, as while the intellectual and popular fascination with fame has a long history (Barker, 2003), it was not really until the 1970s, and in film studies in particular, that the subject was given real academic consideration. Film studies forged the way when it came to the academic study of stardom, and in terms of the volume of work published and the historical knowledge generated, it arguably remains the most developed field. There are good reasons for this which are disciplinary and historical. In Europe and North America, Film studies received earlier establishment as an academic discipline (compared to television studies or popular music studies for example), and a number of scholars have argued that it was cinema, and Hollywood in particular, which provided the context for the establishment of celebrity as a mass industry (Gamson, 1994;

Turner, 2004). In the opening to the collection *Stardom: Industry of Desire* in 1991, Christine Gledhill asserted with some confidence that the 'cinema still provides the ultimate confirmation of stardom' (1991: xiii). This is not something which can be easily subjected to empirical measurement. But the argument that studies from different media and disciplinary contexts can speak to one another in a *broader* dialogue about fame shapes the overall philosophy of this *Reader*. In fact, this premise largely structures the thinking that lies behind the construction of this book. Its aims are shaped, first, by cultural and economic shifts in the circulation of fame, and second, by the related cross and interdisciplinary academic contexts in which these are explored. For example, one can argue that the media contexts for the production and circulation of fame have become less specific (Geraghty, 2000; Holmes and Redmond, 2006). There is now a vast range of media sites through which modern celebrity can emerge. Mass, digital and narrowcast media outlets, often in a synergetic relationship, enable the famous to be pictured, photographed, broadcast, pod cast and filmed in a real-time, offering a 24/7 relay across the globe. Celebrities are now rarely restricted to a single medium, and the commercial and cultural value of the modern star or celebrity is seen to be predicated on their inter- and cross-textual appeal. This process has fuelled a debate about the flattening of distinctions between stars, celebrities and personalities. This is usually articulated with a tone of alarm, forming part of the lament about the decline of status and value which attends modern celebrity. The contemporary media context may indeed have weakened the significance of particular modalities of representation and address where celebrity is concerned, but it would seem rash to deny that significant media distinctions remain (Turner, 2004: 8). As the case studies in this book make clear, many star or celebrity personae do remain associated with a particular media context or role. To suggest that footballers, pop stars, television hosts or 'web-celebs', all foster similar affective relations with their audience is surely a woeful neglect of the ideological, aesthetic and cultural currents through which their public profiles flow. This also encourages us to consider how there are a vast range of different forms of contact with celebrity, shaped in part by different attitudes and investments on the part of the audience (Turner, 2004: 9). Many of the authors in this *Reader* aim to address such specificities, offering what we hope is a diverse account of how celebrity has resonated across different historical, political and cultural contexts.

This broader perspective is also intended to reflect (while it is also made possible by), the expansion of academic interest in stardom and celebrity, across media and cultural studies, popular music, sport and literary studies, sociology, psychology, law studies and beyond. As noted above, film studies played a seminal role in demonstrating the possibilities here, laying important contexts for the later growth of scholarly work in the field. Certainly, as Martin Barker has noted, such analysis did not begin with Richard Dyer's canonical intervention *Stars* (originally published in 1979) (2003: 5), and there is a longer heritage of intellectual comment on fame. But as Barker notes, Dyer did raise new questions about how stars might be studied:

> Famously, he invited examination of stars within representation. What is the meaning of the 'character' that some stars display? How does the endless talk surrounding stars relate to their on-screen personae? What kinds of pleasure, dream and compensation for life do stars offer their audiences? In short, what is their ideological function? (Barker, 2003: 6)

Dyer's work emphasized how stars could be understood as cultural or ideological 'signs' – investigated using the tools of semiotics and contextual and historical analysis. In playing an influential role in mapping the cultural functions of stardom, Dyer placed a particular emphasis on how stars articulated ideas about personhood, and individualism in capitalist society. Although this idea permeates the work of different scholars in different ways, many agree that the cultural and political functions of stardom and celebrity are intimately intertwined with the concept of identity in modern society. In this respect, one of the strengths of Dyer's work was arguably its bid to combine broader ideological issues with the contingent detail of particular case studies. Dyer's *Heavenly Bodies: Film Stars and Society* (1987) went on to offer a more detailed framework (see Section Two) for conceptualizing and researching the star image (see also Holmes, 2006). This was not simply a theory about how the star image worked, but a theory about how a star sign could be understood as dramatizing, disrupting or reconciling contradictory ideas about identity in any given age. His work also offered ambitious methodological tools for the analysis of stardom: an integrated model for mining the cultural significance of a star that involved textual and biographical analysis (assessing the 'on- and off-screen', 'public and private', 'mediated and authentic' life of the star); questions of pleasure and identification; and ideological and historical specificity. This synthetic approach enabled the meaning of the star to emerge out of the cultural world in which they signified.

Nonetheless, a number of subsequent shifts broadened the focus out, ranging from an emphasis on political economy, the history of film stardom, the role of the audience, to issues that explore the impact of new media technologies and embodiment theory on celebrity culture (see Holmes and Redmond, 2006; Willis, 2005; Austin and Barker, 2003). There has also been a challenge to the hegemonic focus on Hollywood as the dominant site of stardom (e.g. Vincendau, 2000; Babington, 2001; Mishra, 2001), while its academic dominance undoubtedly remains. Nevertheless, in film studies in particular, the notion of reading star images still retains an important significance (e.g. Willis, 2005), partly because it has always been more tightly anchored to the study of the film text when compared to media, television or cultural studies (and beyond).

Since this earlier period, perhaps the greatest expansion of the field has occurred in media and cultural studies. That is not to suggest that these spheres are autonomous, although they do exist within certain borders which have mitigated against a more extensive interaction. Media and cultural studies' approaches to stars and celebrities arguably draw on a wider range of political references – particularly with respect to neo-Marxism – and they have used a wider range of methodological tools (including quantitative analysis) which seeks to situate celebrity alongside broader discussions of power; and the sanctity or centrality of the 'text' is questioned. Nonetheless, in a very real sense, the study of stars and celebrities, right from the start, has been founded on interdisciplinary connections and conversations. Richard Dyer, for example, brought together film, media and cultural studies approaches to get to the heart of the matter of stardom. Dyer's work was also concerned with production, with the industry of fame, as well as modes and types of reception and identification (although, as we outline in the introduction to Section Four, Dyer was most concerned with the star-as-text). A great deal of the textual and ideological work that followed adopted this 'articulating approach' to understanding stars and celebrities. More recently, for example, Jackie Stacey (1994) a sociologist, has combined textual, ethnographic and psychoanalytical analysis to explore the pleasure that women got from the Hollywood stars they adored in wartime and post-war Britain.

In effect, then, what this *Reader* hopes to uniquely recognize and achieve is the sense that the different approaches to star and celebrity analysis have always shared a degree of common ground. It aims to show how their distinctive and discrete approaches work to provide a profound commentary on fame, and that when we bring them together 'under one roof', so to speak, there are links, bridges, overlaps and disagreements which are both productive and thought provoking in furthering work in the field.

A star? Minor celebrity? Wannabee? What's in a name?

It is from these relational but different disciplinary contexts that the title of this *Reader* emerges. But in claiming to offer insight into stardom *and* celebrity, does this mean that we are conceiving of them as distinctive categories? Film studies typically used the word 'stardom', and this reflected the historical currency of the term where the cinema is concerned. At a theoretical level, the concept of the star was used to imply a discursive *interaction* between on- and off-screen image (Ellis, 1992: 91). Outside of film studies, the term 'celebrity' has more commonly been employed. This is partly because it encompasses a wider range of spheres, and the term is often used to simply suggest the contemporary state of being famous. For example, we might suggest that 'a celebrity is a name which, once made by the news, now makes news by itself' (Rein et al., 1997: 14).

There has always been what Andrew Tolson refers to as an 'instability and ambiguity' structuring attempts to categorize fame (1996: 129), and academia has to some extent persisted with boundaries which are not always reflected in *public* discourse. In the contemporary moment, the term 'celebrity' arguably has the most popular cultural currency. This may reflect the blurring of different types of fame to which we have referred. But the currently ubiquitous use of the term celebrity, and the connotations it carries, also suggests how these terms cannot be viewed as autonomous academic constructs, divorced from the wider historical and cultural contexts in which they circulate. For example, and as established at the start of this Introduction, despite their blurred boundaries, there is still a hierarchy of cultural values which organizes the meanings of these terms, with the concept of the 'star' positioned above the concept of the 'celebrity' – with its persistent association with fame as more ubiquitous, and thus devalued, currency (see Marshall, 1997).

The derogatory use of the term celebrity emerges from broader debates about shifts in the nature of modern fame – the oft-cited argument (in public commentary in particular) that it has become impoverished through the decline of talent, merit and achievement. The increasing elision of 'work' or profession has certainly been reflected in certain academic definitions, including the suggestion that a celebrity describes someone whose fame rests overwhelmingly on their lifestyle rather than profession – if indeed they are actually known for the latter at all (Geraghty, 2000: 187). Some celebrities are primarily defined by their circulation in celebrity magazines, a sphere that was traditionally conceived as offering a *secondary* text in relation to the primary media role (see Dyer, 1998). This use of the term celebrity is reinforced by the fact that those known for a public role in a particular profession, most notably in cinema or music, are still more likely to carry the title of star: we rarely say 'pop celebrity' or 'film celebrity' (Evans, 2005: 4). But this also foregrounds how terms shift and slide between and across appearances in particular media contexts, as film stars and pop stars occupy the province of celebrity culture when appearing in a celebrity magazine. The key point here, however, is that it is not possible to locate a set of coherent criteria against which these terms are used, and nor is it possible to use them objectively. The title of this *Reader* reflects how the essays use the terms in a range of different ways, while it also deliberately situates the book at the intersection of different disciplinary contexts.

A *Reader* in stardom and celebrity

Stardom and Celebrity: A Reader does not of course offer a definitive overview of academic work on the subject, nor map a definitive, or indeed coherent, history of how stardom and celebrity have developed. This is neither possible nor desirable. We have deliberately selected a range of different arguments, as well as theoretical and methodological approaches, some of which may not be happily reconciled. But across this spectrum, the narrative of the *Reader* does aim to offer insight into how fame has changed over time (both in terms of the focus of individual essays and the collection as a whole), while it also explores the historical trajectory of how *this has been analysed*. It works from the premise that academic texts are themselves historical, shaped by their own disciplinary, political, biographical and cultural contexts. While they may often claim to adopt a distance from the subject, surveying and scrutinizing it through the 'objectivity' of an analytic gaze, the busy circuits of academic comment involve a high degree of intellectual and emotional investment that are always framed in the subjective and *through* the subject. Theoretical and methodological approaches are subject to fashions, critiques and revision, best seen as operating in a dynamic process of fluid negotiation and 'becoming' rather than as occupying a fixed and rigid position from which to approach things. As the *Reader* makes clear, the changing cultural, political and economic contexts of stardom and celebrity also contribute to the on-going revision of ideas, arguments and approaches that attempt to make 'meaning' out of its floating or kinetic characteristics. We suggest that there is a need to continually reflect on the changing relationship between contexts of stardom/celebrity, and the theoretical and methodological frameworks through which they are explored. It is because of a desire to capture this sense of *dynamism* that the *Reader* includes seminal and canonical analyses, alongside a range of innovative (newer) pieces and interventions. In conjunction with the Section Introductions, we hope that the reader forms their own sense of the dialogue which is at work here, and the insights, questions and challenges it might raise.

Journeying through fame: The structure of the *Reader*

The *Reader* aims to take both a theoretical and an illustrative approach to the exploration of stars and celebrities. It opens with three theoretically driven sections. Section One,

Stardom and Celebrity: Theoretical Antecedents, sets out to chart the 'wider' intellectual arguments and positions that have greatly impacted upon star and celebrity analysis. By doing this, the *Reader* is suggesting that to be fully cognoscente with the arguments and issues raised and explored in the study of celebrity culture (and which follow in this *Reader*) one has to be aware of, and familiar with, the meta-theoretical discourses from which this work has developed. This, then, is a foundational section, offering the building blocks for understanding the 'big ideas' that follow. Section Two, The Analysis of Fame: Understanding Stardom, draws upon the major canonical work on star (and celebrity) theory, but also with a new essay by Rebecca Williams that makes an important contribution to the field by reflecting on how a feminist approach to author- ship can be used to read the image of Drew Barrymore. These essays make cultural, ideological, contextual, institutional and textual sense of stars as signifying practices, involved in processes of identification. Section Three, Fame – Remember My Name?: Histories of Stardom and Celebrity, examines what might be described as key historical junctures in how fame has been mapped and recorded. Not only does this section present a selective history of where, how and why stars and celebrities emerged, but it also offers a history of academic thought on this process.

In Sections Four to Six, the *Reader* moves on to explore what it sees as the most important economic, industrial/ commercial and ideological sites for the study of star and celebrity. In a sense, in these sections, the analysis becomes more site- and text specific, with closely focused explorations of the production, meaning and consumption of fame. Section Four, Producing Fame: 'Because *I'm* Worth It', focuses on the political economy of celebrity culture (a field somewhat marginalized in earlier work in star studies). It seems crucial to consider celebrity culture as a business, and not simply the province of 'magic' and wonder – a world in which, as Samuel Goldwyn once commented, 'God makes the stars. It's up to producers to find them' (cited in Dyer, 1998: 16). Essays in this section address the commercial and commodified nature of stardom and celebrity, taking in agents and image makers, Hollywood cinema and the fashion industry, the celebrity CEO, the legal regulation of celebrity, and the celebrification of the literary author. Section Five, Made in Culture: Star and Celebrity Representations, focuses on the way particular star and celebrity images are made up, or put together, to say something pleasurable and ideological about the self and the cultural world. Such representations are not necessarily consciously manipulative; rather they emerge as symbolic signs of the age, addressing social conflicts, divisions and inequalities. The essays in this section read star images at the level of representation and identity, focusing upon how they speak to issues of race, class, gender and nationality. Section Six, Consuming Fame/Becoming Famous?: Celebrity and Its Audience looks at the way stars and celebrities are made sense of by viewers, listeners or fans. Through processes of identification, idolization and emulation (and, occasionally, dislike and envy), the consumers of the famous use and need stars for a variety of social and psychic reasons. Many of the essays in this section employ empirical research into fan's relations with stars and celebrities, and as such, it contains the voices, opinions and desires of 'real' people exploring their own fascination with the famous.

In one sense, the structure of the *Reader* takes what might be described as a conventional 'circuit of culture' (Hall, 1997) approach to the study of stars and celebrities. Sections are devoted to the grand shibboleths of representation (identity), production (distribution) and consumption (reception). However, what one finds in these divisions is a wealth of diverse and divergent material that fluidly moves in and between the territories which have been ascribed. The sections need to be seen as loosely bordered with connections and articulations running in and between them. For this reason, one can actually start reading the *Reader* from back to front or from the middle out, or from any entry point that one wishes to take. In fact, the joy of this *Reader* – of any Reader – is that it warrants returning to, again and again. This is precisely because of the different ways in which it can be approached, enabling the reader to take away something different each time.

Stars and celebrities *do* matter: they 'house' our dreams and fuel our fantasies; they address and represent (often implicitly) some of the most important political issues of the day, and they can give us both ephemeral and lasting pleasure, even if, in the end, this is a pleasure built on artifice and the lie of the possible. This is a *Reader* to enjoy, but it also a *Reader* that seeks to get under the skin of fame and the skin of the reader. In this respect, it aims to make a lasting impression on the field, as well as on the person who engages with its ideas and arguments.

Star and Celebrity Culture: Theoretical Antecedents

Section One

Introduction
Sean Redmond and Su Holmes

> *A speech has two parts. You must state your case and you must prove it.*
> *You cannot either state your case and omit to prove it, or prove it without*
> *first having stated it, since any proof must be proof of something and the*
> *only use of a preliminary statement is the proof that follows it.*

(Aristotle, 1991: 216. Trans. by George A. Kennedy)

When one begins to research something new, or to take up a position on a particular topic or area of analysis, one often does so with a particular theoretical or methodological approach to hand, or with theories and methods in mind that one can or will draw upon. One enters the investigative arena with a research question and a way of working or approaching that question. However, that is not to say that research doesn't also yield unexpected ways of thinking and recording, or epiphany moments that change the direction, focus and approach that one is taking. Good research takes risks and involves accepting challenges to one's original ideas and working practices.

In terms of the research for this *Reader*, such a process of renewal and re-imagining constantly took place: the editors grappled with theoretical, historical, textual and contextual concerns as they systematically began to map the footprints of star and celebrity analysis across time, method and discipline. *But where best to start the journey?* Where does one need to (re) visit to discover the approaches that inform star and celebrity analysis? The answer, in what might loosely be described as an epiphany, came with the editors deciding that to be fully cognoscente with the arguments and issues raised and explored in the study of stars and celebrities, one has to be aware of the wider theoretical and methodological discourses from which this work has developed. One has to actually *leave* the subject–specific field of star and celebrity culture and make a *pathway* to some of the writers who provided the meta-discourse for thinking about fame in the first place.

In this unique section – unique when compared to other academic works on stardom and celebrity – one finds the foundational work from which much star and celebrity work emerges. A great many of the central contributors to this *Reader* utilize the ideas of the writers found in this section. In fact, to be provocative, the editors think that without such cross-referencing and historical and theoretical linkage, one is only ever getting a partial picture of the way (and why) these seminal star and celebrity theorists come to conclusions they do. This is, of course, one of the problems with a *Reader*: it takes a chapter or article out of its original context and situates it in a themed section newly devised by the editors. Through having a theoretical antecedents section the editors hope that such context and lineage is given greater weight and support.

That said, the theoretical and methodological choices made here are themselves open to debate and contestation. The choices are also – in fact they have to be – *selective*. Nonetheless, the editors consider that the essays included in this section have had the most dramatic or lasting effect on star and celebrity analysis, and/or they are currently shaping the discussion of fame in profound and meaningful ways. Selections, then, have been based upon how the work which is found in this section continues to ener-gize the textual, industrial, representational, ideological, psychoanalytic and reception discussions that take place in the star and celebrity universe. As such, the selections made in this section also work to 'speak to' each of the other themed sections, in what might be described as a process of discursive relay, back and forth between writers, methods and critical approaches.

The section opens with Max Weber's highly influential work on 'Charisma'. Weber, an anti-positivist sociologist writing in the late 19th century, concerned himself with the role and function of bureaucracies and authority in industrial society. Weber believed that human action is increasingly regulated, monitored and controlled in bureaucratic organizations, and these enterprises applied the logic of rationalization to every problem and social encounter. According to Weber, the bureaucratic coordination of the action of large numbers of people has become the dominant structural feature of modern societies, and this has consequences for the way authority is mobilized and supported. Weber sees a corresponding shift away from traditional authority (involving patriarchs, patrimonialism and feudalism) and charismatic authority (based on familial and religious identification) to a type of 'Rational legal authority' defined by impersonal rules that have been legally established. However, Weber also suggests that charismatic authority persists because of its powerful allure to those who 'need' spiritual or irrational modes of identification.

Weber defines charismatic authority – which he also called charismatic domination or charismatic leadership – as 'resting on devotion to the exceptional sanctity, heroism or exemplary character of an individual person, and of the normative patterns or order revealed or ordained by him'. Charisma, then, is 'a certain quality of an individual personality, by virtue of which he is set apart from ordinary men and treated as endowed with supernatural, superhuman, or at least specifically exceptional powers or qualities'. Weber argues that charismatic authority is an inherently unstable form of leadership because it relies solely on the belief of followers who may/can switch allegiances, religions and desires to other charismatic individuals. Charismatic authority, then, is dependent on the *relationship* between the deified and the iconic and the followers who invest in such symbolic adulation. This investment, according to Weber, can and does breakdown. One can quickly identify the way Weber's concept of charis-matic authority relates to and has impacted on star and celebrity theory. Stars and celebrities are often argued to be charismatic leaders or trend setters, their celebrification is often also subject to a loss of favour, as their fame wanes, and fans (fandom) construct para-social relationships with them as if they are indeed extraordinary or God-like figures. In this *Reader*, for example, the work of writers such as Francesco Alberoni (1972) and Richard Dyer (1979) are clearly influenced by Weber's ideas.

In his essay 'Art in the Age of Mechanical Reproduction', Walter Benjamin, a Marxist philosopher writing at the turn of the 20th Century, examines what he sees as the loss of 'aura' in an age where new media technologies are re-situating art objects from their spatial and temporal point of origin and allowing endless copies of them to be made. In this context of the mechanical reproduction of art, Benjamin takes a generally critical view of the way film stars are manufactured by the cinema machine. Benjamin suggests that while live theatrical performance has always involved an authentic auratic presence – channelled through the movements and sounds of the emotionally engaged actor on stage – film performance is predicated on self-negation or self-denial because 'aura is tied to his presence: there can be no replica of it'. The commercial film industry, according to Benjamin, 'responds to the shrivelling of the aura with an artificial build-up of the "personality" outside the studio. The cult of the movie star, fostered by the money of the film industry, preserves not the unique aura of the person but the "spell of the personality," the phoney spell of a commodity'. Film stars, then, are given auratic qualities through promotional and marketing activities, but this aura is commodified, with little existential, lasting, meaningful appeal, for performer or fan. In fact, as Benjamin concludes, 'under these circumstances the film industry is trying hard to spur the interest of the masses through illusion-promoting spectacles and dubious speculations'. Benjamin's concept of aura, his understanding of how aura is simulated through the figure of the film star and his exploration of how commercial cinema has the potential to shape the consciousness of the mass audience, has played an important role in approaches to stardom and celebrity. As can be seen in later sections of this *Reader*, whether implicitly or explicitly, these ideas have structured a great deal of work on star or celebrity images, whether we are talking about the negotiation of ideological discourses, or the identificatory processes of fandom.

In the essay, 'The Culture Industry: Enlightenment as Mass Deception', Adorno and Horkheimer also adopt a Marxist perspective to reflect on how film stars function, although their conclusions are much more savagely critical. Writing in the 1940s, against the backdrop of the rise of Fascism and the Nazi propaganda war, and having fled from Germany to America, to escape persecution, they consider the American film industry to be a dominant culture industry that standardizes output and dupes the masses with the false promise of a good life. For Adorno and Horkheimer, Hollywood film offers movie-goers a particularly seductive version of 'pseudo individuality' where minor variations in plot, genre and characterization are made to appear original, masking the fact that in form, style and ideological intent, they are the same as that which has endlessly gone before. Hollywood film serves the economic and political needs of capitalism and film stars are one of its greatest commodity and escapist inventions. The 'exceptional film star whose hair curls over her eye to demonstrate her originality' is in fact 'mass produced like Yale locks, whose only difference can be measured in fractions of millimeters. The peculiarity of the self is monopoly commodity determined by society; it is falsely represented as natural'. According to Adorno and Horkheimer, 'the film star with whom one is meant to fall in love with is from the outset a copy of himself'. Their work has exerted a great deal of influence over the way stars and celebrities have been read, historicized and contextualized. Writers such as Joshua Gamson (1994) and

Richard Dyer (1987), for example, assess the meaning of stars through the filters of capitalism and bourgeois individualism, albeit with different, more optimistic or radical conclusions about the agency that people can have over the texts they consume.

In 'Myth Today', Roland Barthes, a highly influential post-structuralist semiotician, usefully extends the way that the sign systems can be understood to generate 'social ideology'. Barthes argues that connotation, or ideological meaning, emerges in what he calls the environment of myth. According to Barthes myth has, 'a very close communication with culture, knowledge, history, and it is through them, so to speak, that the environmental world of culture invades the system of representation'. Myth *speaks* dominant culture and is imbued with the 'fragments of ideology', but this is always effaced or naturalized within the textual operations so that 'what myth gives back in return is a natural image of this reality'. According to Barthes, myth de-politicizes representation; 'myth does not deny things, on the contrary, its function is to talk about them; simply it purifies them, it makes them innocent, it gives them a natural and eternal justification, it gives them a clarity which is not that of an explanation but that of a statement of fact'. In terms of star and celebrity analysis, Barthes' concept of myth has often been employed to make sense of a particular star's constructed image, and to link ideology and power to the way stars and celebrities signify. In this *Reader*, for example, one finds numerous writers who explore the mythic function of stars.

However, Roland Barthes' theoretical work has impacted on star and celebrity analysis in another way. In 'The Photo Effect', Barthes examines what he sees as the 'here-now and the there-then' paradox of photography. For Barthes, the photograph is always already a record; it makes present something that is absent; and brings that which has already gone into the here-and-now through the illusion of the 'reality' of the image. Photographs, according to Barthes, are based upon a present/absent paradox. This idea has been taken up in the work of a number of authors in this *Reader* (including Ellis, 1992 and Redmond, 2006) in terms of the way film stars are argued to be simultaneously present/absent creatures. The film star, a vision of corporeal perfection, intimately 'there' before the admiring spectator, is also simultaneously not there, a higher extraordinary being, and the trace of an image long gone.

In 'The Ecstasy of Communication', Jean Baudrillard, a leading postmodern theorist, abandons the Barthesian idea that symbols, signs and ideology can refer to anything but the liquid chasm from which they emerge. In the contemporary moment, reality has been surpassed with hyperreality, in a social world of free-floating, media–ignited signifiers. Simulation, according to Baudrillard, is all that there is: 'today the scene and the mirror no longer exist; instead, there is a screen and network. In place of the reflexive transcendence of mirror and scene, there is a non-reflecting surface, an immanent surface where operations unfold – the smooth operational surface of communication'. Baudrillard suggests that there is an obscenity to the way vision, information and simulacra have found their way into every social encounter, and into every power network. It is 'the obscenity of the visible, of the all-too-visible, of the more-visible-than-the-visible. It is the obscenity of what no longer has any secret, of what dissolves completely in information and communication'. Baudrillard's vision of the obscene has had a major impact upon the way stars and celebrities can be read or contextualized. Taken to be the epitome of the ecstasy of communication, the famous elite are argued to be the purest conduits of the obscene. They are at the nexus of the communication highway and they reach into every simulated human encounter.

1 The Nature of Charismatic Domination

Max Weber

The essence of charisma and its workings

Bureaucracy, like the patriarchal system which is opposed to it in so many ways, is a structure of 'the everyday', in the sense that stability is among its most important characteristics. Patriarchal power, above all, is rooted in the supply of the normal, constantly recurring, needs of everyday life and thus has its basis in the economy – indeed, in just those sections of the economy concerned with the supply of normal everyday requirements. The patriarch is the 'natural leader' in everyday life. In this respect, bureaucracy is the counterpart of patriarchalism, only expressed in more rational terms. Bureaucracy, moreover, is a permanent structure and is well adapted, with its system of rational rules, for the satisfaction of calculable long-term needs by normal methods. On the other hand, the supply of all needs which go beyond the economic requirements of everyday life is seen, the further back we go in history, to be based on a totally different principle, that of *charisma*. In other words, the 'natural' leaders in times of spiritual, physical, economic, ethical, religious or political emergency were neither appointed officials nor trained and salaried specialist 'professionals' (in the present-day sense of the word 'profession'), but those who possessed specific physical and spiritual gifts which were regarded as supernatural, in the sense of not being available to everyone.

[...]

In contrast with all forms of bureaucratic administrative system, the charismatic structure recognises no forms or orderly procedures for appointment or dismissal, no 'career', no 'advancement', no 'salary'; there is no organised training either for the bearer of charisma or his aides, no arrangements for supervision or appeal, no allocation of local areas of control or exclusive spheres of competence, and finally no standing institutions comparable to bureaucratic 'governing bodies' independent of persons and of their purely personal charisma. Rather, charisma recognises only those stipulations and limitations which come from within itself. The bearer of charisma assumes the tasks appropriate to him and requires obedience and a following in virtue of his mission. His success depends on whether he finds them. If those to whom he feels himself sent do not recognise his mission, then his claims collapse. If they do recognise him, then he remains their master for as long as he is able to retain their recognition by giving 'proofs'. His right to rule, however, is not dependent on their will, as is that of an elected leader; on the contrary, it is the duty of those to whom he is sent to recognise his charismatic qualification.

[...]

The continued existence of charismatic authority is, by its very nature, characteristically *unstable*: the bearer may lose his charisma, feel himself, like Jesus on the cross, to be 'abandoned by his God', and show himself to his followers as 'bereft of his power', and then his mission is dead, and his followers must hopefully await and search out a new charismatic leader. He himself, however, is abandoned by his following, for pure charisma recognises no 'legitimacy' other than that conferred by personal power, which must be constantly re-confirmed. The charismatic hero does not derive his authority from ordinances and statutes, as if it were an official 'competence', nor from customary usage or feudal fealty, as with patrimonial power: rather, he acquires it and retains it only by proving his powers in real life. He must perform miracles if he wants to be a prophet, acts of heroism if he wants to be a leader in war. Above all, however, his divine mission must 'prove' itself in that those who entrust themselves to him must prosper. If they do not, then he is obviously not the master sent by the gods. This very serious conception of genuine charisma obviously stands in stark contrast with the comfortable pretensions of the modern theory of the 'divine right of kings', with its references to the 'inscrutable' decrees of God, 'to whom alone the monarch is answerable': the genuinely charismatic leader, by contrast, is answerable rather to his subjects. That is, it is for that reason and that reason alone that precisely he personally is the genuine master willed by God.

[...]

Bureaucratic rationalisation can also be, and often has been, a revolutionary force of the first order in its relation to tradition. But its revolution is carried out by *technical* means, basically 'from the outside' (as is especially true of all economic reorganisation); first it revolutionises things and organisations, and then, in consequence, it changes people, in the sense that it alters the conditions to which they must adapt and in some cases increases their chances of adapting to the external world by rational determination of means and ends. The power of charisma, by contrast, depends on beliefs in revelation and heroism, on emotional convictions about the importance and value of a religious, ethical, artistic, scientific, political or other manifestation, on heroism, whether ascetic or military, or judicial wisdom or magical or other favours. Such belief revolutionises men 'from within' and seeks to shape things and organisations in accordance with its revolutionary will. This contrast must, to be sure, be rightly understood. For all the vast differences in the areas in which they operate, the psychological origins of ideas are essentially the same, whether they are religious, artistic, ethical, scientific or of any other kind: this is especially true of the organising ideas of social and political life. Only a purely subjective, 'time-serving' evaluation could attribute one sort of idea to 'understanding' and another to 'intuition' (or whatever other pair of terms one might care to use): the mathematical 'imagination' of a Weierstrass is 'intuition' in exactly the same sense as that of any artist, prophet or, for that matter, of any demagogue: that is not where the difference lies.[1] If we are to understand the true meaning of 'rationalism', we must emphasise that the difference does not lie in general in the person or in the inner 'experiences' of the creator of the ideas or the 'work', but in the manner in which it is inwardly 'appropriated' or 'experienced' by those whom he rules or leads. We have already seen that, in the process of rationalisation, the great majority of those who are led merely appropriate the external technical consequences which are of practical importance to their interests, or else adapt themselves to them (in the same way that we 'learn' our multiplication tables or as all too many jurists learn the techniques of the law): the actual content of their creator's ideas remains irrelevant to them. This is the meaning of the assertion that rationalisation and rational organisation revolutionise 'from the outside', whereas charisma, wherever its characteristic influence is felt, on the contrary exerts its revolutionary power from within, by producing a fundamental change of heart ('*metanoia*') in the ruled.

[...]

The origin and transformation of charismatic authority

Charismatic domination in the 'pure' sense which has just been described is always the offspring of unusual circumstances – either external, especially political or economic, or internal and spiritual, especially religious, or both together. It arises from the excitement felt by all members of a human group in an extraordinary situation and from devotion to heroic qualities of whatever kind. It follows directly from this, however, that it is only in the very early stages that the bearer's own faith in his charisma and that of his disciples (whether the charisma is prophetic or of some other kind) and the devout belief of those to whom he feels himself sent in his mission normally operates with unbroken force, unity and vigour. If the tide which once elevated a charismatically led group out of the routine of everyday life flows back into everyday channels, then charismatic domination, at least in its pure form, is undermined in most cases: it becomes 'institutionalised' and changes course, until it either becomes purely mechanical or is imperceptibly superseded by totally different structural principles or becomes mingled and blended with them in a variety of forms; and when this happens, it becomes in fact inseparably bound up with them, often deformed beyond recognition, an element in the empirical historical structure which can be separated out only in theoretical analysis.

'Pure' charismatic domination is thus unstable in a quite specific sense, and all its transformations derive in the last analysis from one and the same source. It is usually the wish of the master himself, and always that of his disciples and, even more, of his charismatically led followers to change charisma and the charismatic blessings of his subjects from a once-for-all, extremely transitory free gift of grace belonging to extraordinary times and persons into a permanent, everyday possession. The inexorable concomitant of this change, however, is a change in the inner character of the structure. The mode of existence of charisma is always overtaken by the conditions of everyday life and the forces which dominate them, especially economic interests; and this is so whether we consider the development of a war hero's charismatic following into a state, the development of the charismatic community of a prophet, an artist, a philosopher or an ethical or scientific innovator into a church, sect, academy or school, or the development of a charismatically led group of followers of a cultural idea into a party or even a mere apparatus of newspapers and periodicals. The turning-point always comes when the charismatic followers and disciples become first – as in the Frankish king's *'trustis'* – the lord's table companions, marked out by special rights, then vassals, priests, public functionaries, party officials, officers, secretaries, editors and publicists, or publishers, wanting to make a living out of the charismatic movement, or else employees, teachers or other professional interest groups, prebendaries, holders of patrimonial offices and the like. The charismatically ruled, on the other hand, usually become tax-paying 'subjects', contributing members of the church, sect, party or club, soldiers conscripted, drilled and disciplined according to the rules and regulations, or law-abiding 'citizens'. Charismatic preaching inevitably – even despite the Apostle's admonition not to 'damp down the spirit' – declines, according to circumstances, into dogma, doctrine, theory, regulations, legal judgments, or petrified tradition.

[…]

It is the universal fate of all parties, which almost without exception originated as charismatic followings, either of legitimate rulers or of Caesarist pretenders or of demagogues in the style of Pericles or Cleon or Lassalle, when once they slip into the everyday routine of a permanent organisation, to remodel themselves into a body led by *'notables'*. Indeed, one might say that up until the end of the eighteenth century they almost always became federations of nobles. In the Italian cities of the Middle Ages, since the fairly large feudal bourgeoisie was admittedly almost completely Ghibelline, there was often a 'reduction to the ranks' of the *nobili*, equivalent to disqualification from office and deprivation of political rights. Nevertheless, it is very exceptional, even under the *'popolani'*, for a *non*-noble to hold a leading office, even though here, as everywhere, the financing of the parties was bound to be done by the bourgeoisie. The decisive factor at that time was that military support for the parties, which very often aspired to direct power, was provided by the nobility: in the case of the Guelphs, for instance, there was an established register. Any party of the period before the French Revolution – the Huguenots or Catholic League, or any of the English parties, including the 'Roundheads' – reveals the same typical pattern: a transition from a charismatic period of excitement, in which the barriers of class and status group are broken down in the common support of one or more heroes, to the development of associations of notables, led for the most part by nobles. Even the 'bourgeois' parties of the nineteenth century, the Radicals not excepted, always fell into the old pattern of domination by notables for the simple reason that it was only the notables who could direct either the state itself or the party without pay, but also, of course, because of their social or economic influence.

[…]

In Germany, the teachers are the stratum who, because of the 'status' attached to their profession, act as unpaid electoral agents for the specifically 'bourgeois' parties, just as the clergy normally do for the authoritarian parties. In France it has long been the advocates who have acted for the bourgeois parties, partly because of their technical qualifications, and partly, both during and after the Revolutionary period, because of their status.

Some groupings in the French Revolution, which did not, however, exist for long enough to develop a definite structure, show the first signs of bureaucratic organisation, which was beginning to prevail everywhere by the last decades of the nineteenth century. The swing of the pendulum between charismatic obedience and submission to notables has now been replaced by the struggles between the bureaucratic party organisation and the charismatic party leadership. The party organisation has fallen more and more securely into the hands of the professional party officials, the further the process of bureaucratisation has gone and the larger have become the direct and indirect prebendal interests and chances that depend on it, and this is so whether these officials are direct agents of the party or originally free entrepreneurs like the American bosses. In their hands lie the system of personal connexions with ward chairmen, agitators, controllers and other indispensable personnel, the lists, papers and all the other materials which must be known about if the party machine is to be kept under control. It is thus only possible successfully to influence the conduct of the party and, in some cases, successfully to secede from it if one controls such an apparatus.

[. . .]

This more or less consistently developed bureaucracy now determines the behaviour of a party in normal times, including the decisively important choice of candidates. But even in such highly bureaucratised structures as the North American parties, as the last Presidential campaign showed, the charismatic type of leadership occasionally comes to the fore again in times of great excitement. If there is a 'hero' available, he seeks to break the domination of the party machine by imposing plebiscitary forms of designation, and in some cases by transforming the whole machinery of nomination. Whenever charisma gains the ascendancy in this way, it naturally runs up against the resistance of the normally dominant apparatus of the professional politicians, especially the bosses who organise leadership and finance and keep the party functioning and whose creatures the candidates usually are. For it is not only the place-hunters whose material interests depend on the selection of party candidates. The material interests of the party's patrons – banks, contractors and trusts – are also, of course, very deeply involved in the choice of persons. The large contributor who finances a charismatic party leader in particular cases and expects from his electoral success, according to circumstances, state commissions, tax-farming concessions, monopolies or other privileges, but above all the repayment of his advances with appropriate interest, has been a typical figure since the days of Crassus. On the other hand, however, the normal party organisation depends on the support of such patrons. The party's regular income from members' subscriptions and possibly deductions from the salaries of officials who have obtained their posts with the help of the party (as in North America) is seldom sufficient. Direct economic exploitation of the party's power may enrich those directly involved without necessarily filling the party's own coffers at the same time. Frequently, membership subscriptions are for propaganda purposes either abolished altogether or made to depend on self-assessment: when this happens the large contributors become, even in formal terms, the rulers of the party's finances. The regular leader of the party organisation and genuine specialised expert, the boss or party secretary, can only rely on their money completely, however, when he has firm control of the machinery of the party. Every upsurge of charisma is thus a threat to the regular organisation even from the financial point of view. We thus have the frequent spectacle of competing bosses or other leaders of rival parties agreeing amongst themselves in the common interests of business to suppress the rise of charismatic leaders who would be independent of the regular party machines.

It is as a rule easy for the party organisation to achieve this castration of charisma: in America it has been done successfully time and again, even in the conduct of the 'presidential primaries', with their plebiscitary and charismatic character, since the professional organisation, because of its very continuity, remains tactically more than a match for emotional hero-worship in the long run. Only extraordinary conditions can enable charisma to triumph over the organisation. The peculiar relationship of charisma and bureaucracy which split the English Liberal Party over the introduction of the first Home Rule Bill is well known: Gladstone's completely personal charisma, so irresistible in its appeal to puritan rationalism, forced the majority of the caucus-bureaucracy, in spite of the most determined hostility on specific points and dire forebodings about the election, to swing unconditionally behind him, so leading to the split in the machine created by Chamberlain and as a result to the loss of the electoral contest. The same kind of thing happened last year (1912) in America.

We can accept that the chances of charisma in its struggle with bureaucracy in a party depend to some extent on the general character of the party. The chances of charisma are very different in a simple 'unprincipled' party – that is, a party of place-hunters which formulates its programme *ad hoc* in the light of the opportunities offered by the particular electoral contest – from what they are in a party which is primarily an association of notables based purely on status, or a class party, or a party which to a greater extent still preserves its idealistic 'programme' or 'ideology' (all such contrasts being, of course, relative). In certain respects, its chances are greatest in a party which is primarily of the first type, since in such a party it is much easier for impressive personalities to win the necessary following, other things being equal, than in such petty bourgeois organisations of notables as the German parties, especially the liberal parties with their inflexible 'programmes' and 'ideologies', whose adaptations to temporary demagogic opportunities may always signify catastrophe. But it is impossible to generalise about this topic. Each individual case is affected by too close an association between the intrinsic laws of the particular party machine and the economic and social conditions prevailing in the concrete situation.

As these examples show, charismatic domination is by no means only to be found at primitive stages of development: the three basic types of structure of domination cannot simply be arranged in a linear order of development, but are found in the most varied combinations with each other. It must be admitted, however, that charisma is fated to decline as permanent institutional structures increasingly develop. In the early stages of social relationships, as far back as we can reach, every social action which goes beyond the provision of traditional needs in the household economy is charismatic in structure. Primitive man sees in all those influences which determine his life from the outside, the working of specific powers, which belong to things, animate or inanimate, and to men, dead as well as living, and give them power to act for good or ill.

The whole conceptual apparatus of primitive peoples, including their myths about nature and animals, proceeds on such assumptions. Such concepts as *mana* and *orenda*, as interpreted in ethnography, refer to such specific powers, which are 'supernatural' simply in the sense that they are not available to everyone, but are inseparable from their personal or material possessors. Every event which is out of the everyday run allows charismatic powers to blaze up, and every unusual capacity arouses charismatic beliefs, which then again lose some of their meaning in everyday routines. In normal times, the power of the village headman is extremely small: he is little more than an arbitrator and a representative. The members of the community generally speaking do not consider that they have an authentic right to depose him, because his power is based on charisma and not election. But on occasion they may desert him without hesitation and settle elsewhere. This sort of contempt for a king on account of his lack of charismatic qualification is found among the Germanic tribes. Anarchy, regulated only by continued observance of accepted custom, either through lack of thought or through fear of some ill-defined consequences of innovation, may be seen as almost the normal condition of primitive communities. Much the same is true in normal everyday conditions of the social power of the magicians. But when there is some special event – a great hunting expedition, a drought or other threat from the anger of the demons, but especially the danger of war – the charisma of the hero or magician is immediately able to begin to function. The charismatic leader in hunting or war is often a separate figure alongside the peacetime chief, who has primarily economic functions, and hence acts mainly as an arbitrator. If a permanent cult develops in order to influence the gods and demons, then the charismatic prophet and magician evolves into the priest. If the state of war becomes chronic, necessitating the technical development of military leadership to allow for the systematic training and recruitment of warriors, then the charismatic leader of the army becomes the king. The Frankish royal officials, the count and the *sakebaro*, were originally concerned only with military and financial matters: their other functions, especially the administration of justice, which had originally been left entirely to the old charismatic people's arbitrator, were not added until later.

The emergence of a class of war-princes as a permanent structure with a permanent apparatus marks a decisive step to the stage at which the concepts of 'king' and 'state' can appropriately be used, as opposed to that of the 'chief', who may, according to circumstances, exercise primarily economic functions in the interests of the communal economy and the economic regulation of the village or market community, or else may have primarily magical (cultic or medical) or judicial (originally arbitrational) functions. On the other hand, it is arbitrary to follow Nietzsche in making kingship and the state begin with the subjection of another tribe by a victorious people and the creation of a permanent apparatus to hold the subjects in dependence as tributaries. For precisely the same differentiation between those who are fit to serve as warriors and are exempted from tax and those who are not fit and so are liable to tax can easily develop within any tribe which is chronically under military threat – not necessarily in the form of patrimonial dependence of the latter on the former, but very often without that. The following of a chief can then join together into a military guild and exercise political rights as lords, so that an aristocracy of the feudal type emerges; or else the chief may increasingly begin to pay his followers, first in order to make raids for plunder, and then in order to rule the other members of his own people. (There are many examples of the latter, too.) What is true is that kingship is normally what results from the development of the charismatic war-prince into a permanent institution, with an apparatus of domination to control the unarmed subjects by force. Admittedly, and quite naturally, this apparatus is most rigidly developed in foreign territory acquired by conquest, where it is required by the constant threat to the ruling stratum. The Norman states, especially England, were not by accident the only Western feudal states with a genuinely centralised and technically developed administration, and the same is true of the Arabian, Sassanid and Turkish warrior-states, which were most rigidly organised on conquered territory. Exactly the same is true, moreover, in the area of hierocratic power. The rigidly organised centralisation of the Catholic Church developed in the mission-field of the West and was completed after the historic local powers of the Church had been destroyed by the French Revolution: the technical apparatus of the Church was created during its period as the 'church militant'. But royal and high-priestly power in itself may be found even without conquest or mission, if one sees the decisive characteristic as the permanent institutionalisation of domination and therefore the existence of a continuous apparatus of domination, be it bureaucratic, patrimonial or feudal in character.

(*Wirtschaft und Gesellschaft*, 4th edn, Tübingen, 1956, II, pp. 662–79. First published in 1922)

Note

1. And incidentally they correspond completely with each other also in the 'value'-sphere, which does not concern us here, in that they all – even artistic intuition – in order to make themselves objective and so in general to prove their reality, imply 'grasping', or, if it is preferred, being 'grasped' by the claims of the 'work', and not a subjective 'feeling' or 'experience' like any other.

2 The Work of Art in the Age of Mechanical Reproduction

Walter Benjamin

[...]

I

The artistic performance of a stage actor is definitely presented to the public by the actor in person; that of the screen actor, however, is presented by a camera, with a twofold consequence. The camera that presents the performance of the film actor to the public need not respect the performance as an integral whole. Guided by the cameraman, the camera continually changes its position with respect to the performance. The sequence of positional views which the editor composes from the material supplied him constitutes the completed film. It comprises certain factors of movement which are in reality those of the camera, not to mention special camera angles, close-ups, etc. Hence, the performance of the actor is subjected to a series of optical tests. This is the first consequence of the fact that the actor's performance is presented by means of a camera. Also, the film actor lacks the opportunity of the stage actor to adjust to the audience during his performance, since he does not present his performance to the audience in person. This permits the audience to take the position of a critic, without experiencing any personal contact with the actor. The audience's identification with the actor is really an identification with the camera. Consequently the audience takes the position of the camera; its approach is that of testing.[1] This is not the approach to which cult values may be exposed.

II

For the film, what matters primarily is that the actor represents himself to the public before the camera, rather than representing someone else. One of the first to sense the actor's metamorphosis by this form of testing was Pirandello. Though his remarks on the subject in his novel *Si Gira* were limited to the negative aspects of the question and to the silent film only, this hardly impairs their validity. For in this respect, the sound film did not change anything essential. What matters is that the part is acted not for an audience but for a mechanical contrivance—in the case of the sound film, for two of them. "The film actor," wrote Pirandello, "feels as if in exile—exiled not only from the stage but also from himself. With a vague sense of discomfort he feels inexplicable emptiness: his body loses its corporeality, it evaporates, it is deprived of reality, life, voice, and the noises caused by his moving about, in order to be changed into a mute image, flickering an instant on the screen, then vanishing into silence. . . The projector will play with his shadow before the public, and he himself must be content to play before the camera."* This situation might also be characterized as follows: for the first time—and this is the effect of the film—man has to operate with his whole living person, yet forgoing its aura. For aura is tied to his presence; there can be no replica of it. The aura which, on the stage, emanates from Macbeth, cannot be separated for the spectators from that of the actor. However, the singularity of the shot in the studio is that the camera is substituted for the public. Consequently, the aura that envelops the actor vanishes, and with it the aura of the figure he portrays.

It is not surprising that it should be a dramatist such as Pirandello who, in characterizing the film, inadvertently touches on the very crisis in which we see the theater. Any thorough study proves that there is indeed no greater contrast than that of the stage play to a work of art that is completely subject to or, like the film, founded in, mechanical reproduction. Experts have long recognized that in the film "the greatest effects are almost always obtained by 'acting' as little as possible. . . ." In 1932 Rudolf Arnheim saw "the latest trend . . . in treating the actor as a stage prop chosen for its characteristics and . . . inserted at the proper place."[2] With this idea something else is closely connected. The stage actor identifies himself with the character of his role. The film actor very often is denied this opportunity. His creation is by no means all of a piece; it is composed of many separate performances. Besides certain fortuitous considerations, such as cost of studio, availability of fellow players, décor, etc., there are elementary necessities of equipment that split the actor's work into a series of mountable episodes. In particular, lighting and its installation require the presentation of an event that, on the screen, unfolds as a rapid and unified scene, in a sequence of separate shootings which may take hours at the studio; not to mention more obvious montage. Thus a jump from the window can be shot in the studio as a jump from a scaffold, and the ensuing flight, if need be, can be shot weeks later when outdoor scenes are taken. Far more paradoxical cases can easily be construed. Let us assume that an actor is supposed to be startled by a knock at the door. If his reaction is not satisfactory, the director can resort to an expedient: when the actor happens to be at the studio again he has a shot fired behind him without his being forewarned of it. The frightened reaction can be shot now and be cut into the screen version. Nothing more strikingly shows that art has left the realm of the "beautiful semblance" which, so far, had been taken to be the only sphere where art could thrive.

III

The feeling of strangeness that overcomes the actor before the camera, as Pirandello describes it, is basically of the same kind as the estrangement felt before one's own

* Luigi Pirandello, *Si Gira*, quoted by Léon Pierre-Quint, "Signification du cinéma," *L'Art ciné-matographique, op. cit.*, pp. 14–15.

image in the mirror. But now the reflected image has become separable, transportable. And where is it transported? Before the public.[3] Never for a moment does the screen actor cease to be conscious of this fact. While facing the camera he knows that ultimately he will face the public, the consumers who constitute the market. This market, where he offers not only his labor but also his whole self, his heart and soul, is beyond his reach. During the shooting he has as little contact with it as any article made in a factory. This may contribute to that oppression, that new anxiety which, according to Pirandello, grips the actor before the camera. The film responds to the shriveling of the aura with an artificial build-up of the "personality" outside the studio. The cult of the movie star, fostered by the money of the film industry, preserves not the unique aura of the person but the "spell of the personality," the phony spell of a commodity. So long as the movie-makers' capital sets the fashion, as a rule no other revolutionary merit can be accredited to today's film than the promotion of a revolutionary criticism of traditional concepts of art. We do not deny that in some cases today's films can also promote revolutionary criticism of social conditions, even of the distribution of property. However, our present study is no more specifically concerned with this than is the film production of Western Europe.

It is inherent in the technique of the film as well as that of sports that everybody who witnesses its accomplishments is somewhat of an expert. This is obvious to anyone listening to a group of newspaper boys leaning on their bicycles and discussing the outcome of a bicycle race. It is not for nothing that newspaper publishers arrange races for their delivery boys. These arouse great interest among the participants, for the victor has an opportunity to rise from delivery boy to professional racer. Similarly, the newsreel offers everyone the opportunity to rise from passer-by to movie extra. In this way any man might even find himself part of a work of art, as witness Vertov's *Three Songs About Lenin* or Ivens' *Borinage*. Any man today can lay claim to being filmed. This claim can best be elucidated by a comparative look at the historical situation of contemporary literature.

For centuries a small number of writers were confronted by many thousands of readers. This changed toward the end of the last century. With the increasing extension of the press, which kept placing new political, religious, scientific, professional, and local organs before the readers, an increasing number of readers became writers—at first, occasional ones. It began with the daily press opening to its readers space for "letters to the editor." And today there is hardly a gainfully employed European who could not, in principle, find an opportunity to publish somewhere or other comments on his work, grievances, documentary reports, or that sort of thing. Thus, the distinction between author and public is about to lose its basic character. The difference becomes merely functional; it may vary from case to case. At any moment the reader is ready to turn into a writer. As expert, which he had to become willy-nilly in an extremely specialized work process, even if only in some minor respect, the reader gains access to authorship. In the Soviet Union work itself is given a voice. To present it verbally is part of a man's ability to perform the work. Literary license is now founded on polytechnic rather than specialized training and thus becomes common property.[4]

All this can easily be applied to the film, where transitions that in literature took centuries have come about in a decade. In cinematic practice, particularly in Russia, this change-over has partially become established reality. Some of the players whom we meet in Russian films are not actors in our sense but people who portray *themselves*—and primarily in their own work process. In Western Europe the capitalistic exploitation of the film denies consideration to modern man's legitimate claim to being reproduced. Under these circumstances the film industry is trying hard to spur the interest of the masses through illusion-promoting spectacles and dubious speculations.

IV

The shooting of a film, especially of a sound film, affords a spectacle unimaginable anywhere at any time before this. It presents a process in which it is impossible to assign to a spectator a viewpoint which would exclude from the actual scene such extraneous accessories as camera equipment, lighting machinery, staff assistants, etc.— unless his eye were on a line parallel with the lens. This circumstance, more than any other, renders superficial and insignificant any possible similarity between a scene in the studio and one on the stage. In the theater one is well aware of the place from which the play cannot immediately be detected as illusionary. There is no such place for the movie scene that is being shot. Its illusionary nature is that of the second degree, the result of cutting. That is to say, in the studio the mechanical equipment has penetrated so deeply into reality that its pure aspect freed from the foreign substance of equipment is the result of a special procedure, namely, the shooting by the specially adjusted camera and the mounting of the shot together with other similar ones. The equipment-free aspect of reality here has become the height of artifice; the sight of immediate reality has become an orchid in the land of technology.

Even more revealing is the comparison of these circumstances, which differ so much from those of the theater, with the situation in painting. Here the question is: How does the cameraman compare with the painter? To answer this we take recourse to an analogy with a surgical operation. The surgeon represents the polar opposite of the magician. The magician heals a sick person by the laying on of hands; the surgeon cuts into the patient's body. The magician maintains the natural distance between the patient and himself; though he reduces it very slightly by the laying on of hands, he greatly increases it by virtue of his authority. The surgeon does exactly the reverse; he greatly diminishes the distance between himself and the patient by penetrating into the patient's body, and increases it but little by the caution with which his hand moves among the organs. In short, in contrast to the magician—who is still hidden in the medical practitioner—the surgeon at the decisive moment abstains from facing the patient man to man; rather, it is through the operation that he penetrates into him.

Magician and surgeon compare to painter and cameraman. The painter maintains in his work a natural distance from reality, the cameraman penetrates deeply into its web.[5] There is a tremendous difference between the pictures they obtain. That of the painter is a total one, that of the cameraman consists of multiple fragments which are assembled under a new law. Thus, for contemporary man the representation of reality by the film is incomparably more significant than that of the painter, since it offers, precisely because of the thoroughgoing permeation of reality with mechanical equipment, an aspect of reality which is free of all equipment. And that is what one is entitled to ask from a work of art.

V

Mechanical reproduction of art changes the reaction of the masses toward art. The reactionary attitude toward a Picasso painting changes into the progressive reaction toward a Chaplin movie. The progressive reaction is characterized by the direct, intimate fusion of visual and emotional enjoyment with the orientation of the expert. Such fusion is of great social significance. The greater the decrease in the social significance of an art form, the sharper the distinction between criticism and enjoyment by the public. The conventional is uncritically enjoyed, and the truly new is criticized with aversion. With regard to the screen, the critical and the receptive attitudes of the public coincide. The decisive reason for this is that individual reactions are predetermined by the mass audience response they are about to produce, and this is nowhere more pronounced than in the film. The moment these responses become manifest they control each other. Again, the comparison with painting is fruitful. A painting has always had an excellent chance to be viewed by one person or by a few. The simultaneous contemplation of paintings by a large public, such as developed in the nineteenth century, is an early symptom of the crisis of painting, a crisis which was by no means occasioned exclusively by photography but rather in a relatively independent manner by the appeal of art works to the masses.

Painting simply is in no position to present an object for simultaneous collective experience, as it was possible for architecture at all times, for the epic poem in the past, and for the movie today. Although this circumstance in itself should not lead one to conclusions about the social role of painting, it does constitute a serious threat as soon as painting, under special conditions and, as it were, against its nature, is confronted directly by the masses. In the churches and monasteries of the Middle Ages and at the princely courts up to the end of the eighteenth century, a collective reception of paintings did not occur simultaneously, but by graduated and hierarchized mediation. The change that has come about is an expression of the particular conflict in which painting was implicated by the mechanical reproducibility of paintings. Although paintings began to be publicly exhibited in galleries and salons, there was no way for the masses to organize and control themselves in their reception.[6] Thus the same public which responds in a progressive manner toward a grotesque film is bound to respond in a reactionary manner to surrealism.

VI

The characteristics of the film lie not only in the manner in which man presents himself to mechanical equipment but also in the manner in which, by means of this apparatus, man can represent his environment. A glance at occupational psychology illustrates the testing capacity of the equipment. Psychoanalysis illustrates it in a different perspective. The film has enriched our field of perception with methods which can be illustrated by those of Freudian theory. Fifty years ago, a slip of the tongue passed more or less unnoticed. Only exceptionally may such a slip have revealed dimensions of depth in a conversation which had seemed to be taking its course on the surface. Since the *Psychopathology of Everyday Life* things have changed. This book isolated and made analyzable things which had heretofore floated along unnoticed in the broad stream of perception. For the entire spectrum of optical, and now also acoustical, perception the film has brought about a similar deepening of apperception. It is only an obverse of this fact that behavior items shown in a movie can be analyzed much more precisely and from more points of view than those presented on paintings or on the stage. As compared with painting, filmed behavior lends itself more readily to analysis because of its incomparably more precise statements of the situation. In comparison with the stage scene, the filmed behavior item lends itself more readily to analysis because it can be isolated more easily. This circumstance derives its chief importance from its tendency to promote the mutual penetration of art and science. Actually, of a screened behavior item which is neatly brought out in a certain situation, like a muscle of a body, it is difficult to say which is more fascinating, its artistic value or its value for science. To demonstrate the identity of the artistic and scientific uses of photography which heretofore usually were separated will be one of the revolutionary functions of the film.[7]

By close-ups of the things around us, by focusing on hidden details of familiar objects, by exploring commonplace milieus under the ingenious guidance of the camera, the film, on the one hand, extends our comprehension of the necessities which rule our lives; on the other hand, it manages to assure us of an immense and unexpected field of action. Our taverns and our metropolitan streets, our offices and furnished rooms, our railroad stations and our factories appeared to have us locked up hopelessly. Then came the film and burst this prison-world asunder by the dynamite of the tenth of a second, so that now, in the midst of its far-flung ruins and debris, we calmly and adventurously go traveling. With the close-up, space expands; with slow motion, movement is extended. The enlargement of a snapshot does not simply render more precise what in any case was visible, though unclear: it reveals entirely new structural formations of the subject. So, too, slow motion not only presents familiar qualities of movement but reveals in them entirely unknown ones "which, far from looking like retarded rapid movements, give the effect of singularly gliding, floating, supernatural motions."* Evidently a different nature opens itself to the camera than opens to the naked eye—if only because an unconsciously penetrated space is substituted for a space consciously explored by man. Even if one has a general knowledge of the way people walk, one knows nothing of a person's posture during the fractional second of a stride. The act of reaching for a lighter or a spoon is familiar routine, yet we hardly know what really goes on between hand and metal, not to mention how this fluctuates with our moods. Here the camera intervenes with the resources of its lowerings and liftings, its interruptions and isolations, its extensions and accelerations, its enlargements and reductions. The camera introduces us to unconscious optics as does psychoanalysis to unconscious impulses.

Notes

1. "The film . . . provides—or could provide—useful insight into the details of human actions. . . . Character is never used as a source of motivation; the inner life of the persons never supplies the principal cause of the plot and seldom is its main result."

* Rudolf Arnheim, *loc. cit.*, p. 138.

(Bertolt Brecht, *Versuche*, "Der Dreigroschenprozess," p. 268.) The expansion of the field of the testable which mechanical equipment brings about for the actor corresponds to the extraordinary expansion of the field of the testable brought about for the individual through economic conditions. Thus, vocational aptitude tests become constantly more important. What matters in these tests are segmental performances of the individual. The film shot and the vocational aptitude test are taken before a committee of experts. The camera director in the studio occupies a place identical with that of the examiner during aptitude tests.

2. Rudolf Arnheim, *Film als Kunst*, Berlin, 1932, pp. 176 f. In this context certain seemingly unimportant details in which the film director deviates from stage practices gain in interest. Such is the attempt to let the actor play without make-up, as made among others by Dreyer in his *Jeanne d'Arc*. Dreyer spent months seeking the forty actors who constitute the Inquisitors' tribunal. The search for these actors resembled that for stage properties that are hard to come by. Dreyer made every effort to avoid resemblances of age, build, and physiognomy. If the actor thus becomes a stage property, this latter, on the other hand, frequently functions as actor. At least it is not unusual for the film to assign a role to the stage property. Instead of choosing at random from a great wealth of examples, let us concentrate on a particularly convincing one. A clock that is working will always be a disturbance on the stage. There it cannot be permitted its function of measuring time. Even in a naturalistic play, astronomical time would clash with theatrical time. Under these circumstances it is highly revealing that the film can, whenever appropriate, use time as measured by a clock. From this more than from many other touches it may clearly be recognized that under certain circumstances each and every prop in a film may assume important functions. From here it is but one step to Pudovkin's statement that "the playing of an actor which is connected with an object and is built around it...is always one of the strongest methods of cinematic construction." (W. Pudovkin, *Filmregie and Filmmanuskript*, Berlin, 1928, p. 126.) The film is the first art form capable of demonstrating how matter plays tricks on man. Hence, films can be an excellent means of materialistic representation.

3. The change noted here in the method of exhibition caused by mechanical reproduction applies to politics as well. The present crisis of the bourgeois democracies comprises a crisis of the conditions which determine the public presentation of the rulers. Democracies exhibit a member of government directly and personally before the nation's representatives. Parliament is his public. Since the innovations of camera and recording equipment make it possible for the orator to become audible and visible to an unlimited number of persons, the presentation of the man of politics before camera and recording equipment becomes paramount. Parliaments, as much as theaters, are deserted. Radio and film not only affect the function of the professional actor but likewise the function of those who also exhibit themselves before this mechanical equipment, those who govern. Though their tasks may be different, the change affects equally the actor and the ruler. The trend is toward establishing controllable and transferrable skills under certain social conditions. This results in a new selection, a selection before the equipment from which the star and the dictator emerge victorious.

4. The privileged character of the respective techniques is lost. Aldous Huxley writes:

> "Advances in technology have led...to vulgarity....Process reproduction and the rotary press have made possible the indefinite multiplication of writing and pictures.

Universal education and relatively high wages have created an enormous public who know how to read and can afford to buy reading and pictorial matter. A great industry has been called into existence in order to supply these commodities. Now, artistic talent is a very rare phenomenon; whence it follows...that, at every epoch and in all countries, most art has been bad. But the proportion of trash in the total artistic output is greater now than at any other period. That it must be so is a matter of simple arithmetic. The population of Western Europe has a little more than doubled during the last century. But the amount of reading—and seeing—matter has increased, I should imagine, at least twenty and possibly fifty or even a hundred times. If there were n men of talent in a population of x millions, there will presumably be 2n men of talent among 2x millions. The situation may be summed up thus. For every page of print and pictures published a century ago, twenty or perhaps even a hundred pages are published today. But for every man of talent then living, there are now only two men of talent. It may be of course that, thanks to universal education, many potential talents which in the past would have been stillborn are now enabled to realize themselves. Let us assume, then, that there are now three or even four men of talent to every one of earlier times. It still remains true to say that the consumption of reading—and seeing—matter has far outstripped the natural production of gifted writers and draughtsmen. It is the same with hearing-matter. Prosperity, the gramophone and the radio have created an audience of hearers who consume an amount of hearing-matter that has increased out of all proportion to the increase of population and the consequent natural increase of talented musicians. It follows from all this that in all the arts the output of trash is both absolutely and relatively greater than it was in the past; and that it must remain greater for just so long as the world continues to consume the present inordinate quantities of reading-matter, seeing-matter, and hearing-matter."— Aldous Huxley, *Beyond the Mexique Bay. A Traveller's Journal*, London, 1949, pp. 274 ff. First published in 1934.

This mode of observation is obviously not progressive.

5. The boldness of the cameraman is indeed comparable to that of the surgeon. Luc Durtain lists among specific technical sleights of hand those "which are required in surgery in the case of certain difficult operations. I choose as an example a case from oto-rhino-laryngology;...the so-called endonasal perspective procedure; or I refer to the acrobatic tricks of larynx surgery which have to be performed following the reversed picture in the laryngoscope. I might also speak of ear surgery which suggests the precision work of watchmakers. What range of the most subtle muscular acrobatics is required from the man who wants to repair or save the human body! We have only to think of the couching of a cataract where there is virtually a debate of steel with nearly fluid tissue, or of the major abdominal operations (laparotomy)."—Luc Durtain, *op. cit.*

6. This mode of observation may seem crude, but as the great theoretician Leonardo has shown, crude modes of observation may at times be usefully adduced. Leonardo compares painting and music as follows: "Painting is superior to music because, unlike unfortunate music, it does not have to die as soon as it is born....Music which is consumed in the very act of its birth is inferior to painting which the use of varnish has rendered eternal." (Trattato I, 29.)

7. Renaissance painting offers a revealing analogy to this situation. The incomparable development of this art and its significance rested not least on the integration of a number of new sciences, or at least of new scientific data. Renaissance painting made use of anatomy and perspective, of mathematics, meteorology, and chromatology. Valéry writes: "What could be further from us than the strange claim of a Leonardo to whom painting was a supreme goal and the ultimate demonstration of knowledge? Leonardo was convinced that painting demanded universal knowledge, and he did not even shrink from a theoretical analysis which to us is stunning because of its very depth and precision...."—Paul Valéry, *Pièces sur l'art*, "Autour de Corot," Paris, p. 191.

3 The Culture Industry: Enlightenment as Mass Deception

Theodor W. Adorno and Max Horkheimer

[…]

Real life is becoming indistinguishable from the movies. The sound film, far surpassing the theater of illusion, leaves no room for imagination or reflection on the part of the audience, who is unable to respond within the structure of the film, yet deviate from its precise detail without losing the thread of the story; hence the film forces its victims to equate it directly with reality. The stunting of the mass-media consumer's powers of imagination and spontaneity does not have to be traced back to any psychological mechanisms; he must ascribe the loss of those attributes to the objective nature of the products themselves, especially to the most characteristic of them, the sound film. They are so designed that quickness, powers of observation, and experience are undeniably needed to apprehend them at all; yet sustained thought is out of the question if the spectator is not to miss the relentless rush of facts. Even though the effort required for his response is semi-automatic, no scope is left for the imagination. Those who are so absorbed by the world of the movie—by its images, gestures, and words—that they are unable to supply what really makes it a world, do not have to dwell on particular points of its mechanics during a screening. All the other films and products of the entertainment industry which they have seen have taught them what to expect; they react automatically. The might of industrial society is lodged in men's minds. The entertainments manufacturers know that their products will be consumed with alertness even when the customer is distraught, for each of them is a model of the huge economic machinery which has always sustained the masses, whether at work or at leisure—which is akin to work. From every sound film and every broadcast program the social effect can be inferred which is exclusive to none but is shared by all alike. The culture industry as a whole has molded men as a type unfailingly reproduced in every product. All the agents of this process, from the producer to the women's clubs, take good care that the simple reproduction of this mental state is not nuanced or extended in any way.

[…]

As naturally as the ruled always took the morality imposed upon them more seriously than did the rulers themselves, the deceived masses are today captivated by the myth of success even more than the successful are. Immovably, they insist on the very ideology which enslaves them. The misplaced love of the common people for the wrong which is done them is a greater force than the cunning of the authorities. It is stronger even than the rigorism of the Hays Office, just as in certain great times in history it has inflamed greater forces that were turned against it, namely, the terror of the tribunals. It calls for Mickey Rooney in preference to the tragic Garbo, for Donald Duck instead of Betty Boop. The industry submits to the vote which it has itself inspired. What is a loss for the firm which cannot fully exploit a contract with a declining star is a legitimate expense for the system as a whole. By craftily sanctioning the demand for rubbish it inaugurates total harmony. The connoisseur and the expert are despised for their pretentious claim to know better than the others, even though culture is democratic and distributes its privileges to all. In view of the ideological truce, the conformism of the buyers and the effrontery of the producers who supply them prevail. The result is a constant reproduction of the same thing.

[…]

The culture industry remains the entertainment business. Its influence over the consumers is established by entertainment; that will ultimately be broken not by an outright decree, but by the hostility inherent in the principle of entertainment to what is greater than itself. Since all the trends of the culture industry are profoundly embedded in the public by the whole social process, they are encouraged by the survival of the market in this area. Demand has not yet been replaced by simple obedience. As is well known, the major reorganization of the film industry shortly before the First World War, the material prerequisite of its expansion, was precisely its deliberate acceptance of the public's needs as recorded at the box-office—a procedure which was hardly thought necessary in the pioneering days of the screen. The same opinion is held today by the captains of the film industry, who take as their criterion the more or less phenomenal song hits but wisely never have recourse to the judgment of truth, the opposite criterion. Business is their ideology. It is quite correct that the power of the culture industry resides in its identification with a manufactured need, and not in simple contrast to it, even if this contrast were one of complete power and complete powerlessness. Amusement under late capitalism is the prolongation of work. It is sought after as an escape from the mechanized work process, and to recruit strength in order to be able to cope with it again. But at the same time mechanization has such power over a man's leisure and happiness, and so profoundly determines the manufacture of amusement goods, that his experiences are inevitably after-images of the work process itself. The ostensible content is merely a faded foreground; what sinks in is the automatic succession of standardized operations. What happens at work, in the factory, or in the office can only be escaped from by approximation to it in one's leisure time. All amusement suffers from this incurable malady. Pleasure hardens into boredom because, if it is to remain pleasure, it must not demand any effort and therefore moves rigorously in the worn grooves of association. No independent thinking must be expected from the audience: the product prescribes every reaction: not by its natural structure (which collapses under reflection), but by signals. Any logical connection calling for mental effort is painstakingly avoided. As far as possible, developments must follow from the immediately preceding situation and never from the idea of the whole. For the attentive movie-goer any individual scene will give him the whole thing. Even the set pattern itself still seems dangerous, offering some meaning—wretched as it might be—where only meaninglessness is acceptable. Often the plot is maliciously deprived of the development demanded by characters and matter according to the old pattern. Instead, the next step is what the script writer takes to be the most striking effect in the particular situation. Banal though elaborate surprise interrupts the story-line. The tendency mischievously to fall back on pure nonsense, which was a legitimate part of popular art, farce and clowning, right up to Chaplin and the Marx Brothers, is most obvious in the unpretentious kinds. This tendency has completely asserted itself in the text of the novelty song, in the thriller movie, and in cartoons, although in films starring Greer Garson and Bette Davis the unity of the socio-psychological case study provides something approximating a claim to a consistent plot. The idea itself, together with the objects of comedy and terror, is massacred and fragmented. Novelty songs have always existed on a contempt for meaning which, as predecessors and successors of psychoanalysis, they reduce to the monotony of sexual symbolism. Today detective and adventure films no longer give the audience the opportunity to experience the resolution. In the non-ironic varieties of the genre, it has also to rest content with the simple horror of situations which have almost ceased to be linked in any way.

Cartoons were once exponents of fantasy as opposed to rationalism. They ensured that justice was done to the creatures and objects they electrified, by giving the maimed specimens a second life. All they do today is to confirm the victory of technological reason over truth. A few years ago they had a consistent plot which only broke up in the final moments in a crazy chase, and thus resembled the old slapstick comedy. Now, however, time relations have shifted. In the very first sequence a motive is stated so that in the course of the action destruction can get to work on it: with the audience in pursuit, the protagonist becomes the worthless object of general violence. The quantity of organized amusement changes into the quality of organized cruelty. The self-elected censors of the film industry (with whom it enjoys a close relationship) watch over the unfolding of the crime, which is as drawn-out as a hunt. Fun replaces the pleasure which the sight of an embrace would allegedly afford, and postpones satisfaction till the day of the pogrom. In so far as cartoons do any more than accustom the senses to the new tempo, they hammer into every brain the old lesson that continuous friction, the breaking down of all individual resistance, is the condition of life in this society. Donald Duck in the cartoons and the unfortunate in real life get their thrashing so that the audience can learn to take their own punishment.

The enjoyment of the violence suffered by the movie character turns into violence against the spectator, and distraction into exertion. Nothing that the experts have devised as a stimulant must escape the weary eye; no stupidity is allowed in the face of all the trickery; one has to follow everything and even display the smart responses shown and recommended in the film. This raises the question whether the culture industry fulfills the function of diverting minds which it boasts about so loudly. If most of the radio stations and movie theaters were closed down, the consumers would probably not lose so very much. To walk from the street into the movie theater is no longer to enter a world of dream; as soon as the very existence of these institutions no longer made it obligatory to use them, there would be no great urge to do so. Such closures would not be reactionary machine wrecking. The disappointment would be felt not so much by the enthusiasts as by the slow-witted, who are the ones who suffer for every-thing anyhow. In spite of the films which are intended to complete her integration, the housewife finds in the darkness of the movie theater a place of refuge where she can sit for a few hours with nobody watching, just as she used to look out of the window when there were still homes and rest in the evening. The unemployed in the great cities find coolness in summer and warmth in winter in these temperature-controlled locations. Otherwise, despite its size, this bloated pleasure apparatus adds no dignity to man's lives. The idea of "fully exploiting" available technical resources and the facilities for aesthetic mass consumption is part of the economic system which refuses to exploit resources to abolish hunger.

The culture industry perpetually cheats its consumers of what it perpetually promises. The promissory note which, with its plots and staging, it draws on pleasure is endlessly prolonged; the promise, which is actually all the spectacle consists of, is illusory: all it actually confirms is that the real point will never be reached, that the diner must be satisfied with the menu. In front of the appetite stimulated by all those brilliant names and images there is finally set no more than a commendation of the depressing everyday world it sought to escape. Of course works of art were not sexual exhibitions either. However, by representing deprivation as negative, they retracted, as it were, the prostitution of the impulse and rescued by mediation what was denied. The secret of aesthetic sublimation is its representation of fulfillment as a broken promise. The culture industry does not sublimate; it represses. By repeatedly exposing the objects of desire, breasts in a clinging sweater or the naked torso of the athletic hero, it only stimulates the unsublimated forepleasure which habitual deprivation has long since reduced to a masochistic semblance. There is no erotic situation which, while insinuating and exciting, does not fail to indicate unmistakably that things can never go that far. The Hays Office merely confirms the ritual of Tantalus that the culture industry has established anyway. Works of art are ascetic and unashamed; the culture industry is pornographic and prudish. Love is down-graded to romance. And, after the descent, much is permitted; even license as a marketable speciality has its quota bearing the trade description "daring." The mass production of the sexual automatically achieves its repression. Because of his ubiquity, the film star with whom one is meant to fall in love is from the outset a copy of himself. Every tenor voice comes to sound like a Caruso record, and the "natural" faces of Texas girls are like the successful models by whom Hollywood has typecast them. The mechanical reproduction of beauty, which reactionary cultural fanaticism wholeheartedly serves in its methodical idolization of individuality, leaves no room for that unconscious idolatry which was once essential to beauty. The triumph over beauty is celebrated by humor—the *Schadenfreude* that every successful deprivation calls forth. There is laughter because there is nothing to laugh at. Laughter, whether conciliatory or terrible, always occurs when some fear passes. It indicates liberation either from physical danger or from the grip of logic. Conciliatory laughter is heard as the echo of an escape from power; the wrong kind overcomes fear by capitulating to the forces which are to be feared. It is the echo of power as something inescapable. Fun is a medicinal bath. The pleasure industry never fails to prescribe it. It makes laughter the instrument of the fraud practised on happiness. Moments of happiness are without laughter; only operettas and films portray sex to the accompaniment of resounding laughter. But Baudelaire is as devoid of humour as Hölderlin. In the false society laughter is a disease which has attacked happiness and is drawing it into its worthless totality. To laugh at something is always to deride it, and the life which, according to Bergson, in laughter breaks through the barrier, is actually an invading barbaric life, self-assertion prepared to parade its liberation from any scruple when the social occasion arises. Such a laughing audience is a parody of humanity. Its members are monads, all dedicated to the pleasure of being ready for anything at the expense of everyone else. Their harmony is a caricature of solidarity.

[...]

Amusement, if released from every restraint, would not only be the antithesis of art but its extreme role. The Mark Twain absurdity with which the American culture industry flirts at times might be a corrective of art. The more seriously the latter regards the incompatibility with life, the more it resembles the seriousness of life, its antithesis; the more effort it devotes to developing wholly from its own formal law, the more effort it demands from the intelligence to neutralize its burden. In some revue films, and especially in the grotesque and the funnies, the possibility of this negation does glimmer for a few moments. But of course it cannot happen. Pure amusement in its consequence, relaxed self-surrender to all kinds of associations and happy nonsense, is cut short by the amusement on the market: instead, it is interrupted by a surrogate overall meaning which the culture industry insists on giving to its products, and yet misuses as a mere pretext for bringing in the stars. Biographies and other simple stories patch the fragments of non-sense into an idiotic plot. We do not have the cap and bells of the jester but the bunch of keys of capitalist reason, which even screens the pleasure of achieving success. Every kiss in the revue film has to contribute to the career of the boxer, or some hit song expert or other whose rise to fame is being glorified. The deception is not that the culture industry supplies amusement but that it ruins the fun by allowing business considerations to involve it in the ideological clichés of a culture in the process of self-liquidation. Ethics and taste cut short unrestrained amusement as "naïve"—naïveté is thought to be as bad as intellectualism—and even restrict technical possibilities. The culture industry is corrupt; not because it is a sinful Babylon but because it is a cathedral dedicated to elevated pleasure. On all levels, from Hemingway to Emil Ludwig, from Mrs. Miniver to the Lone Ranger, from Toscanini to Guy Lombardo, there is untruth in the intellectual content taken ready-made from art and science. The culture industry does retain a trace of something better in those features which bring it close to the circus, in the self-justifying and nonsensical skill of riders, acrobats and clowns, in the "defense and justification of physical as against intellectual art."[1] But the refuges of a mindless artistry which represents what is human as opposed to the social mechanism are being relentlessly hunted down by a schematic reason which compels everything to prove its significance and effect. The consequence is that the nonsensical at the bottom disappears as utterly as the sense in works of art at the top.

The fusion of culture and entertainment that is taking place today leads not only to a depravation of culture, but inevitably to an intellectualization of amusement. This is evident from the fact that only the copy appears: in the movie theater, the photograph; on the radio, the recording. In the age of liberal expansion, amusement lived on the unshaken belief in the future: things would remain as they were and even improve. Today this belief is once more intellectualized; it becomes so faint that it loses sight of any goal and is little more than a magic-lantern show for those with their backs to reality. It consists of the meaningful emphases which, parallel to life itself, the screen play puts on the smart fellow, the engineer, the capable girl, ruthlessness disguised as character, interest in sport, and finally automobiles and cigarettes, even where the entertainment is not put down to the advertising account of the immediate producers but to that of the system as a whole. Amusement itself becomes an ideal, taking the place of the higher things of which it completely deprives the masses by repeating them in a manner even more stereotyped than the slogans paid for by advertising interests. Inwardness, the subjectively restricted form of truth, was always more at the mercy of the outwardly powerful than they imagined. The culture industry turns it into an open lie. It has now become mere twaddle which is acceptable in religious bestsellers, psychological films, and women's serials as an embarrassingly agreeable garnish, so that genuine personal emotion in real life can be all the more reliably controlled. In this sense amusement carries out that purgation of the emotions which Aristotle once attributed to tragedy and Mortimer Adler now allows to movies.

The stronger the positions of the culture industry become, the more summarily it can deal with consumers' needs, producing them, controlling them, disciplining them, and even withdrawing amusement: no limits are set to cultural progress of this kind. But the tendency is immanent in the principle of amusement itself, which is enlightened in a bourgeois sense. If the need for amusement was in large measure the creation of industry, which used the subject as a means of recommending the work to the masses—the oleograph by the dainty morsel it depicted, or the cake mix by a picture of a cake—amusement always reveals the influence of business, the sales talk, the quack's spiel. But the original affinity of business and amusement is shown in the latter's specific significance: to defend society. To be pleased means to say Yes. It is possible only by insulation from the totality of the social process, by desensitization and, from the first, by senselessly sacrificing the inescapable claim of every work, however inane, within its limits to reflect the whole. Pleasure always means not to think about anything, to forget suffering even where it is shown. Basically it is helplessness. It is flight; not, as is asserted, flight from a wretched reality, but from the last remaining thought of resistance. The liberation which amusement promises is freedom from thought and from negation. The effrontery of the rhetorical question, "What do people want?" lies in the fact that it is addressed—as if to reflective individuals—to those very people who are deliberately to be deprived of this individuality. Even when the public does—exceptionally—rebel against the pleasure industry, all it can muster is that feeble resistance which that very industry has inculcated in it. Nevertheless, it has become increasingly difficult to keep people in this condition. The rate at which they are reduced to stupidity must not fall behind the rate at which their intelligence is increasing. In this age of statistics the masses are too sharp to identify themselves with the millionaire on the screen, and too slow-witted to ignore the law of the largest number. Ideology conceals itself in the calculation of probabilities. Not everyone will be lucky one day—but the person who draws the winning ticket, or rather the one who is marked out to do so by a higher power—usually by the pleasure industry itself, which is represented as unceasingly in search of talent. Those discovered by talent scouts and then publicized on a vast scale by the studio are ideal types of the new dependent average. Of course, the starlet is meant to symbolize the typist in such a way that the splendid evening dress seems meant for the actress as distinct from the real girl. The girls in the audience not only feel that they could be on the screen, but realize the great gulf separating them from it. Only one girl can draw the lucky ticket, only one man can win the prize, and if, mathematically, all have the same chance, yet this is so infinitesimal for each one that he or she will do best to write it off and rejoice in the other's success, which might just as well have been his or hers, and somehow never is. Whenever the culture industry still issues an invitation naïvely to identify, it is immediately withdrawn. No one can escape from himself any more. Once a member of the audience could see his own wedding in the one shown in the film. Now the lucky actors on the screen are copies of the same category as every member of the public, but such equality only demonstrates the insurmountable separation of the human elements. The perfect similarity is the absolute difference. The identity of the category forbids that of the individual cases. Ironically, man as a member of a species has been made a reality by the culture industry. Now any person signifies only those attributes by which he can replace everybody else: he is interchangeable, a copy. As an individual he is completely expendable and utterly insignificant, and this is just what he finds out when time deprives him of this similarity.

[...]

The culture industry tends to make itself the embodiment of authoritative pronouncements, and thus the irrefutable prophet of the prevailing order. It skilfully steers a winding course between the cliffs of demonstrable misinformation and manifest truth, faithfully reproducing the phenomenon whose opaqueness blocks any insight and installs the ubiquitous and intact phenomenon as ideal. Ideology is split into the photograph of stubborn life and the naked lie about its meaning—which is not expressed but suggested and yet drummed in. To demonstrate its divine nature, reality is always repeated in a purely cynical way. Such a photological proof is of course not stringent, but it is overpowering. Anyone who doubts the power of monotony is a fool. The culture industry refutes the objection made against it just as well as that against the world which it impartially duplicates. The only choice is either to join in or to be left behind: those provincials who have recourse to eternal beauty and the amateur stage in preference to the cinema and the radio are already—politically—at the point to which mass culture drives its supporters. It is sufficiently hardened to deride as ideology, if need be, the old wish-fulfillments, the father-ideal and absolute feeling. The new ideology has as its objects the world as such. It makes use of the worship of facts by no more than elevating a disagreeable existence into the world of facts in representing it meticulously. This transference makes existence itself a substitute for meaning and right. Whatever the camera reproduces is beautiful. The disappointment of the prospect that one might be the typist who wins the world trip is matched by the disappointing appearance of the accurately photographed areas which the voyage might include. Not Italy is offered, but evidence that it exists. A film can even go so far as to show the Paris in which the American girl thinks she will still her desire as a hopelessly desolate place, thus driving her the more inexorably into the arms of the smart American boy she could have met at home anyhow. That this goes on, that, in its most recent phase, the system itself reproduces the life of those of whom it consists instead of immediately doing away with them, is even put down to its credit as giving it meaning and worth. Continuing and continuing to join in are given as justification for the blind persistence of the system and even for its immutability. What repeats itself is healthy, like the natural or industrial cycle. The same babies grin eternally out of the magazines; the jazz machine will pound away for ever. In spite of all the progress in reproduction techniques, in controls and the specialities, and in spite of all the restless industry, the bread which the culture industry offers man is the stone of the stereotype. It draws on the life cycle, on the well-founded amazement that mothers, in spite of everything, still go on bearing children and that the wheels still do not grind to a halt. This serves to confirm the immutability of circumstances. The ears of corn blowing in the wind at the end of Chaplin's *The Great Dictator* give the lie to the anti-Fascist plea for freedom. They are like the blond hair of the German girl whose camp life is photographed by the Nazi film company in the summer breeze. Nature is viewed by the mechanism of social domination as a healthy contrast to society, and is therefore denatured. Pictures showing green trees, a blue sky, and moving clouds make these aspects of nature into so many cryptograms for factory chimneys and service stations. On the other hand, wheels and machine components must seem expressive, having been degraded to the status of agents of the spirit of trees and clouds. Nature and technology are mobilized against all opposition; and we have a falsified memento of liberal society, in which people supposedly wallowed in erotic plush-lined bedrooms instead of taking open-air baths as in the case today, or experiencing breakdowns in prehistoric Benz models instead of shooting off with the speed of a rocket from A (where one is anyhow) to B (where everything is just the same). The triumph of the gigantic concern over the initiative of the entrepreneur is praised by the culture industry as the persistence of entrepreneurial initiative. The enemy who is already defeated, the thinking individual, is the enemy fought.

[…]

The morality of mass culture is the cheap form of yesterday's children's books. In a first-class production, for example, the villainous character appears as a hysterical woman who (with presumed clinical accuracy) tries to ruin the happiness of her opposite number, who is truer to reality, and herself suffers a quite untheatrical death. So much learning is of course found only at the top. Lower down less trouble is taken. Tragedy is made harmless without recourse to social psychology. Just as every Viennese operetta worthy of the name had to have its tragic finale in the second act, which left nothing for the third except to clear up misunderstandings, the culture industry assigns tragedy a fixed place in the routine. The well-known existence of the recipe is enough to allay any fear that there is no restraint on tragedy. The description of the dramatic formula by the housewife as "getting into trouble and out again" embraces the whole of mass culture from the idiotic women's serial to the top production. Even the worst ending which began with good intentions confirms the order of things and corrupts the tragic force, either because the woman whose love runs counter to the laws of the game plays with her death for a brief spell of happiness, or because the sad ending in the film all the more clearly stresses the indestructibility of actual life. The tragic film becomes an institution for moral improvement. The masses, demoralized by their life under the pressure of the system, and who show signs of civilization only in modes of behavior which have been forced on them and through which fury and recalcitrance show everywhere, are to be kept in order by the sight of an inexorable life and exemplary behavior. Culture has always played its part in taming revolutionary and barbaric instincts. Industrial culture adds its contribution. It shows the condition under which this merciless life can be lived at all. The individual who is thoroughly weary must use his weariness as energy for his surrender to the collective power which wears him out. In films, those permanently desperate situations which crush the spectator in ordinary life somehow become a promise that one can go on living. One has only to become aware of one's own nothingness, only to recognize defeat and one is one with it all.

[...]

In the culture industry the individual is an illusion not merely because of the standardization of the means of production. He is tolerated only so long as his complete identification with the generality is unquestioned. Pseudo individuality is rife: from the standardized jazz improvization to the exceptional film star whose hair curls over her eye to demonstrate her originality. What is individual is no more than the generality's power to stamp the accidental detail so firmly that it is accepted as such. The defiant reserve or elegant appearance of the individual on show is mass-produced like Yale locks, whose only difference can be measured in fractions of millimeters. The peculiarity of the self is a monopoly commodity determined by society; it is falsely represented as natural. It is no more than the moustache, the French accent, the deep voice of the woman of the world, the Lubitsch touch: finger prints on identity cards which are otherwise exactly the same, and into which the lives and faces of every single person are transformed by the power of the generality. Pseudo individuality is the prerequisite for comprehending tragedy and removing its poison: only because individuals have ceased to be themselves and are now merely centers where the general tendencies meet, is it possible to receive them again, whole and entire, into the generality. In this way mass culture discloses the fictitious character of the "individual" in the bourgeois era, and is merely unjust in boasting on account of this dreary harmony of general and particular. The principle of individuality was always full of contradiction. Individuation has never really been achieved. Self-preservation in the shape of class has kept everyone at the stage of a mere species being. Every bourgeois characteristic, in spite of its deviation and indeed because of it, expressed the same thing: the harshness of the competitive society. The individual who supported society bore its disfiguring mark; seemingly free, he was actually the product of its economic and social apparatus. Power based itself on the prevailing conditions of power when it sought the approval of persons affected by it. As it progressed, bourgeois society did also develop the individual. Against the will of its leaders, technology has changed human beings from children into persons. However, every advance in individuation of this kind took place at the expense of the individuality in whose name it occurred, so that nothing was left but the resolve to pursue one's own particular purpose. The bourgeois whose existence is split into a business and a private life, whose private life is split into keeping up his public image and intimacy, whose intimacy is split into the surly partnership of marriage and the bitter comfort of being quite alone, at odds with himself and everybody else, is already virtually a Nazi, replete both with enthusiasm and abuse; or a modern city-dweller who can now only imagine friendship as a "social contact": that is, as being in social contact with others with whom he has no inward contact. The only reason why the culture industry can deal so successfully with individuality is that the latter has always reproduced the fragility of society. On the faces of private individuals and movie heroes put together according to the patterns on magazine covers vanishes a pretense in which no one now believes; the popularity of the hero models comes partly from a secret satisfaction that the effort to achieve individuation has at last been replaced by the effort to imitate, which is admittedly more breathless. It is idle to hope that this self-contradictory, disintegrating "person" will not last for generations, that the system must collapse because of such a psychological split, or that the deceitful substitution of the stereotype for the individual will of itself become unbearable for mankind. Since Shakespeare's *Hamlet*, the unity of the personality has been seen through as a pretense. Synthetically produced physiognomies show that the people of today have already forgotten that there was ever a notion of what human life was. For centuries society has been preparing for Victor Mature and Mickey Rooney. By destroying they come to fulfill.

The idolization of the cheap involves making the average the heroic. The highest-paid stars resemble pictures advertising unspecified proprietary articles. Not without good purpose are they often selected from the host of commercial models. The prevailing taste takes its ideal from advertising, the beauty in consumption. Hence the Socratic saying that the beautiful is the useful has now been fulfilled—ironically. The cinema makes propaganda for the culture combine as a whole; on radio, goods for whose sake the cultural commodity exists are also recommended individually. For a few coins one can see the film which cost millions, for even less one can buy the chewing gum whose manufacture involved immense riches—a hoard increased still further by sales. *In absentia*, but by universal suffrage, the treasure of armies is revealed, but prostitution is not allowed inside the country. The best orchestras in the world—clearly not so— are brought into your living room free of charge. It is all a parody of the never-never land, just as the national society is a parody of the Human society. You name it, we supply it. A man up from the country remarked at the old Berlin Metropol theater that it was astonishing what they could do for the money; his comment has long since been adopted by the culture industry and made the very substance of production. This is always coupled with the triumph that it is possible; but this, in large measure, is the very triumph. Putting on a show means showing everybody what there is, and what can be achieved. Even today it is still a fair, but incurably sick with culture. Just as the people who had been attracted by the fairground barkers overcame their disappointment in the booths with a brave smile, because they really knew in advance what would happen, so the movie-goer sticks knowingly to the institution. With the cheapness of mass-produce luxury goods and its complement, the universal swindle, a change in the character of the art commodity itself is coming about. What is new is not that it is a commodity, but that today it deliberately admits it is one; that art renounces its own autonomy and proudly takes its place among consumption goods constitutes the charm of novelty.

Note

1. Frank Wedekind, *Gesammelte Werke*, Vol. IX (Munich, 1921), p. 426.

4 Myth Today

Roland Barthes

Myth as a semiological system

[...]

Let me therefore restate that any semiology postulates a relation between two terms, a signifier and a signified. This relation concerns objects which belong to different categories, and this why it is not one of equality but one of equivalence. We must here be on our guard for despite common parlance which simply says that the signifier *expresses* the signified, we are dealing, in any semiological system, not with two, but with three different terms. For what we grasp is not at all one term after the other, but the correlation which unites them: there are, therefore, the signifier, the signified and the sign, which is the associative total of the first two terms. Take a bunch of roses: I use it to *signify* my passion. Do we have here, then, only a signifier and a signified, the roses and my passion? Not even that: to put it accurately, there are here only 'passionified' roses. But on the plane of analysis, we do have three terms; for these roses weighted with passion perfectly and correctly allow themselves to be decomposed into roses and passion: the former and the latter existed before uniting and forming this third object, which is the sign. It is as true to say that on the plane of experience I cannot dissociate the roses from the message they carry, as to say that on the plane of analysis I cannot confuse the roses as signifier and the roses as sign: the signifier is empty, the sign is full, it is a meaning.

[...]

In myth, we find again the tri-dimensional pattern which I have just described: the signifier, the signified and the sign. But myth is a peculiar system, in that it is constructed from a semiological chain which existed before it: it *is a second-order semiological system*. That which is a sign (namely the associative total of a concept and an image) in the first system, becomes a mere signifier in the second. We must here recall that the materials of mythical speech (the language itself, photography, painting, posters, rituals, objects, etc.), however different at the start, are reduced to a pure signifying function as soon as they are caught by myth. Myth sees in them only the same raw material; their unity is that they all come down to the status of a mere language. Whether it deals with alphabetical or pictorial writing, myth wants to see in them only a sum of signs, a global sign, the final term of a first semiological chain. And it is precisely this final term which will become the first term of the greater system which it builds and of which it is only a part. Everything happens as if myth shifted the formal system of the first significations sideways. As this lateral shift is essential for the analysis of myth, I shall represent it in the following way, it being understood, of course, that the spatialization of the pattern is here only a metaphor:

It can be seen that in myth there are two semiological systems, one of which is staggered in relation to the other: a linguistic system, the language (or the modes of representation which are assimilated to it), which I shall call the *language-object*, because it is the language which myth gets hold of in order to build its own system; and myth itself, which I shall call *metalanguage*, because it is a second language, *in which* one speaks about the first. When he reflects on a metalanguage, the semiologist no longer needs to ask himself questions about the composition of the language-object, he no longer has to take into account the details of the linguistic schema; he will only need to know its total term, or global sign, and only inasmuch as this term lends itself to myth. This is why the semiologist is entitled to treat in the same way writing and pictures: what he retains from them is the fact that they are both *signs*, that they both reach the threshold of myth endowed with the same signifying function, that they constitute, one just as much as the other, a language-object.

[...]

I am at the barber's, and a copy of *Paris-Match* is offered to me. On the cover, a young Negro in a French uniform is saluting, with his eyes uplifted, probably fixed on a fold of the tricolour. All this is the *meaning* of the picture. But, whether naïvely or not, I see very well what it signifies to me: that France is a great Empire, that all her sons, without any colour discrimination, faithfully serve under her flag, and that there is no better answer to the detractors of an alleged colonialism than the zeal shown by this Negro in serving his so-called oppressors. I am therefore again faced with a greater semiological system: there is a signifier, itself already formed with a previous system (*a black soldier is giving the French salute*); there is a signified (it is here a purposeful mixture of Frenchness and militariness); finally, there is a presence of the signified through the signifier.

Before tackling the analysis of each term of the mythical system, one must agree on terminology. We now know that the signifier can be looked at, in myth, from two points of view: as the final term of the linguistic system, or as the first term of the mythical system. We therefore need two names. On the plane of language, that is, as the final term of the first system, I shall call the signifier: *meaning* (*a Negro is giving the French salute*); on the plane of myth, I shall call it: *form*. In the case of the signified, no ambiguity is possible: we shall retain the name *concept*. The third term is the correlation of the first two: in the linguistic system, it is the *sign*; but it is not possible to use this word again without ambiguity, since in myth (and this is the chief peculiarity of the latter), the signifier is already formed by the *signs* of the language. I shall call the third term of myth the *signification*. This word is here all the better justified since myth has in fact a double function: it points out and it notifies, it makes us understand something and it imposes it on us.

The form and the concept

The signifier of myth presents itself in an ambiguous way: it is at the same time meaning and form, full on one side and empty on the other. As meaning, the signifier already postulates a reading, I grasp it through my eyes, it has a sensory reality (unlike the linguistic signifier, which is purely mental), there is a richness in it. As a total of linguistic signs, the meaning of the myth has its own value, it belongs to a history, that of the Negro: in the meaning, a signification is already built, and could very well be self-sufficient if myth did not take hold of it and did not turn it suddenly into an empty, parasitical form. The meaning is *already* complete, it postulates a kind of knowledge, a past, a memory, a comparative order of facts, ideas, decisions.

It is this constant game of hide-and-seek between the meaning and the form which defines myth. The form of myth is not a symbol: the Negro who salutes is not the symbol of the French Empire: he has too much presence, he appears as a rich, fully experienced, spontaneous, innocent, *indisputable* image. But at the same time this presence is tamed, put at a distance, made almost transparent; it recedes a little, it becomes the accomplice of a concept which comes to it fully armed, French imperiality: once made use of, it becomes artificial.

Let us now look at the signified: this history which drains out of the form will be wholly absorbed by the concept. As for the latter, it is determined, it is at once historical and intentional; it is the motivation which causes the myth to be uttered. Grammatical exemplarity, French imperiality, are the very drives behind the myth. The concept reconstitutes a chain of causes and effects, motives and intentions. Unlike the form, the concept is in no way abstract: it is filled with a situation. Through the concept, it is a whole new history which is implanted in the myth. For the Negro-giving-the-salute as form, its meaning is shallow, isolated, impoverished; as the concept of French imperiality, here it is again tied to the totality of the world: to the general History of France, to its colonial adventures, to its present difficulties. Truth to tell, what is invested in the concept is less reality than a certain knowledge of reality; in passing from the meaning to the form, the image loses some knowledge: the better to receive the knowledge in the concept. In actual fact, the knowledge contained in a mythical concept is confused, made of yielding, shapeless associations. One must firmly stress this open character of the concept; it is not at all an abstract, purified essence; it is a formless, unstable, nebulous condensation, whose unity and coherence are above all due to its function.

In this sense, we can say that the fundamental character of the mythical concept is to be *appropriated*: grammatical exemplarity very precisely concerns a given form of pupils, French imperiality must appeal to such and such a group of readers and not another. The concept closely corresponds to a function, it is defined as a tendency.

[…]

As I said, there is no fixity in mythical concepts: they can come into being, alter, disintegrate, disappear completely. And it is precisely because they are historical that history can very easily suppress them. This instability forces the mythologist to use a terminology adapted to it, and about which I should now like to say a word, because it often is a cause for irony: I mean neologism. The concept is a constituting element of myth: if I want to decipher myths, I must somehow be able to name concepts. The dictionary supplies me with a few: Goodness, Kindness, Wholeness, Humaneness, etc. But by definition, since it is the dictionary which gives them to me, these particular concepts are not historical. Now what I need most often is ephemeral concepts, in connection with limited contingencies: neologism is then inevitable. China is one thing, the idea which a French petit-bourgeois could have of it not so long ago is another: for this peculiar mixture of bells, rickshaws and opium-dens, no other word is possible but *Sininess*.[1] Unlovely? One should at least get some consolation from the fact that conceptual neologisms are never arbitrary: they are built according to a highly sensible proportional rule.

The signification

[…]

What must always be remembered is that myth is a double system; there occurs in it a sort of ubiquity: its point of departure is constituted by the arrival of a meaning. To keep a spatial metaphor, the approximative character of which I have already stressed, I shall say that the signification of the myth is constituted by a sort of constantly moving turnstile which presents alternately the meaning of the signifier and its form, a language-object and a metalanguage, a purely signifying and a purely imagining consciousness. This alternation is, so to speak, gathered up in the concept, which uses it like an ambiguous signifier, at once intellective and imaginary, arbitrary and natural.

I do not wish to prejudge the moral implications of such a mechanism, but I shall not exceed the limits of an objective analysis if I point out that the ubiquity of the signifier in myth exactly reproduces the physique of the *alibi* (which is, as one realizes, a spatial term): in the alibi too, there is a place which is full and one which is empty, linked by a relation of negative identity ('I am not where you think I am; I am where you think I am not'). But the ordinary alibi (for the police, for instance) has an end; reality stops the turnstile revolving at a certain point. Myth is a *value*, truth is no guarantee for it; nothing prevents it from being a perpetual alibi: it is enough that its signifier has two sides for it always to have an 'elsewhere' at its disposal. The meaning is always there to *present* the form; the form is always there to *outdistance* the meaning. And there never is any contradiction, conflict, or split between the meaning and the form: they are never at the same place. In the same way, if I am in a car and I look at the scenery through the window, I can at will focus on the scenery or on the window-pane. At one moment I grasp the presence of the glass and the distance of the landscape; at another, on the contrary, the transparence of the glass and the depth of the landscape; but the result of this alternation is constant: the glass is at once present and empty to me, and the landscape unreal and full. The same thing occurs in the mythical signifier: its form is empty but present, its meaning absent but full. To wonder at this contradiction I must voluntarily interrupt this turnstile of form and meaning, I must focus on each separately, and apply to myth a static method of deciphering; in short, I must go against its own dynamics: to sum up, I must pass from the state of reader to that of mythologist.

[...]

One last element of the signification remains to be examined: its motivation. We know that in a language, the sign is arbitrary: nothing compels the acoustic image *tree* 'naturally' to mean the concept *tree:* the sign, here, is unmotivated. Yet this arbitrariness has limits, which come from the associative relations of the word: the language can produce a whole fragment of the sign by analogy with other signs (for instance one says *aimable* in French, and not *amable*, by analogy with *aime*). The mythical signification, on the other hand, is never arbitrary; it is always in part motivated, and unavoidably contains some analogy. For Latin exemplarity to meet the naming of the lion, there must be an analogy, which is the agreement of the predicate; for French imperiality to get hold of the saluting Negro, there must be identity between the Negro's salute and that of the French soldier. Motivation is necessary to the very duplicity of myth: myth plays on the analogy between meaning and form, there is no myth without motivated form. In order to grasp the power of motivation in myth, it is enough to reflect for a moment on an extreme case. I have here before me a collection of objects so lacking in order that I can find no *meaning* in it; it would seem that here, deprived of any previous meaning, the form could not root its analogy in anything, and that myth is impossible. But what the form can always give one to read is disorder itself: it can give a signification to the absurd, make the absurd itself a myth. This is what happens when commonsense mythifies surrealism, for instance. Even the absence of motivation does not embarrass myth; for this absence will itself be sufficiently objectified to become legible: and finally, the absence of motivation will become a second-order motivation, and myth will be re-established.

'THAT-HAS-BEEN'; The Pose; The Luminous Rays, Colour; Amazement; Authentification

Roland Barthes

First of all I had to conceive, and therefore if possible express properly (even if it is a simple thing) how Photography's Referent is not the same as the referent of other systems of representation. I call 'photographic referent' not the *optionally* real thing to which an image or a sign refers but the *necessarily* real thing which has been placed before the lens, without which there would be no photograph. Painting can feign reality without having seen it. Discourse combines signs which have referents, of course, but these referents can be and are most often 'chimeras.' Contrary to these imitations, in Photography I can never deny that *the thing has been there*. There is a superimposition here: of reality and of the past. And since this constraint exists only for Photography, we must consider it, by reduction, as the very essence, the *noeme* of Photography. What I intentionalize in a photograph (we are not yet speaking of film) is neither Art nor Communication, it is Reference, which is the founding order of Photography.

The name of Photography's *noeme* will therefore be: 'That-has-been,' or again: the Intractable. In Latin (a pedantry necessary because it illuminates certain nuances), this would doubtless be said: *interfuit*: what I see has been here, in this place which extends between infinity and the subject (*operator or spectator*); it has been here, and yet immediately separated; it has been absolutely, irrefutably present, and yet already deferred. It is all this which the verb *intersum* means.

In the daily flood of photographs, in the thousand forms of interest they seem to provoke, it may be that the *noeme* 'That-has-been' is not repressed (a *noeme* cannot be repressed) but experienced with indifference, as a feature which goes without saying. It is this indifference which the Winter Garden Photograph had just roused me from. According to a paradoxical order—since usually we verify things before declaring them 'true'—under the effect of a new experience, that of intensity, I had induced the truth of the image, the reality of its origin; I had identified truth and reality in a unique emotion, in which I henceforth placed the nature—the genius—of Photography, since no painted portrait, supposing that it seemed 'true' to me, could compel me to believe its referent had really existed.

I might put this differently: what founds the nature of Photography is the pose. The physical duration of this pose is of little consequence; even in the interval of a millionth of a second there has still been a pose, for the pose is not, here, the attitude of the target or even a technique of the *Operator*, but the term of an 'intention' of reading: looking at a photograph, I inevitably include in my scrutiny the thought of that instant, however brief, in which a real thing happened to be motionless in front of the eye. I project the present photograph's immobility upon the past shot, and it is this arrest which constitutes the pose. This explains why the Photograph's *noeme* deteriorates when this Photograph is animated and becomes cinema: in the Photograph, something *has posed* in front of the tiny hole and has remained there forever (that is my feeling); but in cinema, something *has passed* in front of this same tiny hole: the pose is swept away and denied by the continuous series of images: it is a different phenomenology, and therefore a different art which begins here, though derived from the first one.

In Photography, the presence of the thing (at a certain past moment) is never metaphoric; and in the case of animated beings, their life as well, except in the case of photographing corpses; and even so: if the photograph then becomes horrible, it is because it certifies, so to speak, that the corpse is alive, as *corpse*: it is the living image of a dead thing. For the photograph's immobility is somehow the result of a perverse confusion between two concepts: the Real and the Live: by attesting that the object has been real, the photograph surreptitiously induces belief that it is alive, because of that delusion which makes us attribute to Reality an absolutely superior, somehow eternal value; but by shifting this reality to the past ('this-has-been'), the photograph suggests that it is already dead. Hence it would be better to say that Photography's inimitable feature (its *noeme*) is that someone has seen the referent (even if it is a matter of objects) *in flesh and blood*, or again *in person*. Photography, moreover, began, historically, as an art of the Person: of identity, of civil status, of what we might call, in all senses of the term, the body's *formality*. Here again, from a phenomenological viewpoint, the cinema begins to differ from the Photograph; for the (fictional) cinema combines two poses: the actor's 'this-has-been' and the role's, so that (something I would not experience before a painting) I can never see or see again in a film certain actors whom I know to be dead without a kind of melancholy: the melancholy of Photography itself (I experience this same emotion listening to the recorded voices of dead singers).

[...]

It is often said that it was the painters who invented Photography (by bequeathing it their framing, the Albertian perspective, and the optic of the *camera obscura*). I say: no, it was the chemists. For the *noeme* 'That-has-been' was possible only on the day when a scientific circumstance (the discovery that silver halogens were sensitive to light) made it possible to recover and print directly the luminous rays emitted by a variously lighted object. The photograph is literally an emanation of the referent. From a real body, which was there, proceed radiations which ultimately touch me, who am here; the duration of the transmission is insignificant; the photograph of the missing being, as Sontag says, will touch me like the delayed rays of a star. A sort of umbilical cord links the body of the photographed thing to my gaze: light, though impalpable, is here a carnal medium, a skin I share with anyone who has been photographed.

It seems that in Latin 'photograph' would be said 'imago lucis opera expressa'; which is to say: image revealed, 'extracted', 'mounted', 'expressed' (like the juice of a lemon) by the action of light. And if Photography belonged to a world with some residual sensitivity to myth, we should exult over the richness of the symbol: the loved body is immortalized by the mediation of a precious metal, silver (monument and luxury); to which we might add the notion that this metal, like all the metals of Alchemy, is alive.

Perhaps it is because I am delighted (or depressed) to know that the thing of the past, by its immediate radiations (its luminances), has really touched the surface which in its turn my gaze will touch, that I am not very fond of Color. An anonymous daguerreotype of 1843 shows a man and a woman in a medallion subsequently tinted by the miniaturists on the staff of the photographic studio: I always feel (unimportant what actually occurs) that in the same way, color is a coating applied *later on* to the original truth of the black-and-white photograph. For me, color is an artifice, a cosmetic (like the kind used to paint corpses). What matters to me is not the photograph's 'life' (a purely ideological notion) but the certainty that the photographed body touches me with its own rays and not with a superadded light.

[...]

The Photograph does not call up the past (nothing Proustian in a photograph). The effect it produces upon me is not to restore what has been abolished (by time, by distance) but to attest that what I see has indeed existed. Now, this is a strictly scandalous effect. Always the Photograph *astonishes* me, with an astonishment which endures and renews itself, inexhaustibly. Perhaps this astonishment, this persistence reaches down into the religious substance out of which I am molded; nothing for it: Photography has something to do with resurrection: might we not say of it what the Byzantines said of the image of Christ which impregnated St. Veronica's napkin: that it was not made by the hand of man, *acheiropoietos*?

[...]

The Photograph does not necessarily say *what is no longer*, but only and for certain *what has been*. This distinction is decisive. In front of a photograph, our consciousness does not necessarily take the nostalgic path of memory (how many photographs are outside of individual time), but for every photograph existing in the world, the path of certainty: the Photograph's essence is to ratify what it represents. One day I received from a photographer a picture of myself which I could not remember being taken, for all my efforts; I inspected the tie, the sweater, to discover in what circumstances I had worn them; to no avail. And yet, *because it was a photograph* I could not deny that I had been *there* (even if I did not know *where*). This distortion between certainty and oblivion gave me a kind of vertigo, something of a 'detective' anguish (the theme of *Blow-Up* was not far off); I went to the photographer's show as to a police investigation, to learn at last what I no longer knew about myself.

No writing can give me this certainty. It is the misfortune (but also perhaps the voluptuous pleasure) of language not to be able to authenticate itself. The *noeme* of language is perhaps this impotence, or, to put it positively: language is, by nature, fictional; the attempt to render language unfictional requires an enormous apparatus of measurements: we convoke logic, or, lacking that, sworn oath; but the Photograph is indifferent to all intermediaries: it does not invent; it is authentication itself; the (rare) artifices it permits are not probative; they are, on the contrary, trick pictures: the photograph is laborious only when it fakes. It is a prophecy in reverse: like Cassandra, but eyes fixed on the past, Photography never lies: or rather, it can lie as to the meaning of the thing, being by nature *tendentious*, never as to its existence.

Perhaps we have an invincible resistance to believing in the past, in History, except in the form of myth. The Photograph, for the first time, puts an end to this resistance: henceforth the past is as certain as the present, what we see on paper is as certain as what we touch. It is the advent of the Photograph—and not, as has been said, of the cinema—which divides the history of the world.

It is precisely because the Photograph is an anthropologically new object that it must escape, it seems to me, usual discussions of the image. It is the fashion, nowadays, among Photography's commentators (sociologists and semiologists), to seize upon a semantic relativity: no 'reality' (great scorn for the 'realists' who do not see that the photograph is always coded), nothing but artifice: *Thesis*, not *Physis*; the Photograph, they say, is not an *analogon* of the world; what it represents is fabricated, because the photographic optic is subject to Albertian perspective (entirely historical) and because the inscription on the picture makes a three-dimensional object into a two-dimensional effigy. This argument is futile: nothing can prevent the Photograph from being analogical; but at the same time, Photography's *noeme* has nothing to do with analogy (a feature it shares with all kinds of representations). The realists, of whom I am one and of whom I was already one when I asserted that the Photograph was an image without code—even if, obviously, certain codes do inflect our reading of it—the realists do not take the photograph for a 'copy' of reality, but for an emanation of *past reality*: a *magic*, not an art. To ask whether a photograph is analogical or coded is not a good means of analysis. The important thing is that the photograph possesses an evidential force, and that its testimony bears not on the object but on time. From a phenomenological viewpoint, in the Photograph, the power of authentication exceeds the power of representation.

Note

1. Or perhaps *Sinity?* Just as if Latin/Latinity = Basque/x, x = Basquity.

5 The Ecstasy of Communication

Jean Baudrillard

There is no longer any system of objects. My first book contains a critique of the object as obvious fact, substance, reality, use value.[1] There the object was taken as sign, but as sign still heavy with meaning. In this critique two principal logics interfered with each other: a phantasmatic logic that referred principally to psychoanalysis—its identifications, projections, and the entire imaginary realm of transcendence, power and sexuality operating at the level of objects and the environment, with a privilege accorded to the house/automobile axis (immanence/transcendence); and a differential social logic that made distinctions by referring to a sociology, itself derived from anthropology (consumption as the production of signs, differentiation, status and prestige). Behind these logics, in some way descriptive and analytic, there was already the dream of symbolic exchange, a dream of the status of the object and consumption beyond exchange and use, beyond value and equivalence. In other words, a sacrificial logic of consumption, gift, expenditure (dépense), potlatch, and the accursed portion.[2]

In a certain way all this still exists, and yet in other respects it is all disappearing. The description of this whole intimate universe—projective, imaginary and symbolic—still corresponded to the object's status as mirror of the subject, and that in turn to the imaginary depths of the mirror and "scene": there is a domestic scene, a scene of interiority, a private spacetime (correlative, moreover, to a public space). The oppositions subject/object and public/private were still meaningful. This was the era of the discovery and exploration of daily life, this other scene emerging in the shadow of the historic scene, with the former receiving more and more symbolic investment as the latter was politically disinvested.

But today the scene and mirror no longer exist; instead, there is a screen and network. In place of the reflexive transcendence of mirror and scene, there is a nonreflecting surface, an immanent surface where operations unfold—the smooth operational surface of communication.

Something has changed, and the Faustian, Promethean (perhaps Oedipal) period of production and consumption gives way to the "proteinic" era of networks, to the narcissistic and protean era of connections, contact, contiguity, feedback and generalized interface that goes with the universe of communication. With the television image—the television being the ultimate and perfect object for this new era—our own body and the whole surrounding universe become a control screen.

If one thinks about it, people no longer project themselves into their objects, with their affects and their representations, their fantasies of possession, loss, mourning, jealousy: the psychological dimension has in a sense vanished, and even if it can always be marked out in detail, one feels that is not really there that things are being played out. Roland Barthes already indicated this some time ago in regard to the automobile: little by little a logic of "driving" has replaced a very subjective logic of possession and projection.[3] No more fantasies of power, speed and appropriation linked to the object itself, but instead a tactic of potentialities linked to usage: mastery, control and command, an optimization of the play of possibilities offered by the car as vector and vehicle, and no longer as object of psychological sanctuary. The subject himself, suddenly transformed, becomes a computer at the wheel, not a drunken demiurge of power. The vehicle now becomes a kind of capsule, its dashboard the brain, the surrounding landscape unfolding like a televised screen (instead of a live-in projectile as it was before).

(But we can conceive of a stage beyond this one, where the car is still a vehicle of performance, a stage where it becomes an information network. The famous Japanese car that talks to you, that "spontaneously" informs you of its general state and even of your general state, possibly refusing to function if you are not functioning well, the car as deliberating consultant and partner in the general negotiation of a lifestyle, something—or someone: at this point there is no longer any difference—with which you are connected. The fundamental issue becomes the communication with the car itself, a perpetual test of the subject's presence with his own objects, an uninterrupted interface.

It is easy to see that from this point speed and displacement no longer matter. Neither does unconscious projection, nor an individual or social type of competition, nor prestige. Besides, the car began to be de-sacralized in this sense some time ago: it's all over with speed—I drive more and consume less. Now, however, it is an ecological ideal that installs itself at every level. No more expenditure, consumption, performance, but instead regulation, well-tempered functionality, solidarity among all the elements of the same system, control and global management of an ensemble. Each system, including no doubt the domestic universe, forms a sort of ecological niche where the essential thing is to maintain a relational decor, where all the terms must continually communicate among themselves and stay in contact, informed of the respective condition of the others and of the system as a whole, where opacity, resistance or the secrecy of a single term can lead to catastrophe.[4]

Private "telematics": each person sees himself at the controls of a hypothetical machine, isolated in a position of perfect and remote sovereignty, at an infinite distance from his universe of origin. Which is to say, in the exact position of an astronaut in his capsule, in a state of weightlessness that necessitates a perpetual orbital flight and a speed sufficient to keep him from crashing back to his planet of origin.

This realization of a living satellite, *in vivo* in a quotidian space, corresponds to the satellitization of the real, or what I call the "hyperrealism of simulation"[5]: the elevation of the domestic universe to a spatial power, to a spatial metaphor, with the satellitization of the two-room-kitchen-and-bath put into orbit in the last lunar module. The very quotidian nature of the terrestrial habitat hypostasized in space means the end of metaphysics. The era of hyperreality now begins. What I mean is this: what was projected psychologically and mentally, what used to be lived out on earth as metaphor, as mental or metaphorical scene, is henceforth projected into reality, without any metaphor at all, into an absolute space which is also that of simulation.

This is only an example, but it signifies as a whole the passage into orbit, as orbital and environmental model, of our private sphere itself. It is no longer a scene where the dramatic interiority of the subject, engaged with its objects as with its image, is played out. We are here at the controls of a micro-satellite, in orbit, living no longer as an actor or dramaturge but as a terminal of multiple networks. Television is still the most direct prefiguration of this. But today it is the very space of habitation that is conceived as both receiver and distributor, as the space of both reception and operations, the control screen and terminal which as such may be endowed with telematic power—that is, with the capability of regulating everything from a distance, including work in the home and, of course, consumption, play, social relations and leisure. Simulators of leisure or of vacations in the home—like flight simulators for airplane pilots—become conceivable.

Here we are far from the living-room and close to science fiction. But once more it must be seen that all these changes—the decisive mutations of objects and of the environment in the modern era—have come from an irreversible tendency toward three things: an ever greater formal and operational abstraction of elements and functions and their homogenization in a single virtual process of functionalization; the displacement of bodily movements and efforts into electric or electronic commands, and the miniaturization, in time and space, of processes whose real scene (though it is no longer a scene) is that of infinitesimal memory and the screen with which they are equipped.

There is a problem here, however, to the extent that this electronic "encephalization" and miniaturization of circuits and energy, this transistorization of the environment, relegates to total uselessness, desuetude and almost obscenity all that used to fill the scene of our lives. It is well known how the simple presence of the television changes the rest of the habitat into a kind of archaic envelope, a vestige of human relations whose very survival remains perplexing. As soon as this scene is no longer haunted by its actors and their fantasies, as soon as behavior is crystallized on certain screens and operational terminals, what's left appears only as a large useless body, deserted and condemned. The real itself appears as a large useless body.

This is the time of miniaturization, telecommand and the microprocession of time, bodies, pleasures. There is no longer any ideal principle for these things at a higher level, on a human scale. What remains are only concentrated effects, miniaturized and immediately available. This change from human scale to a system of nuclear matrices is visible everywhere: this body, our body, often appears simply superfluous, basically useless in its extension, in the multiplicity and complexity of its organs, its tissues and functions, since today everything is concentrated in the brain and in genetic codes, which alone sum up the operational definition of being. The countryside, the immense geographic countryside, seems to be a deserted body whose expanse and dimensions appear arbitrary (and which is boring to cross even if one leaves the main highways), as soon as all events are epitomized in the towns, themselves undergoing reduction to a few miniaturized highlights. And time: what can be said about this immense free time we are left with, a dimension henceforth useless in its unfolding, as soon as the instantaneity of communication has miniaturized our exchanges into a succession of instants?

**

Thus the body, landscape, time all progressively disappear as scenes. And the same for public space: the theater of the social and theater of politics are both reduced more and more to a large soft body with many heads. Advertising in its new version—which is no longer a more or less baroque, utopian or ecstatic scenario of objects and consumption, but the effect of an omnipresent visibility of enterprises, brands, social interlocuters and the social virtues of communication—advertising in its new dimension invades everything, as public space (the street, monument, market, scene) disappears. It realizes, or, if one prefers, it materializes in all its obscenity; it monopolizes public life in its exhibition. No longer limited to its traditional language, advertising organizes the architecture and realization of super-objects like Beaubourg and the Forum des Halles, and of future projects (e.g., Parc de la Villette) which are monuments (or anti-monuments) to advertising, not because they will be geared to consumption but because they are immediately proposed as an anticipated demonstration of the operation of culture, commodities, mass movement and social flux. It is our only architecture today: great screens on which are reflected atoms, particles, molecules in motion. Not a public scene or true public space but gigantic spaces of circulation, ventilation and ephemeral connections.

***

It is the same for private space. In a subtle way, this loss of public space occurs contemporaneously with the loss of private space. The one is no longer a spectacle, the other no longer a secret. Their distinctive opposition, the clear difference of an exterior and an interior exactly described the domestic *scene* of objects, with its rules of play and limits, and the sovereignty of a symbolic space which was also that of the subject. Now this opposition is effaced in a sort of *obscenity* where the most intimate processes of our life become the virtual feeding ground of the media (the Loud family in the United States, the innumerable slices of peasant or patriarchal life on French television). Inversely, the entire universe comes to unfold arbitrarily on your domestic screen (all the useless information that comes to you from the entire world, like a microscopic pornography of the universe, useless, excessive, just like the sexual close-up in a porno film): all this explodes the scene formerly preserved by the minimal separation of public and private, the scene that was played out in a restricted space, according to a secret ritual known only by the actors.

Certainly, this private universe was alienating to the extent that it separated you from others—or from the world, where it was invested as a protective enclosure, an imaginary protector, a defense system. But it also reaped the symbolic benefits of alienation, which is that the Other exists, and that otherness can fool you for the better or the worse. Thus consumer society lived also under the sign of alienation, as a society of the spectacle.[6] But just so: as long as there is alienation, there is spectacle, action, scene. It is not obscenity—the spectacle is never obscene. Obscenity begins precisely when there is no more spectacle, no more scene, when all becomes transparent and immediately visible, when everything is exposed to the harsh and inexorable light of information and communication.

We are no longer a part of the drama of alienation; we live in the ecstasy of communication. And this ecstasy is obscene. The obscene is what does away with every mirror, every look, every image. The obscene puts an end to every representation. But it is not only the sexual that becomes obscene in pornography; today there is a whole pornography of information and communication, that is to say, of circuits and networks, a pornography of all functions and objects in their readability, their fluidity, their availability, their regulation, in their forced signification, in their performativity, in their branching, in their polyvalence, in their free expression. . . .

It is no longer then the traditional obscenity of what is hidden, repressed, forbidden or obscure; on the contrary, it is the obscenity of the visible, of the all-too-visible, of the more-visible-than-the-visible. It is the obscenity of what no longer has any secret, of what dissolves completely in information and communication.

Marx set forth and denounced the obscenity of the commodity, and this obscenity was linked to its equivalence, to the abject principle of free circulation, beyond all use value of the object. The obscenity of the commodity stems from the fact that it is abstract, formal and light in opposition to the weight, opacity and substance of the object. The commodity is readable: in opposition to the object, which never completely gives up its secret, the commodity always manifests its visible essence, which is its price. It is the formal place of transcription of all possible objects; through it, objects communicate. Hence, the commodity form is the first great medium of the modern world. But the message that the objects deliver through it is already extremely simplified, and it is always the same: their exchange value. Thus at bottom the message already no longer exists; it is the medium that imposes itself in its pure circulation. This is what I call (potentially) ecstasy.

One has only to prolong this Marxist analysis, or push it to the second or third power, to grasp the transparence and obscenity of the universe of communication, which leaves far behind it those relative analyses of the universe of the commodity. All functions abolished in a single dimension, that of communication. That's the ecstasy of communication. All secrets, spaces and scenes abolished in a single dimension of information. That's obscenity.

The hot, sexual obscenity of former times is succeeded by the cold and communi-cational, contactual and motivational obscenity of today. The former clearly implied a type of promiscuity, but it was organic, like the body's viscera, or again like objects piled up and accumulated in a private universe, or like all that is not spoken, teeming in the silence of repression. Unlike this organic, visceral, carnal promiscuity, the promiscuity that reigns over the communication networks is one of superficial saturation, of an incessant solicitation, of an extermination of interstitial and protective spaces. I pick up my telephone receiver and it's all there; the whole marginal network catches and harasses me with the insupportable good faith of everything that wants and claims to communicate. Free radio: it speaks, it sings, it expresses itself. Very well, *it* is the sympathetic obscenity of its content. In terms a little different for each medium, this is the result: a space, that of the FM band, is found to be saturated, the stations overlap and mix together (to the point that sometimes it no longer communicates at all). Something that was free by virtue of space is no longer free. Speech is free per-haps, but I am less free than before: I no longer succeed in knowing what I want, the space is so saturated, the pressure so great from all who want to make themselves heard.

I fall into the negative ecstasy of the radio.

There is in effect a state of fascination and vertigo linked to this obscene delirium of communication. A singular form of pleasure perhaps, but aleatory and dizzying. If we follow Roger Caillois[7] in his classification of games (it's as good as any other)— games of expression (*mimicry*), games of competition (*agon*), games of chance (*alea*), games of vertigo (*ilynx*)—the whole tendency of our contemporary "culture" would lead us from a relative disappearance of forms of expression and competition (as we have remarked at the level of objects) to the advantages of forms of risk and vertigo. The latter no longer involve games of scene, mirror, challenge and duality; they are, rather, ecstatic, solitary and narcissistic. The pleasure is no longer one of manifestation, scenic and aesthetic, but rather one of pure fascination, aleatory and psychotropic. This is not necessarily a negative value judgment: here surely there is an original and profound mutation of the very forms of perception and pleasure. We are still measuring the consequences poorly. Wanting to apply our old criteria and the reflexes of a "scenic" sensibility, we no doubt misapprehend what may be the occurrence, in this sensory sphere, of something new, ecstatic and obscene.

One thing is sure: the scene excites us, the obscene fascinates us. With fascination and ecstasy, passion disappears. Investment, desire, passion, seduction or again, according to Caillois, expression and competition—the hot universe. Ecstasy, obscenity, fascination, communication or again, according to Caillois, hazard, chance and vertigo—the cold universe (even vertigo is cold, the psychedelic one of drugs in particular).

* * *

In any case, we will have to suffer this new state of things, this forced extroversion of all interiority, this forced injection of all exteriority that the categorical imperative of communication literally signifies. There also, one can perhaps make use of the old metaphors of pathology. If hysteria was the pathology of the exacerbated staging of the subject, a pathology of expression, of the body's theatrical and operatic conversion; and if paranoia was the pathology of organization, of the structuration of a rigid and jealous world; then with communication and information, with the immanent promiscuity of all these networks, with their continual connections, we are now in a new form of schizophrenia. No more hysteria, no more projective paranoia, properly speaking, but this state of terror proper to the schizophrenic: too great a proximity of everything, the unclean promiscuity of everything which touches, invests and penetrates without resistance, with no halo of private protection, not even his own body, to protect him anymore.

The schizo is bereft of every scene, open to everything in spite of himself, living in the greatest confusion. He is himself obscene, the obscene prey of the world's obscenity. What characterizes him is less the loss of the real, the light years of estrangement from the real, the pathos of distance and radical separation, as is commonly said: but, very much to the contrary, the absolute proximity, the total instantaneity of things, the feeling of no defense, no retreat. It is the end of interiority and intimacy, the overexposure and transparence of the world which traverses him without obstacle. He can no longer produce the limits of his own being, can no longer play nor stage himself, can no longer produce himself as mirror. He is now only a pure screen, a switching center for all the networks of influence.

Translated by John Johnston

Notes

1. *Le Système des objets* (Paris: Gallimard, 1968). [Tr.]
2. Baudrillard is alluding here to Marcel Mauss's theory of gift exchange and Georges Bataille's notion of *dépense*. The "accursed portion" in the latter's theory refers to whatever remains outside of society's rationalized economy of exchanges. See Bataille, *La Part Maudite* (Paris: Editions de Minuit, 1949). Baudrillard's own conception of

symbolic exchange, as a form of interaction that lies outside of modern Western society and that therefore "haunts it like its own death," is developed in his *L'échange symbolique et la mort* (Paris: Gallimard, 1976). [Tr.]

3. See Roland Barthes, "The New Citroën," *Mythologies*, trans. Annette Lavers (New York: Hill and Wang, 1972), pp. 88–90. [Tr.]

4. Two observations. First, this is not due alone to the passage, as one wants to call it, from a society of abundance and surplus to a society of crisis and penury (economic reasons have never been worth very much). Just as the effect of consumption was not linked to the use value of things nor to their abundance, but precisely to the passage from use value to sign value, so here there is something new that is not linked to the end of abundance.

Secondly, all this does not mean that the domestic universe—the home, its objects, etc.—is not still lived largely in a traditional way—social, psychological, differential, etc. It means rather that the stakes are no longer there, that another arrangement or life-style is virtually in place, even if it is indicated only through a technologistical discourse which is often simply a political gadget. But it is crucial to see that the analysis that one could make of objects and their system in the '60s and '70s essentially began with the language of advertising and the pseudo-conceptual discourse of the expert. "Consumption," the "strategy of desire," etc. were first only a metadiscourse, the analysis of a projective myth whose actual effect was never really known. How people actually live with their objects—at bottom, one knows no more about this than about the truth of primitive societies. That's why it is often problematic and useless to want to verify (statistically, objectively) these hypotheses, as one ought to be able to do as a good sociologist. As we know, the language of advertising is first for the use of the advertisers themselves. Nothing says that contemporary discourse on computer science and communication is not for the use alone of professionals in these fields. (As for the discourse of intellectuals and sociologists themselves . . .)

5. For an expanded explanation of this idea, see Baudrillard's essay "La précession des simulacres," *Simulacres et Simulation* (Paris: Galilée, 1981). An English translation appears in *Simulations* (New York: Foreign Agent Series, Semiotext(e) Publications, 1983). [Tr.]

6. A reference to Guy Debord's *La société du spectacle* (Paris: Buchet-Chastel, 1968). [Tr.]

7. Roger Caillois, *Les jeux et les hommes* (Paris: Gallimard, 1958). [Tr.]

The Analysis of Fame: Understanding Stardom

Introduction
Sean Redmond and Su Holmes

In terms of popular media discourse and everyday 'common sense' reasoning, the idea that there is *anything much* to understand about stardom would be met with widespread disbelief. What is there to understand? Stars are just naturally charismatic; essentially beautiful; the camera adores them; light pours out from the centre of their beings. They live glamorous lives. They sometimes make (bad) mistakes. A number of them are phoney (not truly beautiful). We want to be like them, sometimes to the point of obsession. Stars are the main actors in a film, or the leading performers in a (music) video. They are 'faces' and 'bodies' in magazines, newspapers, posters and numerous advertisements. Stars are . . . just 'stars' . . . right?

Of course, at least in an academic context, stars are a great deal more than shafts of light or filmic entities (although all the qualities listed above *do* require greater understanding since they involve ideological, political and economic issues that lurk below the surface of their myth-like rhetoric). One needs to understand stardom because its pleasures, representations, productions and affects/effects have a dramatic impact on social life. As Richard Dyer eloquently writes

> Stars articulate what it is to be human being in contemporary society; that is, they express the particular notion we hold of the person, of the 'individual. They do so complexly, variously – they are not straightforward affirmations of individualism. On the contrary, they articulate both the promise and the difficulty that the notion of individuality presents for all of us who live by it'. (Dyer, 1987: 10)

Of course, when one puts 'media' celebrities or 'television personalities' into the equation, one begins to address issues of cultural value, appeal and desire, circulation and reception. One begins to get to the heart of understanding fame in all its complex manifestations. The purpose of this section, then, is to go some way to understanding how academia – across disciplines and historical periods – has made sense of stardom. In terms of the imagined trajectory of this *Reader*, this section focuses upon film stars and stardom as the very first 'cluster' of texts and contexts that found a mass marketplace, interested academics, and led to new analysis and ways of thinking about power, desire and identification in the modern world. The film industry is often credited with creating the iconic figure of the star-celebrity, and the marketing and publicity strategies for commodifying them. And at an intellectual level one can approximately argue that film studies brings into being the academic study of stars.

In terms of a defining moment, then, the academic analysis of stardom is closely associated with the work of film studies and Richard Dyer's work in particular. Although considered at first to be a radical departure from the 'normal' or accepted research areas in film, such as film authorship, the analysis of stardom gathered support from a new generation of scholars interested in examining popular cinema and pleasure. As James Donald noted, prior to this

> **there seemed to be little inclination by film theorists to engage with the topic…a sign, perhaps, of the gulf between theory and popular experience, but more significantly of the difficult problems posed for the academic study of film, at whatever level, by the phenomenon of stardom. (1999: 33)**

Richard Dyer's groundbreaking *Stars* (1979) is credited with introducing the first full-scale textual and ideological examination of this phenomena. However, the analysis of stars predates Richard's book, as he makes clear (Austin and Barker, 2003: 5). Essay length studies had actually emerged in (media) sociology and communications, psychology, philosophy and anthropology. Consequently, in understanding stardom one has to largely situate oneself in the field of film studies, and yet one also has to recognize the other fields that have influenced its critical orbit. So the selections in this section have been made with the 'weight' of these issues in mind.

Francesco Alberoni's 'The Powerless "Elite": Theory and Sociological Research and the Phenomenon of Stars' is the opening essay to this section. Alberoni, an Italian sociologist, explores the complex role and function that stars perform in contemporary life. Drawing on Weber's concept of charisma (see Section One), Alberoni argues that stars are charismatic figures or leaders but their power to direct action or influence decision making is decidedly limited. Stars are clearly role defined and 'skill' specific, and they 'do not occupy institutional positions of power'. Their charisma emanates from a restricted field of attraction and desire, which removes them from the established (State directed) power base where decisions about the economy and politics are made. According to Alberoni, stars are an elite group, a 'remarkable' social phenomenon, 'whose institutional power is very limited or non-existent, but whose doings and way of life arouse a considerable and sometimes even a maximum degree of interest'. Alberoni's essay has been widely referenced in subsequent studies of stardom, and given the argument that stars and celebrities now fully occupy the social centre (see Nick Couldry's essay in Section Six) his work remains essential reading for those interested in issues of power and authority.

Excerpts from Richard Dyer's 'Stars' and 'Heavenly Bodies' are intended to mark the shift toward the academic interest in stars in the context of representation, myth and ideology. Dyer's work pays careful attention to the construction of star images, their mythic nature, their role in 'speaking' about what it means to be an individual, and their historical specificity in terms of the way address (make safe) conflicts and issues that circulate in the social world. Dyer's work then notably questions Alberoni's thesis by demonstrating that the political and ideological are core values of stardom at least in the 'everyday' context of meaning-generation. In 'Charisma', Richard Dyer returns us to Weber's concept but through the conjoining of 'social function', 'social instability' and 'ideology'. For Dyer, as with Weber, 'charismatic appeal is effective especially when the social order is uncertain, unstable and ambiguous and when the charismatic figure or group offers a value, order or stability to counterpoise this'. Dyer uses the star charisma of Marilyn Monroe to show how she 'seemed to be the very tensions that run through the ideological life of 50s America'. In the 'Introduction' to *Heavenly Bodies* Dyer sets up his dual hypothesis that first, 'Images have to be made. Stars are produced by the media industries, film stars by Hollywood (or its equivalent in other countries)' and that second, star images relate to 'notions of personhood *Di* and social reality'. Dyer suggests that it is only through combining textual and intertextual analysis of stars with ideological and historical contexts that one gets close to understanding their fascination for the audience and their power to affect ordinary people's lives.

The intertextual and ideological circulation of the star image is also examined in John Ellis' 'Stars as a Cinematic Phenomenon'. However, Ellis' essay is considered to be particularly important because of the original use he makes of Roland Barthes' concept of the 'photo effect' to explore what he sees as the absent/present paradox of stardom. He uses this to explore what he sees as important qualitative differences between cinematic and televisual fame – a position which has exerted a considerable influence on the field of star analysis at the level of medium specificity. Ellis argues that 'the star is at once ordinary and extraordinary, available for desire and unattainable. *Fam* This paradox is repeated and intensified in cinema by the regime of presence-yet absence that is the filmic image'. In this way, the 'this is was' nature of the star 'awakens a series of psychic mechanisms which involve various impossible images' including 'the narcissistic experience of the mirror phase'. Ellis then goes on to set up his position on television fame which he considers being that much more present or 'immediate' than cinema stardom. For Ellis, 'What television does present is the "personality". The personality is someone who is famous for being famous and is famous only in so far as he or she makes frequent television appearances.... In some ways, they are the opposite of stars, agreeable voids rather than sites of conflicting meanings'. One can clearly take issue with Ellis here, particularly since the multi-media, digital landscape of the contemporary age suggests a much more polymorphous and slippery relationship between images of any kind.

This is something that Christine Geraghty addresses in 'Re-examining Stardom: Questions of Texts, Bodies and Performance'. In this essay, Geraghty suggests that one needs to 'rethink the categories' through which stars are examined and understood because the flow and flux of the contemporary representation of the famous differently shape 'how film stars make meaning in contemporary cinema and contemporary culture'. Geraghty locates three meta categories through which stars generate meaning. First, there is the 'Star-as-celebrity', he or she who is primarily represented in terms of their leisure pursuits and lifestyle, and who 'literally interact with those from other areas. Thus, our knowledge that Johnny Depp goes out with the model Kate Moss is in the same register as the news of footballer David Beckham marrying a Spice Girl'. Second, there is the 'Star-as-professional', he or she who can be identified according to their professional role. Geraghty suggests that this is best understood in terms of the way stars are associated with a particular genre in terms of marketing and film and video classification. However, it is also to do with textual enunciation *on screen*, so that in the case of Harrison Ford, 'enjoyment . . . very much depends on watching the contrast between easy expressions of his body movements and the impassive face with its limited range of expressions'. Third, there is the 'Star-as-performer', 'marked by an emphasis on 'impersonisation', on a distinction between star and role which is effaced in the 'Star-as-professional'. Geraghty suggests that this has particular resonance in a contemporary cinematic age where special effects and spectacle are often argued to deny the star-actor a chance to shine. In this context, 'acting has become a way of claiming back the cinema for human stars and it is not accidental that method acting has become so strongly associated with certain modes of film stardom'.

In 'Gender, Sexuality and Power', an essay written exclusively for this collection, Rebecca Williams explores the ways in which approaches to film stardom are intertwined with (and can productively be explored through) 'third wave' feminism and auteur theory. In drawing on these perspectives, and assessing their implications for approaches to stardom, Williams argues that certain female stars can be identified both as empowered figures and as 'disruptive' agents who subvert the patriarchal celebrity culture from which they emerge. Williams uses Drew Barrymore as her primary case study, arguing that, 'her status as a producer/auteur and the inextricability of her on-screen and "real life" personas make her a unique example of a female celebrity: one that ensures a feminist reading is now possible'. In Williams' essay, then, Barrymore emerges as someone who 'authors' her own image, particularly in terms of wanting to be seen as an 'auteur' through the work of her production company and the well publicized commentary on the directors she has worked with. However, it is her 'performed agency', on screen, that enables one to 'explore the ways in which she subverts or reinforces hegemonic ideas about gender and sexuality, rendering a complex and ambiguous feminist reading of her star persona possible'.

The last two essays in this section move the analysis of stardom into new textual and theoretical areas – stars become explicitly connected to celebrity, to authorship, to new theoretical interventions. But they also begin to recognize the shifting and historical nature of the star and celebrity universe – a critical issue taken up and extended in the next section.

6

The Powerless 'Elite': Theory and Sociological Research on the Phenomenon of the Stars[1]

Francesco Alberoni

General conditions for the existence of the phenomenon

In every society are to be found persons who, in the eyes of other members of the collectivity, are especially remarkable and who attract universal attention. This applies most often to the king and nobles, to priests, prophets and men of power, although often in very diverse ways and in varying degrees. In general it is a question of persons who hold power (political, economic or religious) – that is to say, of persons whose decisions have an influence on the present and future fortunes of the society which they direct. This rule holds true even in modern western society. However, besides these persons, one finds others, *whose institutional power is very limited or non-existent, but whose doings and way of life arouse a considerable and sometimes even a maximum degree of interest*. This interest is not related to the consequences which the activities and decisions of these particular individuals (stars, idols, *'divi'*) can have on the lives and future expectations of members of the society. They belong to another sphere of evaluation.

The existence, at the heart of a society, of two categories of persons whose behaviour is an object of great attention, is accompanied effectively by a difference *in orientations and in criteria of evaluation*. Because the holders of power are 'evaluated' almost exclusively according to the direct or indirect consequences of their activities for the attainment of societal goals and for the organization of the community, with them it is a question of a specific criterion of evaluation. With the second group, a more complex system, which we are going to analyse in the course of the present research, is involved.

A phenomenon like 'stardom' does not exist unless certain systems of action are institutionally considered as *unimportant from a political point of view*. In other words 'stars' exist in that measure to which their activities are not mainly evaluated according to the consequences which they involve for the collectivity. There is a social mechanism of separation which, put schematically, holds that the 'stars' do not occupy *institutional positions of power*. One may note that this situation could not, in theory, hold in a marxist social system where every member of a social group has a function for the collectivity and is responsible for the consequences of his action. It could, however, hold in these circumstances in respect of persons who, living outside the system and belonging to the capitalist world, have no power over the system itself.

Besides these two conditions which we have indicated, we can mention several others: the degree of structuring of the social system; the growth in size of societies; the increase in economics wealth and, social mobility.

As far as the *structuring* of the social system is concerned, what we have already said has implied this. The separation out of specific principles of evaluation, important for the growing institutional cadres of decision-making power, cannot help but produce a complex structure in a society.

As to the size of the social system, we observe that in public–star relationships, each individual member of the public knows the star, but the star does not know any individual. The star views the public as a collectivity. This does not mean that personal relationships between the star and other actors cannot exist, but that it is not these personal relationships which characterize the phenomenon. For a relationship of this kind to be set up, one must presuppose a large number of spectators and the existence of certain specific social mechanisms. Even if the star is perceived in his or her individuality, the spectators cannot be perceived in theirs. This situation is best exemplified in a large-scale society, with a high level of interdependence, at the core of which and by virtue of its very large size, only a small number of persons can provide a point of reference for all. In a more restricted community, the same process would be possible, bearing in mind the existence of those institutional barriers of the type which separate the king, or certain priests or nobles. In this case, the phenomenon would be something other than 'stardom', since for the latter there is no institutional barrier. On the contrary, the obstacle arises in most cases either because observation of the person concerned cannot be direct or because of the sheer number of aspirants to such a type of relationship. We can see that the relationship between star and public lacks an element which we would label 'mutuality'.

An increase of economic wealth is a third basic condition. In effect, only an income above subsistence level allows the mobilization of interests and attention which gives rise to the phenomenon of stardom. Nevertheless, one must be cautious in establishing a correlation between these two orders of phenomena. On the one hand, the rise in income above subsistence level is always the fruit of an economic and structural trans-formation of society – a point which connects with the two earlier conditions – on the other hand, we can find the phenomenon of 'stars' at very low levels of income and economic development (football-players in South America; cinema actors in India). One might even wonder whether the phenomenon in its most accentuated form is not peculiar to societies which are socially and economically underdeveloped.

Social mobility, which is dependent on the transformation of the system, is also a fundamental condition for enabling one to have admiration, rather than envy, for the star.

Stardom and charisma

We will use the word 'stars' and 'stardom' with a rather wider meaning than common usage allows, especially in Italy.[2] Following Panzini's definition (1963, p. 202), one would understand by this word the phenomenon by which a certain individual attracts, in the eyes of many others, an unconditional admiration and interest. The cry of the crowd to the victorious champion 'you are a god' provides a typical example. The champion is credited with capacities superior to those of all other men, and thus with super-human qualities. Weber defined this situation as *charismatic* (1968, vol. 1, p. 241).

According to Max Weber, charisma leads to a power relationship by virtue of the fact that the possessor of charisma is perceived as a leader or chief (thus producing an internalized feeling of obligation); under his leadership, those who submit derive benefits which constitute proof of charisma. In the definition of 'stardom' we have made it clear that the star is not endowed with authoritative power and that his decisions are not collectively felt to have any influence on the life and the future of members of the collectivity. How is it that the charismatic element of 'stardom' does not get transformed into a power relationship? The explanation must be sought in the mechanisms which, in a highly structured society, give rise to the specificity of social roles. Whoever occupies a social position is appraised according to the specific content of the function which characterizes this position (see Parsons, 1949). In the case of a multiple classification, the specificity of the function and of the evaluation does not disappear (see Alberoni, 1960, pp. 37–42).

In other words, a bank employee is judged in the light of specific criteria which relate to the kind of work he does. If at the same time he is a member of some association, the kind of normative qualities required of him in the second system and the evaluative criteria used in relation to it, are not only specific, but often will not relate to the former. It is exactly this independence of social roles which, in modern societies, leads to conflicts between the roles themselves. Thus the bank employee or the unattached person who rejoices at the victory of his sporting hero and who calls out 'you are a god' does not cease to be a bank employee or a private citizen in order to follow his idol and share in his idol's charisma. The behaviour in which charisma is expressed is in reality behaviour in a particular role, while the behaviour of the spectator is defined by exclusion from this role and by the retention of his ordinary roles. The spectator is present at, shares in, but does not act. The manifestation of charisma which concerns us presupposes, therefore, a stable social structure – that is, a system of pre-established and internalized roles, of such a kind that the sharing in charisma does not result in the restructuring of habitual systems of action. In this way, the charisma is highly specific.

The racing cyclist who is a demi-god in the eyes of his enthusiastic admirer does not necessarily show competence in other fields. The specificity of charisma should be understood as a specificity relating to one class of actions, all requiring the same kind of skill. This is why a great racing cyclist can also be a great athlete. Specialization lies at the heart of any particular field. Besides, a champion's superiority in fields different from his speciality, but within the same category, can furnish confirmation of his true charismatic nature.

By contrast, in a society where there is no complexity of social structures, nor mechanisms for separating out social roles, charisma tends to become generalized. This is one of the reasons why stardom does not exist in small-scale societies. The exceptional man raises himself to a charismatic level and becomes a hero. He thus acquires over the community a power which, at the same time, exposes him to aggressively violent reactions on the part of his opponents and to the envy of those who are less adept than he. Change occurs within two limiting points: either the hero is overthrown by envy and aggression, or he succeeds over his enemies and his power is institutionalized. Neither case would be expected in large-scale societies with a high level of structuring. In such cases, charisma is not generalized, the star does not acquire power and as a result is not exposed to envy or aggression. The sharp separation between roles which prevents the stars from acquiring an institutionalized position of power in a highly structured society is the social system's protection mechanism against the menace of generalized charisma. The separation of roles in this respect offers much stronger guarantees than does simply specificity of roles. In the case of multiple allocation, the specification of roles is only efficacious up to the point where the corresponding modes of evaluation are deeply internalized. If the specificity of evaluation were strongly internalized, the star would be able to occupy a power position because he or she would be evaluated quite differently as a holder of power than as artist, football champion, etc. But if the internalization is shallow, there is always the danger in this situation that charisma will become generalized. The great actor, the great athlete, the personage known to all, sympathetic, attractive – all these could be raised to power, not independently of the fact of their being actors, cyclists or well-known figures, but precisely because they are such. This would occur especially in countries where the structuring is still weak and where specific and rational modes of evaluation are little internalized.

[. . .]

The mechanism by which social roles are sharply separated seems therefore to have the function of a defence against the generalization of charisma. In the light of these considerations one may assume that the condition of sharp separation of roles will lose its importance along with a greater internalization of specific modes of evaluation.

The 'stars' as an elite

In any society which is socially stratified, normal methods for the study of stratification always enable us to identify a more exalted social stratum which has sharply different characteristics from other social strata. A primary feature of this difference is the existence, amongst members of this particular stratum, of a higher degree of interaction than is found between members of other strata.

A second feature derives from the fact that in this group, competition, and often very active competition, always takes place with a high regard for the rules and mores of the group, thus ensuring that the decisions of members of the 'elite' do not have too sudden and sharp repercussions on the non-privileged.

The third feature is a certain degree of isolation, compared with other strata and groups. In general this is a question of ensuring a degree of secrecy for the activities of competition and cooperation, since these might not accord with the those of the non-privileged. The reduction in what we will call observability has the effect of enabling those who hold power to follow strategies for conserving it, and sometimes constitutes a means for preserving privilege. In contrast, an increase in observability is often an expression of the diminution of power. All of which comes back to the point that a power elite can never be exposed to a high degree of observability. In any case, the forms and the nature of observability, as far as the holders of institutional power are concerned, are institutionally established (in democracy in very liberal measure); this characteristic, which is most important, is respected even when there is a high degree of observability. In the case of the stars, on the contrary, observability is practically unlimited.

[. . .]

In long-established and well-consolidated democracies, where the internalization of the values of the social system is deepest, observability is greater and more diffused. This probably stems from the fact that the danger represented by the generalization of charisma is least; the institutionalized rules coincide in greater measure with the mores of the community. The limitation of evaluations within highly specific limits here loses its importance. In England, or in the United States, politicians are evaluated (in a greater measure than in Italy, for example) with regard to activities which are not strictly or specifically political. The President of the United States, in order to be elected, must present a total image of his private life, of his relations with the community, etc., something which is inconceivable in a democracy of recent origin, menaced by the generalization of charisma. The mode of behaviour in the community becomes the object of evaluation in order to demonstrate the adherence of the candidate to the mores of the society, mores which constitute the fundamental basis of evaluation internalized from the political system. The President will become a symbol for the nation, an ideal model for universal reference; he crystallizes in himself many of the characteristics belonging to stardom. Hence a necessity for an *a priori* evaluation of his manner of life and of his capacities in office. The latter is possible when the values inspired by the political system are widely shared and deeply internalized. A very slight deviation can then rapidly provoke the condemnation of the person, whatever may be his institutional power position. The case is very different if this internalization does not exist. Satisfaction can easily transform itself into admiration, qualities into superhuman properties, superiority into charisma, and admiration into devotion.

[. . .]

We can say that the stars are, like the power elite, an object of reference for the community, but of a different kind. It seems to us useful to stress that a good many of these stars appear in the eyes of the public as being in close interaction and making up a true elite which occupies a central place (although without power) in a community of an industrialized kind. They constitute a genuine core of the community, and although deprived of any fixed or stable location, they do at least partially congregate as a group in certain privileged places.[3]

If we were to choose any list whatsoever of people of this kind, based on a sampling of weekly magazines, we would soon find that the majority has been or is effectively in interaction. We are here concerned with a world of entertainment, related to everyday society by reason of business or profession, or because they frequent the same fashionable places, the same receptions, etc.

In the eyes of the public, this commonality probably seems higher than it really is, either by reason of the false impression of proximity suggested by television shows, or through the juxtaposition of photographic evidence with press articles, or because of the care which is taken to present to the public friendly and cooperative forms of interaction and to soften hostile and competitive forms. The members of this elite thus appear, contrary to fact, as being potentially in interaction.

One can say that the stars form a social group with very fluid and uncertain limits. The group is not structured, but it shows certain centres of interaction which sometimes take on the character of sub-group or sub-community: for example, the community group of the Via Veneto in Rome, the Frank Sinatra clan, etc. Those who make up a lower group (the fringe constituted by those who, in the eyes of the public, interact only occasionally with the group, like certain writers, painters or fashionable thinkers) do not, however, exhaust the totality of these personages who are 'significant', *although lacking in power or authority*. The protagonists in national scandals those accused of famous crimes are not part of this elite: participants in televised competitions or television plays enter it in a rather fleeting manner. Even when they lack interactive relationships with the community core, or when they are institutionally excluded from it, these people (even the criminals) are nevertheless potential members of it in the eyes of the public.

Evaluation of modes of conduct in the community

We have said that the stars are those members of the community whom *all* can evaluate, love or criticize. They are the chosen objects of collective gossip, the channels of which are the mass media of communication.

To fulfil such a social function, they must be observable to people of all degrees. In a small-scale community, observability is very much heightened, and the tension which accompanies observability is very great, but there also exist specific mechanisms for reducing observability and for preserving an area of privacy. All members of the social groups are subject to continual observation and other members of the group evaluate their behaviour (often by means of gossip) in order to:

1. Decide whether, according to group values and rules, their morality or character is deviant.
2. Compare performance with expectation.
3. Verify culturally established predictions and expectations, based on earlier behaviour and the pressures exerted by the milieu.
4. Assess the influence of their behaviour on the community (for instance, the effect of their example on morals).

   The result is to encompass behaviour in a system of value-norms and procedure-results, which is predetermined but also in a continual, if rather slow, state of revision. Each behaviour is, therefore, a matter to be experienced by the collectivity and the result serves to test the systems of expectation (normative or not) of the group under consideration.
5. One other source of tension associated with observability lies in its direct correspondence with conscious or unconscious desires or impulses (voyeurism, release of aggression, love, etc.).

6. There is, finally, one class of evaluations from which several advantages might be expected in connection with interactive relations. In this case observation is useful to an individual to the extent that the behaviour is particularly instrumental for him.

[...]

As far as the evaluative orientation of the sixth type is concerned, it can apply to persons with whom the subject is in interaction (members of his family, friends, acquaintances, rivals, etc.) and persons who hold power in the community (the power elite). Orientations of types 1, 2, 3, and 5 are, in a large-scale community, directed towards the stars, while orientations of types 4 and 6 are specifically directed towards the power elite. We can note that, even when limited to evaluations of types 1, 2, 3, and 5, there is a profound difference between the gossip which goes on in small villages and that which applies to the stars. The former is more critical, aggressive, scandalous than the latter. The majority of the stars chooses freely, or at least accepts its collective role, and the group to which they belong retains a sufficient degree of stability. These two conditions would not be realizable if the aggressive and competitive components which develop in community life were free to attach to them.

One other interesting fact is that the stars are not objects of envy. Further, the elite of the stars is not in general perceived as a privileged class; their very existence is not regarded as a clear and brutal witness to social injustice.

The lack of slander, of envy and of class demands – these are the phenomena between which one can see a correlation, but which, from a sociological point of view, are not necessarily linked.

In general, scandal occurs without those who are its object being considered as a privileged group. It consists essentially in sharing with someone else the knowledge and reprobation of some moral act of another known to both, and in deriving a satisfaction from the condemnation which compensates for a personal aggressiveness in relation to the person who is the object of scandal. Such a satisfaction exists when, in a small community, the shared condemnation effectively harms the intended person; from this condemnation issue collective punitive acts (sanctions). The fact that such a condemnation is made according to shared standards of evaluation avoids, on the other hand, any feelings of guilt which might be provoked by the consciousness of personal aggression. The unconscious aggression which is the driving force of the action is transformed in this manner into 'moral disdain'. From the point of view of the community, this process functions as a mechanism for assessing all behaviour according to the values and rules of the group. This mechanism presupposes the existence of rigorous principles of evaluation and the possibility of an effective prejudice against the deviant person (sanction), and moreover the existence of prior motives of aggressiveness. In relation to the stars these three conditions exist only in very small measure.

[...]

We thus arrive at a discussion of envy. In envy an acquisition of some kind, or an advantage obtained by a person, is considered by some other person as an injustice. The roots of envy, as psychologists have demonstrated, lie in infancy. In most cases it is the *transfer* from competitive infantile situations concerning a frustrated love object, which is internalized to allow its exclusive possession. An analogous mechanism can be found in static societies. Competition for some good in limited supply (like land) develops on the supposition that acquisition of one part of the good by an individual automatically implies the potential deprivation of all other individuals.[4] This mechanism tends to disappear in an economic system in which goods are capable of accumulation without limit by means of rationally controlled individual and collective action (following the principle of efficiency). In such a reference system, any action which is revealed as efficient for attaining an end is judged as likely not to diminish but to increase the probability that other individuals can attain the same result. In place of the mechanism of envy there is released the mechanism of admiration.

A powerful component of stardom is the admiration for the success achieved by the stars. Gina Lollobrigida, Sophia Loren, Marilyn Monroe bear witness, by their existence, to the large possibilities for social mobility. From the point of view of communal orientations of evaluation, the problem is to demonstrate that such a great improvement of status has been obtained not by illicit means but thanks to meritorious conduct and to exceptional or charismatic qualities. A major part of 'gossip' about stars performs this function. It is evident that this interpretation depends on the existence of a certain degree of social distance between the star and the public, so as to permit only an indirect or partial confrontation between the one and the other. This can be verified without difficulty when information is provided by the more remote means of communication, and in particular by mass communication. This absence of direct inter-action is often felt by the public as a limitation, a hindrance to full and entire knowledge of the stars. But this last aspiration, if it were satisfied, would lead to a complete development of a moral critique and the freeing of components of aggression and envy which exist all the time, but under control. These components would threaten the existence even of the stars.

Let us conclude this point with a last observation. We have noted in passing, and it has been verified in our experimental research, that the moral evaluation of the stars is more 'indulgent' than that reserved by the public for those who are socially nearer to them. This shows itself particularly in the case of small communities where social control is rigorous and where the contrast is very obvious between this control and the tolerance shown towards the stars. This phenomenon can be explained in part by the absence of those aggressive components which underlie slander and envy, and in equal part by social distance. On the basis of previously stated considerations, we can understand the reasons for this fact in sociological terms. Amongst the modes of evaluation already discussed, the fourth type has, in small communities, a very great importance where the evaluation aims to test the consequences of a way of acting for the community (the influence of example on morals). Moral vigilance and negative evaluation equally function to protect the community against the threat represented by the example of deviant behaviour which goes unpunished. In the case of stars, this category of evaluation loses its importance because they are not judged institutionally responsible for the results of their actions on the community. In small communities, there is an awareness of the potentially scandalous and corrupting character of their behaviour, but there is no possibility of applying sanctions. In the more generalized community, the separation of roles has such an important function that it makes this danger pass to a second level. As a result, a strong component of moral evaluation disappears or is attenuated. At the psychological level, this reduction is achieved by a relative evaluation: in effect each person judges, not in relation to the standards of his own community, but in relation to those of the stars (elite) who serve as a reference group. A big gap between the rules of the community of membership and those of the reference group requires continual recourse to a mechanism of separation between 'us' and our community and 'them' and their community. This can lead to an opposition between the reference group and the community of membership. We will see how strong are the critico-aggressive components which are then released.

Action within the community and action on the part of the community

Taken together, these factors which we have illustrated strongly reduce the aggressive and competitive components which develop in action in a community. However, they do not suffice to explain why the elite of stars is not considered as a privileged class, witness to the injustice of the social system. Their wealth, the manner of life they lead, constitute evident affronts to egalitarian ideals. The most commonly given explanations of this phenomenon appeal on the one hand to the mechanisms of the 'star system' and on the other to the 'narcotizing illusion'.

In the former case, one observes that stardom is the product of an important publicity organization which is useful to the entertainment industry. Thanks to the media of communication, the public are presented with the image of the person who has most chance of attracting attention and sympathy, of exciting human warmth or curiosity. The whole life of the stars is thus astutely orchestrated and arranged, so that nothing is left to chance. This type of explanation suffers from a certain naiveté. It is simplistic and naive to think that a phenomenon like stardom can be the intentional result of artful manoevres. Publicity agents, by their actions, do no more than facilitate and direct into a chosen path, a phenomenon which is an expression of the society as a whole. They are no more than part of the social mechanism which they are supposed to create.

Moreover, this thesis is contradicted by the history of stardom. In the early days film producers were opposed to the development of the system which nevertheless became established; and it was only after the event that they came to favour it, realizing that they could exploit it to their own ends, rather than find themselves crushed by opposing it. Furthermore, one cannot say that the star system has tended to cover up the wealth of the stars, their luxury, or their extraordinary earnings, in order to stress their social merits and their social function, etc. The star system has never, indeed, sought to legitimate the position of the stars on any other basis than their personality, their private life, their friends, their intimate tragedies and their eccentricities. Without any doubt it has attenuated the competitive elements of their ways of acting in the community, and has proclaimed the existence of amicable relations between such and such amongst them, and between them and the public. That could have contributed, marginally, to the avoidance of any growth of class resentment, but it certainly would not have been possible so to act if resentment of this kind was clearly manifested.

The theory of the 'narcotizing illusion' sees in the star system a cultural product of the economic power elite, having as its object to supply the masses with an escape into fantasy and an illusion of mobility, in such a way as to prevent their taking stock of their real condition as exploited masses. Against this theory, which has achieved considerable success, there is the fact that the star system has prospered, and prospered in nearly all countries and at all social levels – even amongst groups which adopt a marxist perspective. Interest in stars can be found through the whole range of the political keyboard, without any distinction. It would be interesting to make a closer study of the changing attitude of the press, and especially of the communist press, towards the stars. Immediately after the war (until about 1950) the stars were criticized or condemned. Subsequently they, and their way of life, were given a warm welcome. Many amongst them were men of the left who had never in their lives sought to become stars and who, on the contrary, had even denounced the phenomenon. The stars are proclaimed as such by the collectivity. It is not they themselves who impose themselves on the latter by a power acquired independently of the collectivity. This does not stem only from the fact that the stars are an open elite. Things would not be different if the stars were self-perpetuating, and if what is the case for some individuals like, for example, Greta Garbo and Clark Gable, were a universal rule. What counts is the fact that their *status* is always potentially revocable: by the public. The star system thus never creates the star, but it proposes the candidate for 'election', and helps to retain the favour of the 'electors'. Certainly those who activate the star system have an ascendancy of power which they hold over the public, but that is precisely why it is towards them and not towards the stars, that there can and does form some class resentment. In the eyes of the public, the producer is someone of quite a different order from the star whom he launches. Even when he enters into the elite of the stars he always remains an ambivalent figure, and the public forgets his power only when his personal affairs, as also his way of acting in the community, assume an autonomous interest.[5]

We can now appreciate a last and interesting phenomenon peculiar to stardom. Although most stars are not dispersed, but grouped together, the evaluative orientation is not directed towards the group. It is almost always the individual and not the group, that is, the ways of acting within the community and not the community itself, which become the object of evaluation. It can turn out that the community itself becomes an object of evaluation, but in this case the framework changes completely and the critical-aggressive components of which we have spoken are released.

In this case, the elite of the stars, instead of becoming the centre of the community as a whole, is detached from it and is differentiated as a distinct and privileged community, an expression of organized social forces and, as a result a holder of power. In such a case the star no longer belongs to the wider community, that is to say to ours, but to an opposed community.

The innumerable denunciations of the moral poverty and the corruption of Hollywood, together with marxist critiques, or again films like *La Dolce Vita*, tend towards the production of a frame of meaning of this kind. But this restructuring does not persist and tends quickly to dissolve. It gives way, on the whole, to an evaluation of each individual and his influence on the community. That is why men can scorn and condemn the morals of Hollywood, the way of life of the Via Veneto and of criminal circles, and continue meanwhile to be touched by the vicissitudes which affect Carla Gravina and Sacha Distel, to admire Lana Turner, to express sympathy for Frank Sinatra and to respect the memory of Clark Gable.

Meaning and perspectives of stardom

In the light of the foregoing considerations, stardom appears as a phenomenon appropriate to a certain moment in the development of industrial societies, in which it fulfils certain variable functions which depend on the socio-political configuration of the society. Stardom carries a time dimension, which enables us to make a dynamic study of it.

The development of industry, the rise in population, urbanization, the increasing interdependence of the economic system and the appearance of the means of mass communication all tend to break down traditional social relationships. Society becomes differentiated and develops associations and organizations which are impersonal, rational and variable, controlled by a limited number of men who possess particular qualities and who monopolize the instruments of control. The information which, transmitted by the traditional channels of communication, sufficed in more limited communities to provide the coordinates of orientation in the heart of the general system, rapidly became insufficient because of the increasing complexity of the latter, because of its novelty and variability. The political organization of the whole society and of the state is largely controlled by new strata and by classes under formation; in addition the society and the state become rationalized according to the model of economic arrangements. The system presents a new structure formed from an articulated assemblage of positions defined in universalist ways, to which correspond specific roles, which are themselves universal, neutral and subject to the criteria of efficiency. The culture ceases to be a collection of pre-ordained solutions to recurring problems; it is differentiated in two directions. On the one hand it becomes a science capable of obtaining results wished for by means of procedures open to theoretical deduction; on the other hand the culture depends on a large area of consensus concerning the implicit meaning of given situations or about the possibility of attaining certain ends and realizing certain values. In this process the horizon of the community widens. The symbols of power of the community constitute the emotional centre of the social system as a whole. Sometimes one might see the emergence of national fascism, sometimes, when conflict between classes occurs in the absence of a dominant class, the community is identified with the class.

In such a case the community sees itself in those individuals who have symbolic value, and who at the same time occupy positions of symbolic power. They are the charismatic leaders who interpret new and former values of the whole community; on this basis they give unity to the experiences and expectations of members of the community, while creating the consensus which permits the whole process to go forward. In other countries with a democratic tradition, representative institutions are modified so as to welcome and meet the new demands which continually arise.

In those countries (an example is provided by Italy before the rise of fascism) the daily demands for orientation of community life (met in the small community by relations of neighbourhood, by gossip, by the exercise of applied morals, etc.) begin to be met at the level of a more general community life. The media of mass communication begin to present to the public persons who belong to the extended community and who become an object of interest, identification and collective evaluation. With the progress of visual information, persons of the entertainment world begin, to an increasing degree, to make their mark. Their lives, their social relationships, become an object of identification or a projection of the needs of the mass of the population, a benchmark for positive or negative evaluation, the chance to have experience in the domain of the morally possible, and a living testimony to the possibility of achieving a rise in personal status. Thanks to a collective consensus, their capacity and their skill readily acquire a charismatic dimension. However, the generalization of charisma is impeded by the simultaneous articulation of the structuring in the form of specific roles. Correspondingly, a preponderance is established of modes of evaluation which are impersonal, neutral and specific. On the other hand, since the danger of charisma exists in a much higher degree where the internalization of new evaluative orientations is shallowest (that is to say that it exists especially when the process of nation-forming is at its beginning) one also sees appearing mechanisms for the rigorous separation of roles. For this reason one must posit a more or less sharp distinction between the elite of power and the elite of stars. This mechanism of separation acquires a particular importance in countries which, after an experience of charismatic power, becomes democratic again (like Italy) at the moment when the process of economic development and rationalization is unleashed.

[...]

Our account has been concerned with progress towards a particularly interesting stage of transition, where a society is both rationalized and democratic, where the manifestations of charisma are henceforth under control, where the mythic forms of stardom tend to disappear and where regard for the wider society is strong and has already lost the implication of a euphoric participation in its 'power', although it has not yet become a responsible participation. How should this phenomenon be projected into the future? It is difficult to predict future developments, but it is at least very probable that the stars will continue to exist, both as privileged members of the wider community and as an object of reference for members of the latter. This might follow from the great extension of the wider community which only allows a few members to be a collective object of reference; or it could be so because, in a society under transition, there is always some insufficiency in the culture and consequently a need for a collective consensus about the new implications of reality and new solutions to be found to the problems of family, neighbourhood, of production and consumption, etc.

The progressive increase in interdependence in industrial society ought to lead us to take account of the responsibilities of all public personages, with rather more rigour than one finds in practice. We have seen that the stars are not held institutionally responsible for the consequences of their own actions on the community, since this responsibility rests uniquely on those men who occupy positions of institutional power. A decrease in the sharp separation of social roles and in their specificity can create the necessary conditions for opening to evaluation the 'private' life of the stars as well as of men engaged in politics, according to the consequences which their actions have for the collectivity.

Other likely changes can be foreseen if the tension of aspirations is reduced: this might create, or add to, the chances for individuals to satisfy personal ambition while at the same time supporting the institutional mechanisms provided by the society.

Notes

1. Extract from research conducted for the Institute of Sociology of the Catholic University of Milan, with financial help from UNESCO.
2. In French, the word *'divismō'* has been retained as a concept, and 'divi', in the plural as a related term; but the word 'vedette' has usually been used instead of the singular 'divo'.

   Translator's note: In this English translation, 'divi' has been rendered as 'stars'; similarly, the key term 'divismo', for which there is no English synonym, has been translated usually as 'stardom', and occasionally as 'star system' or 'phenomenon of the stars' (as in the title). It is hoped that the context fully conveys the intended meaning of these related concepts.
3. These are the star 'communities', as in Hollywood, or the Via Veneto, Rome, and all other places where the fashionable set meet. The most frequent occasions are for film premières, festivals, exhibitions, cruises, receptions and presentations of literary and artistic prizes, etc.
4. Alberoni (1961, pp. 69–80). This phenomenon is well described in Banfield (1961).
5. What we have just said is of great sociological interest, since we can establish in the same way that class resentment and the experience of injustice do not depend on the fact of contrasting inequalities with egalitarian ideals, but that they depend essentially on the fact that one perceives the existence of an autonomous illegitimate power underpinning the inequality. If the autonomous power goes by default (as in stardom) class resentment and the experience of injustice are consequently lacking.

References

Alberoni, F. (1960), *Contributo all' Integrazione sociale dell' Immigrato*, Milano, Vita e Pensiero.

Alberoni, F. (1961), 'Saggio critico delle differenze socioculturali tra due region meridionali', *Internat. soc. Science Rev.*, vols. 1 and 2.

Banfield, E. (1961), *Una Communita del Mezzogiorno, Bologna*, Il Mulino.

Panzini, A. (1963), *Modern Dictionary of Words which are not Found in Ordinary Dictionaries*, Milano, Hoepli.

Parsons, T. (1949), *The Social System*, Free Press.

Weber, M. (1968), *Economy and Society*, Bedminster Press.

7 Stars

Richard Dyer

[...]

Stars and the status quo

[...]

In his *Collective Search for Identity* Klapp suggests that stars (and other celebrities) can have one of three different relationships to prevalent norms – *reinforcement, seduction* and *transcendence*.

'To reinforce a person in social roles – encourage him [sic] to play those which are highly valued – and to maintain the image of the group superself are presumably the classic functions of heroes in all societies' (p. 219). Given Klapp's alternative, but necessarily exceptional, categories of seduction and transcendence (see below), this is acceptable. His elaboration of the concept is more problematic:

> **The beauty of heroes as a character-building force is that the individual, daydreaming, *chooses for himself* [sic], within the opportunities the available models provide – which, fortunately for the social order, usually 'just happen to be' more supporting than erosive or subversive. (p. 220)**

We might want to question here the extent to which the individual is not so shaped by the ideologies of her/his culture, or so structurally placed within her/his society, that choice becomes very delimited and predefined indeed. Equally, Klapp does not explore the implications of his view that models 'just happen to be' supportive of the *status quo* – his inverted commas show he is aware of the problem, but his liberalism does not allow him to ask who fashions the *status quo* or who controls the provision of models.

In the seduction scenario the hero breaks the rules or norms, but in a charming way. Klapp's examples are Mickey Spillane or James Bond, who demonstrate that 'it is possible, permissible, even admirable, to romp in the forbidden pasture' (p. 227).

In the case of transcendence, the hero 'produces a fresh point of view, a feeling of integrity, and makes a new man [sic]' (p. 229). This is more than just getting away with something, as in the previous category, since it does 'redefine and recreate standards by which experience is to be judged'. One of Klapp's examples in this category is Jean-Paul Belmondo, whose popularity with college students he sees as epitomising their discovery of a radical new lifestyle. Another example is I think more interesting, since it suggests the possibility of transcendence in a much less intellectually respectable instance. He quotes an account by a woman student recalling her enjoyment of Sandra Dee in *Gidget*, particularly her perseverance in learning to be a surfer, despite mockery, setbacks, etc. Here is an example, Klapp suggests, of a star offering 'a springboard by which a girl can vicariously leap from femininity into a role usually reserved for boys' (p. 234). There are problems with Klapp's categories of seduction and transcendence. How, for instance, can one actually distinguish with any rigour between the two? Can one not see both, and especially transcendence, as simply providing a 'safety-valve' for discontent, and by providing expression of it siphoning it off as a substantial subversive force? The answer to that depends on how hermetic your conception of the mass media, and of ideology, is. My own belief is that the system is a good deal more 'leaky' than many people would currently maintain. In my view, to assert the total closure of the system is essentially to deny the validity of class/sex/race struggles and their reproduction at all levels of society and in all human practices.

Reinforcement of values under threat

Klapp's category of reinforcement suggests only that heroes reinforce by embodying dominant values. Two studies of individual stars, William R. Brown on Will Rogers and Charles Eckert on Shirley Temple, suggest that stars embody social values that are to some degree in crisis.

In *Imagemaker: Will Rogers and the American Dream* Brown shows how Rogers embodied the four strands of the American Dream (the dignity of the common individual, democracy as the guarantee of freedom and quality, the gospel of hard work and the belief in material progress) at a point in time when the dream was becoming increasingly hard to believe in. Thus the 'dignity of the common individual' strand of the dream was linked in Rogers's image with that of the 'sturdy yeoman' at a time when farmers were suffering from a decline in their purchasing power as compared to other groups in the economy and from their gradual incorporation into a vast market economy. There was concurrently 'governmental corruption, financial greed, crime and a revolution in morals' (p. 60) and the emergence of anti-heroes, notably Al Capone.

In the face of this experience, Brown argues, Rogers reaffirmed the reality and validity of the 'sturdy yeoman', and similarly with the other values of the American Dream. One could say that at a time when the American value system might have been redirected, the old goals appearing inadequate, Rogers was there to demonstrate that there was life still in the traditional values and attitudes.

Eckert's article, 'Shirley Temple and the House of Rockefeller', uses a similar model, but with greater attention to the specificities of ideology. This leads him to stress the function of Temple for dominant ideology and interests, rather than for the reassurance of the audience as in Brown's approach. Eckert links Temple to the political solutions offered by the Republicans and Democrats to the poverty born of the Depression – the former stressed the role of individual charity (giving to the poor), seeing the federal relief programme proposed by the Democrats as an attack on the American ideals of initiative and individualism. By 1934, says Eckert, there was a deadlock – federal relief was not really working, yet its introduction had 'utterly demoralised charity efforts'. Into this situation comes Temple. The emphasis in her films is on love as a natural, spontaneous opening of one's heart so that 'the most implacable realities alter and disperse'; it is a love that is not universal but rather elicited by need.

Eckert stresses that one has to take other elements into account to understand fully Temple's star status – e.g. 'the mitigation of reality through fantasy, the exacerbated emotions relating to insufficiently cared for children, the commonly stated philosophy of pulling together to whip the Depression', but none the less insists that 'Shirley and her burden of love appeared at a moment when the official ideology of charity had reached a final and unyielding form and when the public sources of charitable support were drying up' (ibid.). I would generalise from this the notion of the star's image being related to contradictions in ideology – whether within the dominant ideology, or between it and other subordinated/revolutionary ideologies. The relation may be one of displacement, or of the suppression of one half of the contradiction and the fore-grounding of the other, or else it may be that the star effects a 'magic' reconciliation of the apparently incompatible terms. Thus if it is true to say that American society has seen sexuality, especially for women, as wrong and, in effect, 'extraordinary', and yet has required women to be both sexy and pure and ordinary, then one can see Lana Turner's combination of sexuality and ordinariness, or Marilyn Monroe's blend of sexiness and innocence, as effecting a magical synthesis of these opposites. This was possible partly through the specific chains of meaning in the images of those two stars, and partly through, once again, the fact of their real existence as individuals in the world, so that the disunity created by attaching opposing qualities to their images was none the less rendered a unity simply by virtue of the fact that each was only one person. So far I have been discussing the way stars may reinforce aspects of ideology simply by repeating, reproducing or reconciling them. However, both Barry King and Eckert (in his article on Shirley Temple) suggest that reinforcement may be achieved not so much by reiterating dominant values as by concealing prevalent contradictions or problems.

King discusses this in general terms. What he calls 'Hollywood studio realism' is built around 'the centrifuge of the hero', and is, he claims, 'inescapably social commentary' – yet it must not offend the audience (for else it would not sell). The star solves this problem 'because he or she converts the opinion expressed in the film to an expression of his being... he converts the question "why do people feel this way?" to "how does it feel to have such feelings?" ' This works in terms of the producers: 'The stars... ease the problem of judgement (which would politicise media) off the shoulders of those controlling the media by throwing it onto the realm of personal experience and feelings.' Equally it works for the audience, depoliticising their consciousness by individualising it, rendering the social personal.

The stars serve to mask people's awareness of themselves as class members by reconstituting social differences in the audience 'into a new polarity pro-star/ anti-star... collective experience is individualised and loses its collective insignificance'. In all these ways then stars, by virtue of being experienced (that is they are a phenomenon of experience not cognition) and individuated (embodying a general social value/norm in a 'unique' image), and having an existence in the real world, serve to defuse the political meanings that form the inescapable but potentially offensive or explosive point of departure of all media messages. King has not argued this through in the case of a specific star, but the argument might run that John Wayne or Jane Fonda, both stars with obvious political associations, act unavoidably to obscure the political issues they embody simply by demonstrating the lifestyle of their politics and displaying those political beliefs as an aspect of their personality. This means that films and stars are ideologically significant in the most general sense of cutting audiences off from politics, rendering them passive (cf. Lowenthal), but not ideologically significant in the narrower sense of reinforcing a given political standpoint. The specific politics of Wayne and Fonda would thus be irrelevant in discussing their ideological function, which is identical with that of all stars.

Whilst I would certainly share King's view as a description of a *tendency* of the star phenomenon, nevertheless I find it hard to discount the specific ideological meaning/function of given stars. King's view depends upon dismissing as politically irrelevant such things as lifestyles, feelings and 'the personal'. Obviously whether or not one regards these things as political depends upon one's politics. My own feeling is that we are so shaped and penetrated by our society that the personal is always political.

Charles Eckert's discussion of Shirley Temple stresses the way in which Temple's image both 'asserts and denies' problem aspects of Depression-capitalist society. Money, in the Republican ideological complex to which Temple's films belong, was a problematic issue: 'as a charitable gift [it] was benevolent, whereas [money] in the form of dole was destructive'. Charity and initiative were the values to be foregrounded, while money was 'ambivalent and repressed'.

Eckert's analysis seems to me to be in many respects exemplary for its linking of the produced image to the specific ideological realities of its time. Of course, not all stars will require the concept of displacement to account for their ideological functioning, but many will and Temple is a good example of the usefulness of the concept, since she is the kind of star so apparently without ideological significance.

Compensation

The notion of stars compensating people for qualities lacking in their lives is obviously close to the concept of stars embodying values that are under threat. The latter are presumably qualities which people have an idea of, but which they do not experience in their day-to-day lives. However, compensation implies not that an image makes one believe all over again in the threatened value, but that it shifts your attention from that value to some other, lesser, 'compensatory' one.

Leo Lowenthal sees the shift as one from active involvement in business, politics, the productive sphere, to active involvement in leisure and consumption. Lowenthal sees that this is a problem of real structural failures in society, not just a crisis of belief in an ideology. This perspective also informs Robert K. Merton's study of Kate Smith in his book *Mass Persuasion*. This is a study of the enormously successful war-bond drive conducted by Kate Smith on 21 September 1943. Many factors contributed to this success (length of broadcast, its special build-up, the content of what Smith said, etc.), but none more so than the image of Smith herself. Merton suggests that there was a congruence between Smith's image and the themes used to sell the bonds (e.g. partriotism, self-sacrifice, etc.), but above all notes that interviewees for his study stressed time and again Smith's sincerity. The radio broadcast itself 'corroborated' Smith's image of sincerity by the fact that she was doing it for nothing and that it went on for so long and yet she never flagged. Equally her image had been built up by the convergence of a variety of factors:

> published accounts of her charities; inadvertent and casual radio references to her contributions; expressions of her identification with other plain people; the halo transferred from the kind of people she talks about to herself – all these contribute to her established reputation as a doer of good. (p. 100)

Smith's image is then a condensation of various traditional values, 'guaranteed' by the actual existence of Smith as a person, producing her as an incarnation of sincerity.

Merton's interviewees contrasted Smith's sincerity with 'the pretenses, deceptions and dissembling which they observe in their daily experience' (p. 142). Merton suggests that the experience of being manipulated characterises contemporary society, it is one of 'the psychological effects of a society which, focused on capital and the market, tends to instrumentalise human relationships' (p. 143).

Although one could quarrel with aspects of Merton's formulation (the notion of 'a person' should not be taken as a given or an absolute, since notions of what it is to be human are culturally and historically specific; it may be that the discrepancy between appearance and reality in human relationships is necessary and inescapable, Smith's appeal therefore being unrealisably utopian), at the level of description it seems very persuasive.

Merton also explores other aspects of Smith's image, unfortunately in less detail. Thus he suggests that Smith embodies the first of the 'three prevailing models for the feminine sex role: the domesticity pattern, the career pattern, and the glamour pattern' at the expense of the other two. By reinforcing and therefore legitimating the domesticity pattern, she 'serves to mitigate the strain and conflict' these contradictory roles impose on women.

Charisma

Merton's ideas, as well as those of Eckert and Brown, all relate to the notion of 'charisma' as developed by Max Weber in the field of political theory. I'd like to end Part One by discussing Weber's theories and their relevance to the star phenomenon, as, in a suitably modified form, the notion of charisma (in the Weberian sense, not just meaning 'magic', etc.) does combine concepts of social function with an understanding of ideology.

Weber was interested in accounting for how political order is legitimated (other than by sheer force), and suggested three alternatives: tradition (doing what we've always done), bureaucracy (doing things according to agreed but alterable, supposedly rational rules) and charisma (doing things because the leader suggests it). Charisma is defined as 'a certain quality of an individual personality by virtue of which he [sic] is set apart from ordinary men and treated as endowed with supernatural, superhuman or at least superficially exceptional qualities' (*On Charisma and Institution Building*, p. 329).

There are certain problems about transferring the notion of charisma from political to film theory. As Alberoni has pointed out, the star's status depends upon her/his not having any institutional political power. Yet there is clearly some correspondence between political and star charisma, in particular the question of how or why a given person comes to have 'charisma' attributed to him/her. E. A. Shils in 'Charisma, Order and Status' suggests that

The charismatic quality of an individual as perceived by others, or himself [sic] lies in what is thought to be his connection with (including possession by or embedment in) some *very central* feature of man's existence and the cosmos in which he lives. The centrality, coupled with intensity, makes it extraordinary.

One does not have to think in terms of 'man's existence' and 'the cosmos', somewhat suspect eternal universals, to accept the general validity of this statement, especially as it is probably very often the case that what is culturally and historically specific about the charismatic person's relationship to her/his society may none the less present itself, or be read, as being an eternal universal relationship.

S. N. Eisenstadt in his introduction to Weber's *Charisma and Institution Building* has taken this one stage further by suggesting, on the basis of a survey of communications research, that charismatic appeal is effective especially when the social order is uncertain, unstable and ambiguous and when the charismatic figure or group offers a value, order or stability to counterpoise this. Linking a star with the whole of a society may not get us very far in these terms, unless one takes twentieth-century western society to have been in constant instability. Rather, one needs to think in terms of the relationships (of the various kinds outlined above) between stars and specific instabilities, ambiguities and contradictions in the culture (which are reproduced in the actual practice of making films, and film stars).

This model underlines one of the earliest attempts to analyse a star image, Alistair Cooke's *Douglas Fairbanks: The Making of a Screen Character*, published in 1940. Cooke accounts for Fairbanks's stardom in terms of the appropriateness of his 'Americanness' to the contemporary situation of America.

Marilyn Monroe provides another example. Her image has to be situated in the flux of ideas about morality and sexuality that characterised the 50s in America and can here be indicated by such instances as the spread of Freudian ideas in post-war America (registered particularly in the Hollywood melodrama), the Kinsey report, Betty Friedan's *The Feminine Mystique*, rebel stars such as Marlon Brando, James Dean and Elvis Presley, the relaxation of cinema censorship in the face of competition from television, etc. (In turn, these instances need to be situated in relation to other levels of the social formation, e.g. actual social and sexual relations, the relative economic situations of men and women, etc.) Monroe's combination of sexuality and innocence is part of that flux, but one can also see her 'charisma' as being the apparent condensation of all that within her. Thus she seemed to 'be' the very tensions that ran through the ideological life of 50s America. You could see this as heroically living out the tensions or painfully exposing them.

Just as star charisma needs to be situated in the specificities of the ideological configurations to which it belongs, so also virtually all sociological theories of stars ignore the *specificities* of another aspect of the phenomenon – the audience.

(Assumptions about the audience as a generalised, homogenous collectivity abound in the material surveyed above.) The importance of contradictions as they are lived by audience members in considering the star phenomenon is suggested by asides in J. P. Mayer, Andrew Tudor and Edgar Morin to the effect that particularly intense star/audience relationships occur among adolescents and women. They point to some empirical evidence for this. I would also point out the absolutely central importance of stars in gay ghetto culture. These groups all share a peculiarly intense degree of role/identity conflict and pressure, and an (albeit partial) exclusion from the dominant articulacy of, respectively, adult, male, heterosexual culture. If these star/audience relationships are only an intensification of the conflicts and exclusions experienced by everyone,[1] it is also significant that, in the discussion of 'subversive' star images in the next part, stars embodying adolescent, female and gay images play a crucial role.

Note

1. I do not know of any research which looks at the differences in star/audience relationships according to class and race.

Heavenly Bodies

Richard Dyer

[...]

Making Stars

The star phenomenon consists of everything that is publicly available about stars. A film star's image is not just his or her film, but the promotion of those films and of the star through pin-ups, public appearances, studio hand-outs and so on, as well as interviews, biographies and coverage in the press of the star's doings and 'private' life. Further, a star's image is also what people say or write about him or her, as critics or commentators, the way the image is used in other contexts such as advertisements, novels, pop songs, and finally the way the star can become part of the coinage of everyday speech. Jean-Paul Belmondo imitating Humphrey Bogart in *A bout de souffle* is part of Bogart's image, just as anyone saying; in a mid-European accent, 'I want to be alone' reproduces, extends and inflects Greta Garbo's image.

[...]

Images have to be made. Stars are produced by the media industries, film stars by Hollywood (or its equivalent in other countries) in the first instance, but then also by other agencies with which Hollywood is connected in varying ways and with varying degrees of influence. Hollywood controlled not only the stars' films but their promotion, the pin-ups and glamour portraits, press releases and to a large extent the fan clubs. In turn, Hollywood's connections with other media industries meant that what got into the press, who got to interview a star, what clips were released to television was to a large extent decided by Hollywood. But this is to present the process of star making as uniform and oneway. Hollywood, even within its own boundaries, was much more complex and contradictory than this. If there have always been certain key individuals in controlling positions (usually studio bosses and major producers, but also some directors, stars and other figures) and if they all share a general professional ideology, clustering especially around notions of entertainment, still Hollywood is also characterised by internecine warfare between departments, by those departments getting on with their own thing in their own ways and by a recognition that it is important to leave spaces for individuals and groups to develop their own ideas (if only because innovation is part of the way that capitalist industries renew themselves). If broadly everyone in Hollywood had a sense of what the Monroe, Robeson and Garland images were, still different departments and different people would understand and inflect the image differently. This already complex image-making system looks even more complex when one brings in the other media agencies involved, since there are elements of rivalry and competition between them and Hollywood, as well as co-operation and mutual influence. If the drift of the image emanates from Hollywood, and with some consistency within Hollywood, still the whole image-making process within and without Hollywood allows for variation, inflection, and contradiction.

[...]

Stars are made for profit. In terms of the market, stars are part of the way films are sold. The star's presence in a film is a promise of a certain kind of thing that you would see if you went to see the film. Equally, stars sell newspapers and magazines, and are used to sell toiletries, fashions, cars and almost anything else.

This market function of stars is only one aspect of their *economic importance*. They are also a property on the strength of whose name money can be raised for a film; they are an asset to the person (the star him/herself), studio and agent who controls them; they are a major part of the cost of a film. Above all, they are part of the labour that produces film as a commodity that can be sold for profit in the market place.

Stars are involved in making themselves into commodities; they are both labour and the thing that labour produces. They do not produce themselves alone. We can distinguish two logically separate stages. First, the person is a body, a psychology, a set of skills that have to be mined and worked up into a star image. This work, of fashioning the star out of the raw material of the person, varies in the degree to which it respects what artists sometimes refer to as the inherent qualities of the material; make-up, coiffure, clothing, dieting and body-building can all make more or less of the body features they start with, and personality is no less malleable, skills no less learnable. The people who do this labour include the star him/herself as well as make-up artistes, hairdressers, dress designers, dieticians, body-building coaches, acting, dancing and other teachers, publicists, pin-up photographers, gossip columnists, and so on. Part of this manufacture of the star image takes place in the films the star makes, with all the personnel involved in that, but one can think of the films as a second stage. The star image is then a given, like machinery, an example of what Karl Marx calls 'congealed labour', something that is used with further labour (scripting, acting, directing, managing, filming, editing) to produce another commodity, a film.

Stars are examples of the way people live their relation to production in capitalist society. The three stars examined in subsequent chapters all in some measure revolted against the lack of control they felt they had – Robeson by giving up feature film-making altogether, Monroe by trying to fight for better parts and treatment, Garland by speaking of her experiences at MGM and by the way in which her later problems were credited to the Hollywood system. These battles are each central parts of the star's image and they enact some of the ways the individual is felt to be placed in relation to business and industry in contemporary society. At one level, they articulate a dominant experience of work itself under capitalism – not only the sense of being a cog in an industrial machine, but also the fact that one's labour and what it produces seem so divorced from each other – one labours to produce goods (and profits) in which one either does not share at all or only in the most meagre, back-handed fashion. Robeson's, Monroe's, Garland's sense that they had been used, turned into something they didn't control is particularly acute because the commodity they produced is fashioned in and out of their own bodies and psychologies.

[...]

Living Stars

Stars articulate what it is to be a human being in contemporary society; that is, they express the particular notion we hold of the person, of the 'individual'. They do so complexly, variously – they are not straightforward affirmations of individualism. On the contrary, they articulate both the promise and the difficulty that the notion of individuality presents for all of us who live by it.

'The individual' is a way of thinking and feeling about the discrete human person, including oneself, as a separate and coherent entity. The individual is thought of as separate in the sense that she or he has an existence apart from anything else – the individual is not just the sum of his or her social roles or actions. He or she may only be perceived through these things, may even be thought to be formed by them, yet there is, in this concept of the person, an irreducible core of being, the entity that is perceived within the roles and actions, the entity upon which social forces act. This irreducible core is coherent in that it is supposed to consist of certain peculiar, unique qualities that remain constant and give sense to the person's actions and reactions. However much the person's circumstances and behaviour may change, 'inside' they are still the same individual; even if 'inside' she or he has changed, it is through an evolution that has not altered the fundamental reality of that irreducible core that makes her or him a unique individual.

At its most optimistic, the social world is seen in this conception to emanate from the individual, and each person is seen to 'make' his or her own life. However, this is not necessary to the concept. What is central is the idea of the separable, coherent quality, located 'inside' in consciousness and variously termed 'the self', 'the soul', 'the subject' and so on. This is counterposed to 'society', something seen as logically distinct from the individuals who compose it, and very often as inimical to them. If in ideas of 'triumphant individualism' individuals are seen to determine society, in ideas of 'alienation' individuals are seen as cut adrift from and dominated, battered by the anonymity of society. Both views retain the notion of the individual as separate, irreducible, unique.

[...]

Stars articulate these ideas of personhood, in large measure shoring up the notion of the individual but also at times registering the doubts and anxieties attendant on it. In part, the fact that the star is not just a screen image but a flesh and blood person is liable to work to express the notion of the individual.

[...]

It can be enough just to know that there was one such person, but generally our sense of that one person is more vivid and important than all the roles and looks s/he assumes. People often say that they do not rate such and such a star because he or she is always the same.

This coherent continuousness within becomes what the star 'really is'. Much of the construction of the star encourages us to think this. Key moments in films are close-ups, separated out from the action and interaction of a scene, and not seen by other characters but only by us, thus disclosing for us the star's face, the intimate, transparent window to the soul. Star biographies are devoted to the notion of showing us the star as he or she really is. Blurbs, introductions, every page assures us that we are being taken 'behind the scenes', 'beneath the surface', 'beyond the image', there where the truth resides. Or again, there is a rhetoric of sincerity or authenticity, two qualities greatly prized in stars because they guarantee, respectively, that the star really means what he or she says, and that the star really is what she or he appears to be. Whether caught in the unmediated moment of the close-up, uncovered by the biographer's display of ruthless uncovering, or present in the star's indubitable sincerity and authenticity, we have a privileged reality to hang on to, the reality of the star's private self.

[...]

The private self is not always represented as good, safe or positive. There is an alternative tradition of representing the inner reality of men, especially, which stretches back at least as far as the romantic movement. Here the dark, turbulent forces of nature are used as metaphors for the man's inner self: Valentino in *The Son of the Sheik*, the young Laurence Olivier as Heathcliff in *Wuthering Heights* and as Maxim de Winter in *Rebecca*. In the forties and fifties the popularisation of psychoanalysis added new terms to the private:public opposition. Thus:

private	public
subconscious	conscious
Id	Ego

and in the still more recent Lacan inflection:

Imaginary	Symbolic

These have been particularly important in the subsequent development of male stars, where the romantic styles of brooding, introspective, mean-but-vulnerable masculinity have been given Oedipal, psychosexual, paranoid or other crypto-psycho-analytical inflections with stars like Montgomery Clift, James Dean, Marlon Brando, Anthony Perkins, Jack Nicholson, Richard Gere. Recent black male stars such as Jim Brown, Richard Roundtree and Billy Dee Williams are interesting in that their fiercely attractive intensity seems closer to the 'dangerous' romantic tradition proper; at the same time they also draw on the old stereotype of the black man as brute, only now portraying this as attractive rather than terrifying; and they are almost entirely untouched by the psychoanalytical project of rationalising and systematising and naming the life of the emotions and sensations. All these male stars work variations on the male inner self as negative, dangerous, neurotic, violent, but always upholding that as the reality of the man, what he is really like.

[...]

What is at stake in most of the examples discussed so far is the degree to which, and manner in which, what the star really is can be located in some inner, private, essential core. This is how the star phenomenon reproduces the overriding ideology of the person in contemporary society. But the star phenomenon cannot help being also about the person in public. Stars, after all, are always inescapably people in public. If the magic, with many stars, is that they seem to be their private selves in public, still they can also be about the business of being in public, the way in which the public self is endlessly produced and remade in presentation.

[...]

The private/public, individual/society dichotomy can be embodied by stars in various ways; the emphasis can fall at either end of the spectrum, although it more usually falls at the private, authentic, sincere end. Mostly too there is a sense of 'really' in play – people/ stars are really themselves in private or perhaps in public but at any rate somewhere. However, it is one of the ironies of the whole star phenomenon that all these assertions of the reality of the inner self or of public life take place in one of the aspects of modern life that is most associated with the invasion and destruction of the inner self and corruptibility of public life, namely the mass media. Stars might even seem to he the ultimate example of media hype, foisted on us by the media's constant need to manipulate our attention. We all know how the studios build up star images, how stars happen to turn up on chat shows just when their latest picture is released, how many of the stories printed about stars are but titillating fictions; we all know we are being sold stars. And yet those privileged moments, those biographies, those qualities of sincerity and authenticity, those images of the private and the natural can work for us. We may go either way.

8 Stars as a Cinematic Phenomenon

John Ellis

[…]

There is always a temptation to think of a 'star image' as some kind of fixed repertory of fixed meanings (Joan Crawford = tough, independent, ruthless, threateningly sexy, etc.). However, this seems to simplify the process, and to misstate the role of the star in producing meanings in films and beyond films. Star images are paradoxical. They are composed of elements which do not cohere, of contradictory tendencies. They are composed of clues rather than complete meanings, of representations that are less complete, less stunning, than those offered by cinema. The star image is an *incoherent* image. It shows the star both as an ordinary person and as an extraordinary person. It is also an *incomplete* image. It offers only the face, only the voice, only the still photo, where cinema offers the synthesis of voice, body and motion. The star image is paradoxical and incomplete so that it functions as an invitation to cinema, like the narrative image. It proposes cinema as the completion of its lacks, the synthesis of its separate fragments.

The relationship is not, however, only that of star-image = incomplete: film performance = completion. It is also one where the process of the star image echoes, repeats and develops a fundamental aspect of cinema itself. The star image rests on the paradox that the star is ordinary and extraordinary at the same time. The cinematic image (and the film performance) rests on the photo effect, the paradox that the photograph presents an absence that is present. In this sense, the star image is not completed by the film performance, because they both rest on the same paradox. Instead, the star image promises cinema. It restates the terms of the photo effect, renews the desire to experience this very particular sense of present-absence. So the star image is incomplete and paradoxical. It has a double relationship to the film performance: it proposes that the film performance will be more complete than the star image; and it echoes and promotes the photo effect which is fundamental to cinema as a regime of representation.

The process of circulation of a star image has been broadly the same whether it has been undertaken by a centralised studio agency (the form of classic Hollywood) or by a specialised enterprise contracted by the star themselves (the current form). The star's activities are presented in a number of media, some associated quite directly with the film industry, others using the film industry as one raw material amongst many. In the classic period of Hollywood, stars would 'feature' both in newspapers and magazines of general interest, and in magazines associated with cinema, fan magazines (or as we can now call them, fanzines). They appeared in advertisements, endorsing products. They appeared on radio, both in news, chat-shows and fiction. At certain points, they appeared directly as products and merchandise effects. The first star to do so was (probably) Mickey Mouse. In all of these media, the star appears directly as face, body and voice; and as a figure constructed by writing. There are photographs of the star; there are written descriptions of the star's activities; there are the voices of stars speaking (or singing) on the radio, from the mid-1920s onward. Each of these forms of appearance is less than that offered by sound cinema, which will present the animated, talking figure of the star. So on the simplest level, through the presentation of the star in photos, writing and radio, the elements of the star's person are offered to the public, but in discrete bits and without movement. The promise of these various presentations is that the film performance will present the completeness of the star, the real mystery at which these only hint. Hence the presentation of Marlene Dietrich to the American audience. Already a star in Europe because of *The Blue Angel* (1930), a film not then released in America, she arrived to film *Morocco* (1930). Her image (photographic and written) appeared in the press; she had already 'proved' herself in another unavailable film; her mystery was well cultivated. So *Morocco* appeared, its narrative multiply punning on that of *The Blue Angel*, and its publicity announced: 'Now you can see . . .'. The film revealed what the star image in its subsidiary circulation could only hint at or describe in a veiled meta-language.

The particular nature of the copy, the photos and the broadcasts made by/from stars reveals the other side of the star image's relation to the cinema. The stars are presented both as stars and as ordinary people: as very special beings, and as beings just like the readers. This seems to be the case both for male and for female stars, but sexual difference inevitably colours what kinds of roles are shown. Thus we have Bette Davis's recipes but Tyrone Power's baseball achievements; Audrey Hepburn's affinity for Givenchy clothes but Errol Flynn's big game hunting. Photographs similarly will show stars in the most mundane of postures, feeding babies or just relaxing in old clothes; and then in the most exotic, performing stunts at a lavish party or meeting the King of England.

These general characteristics of the coverage are inflected in different ways by the different kinds of publications which make use of stars. It could be said that mass circulation daily and sunday newspapers tend to use stars as a kind of moral barometer, whereas fanzines push the paradoxical constitution of the star image to its limits. Mass newspapers use stars for their own ends: they can be the occasion of scandals, and they provide a repertory of figures who are in the public eye, yet have no political power. Stars provide newspapers with the vehicle for discussion of sexuality, of the domain of the personal and the familial. This is relatively absent from public political life, so the stars perform a valuable function in newspapers: they provide the dimension of the personal. This dimension is that which is inhabited by most of their readers, yet is not that of the events portrayed in the news. Stars have a soldering function: they hold the news and the personal together by being both public and intimate, by being news only in so far as they are persons.

Fanzines are a different kind of publication, very much more directly linked in to the industry itself. They emphasise stars-as-workers much more than other publications, with details of the punishing studio schedules, the indignities of make-up and costume for some parts, the hard training for dancing and stunts, even the lousy facilities offered by studios. Yet at the same time they can present the extraordinary aspects of the star as well, because they are generally high-quality printing jobs with glossy, high-definition full-page photos. These photos present both male and female stars with all the sophisticated techniques that are available. These are images of faces (sometimes bodies as well) in all their impossibility: smooth, free of blemishes, clear-eyed, every feature perfect. Often, the two aspects cross over each other in the same feature: pieces about the hard work of rehearsal dive into sentences which stress 'nevertheless' the exceptional talent of the performer.

[...]

The star image functions in two ways. First it is the invitation to cinema, posing cinema as synthesising all the disparate and scattered elements of the star image. Second, it repeats the cinematic experience by presenting an impossible paradox: people who are both ordinary and extraordinary. This is the same paradox as the photo effect. The oscillation between the ordinariness and the extraordinariness of the star implies a whole series of features which echo the photo effect. The star is ordinary, and hence leads a life like other people, is close to them, shares their hopes and fears: in short, the star is present in the same social universe as the potential film viewer. At the same time the star is extraordinary, removed from the life of mere mortals, has rarified and magnified emotions, is separate from the world of the potential film viewer. The circulation of the contradictory star image therefore operates a kind of summary or reminder of the photo effect of cinema. Yet it is more than that as well. The figure of the star crystallises the equivocal relationship to the viewer's desire that can be said to be produced by the photo effect.

By presenting a present-absence, by making statements in the impossible mode of 'this is was', the photo effect awakens a series of psychic mechanisms which involve various impossible images: the narcissistic experience of the mirror phase; the masculine fetishistic refusal (yet acknowledgment) of the fact of sexual difference; and at the same time, a particular variant of the voyeuristic contract. The photo effect can be said to be involved with a series of psychic mechanisms which participate in the construction of the polyvalent desires of both male and female viewers. The star is an impossible image, like the cinematic image. The star is tantalisingly close and similar, yet at the same time remote and dissimilar. Further, the star is a legitimate object for the desire of the viewer in so far as the star is like the viewer, and an impossible object for the desire of the viewer in so far as the star is extraordinary, unlike the viewer. There is a complicated game of desires that plays around the figure of the star: every feature in it is counteracted by another feature. The male and female star can be desired by either sex, yet that desire has access to its object only on condition that its object is presented as absent. Desire is both permitted and encouraged, yet knows it cannot achieve any tangible form of satisfaction, except the satisfactions of looking. The phenomenon of stardom relies on the photo effect for its full expression; it is equally a summary of the photo effect, making explicit the relationship between the photographic and the realm of desire. Constituted by a central paradox, the star system is both a promise of cinema ('this is the photo effect'), and an invitation to cinema ('these are clues; cinema synthesises them'). The film performance of a star both animates the desire that plays around the star's published image, yet holds that desire in place by the operations of the fiction. The use of the fiction always exceeds the star's image and the star's presence in a film, except at that single point where the fiction is suspended in favour of the pure performance: the 'fetishistic' moment.

The star's performances in individual films have a particular relationship with the images in subsidiary circulation. In the period of classic Hollywood at least, each star's figure was around all the time in subsidiary forms of circulation, but was seen in the cinema only occasionally: in two or three films a year. The film performance was therefore rare; the subsidiary circulation was commonplace. The film performance was a, special event. The film performance of a star also involved a large degree of overt fiction, which the star in circulation outside the cinema did not. The construction of a star's image in subsidiary circulation must have routinely involved forms of fiction, but these were offered as though they were true facts. The fictional element of a star's film performance is acknowledged by all concerned, performers, film-makers and audiences alike.

[...]

The film performance of the star takes up and furthers the star image from other media. The relation between the figure of the star and the desire of the spectator is animated and intensified. The play between the possibility and impossibility of the star as an object of desire is intensified by the photo effect of presence-absence. The star finally appears as a physical figure observable over an extended period by the film audience: no longer a disembodied radio voice, a frozen photo image or a character in a piece of journalistic writing. Introduced here is a whole new dimension of the star: not just the star-in-movement, but also the incidental aspects of that movement. The star's performance in a film reveals to the viewer all those small gestures, particular aspects of movement and expression, unexpected similarities to acquaintances or even to self. The journalistic apotheosis of these moments witnesses the feeling that the star is caught unawares in them. They are things, it seems, that could hardly have been planned or foreseen. They mark the absorption of the star into the fictional character. The star seems to be feeling the emotion of the role at that point as his or her own emotion. The star is not performing here, so much as 'being'. In other words, what the film performance permits is moments of pure voyeurism for the spectator, the sense of overlooking something which is not designed for the onlooker but passively allows itself to be seen. This is different from the star's image in other forms of circulation, where the elements of intentionality are very marked. The fanzine photo is obviously constructed for the look; the magazine interview or the radio broadcast participate in forms of direct address where the star is present as an intentional 'I'.

This sense of overlooking the incidental and the unmotivated aspects of the star's figure has two consequences which tend to outrun the film-as-fiction. First, it pushes the photo effect to its limits, especially with a star who is dead. This effect is an epidemic with stars like Garland or Monroe, whose presence on the screen brings with it the widespread myths of their tragic lives, the stories of their absence. In both cases, the combination of the extra-filmic circulation of a star's tragic story with their film performance promotes a voyeuristic relation to the performance. Rather than identifying the role in the fiction with the life of the star (a comparatively rare possibility), the incidental moments are promoted to the forefront of attention. These 'poignant' moments thus become the only remaining route to the truth or the essence of the star's personality. The incidental moments of the star caught unawares seem to provide a glimpse of the secret personality that disappeared (or destroyed itself) leaving behind the perpetual, unresolvable paradox of the star image. The film photograph constructs the possibility of a voyeuristic effect of catching the star unawares. The paradox of the star's image (especially Monroe's) exacerbates this effect, sending the desiring viewer off to the film itself as the only remaining physical manifestation of the star amid the welter of photo sessions, TV and film biographies, memoirs of associates both would-be and real. The viewer glimpses something, perhaps only a trick of the light. But it is only glimpsed during the film performance. Then the circuit begins again: more consumption of forms of subsidiary circulation, the desire to see more films, and even films-that-never-were: the out-takes, the screen-tests and so on.

There is one further effect that can result from the star's performance being taken as the indicator of some kind of psychic truth. This is a more fetishistic tendency. At its limits, this results in the expression of the desire to halt the movement of the film, to freeze one of the actions of the star. Hence some films come in damaged prints simply because some fetishist has cut out a favourite section. Sometimes this effect can be seen in the construction of the film itself: in the performances of songs by Marlene Dietrich which litter Von Sternberg's films. Further, the plots of some Von Sternberg films can be seen as cyclic rather than progressing from beginning to end. They repeat the same scenarios of desire, circling around a neuralgic point. That point is the figure of the star, and of the female star rather than the male star.

These examples indicate how a star's film performance can expand the realm of desire, the incidental relations between audience and photo effect, to proportions that can be deemed arcane or even anti-social. As a rule, it is the fact of fiction in the film which contains the star's performance. The star's performance is held in place by the fiction. Fiction provides a double perspective. The fiction is always more than the star or the stars (sometimes only just, though, e.g. *Hollywood Canteen* (1944)), and provides the star with a role that is to a greater or lesser extent different from the star's public image. The public image consists of a series of more or less paradoxical attributes; very little of a stable identity emerges from them apart from that of the star-paradox itself, ordinary and extraordinary. In the fiction, however, the star has to incarnate some kind of identity, be it Mildred Pierce, Sam Spade, La Bessière (or is it Le Bessier?), Stuart McIver. These names (rather more than those of the stars) designate stable points of identity, characters caught in webs of narrative circumstance through which they chart a path. To this extent, then, the fiction imposes a different regime of being upon the star. We have to know where the fictional character incarnated by the star actually stands. So there is a certain attenuation of the star image in the star's film performance. Certainly, there is still some element of the oscillation between the extraordinary and the ordinary, but this oscillation is fixed for the duration of the film to provide fairly stable reference points.

The star performance in the fiction can have three kinds of relation to the star image in subsidiary circulation. The fiction can content itself with performing the image in those rare cases where the star's image outside of cinema is fairly stable. This is perhaps more possible for male stars, whose characters can be defined by their activities. Such is the case perhaps with Errol Flynn, whose roles seem to a large extent the kind of exploit for which he became famous. The second, more usual, relation is that in which the fiction exceeds the circulated image. At its limits, the fictional figure can go against the grain of the circulated image, creating a specific tension in the film. Such is the case with Hitchcock's *Suspicion* (1941) where Cary Grant is cast as the likely murderer and swindler. The whole film is constructed on this dislocation in order to render Joan Fontaine's suspicions incongruous at first, and then increasingly irrefutable even to the most incredulous audience as the 'evidence' mounts. Despite the reconciliatory ending, this film represents something more than 'casting against type'. *Suspicion* needs the star image of Cary Grant in order to function at all.

More usually, the fictional figure is 'to one side' of the star's general image, where this can be established. Certain elements of the publicly circulated star image complex are used by the film, other elements are refused, further elements are added. Doris Day's films display her in a much wider range of characters than her image would suggest. Certain elements of her image are always present (sometimes her pervasive ordinariness or directness of approach to people), but they are not always the same elements. Further characteristics are accumulated to her fictional personas that have little or nothing to do with her star images. Yet the star image continues in circulation, feeding off the films where it can, trying to ignore aspects of her past as well as aspects of her fictional roles. The importance of Doris Day as a star phenomenon is the way in which her star images have obliterated the memory of her films. Doris Day's fictional roles are very much 'to one side' of her circulated images.

The star's place in a film thus seems to be a difficult one. The film is constructed by the process of the star image as the point at which the paradox of the image will be explicated, and the disparate elements of the image will come together. The star performance thus animates the star image, and animates the desire which circulates in it. In doing so, the performance exceeds the circulated image in two usually mutually compensating ways. First, the performance is fictional, placing the star in a role whose characteristics have to be fairly stable. This role can have a number of different relationships to the circulated image: it can resemble it to a large degree; it can contradict it; it can be to one side of it. In most cases, the fictional context of the star's performance is enough to hold in check or to balance a second way in which the star's performance exceeds the star's circulated image. This second excess is the way in which desire is animated towards the performing figure. The performance produces the effect that, in its incidental rather than intended moments, it reveals something of the essence of the star's personality.

For the fiction film, the star and the places that the star can adopt produce a commendable narrative economy. Stars are recognisable; stars are the centre of the action. So the narration need waste very little time and space in pointing out who the central characters are. The regime of stardom that I have described here is found in its most straightforward form in the commercial cinema, and particularly in that of classic Hollywood. It is qualitatively different from any phenomenon found in television. Television has used the word 'star' to apply to anybody who appeared on its screen: even the weather forecasters. But television does not produce a play between the ordinariness and extraordinariness of its performers because it does not participate in the photo effect, and it cannot present the lives of its performers as anything particularly glamorous. The *TV Times* (29/1/1981) feature on Susannah York, appearing in the series *Second Chance* was revealing. Here is a woman who lives by Wandsworth Common and has gone through a divorce, just like the character she is playing. The profile was unable to generate any other sense of Susannah York: no sense of the extraordinary, no sense of glamour, even. There was a sense in which the dimension of desire was being written out of the piece. The institution of television (at least in Britain) seems at pains to reduce the star phenomenon by reducing the extraordinariness of its performers, and their status as figures of an equivocal attraction and identification by viewers both male and female.

Centrally lacking in television is the photo effect. Television presents itself as an immediate presence, except when it is borrowing the cinema with transmissions that are labelled 'films'. Television pretends to actuality, to immediacy; the television image in many transmissions (news, current affairs, chat shows, announcements) behaves as though it were live and uses the techniques of direct address. Its narrative regime is different. It hardly ever presents its performers in comparison to their presence in subsidiary forms of circulation in the way that is characteristic of cinema's use of its stars. Instead, the television performer appears regularly for a series which itself is constituted on the basis of repetition of a particular character and/or situation. The television performer appears in subsidiary forms of circulation (newspapers, magazines) mostly during the time that the series of performances is being broadcast. The result is a drastic reduction in the distance between the circulated image and the performance. The two become very much entangled, so that the performer's image is equated with that of the fictional role (rather than vice versa). The television performer exists very much more in the same space as the television audience, as a known and familiar person rather than as a paradoxical figure, both ordinary and extraordinary.

There is no way that the image in subsidiary circulation is a promise of television as the synthesis of its disparate parts. The image in subsidiary circulation is present in the culture rather less than the television performance, which has no real rarity value. The exchange is the other way about than in cinema: the television performance provides the basic materials and the basic enigma ('Is there a person different from the role in the fiction?') and the magazine profile provides the solution of it. Television's regime is rather more straightforward than cinema's, and its stress is rather more on the ordinariness of its performers, using them with greater abandon than cinema could ever conceive, presenting them as much more of an immediate presence.

What television does present is the 'personality'. The personality is someone who is famous for being famous, and is famous only in so far as he or she makes frequent television appearances. Such is the case of Zsa Zsa Gabor, often mistaken as a cinema star. The personality on British television has been taken to new heights by Michael Parkinson and Russell Harty, whose secret is that they have no known identity of any kind. In some ways, they are the opposite of stars, agreeable voids rather than sites of conflicting meanings. More usually, the television personality is equated with a particular genre of character in fiction, or a particular area of knowledge or interest in factual programmes. Hence the scientist-personalities of Magnus Pyke or Patrick Moore; the political personality of Robin Day. These are personalities or celebrities rather than stars in the cinematic sense. Their notoriety results from their fairly constant presence on the medium rather than their rarity; they are familiar rather than remote; they are present in the actuality of the television image rather than the photo effect of the cinema image; they activate no conflict of meanings and no real enigmas; they bear a fairly minimal relationship to the desire of the spectator, the subsidiary circulation of material about them is more concerned with discovering if there is a personality separate from that of the television role than it is with the paradox of ordinary-but-extraordinary.

Television may yield personalities rather than stars, but the structure of the star system seems still to be present in the rock music industry. Here, the live performance takes the place of the film performance. It, too, is rare compared to other forms of circulation; it, too, is more complete in relation to other forms, including that of the disc (some groups excepted) and the tantalising television appearance. The journalism that surrounds the rock star works in a similar paradoxical register to that of film star journalism. Mick Jagger is one of its outstanding creations: the uncouth lad integrated with the jet-set. More often, journalism provides its sense of the ordinariness of the star through pronouncements like 'I mostly eat baked beans when it comes down to it, really' balanced against details of musicianship and statistical information ('Number one for six weeks', 'two gold discs', 'three-quarters of a million pounds').

Stars in classic Hollywood cinema exist as marketing devices, specifying a film in order to encourage attendance at its performances. As a marketing device, the star image in subsidiary forms of circulation is not a complete and settled identity. If it was, it would be a satisfactory phenomenon and would not produce the curiosity necessary to encourage cinema attendances. This curiosity seems to be produced in two ways: first by the enigma of star paradox (ordinary-extraordinary) and second by the resultant promise of cinema (of presence-absence). In its turn, this star phenomenon outside the film has certain effects within the film. It produces the star's film performance as the completion and potential explanation of the star phenomenon. It produces a relationship of desire between spectator and star performer that is intensified by the photo effect of cinema itself. These effects are almost always held in place by the operation of the fiction which suspends the oscillations of the star paradox in favour of a relatively stable fictional identity for the star performer. On rare occasions, whose reasons are both textual and extra-textual, the effects of desire outrun the effects of the fiction, producing cultism or fetishism. Finally, the star's film performance does not exhaust the paradoxes of the star's circulated image.

9 Re-examining Stardom: Questions of Texts, Bodies and Performance

Christine Geraghty

[...]

Defining stars

Definitions of stars in film studies have emphasised that the concept of stardom is sustained by a contrast between the performing presence and what happens 'off-stage'. Dyer writes of stars having 'an existence in the world independent of their screen/ "fiction" appearances' (1979: 22) and describes stardom as 'an image of the ways stars live' (1979: 39). Allen and Gomery talk of 'a duality between actor and character' and, citing Edgar Morin, refer to stars as 'actors "with biographies"' (1985: 172), whereas Tasker in her work on New Hollywood describes stars as 'complex personas made up of far more than the texts in which they appear' (1993: 74).

[...]

The contrast between the public and private, the ordinary and the extraordinary is made available through a wide range of texts which goes well beyond the films into the newspapers, fan magazines, television shows and exchanges of information and rumour between fans. Dyer's influential notion of 'the structured polysemy' of the star image (1979: 3) drew attention to this wide range of source material and emphasised the contradictory ideals which stars embody. Dyer identified 'multiple *but finite* meanings' (1979: 72, my emphasis) but later commentators have concentrated on the instability of star images. Judith Mayne is typical in arguing that 'inconsistency, change and fluctuation are characteristic of star images' (1993: 128) and suggests that the very appeal of stardom is based on 'constant reinvention, the dissolution of contraries, the embrace of widely opposing terms' (1993: 138). The emphasis on instability has been particularly strong because stars in film studies have been strongly associated with questions of identity – 'being interested in stars is being interested in how we are human now' (Dyer, 1987: 17). Psychoanalytic theory, influential in film studies, has emphasised the instability of the subject and the contradictory nature of identity. Links with cultural studies have also contributed to this sense of instability and resistance, emphasising the role of fans in making different and contested meanings.

[...]

Generally, then, the model for work on stars and their audiences has been that of an unstable and contradictory figure, constructed both intertextually (across different films) and extratextually (across different types of material). The relationship between the audience and star is deemed to be best figured by the fan whose knowledge comes from a wide variety of sources and who reworks the material in the interests of working through contradictory questions of identity. This emphasis on the duality of the film star and the relationship with the fan has also become established for work in popular culture more generally. In music, television, sport and beyond, the model is one of a relationship between the public sphere of performance and work and the private sphere of personal lives, of the home and personal relationships as 'revealed' through the media. Sometimes this relationship is heavily managed as can be seen in the pages of *Hello!*, the British photomagazine which invites us into the tranquil and polished homes of a range of celebrities and is always careful to emphasise the value of their work. Elsewhere, the less respectful press publicises claims of drug use, marital difficulties and personal disasters, often with an implied contrast between the control and skill of the public performance and the lack of control 'off-stage'. Princess Diana entered into the realm of stardom when knowledge of her unhappy private life could act as a counter to the glamorous public 'work'.

Rethinking the categories

In thinking about how film stardom now operates in popular US cinema in particular, we need to unpack this model of stardom and look at the different ways in which meaning is made through a star. In this section, I want to look at other categories – celebrity/professional/performer – which also contribute to a paradigm of the different ways in which well-known individuals 'appear' in the media and to suggest that these distinctions better help us to understand what film stars have in common with and how they differ from other mass media public figures.

The term celebrity indicates someone whose fame rests overwhelmingly on what happens outside the sphere of their work and who is famous for having a lifestyle. The celebrity is thus constructed through gossip, press and television reports, magazine articles and public relations.

[...]

Celebrities may be contrasted to 'professionals'. These are people whose fame rests on their work in such a way that there is very little sense of a private life and the emphasis is on the seamlessness of the public persona. In television, this kind of consistency has been associated by Langer with television's personalities which 'exist as more or less stable "identities" within the flow of events, situations and narratives' (1981: 357). This consistency is evident with newsreaders, journalists, chat-show hosts and sports commentators who are particularly associated with modes of direct address to the audience. It can also be seen in fictional shows which depend on the regular appearance of recognisable fictional characters so that the actor is hidden behind the character and recognised only through that association. Regular soap and situation comedy actors would fall into this category since their fame depends on particular professional roles.

The professional lacks the double image of the star though, as the case of Roseanne illustrates, the move can be made to star status when a 'biography' is brought to the audience's attention.

The third category, that of performer, is also associated with work and the public element of the star duality rather than the private life of the celebrity. In this category though, unlike that of the professional, skills and performance elements are not hidden but drawn attention to and the emphasis is on the showcasing or demonstration of skills. Tasker, in her work on action films, contrasts performers such as Chuck Norris and Claude Van Damme to stars, suggesting that the performer is characterised by the focus on particular skills such as martial arts which are showcased by the text (1993: 74). In this context, certain kinds of actors can be seen as performers whose acting skills are showcased in theatre, film and television. The actor as a performer is defined by work and is often associated with the high cultural values of theatrical performance, even when that performance takes place in film or television.

Film stardom then has to be seen in the context of the drive in the media to create and exploit the status of being famous across the whole range of entertainment formats. Film, a medium in its own right, becomes also a site to be mined by other media. But cinema is a relatively inefficient way of delivering fame compared with some other formats. Cinema is slow to produce new products and while this can generate a sense of anticipation ('Batman is back') and huge audiences for the first weekend's screening the gaps between films for individual stars can be very long. Committed fans may be happy to re-view during the absence but the more regular appearances of those from spheres such as television, music or sport makes them more available to function as stars whether as pin-ups in teen magazines or as recognisable figures in press stories. I want to suggest that, in this situation, the emphasis on the polysemic film star as a site of resistance can no longer, if it ever could, account for the variety of ways in which film stars function. In a situation of intense competition for the extratextual attention of the media, there are choices, for audiences and stars, about whether to exploit the full range of mass media exposure or to establish pleasures around stardom which are specifically related to the film text and to cinema. It is these questions I wish to explore through an examination of the way in which film stars can be analysed through the categories I have outlined here.

Star-as-celebrity

The dual nature of film stardom continues to be important but in certain contexts the emphasis is almost entirely on 'biography' or the celebrity element of stardom. Films stars share this terrain with others from sport, television, fashion and music, and the material found in the press, in particular, emphasises not the work but the leisure and private life of the star. This is the area where the intertextuality may be most important since knowledge of the star's 'real' life is pieced together from gossip columns and celebrity interviews, establishing a range of discourses in which the star features. In the discourse of celebrity, film stars literally interact with those from other areas. Thus, our knowledge that Johnny Depp goes out with the model Kate Moss is in the same register as the news of footballer David Beckham marrying a Spice Girl. For young fans, in particular, the celebrity mode may be the most accessible way into film stardom precisely because it links together different entertainment formats – magazines, videos, photography, film – and reworks distant film stars into the boyfriend of the girl next door; the teenage magazine *Sugar* (Issue 32, June 1997) remarked that Gwyneth Paltrow was 'as nervous as the rest of us' at having her long hair cut. 'Only difference is, she had Brad to sit in the salon, reassuringly holding her mitt throughout her hideous ordeal!'

This emphasis on the private sphere and the interaction with other forms of fame means that in the celebrity mode the films are relatively unimportant and a star can continue to command attention as a celebrity despite failures at the box office. For Julia Roberts and Richard Gere, for instance, the balance of their star constructions shifted away in the 1990s from their relatively unsuccessful films to the complications of their personal lives. In such circumstances, the dual nature of the star construction has diminished and the balance has shifted towards that of the celebrity where there is no work to back up the emphasis on the private life. In this construction of the celebrity, it no longer makes sense to see this circulation of information and images as subsidiary or secondary to the films or indeed to see cinema as different from other entertainment arenas. It is the audience's access to and celebration of intimate information from a variety of texts and sources which are important here.

Star-as-professional

By contrast, the other categories of stardom construct a rather different relationship between star and audience, one which is based much more substantially on the film text. In these categories – the star-as-professional and the star-as-performer – it is quite possible to understand and enjoy the meaning of the star without the interdiscursive knowledge which the star-as-celebrity relies on.

The star-as-professional makes sense through the combination of a particular star image with a particular film context. It arises when we check 'whether an actor's presence in a film seems to correspond with his or her professional role' (Naremore, 1990: 262) and often involves the star's identification with a particular genre. Thus, certain stars such as Steve Martin, Eddie Murphy and Jim Carrey are linked to certain forms of comedy whereas the stars whom Tasker discusses – Stallone, Schwarznegger and Van Damme – are associated with quite precise variations of the action film and displays of masculine prowess.

I would suggest that for the star-as-professional a stable star image is of crucial importance. Too much difference from established star image may lead to disappointment for the intended audience. Stallone offers an interesting example of the difficulties facing a professional star who wants to change. In her study of action heroes such as Stallone, Tasker emphasises the instability of stardom, arguing that the 'truth' of a star is tied to identity which is never secured (1993: 76) and that stars work by creating space for contradictory and ambivalent identifications in the audience. She suggests that a star such as Schwarznegger managed to work on this instability by introducing an element of comedy, thus effecting a change in image away from bodybuilding and a shift into more mainstream work. But Tasker also cites the example of Stallone whose star image embodies the immigrant who achieves success in the face of the establishment. Films such as *Rocky* (1976) and *First Blood* (1982) crucially conflated fictional narratives and the story of the actor, so that certain themes – 'rags to riches', 'achievement through struggle', 'determination to succeed against all odds' – became 'central aspects of Stallone's star image' (1993: 84). Tasker's account suggests, however, that far from being unstable this image is critical to the success of his films and that repetition of the 'underdog' (1993: 84) figure is essential to the success of his work.

If Stallone has had difficulties settling for being a professional star linked to particular genres, Harrison Ford is probably the most successful current exponent of this approach, a man described by *Screen International* as having 'a near perfect track record and probably the most consistent box office draw in the world' (15 December, 1995, p. 18). Ford operates in a wider generic field than many professional stars, moving smoothly between action films, thrillers and detective films with the occasional aside into comedy. Given this variation, it is noteworthy that Ford is absolutely consistent in performance, and enjoyment of a Ford film very much depends on watching the contrast between easy expressiveness of his body movements and the impassive face with its limited range of expressions. In this respect, Ford represents a continuation of the Hollywood studio style which Dyer analyses in his study of stars. He distinguished between acting styles in which the actor appears to be playing himself or herself (the radio or Hollywood studio style) and those in which there is a clear distinction between actor and character (the repertory or Broadway style) (1979: 156–60). Barry King also differentiates between 'impersonation' in which the actor's ' "real" personality ... should disappear into the part', and 'personification' in which the actor's personality is consonant with the part (1991: 168). The Hollywood star system was very much associated with personification, with the notion that the stars did not act but were themselves and that the pleasurably recognisable repertoire of gestures, expressions and movements were the property of the star not of any individual character.

So seamless is this style in Ford's case that it is easier to describe it by talking about the rare points where it is put at risk or seems to be not going to happen. Part of the power of the dance scene in *Witness* (Weir, 1985) lies in the way in which Ford is transformed, the shift from thriller to romance being marked through performance. As he approaches Rachel (Kelly McGinnis), his face is stiff and his eyes intense. Then his eyes widen, a smile breaks up the planes of his face and as he holds her and begins to move, rather stiffly and carefully, he puts the dance in quotation marks with the movement of his hands and a shrug of his shoulders. The intense, impassive expression returns as the pair nearly kiss; then, he moves his body fractionally before he turns his gaze away from her, softens his face muscles, widens his eyes and resumes the dance until it is interrupted by the arrival of Rachel's father. The tenderness of the scene depends upon the revelation, through gesture, of feeling which is normally hidden behind the Ford mask.

[...]

Ford and others in this category represent a continuation of the performance methods of, for instance, John Wayne (Dyer, 1979: 165–7) and Clint Eastwood.[1] The difference may only be one of degree in that for stars such as Ford the range seems to be getting narrower given the market demands for an association of the professional star with particular characters or 'franchises'; *Screen International* (9 December 1994, p. 24) commented approvingly that Ford 'has established himself as Jack Ryan in another successful franchise'. This narrowing of range is a way of giving to film the stability normally associated with long-running television series. It is usual to *contrast* the television personality and the cinema star as Langer does in suggesting that in cinema 'the star absorbs the identity of the film character' whereas on television it is the characters who are the 'memorable identities' (1981: 359). I am suggesting instead that film stars such as Ford, who work within the star-as-professional category, operate for cinema/video in the same way as a character in a television series, providing the pleasures of stability and repetition and the guarantee of consistency in the apparent plethora of choice offered by the expanding media.

Star-as-performer

This emphasis on a consistent persona underlines the claim to the uniqueness of the star-as-professional but, because of the emphasis on 'being' rather than acting, little attention is paid to the work done unless it be to the difficulties of filming hazardous action sequences. In this final category, though, attention is deliberately drawn to the work of acting so that, in a reversal of the celebrity category, it is performance and work which are emphasised, not leisure and the private sphere. This has always been a factor for certain, often theatrically based, stars, but I would suggest that it now takes on particular importance as a way for film stars to claim legitimate space in the overcrowded world of celebrity status. The expansion of the celebrity side means that film stars no longer dominate that arena and indeed the fact that soap stars and pop musicians can gain such celebrity may precisely, as Allen and Gomery note, have devalued the process. As a response to this there has been quite a pronounced shift towards performance as a mark of stardom and the concept of star-as-performer has become a way of re-establishing film-star status through a route which makes its claim through the film text rather than appearances in the newspapers. Method acting, in particular, claims cultural status by making the celebrity trappings part of the detritus which has to be discarded if the performance is to be understood; Naremore comments that De Niro, 'since becoming a famous actor, has avoided tacky celebrity interviews' (1990: 280).

[. . .]

This anxiety about the possibilities of acting in cinema has been reinforced in the 1980s and 1990s by the emphasis on blockbusters, special effects and computer graphics. Outside the cinema, stars compete for celebrity status with the glitterati from other fields; inside, they have to contend with dinosaurs, twisters and animated rabbits.

In this situation, acting has become a way of claiming back the cinema for human stars and it is not accidental that method acting has become so strongly associated with certain modes of film stardom. Colin Counsell describes the method as 'a pre-eminently *realistic* style of acting' (1996: 53) and outlines the key signs of the method as 'a new ease or "naturalness" on-stage' (1996: 54); an increased emphasis on the significance of a character's inner life and the signs by which it could be deduced; a 'heightened emotionalism' (1996: 56) which is expressed in intense outbursts of expression; and 'an underlying vision of the individual as divided between an "authentic" inner and a potentially repressed/repressive outer self' (1996: 63).

[. . .]

The significance of method acting for concepts of film stardom has been recognised. Both Dyer and King discuss method acting as a particularly important feature of Hollywood cinema. Gledhill, in her discussion of melodrama and stars, draws attention to the way in which the method actor *'embodies* conflicts' and suggests that this emphasis on the bodily manifestation of moral dilemmas makes 'the Method...the contemporary performance mode most able to deliver "presence"' (1991b: 224). The emphasis on the body, the promise that every gesture and grimace carries meaning in terms of character if not of narrative, the inarticulate speech which the audience has to strain for, the moments of stillness and silence where action might be anticipated – these are signs of performance which audiences now expect and understand.

[...]

I am not suggesting that cinema audiences now recognise 'the Method' by name but that they do recognise modes of performing in ways which have implications for understanding how some stars (not all of whom can be directly associated with the Method) make meaning. As Lesley Stern suggests in her extremely interesting account, De Niro is not 'narrowly Method' (1995: 209) and he appears 'to relish the very game of performance' (1995: 210); it is this method-related emphasis on performance which is apparent in the work of a number of male stars.

[...]

This emphasis on performance works well, in fact, for the ageing star since it has the added merit of valuing experience and allowing a career to continue well beyond the pin-up stage. Method acting directs attention to the body of the star but shifts it away from the body as spectacle (the way in which Ford and Stallone move, for instance) to the body as site of performance, worked over by the actor. In a quite conscious way, the audience is invited to recognise and admire what the actor is doing with his face and body. The revival of Al Pacino's career and the continuance of De Niro's owes much to the sense of older performers displaying well-honed skills and passing on their knowledge to the younger actors around them. Even for young male stars who are teenage pin-ups (and thus operate as celebrities) the adoption of the method approach can work as a sign of more serious intentions. Depp's shift (the thickening body, the incoherent explanations) in *Donnie Brasco* (Newell, 1997) may be an early move in that process while the languid sexuality of Brad Pitt in *Thelma and Louise* (1991) has been replaced by a more self-aware attention to the details of accent and gesture in *Se7en* (Fincher, 1995) and *The Devil's Own* (1997).

The more widespread recourse to method acting has also affected the relationship between the star and others in the film. The hierarchy of performance was always clear in classic Hollywood films in which stars were surrounded and supported by character actors and second-rank sidekicks. In acting terms, there was a difference between the personification mode of the stars and the character acting which surrounded them. That difference is now much less pronounced and this change explains what would otherwise seem to be quite a contradictory shift, on the one hand to ensemble playing and on the other to acting as confrontation and contrast. In the emphasis on ensemble, the gangster film has played a key role. Unlike the western, the gangster film has remained a consistently strong genre and its stories of male groups, explosive violence and narcissism have meshed with cinematic method acting's characteristic emphasis on internal conflict expressed through the body. An early and influential example of this can be found in *The Godfather* (Coppola, 1972) where the stars Marlon Brando and Al Pacino are surrounded by actors whose performances are similarly expressive in their apparently inarticulate reliance on gesture and facial expression. An interesting variant on this occurs in *Goodfellas* (Scorsese, 1990) where the major star, De Niro, is one of the group who supports the relatively unknown Ray Liotta, and also in *Reservoir Dogs* (Tarantino, 1991) where each of the group is given moments of playing centre stage.

The ensemble playing, which tends to position the star as 'one of the boys', is paralleled by a strong sense of performance as competition which is generated when actors, operating in the same performance mode (which itself emphasises internal conflict), are given equal weight in narratives which hinge on external conflict and opposition between them. This rivalry is internally generated by the text and its power comes from the appeal to aesthetic judgements (which is the better actor?) rather than from stories of off-screen rivalry or different fan allegiances. This aesthetic dimension is underpinned by strong associations with similar contests in sport and particularly boxing, an unsurprising analogy given method acting's strong association with issues of masculinity. The encounter between Pacino and De Niro in *Heat* (Mann, 1995) is a vivid example of this kind of contest. Both are well known as cinematic method actors. The narrative sets them in opposition as policeman and criminal and they watch, follow and photograph each other until, well over halfway through the film, they meet face to face in a coffee bar. The shot/reverse-shot system concentrates on faces, framing tighter as the scene goes on. Though both give highly restrained performances, Pacino is the more edgy, his head stretched from his shoulders like a watchful bird, his eyes more open and alert. He leans towards De Niro and the camera whereas De Niro leans back, more hunched down, his eyes narrowed. Their bodies thus mirror each other as in the dialogue they discuss how they are locked together through their work. Difference is thus displayed but a strong sense of complementary performances is also established. The cultural value of such acting was neatly summed up by the *Sight and Sound* reviewer who searched for a comparison and suggested that 'if *Heat* were a play you could imagine De Niro and Pacino swapping roles every night like Olivier and Richardson in *Othello*' (Wrathall, 1996: 44).

[…]

The development of the star-as-performer as a means of reclaiming the cultural value means that we need perhaps to look again at how we understand the audience's activity in relation to stars. Dyer's emphasis on stars as a means of exploring social identity ['We're fascinated by stars because they enact ways of making sense of the experience of being a person' (1987: 17)] has been combined with an emphasis in cultural studies on the extratextual work of fans, which I discussed earlier. Polysemy and resistance thus became key terms in thinking about film stars, and the fan position, which is strongly associated with the star-as-celebrity, was assumed to be the ideal position from which to understand a star. For some kinds of stars and for some performances, however, this emphasis on the extratextual is not necessary and it is the audience's understanding of the specifically cinematic pleasures of genre and performance which needs to be foregrounded. The different modes of stardom I have described require different kinds of knowledge from audiences and although some film stars do operate as celebrities, knowledge of this is not essential to understanding their film appearances. The construction of Johnny Depp as a celebrity relies on extratextual knowledge of his bad behaviour and his stormy on/off affair with Kate Moss. For the category of performer, this extratextual information is largely irrelevant. Understanding Depp's significance in *Donnie Brasco* comes instead from textual knowledge of the performance itself, from its contrast to the rather fragile and whimsical acting styles Depp adopted in *Edward Scissorhands* (Burton, 1990) and *What's Eating Gilbert Grape?* (Hallstrom, 1993) and from the comparisons to be made with the performances of other male stars, such as De Niro and Pacino, who have used this method-influenced approach.

Analysing the female star

My discussion so far, particularly on the professional and the performer, has concentrated on male stars. I want to look now at how these categories might be applied to women film stars. In doing so, I think it is important to recognise that women stars do operate in a different context from their male counterparts. This is expressed both by the stars themselves in, for instance, complaints about the lack of good parts, and in the 'common sense' of the industry. A striking example of the common assumptions about female stars can be found in *Screen International*'s yearly assessment (since 1992) of the 'top actors' or key 'power players'. Women are both in a marked minority in the lists and the subject of generalised comments about the sheer unlikliness of women as stars. Thus, the failure of *The Scarlet Letter* (Joffe, 1995) becomes the failure of Demi More as a star, and then a question about women more generally; it raised 'the same ugly question: can she carry a film? Can *any* actress carry a film?' (*Screen International*, 15 December 1995, p. 19).

The category of celebrity is one which works well for female stars. Women function effectively as spectacle in the press and on television as well as in the cinema. In addition, the common association in popular culture between women and the private sphere of personal relationships and domesticity fits with the emphasis, in the discourse of celebrity, on the private life and the leisure activity of the star. The 'biography' of the woman star then can be appropriately used to make a star-as-celebrity out of her. Drew Barrymore offers an extreme but by no means unique example of an actress whose film appearances are set in the context of a turbulent private life. Stories of love affairs, weddings and divorces bring women stars into the arena of tabloid journalism while in more staid (and stage-managed) interviews stars such as Demi Moore stress the importance of creating domestic space in which their children can grow up. Julia Roberts offers a particularly interesting example of the way in which stardom can be built on and around celebrity. Charlotte Brunsdon's analysis of Robert's most famous role, as Vivian in *Pretty Woman* (Marshall, 1990), draws attention to the way in which her nervy awkwardness is transformed by her naturalness and the unconscious 'power of her beauty' (1997: 99). Since then, her film performances have been patchy but her celebrity status is based precisely on this contrast between the successful life her beauty seems to deserve and the disasters to which her natural impulses lead her. As Brunsdon suggests, there are strong possibilities for identification in the way in which Roberts lives out of the difficulties of femininity and I would suggest that the intermittent success of her films (*Screen International*, 12 December 1998, speaks of 'yet another comeback') is less important for her role as a star than her consistent extratextual interest as a celebrity.[2]

[...]

While the celebrity category may flourish on inconsistent behaviour in the personal sphere and contradictions between public and private selves, the professional star depends on a consistent sense of self and the willingness of the industry to franchise a role. Female candidates for this category might be Sigourney Weaver in her Ripley role and Linda Hamilton as Sarah Connor in the Terminator films. Both films offered a strong female character who was identified with the actress playing it and had the emphasis on action associated with the professional category. Despite the strong sense of identification many fans felt with these actresses/characters, neither did well enough, in the industry's terms, to feature in *Screen International*'s lists or establish a secure franchise. Hamilton did not make enough films to demonstrate a consistent personna and Weaver seems to have actively tried to avoid the typing associated with the professional category. She has starred in other genres – comedy, for instance, in *Working Girl* (Nicholls, 1988), a biopic in *Gorillas in the Mist* (Apted, 1988) and artistic drama in *Death and a Maiden* (Polanski, 1994). The difference between her and Harrison Ford in *Working Girl* is instructive; while Ford maintains his professional mode by playing the hero with silent bemusement, Weaver gives a broad and excessively villainous sweep to her portrayal of Katherine, turning herself into the monster against whom the heroine struggles. Although she maintains a consistent star image as a strong woman, Weaver as an actress appears to refuse the restrictions of the professional category and hence the kind of stardom which the male action heroes have established.

The female star who comes closest to success as a professional is perhaps Whoopi Goldberg. *Screen International* commented on her success in *Sister Act* (Ardolino, 1992) by describing her as 'an unlikely star', which would seem to be a reference to her race and gender since the consistency of her roles and her identification with comedy are comparable to a male comedy star. *Screen International* indeed half recognises this by emphasising her financial worth: 'by making sure she gets her worth – namely 7 million dollars for *Sister Act II* – she also became a landmark of a different kind: an actress with the clout of a male star' (10 December 1993, p. 21). The association of money and power with masculinity even when discussing a black, female star is entirely typical. The cost for Goldberg, though, has been the restriction of her image to that of an outsider whose asexual appearance and comic mannerisms diminish any threat to white audiences (Mayne, 1993; Stuart, 1993).

It may seem easier for women to develop into stars through the category of performers, a mode in which cultural value is more important than financial pulling power. However, the codification of cinematic method acting that has worked so well for male stars has not been so helpful for their female counterparts. Counsell suggests that the method's emphasis on the divided self worked against women in that while 'the iconography of neurosis quickly became an acceptable way of representing men', the neurotic woman was 'demonised ... as victim or villainess'. 'The Method actress' he concludes 'could not be "normal" enough' for Hollywood's restricted vision of appropriate female behaviour (1996: 76).[3] Two other factors may also be at play. The method approach, emphasising as it did the repression and release of emotion, gave male actors the task of expressing feelings as well as providing action. In some senses, male stars took over the traditional role of women and provided the tears as well as the punches. In addition, the emphasis on ensemble playing has perhaps worked rather differently for women stars. While ensemble playing by women is a feature of certain kinds of women's film, such as *How to make an American Quilt* (Moorhouse, 1995), the emphasis on male groups in the more prestigious gangster and thriller genres has tended to take attention away from the actresses' performance. Thus, even in *Goodfellas* (Scorsese, 1990), a gangster film which is highly unusual in its emphasis on the home life of the gangster, Lorraine Bracco's performance as the wife cannot match the weight of the ensemble playing of De Niro, Pesci, Liotta and the rest of the gang.

It is possible, however, to see cinematic method acting in some performances by contemporary women stars. Jodie Foster's performances, for instance, in *The Accused* (Kaplan, 1988) and *The Silence of Lambs* (Demme, 1991) are marked by the way in which internal division and doubt are expressed in gestures, silences, explosions of emotion comparable to that of male stars. It is not accidental that these critically successful performances were given in thrillers/court-room dramas since in these films Foster was given access, which generally women stars do not have, to the gangster/ thriller genres where the method has worked most successfully for male stars. Foster's performances in other genres – *Sommersby* (Amiel, 1993), *Nell* (Apted, 1994) – were less well received and her strong track record rests on her position as a producer and director as well as an actor though, as with Whoopi Goldberg, her success is expressed in the industry through male comparisons: 'if this is a boy's game, then Jodie plays it like the boys: with a balance of caution and boldness' *(Screen International*, 10 December 1993, p. 21). A more unusual example of a method-influenced performance, in that it occurred in a literary adaptation, was that of Nicole Kidman in *Portrait of a Lady* (Campion, 1996). Here Campion's visceral direction with its dramatic use of close-ups focused attention on Kidman's physical expression of Isabel Archer's voluntary entrapment in the way she walked, stammered and even struggled for breath.

[…]

Conclusions

A final example illustrates the different way in which stars make meaning through the categories I have outlined and how gender and race inflect these categories. *The Bodyguard* (Jackson, 1992) was critically derided but was a huge commercial success. bell hooks (1994) has pointed out that the film's doomed romance between the black singer Rachel Marron (Whitney Houston) and her white bodyguard Frank Farmer (Kevin Costner) is predicated on its unspoken assumptions about the impossibility of successful interracial relationships in Hollywood films. But *The Bodyguard* is also worth considering in terms of stars as well as narrative for what we get is a contest between the two stars which throws interesting light on film stardom in 1990s' Hollywood. The film's huge grosses put Houston into 11th position on *Screen International*'s 1996 list of top-20 screen stars, making her the first of only three female stars included. She brings to the film her star status as a singer/celebrity which is treated respectfully. The camera circles her, giving the audience both her beautiful face and long shots of her dancing, exercising and singing. The narrative makes her vulnerable and potentially a victim but we are continually reminded of her (invulnerable) star status by the songs and her composed demeanour. Costner, on the other hand, still carries with him the success of *Dances with Wolves* (Costner, 1990). Although he had a reputation as a pin-up, the film seems more concerned to emphasise his performance. He thus seeks to express his character's ambivalent obsession with his job and his fear that exposing his vulnerability in love will make him less good at it. This narrative motivation may not, as Hooks indicates, be very strong but it gets its resonances from our familiarity with such internal conflicts as performed by a succession of male stars. The film thus neatly demonstrates how two big stars can be so different and need different analysis to account for their meaning. Houston is treated as a pin-up who sings; Costner is giving an acting performance. Houston is given very little space to express any feeling; Costner uses cinematic method techniques to indicate that he is trying to express the inexpressible. Houston's star status is secure in the popular enjoyment of her voice and songs; Costner is trying to claim cultural status of a different order as a serious actor. And, of course, Houston as a black woman would find it almost impossible to claim the ground on which Costner is staking his claim to stardom. In the end, it is not just the narrative but the different concepts attached to stardom which reinforce their separate worlds and send Houston back to her singing and Costner back to his work.

Acknowledgements

With thanks to Jim Cook for making very helpful comments on early drafts of this chapter and to Christine Gledhill for her perceptive and thoughtful work as an editor.

Notes

1. As is indicated here, Dyer did recognise consistency in a star image. I am suggesting that the interest in difference in film and cultural studies has overemphasised the notion of star instability in his work.
2. Brunsdon (1997: 100) draws on Jennifer Wicke's concept of 'celebrity feminism' in her analysis. The category interestingly links film stars with women academics and writers in a way which illustrates the fluidity of the star category.
3. Counsell (1996) suggests that, in an earlier period, Jane Fonda was the only method actress to be offered high-profile parts in films and compares this to the success of method actors from the 1950s onwards.

References

Allen, R. C. and Gomery, D. 1985: *Film history: theory and practice*. New York: Random House.

Balio, T. 1988: 'A major presence in all of the world's most important markets': the globalization of Hollywood in the 1990s. In Neale, S. and Smith, M. (eds), *Contemporary Hollywood cinema*. London: Routledge, pp. 58–73.

Brunsdon, C. 1997: Post-feminism and shopping films. In *Screen tastes: soap opera to satellite dishes*. London: Routledge, pp. 81–102.

Counsell, C. 1996: *Signs of performance*. London: Routledge.

Dyer, R. 1979: *Stars*. London: British Film Institute.

Dyer, R. 1987: *Heavenly bodies; film stars and society*. London: British Film Institute.

Gledhill, C. 1991b: Signs of melodrama. In Gledhill, C. (ed.), *Stardom: industry of desire*. London: Routledge, pp. 207–29.

Hooks, B. 1994: Seduction and betrayal: *The Crying Game meets The Bodyguard*. In *Outlaw culture: resisting representations*. New York: Routledge, pp. 53–62.

King, B. 1991: Articulating stardom. In Gledhill, C. (ed.), *Stardom: industry of desire*. London: Routledge, pp. 167–82.

Langer, J. 1981: Television's personality system. *Media Culture and Society* 3(4), 351–65.

Mayne, J. 1993: *Cinema and spectatorship*. London: Routledge.

Naremore, J. 1990: *Acting in the cinema*. Berkeley, CA: University of California Press.

Stern, L. 1995: *The Scorsese connection*. London: British Film Institute.

Stuart, A. 1993: The outsider: Whoopi Goldberg and shopping mall America. In Dodd, P. and Cook, P. (eds), *Women and film: a sight and sound reader*. London: Scarlet Press, pp. 62–7.

Tasker, Y. 1993: *Spectacular bodies*. London: Routledge.

Wrathall, J. 1996: Review of *Heat. Sight and Sound* 6(2), 42–4.

From *Beyond Control* to In Control: Investigating Drew Barrymore's Feminist Agency/Authorship

Rebecca Williams

In this essay, I shall consider the actress Drew Barrymore, one of Hollywood's most successful female stars, able to command $15million dollars per appearance (Kurtzberg, 2004) and responsible for producing numerous box office hits. Approaching this from a broadly feminist perspective, I will first offer a brief overview of previous theories of stardom, feminism and agency. In this discussion I will move on to outline the arguments made by Melissa Pearl Friedling (2000) who suggested that throughout the early to mid-1990s, secondary materials surrounding Drew Barrymore emphasized her status as a former drug and alcohol addict to present a limited, often contradictory feminist reading of her star persona. I will counter this argument, suggesting that Barrymore is no longer denied agency by her former addiction and that her recent successes suggest that she promises the possibility of star 'authorship'. I will go on to illustrate how she is able to display active agency by regulating and circulating her own public persona and exercising considerable control over the projects she is involved in and via her position as an active producer in her company Flower Films. I will move on to offer a broad discussion of her ambivalent feminist status via analysis of her films and secondary publicity materials suggesting that, as Friedling argued, this remains complex and contradictory. However, in conclusion. I will argue that this is now due not to Barrymore's status as a former addict. Rather, it emerges from an interplay between her relative power in the Hollywood industry, and the constraints of its economic frameworks – including generic expectation, agents and managers, and the mass media.

Theorizing female stars

Recent studies have begun to offer serious critical attention to mainstream movie stars of the typically culturally devalued blockbuster genre, such as Jim Carrey (Drake, 2004). Jackie Chan (Gallagher, 2004), Will Smith (King, 2003) and Keanu Reeves (Rutsky, 2001). However, with a few exceptions (Geraghty, 2003; Kramer, 2004; Zuk, 1998), there persists a neglect of the mainstream female star, with discussions remaining highly gendered. The notion of star agency is clearly demarcated between those who have 'too much' control and those who do not possess enough. The excessively controlling star is often pathologized and demonized for their strict enforcing of their public persona and is routinely typified as a 'control freak', such as the characterization of the apparently controlling Jennifer Lopez as a 'diva', or the endless discussions of Madonna's masculinized power (Seigworth, 1993; Penaloza, 2004). In contrast, stars lacking agency are caricatured as puppets, controlled by agents, managers and the media that created them, and unable to exercise any influence over their careers or public selves (Doss, 1999). Unsurprisingly, these opposing positions are highly gendered: the controlled, excessive celebrity is masculinized while the passive, powerless figure is feminized.

In those rare instances when female celebrities are seen to exercise control over their public personas and have 'serious' careers, they are often masculinized, whilst those who are explicitly coded via female sexuality are presumed to lack agency and the ability to control their own careers. For example, discussion of Jodie Foster most often considers her transgressive femininity and sexuality, her possession of culturally masculinized traits and her alleged 'toughness' (Dubois, 2001; Innes, 1998; Kramer, 2003; Staiger, 1993). However, Foster's masculinization privileges her and, together with her status as a 'serious' award-winning actress, producer and director, allows her to be considered 'worthy' of consideration as a star. A contrast is Sharon Stone, who is routinely depicted as sexualized, dumb, passive and lacking the agency to control her own star image. As an attractive, eroticized spectacle Stone's supposed lack of talent is articulated via derision toward her acting proficiency (Feasey, 2003, 2004). Furthermore. Stone frequently negotiates her own public persona through victimization and sensuality, but it is possible to argue that Stone understands and exploits the mechanisms of Hollywood publicity to represent her own persona, which she constructs by correlating herself with the parts she plays (Feasey, 2004: 200–202).

Star authorship and agency

Such issues highlight the prevalent 'assumptions concerning identity that underlie a good deal of "serious" film – and cultural – studies, including the often unstated idea that "auteurs" and "actors" are active, thinking subjects (i.e. artists) while "movie stars" are passive objects, mere products of the culture industry' (Rutsky, 2001: 185). Work on star agency was most famously undertaken by Richard Dyer (1979, 1986) who argued that stars performed ideological functions, representing dominant or oppositional views on sexuality, gender, race and so on. Furthermore, in his analysis of the ways in which star personas were constructed he noted that, 'it is certainly possible to establish, as "auteur theory" enjoins us, continuities, contradictions and transformations either in the totality of a star's image or in discrete elements such as dress or performance style, roles, publicity, iconography' (Dyer, 1979: 174).

I am drawing broadly upon Dyer's framework to argue that it is not that movie stars should be considered authors or auteurs, but rather that the social and cultural patterns that such stars embody should be considered worthy of scrutiny. However, the idea of the active star endures, with Marshall arguing that 'In their often "unique" – or perhaps idiosyncratic – personalities and in their attempts to achieve autonomous status, one can see the work of active human agency' (Marshall 1997: 242). It can be argued that stars such as Barrymore can be seen as authors of their own images and star personas, particularly through the active creation of a publicly circulated star persona in 'secondary texts' (Fiske, 1991: 85).

Consideration of Drew Barrymore as a star able to demonstrate active agency is, Melissa Friedling argues, complicated by her status as a former drug and alcohol addict. In early publicity material, she was 'never understood to be author of her own image. Intentionality or voluntarity is the very thing that is denied of both the addict and of the star' (Friedling, 2000: 50). Friedling argues that addiction and agency are mutually exclusive as 'addiction constitutes a crisis in the reproduction of dominant norms... [and] representations of addiction become the stage for repeated recoveries of "normality" ' (Friedling, 2000: 30). Therefore, she asserts, a feminist reading of Drew Barrymore's star persona is restricted by the emphasis on her status as addicted, dirty and as 'other' in publicity materials, and by the attempts of such articles to recuperate her into heteronormativity. Despite her argument that this ultimately deprives her of agency, feminists have openly championed 'bad girls' who transgress normative female sexuality and represent empowerment (Lumby, 1997; Nicolini, 1995). Friedling thus appears to make judgements regarding the value of certain forms of feminism, dismissing 'do me' feminism as an artificial media construct, designed to perpetuate the sexualization and control of women who believed themselves to be emancipated through their sexual freedom. Furthermore, Friedling's analysis only accounts for Barrymore's career until 1995, and her association with addiction and a 'bad girl' persona has long since been diminished by her penchant for appearing in high-grossing romantic comedies.

Barrymore's very real power within Hollywood is one indicator of the potential for a reading of the star as a successful female role model. Although the trend for stars to develop their own production companies is widespread and such arrangements have long been beneficial for stars and studios alike (King, 2003: 69–70), most of these production companies are so-called vanity projects, established to bolster a star's ego whilst simultaneously tying them to a particular studio (Ellis and Sutherland, 2004: 191). In contrast, Barrymore is an active producer for her company Flower Films, having produced or executive produced several of her own films, and frequently ranking as one of the most powerful actresses in entertainment (Furman and Furman. 2000: 182). Barrymore's status as a producer on many of her movies means that she can exert control over various elements of these films, such as her insistence that guns not be used in *Charlie's Angels* (Heath, 2000: 72) or her artistic input into the tracks on the *Never Been Kissed* soundtrack (Barrymore et al., 1999). Furthermore, she frequently attests that she aggressively fights for parts that she wants (Furman and Furman, 2000: 152; Grobel, 2003: 50; Donofrio, 2001: 98) and also claims to be pro-active when recruiting those she wishes to co-star with, persuading Cameron Diaz to appear in *Charlies' Angels* (Juvonen et al., 2001: 118) and lobbying for the casting of the unknown Michael Vartan in *Never Been Kissed* (Ellis and Sutherland, 2004: 212).

Whilst I am not arguing that Barrymore can be seen as an auteur figure through her status as a producer, the creation of Flower Films has certainly enabled her to exert greater control over the projects she is involved in and to change some aspects of films that she is dissatisfied with (Lotz and Ross, 2004: 193). Furthermore, she discursively positions herself as a potential auteur in numerous ways. First, she frequently praises her various directors such as Penny Marshall or George Clooney, speaking about each one effusively and deferentially (Blosdale, 2001; Grobel, 2003). Indeed, the 'notion of the star and the director mutually bringing something out in each other informs much auterist criticism' (Dyer, 1979: 177) and by aligning herself closely with the directors of various projects and emphasizing the reciprocal nature of their relationship. Barrymore discursively constructs herself as active and able to control the parts she is playing. Furthermore, her recent foray into directing (*The Best Place to Start*, 2004) means that Barrymore may yet develop into an auteur figure.

Christine Geraghty usefully distinguishes between different types of star; the 'professional' (whose fame relies upon their work whilst their private life remains hidden), the 'performer' (who displays their skills via their performances), and the 'celebrity', categorized as being famous primarily for what happens in their private life and for having a 'lifestyle', and being 'constructed through gossip, press and television reports, magazine articles and public relations' (Geraghty, 2000: 187). Female stars, such as Barrymore, are usually defined as celebrities due to their function as attractive 'spectacle' and because of their association with the 'private sphere' or romantic attachments and relationships. Barrymore also fulfils the notion of a star as 'a performer in a particular medium whose figure enters into subsidiary forms of circulation and then feeds back into future performance' (Ellis, 1982: 1). Her on-screen roles often inextricably recall the star persona created in secondary texts which establish her as 'an icon, a living embodiment of tragedy and survival' (Mundy, 1995: 314), and she frequently highlights similarities between herself and the characters she plays, discussing how she 'becomes' characters (Barrymore, 2001; Heath, 2000: 72), 'gets to know' them (Deitch Rohrer, 1994: 52), or what she has learned from playing them (Furman and Furman, 2000: 147).

In the old star system, studios were keen to merge the on- and off-screen personas of their stars, and 'the star's life became available as a narrative paralleling and (at the same time) reinforcing the on-screen image' (Gaines, 1992: 37), depriving the stars of agency to create their own narratives. Whilst many contemporary Hollywood stars are keen to actively construct their own star narratives, such a task is normally undertaken by the media via secondary or in academic analyses of celebrity figures. Thus, celebrity agency is circumvented by the media's creation of star narratives, and such agency thus 'needs to be viewed as *situated*: that is ... performances of "active agency" constantly reflect upon [their] role[s] within hierarchies of production' (Hills and Williams, 2005: 347), whilst also negotiating their desire to offer their own interpretations of characters and to actively demonstrate their autonomy and individuality. Accepting Barrymore's performed agency enables us to explore the ways in which she subverts or reinforces hegemonic ideas about gender and sexuality, rendering a complex and ambiguous feminist reading of her star persona possible.

'Beyond control'?: Barrymore's transgressive comeback

In her early post-rehab films, Barrymore often plays the role of temptress or vamp, and she is often objectified and shown semi-naked, although her explicit sexuality is often aggressive and transgressive. Such films emphasized unexpected female deviancy, recalling Barrymore's early experiences and her widely circulated image as 'wild' or 'out of control'. In *Poison Ivy* (1992), Barrymore's character infiltrates the home of her friend Cooper, killing her mother and seducing her father. Ivy is presented as a threat due to her demarcation as sexually deviant, highlighted by her costuming in mini skirts, cowboy boots and her piercings and tattoos. Furthermore, her barely suppressed lesbian desire for Cooper and her seduction of the household patriarch symbolise Ivy's threat to the heteronormative stability of the nuclear family (Woodward, 2002: 313). In 1992's *Guncrazy*, she plays the abused, promiscuous teenager Anita who falls in love with a recently paroled prisoner. The film is one of Barrymore's most overtly feminist roles, incorporating 'a feminist morality and a philosophical discussion of violence' (Lane, 2000: 192) through its identification with the abused central character of Anita.

In *Doppelganger* (1993) Barrymore's character is again stigmatized through her threatening sexuality and the possibility of her 'splitting' into two, either via the existence of an evil twin or her own schizophrenia. Furthermore, in *Beyond Control* (1993), Barrymore plays Amy Fisher; the notorious teen who shot and paralysed the wife of her married lover, and subsequently served a lengthy jail sentence. Again the film eroticizes Barrymore's teenage body, depicting her as the protagonist in the seduction of her married lover in one particularly graphic scene halfway through the film. However, her role in *Beyond Control* proved contentious, as the Amy Fisher case prompted much controversy with many hailing her as a feminist icon whilst others derided her as a deranged teen and despaired of the celebrity culture that had turned her into a media star (Wurtzel, 1998: 91–95). In each of these four 'comeback' films, Barrymore is

> **consistently acting in retaliation against patriarchal gender expectations...she appeared to represent the threat of a feminist critique of culture...Narrative closure is achieved in all three cases with the punishing of bad, abusive men who take advantage of young girls, supplying all the movies with an explicit, albeit naïve, feminist spin. (Friedling, 2000: 34)**

In the second wave of 'vamp' roles (1994–1995) Barrymore is less objectified and less often shown naked or engaged in sexual acts. Whether playing a prostitute in a female Western (*Bad Girls*, 1994), a psychiatric patient (*Mad Love*, 1995) or an accidental murderess (*Boys On The Side*, 1995), such roles appeared to draw on her personal history, casting her in parts that emphasized collective female action and 'themes of *accidental* criminality...[in which her characters were] recuperated into a straight white patriarchal order as narrative resolution is achieved with her contentment in the arms of a protective man' (Friedling, 2000: 50–51). However, this is not necessarily so. Although Holly in *Boys on the Side* eventually marries a policeman and has a child, the ambiguous endings of both *Bad Girls* and *Mad Love* do not allow us to easily make the same assumptions. *Mad Love's* conclusion depicts Casey's return to institutionalization and the final scenes highlight the distance between her and her boyfriend, with little indication that their relationship will continue. Furthermore, despite the eradication of the overt feminism of *Bad Girls* when the studio replaced director Tamra Davis with Jonathan Kaplan (Lane, 2000), Barrymore's character Lilly remains subtextually coded as bisexual and the film's denouement depicts her riding off into the sunset with her female companions.

Throughout this period Barrymore continued to intertwine her 'real life' self with her on-screen roles in numerous contemporary interviews, relating the character of troubled, institutionalized Casey in *Mad Love* to her own experiences in, and on the run from, rehab (Broughton, 1995: 42), but acknowledging that 'when it was over, the cathartic aspect of it kicked in, and I felt freer than I've ever felt' (Furman and Furman, 2000: 119). Finally, her small roles in *Wayne's World 2* (as a nymphomaniac Swedish secretary) and *Batman Forever* (as 'good girl' Sugar to the vampish Spice in a typical good girl/bad-girl dichotomy) seem to parody her previous tendency towards playing vamps and also her sexualized star persona.

Screaming and kissing: Barrymore's 'appropriate femininity'

If her roles in *Wayne's World 2* and *Batman Forever* poked fun at her history of 'vamp' roles, her part in *Scream* (1996) allowed her to exorcise those associations for good. It is well documented that Barrymore rejected the lead role of Sydney Prescott, opting instead for the part of Casey Becker who dies in the opening scenes, in order to shock and unnerve the audience (Juvonen et al., 2001: 118). Thus, the film draws on Barrymore's 'personal history of exploitation and victimisation then kill[s] her within the first fifteen minutes' (Rowe Karlyn, 2003), suggesting that even in a cameo role Barrymore's characters and her star persona cannot be easily disentangled. Her star agency is evidenced by her ability to suggest to the director that she take a different part but it is also perhaps demonstrated if we read this role as a transition between her early career and its next phase. This role can be viewed as her attempt to kill off her previously sexualized 'vamp' characters as, 'by killing off this character so decisively, the film also kills off a certain model of femininity – dumb, passive, dependent, victimized – in order to replace it with another that is more knowing, less glamorous and far more capable' (Rowe Karlyn, 2003).

Following her on-screen death in *Scream*, Barrymore was reborn through starring roles in high budget romantic comedies or supporting parts in independent movies. Each of these roles showed a marked departure from her previously sexualized characters, featuring Barrymore as characters who were, if not literal virgins, at least innocent and desexualized. For example, in *The Wedding Singer* (1998) she plays Julia, another resolutely sweet, 'innocent' character. Julia is routinely depicted through opposition with other female characters; primarily her promiscuous cousin Holly, but also the women with whom her fiancé Glen cheats on her. The film devalues those characters who represent unacceptable femininity; thus women who are promiscuous, 'easy' or simply showing too much flesh can be mocked and dismissed, allowing the film to foreground the appropriate 'girlish', romantic femininity which Julia represents. Furthermore, Barrymore's character Danielle in *Ever After*, a modern retelling of the Cinderella tale, is clearly demarcated as a virgin until she falls in love with her Prince. Despite this embodiment of innocent sexuality, Danielle is not depicted as a victim and, at the movie's climax, actively escapes from the villain rather than waiting to be rescued, providing a knowing post-feminist spin on the traditional tale. All the while, Barrymore's extra-textual identification with her roles continues, likening the relationship between her Cinderella character and her stepmother in *Ever After* to her strained relationship with her own estranged mother and consistently enthusing about her relation to each of her roles, attesting that she feels like she learns something from each of them (Furman and Furman, 2000: 147).

The commercial success of these films enabled her to form her production company 'Flower Films' and to produce the successful high school movie *Never Been Kissed* (1999). Barrymore's character, Josie, is a literal virgin; having never experienced a proper kiss, let alone engaged in any type of sexual activity. She is initially coded as unattractive and despite her intellect and success in being the *Chicago Sun Times'* youngest ever copy-editor, she is unpopular, awkward and deeply unhappy. Returning to school as an undercover reporter, she eventually learns that it is best to be yourself and is accepted by her peers as well as finds love in the arms of schoolteacher Sam Coulson (Shary, 2002: 243).

Nonetheless, the film's moralizing falls short as, despite preaching that individuality is the route to happiness, Josie still has to conform to stereotypical femininity by bleaching her hair, wearing fashionable clothing and beginning a heterosexual romance in order to be accepted, normal and happy. However, the potentially contentious aspects of the film are circumvented in Barrymore's extratextual comments. Claiming an affinity with Josie whilst refuting the allegation that the film is merely about an 'unattractive girl getting a miracle makeover' (Furman and Furman, 2000: 166), Barrymore is able to undermine potential accusations about the film's harmful message from her position *as* Josie, established by emphasizing her similarities with the character. Thus, she attempts to foreclose alternative readings of the character by offering her own apparently authoritative interpretation.

Both *Charlie's Angels* (2000) and its sequel *Full Throttle* (2003) have prompted debate about the films' representation of its stars Barrymore, Cameron Diaz and Lucy Liu as whilst the Angels are portrayed as intelligent and multi-skilled, they are also depicted as sexualized objects who depend upon their looks to manipulate men (Gauntlett, 2003: 67). Despite the character's sexuality and physical attractiveness, one can read the film as a testament to contemporary post-feminism and the promise that women do not have to choose between brains and beauty. The films offer alternate models of femininity – the 'bad girl', the 'brainy girl' or the 'romantic', acknowledging that all three are acceptable lifestyle choices and avoiding the privileging of one over the others. However, Barrymore's Angel is the most sexually promiscuous and deviant, cheating on her boyfriend and suitably punished by the revelation that she has slept with the enemy. Such intertextual cues recall Barrymore's chequered personal history although, as Executive Producer of the film, we are assured that this is done with her full consent and that she is in on the joke.

Most recently, Barrymore starred in *50 First Dates* (2004) playing Lucy, a woman with no short-term memory who must be wooed every day by love interest Henry (Adam Sandler). Despite this return to playing innocent, 'good' characters, the film's depiction of Lucy as a disenfranchised, abnormal character 'who will always be a childish girl, never have agency, never be able to make an informed decision that she can count on lasting' (Fuchs, 2004) is problematic. For, rather than taking control and developing her own system for remembering events and coping with her disability, Lucy remains reliant upon Henry's interpretation of previous events. It seems that as Barrymore's roles become more commercially successful, feminist readings of them become increasingly contradictory and complex.

What this group of roles also highlights is the importance of generic expectation, and how this can undermine the notion of the star as author of their own image, as each of the characters Barrymore plays clearly fulfils typical expectation of the romantic-comedy or action genre. Indeed, issues of authorship and genre have often clashed, with authorship often aligned with high or legitimate notions of art, whilst genre has been perceived as formulaic and commerce-based (Neale, 1980: 8). Thus, generic necessity restricts Barrymore's ability to fully articulate her own star agency through construction of a narrative that aligns her with these types of characters, further complicating a reading of her star persona. However, it can be argued that Barrymore still possesses 'potentially disruptive queer agency' (Friedling, 2000: 33) through the way in which her star persona transgresses boundaries regarding appropriate femininity and questions normative ideas regarding gender and sexuality. Her feminism remains contradictory and ambivalent, although this is now due to economic and industry factors, such as generic expectation or the need to avoid the alienation of audience members, rather than the stigma of her addiction.

"I'm not a torch-carrying feminist,": Barrymore's ambivalent feminism

In secondary material Barrymore articulates her political stance and suggests some pro-feminist leanings. Stars' ability to represent the everyday concerns of the public designates them as 'active agents that in the public spectacle stand in for the people. The assuming of this secondary agency role has led many stars to become spokespersons for political causes and issues' (Marshall, 1997: 244). For example, Barrymore wrote, produced, directed and starred in the documentary *The Best Place to Start* (2004) about young people's voting habits, and encouraging women into political activity, particularly regarding issues surrounding their own bodies and sexuality (Bried, 2004; Finke, 2004; Schulte-Hillen, 2004). Barrymore further demonstrates her agency by acting as a spokesperson for the Female Health Foundation (Ellis and Sutherland, 2004: 1999) and in regularly attending Hollywood celebrations of female actors and producers. She frequently advocates a 'girl power' attitude, encouraging women to 'go after what they want' (Collins, 2004: 193) and to make the first move with men (Juvonen, 2004). However, she has distanced herself from overtly feminist views, noting that

> I'm not a torch-carrying feminist, but I love women. All of my good friends are women, and I try to respect myself as a woman . . . I think what's great is if you can have intelligence and capability as your foundation and be fun and sexy on top of it. (Fowler, 2002)

As Marshall notes, celebrity agency rarely equates with an overt political or social movements as is often 'reduced to a privatized, psychologized representation of activity and transformation' (Marshall, 1997: 244). Fittingly, Barrymore's feminism is less an encouragement towards political or social action and more a 'popular feminism' (McRobbie, 1999), 'third wave feminism' (Findlen, 1995; Karras, 2002; Orr, 1997), or 'post-feminism' which focuses upon independence, confidence and autonomy. Despite the challenges from traditional feminists regarding the usefulness of such forms of feminism (Detloff, 1997; Baumgardner and Richards, 2000: 222–224), they remain widely circulated in the media, often through celebrities such as Barrymore.

This overview of Barrymore's roles and secondary material over the past 15 years allows us to chart the progression of her characters from threateningly transgressive and sexualized, women caught up in accidental criminality, to 'good girls' who obey heteropatriarchal norms. The assumption that Barrymore possesses agency to control her own image enables us to 'read' her career and suggest moments where she may display astute self-awareness with regard to her star persona, self-reflexively drawing upon her personal history to inform a role (e.g. *Guncrazy*) or parodying it (e.g. *Wayne's World* 2). The presumption of Barrymore's star agency also allows us to look for moments of subversion of feminist ideas where her characters are recuperated into heteropatriarchal norms, 'indicating points of resistance as well as managing resistance and anxiety' (Friedling, 2000: 44).

In control?: Refuting celebrity agency/authorship

The above analysis positions Drew Barrymore as an independent star, able to display active agency by regulating and circulating her own public persona and exercising considerable control over the projects she is involved in. However, this is an overly individualist view of celebrity which does not account for the activities of other players in the cultural industry of Hollywood and the mass media which promotes it. In this section, I will examine how a feminist reading of Barrymore remains contradictory and unstable due to the ideological and institutional constraints of the industry she works within.

First, it has been argued that stars seek to avoid correlating themselves with their most recent characters, to avoid any potential threat to their independent agency (Gamson, 1994; King, 2003; Turner, 2004). Whilst many stars promote 'their latest work as a means of enhancing their cultural value in general and so it is possible that they will be reluctant to closely tie this publicity to the particular performance vehicle' (Turner, 2004: 36). Barrymore instead makes discursive bids for star agency by constructing a narrative of her own 'real-life' which is reflected in the progression between the various parts she plays. This is evidenced by the examples of her extra-textual attempts to conflate herself with her roles. Whilst, as noted above, she effusively identifies with her characters in films such as *Never Been Kissed*, when she later moves on to play the more rebellious Dylan in *Charlie's Angels*, she declares this to be a conscious, rational choice:

> I fancied it because I have just played so many nice girls and losers and girls who have never been kissed or barely know how to kiss or puritans or these valiant, pure intentioned, rarely-make-a-mistake characters ... I wanted to play a little bit of a badass, I wanted to play someone who was unashamed and was in touch with her sexuality and in touch with her bravery. (Heath, 2000: 72)

Although when promoting a specific movie, Barrymore may effusively declare her identification with and similarity to that character, as her career progresses she necessarily needs to continually negotiate the aspects of her star persona which she conflates with each role. This is closely related to the economic necessities of the industry and the need for the star to market themselves as a malleable, versatile commodity whilst simultaneously promoting their current film. Thus, in the earlier example of disavowing her 'good girl' roles when starring in *Charlie's Angels*, Barrymore assesses which traits are most appropriate for that character and discursively aligns herself with Dylan whilst covertly devaluing her previous characters. Such a negotiation between maintaining one's own star persona and aligning oneself with a given character often results in 'a push in different directions: both towards and away from a celebrity divorced from her particular vehicles and roles, known for her self alone; and both toward and away from interchangeability' (Gamson, 1994: 81).

Furthermore, stars are often perceived as the sole 'creator' of their star persona. The collaborative nature of a star's profession is often negated. For example, in a study of Madonna, Francis Wasserlein noted that there is little interest in 'the names of the players and technical people on Madonna's recordings ... The Madonna business is about marketing Madonna' (Wasserlein, in Hills, 2002: 179). Such figures undermine the notion of 'celebrity-as-author' as they belie the assumption that celebrities are the sole authors of their own images, free to present whatever persona they alone see fit. Furthermore, publicists can circulate their own, sometimes contradictory, readings of stars' various roles and films as they 'distribute their preferred meaning of films (cognitive and affective) through an independent agency (the mass media) to audiences' (Moloney, 1999: 47). However, such work is usually behind the scenes in order to perpetuate the idea of the celebrity as an autonomous, active agent. Therefore, star agency is best thought of as 'performed agency'. It foregrounds the representation of the celebrity as sole author of their star persona (their ability to select roles) without acknowledging the collaborative nature of the film-making process and the multi-faceted publicity industries within which it operates.

Second, I have argued that stars such as Barrymore, who own production companies, can exercise greater control over their projects and that this enables them to produce movies they have a greater sense of involvement in. This, I have suggested, may enable us to read Barrymore not as author of her produced films but as able to discursively position herself as an active agent through her identification with her directors and her suggestion that she may develop her interest in behind the camera work.

Third, I have suggested that celebrities who repeatedly play similar characters are exercising their agency by choosing roles that reflect 'themselves', that form some coherent ideology, and express some of the stars' own ideas and beliefs, which in Barrymore's case is a form of feminism. However, playing the same types of characters perhaps demonstrates a distinct lack of agency and suggests instead that the particular star is being typecast into similar roles by the industry they work for. Thus, Barrymore's initial string of 'vamp' roles was less a matter of choice than indicative of the characters that reluctant studios felt she could effectively play (Heath, 1993). Furthermore, I have argued that Barrymore's active decision to 'kill off' her previous vamp characters through her role in *Scream* and the subsequent move into big-budget romantic comedies indicates her agency to construct her star narrative. However, this suggests that she was able to pre-empt the film's success and choose her role accordingly. It is perhaps more likely that her post-*Scream* success was a result of the critical view that it was the subversion of Barrymore's presence as the apparent star of the film that provided the 'hook that captures the audience' (Muir, 1999: 208). This was widely perceived to have contributed to the film's success and thus increased Barrymore's star status within Hollywood and leading onto bigger roles.

Barrymore's ability to select the roles she wishes to play is also constrained by the competitive nature of the film industry, which often means that other actresses or production companies take on projects she desires. Her wish to play Lolita in Adrian Lyne's remake was thwarted (Lindquist, 1991) and her oft-reiterated intention to play Brandon Teena was undermined by the production of the Oscar-winning *Boys Don't Cry*, based upon the same story. As well as restricting Barrymore's ability to select those projects she wishes to become involved in, this also threatens her ability to construct a satisfactory star narrative regarding the progress of her career. Her desire to play Teena was articulated in secondary materials as a wish to engage in serious acting (van Meter, 1996: 72), indicating a narrative development in her own career and a 'moving onto' more respectable roles. Thus, Barrymore's ability to construct herself as an active agent – able to control her star persona and select her own roles according to a star narrative – is thwarted by the constraints of both parent and rival studios, publicists and agents, and the involvement of writers/directors and production personnel.

Conclusion

This analysis of Drew Barrymore's star persona through her film appearances and secondary materials has sought to challenge conventional theories of stardom and celebrity which either neglect female stars or polarize them according to highly gendered categories of masculine (active agents) or feminine (passive, disempowered, sexualized). I have sought to concur with Melissa Friedling's assertion that feminist readings of the star are complex and ambivalent but have sought to argue that, as Barrymore's career has developed, this contradiction is a result, not of her status as a former addict, but due to her increased involvement within the Hollywood industry. Thus, whilst Barrymore can be considered to be the author of her own star persona and of her career trajectory, we cannot fail to acknowledge that the agency she displays when constructing her star narrative, is a performed agency which the star discursively articulates. Despite her frequent entwining of herself with her roles and her apparently frank discussion of her 'real-life', she is never truly revealing her 'self': as one Hollywood producer noted, 'She's an actress. She knows how much to give so that you feel that way' (Juvonen et al., 2001: 118). Thus, although the star narrative she constructs and circulates in secondary materials suggests that she is actively able to choose her roles in order to represent a coherent feminist ideology and reflect her 'real-life', the economics of the industry in which Barrymore works cannot be underestimated. It is the influence of 'cultural intermediaries', film studios, colleagues, production personnel and generic constraints that contribute to the continuation of Barrymore's image as 'neither emancipatory nor conciliatory, neither positive nor negative, but rather as ambivalent' (Friedling, 2000: 44).

References

Barthes, Roland (1977) *Image Music Text*, London: Fontana Press.
Baumgardner, Jennifer and Amy Richards (2000) *Manifesta: Young Women, Feminism, and the Future*, New York: Farrar, Straus and Giroux.

Blosdale, Christine (2001) 'Celebetty Drew Barrymore', available at http://www.
  drewheaven.com/print/article03.php [accessed 8 January 2005].

Bried, Erin 'Drew Barrymore's Not-So-Secret Passion', *Self* September 2004: 178.

Broughton, Frank 'Pretty on the Inside', *i-D* March 1995: 42.

Cassetta, Debbie (2000) 'When fans collide: net celebrity in the Xenaverse', *Whoosh:
  The Journal of the International Association of Xena Studies* 50, available at
  http://www.whoosh.org/issue50/cassettal.html [accessed 12 June 2005].

Collins, Nancy 'Drew Grows Up', *Bazaar* April 2004: 193.

Deitch Rohrer, Trish 'Wild Honey', *Arena* July 1994: 52.

Detloff, Madelyn (1997) 'Mean Spirits: The Politics of Contempt Between Feminist
  Generations', *Hypatia*, 12 (3): 76–100.

Donofrio, Beverly 'The Risk I Took for Love', *Marie Claire* October 2001: 98.

Doss, Erika (1999) *Elvis Culture: Fans, Faith and Image*, Lawrence, Kansas: University
  Press of Kansas.

Drake, Philip (2004) 'Jim Carrey: The Cultural Politics of Dumbing Down', in
  Andrew Willis (ed.), *Hollywood, Film Stars and Beyond*, Manchester: Manchester
  University Press, pp. 71–88.

Dubois, Diane (2001) 'Seeing the Female Body Differently: Gender Issues in *The Silence
  of the Lambs*', *Journal of Gender Studies* 10 (3): 297–310.

Dyer, Richard (1979) *Stars*, London: BFI.

—— (1986) *Heavenly Bodies: Film Stars and Society*, Basingstoke: Macmillan Education.

Ellis, John (1982) *Visible Fictions: Cinema, Television, Video*, London: Routledge.

Ellis, Lucy and Bryony Sutherland (2004) *Drew Barrymore: The Biography*, London:
  Aurum Press.

Feasey, Rebecca (2003) "Sharon Stone, Screen Diva': Stardom, Femininity and Cult
  Fandom' in Mark Jancovich, Antonio Lazovo Reboll, Julian Stringer and Andrew
  Willis (eds.), *Defining Cult Movies: The Cultural Politics of Oppositional Taste*,
  Manchester: Manchester University Press, pp. 172–184.

—— (2004) 'Stardom and Sharon Stone: Power as Masquerade', *Quarterly Review of
  Film and Video* 21 (3): 199–207.

Findlen, Barbara (1995) *Listen Up: Voices from the Next Feminist Generation*, USA:
  Seal Press.

Finke, Nikki, 'Angel on the Bus', *LA Weekly* 24 September 2004.

Fiske, John (1991) *Television Culture*, London: Routledge.

Fowler, H. W. (2002) 'A Three-on-One with *Charlie's* Booty-Shakin', Drag-Dressin',
  Ass-Kickin' Angels', available at http://www.eonline.com/Features/Features/
  Charliesangels/Qa/ [accessed 6 January 2005].

Friedling, Melissa Pearl (2000) *Recovering Women: Feminisms and the Representation
  of Addiction*, Boulder, Colorado: Westview Press.

Fuchs, Cynthia (2004) 'Keep Running: Review of *50 First Dates*', available at http://www.
  popmatters.com/film/reviews/f/50-first-dates.shtml [accessed 11 January 2004].

Furman, Leah and Elina Furman (2000) *Happily Ever After: The Drew Barrymore
  Story*, New York: Ballantine.

Gaines, Jane M. (1992) *Contested Culture: The Image, the Voice and the Law*, London: BFI.

Gallagher, Mark (2004) 'Rumble in the USA: Jackie Chan in Translation', in
  Andrew Willis (ed.), *Hollywood, Film Stars and Beyond*, Manchester: Manchester
  University Press, pp. 113–139.

Gamson, Joshua (1994) *Claims to Fame*: *Celebrity in Contemporary America*, California: University of California Press.

Gauntlett, David (2002) *Media, Gender and Identity: An Introduction*, London: Routledge.

Geraghty, Christine (2000) 'Re-examining Stardom: Questions of Texts, Bodies and Performance', in Christine Gledhill and Linda Williams (eds.), *Reinventing Film Studies*, London: Arnold, pp. 183–202.

—— (2003) 'Performing as a Lady and a Dame: Reflections on Acting and Genre', in Thomas Austin and Martin Barker (eds.), *Contemporary Hollywood Stardom*, London: Arnold, pp. 105–117.

Gledhill, Christine (1991) *Stardom: Industry of Desire*, London: Routledge.

Grobel, Lawrence (2003) 'The Latest Drew Stories', *Movieline* March: 50.

Heath, Chris (1993) 'Drew Love, Drew Grit', *Details* June, 32–33.

—— 'The Naughty Adventures of Miss Drew Barrymore' *Rolling Stone* 23 November 2000: 72.

Hills, Matt (2002) *Fan Cultures*, London: Routledge.

Hills, Matt and Rebecca Williams (2005) 'It's all my interpretation: reading spike through the 'subcultural celebrity' of James Marsters', *European Journal of Cultural Studies* 8 (3): 345–365.

Innes, Sherrie A (1998) *Tough Girls: Women Warriors and Wonder Women in Popular Culture*, Philadelphia, PA: University of Pennsylvania Press.

Internet Movie Database (2005) 'Drew Barrymore', available at http://www.imdb.com/name/nm0000106/ [accessed 3 February 2005].

Juvonen, Nancy (2004) 'True Drew', *Glamour* March, 12–13.

—— (2004) 'Interview', available at http://www.drew-barrymore.org/php/interviews.php [accessed 8 January 2005].

Juvonven, N., A. Heckerling, J. Baddeley and M. Bochco 'Women We Love: Drew Barrymore'. *Esquire* October 2001: 118.

Karras, Irene (2002) 'The Third Wave's Final Girl: *Buffy the Vampire Slayer*', available at http://www.thirdspace.ca/articles/karras.htm [accessed 13 January 2005].

King, Barry (2003) 'Embodying An Elastic Self' The Parameters of Contemporary Stardom', in Thomas Austin and Martin Barker (eds.), *Contemporary Hollywood Stardom*, London: Arnold, pp. 45–61.

King, Geoff (2003) 'Stardom in the Willennium' in Thomas Austin and Martin Barker (eds.), *Contemporary Hollywood Stardom*, London: Arnold, pp. 62–73.

Kramer, Peter (2004) 'The Rise and Fall of Sandra Bullock: Notes on Starmaking and Female Stardom in Contemporary Hollywood', in Andrew Willis (ed.), *Hollywood, Film Stars and Beyond*, Manchester: Manchester University Press, pp. 89–112.

Kurtzberg, Brad (2004) '"Pretty Woman" is also Highest Paid Actress', available at http://www.elitestv.com/pub/2004/Dec/EEN41b61d10c8555.html [accessed 4 January 2005].

Lacey, Joanne (2003) ' "A galaxy of Stars to Guarantee Ratings": Made-for-Television Movies and the Female Star System', in Thomas Austin and Martin Barker (eds.), *Contemporary Hollywood Stardom*, London: Arnold, pp. 187–198.

Lane, Christina (2000) *Feminist Hollywood: From Born in Flames to Point Break*, Detroit: Wayne State University Press.

Lindquist, Mark (1991) 'Woman Child', available at http://www.drew-barrymore.org/php/print.php?key=ifl991&act=detail [accessed 6 January 2005].

Lotz, A.D. and S.M. Ross (2004) 'Bridging Media-Specific Approaches: The Value of Feminist Television Criticism's Synthetic Approach', *Feminist Media Studies* 4 (2): 185–202.

Lumby, Catharine (1997) *Bad Girls: Media, Sex and Feminism in the 90s*, St. Leonards, NSW: Allen & Unwin.

Marshall, P. David (1997) *Celebrity and Power: Fame in Contemporary Culture*, Minneapolis: University of Minnesota Press.

McRobbie, Angela (1999) *In the Culture Society: Art, Fashion and Popular Music*, London and New York: Routledge.

Moloney, Kevin (1999) 'Publicists – Distribution Workers in the Pleasure Economy of the Film Industry', in Jonathan Bignell (ed.), *Writing and Cinema*, London: Longman, pp. 43–56.

Moseley, Rachel (2002a) 'Glamorous Witchcraft: Gender and Magic in Teen Film and Television', *Screen* 43 (41): 403–422.

—— (2002b) *Growing Up With Audrey Hepburn*, Manchester and New York: Manchester University Press.

Muir, John Kenneth (1999) *Wes Craven: The Art of Horror*, Jefferson, North Carolina and London: McFarland and Company.

Mundy, Chris (1995) 'Drew Barrymore', in Peter Travers (ed.), *The Rolling Stone Film Reader: From 1967 to 1996*, New York: Pocket Books, pp. 313–319.

Neale, Stephen (1980) *Genre*, London: BFI.

Negra, Diane (2001) 'Introduction: Female Stardom and Early Film History', *Camera Obscura* 16 (3): 1–7.

Nicolini, Kim (1995) 'Staging the Slut: Hyper-Sexuality in Performance', *Bad Subjects* 20, available at http://eserver.org/bs/20/Nicolini.html [accessed 16 February 2005].

Orr, Cathryn (1997) 'Charting the Currents of the Third Wave', *Hypatia* 12 (3): 29–45.

Penaloza, Lisa (2004) 'Consuming Madonna Then and Now: An Examination of the Dynamics and Structuring of Celebrity Consumption', in Santiago Fouz-Hernandez and Freya Jarman-Ivens (eds.) *Madonna's Drowned Worlds: New Approaches to her Cultural Transformations 1983–2003*, Aldershot, Hants: Ashgate Publishing, pp. 176–192.

Rowe Karlyn, Kathleen (2003) 'Scream, Popular Culture, and Feminism's Third Wave: "I'm Not My Mother"', *Genders On-Line Journal* 38, available at http://www.genders.org/g38/g38_rowe_karlyn.html [accessed 10 January 2005].

Rutsky, R. L. (2001) 'Being Keanu', in Jon Lewis (ed.), *The End of Cinema as we Know It: American Film in the Nineties*, New York: New York University Press, pp. 185–194.

Schulte-Hillen, Sophie (2004) 'Drew wants YOU to VOTE (or at least make some noise)', *Elle Girl* September: 116.

Seigworth, Greg (1993) 'The Distance Between Me and You: Madonna and Celestial Navigation (or You Can Be My Lucky Star)', in Cathy Schwichtenberg (ed.) *The Madonna Connection: Representational Politics, Subcultural Identities, and Cultural Theory*, Oxford: Westview Press, pp. 291–318.

Shary, Timothy (2002) 'The Nerdly Girl and her Beautiful Sister', in Frances Gateward and Murray Pomerace (eds.), *Sugar, Spice, and Everything Nice: Cinemas of Girlhood*, Wayne State University Press, pp. 235–352.

Stacey, Jackie (1994) *Star Gazing: Hollywood Cinema and Female Spectatorship*, London: Routledge.

Staiger, Janet (1993) 'Taboos and Totems: Cultural Meanings of *Silence of the Lambs*', in Jim Collins, Hilary Radner and Ava Preacher Collins (eds.), *Film Theory Goes to the Movies*, London: Routledge, pp. 142–154.

Tasker, Yvonne (1998) *Working Girls: Gender and Sexuality in Popular Cinema*, London: Routledge.

Turner, Graeme (2004) *Understanding Celebrity*, London: Sage.

van Meter Jonathan (1996) 'Drew on Top', *Bazaar* December 1996: 178.

Woodward, Steven (2002) 'She's Murder: Pretty Poisons and Bad Seeds', in Frances Gateward and Murray Pomerace (eds.), *Sugar, Spice, and Everything Nice: Cinemas of Girlhood*, Detroit, MI: Wayne State University Press, pp. 303–322.

Wurtzel, Elizabeth (1998) *Bitch: In Praise of Difficult Women*, London: Quartet Books.

Zuk, Rhoda (1998) 'Entertaining Feminism: *Roseanne* and Roseanne Arnold', *Studies in Popular Culture* 20:1 available at http://pcasacas.org/SPC/spcissues/21.1/zuk.htm [accessed 20 June 2005].

Fame – Remember My Name?: Histories of Stardom and Celebrity

Introduction
Sean Redmond and Su Holmes

Fame is metamorphic.... There can be no single perspective, no secret key by which to unlock what it really is

(Braudy, 1986: 591)

As Braudy's statement suggests, fame is a cultural phenomenon that is constantly *in process*, and this very fluidity demands a multi-faceted and self-reflexive framework of analysis. Section Three explores ways of understanding the historical trajectory of fame, and it acknowledges that the notion of 'history' here is not a simple concept. As established in the Introduction, similar to other sources of commentary we could access, the academic discussion of fame is *historical*. It does not simply offer an 'objective' analysis of the field, but reflects something of the 'culture of fame' in which it was written. History is a social invention, produced by construction and re-construction, a moveable, fluid feast. In relation to the focus of this section, this is a useful perspective to bear in mind, as there is no 'objective' history of fame that we can present here. As Lynn Spigel explains,

History is a kind of knowledge based not only on the historian's subjective determinations regarding evidence but also on the conventions of writing that govern other kinds of textual production.... It is the process of interpretation – and the ways in which we use evidence to produce an argument – that is at stake. (2001: 12)

This 'process of interpretation', and the construction, selection and processing of evidence, is applicable to the subject of fame.

Examining the history of fame has an important role to play in a context where the primary emphasis in on *change* – the idea that fame has changed, and *is* changing, in new and significant ways. In this respect, it is worth considering Braudy's response to the cultural decline thesis, and his suggestion that 'such Golden Ages of true worth and justified fame never existed. And in any case we would never have heard of them, since to trumpet one's disdain for fame ... necessarily follows in the tracks of fame itself' (1986: 8). Braudy's statement beckons a welcome degree of self-reflexivity in thinking about how the history of fame is written. But it also reflects how the impact of the mass media ('we would never have heard of them') is understandably at the centre of discussions about when, how and why fame has changed. Critics such as Daniel Boorstin (1961) insist that achievement and heroism were once recognized for their *own* value, without being refracted through the machines of publicity and promotion (see Evans, 2005: 20). But this position can be questioned. Jessica Evans' (2005) carefully probes the contemporary emphasis on change here by arguing that

> [T]here are continuities between the past and the present: the media, whether the mass media of the twentieth century or that of the pre-print period, are and always have been essential to celebrity. For, in order to be 'known' by many and talked of at a distance and from afar, one needs a medium of dissemination. And these continuities reach back well before the development of the mass media as we know them today. (Evans, 2005: 21)

While there is certainly some agreement that there is an ongoing development to discuss, there is not necessarily a consensus about what this development is. Braudy's *The Frenzy of the Renown* (1986) has offered the most extensive history in this respect, investigating the 'will to fame' from Roman times until (at the time when he was writing) the present day. But this long historical sweep – and its emphasis on conti-nuity – has often been challenged by recent scholarship (Turner, 2004: 9). Others have posited the origins of modern celebrity in a much shorter historical trajectory, as linked to the development of the mass media, and its visual capacities in particular (Turner, 2004: 10; Gamson, 1994; Rojek, 2001). A key site for tracing this development has been the establishment of the star system in classical Hollywood cinema, although this example may again emphasize (at the level of cultural memory at least) the degree to which contradictory perceptions structure how the history of fame is perceived. In the popular imaginary, film stars from this era are often recalled nostalgically, represent-ing a time of more distinguished stardom when compared to the present day. This is despite the fact that they emerged from a structure which represented the consolida-tion of the *mass production* of fame: the Hollywood studio system. There is also debate as to whether the post-World War Two period, with the advent of television and the wider expansion of media outlets, represents the last 'decisive shift' in fame (Braudy, 1986), or whether there are further significant developments since (particularly with the rise of new media – see Lumby in Section Six).

Last, there is the issue of how we access and research the past. While history is always a matter of interpretation – it does not lie still and cannot be brought fully under control – we nevertheless have to select from a range of approaches and sources for mapping its contours. Fame is a very 'elusive' idea (Braudy, 1986: 591), and as celebrity only exists *within representation*, when we talk about the history of fame we are talking about the stories which are written about people, the photographs which are taken or the performances which are captured on light-sensitive film. Thus, many of the authors in this section explore the history of fame by considering the changing ways in which the famous are *represented*. This raises issues of both source and method: what approaches, and indeed types of evidence, are available here? The essays in this section provide examples in this respect, ranging across the use of popular discourse in celebrity magazines, the study of broader social, cultural and political shifts, to the analysis of particular case studies and media texts. Thinking about the history of fame is no simple task, but we hope that the essays in Section Three stimulate debate.

Precisely because of the complexities outlined above, the essays in this section do not aim to offer a coherent or chronological history. Some authors examine broader histories of fame (Gamson, Rojek, Braudy) while others offer specific case studies from particular historical junctures (deCordova, Holmes). At the same time, the essays are intended to give the reader a sense of development.

Richard deCordova's 'The Emergence of the Star System in America' opens the section by tracing how the concept of the star evolved in Hollywood cinema between 1907 and the late teens. The focus here is on the discursive strategies which brought the star into being (drawing on Foucault's (1970) conception of discourse which refers to specific frameworks of thinking which take place within wider systems of social and cultural power). In exploring the intertextual site of the fan magazine, deCordova maps three key stages: the discourse on acting (circa 1907), the emergence of the 'picture personality' (circa 1909) where information was restricted to the professional existence of the actor, to the development of the 'star' (circa 1914), which marked an expansion in the kinds of knowledge that could be produced about the player. Crucially, this encompassed the ways in which 'the private lives of the stars emerged as a new site of knowledge and truth'. Yet while the concept of the star is conceived as a dialectic between on/off-screen identity, deCordova emphasizes how 'the two would ... work to support each other', shoring up an ideologically conservative image of the star at a time when there was intense cultural struggle around the moral reputation of the cinema.

deCordova's more specific historical focus can be linked to a broader historical trajectory in Joshua Gamson's 'The Assembly Line of Greatness: Celebrity in Twentieth-Century America'. Gamson examines the construction of fame both before and beyond the emergence of Classical Hollywood cinema, but like deCordova, he is interested in the intertextual circulation of fame (as found in the press or magazines). Gamson sets out to consider 'the implicit and explicit explanations in popular magazines of why and how people become famous', and his study is motivated by the desire to trace shifts in this discourse: how 'did this ... migrate from fame as the natural result of irrepressible greatness to celebrity as the fleeting product of a vacuum cleaner/sausage maker?' Gamson discerns a constant struggle between two principal 'claims-to-fame' stories: the notion of the mythic, 'authentic, gifted self', and the suggestion that celebrity is simply the product of manufacture. By the late twentieth century, he notes the recurrence of a range of strategies aimed to cope with the 'threat' of the manufacture narrative – the increasing claim to take us 'behind-the-scenes' of celebrity production, the use of irony in celebrity texts and the increased emphasis on the 'power' of the audience. Gamson's framework indeed seems to resonate with many contemporary celebrity texts, ranging from *heat* magazine (Holmes, 2005) to Reality TV.

Although popular debate often insists on abrupt or seismic shifts in fame (usually articulated with a note of alarm), Gamson's analysis is valuable in its emphasis on a continual struggle between competing explanations of fame – as gradually renegotiated through changing cultural and media contexts. But as his analysis also makes clear, television does not fare well in histories of fame. It is often associated with a shift away from meritocratic ideals of stardom, while it is also described as depleting the 'aura' of stardom – whether we refer to television's production of its own 'personalities' (see Ellis, Section Two), or its domestication of stars from other domains. Yet there is still much work to be done from a historical perspective here – especially in the British context in which comparatively little is known about the medium's early circulation of celebrity.[1]

Su Holmes examines what was one of the most controversial programmes on British television in the 1950s: the BBC's version of *This is Your Life*. In popular memory, *This is Your Life* stands as a flattering and reverential celebration of 'great' and 'worthy' celebrities, but in the institutional and cultural contexts of its early circulation (primarily 1955–1962), it carried different discursive meanings. It was variously described as 'Torture-by-TV', and it was seen as transforming 'televiewing into the delight of the Peeping Tom'. Drawing on archival research based on existing programmes, scripts, press reviews and the internal documentation of the BBC, Holmes explores why *This is Your Life* might have been so controversial in the 1950s, reflecting on television's *emerging* role in the circulation of modern fame. Particularly in its negotiation 'of public and private realms', she suggests 'that the programme prefigures the cultural debate which surrounded the advent of talk shows and Reality TV, while it offers a fascinating anticipation of some of their most compelling aesthetic strategies'.

In 'Celebrity and Religion', Chris Rojek returns to a longer historical view, and further probes the idea that changing cultural contexts fundamentally shape the significance of celebrity. His essay is as much about certain forms of audience investment in celebrity (see also Section Six) as it is about the history of fame, and Rojek draws a convincing comparison between celebrity and religious worship, tracing their connections and intersections. In this respect Rojek draws upon Emile Durkheim's (1915) work on the securalization of Western society to account for the deification of stars and celebrities, arguing that 'the growing significance of celebrity culture as … the backcloth of routine existence reinforces the proposition that …"post-God" celebrity is now one of the mainstays of organising recognition and belonging in secular society'. Rojek explores a range of instances where celebrity worship is invested with religious signification, iconography and structures, in ways which have interesting – and often contradictory – relations with other essays in this section. For example, whereas Gamson foregrounds manufacture as the increasingly dominant explanation of fame (and the playful rhetoric of irony this now invokes), Rojek is interested in a history in which celebrities are 'thought to possess God-like qualities' (2001: 53) and are venerated as objects of cult-like worship. Rojek's wider argument here is that although celebrity culture has not simply replaced organized religion, it has emerged as 'one of the replacement strategies that promote new orders of meaning and solidarity'.

Finally, Leo Braudy's highly poetic discussion of 'The Dream of Acceptability' adopts a diachronic gaze across the changing significance of fame. Braudy suggests that since 'Fifth-century Athens, fame has been a way of expressing … the legitimacy of the individual within society' – and indeed working over what this concept of the individual means at any one time (see also Dyer, 1998, 1987 and Marshall, 1997). But while Braudy may foreground a long historical sweep, he also emphasizes the contingent and historical nature of fame. In this respect, he considers a key theme which now permeates contemporary discussion of celebrity, the concept of 'democratization'. In 'the Middle Ages, no peasant thought he could become Richard the Lion-Heart. Later, others might dream of being members of Robin Hood's band, and later still, every young man struggling with his homework nurtured within a potential Abraham Lincoln'.

For the aspirants which covet fame (and the societies in which its promise is nurtured), Braudy foregrounds how fame has historically been imagined as means of control. It is seen as confirming the 'reality' of one's existence in a world where traditional forms of social validation (such as religion, discussed earlier), are in decline.

Note

1. When we compared the volume of work here with that on history of film stardom, it was clear that the difference was considerable.

11 The Emergence of the Star System in America

Richard deCordova

The standard histories of the cinema account for the emergence of the star system through an appeal to a series of four "events."[1]

1. The public wanted to know the names of the film performers. A desire was already there.
2. The producers resisted revealing the performers' names for two reasons: first, they did not want to pay higher salaries to performers; and second, the performers were in reality well-known legitimate actors who would risk their reputation by appearing by name in films.
3. Carl Laemmle, in a move designed to gain an ascendancy over the Patents Trust, introduced the first star, Florence Lawrence. The star system thus emerged out of a struggle between trust members and independents.
4. The independents and the public finally won out and the star system was born.

There is good reason to suspect the accuracy of many of these points.[2] But whether accurate or not this series of events hardly stands as an adequate historical explanation. The forces which put the star system in place are reduced to the play of personal initiative on the one hand and a reified notion of the public desire on the other. The star system is not simply the creation of one person or even one company; nor is the desire for movie stars something that arose unsolicited.

The emergence of the star system can perhaps best be seen as the emergence of a knowledge and analyzed in these terms. Before 1909 virtually none of the players' names were known to the public, but by 1912 most of them had been "discovered."[3] It is clear from this example that the "picture personality" was the result of a particular production and circulation of knowledge. Studio publicity departments, films and fan magazines produced and promulgated this knowledge. What I want to examine in this paper are the rules by which this knowledge was produced and the various transformations these rules underwent.

The emergence of the star system involved a strict regulation of the *type* of knowledge produced about the actor. I will argue that the development of this system was effected through three significant transformations in this regard. These can be listed in the order of their appearance: 1) the discourse on acting, 2) the picture personality and 3) the star.

Before discussing these three stages individually, let me note that the appearance of the second, the picture personality, did not mean the disappearance of the first, the discourse on acting (or for that matter, the third the disappearance of the second). This transformation can best be characterized as a progressive overlaying of discourses and knowledges about a particular site—the actor.

The discourse on acting

It is perhaps misleading to say that this site was *the actor* as if this site was constituted in itself. Before 1907 there was no discourse on the film actor. Textual productivity was focused elsewhere, for the most part on the apparatus itself, on its magical abilities and its capacity to reproduce the real. It was obvious that people were represented on the screen, but the thought that these people were actors was very likely not considered. Acting was a profession of the legitimate stage, quite foreign to the milieu of the cinema's early development. The stage, after all, not only had actors, but also stars. The cinema's complete inobservance of these forms prior to 1907 is a testament to its relatively thoroughgoing disassociation from a theatrical model of representation.

Journalistic discourse of the time focused primarily on the scientific aspects of the apparatus. Eric Smoodin has convincingly demonstrated that this discourse characterized film as a product independent of human labor. This "reification of the apparatus" is clear in the titles of articles such as "Moving Pictures and the Machines which Create Them" and "Revelations of the Camera."[4]

Around 1907 another discourse began to supersede this discourse on the apparatus, one which included and eventually placed into the foreground the role of human labor in the production of film. This should not be viewed as a demystification of the means of production but rather as the regulated appearance of a certain kind of knowledge. This knowledge entered into a struggle destined to resituate the site of textual productivity for the spectator away from the work of the apparatus itself. A number of potential "sites of productivity" were involved in this struggle—the manufacturer, the cinematographer (or director) and the photoplaywright—but of course it was the actor/star that finally became central in this regard.

It is in this context that one must view the earliest appearances of the discourse on acting. In 1907 a series of articles appeared in *Moving Picture World* entitled "The Cinematographer and Some of His Difficulties." These articles, geared towards describing the work of the cinematographer, offered the following definition of the picture performer.

> **Those who make a business of posing for the kinetoscope are called 'picture performers' and many a hard knock they have to take. Practically all of them are professional stage people, and while performing on Broadway at night they pick up a few dollars day times in a moving picture studio. In a variety show, therefore, it sometimes happens that the same tumblers who a moment ago were turning handsprings and somersaults in real life, again appear in such roles as the traditional "Rube" and the "green goods man," but only in a phantom form upon the pictured screen.[5]**

This article and many which follow it use the verb 'pose' to describe the activity of those who appear in films. Before the discourse on acting this activity was understood largely in terms of a photographic tradition. Even after the discourse on acting emerged we can see a sort of struggle between a photographic and a theatrical conception of the body, between posing and acting. There are important links between this contradictory situation and the changes that were taking place in the industry at the time. Robert C. Allen has noted that "between 1907–1908 a dramatic change occurred in American Motion Picture Production; in one year narrative forms of cinema (comedy and dramatic) all but eclipsed documentary forms in volume of production."[6] Even more remarkable is the shift in the percentage of *dramatic* productions from 17% in 1907 to 66% in 1908.[7] There is little doubt that this shift in production supported the contention that people acted in films, but it is not surprising that the suddenness of the documentary's demise left behind powerful vestiges of film's association with a photographic tradition.

The activity of those who appear in films was the subject of a number of stories in this early series of articles. All of these stories followed the same basic pattern. Two examples can be offered here.

The first is a story of the filming of a bank robbery scene:

> In the most realistic way, the "robbers" broke into the bank, held up the cashier, shot a guard "dead" who attempted to come to the rescue, grabbed up a large bundle of money, and made their escape. Thus far all went well. The thieves were running down the street with the police in pursuit, just as the picture had been planned, when an undertaker, aroused by the racket, looked out of his shop. One glance sufficed to tell him that the time had come at last when he might become a hero. The "robbers" were heading toward him, and, leaping into the middle of the sidewalk, he aimed a revolver at the foremost fugitive with the threat: "Stop, thief, or I'll blow your brains out."[8]

The real undertaker apprehended both of the fictional bandits and refused to release them until he was convinced by the head of the bank that the robbery had been staged.

A second story is prefaced by the following statement: "It may sometimes be said that a picture performer becomes so engrossed in his work that he forgets that he is simply shamming." What follows is a story about the filming of a scene in which the hero must rescue a drowning girl. A crowd of bystanders who thought the girl was really drowning jumped into the lake to rescue her. The hero seemed to forget it was all an act and—not to be outdone by his competition—he raced to rescue the girl.[9]

Both of these stories play upon a confusion between the filmic, the profilmic and the real, but they do so primarily as a way of making distinctions between the three. The possibility of these distinctions was a necessary condition for the emergence of what is called here the "picture performer." First of all, this emergence depended upon a knowledge of the performer's existence outside of the narrative of the film itself. By introducing the contingency of the profilmic event into what is otherwise a simple retelling of the planned narrative of the film, these stories differentiate the profilmic from the filmic and ascribe to the former a relatively distinct status. Another narrative is set forth (separable from that of the film) which takes as its subject the performer's part in the production of film.

More obviously perhaps, these stories distinguish the profilmic from the real. In each, a character mistakes the arranged scene for an event in real life. In straightening the two out the character—and the reader—must confront the fictional status of that which is photographed by the camera. This attention to the fact that the scenes enacted in moving pictures were "not real but feigned" had a direct bearing on the status of those who appeared in films; it worked to establish the filmed body as a site of fictional production.

Structured through a play upon the "reality" of filmic representation, these stories refer one to the reality *behind* that representation: that is, to the creative labor of those who appear in films. What I want to turn to now is an examination of the way in which this labor was symbolized through a discourse on acting. This symbolization was somewhat tentative in these early articles. Note, for instance, the use of the term "performer" in the definition quoted previously. Its connotations of popular entertainment undercut any claim that the art of the legitimate actor could be translated directly to the screen. Such claims would proliferate in the next few years, but in 1907 film acting was patently different from legitimate acting. The following quote, from a later installment of "The Cinematographer and Some of His Difficulties," stresses these differences while at the same time valorizing the talent of the film actor.

> [In moving pictures] regular actors are engaged and usually first class actors because they must understand how to express an emotion of a happening perfectly with gestures and action. The actor must understand the trick thoroughly, however, or he is no good for this purpose. The actor who is too reposeful on the stage and expresses his meaning and feeling merely by the tones of his voice or in subtle movements is utterly worthless for the moving picture. Sometimes the actor who has risen no higher than to scrub parts or the chores can be made good use of for the moving pictures because of his great proness to gesture and motion.[10]

Although film acting is identified with stage acting here, it is clear that the film actor's responsibility is to a large extent restricted to his/her function of rendering the action comprehensible. A reviewer of *The Cobbler and the Millionaire* offered one of the earliest assessments of "good acting" precisely on these criteria. "The acting in this film is so good that one could follow the story even without a title."[11] Psychological nuance is not particularly at issue here; the emotion expressed is viewed in broad, unindividuated terms: "the emotion of a happening."

This emphasis on plot and action sharply differentiated film from the legitimate stage, both in the type of acting it required, and, more prominently, in the type of film it implied. Early genres such as the chase film relied wholly on action, casting performers only in broad social types (the policeman, the green goods man, etc.). The disjunction between the types of films being produced and the artistic pretensions of the discourse on acting often manifested itself in a rather ironic treatment of film actors. The words "actor" and "artist" usually appear in quotes in these early articles. In "The Canned Drama" Walter Prichard Eaton parodies the contention that professional actors appear in films by distinguishing between two horses on a movie set—one was a professional actor and the other merely an amateur.[12]

By 1908, a number of films had begun to appear which were used as proof that the art of acting could be translated to the screen. The most important of these, by far, were the French Films d'Art of the Pathé Company. The following quotes point clearly to the importance of these films insofar as the discourse on acting is concerned.

> The greatest improvement at present (and there is still plenty of room for more) is along the line of dramatic structure and significant acting. Does it sound silly to talk thus pedantically, in the

language of dramatic criticism, about moving pictures? If you will watch a poor American picture unroll blinkingly, and then a good French one, you will feel that it is not silly after all.[13]

With reference to the Pathé film d'art, "The Return of Ulysses," to which I referred last
week, it is interesting to point out that the story was written by Jules Lemaître, of the Academie
Française, and the principal characters are taken by Mme. Bartet, MM. Albert Lambert,
Lelauny and Paul Mounet, all of the Comédie Française, Paris. This is equivalent to
David Belasco and his stuyvesant company doing work for the Edison Company. Again I say,
American Manufacturers please note![14]

The aesthetic categories engaged by the discourse on acting and supported by these
films involved a clear articulation of class difference. References to the art of acting in
film worked to legitimize the cinema and dissipate the resistance of those strata of the
middle and upper classes that had been left out of the nickelodeon boom. A new site of
consumption emerged geared very much towards those with pretensions of refinement
and taste.

As I have mentioned, the function of film acting in the earliest descriptions was to
render the action comprehensible. In 1909, however, a number of articles began to appear
which opposed action and acting across class lines. The following quote is virtually
manifesto in this regard.

The majority of "our public" insist on action in a picture. . . . There must be somethin' doin'
every minute. On the other hand there are a large number who demand good acting, who
like "delicate touches," who want to see the heroine LOOK as if her lover's life was in danger
and not as though she were ordering a plate of "beef and" at Dolan's.[15]

The writer goes on to valorize those films which combine both action and acting,
and which therefore appeal to both classes of people. This is significant since it is the
creation of a mass audience that is at issue here, not the expatriation of any particular
segment of it. The discourse on acting was an important part of a larger strategy which
asserted the respectability of the cinema and worked to guarantee the expansion of the
audience during these years.

The discourse on acting was fundamental to the institutionalization of the cinema
in another sense. I have argued that this discourse superseded the discourse on the
apparatus and worked to resituate the site of textual productivity in human labor. This
resituation signalled a new form of product individuation more in keeping with an
increasingly rationalized production system; the audience's appreciation would no
longer be confined to the magic of the machine or to the socio-cultural interest of the
thing photographed but would involve the possibility of discriminating—at the level
of performance—between specific films.

The picture personality

The picture personality was to be the principal site of product individuation throughout
this period. By 1909 picture personalities had begun to appear, either by their own
names or by names the public assigned them. This is usually considered the beginning
of the star system. It is indeed around this time that the star emerges as an economic
reality. However, I have made a distinction between the picture personality and the

star, assigning the emergence of the former to the year 1909 and the latter to 1914. There is a regulation of knowledge specific to the picture personality which distinguishes it significantly from the star.

Three predominant forms of knowledge emerged to produce the picture personality. The first pertained to the circulation of the name. Through a dual movement of concealment and revelation the player's name was constituted as a site of knowledge. The manufacturer's refusal to reveal the names of their players is greatly exaggerated. Biograph is the only company that followed this policy with any consistency. Magazines, newspapers and advertising constantly named names (and obviously with the cooperation of the manufacturers); in fact, there was an intense proliferation of knowledge about the picture personalities during this time.

What has undoubtedly misled many historians is that this knowledge emerged in an explicitly secretive context. The "truth" of the human labor involved in film was constituted as a secret, one whose discovery would be all the more pleasurable since it would emerge out of ostensible attempts to conceal it.[16] One of the major reasons given for the supposed concealment of the players' names, for instance, was that the players were in fact legitimate actors (perhaps well known) who did not want to risk their reputations by being discovered in films. Such an explanation hardly resolves the enigma, however; it only compounds it, doubling its status as secret. Fans who did not know the name of a particular actor were to assume, by this logic, that it was because that actor was well known.

Early fan magazines depended to a large extent on the pleasure the public took in knowing the players' names. Such features as *Moving Picture Story Magazine*'s "Popular Player Puzzle" appealed precisely to this. The following puzzle, for example, was proposed: "A favorite pet of the children."[17] The answer was the actor John Bunny.

The magazine also had a question and answer section. Almost all of the questions asked who had the lead in a particular picture. These sort of questions point to the difficulty of separating the circulation of the players' names and the circulation of the films they were in. What is at stake here is a type of identification in the most usual sense of the word: the identification of an actor in a specific film with a name. However, this identification extended well beyond the single film. What the name designated above all was a form of intertextuality, the recognition and identification of an actor from film to film.

This intertextuality emerged as a measure of the increasing regularity and regulation of the cinematic institution—both in its product (the same actors appeared regularly) and more crucially, in terms of its audience, which had to go to the cinema often for this intertextual meaning to arise. This intertextuality can be posited as the second form of knowledge which constituted the picture personality. This knowledge however, was not produced solely in the cinema; journalistic discourse supported it as well. The most important point to make about this intertextuality is that it restricted knowledge about the players to the textuality of the films they were in. The term "picture personality" is itself evidence of this restriction. The site of interest was to be the personality of the player as it was depicted in film. In one article Frank Lessing explained his success in acting by saying, "one cannot express more than one really is."[18] The correct formulation would have been, "one is no more than one expresses on film," since this defines fairly accurately the tautological existence of the picture personality.

A third type of knowledge that constituted the picture personality pertained to the professional experience of the actor. Insofar as this knowledge related to the actor's previous film experience it worked to establish the intertextual space between films discussed earlier. However, this knowledge often referred to the actor's stage experience and can be seen as a continuation of the discourse on acting.

> **The great success of Miss Lottie Briscoue is not surprising when it is remembered that she was, for years, with that master of dramatic art, Richard Mansfield. Miss Briscoe has already won a host of admirers in the motion picture world by her clever and her pleasing personality.**[19]

I have discussed the way this discourse on acting worked to legitimize film through reference to the acting of the stage. It is important to note that this legitimation was effected entirely at the level of profession. The emergence of the picture personality did not signal any significant shift in this regard. One writer, attempting to explain why people were falling in love with matinee idols, concluded that it proved that the idol's "acting, as well as their personality must be pretty much the same thing."[20] Knowledge about the picture personality was restricted to the player's professional existence—either to his/her representation in films or to his/her previous work in film and theater.

The star

It is along these lines that one can distinguish the star from the picture personality. The star is characterized by a fairly thoroughgoing articulation of the paradigm professional life/private life. With the emergence of the star, the question of the player's existence outside his/her work in films entered discourse.

This question entailed a significant transformation in the regulation of knowledge concerning the player. The manufacturers would no longer be able to restrict knowledge about the players to the textuality of the films they were in. Thus, the absolute control the studios had over the picture personality's image was, in one sense, relinquished, but only so that it could be extended to another sphere. The private lives of the stars emerged as a new site of knowledge and truth.

In 1914 a short story appeared in *Photoplay* entitled "Loree Starr—Photoplay Idol."[21] It is most remarkable for its subtitle—"A Fascinating Serial Story Presenting a New Type of Hero." This new hero is precisely the star as distinguished from the picture personality. It is around this time that the star becomes the subject of a narrative which is quite separable from his/her work in any particular film.

Here is a quote from 1916 which quite explicitly poses the question of the star: "And even in these days of the all-seeing camera-eye there are scores of heroic deeds, of patently self-sacrificing acts, performed by the film folk which never reach pictures or print."[22] It ends by asking—"Is your REEL hero ever a REAL hero?"

So, private and professional become two autonomous spheres that can be articulated in paradigm. It is important to note however, that these two spheres are constituted in what might be called an analogous or redundant relation. The real hero behaves just like the reel hero. The knowledge which emerged concerning the star was restricted to the parameters of this analogy. The private life of the star was not to be in contradiction with his/her film image—at least not in terms of its moral tenor.[23] The two would rather support each other. The power of the cinema was thus augmented by the extension of its textual and ideological functioning into the discourse on the star.

Two related strategies were effected through the star discourse. The first involved a kind of backlash against the theater. The private lives of theatrical stars had quite commonly been associated with scandals of all sorts. The star discourse involved a work which disassociated the film star from this aspect of the theatrical tradition. Harry S. Northrup explains his reasons for not returning to the stage:

> What? The Stage? Not on your life, not if I know myself.... Lock around you here. What more could a man ask than this? A comfortable, attractive home, fifty-two weeks in the year income. Could the stage give me that? It could not.[24]

The following quote is even more explicit.

> Stage life, with its night work, its daytime sleep, its irregular meals, its travelling and close contact, does not make for a natural existence and throws a so-called glamor over many people. Contrast its possibilities with those of the picture studio. In the latter place work is done in regular office hours—daylight work; no glamor of night, of orchestra, of artificial light. A player is located in one neighborhood and is recognized as a permanent and respectable citizen. Evenings can be spent at home, and the normal healthiness of one's own fireside is an atmosphere conductive to refining influences. Healthy outdoor daytime work and a permanent circle of friends make for a sane and non-precarious existence. The restlessness and loneliness attendant on a life of travel is also eliminated.[25]

What is undoubtedly at stake here is the moral healthiness of the cinema as an institution. The discourse on the star worked to assert that the cinema was, "at its source," a healthy phenomenon.

This healthiness was proven largely through reference to the stars' families. One of the major differences between the picture personality and the star is that the latter supports a family discourse. In fact, it doubles the family discourse produced in the films of the day.[26] The narrative which emerged to create the star was entrenched in the same forms of representation as the films in which the stars acted.

The redundancy of these two spheres is linked to the specific articulation of power and knowledge which characterizes the emergence of the star system. As the private lives of the players became a valorized site of knowledge, a work of regulation was effected which kept this knowledge within certain bounds. In this way, the star system worked to support the same ideological project as the films of the day. A great deal of work needs to be done on the apparent failure of this regulation in the star scandals of the early Twenties, and the relation this has to the creation of the Hays Office in 1922.

Notes

1. See, for instance, Alexander Walker, *Stardom: The Hollywood Phenomenon* (New York: Stein and Day, 1970); Arthur Knight, *The Liveliest Art: A Panoramic History of the Movies*, Rev. ed. (New York: New American Library, 1979), and Gerald Mast, *A Short History of the Movies*, 3rd ed. (Chicago: Univ. of Chicago Press, 1981).
2. The opposition between the trust and the independents was simply not a central determinant in the emergence of the star system. Edison and Vitagraph were

extremely active in star promotion from a very early date. Thus, Laemmle's efforts at Imp were neither isolated nor initiatory. Janet Staiger has detailed the early efforts of the Trust companies in "Seeing Stars," *The Velvet Light Trap*, No. 20 (1983), pp. 10–14. Arguments that the development of the star system was impeded by the actors' concerns over their theatrical reputations are equally difficult to sustain. Most of the early film actors had little reputation to lose; those who did seem to have been given publicity from a fairly early date.

3. See Anthony Slide, *Aspects of American Film History Prior to 1920* (Metuchen, N. J.: Scarecrow Press, 1978).

4. Eric Smoodin, "Attitudes of the American Printed Medium Toward the Cinema: 1894–1908," Unpublished Paper, University of California at Los Angeles, 1979.

5. "How the Cinematographer Works and Some of His Difficulties," *Moving Picture World* (hereafter *MPW*), 1, No. 14 (8 June 1907), 212.

6. Robert C. Allen, *Vaudeville and Film 1895–1915: A Study in Media Interaction* (New York: Arno, 1980), p. 212.

7. *Ibid.*, p. 213.

8. "How he Cinematographer Works and Some of His Difficulties," *MPW*, 1, No. 11 (18 May 1907), 166.

9. "How the Cinematographer Works and Some of his Difficulties," *MPW*, 1, No. 14 (8 June 1907), 212.

10. *MPW*, 1, No. 19 (13 July 1907), 298.

11. *MPW*, 5, No. 9 (28 August 1909), 281.

12. Walter Prichard Eaton, "The Canned Drama," *American Magazine*, 68 (September 1909), 493–500.

13. Eaton, p. 499.

14. Thomas Bedding, "The Modern Way in Moving Picture Making," *MPW*, 4, No. 12 (20 March 1909), 326.

15. *MPW*, 5, No. 14 (2 October 1909), 443.

16. This situation is similar to that discussed by Foucault regarding "the secret" of sexuality. See Michel Foucault, *The History of Sexuality*, vol. 1, trans. Robert Hurley (New York: Random House, 1978).

17. *The Motion Picture Story Magazine*, 5, No. 6 (July 1913), 127.

18. *MPW*, 8, No. 5 (4 February 1911), 23.

19. *The Motion Picture Story Magazine*, 1, No. 1 (February 1911), 23.

20. *MPW*, 6, No. 12 (26 March 1910), 468.

21. Robert Kerr, "Loree Starr–Photoplay Idol," *Photoplay*, September 1914.

22. *The Motion Picture Classic*, February 1916, p. 55.

23 Some precision is necessary here. A certain level of contradiction was absolutely essential to the presentation of performance during this period. The force of Mary Pickford's performance in *Stella Maris* (1918), for instance, is dependent upon the discrepancy between Pickford's identity as a wealthy movie star and her appearance in the film (in one of two roles) as a penniless orphan. My argument here is that this field of contradiction did not generally engage moral categories.

24. *Photoplay*, September 1914, p. 70.

25. *Motion Picture Magazine*, February 1915, pp. 85–88.

26. For an interesting discussion of the family discourse in films of the period see Nick Browne, "Griffith and Freud: Griffith's Family Discourse," *Quarterly Review of Film Studies*, 6, No. 1 (Winter 1981), 76–80.

12 | The Assembly Line of Greatness: Celebrity in Twentieth-Century America

Joshua Gamson

This paper traces the history of two intertwining stories in America celebrity texts and their relationship to the development and organization of publicity apparatuses. In one storyline, dominant in the first part of the century, the deserving rise naturally to the top. In the other storyline, stronger in later decades, celebrities are artificially manufactured. As institutional control weakened and publicity mechanisms grew more sophisticated, image-manufacture and celebrity-production became more visible in texts. In each period a balance was struck between the competing explanations of fame through the entry of new narrative elements, most notably through an increase in the power attributed to audiences.

"It is, we are sure," wrote the editor of the movie fan magazine *Silver Screen* in the 1930s, "impossible to be great part of the time and revert to commonplaceness the rest of the time. Greatness is built in" ("Final Fling," 1970, p. 39). In the late 1960s, a *TV Guide* writer (Efron, 1967) took issue with this claim, describing a "peculiar machine" in American culture. "It was conceived by public-relations men," she wrote, "and it is a cross between a vacuum cleaner and a sausage maker. It sucks people in—it processes them uniformly—it ships them briskly along a mechanical assembly line—and it pops them out at the other end, stuffed tight into a shiny casing stamped 'U.S. Celebrity'" (p. 16). Decades later, Andy Warhol's claim that "in the future everyone will be world famous for fifteen minutes" has become the most famous statement on fame. "Well, Andy, the future is now," wrote the editors of "How Fleet It Is," a 1988 *People Weekly* report. "Fame's spotlight darts here and there, plucking unknowns from the crowd, then plunging them back into obscurity" (p. 88). How did this central American discourse migrate from fame as the natural result of irrepressible greatness to celebrity as the fleeting product of a vacuum cleaner/sausage maker?

This is the story of two stories. In one, the great and talented and virtuous and best-at rise to the top of the attended-to, aided perhaps by rowdy promotion, which gets people to notice but can do nothing to actually make the unworthy famous. Fame—from the Latin for "manifest deeds"—is in this story related to achievement or quality. In the other story, the publicity apparatus itself becomes a central plot element, even a central character; the publicity machine focuses attention on the worthy and unworthy alike, churning out many admired commodities called celebrities, famous because they have been made to be. Contrary to ahistorical popular mythology, these two stories have actually coexisted for more than a century, usually in odd but harmonious combinations. Over the course of this century, however, the balance between them has shifted. In this paper, I trace and attempt to make sense of changes in the popular discourse of celebrity—in particular, the implicit and explicit explanations in popular magazines of why and how people become famous.[1] I argue in closing that these stories, built on a long-standing tension between aristocratic and democratic models of fame, raise important questions about public visibility in democratic, consumer-capitalist society.

This is not simply the story of texts, however. Tracing the discourse on celebrity involves tracing as well the history of the mechanisms available and used for garnering attention. A system for celebrity-creation, at times much less systematic than at others, has been in place firmly since the birth of mass commercial culture. Changes both in the concrete organization of publicity and in the technology and media through which recognition is disseminated have had a profound impact on the operation of celebrity in this century.

As technology and publicity apparatuses grew, they became more and more publicly visible, integrated into discussions of celebrity. This visibility increasingly posed a threat, I will argue, to the reigning myth that fame was a natural cream-rising-to-the-top phenomenon. In the first half of the century this threat was largely controlled. It was not entirely muted, however, and a number of changes in the discourse developed, seemingly defusing the challenge. Audiences began to be invited inside the "real lives" of celebrities. Texts affirmed meritocratic fame by "training" audiences in discerning the reality behind an image and by suggesting that publicity apparatuses were in the audience's control. Beginning around 1950, changes in the celebrity-building environment—the breakdown of studio control, the rise of television, a boom in the "supply" of celebrities—significantly destabilized what had been a tightly integrated celebrity system. The publicity enterprise then began a move toward center stage in the celebrity discourse, with manufacture becoming a serious competitor to the organic explanation of fame. A new coping strategy began to show itself in texts: audiences were now invited not only behind the image, but behind the scenes to image *production*. The relationship between image and reality gradually became less a problem than a source of engagement. Previously flattered as the controllers of the direction of publicity spotlights, audiences were now flattered as cynical insiders to the publicity game.

Early fame: Growth of a fault line

As Braudy (1986) amply demonstrates in his history of fame, *The Frenzy of Renown*, the ambition to stand out from the crowd is not at all new in Western culture. One dynamic in particular is relevant here: the long-standing and intertwined strains of aristocratic and democratic fame. At its very early stages, fame-seeking was limited to those with "the power to control their audiences and their images" (p. 28)—that is, to political and religious elites. The early discourses firmly established fame—whether the Roman "fame through public action" (p. 117), the Christian "fame of the spirit" (p. 121), or the literary "fame of the wise" (p. 152)—as the province of the top layer of a natural hierarchy.

Yet with the development of technologies and arts to which many more had access (printing, portraiture, engraving, all widespread by the late sixteenth century), public prominence was gradually detached from an aristocratic social status. "Faces," Braudy (1986) writes, "were appearing everywhere" (p. 267). Both the producers of and audiences for images broadened dramatically, opening "a whole new market in faces and reputations" (p. 305). Discourse began to recognize this as well, suggesting that fame is not the "validation of a class distinction" (p. 371) but the personal possession of any worthy individual. In its democratized version, particularly strong in early America, the discourse is characterized by what Braudy calls "paradoxical uniqueness" (p. 371), a sort of compromise between an elitist meritocracy of the personally distinguished and an egalitarian democracy in which all are deserving. "Praise me because I am unique," went the logic, "but praise me as well because my uniqueness is only a more intense and public version of your own" (p. 372). The "great man" was generally one of distinctive inner qualities, but qualities that could potentially exist in any man. (Women, almost entirely excluded from public life, were also generally excluded from this early mythology of public greatness.)

What is important in this vastly boiled-down history is the existence of a fault line, a pull between aristocracy (in modern form, usually meritocracy) and democracy, that is *built into* modern discourses on fame. The two stories we will be examining are constructed on this fault.

The sucker as expert: Barnum and nineteenth-century celebrity

In the middle of the nineteenth century, a series of dramatic changes in the media of publicity and communication established celebrity as a "mass" phenomenon. Newspapers began to spread with the invention of the steam-powered cylinder press in the early 1800s. By mid-century, new technologies—the telegraph in particular—allowed information to move without necessarily being constrained by space. The idea of "context–free information" began to solidify, such that the value of information was no longer necessarily "tied to any function it might serve in social and political decision-making and action, but may attach itself merely to its novelty, interest, and curiosity" (Postman, 1985, p. 65). Information was now transportable through space and, thus freed, could be bought or sold.

If anyone brought the publicity of surfaces to the American cultural arena, it was P. T. Barnum. Publicity stunts were standard early journalistic fare, and often revealed (Fuhrman, 1989, p. 14); but with Barnum and his claim to cater to the "sucker born every minute," the showman-publicist and the publicity system became active parts of the discourse on fame. Barnum was, first of all, an innovator in the activity of press agentry. His subjects were superlatives—the best, the strangest, the biggest, the only—made superlative through image management. Throughout, "by turning every possible circumstance to [his] account," his main instrument was the press, to which he was "so much indebted for [his] success" (Barnum, 1981 [1869], p. 103).

Barnum was not simply publicly promoting the performers, however; he was publicly performing the promotion. He himself became an international figure for the *way* he focused attention, the way he created fame, and the way he created illusion. "First he humbugs them," a ticket-seller once observed (Toll, 1976) "and then they pay to hear him tell how he did it" (p. 26). Shuttling his audiences between knowing the tricks and believing the illusions, Barnum brought publicity mechanisms and questions of artifice to the forefront.

Film and the early twentieth century star system

Barnum, however, was extraordinary. Although they were common activities, attention-getting and image-management were still relatively unsystematic until the growth of professional public relations and film technology in the early twentieth century. As industrial power grew in the first quarter of the century, so did conscious policies of managing public attitudes in order to retain that power. Corporations "began to *recognize* a public for the first time" (Schudson, 1978, p. 133; see also Carey, 1987). Ivy Lee relentlessly promoted "the art of getting believed in" (Olasky, 1987, p. 49). By the 1920s, led by Edward Bernays (1952), the profession of "counsel on public relations" was well established.

This period also marked the birth of modern American consumer culture (see Fox & Lears, 1983) and, with newly expanded markets (urban, female), a boom in the business of leisure. As celebrity became systematized in early twentieth century America, the leisure-time business of "show" was its primary arena: famous people as entertainment and entertainers as famous people. This new system grew up, of course, around the new technologies of film.

Despite challenges from independent producers, power was in the hands of studios, which were firmly committed to a mass production system. Movie manufacturers adapted the star system to the industry's needs. After unsuccessfully trying to distinguish their products through trademarks and storylines, Klaprat (1985) argues, producers shifted strategies with the discovery that audiences distinguished films by stars (pp. 351–354).

The advantages of the star system had become abundantly clear to film manufacturers, and the studios moved quickly to institutionalize it. By the 1920s, film performers were essentially studio owned-and-operated commodities. The system was extensive and very tightly controlled—successfully so because of the high integration of the industry (see Balio, 1985; Powdermaker, 1950)—encompassing production, distribution, and exhibition of films. Through testing and molding, studios designed star personalities; through vehicles, publicity, promotion, public appearances, gossip, fan clubs, and photography, they built and disseminated the personalities; through press agents, publicity departments, and contracts, they controlled the images.

For the most part, celebrity was built systematically and deliberately through publicity and grooming that merged on- and off-screen personae.

Like the new public relations professionals, the studios turned not only on manipulating attention but on manipulating belief. Critical to the early building of stars was the building of an image that did not *appear* to emanate from the studio. Thus, after test-marketing the image; promoting the personality through advertising, stunts, rumors, and feature stories and photos; and releasing and exhibiting films in premieres and opulent theaters that underlined the stars' larger-than-life images, the studio publicity departments took over to match a star's personal life with the traits of the screen character.

The appetite for films, film stars, and their movie and private lives had by the 1920s become voracious. By the 1930s, Hollywood was the third largest news source in the country, with some 300 correspondents, including one from the Vatican (Balio, 1985, p. 266). The most important outlets for entertainment celebrity stories were the film fan magazines—*Photoplay, Modern Screen*, and *Silver Screen* had monthly circulations of nearly half a million—and the columns of gossip writers such as Hedda Hopper and Louella Parsons (and, publicizing a broader range of people, Walter Winchell in New York). With an eager and sensationalizing press in place by the 1920s, and a fully integrated oligopolistic film industry—by 1930, dominated by the "Big Five" studios—image and information control was not difficult to manage.

Early celebrity texts

Other routes to public visibility still existed, of course, but the process had entered a period of industrialization. This, then, was the state of celebrity in the first half of the twentieth century: the entry of visual media as "the prime arbiters of celebrity and the bestowers of honor" (Braudy, 1986, p. 551), a developed profession of public image-management, and an elaborate and tightly controlled production system mass-producing celebrities for a widely consuming audience. The discourse on celebrity remained in this period, for the most part, in line with the interests of its producers. The theme of the discovery of greatness, earlier termed a greatness of character, was translated into the discovery of a combination of "talent," "star quality," and "personality." The claim was in a different vocabulary—the "culture of personality" (Susman, 1984, pp. 273–277) of consumer capitalism had overtaken the "culture of character" of producer-capitalist republic—but it was still one of an organic, merited rise.

The story of the press agent was alive and well, nearly always harking back to the image of Barnum. The new publicity profession slowly began to get some attention, but in these stories publicity was not a mechanism for creating celebrity but simply a means of bringing the deserving self to the public. At times, however, the new power of publicity media (and studios) to artificially produce fame asserted itself, deepening ambiguities in explanations of claims to fame. The visibility of a publicity "machine" stood as a threat to the notion of naturally derived celebrity status. The simultaneous promotion of audiences to controllers of the publicity machine defused this challenge. Celebrities at the service of the audience, however, brought a new problem: the suspicion that the images presented were constructed to gain an audience. The constant textual exposure of the "real lives" of celebrities—in their more believable, "ordinary" form, supported by a closer audience-celebrity "relationship"—kept this threat at bay.

Discovering the gift: Fame explanations in early texts

These changes were gradual and never seamless. Greatness in its more traditional, aristocratic formulation—virtue, genius, character, or skill that did not depend on audience recognition—remained a strong model in many early magazine texts. "Greatness," asserted Ludwig (1930) in *American Magazine*, "is always productive, never receptive. It is both imagination and will which give the genius his strength" (p. 15). The notion of a correspondence between greatness and fame, however, was clearly threatened in the early consumer culture. The elitist *Vanity Fair*, for example, was forever striving to distinguish the truly "great" from the commercially successful (see Amory & Bradlee, 1960).

These postures were defensive, and understandably so. As Lowenthal (1968) demonstrated, by the 1920s the typical idols in popular magazines were those of consumption (entertainment, sport) rather than production (industry, business, natural sciences). By the 1940s, almost every hero biography featured a hero either "related to the sphere of leisure time" or "a caricature of a socially productive agent" (p. 115). Most writing about famous people reported on their private lives, personal habits, tastes, and romances.

Not only did attention shift to entertainers and their personal lives, but these famous entertainers also underwent a gradual demotion of sorts over the first half of the century. Early on, the stars had been depicted as democratic royalty (with Mary Pickford and Douglas Fairbanks reigning), popularly "elected" gods and goddesses. Lifestyle reports focused on "the good life," the lavish Hollywood homes, the expensive clothing, the glamour those watching could not touch. But, pushed by the development of sound and film realism—and by deeper difficulties—the presentation by the 1930s had become more and more mortal, "prettified versions of the folks who lived just down the block" (Schickel, 1985, p. 99). Rather than the ideal, celebrity was presented in the pages of magazines such as *Life* and *Look* as containing a blown-up version of the typical. "Stars now build homes, live quietly and raise children," a *Life* article ("The New Hollywood," 1940) explained. "Their homes, once gaudy and too ornate, are now as sensible and sound in taste as any in the country" (p. 65). And, as always, *Life* had the pics to prove it: "candid" shots of Merle Oberon playing blind man's bluff with her nephews on a suburban lawn, Brenda Marshall eating her "frugal breakfast" in a simple, bachelorette kitchen (pp. 65–67).

Such ordinariness promoted a greater sense of connection and intimacy between the famous and their admirers. Crucial to this process was the ubiquitous narrative principle of the "inside" journey into the "real lives" of celebrities, lives much like the readers'. Other common themes in entertainment celebrity texts of the time—love lives, the "price they pay for fame," the desire to be just like the reader, the hard work of gaining and retaining success—further tightened the narrative links between the audience and the celebrated.

Decreasing the distance between the celebrated and the celebrators creates a difficulty: If celebrities were so much like the reader, why were they so elevated and so watched? Early celebrity texts updated the American paradox of egalitarian distinction. Rather than for public virtue or action, the celebrity rose due to his or her *authentic, gifted self*. A fame meritocracy was reinscribed in the new consumerist language: the celebrity rises, selected for his personality (revealed through lifestyle choices), an irrational but nonetheless organic "folk" phenomenon. The luck of the lucky star, for example, is that she got the "break" that allowed her to rise. "Nobody knows," an *American Magazine* (Eddy, 1940) article told its readers, "when or where one of these will bob up" (p. 162). Jean Harlow, driving some friends to a studio luncheon, came to fame "quite by accident," moving "from extra to star" (Lee, 1970, p. 43). The stories in their purest form thus suggested that a star would not rise, or bob up, even with a lucky break—unless he had what it took. Fame, apparently, would come to those destined to be famous and pass over the doors of the undeserving.

This tautology (how do we know the famous deserve fame? because they have it) is the core of the dominant early story of fame. Talent was often mentioned but rarely treated as sufficient. The only stars who survived, *Photoplay* suggested (Cohn, 1972), were the ones "who had that rare gift designated as screen charm or personality, combined with adaptability and inherent talent" (p. 33). Clark Gable "deserves his pre-eminent place" because "there's no one else exactly like him" (Maddox, 1970, p. 174). What it took to rise—"star quality," "charisma," "appeal," "personality," or simply "It"—was never defined beyond a label, even "ineffable" (Eddy, 1940, p. 25). Whatever it was, though, the texts made it clear that stars had always had it. Fame, based on an indefinable internal quality of the self, was natural, almost predestined.

The celebrity's background thus took its place as a demonstration that, put simply, a star is born. Ruby Keeler was "born with dancing feet" (Hoyt, 1970, p. 51). Greta Garbo had "a certain force within her" that explained her position "in the vaulted and resplendent cathedral of fame" (Joel, 1970, pp. 172–173).

Greatness is built in; it is *who you are*. If one works at it, or gets a lucky break, it may be discovered. If it is discovered, one becomes celebrated for it, which is evidence that one had it to begin with.

What do we make of the characteristics of these texts—the focus on leisure idols and leisure habits, the gradual move toward ordinariness, the logic of the discovered gift? In many ways these early texts simply reassert in a new cultural vocabulary that those in the public eye are there because they deserve to be. But why not continue to focus on glamorous and extravagant consumption habits? Why increase the intimacy between star and reader through inside stories? A large part of the answer becomes clear when we examine the place of the new publicity professions and the studio system in these early texts.

Exposing the gift: Publicity in the early texts

Initially, this knowledge was not a problem. The studio star system was, for the most part, accommodated quite comfortably into most stories as the final step up the ladder.

The management of publicity was itself generally presented in a way that posed hardly a threat to the notion of natural, deserved celebrity. Stories of Barnum-like "ballyhoo" press agents persisted, claiming that "the old hokum still gets newspaper space better than anything else" (Lockwood, 1940, p. 180); behind each movie premiere, *Reader's Digest* reported (Costello, 1941), was "a group of harried, sardonic studio press agents ... [pulling] the strings" (p. 88). This Barnumesque figure was portrayed as a harmless, amusing promoter—harmless because of the visibility of his tricks. The new public relations counselor had, according to most stories, the same aim as the old showman press agent: to "boost the fame" of public figures.

The dominant notion of publicity in early celebrity texts was of a neutral machine illuminating what "we," the public, wanted to see in the spotlight. The standing model of celebrities as rising organically from the populace would otherwise be jeopardized: if the studios or the newspapers controlled the "machine," people could enter the spotlight not because of popular election but because of manufactured attention by interested elites. The "public" in these stories, modeled as a unified, powerful near-person forever casting its votes for its favorite personalities, became a crucial character in its own right.

As celebrities were being demoted to ordinariness in narratives, then, the audience was being promoted from a position of religious prostration. The public became the final discoverer, the publicity machine shifting the spotlights according to the public's whims. Myrna Loy tells "all you little Marys and Sues and Sarahs who wish you could be movie stars" (Service, 1970) that she is, in fact, *at their service*.

> **I'd like to tell her in good plain English that I am not my own boss. I'd like to tell her that I serve not one boss but several million. For my boss is—the Public. My boss is that very girl who writes me herself and thousands like her. It is the Public that first hired me, and it is the Public that can fire me. The Public criticizes me, reprimands me. (p. 142)**

The celebrity-as-public-servant displaces difficult questions in the relationship between "authentic" greatness and publicity activities. It affirms the notion that celebrities are cream risen to the top while allowing the vague criterion of "personality" to coexist with the newly visible power of the publicity "machine." *You* control the machine, it says. If *you* don't like me, *you* can grab the spotlight and throw it onto someone else more worthy. The anti-democratic implications of both a celebrity elite and elite-controlled publicity are tempered by the emphasis on audience control. Desert and publicity live together.

The more active the audience, the more celebrity is suspect as an artificial image created and managed to pander to that audience. Terms of commerce began to enter the discourse, although still subordinated to terms of greatness and quality. Commercial creation and the marketing of false public images (as opposed to publicizing of true selves) began to surface as an explanation of fame.

This rising skepticism about the connection between celebrity and authenticity was, however, largely muted in most celebrity stories. To a degree, this was simply accomplished through studio control. When Clark Gable suggested in a 1933 *Photoplay* interview, for example, that "I just work here.... The company has an investment in me. It's my business to work, not to think," his statement was considered "frank enough to be dangerous and the studio thereafter began to 'protect' Gable from unguarded utterances" (King, 1986, p. 174).

But the skepticism heightened by increasingly visible publicity activities was contained more commonly by being acknowledged: by pulling down "the expensive mask of glamor." By embracing the notion that celebrity images were artificial products and inviting readers to visit the real self *behind* those images, popular magazines partially defused the notion that celebrity was really derived from *nothing but* images. Celebrity profiling became parked in expose gear, instructions in the art of distinguishing truth from artifice, the real Dietrich from the fake one. Once you get to know the real one, the texts implied, you'll see why you were right to have made her famous.

The at-home-with-the-famous "inside story" was central to this process. The glamorous celebrity was thus sacrificed for the more "realistic" down-to-earth one. Intimacy, bolstering belief, was offered up. Manufactured images, then, would be harmless to allegiances. The public discovers and makes famous certain people because it (with the help of the magazines) *sees through* the publicity-generated, artificial self to the real, deserving, special self. The story of celebrity as a natural phenomenon was shakily joined with the story of celebrity as an artificial one.

Self-owned commodities: Late twentieth century celebrity

In the late 1940s and early 1950s, the film industry was jolted from several sides. In 1948 the Supreme Court unanimously sided with the Department of Justice in its charges against the industry, breaking the Big Five's production-distribution-exhibition monopoly (Balio, 1985, p. 402). The industry was also facing a box office crisis: by 1950, the movie audience had shrunk by two-thirds. The crisis was much aggravated by television, which was fast displacing film as the dominant leisure-time activity.

As studio control was necessarily relaxed and the studio image-maintenance activities became dispersed into an independent publicity profession, film stars in the 1950s became "proprietors of their own image," which they could sell to filmmakers, and subsequently began "to show a distance from their own image" (King, 1986, pp. 169–170). Independent publicists, assistants in the management of public images (and often the controllers in place of the celebrities themselves), became powerful players.

In the meantime, the publicity profession was taking new, more sophisticated shapes. Since World War II, public relations (PR) has grown "from a one-dimensional 'press agentry' function into a sophisticated communications network connecting the most powerful elements of our society" (Blyskal & Blyskal, 1985, p. 27). This growth contained several components that affect celebrity. First, the overall trend toward delineating and targeting specialized market niches in product development, advertising, and sales has made the task of garnering and shaping attention progressively more "scientific." Strategies attempt to zero in on the perceived needs, desires, and knowledge of particular publics, seeking to attract and then sell the attention of segments of the mass markets, matching certain populations to specific messages and vehicles. Second, as the daily practices and interests of PR operatives and journalists, aligned since the 1920s, moved closer over these decades, arenas traditionally perceived as non-entertainment (news in particular) have come to depend on the practices of the entertainment industry, and celebrity in particular. Third, the technologies for providing a visual image that *imitates the representation* of an activity, event, or person, rather than representing it directly, have become highly developed. Finally, the outlets for publicity have exploded with the success, beginning in the early 1970s, of magazine and newspaper writing about "people" and "personality" and, more recently, broadcast "infotainment." This has meant a need for more subject matter, and more opportunities for recognition: literally more editorial space for those aspiring to fame or to regain faded recognition, for star-for-a-day ordinary people, and for celebrities from untapped fields.

Television, with its constant flow, enormous reach, and vast space-filling needs, has from its initial boom provided the most significant new outlet for image-creation. In this world of massive exposure to television's sophisticated image-production, it has become increasingly possible *in a practical sense* to create familiarity with images without regard to content. Boorstin (1961) noted the effect: the celebrity has become familiar for being familiar, "a person who is known for his well-knownness" (p. 57). The economic push to make people known for themselves rather than for their actions remains at the heart of the now-decentralized star system: as sales aids, celebrities are most useful if they can draw attention regardless of the particular context in which they appear. Name recognition in itself is critical for commerce. In fact, the less attached a name is to a context, the more easily it transfers to new markets. As the prime outlet for, disseminator of, and certifier of public images, television has made decontextualized fame a ubiquitous currency.

Celebrity texts in the late twentieth century

The changes in the apparatuses and practices of publicity in the post-glamour, television-dominated era have seeped into celebrity texts. In the later twentieth century several new elements entered gradually into the celebrity discourse. First and most generally, the mechanisms by which images are made and by which celebrity is built have been increasingly exposed. Second, celebrity as a commercial enterprise has been not only acknowledged but often embraced. Third, the audience has been invited to increase its knowledge and its power. Finally, the discourse has brought about an increasing self-consciousness and irony about celebrity.

Although the narratives about and explanations of fame developed in the earlier part of the century have remained commonplace, the challenge from the manufacture-of-fame narrative has been greatly amplified. No longer under institutional guard, it has become a very serious contender in explaining celebrity. Invitations into the process and an ironic stance about it, I argue, operate much like the invitations into the "real lives" of the famous (which continue from the 1920s). They partially defuse the threats the process makes to the notion that fame is rooted in character traits, that admiration of celebrities is grounded in merit.

Celebrity-making revealed

[...]

Visible links between celebrity and selling were certainly not new. Fame as a sales device had been evident within advertising very early on, primarily through endorsements. Beginning in the 1950s, however, celebrity began to be commonly represented not only as *useful to* selling and business, but as a business itself, *created by* selling. Along with the old-style "what success does to the stars" and "life at home with the stars" stories, for example, *TV Guide* showed stars bickering over billing ("Television's Biggest Struggle," 1958), arguing that "I'm a piece of merchandise. The bigger they make my name, the more important I am. And, the more important I am, the more money I'm worth" (p. 21). This stance, which in the early days of studio celebrity was rare and sometimes punished, rapidly became fairly commonplace. Terms began to change: the celebrity was becoming "merchandise," "inventory," "property," a "product," a "commodity," and the fans "markets." Star production, said Kendall (1962) in a *New York Times Magazine* article, "is as ritualistic in its way as a fire dance" (p. 37). Celebrities are an "investment"—"like all raw materials, they often require a good deal of processing before they are marketable"—and that investment "must be protected" (p. 38).

[...]

"Image" has itself become a common term in the texts. In earlier days, an agent was typically shown discovering star quality that simply demanded to be brought to the public, and the subsequent adoration was proof of the quality. Now, a shrewd agent was shown discovering a market and manufacturing a celebrity-product around it. A 1963 series on "Gentlemen of the Pressure" (Morgan, 1963) opened with an illustration of a giant hand holding a television screen on which the word "images" is written. Behind the hand, operating it through a panel marked "networks," is a messy, motley group of people; in front of it, a happy, smiling audience looks at the screen. "A mixed breed of nonobjective salesmen have found a home in the house of TV," the author warned, selling "affection for personalities, products, corporate entities and ideas" (p. 6). Their effects are "a little frightening," and "although they prefer to work in the shadows, they leave their traces on every TV screen in America" (p. 6).

[...]

Throughout these texts, then, is a tremendously heightened self-consciousness about the systematic production of celebrity and celebrity-images for commercial purposes.

Enjoy the hype: Instruction and irony

With such increased visibility, the problem that had surfaced occasionally in the first half of the century has deepened during the second: if celebrities are artificial creations, why should an audience remain attached and lavish attention on their fabricated lives? Along with the gradual foregrounding of artifice have come new narrative elements that, I argue, temper this problem. Texts have brought in what amount to instructions to readers and a new ironic knowingness.

Many such texts have brought to fruition the behind-the-scenes, inside-dope style begun earlier, instructing the reader further in reading performances, finding the "real" behind the "image." This writing acknowledges that a gap between image and reality exists, but denies that bridging it is a problem, especially with television, a medium that can't help but transmit an "accurate, searching image" (Javits, 1960, p. 11). "The TV camera has an X-ray attachment," Arlene Francis told *TV Guide* readers in 1960. "It pierces, it penetrates, it peels away the veneer. It communicates the heart and mind of man" (p. 6). Not surprisingly, this argument runs with the older-style emphasis on a person's "genuine," internal characteristics. If there is a problem peeling away the veneer, viewers need simply be given better viewing tools, and readers can depend on the writer to provide the person underneath. This remains the most common stance in what is still the standard celebrity text, the profile. With the proper guides, one can distinguish true personality from false.

Many texts, though, have become more up-front and unapologetic about artificial authenticity, instructing readers in how to be more sophisticated in recognizing and using it themselves.

An ironic, winking tone in these revelatory texts is one of the clearest later twentieth century developments, not only in "hipster" magazines but also in more mainstream "middle American" ones. The audience has been invited to take its power further with a new, cynical distance from the production of celebrity and celebrity images. In a 1977 report on overcrowding in the "celebrity industry," *Newsweek* ("The People Perplex," 1977) waxed sarcastic, suggesting the foundation of a "National Celebrity Commission to select, at the earliest possible age, a rotating galaxy of Designated People" who would be "scientifically schooled in the art of outrageous behavior" (p. 90). A decade later, an *Esquire* writer (Ephron, 1989) claimed that the strategy of cloaking oneself in goodness by "[buying] a lesser disease, preferably one that primarily affected children," no longer works, since "all the lesser diseases were taken" (p. 104). *Life* magazine ("The Making of Billy Gable," 1989) consulted "industry bigfoots" on how Clark Gable would fare starting out today. The experts recommended plastic surgery ("deflating those wind socks"), publicity control ("a spin doctor"), image building ("have him sitting at ringside for fights and Laker games"), and television series and talk shows. "Were Gable a young actor today," the article concluded, "he would require careful packaging to make him the King of this era" (pp. 53–54).

Irony has also become a common piece of celebrity public personae. "A self-mocking sense of humor," according to casting directors in a *TV Guide* story (Stauth, 1988), "is a key ingredient in star quality" (p. 5). Celebrities are often caught "simultaneously mocking and indulging their icon status," Gitlin (1989) says, describing a collection of *Rolling Stone* photographs. "New-style stars flaunt and celebrate stardom by mocking it, camping it up, or underplaying it (in public!).... The star now stands apart from glamour, and comments (often ironically) on it" (p. 14). In *Esquire* (June 1989), then–Republican Party leader Lee Atwater, joining the posing of entertainment celebrities, saluted the audience with his pants around his ankles.

Why this combination of exposure of the celebrity- and image-manufacturing processes and mockery of it? On one level, the mocking of glamour by celebrities is another star turn, much like tabloid revelations of the "true self," updated to accommodate the visibility of glamour-production: Celebrities invite their admirers to revere them for being "too hip to be reverent or revered" (Gitlin, 1989, p. G14). The constant visibility of publicity mechanisms works similarly on another level, defusing a threat to admiration by offering the audience the position of control. Celebrity audiences are treated to the knowledge of how they, and others, become the "sucker born every minute"—and thus avoid becoming the sucker.

In Barnum, though, the source of tricks was simple and visible. In the later twentieth century texts everyone is a potential trickster, and image-makers and hypesters are everywhere, including in the audience. Who is real? Who really has "star quality" or "talent" or "greatness"? Who actually deserves attention? These questions, still circulating from the earlier fame story, are unanswered—this time because they are largely rendered moot. The notion that fame is based in artifice challenges not only the economics of the celebrity system (if no one is more deserving, consumer loyalty is extremely unstable) but potentially readers as well (if artifice and reality are indistinguishable, one's grounding is extremely unstable). The cynical, knowing, sometimes mocking stance keeps the tension from cracking the story; indeed, it can serve to engage. Through irony, these celebrity texts reposition their readers, enlightened about the falseness of celebrity, to "see the joke" and avoid the disruptive notion that there is nothing behind a fabricated, performed image but layers of other fabricated, performed images.

Conclusion: Democratic celebrity?

The overall history sketched here is of a position switch between two twentieth-century takes on the famous. The struggle by many involved in representing celebrity has been to keep the economics of stardom intact by making celebrity-admiration a coherent enterprise. The economic interests of celebrity producers push toward certain textual characteristics (a coincidence of public and private personae, an explanation of fame as naturally derived and deserved). Celebrity production, when revealed, contains its own potential threat: the explanation of fame as artificially derived. In the early part of the century, the organization of production allowed tight control over the texts. To the degree that the story of artificial production did assert itself, it was accompanied by narrative elements that quieted it (audience control of publicity, the inside story, de-glamorizing). As production organization changed mid-century and "authorship" of the texts was decentralized, the notion of artificial fame was released and intensified in texts. Through discussions of images as images, flattery of audiences' notions of their own knowledge and power, and an ironic stance, celebrity texts have continued to negotiate the tension between the two claims-to-fame stories.

Embedded in these two stories is the long-standing pull between the democratic and the aristocratic in fame discourse. Ought attention go to a naturally deserving elite, or is everyone and no one more deserving? The struggles between these stories described raise important questions about the dynamics of public visibility in democratic, consumer–capitalist society. Do commercial industries dependent on the production of celebrity push in anti-democratic directions by building mystifying myths of meritocratic fame and offering pseudo-participation? Or do they push in democratic directions by empowering audiences, generally in the form of markets, to shape celebrities? Does the embrace of artifice undermine democratic discourse by pushing toward the replacement of reason with image? Or does it support democratic involvement by opening up participation— with lip-synching, anyone can be a star—and decreasing the social gap between the admired and the admirer? The strained and often paradoxical coexistence of the two major storylines examined here does not answer these questions. It may, however, suggest an interesting and critical oddity: that the answer to all of these questions may be yes.

Note

1. Articles from early fan magazines were drawn primarily from two compilations (Gelman, 1972; Levin, 1970). Articles from general-interest periodicals and newspapers

were derived from selected years in the *Reader's Guide to Periodical* and from the archives of the Margaret Herrick Library, Academy of Motion Picture Arts and Sciences, Los Angeles.

References

Amory, C., & Bradlee, F. (Eds.). (1960). *Vanity Fair: Selections from America's most memorable magazine*. New York: Viking.

Balio, T. (Ed.). (1985). *The American film industry*. Madison: University of Wisconsin Press.

Barnum, P. T. (1981). Struggles and triumphs. In C. Bode (Ed.), *Struggles and triumphs*. Middlesex: Penguin Books. [Original work published 1869]

Bernays, E. L. (1952). *Public relations*. Norman, OK: University of Oklahoma Press.

Blyskal, J., & Blyskal, M. (1985). *PR: How the public relations industry writes the news*. New York: William Morrow.

Boorstin, D. J. (1961). *The image: A guide to pseudo-events in America*. New York: Harper and Row.

Braudy, L. (1986). *The frenzy of renown: Fame and its history*. New York: Oxford University Press.

Carey, A. (1987). Reshaping the truth: Pragmatists and propagandists in America. In D. Lazare (Ed.), *American media and mass culture* (pp. 34–42). Berkeley, CA: University of California Press.

Cohn, A. (1972). What every girl wants to know. In B. Gelman (Ed.), *Photoplay treasury* (pp. 32–35). New York: Bonanza Books. [Original work published 1919]

Costello, M. (1941, February). They pronounce it pre-meer. *Reader's Digest*, pp. 88–92.

Eddy, D. (1940, July). Hollywood spies on you. *American Magazine*, pp. 24–25.

Efron, E. (1967, August 11). How to manufacture a celebrity. *TV Guide*, pp. 16–19.

Ephron, N. (1989, June). Famous first words. *Esquire*, pp. 103–105.

Fox, R. W., & Lears, T. J. J. (Eds.). (1983). *The culture of consumption: Critical essays in American history* 1880–1980. New York: Pantheon.

Fuhrman, C. J. (1989). *Publicity stunt!* San Francisco: Chronicle Books.

Gitlin, T. (1989, December 3). Review of *Rolling Stone: The photographs*. *The New York Times*, p. G14.

Hoyt, C. S. (1970) It's Ruby's turn now! In M. Levin (Ed.), *Hollywood and the great fan magazines* (p. 51). New York: Arbor House.

Javits, J. K. (1960, October 1). You can't fool the camera. *TV Guide*, pp. 8–11.

Joel, P. (1970). The first true story of Garbo's childhood. In M. Levin (Ed.), *Hollywood and the great fan magazines* (pp. 14–15). New York: Arbor House.

King, B. (1986). Stardom as an occupation. In P. Kerr (Ed.), *The Hollywood film industry* (pp. 154–184). London: Routledge & Kegan Paul.

Klaprat, C. (1985). The star as market strategy: Bette Davis in another light. In T. Balio (Ed.), *The American film industry* (pp. 351–376). Madison, WI: University of Wisconsin Press.

Lee, S. (1970). Jean Harlow—from extra to star. In M. Levin (Ed.), *Hollywood and the great fan magazines* (pp. 43–44). New York: Arbor House.

Lockwood, A. (1940, February). Press agent tells all. *American Mercury*, pp. 173–180.

Lowenthal, L. (1968). The triumph of mass idols. In L. Lowenthal (Ed.), *Literature, popular culture and society* (pp. 109–140). Palo Alto, CA: Pacific Books.

Ludwig, E. (1930, May). What makes a man stand out from the crowd? *American Magazine*, p. 15.

Maddox. B. (1970). What about Clark Gable now? In M. Levin (Ed.), *Hollywood and the great fan magazines* (pp. 20–21, 173–174). New York: Arbor House.

Morgan. T. (1963. October 19). Gentlemen of the pressure. *TV Guide*, pp. 6–9.

Olasky, M. N. (1987). *Corporate public relations: A new historical perspective*. Hillsdale, NJ: Lawrence Erlbaum.

Postman, N. (1985). *Amusing ourselves to death: Public discourse in the age of show business*. New York: Penguin.

Powdermaker, H. (1950). *Hollywood the dream factory*. Boston: Little, Brown.

Schickel, R. (1985). *Intimate strangers: The culture of celebrity*. New York: Fromm International.

Schudson, M. (1978). *Discovering the news: A social history of American newspapers*. New York: Basic Books.

Service, F. (1970). So you'd like to be a star: Myrna Loy shows you what is back of Hollywood's glamor front. In M. Levin (Ed.), *Hollywood and the great fan magazines* (pp. 142–143). New York: Arbor House.

Stauth, C. (1988, April 2). The secrets of Hollywood's casting directors. *TV Guide*, pp. 2–6.

Susman, W. (1984). *Culture as history*. New York: Pantheon.

Toll, R. C. (1976). *On with the show: The first century of show business in America*. New York: Oxford University Press.

13 'Torture, Treacle, Tears and Trickery': Celebrities, 'Ordinary' People, and *This is Your Life* (BBC, 1955–65)

Su Holmes

This show clearly represents a tasteless affront to the intelligence and sensibility of viewers, a pandering to cheap publicity and the easy acquisition of a mass audience.[1]

It must be stopped. It exploits...human sentiment for the sake of gratifying gutter-like curiosities.[2]

This transforms televiewing into the delight of the Peeping Tom, and those who don't mind should be prevented from indulging in a base and reprehensible desire.[3]

While strongly evocative of the cultural debate which greeted *Big Brother* (2000–, UK), these comments are not a recent condemnation of Reality TV, but refer to the BBC's most popular entertainment programme in the 1950s: *This is Your Life* (hereafter *TIYL*) (BBC, 1955–1964; ITV, 1969–1993; BBC1, 1993–2003). In 2003, the long-running show was axed by the BBC, apparently prompted by the belief that it was outdated (Otzen, 2003) (although it has since been announced that it will return in some form). The *Guardian* reported that in more recent years 'younger celebrities have been non-plussed at the thought of taking part', and rock star Noel Gallagher had snubbed an invitation to appear 'with a gruff "stuff your red book"' (Ibid). Gallagher, arguably better known for head-butting cameras than for graciously accepting awards and tributes, was a rather incongruous choice for 'The Life Treatment', yet the programme indeed seems to belong to a previous era where discourses of celebrity are concerned. Sentimental, nostalgic, reverential and respectful, when it began it did not perhaps anticipate a culture which would hunger for the dramatization of unseemly sexual scandal, delight in 'papping' celebrities sporting scruffy clothes or spots, and where celebrity was the primary marker of a culture in which the public/private boundary has been turned inside out. Or *did* it?

Drawing on archival research based on existing programmes, scripts, press reviews, and the internal documentation of the BBC, this chapter explores why *TIYL* might have been so controversial in the 1950s, reflecting on television's *emerging* role in the circulation of modern fame. Particularly in its negotiation of public and private realms, I suggest that the programme prefigures the cultural debate which surrounded the advent of talk shows and Reality TV, while it offers a fascinating anticipation of some of their most compelling aesthetic strategies.

TIYL was originally derived from an American format. Devised and hosted by Ralph Edwards, it began on US radio in 1948 and transferred to network television in 1952. In 1955, the BBC agreed to take out a two-year option on the format, and with Irishman Eamon Andrews as the host (a personality already well known from his role as a sport commentator on radio, as well as the chairman of the BBC television show *What's My Line?*), it began on British television on 29 July, 1955. The emergence of *TIYL* straddled the new dawn of competition in British broadcasting: the advent of commercial television. It rapidly became an extremely popular show with 12–13 million viewers, and its success was highly valued by the BBC in a climate where the attention of the audience could not be assured. The BBC, however, claimed that it had public service value – most clearly in its bid to take 'ordinary' people, as well as famous people, as its main subjects. The so-called ordinary people ranged across doctors and nurses who had won medals of bravery during the war, heroic military personnel and charity fund-raisers to people who had contributed to their community in other ways. There was a strong attachment to the celebration of national pride and honour, particularly as these related to the past context of war. Within this framework, 'ordinary' people were to be honoured as 'special', and given that the crucial parameters in defining celebrity status are time and space, the aim was to transform them from do-gooders known to their local communities to 'celebrities' on a national scale, however brief their moment of public visibility might be (Desjardins, 2002: 120).

The contributions of celebrities largely emerged from the spheres of British cinema, theatre, literature and sport. The guest would be surprised in the studio (believing they were there for some other reason), or in a public space (during the shooting of a film, in the middle of a theatre performance, or even on a plane). With friends and family emerging to map the subject's journey from childhood to the present day, the succession of witnesses to the *Life* were introduced in gradual succession, linked by the narration of the host.

'The revolting emetic': *TIYL* causes a stir

This was the format that outraged so many press critics in 1950s Britain. First, and perhaps most crucially, there were vehement objections to the *ethics* of the programme, and discussion circled around two key features here: a concern over the 'ambushing' of the subject and its subsequent invasion of their privacy. In the absence of prior consent from the subject themselves, these spheres were inextricably linked. The following comment is highly typical:

> [This programme] now heavily underlines a problem to which I ... urge the BBC to give immediate and critical attention. There is something ethically wrong in luring people to the stage by subterfuge and planting them in front of the cameras to unfold their private lives to the gaze of strangers.... This peering, prying programme is a flagrant invasion of privacy.[4]

Second, such perceptions set the wider context for the argument that the format was akin to torture and victimization. The popular parlance used to describe the subject of the show was always that of the 'victim' (even within the BBC), and critics routinely spoke of *TIYL* as 'torture-by-television' or ranted under headlines which proclaimed 'This is Torture by TV'.[5]

Structuring each of these concerns was urgent discussion about the relationship fostered between programme and viewer. This could express outrage on behalf of the public who were subjected to the 'tasteless affront' of the show – unwillingly turned into 'embarrassed onlookers' or 'impertinent snoopers'.[6] More often, however, there was a clear emphasis on the *complicity* of the audience and the willing and eager pursuit of questionable pleasures and desires. *TIYL* was variously described as 'gobbled up and gloated over', as catering to an 'insatiable addiction to shockers and shocks' and as 'the best-devised show yet for the mass exploitation of morbid curiosity'.[7] The emphasis on a 'mass' haunted descriptions of the 'gawping public', while others worried over its gratification of 'gutter-like curiosities' and the 'delectability of suffering to be watched with glee'.[8]

Third, there emerged the suggestion that the programme was unbearably sentimental, its approach causing critics to report physical symptoms of nausea. If the programme wasn't 'sickly and vulgar' or 'a revolting emetic',[9] it was a 'great gooey meringue',[10] and a 'saccharine encrusted process of personal exposure'.[11] Last, and pervading much of this discussion, was the insistence that *TIYL* was 'utterly UnBritish'.[12] Various assertions regarding the national character were advanced here, but these primarily circled around the suggestion that Britain was a 'private, self-derogatory, shy, modest and honest nation ... [comprising of] people of the grunt and understatement'.[13] These rather contradictory responses, in which *TIYL* is seen to mix torture with a sugary spoonful of flattery, regularly appeared within the same review – as encapsulated by the description that it was a 'high-smelling brew of torture, treacle, tears and trickery'.[14] With a heady mixture of tropes taking in witchcraft, addiction and voyeurism, this indicates something of the heated nature of the programme's reception.

On one level, this simply spoke to fears surrounding the expansion of the mass audience for television. The critics undoubtedly perceived that *TIYL*, screened by the apparently more paternalistic and 'respectable' BBC, was intended to compete with the advent of commercial television. As such, it was invoked as the epitome of commercial fare and what the era of competition might mean for British television. But this context also taps into concern surrounding the 'UnBritish' nature of the format. Given that a range of discursive relations between class and culture are often expressed through the guise of Americanization (Strinati, 1992: 47), the American roots of the format clearly fuelled the critical distaste for the programme. It was commercial television that was most strongly associated with the discourse of Americanization, but precisely because of the powerfully audience-oriented nature of American broadcasting (Camporesi, 1994: 637), the BBC could not afford to ignore the success of its most popular formats. But this did not mean that the disdain for American radio and television was reigned in and perceptions of the American *TIYL* played a central role in shaping its adaptation for British audiences. The BBC initially thought that the format would be completely unsuitable for British television, but after viewing US editions on the telecine, they finally agreed 'that with the necessary precautions this could be made a "BBC" programme'.[15] This process of adaptation (and translation) encompassed the treatment of the subjects and the construction of the narratives to issues of tone, form and aesthetics.

The 'life' narrative: Probing the 'private'?

This process is best dramatized around one of the key 'problems' with *TIYL*, its apparently flagrant invasion of privacy. Albeit on a somewhat abstract level, celebrities can be perceived as the most *visible* figures for dramatizing discourses on privacy, individualism and selfhood at any one time, their existence within a highly mediated framework providing the context for this process to take place (Dyer, 1986). However, the fact that celebrities and ordinary people are *equally* encompassed within the debates surrounding *TIYL* is revealing, pointing to the relative newness of television as the framework organizing these concerns.

The British discussion conveniently obscured the fact that in America, a society which insists upon the freedom of the individual as integral to national identity, *TIYL* had also generated controversy over privacy (see Desjardins, 2002: 127). But this concern does appear to have been more pronounced in Britain, and there were national differences with respect to how the privacy of the subjects was perceived. The Corporation was fully aware of the controversial American reception of the show, but their response was that such critique might be limited if a number of safeguards were implemented. One such framework concerned the narrative material which would animate the celebrity's life on screen:

> **We came to the conclusion that provided the people, the type of story (success not failure) and the incidents (not sordid or embarrassing in any way) were carefully selected, we could avoid the obvious dangers, except the criticism of intruding into the life of a private individual.[16]**

Although this comment may also have encompassed 'ordinary' people, what seems most striking (from a contemporary perspective at least) is that a celebrity could be conceived as a 'private individual' at all. Policed by a rather bourgeois conception of the relationship between privacy, selfhood and questions of (class) 'taste', it seems that the programme's discourse need not be scandalous or embarrassing in order to be intrusive. But while the American version may have linked its origins to the do-gooding rhetoric of 'inspirational shows' (Desjardins, 2002), Mary Desjardins describes how the host Ralph Edwards was also dubbed as a

> **[S]piritual prosecutor, . . . prod[ding] both subjects and witnesses to 'confess' by asking them leading or coercive questions, such as his quizzing of former film star Frances Farmer as to the nature of the 'problem' that landed her in a sanatorium ('Was it drugs? Was it alcohol?'). (2002: 121)**

Although it should be stressed that many of the American editions were similar to the BBC's in their biographical treatment of the subject,[17] the British versions lacked the occasional emphasis on a more confessional rhetoric. The approach detailed above was clearly contrary to the BBC's conception of acceptable material for *TIYL* and their bid to police the boundaries between the 'private' and 'public' self. One of their precautions here was that if after 'four weeks of intensive research, matters are disclosed which might prove embarrassing to the subject, they are either eliminated from the life story or . . . the whole project is dropped'.[18] Just what the BBC considered 'embarrassing' matters are never defined, but the idea of 'scandal' is implicit, and the guidelines operated a process of both repression and censorship. Indeed, just how anathema the 'underside' of celebrity would have been to the BBC is humorously suggested in the edition featuring the amiable British film star, Kenneth More. When Eamon Andrews explains 'Now unfortunately Kenneth, we also have someone that you might *not* be so pleased to see', co-star Kay Kendall appears with the amorous St Bernard dog that had appeared with them in one of their films.

In terms of the 1950s, this indicates a complex regulation of knowledge surrounding the celebrity self – one in which the more unseemly side of human affairs had a certain circulation (it is acknowledged as a 'danger' by the BBC), but which seems to have no place on the familial medium of television. This raises the question as to how television, and then *TIYL*, entered the existing discursive framework of star construction in the 1950s. Drawing on Foucault, Richard deCordova (1990) has famously argued that the construction of stars engages public fascination through the notion of a concealed reality, a discourse which parallels the construction of sexuality in modern western society. Both are organized around a 'will to knowledge' or the incessant effort to 'uncover the truth' (deCordova, 1990: 141), creating a mutually reinforcing structure in the discursive circulation of the star. By the late teens the identity of Hollywood stars was already equated with the private, in so far as the primary focus was what they did off-screen, rather than on. The sexual was afforded the status of 'the most private, and thus the most truthful, locus of identity' (Ibid: 140), even if it was represented by the ultimately conservative ideologies of romance and marriage. But as the star scandals of the 1920s made clear, this actively created a structure in which scandal was always 'the repressed underside' of the star's identity (Ibid: 118) – a repression we literally see enacted in the narrative construction of *TIYL*.

The economic and cultural differences which shaped the circulation of British and Hollywood stars (see Babington, 2001) do not invalidate this argument about the regulation of knowledge. If anything, the moral codes in Britain seemed more restrained: there were no British equivalents to US scandal magazines such as *Confidential* in the 1950s, a time when a number of American stars aimed to sue such publications for their invasion of privacy (see Desjardins, 2002). But in both Britain and America, television was seen to reside at the most conservative end of the continuum where the probing of the 'private' was concerned. Stars from British and Hollywood films, as well as the emerging popular interest in 'continental' cinema, were a constant presence in British cinema programmes in the 1950s, as well as in wider topical and entertainment shows (such as *Picture Page* and *In Town Tonight*). The emphasis here was most clearly on the concept of the star-as-worker (what kind of roles do they enjoying playing? How did they get into acting?), with a subsidiary emphasis on family and domesticity (Holmes, 2005b). Despite the rather conservative nature of its own coverage, the British fan magazine *Picturegoer* complained that television never searched for the 'facts' – 'Nobody ever asks Sinatra if he and Avaare going to patch it up, or if Bacall is really the one'[19] – and attributed this to its address towards a family audience. This brief example is significant in indicating how wider debate did *not* position television as an intrusive apparatus in the construction of the celebrity self – quite the opposite in fact.

Drawing on elements of both the biography and the interview, the narratives on *TIYL* – unfolding from the testimony of the guests and the narration of the host – were universally paradigmatic of the 'success myth' (Dyer, 1998). Although it has been suggested that Britain's more class-bound structure and the cinema's close links with theatre made the idea of the American 'myth of accidental discovery less powerful in the British context' (Babington, 2001: 18), it was perpetually in evidence on *TIYL*. This was perhaps because of its television's aesthetic appetite to offer 'intimate' access to selves that were to be revealed as 'ordinary' (as well as extraordinary), even more so than in the conventional intertextual circulation of the star (see Dyer, 1998). It was usually the case that a combination of talent, 'ordinariness', hard work, setbacks and lucky breaks had functioned to catapult the subject to celebrity status. The edition focusing on the British film star Ronald Shiner[20] begins with an appearance by his friend from scouts, who recalls the mice and rats Shiner kept in his pocket during church. It continues with his friend from his first full-time job as an insurance clerk ('he still liked a laugh and a joke'), and then moves on to introduce a man who had served with Shiner in First World War. An elderly dairyman recalls how Shiner had collected milk by horse and cart in the 1930s ('dear old Dobbin'), before we meet Shiner's wife and 'childhood sweetheart', who recounts the story of their rainy wedding day. Then Andrews explains how 'One day . . . a meeting with a stranger catapults your career into the dizzy stellar regions' (we hear of a talent spotter and then Shiner's time working in theatre), and the story progresses with testimonies from more recent friends and colleagues in the British film industry. In drawing on testimonies spanning both pre- and post-fame stretches of the biography, the programme always presented celebrities as essentially *unchanged* by their fame, a long-standing trope in star construction which pivots on bearing 'witness to the continuousness of the self' (Dyer, 1998: 21). Shiner is praised because his 'cockney ordinariness' stayed with him throughout his life, while Vera Lynn is introduced as 'the international star, now at the peak of her profession, [but who] . . . is still the same unspoiled girl who sang around the house at number three, Thackery Rd, East Ham . . .'.[21] When working-class roots did not provide the context for discourses of 'ordinariness' and authenticity, narratives would still emphasize the fundamental *continuity* of identity. There was actually a seamless intertwining of the personal and the professional self, striving for the ideological coherence that deCordova (1990) associates with the emergence of the Hollywood star system.

When 'ordinary' people were the primary subject for the show, the implications could legitimately be conceived in a different light. Any facet of their biography, from details of childhood, ambitions, to family members, could essentially be conceived as private. In thrusting unsuspecting vicars, nurses or housewives into the television frame, some critics foregrounded these editions as the programme's ultimate intrusion, adding that celebrities at least worked in a profession where the aim 'was to publicise their private lives'.[22] Yet this highly contemporary view was a minority response given that, for most critics, *TIYL* was shamefully intrusive on *both* counts.

The debate surrounding the programme undoubtedly speaks to the shifting and historical nature of how the private is actually perceived (see also Drake in Section Four of this Reader), but at least where celebrities are concerned, the *Life* narratives were still only slightly more detailed than fan magazine or press material. Furthermore, critics complaining of its gross intrusion would then often note in the *same* review that the stories in fact revealed *very little at all*. When commenting on the edition featuring the cricketer David Sheppard, a critic moans 'but it told us little we didn't already know about the man'.[23] How, then, can these comments be reconciled?

The appeal to 'the real': Caught in close-up

The recurrent complaint that *TIYL* exposes the subject's private *life* indicates a discursive act which divulges an off-screen existence. But the problem does not seem to be related to knowledge. The controversy circles around the *visual*, the imaging of the subject by the television apparatus, and the articulation of the self through the particular formal and aesthetic codes of the medium. This foregrounds a tension in the BBC's own perception of the format. They may not have wished to 'intrude' into the subject's life on a discursive level, but they undoubtedly wanted *TIYL* to display *another side* to the person. In the discussion of the edition featuring the comedian Ted Ray, the Controller of Television Programmes complained that 'this was so unemotional as to be dull. [A]fter the first few moments of surprise, [he] used his considerable stage experience ... and simply "gagged" and laughed his way through the programme'.[24] Part of the disappointment is that Ray's performance was too similar to his professional persona. The fact that this pivots on ideas about a visual performance is expanded in the reception of the second edition, featuring the wartime resistance worker, Yvonne Bailey. While 'ordinary' participants were not known by a pre-existing public persona, the idea of what made for a 'good' performance was seen to transfer. The Viewer Research Report claimed that many found the edition disappointing as 'Mrs Bailey's unresponsive personality [was] ... a severe blight to the proceedings. They felt the main attraction of this programme must lie in watching the reactions of the "victim" and on this occasion they felt considerably cheated'.[25] The BBC may have claimed that the show's uplifting narratives lay at the core of its function and appeal,[26] but other evidence suggests that they were well aware of where the real attraction lay.

When it first began the Controller of Television Programmes emphasized that there is no doubt that 'the success of *This is Your Life* is due to "shock" and "stunt value"',[27] and it was later agreed that the confrontation between host and subject 'was the great dramatic moment' of the programme.[28] This moment clearly pivoted on a rhetoric of liveness and spontaneity, and the element of risk this then involved. (After all, nobody knew how the person would actually react.) On one level, *TIYL* was an extensively planned and crafted arena (after weeks of research the host and witnesses rehearsed twice before the live broadcast), with an appeal to the unscripted and the unpredictable at its core. Perhaps like Reality TV today, it crucially orches-trated a space to both *produce and capture* 'the real'. While this term was never used in discussion of *TIYL*, it was implicit in the BBC's initial description of the programme which observed that 'as a *documentary method* it is strikingly dramatic [my emphasis]'.[29] This appeal to 'the real' was precisely what made the programme so controversial. Indeed, certain critics noted that the use of emotion, and the visual strategies which captured it, were entirely legitimate in drama. As Jason Jacobs expands in relation to early television drama, the emergence of the televisual close-up was discussed in terms of a penetrating realism – with the 'intimate' camera observing closely with its X-ray eyes (2000: 120). But outside of fiction, and the buffer of an acknowledged (planned) performance, *TIYL* seemed only *too real*.

Film fan magazines had already debated the damaging effect of television's aesthetic on the public persona of the film star (*Picturegoer* described how stars on television 'writhe nervously, held in enormous and frequently unflattering close-up')[30] (see Holmes, 2005b). While in interviews the audience might witness the stars' nervousness and uncertainty once situated in the new live performance space of television, on *TIYL* they were to apparently witness 'ordinary' emotion and surprise. As one viewer noted of the edition featuring the British film star, Anna Neagle, 'It was a nice feeling to know that such a grand person ... could be so emotionally roused'.[31] But unlike the television interviews, and offering its own particular spin on the ever-present attempt to negotiate authenticity in the celebrity image, *TIYL* specifically aimed to capture them *off-guard*. This now has a staunch place in the tabloid rhetoric of paparazzi photographs: *heat* magazine initially promised to capture celebrities 'off-guard, unkempt, unready, unsanitized' (Llewellyn-Smith, 2001: 120, cited in Holmes, 2005a: 23). The ethos of *TIYL* may not have been so aggressively and boisterously 'democratic' in its treatment of the subject (*heat* is of course also 'the province of the cellulite bottom, the rogue nipple') (Ibid), but it does share the visual desire to penetrate the more polished nature of the public facade. Yet while evocative of the 'unauthorized' discourse of the paparazzi image, this moment also echoes the now familiar rhetoric of talk shows, makeover programmes and Reality TV in which we are constantly solicited to search for the moments when both 'ordinary' people and celebrities are 'really themselves in an unreal environment' (Hill, 2002: 337). Indeed, the spectacle of the face in the grip of apparently spontaneous emotion has come to represent *the* privileged moment of truth-telling in television.

For example, in discussing the concept of 'the reveal' at the end of makeover shows (when participants first witness their transformed home), Rachel Moseley describes its specific blurring of public and private space in ways which seem highly relevant. With personal reaction displayed as public spectacle, public and private 'break open ... [and] emotion, feelings and anger threaten to explode in close-up' (2000: 307). Key to both the power and appeal of such shows is that, despite its careful planning and orchestration, there is a 'potential danger [in] ... this moment which television might not quite contain' (Ibid). Catching the subject in the 'raw', and enjoying the quite real risk of anticipating their reaction, is key to *TIYL*, as the Viewer Research Reports make only too clear.

Moseley also emphasizes the relationship between aesthetics and taste here – that the close-up displays a 'kind of threatening excess' that offends a 'position of class and taste-based superiority' (2000: 314). The BBC's conception of *TIYL* suggests a competing struggle between what, on the one hand, they perceived would make 'good TV', and on the other, questions of taste, ethics and integrity. One of the Corporation's precautions in adapting the format from America specifically concerned its use of the close-up. As the Producer, T. Leslie Jackson explained, the British *TIYL* is more 'tactful and sober ... I never use a close-up on a face that is obviously overcome with emotion if I can avoid it. Sensationalism doesn't pay'.[32] But the introduction of each witness by voice ('Hello Kenneth ... Remember me ... ?'), specifically enabled the camera to linger on the participant's face as it expressed a mixture of anticipation, emotion and confusion.

Many critics disagreed that the BBC aimed for a 'tactful and sober' treatment, and their discussions dwelled on what they saw as its distasteful aesthetic form. The most controversial edition here featured Anna Neagle. Under newspaper headlines such as 'Anna Neagle Weeps Before TV Millions',[33] critics talked for days of the

> [U]nnecessary spectacle of an adult, mature woman being moved to tears, trying to hide her face from the relentless cameras which ... would not spare her the discomfort of being exposed ... and us the sensation of being made into impertinent snoopers.[34]

While on this occasion the celebrity was female, one of the affronts of *TIYL* was that it transgressed not only class but also gendered codes of public conduct. Discourses of feminization were barely even a subtext here (see also Spigel, 1992), with the domestic, intimate medium of television indiscriminately causing men and women, celebrities and 'ordinary' people, to weep before the public gaze. Just as Eamon Andrews was sometimes described as trying to offer a 'calming, rational influence on the proceedings',[35] it was preferred if a middle-class and masculine restraint prevailed. But watching the Neagle programme today, the evidence seems to both support and undermine the BBC's claims to a sober restraint. Neagle begins to cry after viewing a clip of her recently deceased co-star, Jack Buchanan. The kindly host seems slightly embarrassed at this and carries on with his verbal narrative. Rather caught off-guard by Neagle's expressive reaction, the camera at first seems unsure *where* to go and *what* to do. Although not in close-up, it at first remains fixed on Neagle as she tries to hide her face behind her husband's arm – the producer/director Herbert Wilcox. The decision is then made to cut to Wilcox while Anna composes herself off-screen. This takes some time, and as Wilcox tries to string out his narrative about the 'wonderful' Anna, the viewer is acutely aware of her trembling presence – her shaking body can be discerned at the margins of the frame. The decision to *cut* is what differentiates this scenario from today when we expect close-ups of celebrities in distress in Reality TV. But the hesitation of the camera (*should* we cut?) also plays out a competing struggle between what, on the one hand, the BBC instinctively perceived would make 'good TV', and on the other, their role as guardians of 'taste', ethics and integrity.

While the critical debate often invoked the term 'private life' to describe the programme's perceived transgression of public and private spheres, concern most clearly came back to the 'private' *self* – revealed *in the moment* through the unpredictable, spontaneous rhetoric of the television image. The concern surrounding revelation here was quite specifically linked to the viewing experience and its consequent implication of the audience beyond the screen. Critics described being both 'repelled but fascinated', while one critic confessed that 'I find it so often uncomfortable that ... while I am watching ... I feel a little guilty I switched on.'[36] This oscillation between repulsion and fascination was also captured in many BBC Viewer Research Reports. After the first edition in 1955 the BBC recorded that 'A customs officer was more candid than most when he wrote: "Although I would definitely watch another programme of this out of ghoulish curiosity I think we'd be better off without it" '.[37]

In inverting the spatial organization of film viewing and other public entertainments, the viewer was now physically isolated from the crowd, while at the same time, television of course also promised 'to make the viewer feel as if he or she was taking part in a public event' (Spigel, 1992: 116). As Lynn Spigel has explored, this inversion was fraught with a number of contradictions, not least of all because television's promise of spatial mobility had to negotiate the idea that there should still be a 'distance between public sphere and private individual', particularly with respect to middle-class ideals of reception (Spigel, 1992: 117). But there also seems to be a key difference here, and the responses to *TIYL* are prompted by its own particular negotiation of the boundary between public/private self. Despite the fact that the images are solely staged for mass screen consumption, they do not feel like they are part of a 'public event' at all. What is seen by critics and viewers as the 'intimate' nature of the events, encourages the feeling that this is a *private* space being cracked open for public view. The sensation of guilt which emerges, the feeling that this is compelling but it *shouldn't* be, is linked to the notion that *TIYL* 'is like looking through a window at something we had no business to see'.[38] It is in part this which perpetuates the descriptions of the programme as 'keyhole', 'peepshow' and 'voyeuristic TV'. While the still newly privatized nature of viewing no doubt accentuated this sensation, we are hardly unfamiliar with these descriptions today. Although the language may have changed (the contemporary term might be 'car crash' TV), we can recognize such contradictory viewing experiences. From watching surprise reunions on *Surprise Surprise!* or talk shows (most closely mirroring the events on *TIYL*) to viewing 'pore-close' (Jones, 2003) images of distressed contestants on *Big Brother*, there is much that is familiar here.

But, particularly when we try to account for the hysterical reception of the show, the idea of voyeurism still carries a sexual subtext. Indeed, the suggestion that stars on *TIYL* are compelled to 'expose themselves' links the private to the *sexual* (Desjardins, 2002: 127). There are also obvious connections to the sexual in descriptions of the subjects being 'overcome', from the suggestion that a common reaction 'when thrust in front of the camera is ... a gasp of surprise', to reactions such as 'you tell them what you like ... I've *lost control* [my emphasis]'.[39] There are suggestive visual recollections of particular images such as 'last week's issue ... ended with a huge close-up of a wet-eyed, quivering lipped A.E. Matthews.'[40] But the subtext of the sexual is most clearly linked to the stimulation of the viewer's curiosity and fascination, ranging from such descriptions as 'one of the sensations enjoyed by connoisseurs of this programme ... is the titillating disclosure',[41] to the recurrent insistence on 'guilty' viewing – Peeping Toms, peepshows and the programme catering to 'base and reprehensible desire[s]'.[42]

These responses can be linked to a long line of texts, as Laura Grindstaff describes, 'whose sensational and visceral appeal ... offends bourgeois sensibility' (Grindstaff, 1997: 195). But most useful here is the analogy that Grindstaff makes between the public exposure of the 'private' self on talk shows, and the visual address of pornography. She describes the 'money shot' of the text, the image of 'raw emotion ... [or] tearful confession', as the moment of 'ejaculation and orgasm' (Ibid: 169). The camera seeks out 'external, visible proof of a guest's inner emotional state, and the money shot – the dramatic climax – is the linchpin of the discourse' (1997: 169). From this perspective it is significant that when there was later the suggestion of removing the confrontation in *TIYL*, the producer objected, 'but is this not going to emasculate the programme entirely?'.[43] Yet this shot of course came at the *opening* impact of the show. Moseley's 'reveal' or Grindstaff's 'money shot' come at the end of a sequence or programme, unveiled as the great '*climatic* moment [my emphasis]' of the narrative (Moseley, 2000: 312). But it could be argued that *TIYL* was an equally sophisticated format in its distribution of exposure and revelation and its bid to hold the audience in a competitive television environment. *TIYL* offered what the Assistant Head of Light Entertainment,

Eric Maschwitz, described as the 'big confrontation, and then the even succession of surprises which keeps the momentum going'.[44]

It is not so much that the viewing pleasures are sexual in themselves, but rather that the aesthetic organization of the text pivots on structures of anticipation, build-up and 'climax'. At the same time, and at least where the stars were concerned, even the most popular reading of Freud would acknowledge that what is 'repressed' in the text will resurface elsewhere. deCordova describes the 'sexual scandal as the primal scene of all star discourse, the only scenario that offers the promise of a full and satisfying disclosure of the star's identity' (1990: 141). The programme did not offer this 'satisfying disclosure', *far from it*, yet it still beckoned the viewer with the promise of a privileged access to the star's private self. It seems that these rather contradictory impulses meant that the (always implicitly sexual) incitement to the private reality was channelled elsewhere.

'This is cruelty': Torture by TV

It was not simply the capturing of emotion which provoked debate but the power relations in which it unfolded. Unlike the active exchange of an interview, the position constructed for the subject was passive: it demanded they react *to* the narrative as it was presented before their eyes. But it is worth noting that the emphasis on torture/ victimization had a wider currency in relation to television appearances at this time. This was the case with regard to quiz and game shows and their use of 'ordinary' people (also often involving elements of 'ambush') – and the genre received something of a controversial reception on both channels in the 1950s (see Holmes, 2006). It was not so much that the formats themselves were tortuous, but that the antics, often derived from domestic party games, were held up for *public view*. Similarly, it is not that the format of *TIYL* is a mechanism of torture in its own right (meeting friends and relatives and receiving a nice red book) but that its unfolding as a public spectacle is. Clearly, the idea that visibility takes place within regimes of power and control is hardly new (cf Foucault, 1975), and this also has a particular significance with regard to celebrity and a long history in which privacy and autonomy can be sacrificed for public acclaim. On an everyday level, the reaction to such constant surveillance has become increasingly playful (*heat*'s 'Spotted' column sports the tagline 'They Can't Get Away from Us!'), and the celebrity is often perceived as an active agent in a game of public performance. Certainly, one of the most striking differences between now and then is the complete evacuation of the subject's *agency* in relation to *TIYL*: they were never positioned as either willing or complicit, but were more often discussed as vulnerable and exploited and in need of public help. But as suggested at the start of the article, the fact that both 'ordinary' people and celebrities are invoked as an equal focus of concern, with often only minor distinctions drawn, is revealing. In traversing the boundaries between public and private, it seems to point back to television as the troubling framework here.

Despite television's increasingly mass status, there was still an implicit lack of familiarity with, and distrust of, a new and alien technology (see also Spigel, 1992). For example, it is hard to imagine the television camera being conceptualized as a 'three-eyed monster slithering in for a close-up'[45] in later years. While the previous section focused on the fear that the 'nosey sociability' (Corner, 2000) of television would have it peering *into* scenes which should not even be made available for public view, there was also the opposite sense – that television's gaze might be omnipresent and unstoppable, rampaging *out* into the public sphere and *back* into the domestic sphere of the home. Spigel (1992) has explored the variety of ways in which the arrival of (American) television was figured within fears about the blurring of public/private space. While it might promise to offer a 'window' on the world, there was also the sense that its visual field could not be entirely 'screened out', and that in a surveillance-like move, the 'new TV eye threatens to turn back on itself', penetrating the space of apparently 'private' viewing (1992: 118). (This of course also reflects back on the idea of being 'caught' viewing, and the subtext of the sexual on which it pivots.)

The idea of television being out of control was most vividly dramatized in the recollection of one celebrity 'being chased down the passages of Broadcasting House by BBC employees, running in the hope that [their] ... dignity and privacy might be saved'.[46] This was the footballer Danny Blanchflower who, after being confronted by the host, was the first subject to refuse to participate in the show. It was now 1961, and critics had been eagerly anticipating this moment for some time. Blanchflower's actions received a great deal of media coverage (and media support). The *Daily Mail* featured a cartoon in which the footballer kicked 'a television cameraman out of his house', with the camera sporting the label 'TV intrusion'.[47] The fact that the camera is now imaged as having strayed from the BBC studios into *his home* is notable here. Furthermore, the significance of this for the public 'at large' was articulated by such comments as 'We've now reached a highly dangerous position where it is possible to haul anyone – be he butcher, baker or candlestick maker – before the cameras',[48] or

> **With TV cameras poking their glassy snouts into everything from football matches, ... to mothers' meetings, who knows where, or who, is next. You're almost bound to be on television at least once in the next ten years. The whole country is. So I'll be seeing you ... on my screen'.[49]**

There is a slippage here between public and private (and thus also gendered) space, as the camera ranges across the television studio, Danny's home, to sports events and mothers' meetings. This plays out precisely a confusion over *where* it is permissible for the television camera to go, as well as concern over the events which might be vicariously witnessed through it. Perhaps most significantly, the television camera here indiscriminately fixes its gaze on celebrities and 'ordinary' people alike. In 1961, this is apparently a terrifying thought.

Fortunately for the BBC, the programme had just shifted from live transmission to film, so the footage of Blanchflower's refusal was never transmitted. But what became known as 'The Danny Blanchflower Incident' prompted vehement calls for the programme to be axed, and it was this, as well as the programme's long history of courting criticism, which finally prompted a change in the format. As the BBC Board of Directors quickly enquired, 'Would it not be possible to consider informing the victim in advance, while keeping secret what will actually happen in the programme?'[50] While some objected that this would be 'Hamlet without any prince at all!'.[51] it was ultimately agreed that the opening confrontation between host and subject would be filmed at an earlier date. Given the argument about a sexual subtext, this was rather intriguingly known as 'the pick-up', and it would display the subject consenting to participate. The main programme would then be filmed in the studio, with everyone secure in the knowledge that the person was willing to appear. This in many ways confirms that the controversy over *TIYL*, as well as its frisson of excitement, was intrinsically related to *live* television. At a public level, ethical reasons may have prompted the BBC to change the format at this stage. But the decision also emphasized how the significance of its claim to spontaneity and authenticity was gradually being eroded as the era of live television was passing.

***

On one level, the initial critical reception of *TIYL* points to a quite different set of attitudes towards celebrity culture, and thus the continually changing nature of its contours. There *is* a greater expression of respect and reverence here, and the fact that a celebrity could even be conceived as a 'private individual'[52] points to the progressive blurring of public and private spheres. Indeed, public visibility here is more often conceptualized as depleting and diminishing the self, not representing the ultimate validation of one's social existence. But this also suggests that *TIYL* does not straight-forwardly offer us insight into attitudes towards fame and celebrity at this time. Rather, it tells us about how this was refracted through the emerging mass medium of television, and its particular institutional, aesthetic and cultural contexts in Britain.

However, this article began from the premise that the cultural meanings of *TIYL* had shifted significantly over time and that, from a contemporary perspective, its early reception was intriguing for rendering the programme 'strange'. In fact, it is not that there is radical disjuncture between then and now, but rather that its highly contro-versial reception makes a little more sense when situated in relation to the horizon of the contemporary media environment – particularly the relations between popular television, 'ordinary' people and celebrity culture. In this respect, it may well be significant that *TIYL* was axed after the decade that saw the very rapid growth of talk shows, Reality formats and popular celebrity magazines. *TIYL* pivoted on the germ of the desire to capture the self unguarded, to probe into the interior, 'private' space that resides behind the masquerade of public performance, particularly as mediated through the apparent intimacy of emotional response. The explosion and acceleration of this fascination in other media made *TIYL* look rather tame. But in trying to explore just what the problem *was* with *TIYL* it seems that, far from belonging to an earlier era, it perhaps appeared before its time.

Notes

1. Untitled press clipping, 12 June, 1956. Box 663, BBC Written Archives (WAC).
2. *Daily Mail*, 18 April, 1957. Box 663.
3. *Manchester City News*, 4 April, 1956. Box 663.
4. *The Daily Mail*, 8 February, 1961. Box 670.
5. *The Western Mail*, 25 March, 1958. Box 663.
6. *Manchester City News*, 4 April, 1958. Box 663.
7. *Stage*, 4 December, 1958. Box 663.
8. *Manchester City News*, 4 April, 1956. Box 663.
9. *Daily Mirror*, 6 January, 1959. Box 670.
10. *Daily Mirror*, 18 February, 1960. Box 670.
11. *Daily Mirror*, 7 January, 1959. Box 670.
12. *Daily Mail*, 30 July, 1955. Box 771.

13. *Sunday Telegraph*, 14 May, 1961. Box 670.
14. Untitled press clipping, 15 October, 1958. Box 663.
15. C.T.P to D.Tel.B, 21 November, 1955. T12/522/1.
16. C.T.P to D.Tel.B, 21 November, 1955. T12/522/1.
17. *This is Your Life: The Collector's Edition*, Volume One, is available on DVD. My comparison here is based on this material.
18. Assistant H.L.E to D.Tel.B, 'Policy', 12 June, 1960. T16/590.
19. *Picturegoer*, 26 October, 1957, p. 15.
20. Transmitted 11 March, 1958.
21. Transmitted 14 October, 1957.
22. *Yorkshire Evening Post*, 22 January, 1958. Box 663.
23. *Daily Herald*, 4 October, 1960. Box 670.
24. C.T.P to D.Tel.B, 21 November, 1955. T12/522/1.
25. Viewer Research Report, *This is Your Life*, 25 September, 1955.
26. 'Policy', Stuart Hood to D, Tel. B, 9 March, 1961. T16/590.
27. C.P.T to H.L.E, 29 November, 1955. T12/522/1.
28. Michael Mills to H.L.E, 20 January, 1965. T12/1,302/1.
29. C.T.P to D.Tel.B, 21 November, 1955. T12/522/1.
30. *Picturegoer*, 26 March, 1955, p. 18.
31. Viewer Research Report, *This is Your Life*, 17 February, 1958.
32. *Sunday Dispatch*, 11 May, 1958. Box 663.
33. *Daily Express*, 18 February, 1958. Box 663.
34. *Manchester City News*, 4 April, 1958. Box 663.
35. *Sunday Dispatch*, 29 May, 1956. Box 663.
36. *Daily Express*, 19 February, 1958. Box 663.
37. BBC Viewer Research Report, 29 July, 1955.
38. *Daily Sketch*, 19 February, 1958. Box 663.
39. *Daily Sketch*, 30 July, 1955. Box 658.
40. *Sunday Dispatch*, 5 November, 1958. Box 663.
41. *Manchester Guardian*, 22 January, 1957. Box 663.
42. *Manchester City News*, 4 April, 1956. Box 663.
43. Michael Mills to H.L.E, 20 January, 1965. T12/1,302/1.
44. Assistant H.L.E to D.Tel.B, 'Policy', 12 June, 1960. T16/590.
45. *Picturegoer*, 19 September, 1953, p. 18.
46. Untitled press report, 9 February, 1961. Box 670.
47. 'General Press Comment on This is Your Life', T16/590.
48. *Yorkshire Evening Post*, 3 March, 1961. Box 663.
49. *Everybody's*, 1 November, 1958.
50. 'TV Policy, This is Your Life', undated memo, T16/590.
51. Michael Mills to H.L.E, 20 January, 1965. T12/1,302/1.
52. C.T.P to D.Tel.B, 21 November, 1955. T12/522/1.

References

Babington, Bruce (2001) (ed.), *British Stars and Stardom*, Manchester: MUP.
Camporesi, Valeria (1994) 'The BBC and American Broadcasting, 1922–55', *Media, Culture and Society*, 16: 625–639.

Corner, John (2000) 'What Do We Know About Documentary?', *Media, Culture and Society*, 22 (5): 681–688.

deCordova, Richard (1985) 'The Emergence of the Star System in America', *Wide Angle*, 6 (4): 5–13.

—— (1990) *Picture Personalities: The Emergence of the Star System in America*, Urbana and Chicago: University of Illinois Press.

Desjardins, Mary (2002) 'Maureen O'Hara's "Confidential" Life': Recycling Stars Through Gossip and Moral Biography', in Janet Thumim (ed.), *Small Screen, Big Ideas: Television in the 1950s*, London: I.B. Tauris, pp. 118–130.

Dyer, Richard (1986) *Heavenly Bodies: Film Stars and Society*, London: BFI.

—— (1998) *Stars*, (second edition), London: BFI.

Foucault, Michel (1975) *Discipline and Punish: The Birth of the Prison*, Harmondsworth: Penguin.

Grindstaff, Laura (1997) 'Producing Trash, Class and the Money Shot: A Behind-the-scenes account of daytime TV talk', in James Lull and Stephen Hinerman (eds.), *Media Scandals*, Oxford: Polity, pp. 164–202.

Hill, Annette (2002) 'Big Brother: The Real Audience', *Television and New Media*, 3 (3): 323–341.

—— (2005) *Reality TV: Audiences and Popular Factual Television*, London: Routledge.

Holmes, Su (2005a) ' "Off guard, Unkempt, Unready?": Deconstructing Contemporary Celebrity in *heat* Magazine', *Continuum: Journal of Media and Cultural Studies* 19 (1): 21–38.

—— (2005b) *British Television and Film Culture in the 1950s: Coming to a TV Near You!*, Bristol: Intellect Books.

—— (2006) 'The "Give-Away" Shows – Who is Really Paying?': 'Ordinary' People and the Development of the British Quiz Show', *Journal of British Cinema and Television*, 3 (2): 284–303.

Jacobs, Jason (2000) *The Intimate Screen: Early British Television Drama*, Oxford: Clarendon Press.

Jones, Janet (2003) 'Show Your Real Face': A Fan Study of the UK Big Brother Transmissions', *New Media and Society*, 5 (3): 400–421.

Llewellyn-Smith, Caspar (2002) Poplife: *A Journey by Sofa*, London: Sceptre.

Moseley, Rachel (2000) 'Makeover Takeover on British Television', *Screen*, 41 (3): Autumn, 299–314.

Otzen, Ellen (2003) 'This is Your Life', *Guardian*, 15 May, available at http://www.guardian.co.uk [accessed 3 June, 2005].

Spigel, Lynn (1992) *Make Room for TV: Television and the Family Ideal in Postwar America*, Chicago: University of Chicago Press.

Strinati, Dominic (1992) '"The Taste of America": Americanization and Popular Culture in Britain', in Dominic Strinati and Stephen Wagg (eds.), *Come On Down: Popular Culture in Post-War Britain*, London: Routledge, pp. 30–49.

14 | Celebrity and Religion

Chris Rojek

Celebrity worship is regularly condemned in public as idolatry, which carries connotations of slavery, false consciousness and 'the Devil's work'. More prosaically, it is bracketed with triviality and superficiality. Certainly, relationships between fans and celebrities frequently involve unusually high levels of non-reciprocal emotional dependence, in which fans project intensely positive feelings onto the celebrity. The obsessed fan participates in imaginary relations of intimacy with the celebrity. In extreme cases these relations may be a substitute for the real relations of marriage, family and work. For example, Fred and Judy Vermorel,[1] who interviewed many fans in order to question them about the reasons and motives behind their devotion, reported that Joanne, a middle-aged Barry Manilow fan with three children, admitted that when she made love with her husband she imagined him to be Barry. She compared her devotion to Barry with religious experience, in as much as it provided a grounded, affirming quality to her life. Other respondents declared that they regularly engaged in mind-voyaging or mild fantasy-work with the celebrity as the precious other. That is, streams-of-identity thought that imaginatively projected them into the experience of the celebrity to whom they found themselves attracted. High levels of identification are reflected in the wardrobe, vocabulary and leisure practice of such fans. In rare cases they undergo cosmetic surgery to acquire a simulacrum of the celebrity's public face. More generally, the celebrity is an imaginary resource to turn to in the midst of life's hardships or triumphs, to gain solace from, to beseech for wisdom and joy. Piquantly, one ventures that hatred is never far from the surface of adulation because the fan's desire for consummation is doomed to fail.

For fans like Joanne, the emotions aroused by the celebrity do not belong to the levels of trivial or superficial experience.

[...]

It is as if the celebrity provides a path into genuine meaningful experience, and the routine order of domesticity and work is the domain of inauthenticity.

The term 'para-social interaction' is used to refer to relations of intimacy constructed through the mass-media rather than direct experience and face-to-face meetings. This is a form of second-order intimacy, since it derives from representations of the person rather than actual physical contact. None the less, in societies in which as many as 50 per cent of the population confess to sub-clinical feelings of isolation and loneliness, para-social interaction is a significant aspect of the search for recognition and belonging. Celebrities offer peculiarly powerful affirmations of belonging, recognition and meaning in the midst of the lives of their audiences, lives that may otherwise be poignantly experienced as under-performing, anti-climactic or sub-clinically depressing. A peculiar tension in celebrity culture is that the physical and social remoteness of the celebrity is compensated for by the glut of mass-media information, including fanzines, press stories, TV documentaries, interviews, newsletters and biographies, which personalize the celebrity, turning a distant figure from a stranger into a significant other. The tension has inescapable parallels with religious worship, and these are reinforced by the attribution by fans of magical or extraordinary powers to the celebrity. Celebrities are thought to possess God-like qualities by some fans, while others – experiencing the power of the celebrity to arouse deep emotions – recognize the spirit of the shaman.

Anthropological studies of comparative religion and shamanism demonstrate that all cultures possess rites, myths, divine forms, sacred and venerated objects, symbols, consecrated men and sacred places. Each category is attached to a distinctive morphology that organizes experience and bestows sacred or extraordinary meaning on certain types of conduct and experience. It is reasonable to think of these morphologies as establishing principles of inclusion and exclusion. Indeed, all religious systems are ultimately founded on these principles. In secular society, the sacred loses its connotation with organized religious belief and becomes attached to mass-media celebrities who become objects of cult worship. Magic is often associated with celebrities, and powers of healing and second sight are frequently attributed to them. Rock concerts can generate ecstasy and swooning in the audience, which is comparable to some rites of magic.

[…]

Religion, collective effervescence and celebrity

Might we postulate a connection between celebrity culture and religion? After all, in his classical study of religion, Emile Durkheim, anticipating later anthropological findings, proposed that the religious ceremony both consecrates the sacred belief system of the community and provides an outlet for 'collective effervescence'.[2] The latter condition refers to a state of popular excitement, frenzy, even ecstasy. Durkheim argued that the growth of moral individualism is bound to reduce the significance of organized religion. However, since social equilibrium demands structured breaks from routine, the state must assume responsibility for organizing a series of regular secular holidays in which collective effervescence can be released and the bonds of collective life reaffirmed.

Durkheim's prediction about the decline in popularity of organized religion has proved to be accurate. However, his proposition that state policy should increase the number of secular holidays never came to pass. To be sure, secular holidays increased in the twentieth century, but they rarely adopted the programmatic form of organized collective effervescence. With notable exceptions, such as New Year's Eve celebrations, Bastille Day, Mardi Gras and so forth, days off have tended to be interpreted as time spent with partners and kids, rather than as opportunities for remaking a moral life with others.

The secularization thesis usefully draws attention to the deregulation and de-institutionalization of religion. However, it exaggerates the degree to which religion has been replaced by science and legal–rational systems of thought. Religious belief has certainly been partly restructured around nature and culture. For example, spectator sports, the animal rights campaign and various ecological movements clearly arouse intense collective effervescence that has religious qualities. That is, they replicate clear principles of inclusion and exclusion, they are faithful to transcendent spiritual beliefs and principles, and they identify sacred and profane values. There appears, then, to have been substantial convergence between religion and consumer culture. For our purposes, the decisive question is the degree of convergence.

Neal Gabler posits a 'moral equivalence' between the dedication to God and the worship of celebrity.[3] In doing so, he suggests that celebrity culture is secular society's rejoinder to the decline of religion and magic. Celebrity culture is now ubiquitous, and establishes the main scripts, presentational props, conversational codes and other source materials through which cultural relations are constructed. Gabler's account suggests not so much a convergence between consumer culture and religion as a one-way takeover, in which commodities and celebrity culture emerge as the lynchpins of belonging, recognition and spiritual life. Does this view stand up?

Theologians submit that religion is our 'ultimate concern'. By this is meant that religion addresses the fundamental questions of being in the world. Even if traditional organized religion declines, these questions do not disappear. Since the 1960s, the revival of Spiritualism and New Age cultism suggests that these questions remain prominent in culture. But the growing significance of celebrity culture as, so to speak, the backcloth of routine existence reinforces the proposition that, as it were, 'post-God' celebrity is now one of the mainstays of organizing recognition and belonging in secular society.

Celebrity reliquaries and death rites

There are many striking parallels between religious belief and practice and celebrity cultures that reinforce the hypothesis that considerable partial convergence between religion and celebrity has occurred. In secular society fans build their own reliquaries of celebrity culture. Always, the organizing principle behind the reliquary, from the standpoint of the fan, is to diminish the distance between the fan and the celebrity. From Hollywood's earliest days there are reports of fans requesting film stars' soap, a chewed piece of gum, cigarette butts, lipstick tissues and even a blade of grass from a star's lawn. One wonders how many unrecorded incidents there are of individuals sifting through celebrity dustbins in search of a discarded accessory of fame.

Anthropologists observe that ancestor worship and cults organized around the dead are prominent features of shamanism in Asia and Africa. Relics of the dead often form a part of rites of initiation and worship. The Melanesians believe that a dead man's bone possesses *mana* because the spirit inheres in the bone. They also believe that the excretions of the shaman are receptacles of power because they externalize embodied *mana*. Christians also believe that the blood, sweat, hair and semen of the saints possess healing powers. The preservation of relics from the bodies and possessions of the saints is a common feature of religious practice.

In secular society, celebrity reliquaries range from items from public sales of Andy Warhol's collection of junk to Jacqueline Kennedy's possessions and Princess Diana's dresses. All fetched astounding prices. Swatch watches collected by Warhol that cost $40 were sold for thousands of dollars. President Kennedy's golf clubs were sold for $772,500 (858 times Sotheby's estimate); $453,500 was paid for his rocking-chair, which Sotheby's estimated would be sold for $3,000–5,000.

[. . .]

Cemeteries that contain the remains of celebrities are also popular tourist attractions, just as cathedrals housing the graves of saints were once popular places of pilgrimage. Père Lachaise in Paris, Highgate in London, the Hollywood and Westwood cemeteries in Los Angeles, are among the most popular destinations. Highgate now even charges an entry fee. Paying to visit the graves of George Eliot, Ralph Richardson and Karl Marx in Highgate cemetery may prove that death provides no obstacle to the commodification of the celebrity. But it is eclipsed by the product innovation now available at the Hollywood Memorial Cemetery in Los Angeles. Colloquially known as the Valhalla of Hollywood, it is the final resting place of Rudolph Valentino, Tyrone Power, Cecil B. DeMille, Douglas Fairbanks, Nelson Eddy, Bugsy Siegel, Peter Lorre, John Huston, Mel Blanc, Peter Finch and several other stellar Hollywood *habitués*. Facing bankruptcy at the end of the 1990s, the site was taken over, rebranded as 'Forever Hollywood', and marketed as the Valhalla of the stars. Budget internment in the 60-acre site currently costs $637, which includes a specially made video of the deceased that is replayed on a big screen during the ceremony, incorporating highlights from home videos. For executive interment, in the vicinity of a Hollywood star grave, prices currently fetch as much as $5,000. The move has transformed the finances of Forever Hollywood. The number of funerals has increased twenty-fold since the marketing campaign began.

Forever Hollywood offers the fan the ultimate *kitsch* experience – becoming a posthumous neighbour of the celebrity in afterlife. The desire to be joined to a celebrity, even in death, further underlines the peculiar seduction of celebrity culture. At the death of a celebrity, it is quite common for fans to carry away flowers and message tags from wreaths and even handfuls of burial earth as relics. The headstones of James Dean, Dylan Thomas, Sylvia Plath, Buddy Holly and Jim Morrison have all been stolen.

Interestingly, celebrity bears no moral connection with moral elevation. Notoriety is an equivalent source of public fascination. For example, members of the families of Jeffrey Dahmer's victims planned to auction the serial killer's instruments of torture and divide the proceeds. Although their plan was thwarted, public interest in owning the artefacts was considerable. In Britain, similar controversy was aroused by plans to sell 25 Cromwell Street, Gloucester. This was the so-called 'house of horror' in which the serial killers Fred and Rosemary West tortured and murdered their victims. The controversy turned on commercial interests that aspired to memorialize the site as a 'museum' to caution the public against the infernal wiles of transgression. The local council eventually decided to demolish the house. Disposal arrangements for the bricks, timber and mortar were shrouded in secrecy so as to deter ghoulish souvenir hunters.

[. . .]

Celebrity and death

The pilgrims who flock to Graceland, the burial place and former home of Elvis Presley, do not so much honour a dead God as proclaim the presence of a living secular one in popular culture. Many fans believe that Elvis faked his death so as to retire from the intrusions of celebrity culture. Even those who accept his death as a literal fact regard him as a living cultural presence.

Conversely, the death of John Lennon is not disputed, either by fans or the mass-media. Even so, he remains a superhuman, inspirational figure for millions. Lennon was certainly conscious of the extraordinary power of celebrity in popular culture. His comment in the 1960s – that The Beatles were more popular than Jesus Christ – drew outrage in the press and led to public burnings of Beatles records by some religious groups in America. However, it was arguably true. Like religion, Beatles music in the 1960s seemed to communicate the incommunicable.

Lennon clearly found it difficult to cope with fame. His lyric in *The Ballad of John & Yoko* – that 'the way things are going they're gonna crucify me' – suggests he was suffering from a Christ complex. Certainly, the ill-thought-out interventions into politics during the 1970s suggested that he was consciously trying to save the world. Was not Lennon's journey from working-class Liverpool to celestial stardom in the 1960s and '70s a parallel of Christ's journey from the wayside inn's manger to become the 'light of the world'? And did not Lennon's assassination in 1980, at the hands of a deranged fan, echo Christ's death on the cross? For some people, the spiritual comparisons are unmistakable. Against this, if Lennon sometimes presented himself as a messiah-like figure, his sense of the absurdity of celebrity and his irreverence nearly always deflated this public 'face'. While Lennon's ability to engender collective effervescence in audiences is legendary, his worldliness was never an issue. Figuratively speaking, Lennon may have transported audiences to sky and underworld, but he was emphatically of the earth.

[...]

Celebrity ceremonies of ascent

Celebrity culture is secular. Because the roots of secular society lie in Christianity, many of the symbols of success and failure in celebrity draw on myths and rites of religious ascent and descent.

Celebrity culture is not organized around a system of ecumenical values that link this-worldly conduct to salvation. Nor should one underestimate the complexity of modalities of celebrity culture, each with its specific beliefs, myths, rites and symbols. The variety and diversity of celebrity culture is a constant barrier to meaningful generalization. Yet, without wishing to minimize these analytical problems, honour and notoriety are, very often, prominent features of the celebrity status economy, and money is typically the currency in which honour and notoriety are measured.

The rise of celebrity culture is, indeed, intimately connected with the rise of a money economy and the growth of populations concentrated in urban–industrial locations.

It is partly a product of the world of the stranger, wherein the individual is uprooted from family and community and relocated in the anonymous city, in which social relations are often glancing, episodic and unstable. Just as the Puritan in the seventeenth century looked to Christ for comfort and inspiration, fans today, like Joanne mentioned at the beginning of this chapter, seek out celebrities to anchor or support personal life. The dominant motive here is not salvation. Fans are attracted to celebrities for a variety of reasons, with sexual attraction, admiration of unique personal values and mass-media acclaim being prominent. Hardly any believe that celebrities can 'save' them in an orthodox religious or quasi-religious sense. But most find comfort, glamour or excitement in attaching themselves to a celebrity. Through this attachment a sense of glamorous difference is enunciated.

[...]

Elevation refers to the social and cultural processes involved in raising the celebrity above the public. Elevation is literally achieved in Hollywood celebrity because the magnified screen and billboard images are raised above the eye-level of cinema-goers. The wealth and luxury of celebrities are staple, and instantly recognized, symbols of success in market society.

Further evidence of elevation is found in the ubiquity of celebrity biographies in popular culture. Popular, mass-circulation magazines like *Hello* and *OK* are largely devoted to glossy photo-journalism, documenting the marriages, houses, holidays, divorces, births, medical operations, and deaths of celebrities. The TV talk show, such as *Parkinson, Larry King Live, The Late Show with David Letterman* and the *Jay Leno Show*, enhances the image of celebrities as figures of significance by affording them the opportunity to present a variation on the public face in, so to speak, 'out of role' contexts.

[...]

Elevation is a perpetual feature of the honorific status of celebrity. Generally, it is geared to market requirements. Thus, when Tom Cruise, Tom Hanks, Britney Spears, Janet Jackson, John Grisham or Will Self has a new film, album or book to plug, they become the subject of a media saturation campaign by the companies selling the product. A common technique in marketing campaigns is to require the celebrity to participate in out-of-face encounters with chat-show hosts. Plugging a product on TV is more effective if celebrities use the occasion to open up, and reveal personality layers that are hidden from the screen persona. However, celebrity interviews are only effective if the essential role distance between the celebrity and the audience is maintained. Celebrities may slip out of role in chat show interviews so as to appear more human. But if they do so continuously they neutralize the charisma on which their status as exalted and extraordinary figures depends.

[...]

Magic, the second theme, is invoked by the shaman, who partly asserts and reinforces his power through the performance of various tricks and undertakings. Celebrities cultivate the same practice. Hollywood celebrities are able to perform magical feats on celluloid. Action-movie stars like John Wayne, Robert Mitchum, Harrison Ford, Bruce Willis, Mel Gibson and Pierce Brosnan are frequently required to perform remarkable and magical feats on screen. Sports celebrities like David Beckham, Romario, Ronaldo, Wayne Gretsky, Brian Lara, Kapil Dev, Mark McGwire, Conchita Martinez, Venus Williams, Tiger Woods and Anna Kournikova are expected to do the same thing in the sports arena.

[…]

Yet face-to-face encounters are so rare as to belong to the realm of exotica. Bodyguards, publicists and 'impression managers' constitute key elements in the celebrity retinue that manage the presentation of the celebrity face to the public. Public appearances of celebrities are not always accompanied with a roll of drums, although, interestingly, heavy drumbeats are often used in shamanic rites to summon spirits. However, public appearances of celebrities are generally staged events in which publicists, bodyguards and public relations staff announce and manage contact between the celebrity and fans. The celebrity retinue enhances the aura of magic that surrounds the celebrity. Their pomp and mass announces to the public that a figure of significance has descended to – so to speak – break bread with them.

[…]

As for *immortality*, the third theme, in secular society the honorific status conferred on certain celebrities outlasts physical death.

[…]

Celebrity immortality is obviously more readily achieved in the era of mass communications, since film footage and sound recordings preserve the celebrity in the public sphere. Mass communication preserves the cultural capital of celebrities and increases their chances of becoming immortal in the public sphere. Graham McCann, pondering the immortality of Marilyn Monroe, notes the central paradox of celebrity immortality: 'Monroe is now everywhere yet nowhere: her image is on walls, in movies, in books – all after-images, obscuring the fact of her permanent absence.'[4]

Descent and falling

Celebrities take themselves and their fans higher. They are the ambassadors of the celestial sphere. But they can also descend to the underworld, and drag their fans down with them.

[…]

Descent and falling are twinned with ascent and rising. Elevation is, in itself, a source of envy as well as approval. Celebrities acquire so much honorific status and wealth that their downfall becomes a matter of public speculation and, on occasion, is even desired. The mass-media who build up celebrities are often unable to resist engineering their downfall.

Celebrities, however, also collude in bringing about their own descent. The inventories of alcoholism, drug addiction, mania and depression constructed by Kenneth Anger, Gary Herman and Dave Thompson of celebrities in film and rock support the commonsense intuition that constantly being in the public eye produces psychological difficulties and trauma.

[...]

Celebrities often feel both personally unworthy after receiving public adulation and out of control of their own careers. Celebrities suffer an abnormally high incidence of mania, schizophrenia, paranoia and psychopathic behaviour.

The theme of mortification in the rites surrounding celebrity descent seems to take three general forms: scourging, disintegration and redemption. *Scourging* refers to a process of status-stripping in which the honorific status of the celebrity is systematically degraded. It has two forms: *auto-degradation*, in which the primary exponent of status-stripping is the celebrity, and *exo-degradation*, in which external parties, usually situated in the mass-media, are the architects of the status-stripping process. In general the ceremonies surrounding both forms interrelate and are mutually reinforcing.

The celebrated 1960s soccer star George Best was arguably the greatest player of his generation. However, the media and fan expectations of producing a world-class performance every week resulted in gambling and drink problems. After Manchester United won the European Cup in 1968, Best felt strongly that aging players in the team should be replaced. When the manager, Matt Busby, proved reluctant to buy new stars, Best became disenchanted. This reinforced his alcohol dependence and alienated him from other members of the team, and eventually from the manager too. Best became prone to temper tantrums and unpredictable behaviour. Gradually, he became a liability to the team and in his late twenties decided to retire from soccer. Best blamed himself for not being able to withstand the pressures of soccer stardom, but he was also condemned by the media for squandering his gifts.

[...]

Lena Zavaroni, the British child star, died from anorexia in adulthood. Margaux Hemingway and Princess Diana suffered from bulimia. Media speculation about apparent dramatic weight loss has surrounded Calista Flockhart and Portia de Rossi of *Ally McBeal*, Jennifer Aniston of *Friends* and Victoria Beckham of The Spice Girls. Richey Edwards of the Manic Street Preachers engaged in self-mutilation, suffered from depression and alcohol problems, and in 1995 abruptly vanished and is presumed dead. Sid Vicious and Kurt Cobain displayed erratic drug-related behaviour, seemed unable to cope with fame, and both committed suicide, one by a heroin overdose, the other by means of a bullet to the head. Elizabeth Taylor, Elvis Presley, Marlon Brando, Roseanne Barr, Elton John and Oprah Winfrey fought highly public battles with their weight.

Examples of celebrity auto- and exo-degradation could be endlessly added. The point that needs to be re-emphasized here is that status-stripping ceremonies are typically focused on the body. The mortification of idealized masculine and feminine celebrity constructions centres on the scourging of the body, which includes ripping, cutting, shedding, flailing and, conversely, overeating, addiction, agoraphobia and claustrophobia.

[...]

Redemption

[...]

Redemption is the ritualized attempt by a fallen celebrity to re-acquire positive celebrity status through confession and the request for public absolution. In admitting to battles with alcoholism, Elizabeth Taylor, Richard Burton, Paul Merson, Tony Adams, Alex 'Hurricane' Higgins and George Best counterposed their idealized status with the public face of vulnerability. They appealed for compassion from the public rather than blind worship.

Redemption bids carry no guarantee of success. Political commentators usually agree that Clinton's confession and request for forgiveness over the Lewinsky affair hobbled his claim to be the moral leader of the nation. Curiously, for a nation that sets such outward store on cultural probity, Clinton's revelations did not fatally damage his position. His leadership of the longest bull market in postwar history deflected much of the criticism. He left the office of President in 2001 with the highest public approval ratings on record. Then again, he never regained the reputation of a 'Teflon President', one able to withstand moral taint. Clinton was branded as an amoral leader, an iconic status that fittingly summed up the hypocrisy and empty meretriciousness of the 1990s.

The fallen celebrity may never regain the former level of elevation in the public sphere. But confession can produce a more nuanced relationship with the public, in which frailty and vulnerability are recognized as the condition of embodiment, common to celebrity and fan alike. A sort of democracy is established between the celebrity and the fan on the basis of common embodiment, and the vulnerability that is the corollary of embodiment.

Redemption processes involve the active complicity of the audience. For fans are requested either to grant forgiveness in respect of personality weaknesses or negative behaviour that contrasts with the idealized image of the celebrity, or acknowledge the vulnerability and weakness of celebrity.

[...]

But the redemption script is high risk, since it acknowledges personality defects and depends on avoiding slipping back into the pattern of behaviour that provoked the public censure and punishment.

[...]

Celebrity culture is no substitute for religion. Rather, it is the milieu in which religious recognition and belonging are now enacted. The ubiquity of the milieu is the real issue. Today perhaps only the family rivals celebrity culture in providing the scripts, prompts and supporting equipment of 'impression management' for the presentation of self in public life. Indeed, a good deal of evidence, notably the high rate of divorce and the rising number of single-person households, suggests that the family is in decline, while celebrity culture seems to be triumphantly ascendant.

[...]

Celebrity culture motivates intense emotions of identification and devotion, but it is basically a fragmented, unstable culture that is unable to sustain an encompassing, grounded view of social and spiritual order. None the less, some elements of celebrity culture do have a sacred significance for spectators. To the extent that organized religion has declined in the West, celebrity culture has emerged as one of the replacement strategies that promote new orders of meaning and solidarity. As such, notwithstanding the role that some celebrities have played in destabilizing order, celebrity culture is a significant institution in the normative achievement of social integration.

Notes

1. See F. Vermorel & J. Vermorel, *Starlust* (London, 1985).
2. E. Durkheim, *The Elementary Forms of Religious Life* (New York, 1915).
3. In N. Gabler, *Life: The Movie* (New York, 1998).
4. G. McCann, *Marilyn Monroe* (London, 1996), p. 199.

15 The Dream of Acceptability

Leo Braudy

I found it possible to concentrate. It worried me. I remember staring at my reflection in the mirror on the medicine cabinet. "Here you are, nine years old," I told my image. "And what have you done? You're nothing…nothing but a failure."

(Vincente Minnelli, *I Remember It Well*)

[I]t was clear to me that no one had looked at me in years. All of the other attentions had been fleeting, partial, obstructed: now, at a moment's notice, now and at last I was.

(Scott Spencer, *Endless Love*)

[…]

Since fifth-century Athens, fame has been a way of expressing either the legitimacy of the individual within society or (in the Christian and spiritual model) the legitimacy of the individual as opposed to the illegitimacy of the social order. Thus the urge for fame mingles one's acceptance of oneself with the desire for others (or the Other) to recognize that one is special. It is the most immediate effort individuals make to reach beyond themselves, their families, and their place in a traditional order to claim a more general approval of their behavior and nature, whether that approval comes from within the world or outside it. The characteristic fame of an era cannot therefore be reduced to the currently available media or to abstract forces often perceivable in retrospect. It is instead a crucial connective between those forces—a much more immediately comprehensible and explicit goal for people living in history as well as a humanly more fruitful way to consider the interplay between individual will and historical movement.

Like many of the fevers, frenzies, and desires of the past, the longing for old standards of "true" fame reflect a feeling of loss and nostalgia for a mythical world where communal support for achievement could flourish. But in such societies that did exist, it was always only certain groups who had an exclusive right to call the tunes of glory, and both visual and verbal media were in the hands of a few. Until the decline of monarchy in the late eighteenth century, the standards of Western fame were generally those of particular classes and groups who had both the social power and the polemical insecurity to want to argue about them. Republican Rome took the fame that Alexander asserted for himself and made it the standard of behavior for an entire oligarchy of politicians and generals. To such formulations Christianity most successfully asserted that the rules of classical fame, with their emphasis on military and political ostentation for the good of state power, were wrong; or, more politely, that they were right only in the most limited, material, and earthbound way. Throughout the medieval reign of Christianity in Europe, and even into the Renaissance revival of Roman styles of aspiration, there is an interplay between the Christian and the Roman views of what constitutes an ideal person, shaped by a debate over what qualities define human character and activity in general.

The history of fame is inseparable from the history of human self-consciousness, on the part of both the aspirant and the audience. With the eighteenth century, we first discover an urge that seems comparable to our own. The decline in the respect paid to aristocratic military and political fame that is the fruit of the American and French revolutions follows more than a century after Oliver Cromwell's victory over the armies of Charles I had demonstrated that the upper classes had no special monopoly over either military effectiveness or the ability to make England a nation respected throughout Europe. Fame was beginning to be a matter of talent, learning, and personal virtue rather than of birth and inherited rank. With the rise of Washington and later Napoleon, that personal virtue became transformed into the star, the destiny, that singles out the most extreme aspirations. Modern fame, whether ostentatious or evasive, is thus predicated on the Industrial Revolution's promise of increasing progress and the Enlightenment's promise of ever-expanding individual will. Both will and energy, goes the assumption, are boundless, and both are undoubtedly connected to the good of the larger community, because God would not have it otherwise. In the saying popularized by Benjamin Franklin, one of the great exemplars of the new fame, "God helps them that help themselves."

The desire for recognition is *a part of human nature especially* sensitive both to social structures and to the mode and extent of communications within a society. Achievement and success are therefore generally defined primarily in terms of what other people think is worthy of admiration, and self-help in Franklin's formulation as well as many of its descendants is inseparable from the approval of an audience. Of course, many modern aspirants to fame seek a status opposed to widespread standards of approval and admiration. But whatever their nonsocial or antisocial imagery and aspirations, these urges are still expressed through socially and historically learned behavior, setting one tradition against another. The roots of this counterfame are deep in the challenge of Christianity to the classical idea of what constitutes a person. In their modern and secular form they illustrate the crucial awareness of audience that marks our time. The urge to fame is the urge to play an important, a noticed part in the great human drama, even for turning away. As more sensitivity to the different ways that can be accomplished grows, so do the number of aspirants. In the Middle Ages, no peasant thought he could become Richard the Lion-Heart. Later, others might dream of being members of Robin Hood's band, and later still, every young man struggling with his homework nurtured within a potential Abraham Lincoln.

When daily life is perceived in great part as a constant performance before an audience of others, and the popular media are preoccupied with discussions of the proper and improper way to behave, individual self-consciousness about performance is unavoidable. Our beings have taken on a deep dye from the media romance with the eye. Especially for those whose belief in a personal or a cultural past has been eroded or destroyed, the lives being played out before the cameras and typewriters supply a variety of alternatives to follow and avoid, admire and loathe. From the wardrobe of visual styles and antistyles that the business of showing has developed over the last few hundred years, we each put together our own costume. It is not therefore the separation of fame from achievement that is the crucial moral issue, but the definition of achievement itself as something primarily external. Such is the nature of fame in a media world, where honor becomes less a matter of personal satisfaction and personal values than of an external recognition that makes that inner honor "real." But no such acceptance is final, and it should not seem paradoxical if the famous seem shy and private. For fame implies that one deeply knows the rules for socially significant behavior, not necessarily that one's temperament is in accord with them. In fact the greater one's talent for fame, the greater may be one's temperamental distaste for society, since it is easier to understand and manipulate social expectations if one is somehow outside to begin with. To be entrepreneurial about one's work or one's public self does not mean that one is an entrepreneur; it means that one knows how to survive in an entrepreneurial world, even to the extent of satirizing it by selling what is essentially intangible.

As Tocqueville frequently observed, the rise of the democratic political systems in the late eighteenth century posed important questions about the survival not just of old but of any form of status and striving. Observing the fame world of today, we might add that democracy is also characterized by greater and greater disagreement over what constitutes worthy activity—worth doing, worth knowing about, and worth conveying to others.

[. . .]

The most striking effect of the democratization of fame has therefore been the transformation of two of its essential aspects: the connection to a world of spiritual value beyond and the connection to a world of human value through the individual. Unlike the ideal Renaissance theater that mirrored the social structure of society, the theater of modern fame is frequently an alternative to the more restrictive roles of the social world. The fame that is spiritually justifying purports to compensate for the social uneasiness of being successful. By now, almost everyone has heard the innumerable stories of the trap of fame and glory. But most still strive, for part of the promise of modern fame is that you and you alone will be able to do it differently, surmounting the past because you have learned from or ignored its examples. Once the spiritual fulfillment promised by modern fame is given, goes its myth, it can never be taken away. In the face of the myriad identities and demands of a more populous world, the spiritual glow conveyed by being recognized means finally not having to say who you are. Touched by the magic wand of this secular religion, the aspirant moves beyond the usual social context of achievement to a place where there is no career, no progress, no advance, no change—only the purity of being celebrated for being oneself.

The aspiration to such purity restates the close relation fame has always had to both death and transfiguration: the desire to find a place where one may live untarnished and uncorrupted throughout the ages. To study the past shapes of fame makes apparent the simultaneous modern desire to be singled out within time and to survive beyond it, that is, beyond death, whether through the Nobel Prize or *The Guinness Book of Records* or a piece of graffiti in the Times Square IRT station. Especially in the present, when more individuals than ever are trying to justify themselves by the approval of the public world, personal fame promises the ultimate means of taking control. In a world of increasing anonymity and powerlessness, where every day on the news life goes on without you, your name in print or your picture in the papers promises at least a moment of respite from despair. For, if an image lasts beyond death, it implies that its possessor is more than human.

But to be more than human is to have become somewhat impersonal; and the desire to be complete and whole through fame seeks a static perfection possible only when life is gone, even if the famous person still in fact seems to breathe. Many seek fame because they believe it confers a reality that they lack. Unfortunately, when they become famous themselves, they usually discover that their sense of unreality has only increased. The audience that awards the famous the ultimate accolade of its attention is less interested in what they think they "really" are than in what role they play in the audience's continuing drama of the meaning of human nature. In such a drama, change is not very welcome, nor is the "real me," unless that role is also fairly fixed. What to the audience is an icon to admire and even worship to the actual person involved can easily become an embalming above ground. Only those willing to act in accord with those expectations—or who can philosophically accept the brief period in which they accord with public taste—will survive the pressure unwarped.

For most of us the final justification of a transcendent social fame is out of reach. Like Sisyphus struggling to push the rock uphill—or the itsy-bitsy spider crawling up the water spout—every time we take one step up, we are in danger of falling two steps back. We are in danger, that is, so long as the model of society is a ladder, on which the myth of absolute individual opportunity is balanced by the companion myth of the precariousness of all uninherited social position. As Elizabeth I and Napoleon and Hitler established their political legitimacy by connecting themselves to past heroic genealogies, so we assume the guise of the famous to organize and legitimize our own uncertain aspirations and ambitions. Especially in America, with its strong self-help and how-to traditions, the selective emulation of public models is part of the national character. If you cannot get fame yourself, then you can become a fan, gathering reflected glory by carefully monitoring the rise and fall of those more avid for the absolute prizes, but allaying the ambition to be personally great by assuming a pose of involved detachment from their triumphs and tragedies.

Fandom mediates the disparity between the aspirations fostered by the culture and the relatively small increments of personal status possible in a mass society. On the one hand appear the gossip columns and "personality" magazines, continually restaging the same drama: The famous may have enormous personal problems, but they prevail because they have completeness to burn. On the other are innumerable gurus whose messages of Eastern spiritualism mingled with Western self-help release their followers from the burden of emptiness by filling it with themselves. But even for the nonfan, there is a larger sense in which the expansion of the possibility for fame and the preoccupation with those who achieve it indicates a deep-seated uncertainty about the survival of individuality itself. Does the increasing complexity and sheer connectedness of the world—the question might run—mean more uniformity or does it mean that self-assertion might be taking on different shapes, unforeseen in the individualities of the past but somehow linked to them? What is the feeling of human presence in a technological world? Can that world be made more intimate by widening the appeal to a communal validation of individual uniqueness? Now that there are more and more people on earth, and social class has become a matter of finer and finer distinctions, in what dictionary do we find self-definitions?

[...]

Fame may bring wealth, but wealth is insufficient cause for fame. The tangible power of the money that runs the world is to a great extent invisible, while everyone clamors for the reputedly greater spiritual power of fame. Only if businessmen are clearly self-made men (in the manner argued by Bruce Barton) or if, like Howard Hughes, their wealth reaches some figure so outlandish that it can no longer be considered "money," can they demand or receive that extra helping of attention that fame rather than mere name recognition entails. Similarly, the transfiguration of fame, or the need for fame to be a form of social purity, makes the old-style fame of civic life more problematic. It is difficult to be elected to fame. Ronald Reagan may have been somewhat famous in the past. But it sounds odd to use the word to refer to him in his public role, as it would sound even stranger if we were referring to less iconographic public officials. John Hinckley implies as much when he is willing to sacrifice Reagan, the actor turned politician, to his love for Jodie Foster, the actress who has preserved her relation to fame untarnished and even enhanced.

* * *

How should a history of fame end? Fame is an elusive idea that I have here tried to set to words ... But because the nature of fame is defined by the context, both historical and immediate, in which it appears, no pattern traced here has the force of a determining causality. *Fame is metamorphic.* It arises from the interplay between the common and the unique in human nature, the past and what we make of it. There can be no single perspective, no secret key by which to unlock what it really is. Instead of seeking to determine its unchanging essence, we have been looking at a less precise history, in which people tell stories about themselves and stories are told about them. Rather than take a pessimistic attitude toward the contemporary preoccupation with fame, which seems to me to depend always on some nostalgia for a past where standards were adhered to because values were fixed, I prefer to wonder what the future of fame will bring?

[...]

At its best, the urge to fame is a desire for recognition and appreciation that is interwoven with the nature of the human community, both socially valuable and personally enriching, beyond the rewards of comfort and status, in a worth inseparable from the good opinion of others. The urge for fame, one recent aspirant has said, is "the dirty secret." But in Western society, it has also been intertwined with ideals of personal freedom that have animated so much political, social, and economic change in the last two hundred years. The difficulty arises when to be free is defined by being known to be free, because then one might be more known than free. When visibility becomes crucial to the way individuals situate themselves in the world, the display of fame, with its Roman progenitors, redirects its selfless aspects to celebrity sponsorship of charity drives and political gestures toward public duty. As the media of communications cover more of the world and take up more time in the day, to be famous means to be talked about. *Fama* flies through the skies once more.

But to be talked about is to be part of a story, and to be part of a story is to be at the mercy of storytellers—the media and their audience. The famous person is thus not so much a person as a story about a person—which might be said about the social character of each one of us. Like some special aspect of ourselves, the famous person also holds out the possibility that there is another self inside, one not totally defined by that social story. In the incessant spotlight the constant tension between those stories—of the talked-of self and the unexpressed self—becomes more acute. Similarly, the basic conflict of modern fame is between the ideal isolation that has been the propaganda of the famous since the eighteenth century and the expanded urge to recognition that has developed in the pressure of democratization and the widening franchise. In one view, the famous exist on a solitary eminence; in the other, they are part of the audience's story about itself. The celebrity goes it alone, even while he praises the audience who has gone along with him.

To the extent that the desire for fame demands a solitary eminence, it too easily becomes a rejection of fellowship, a threat to a just society, a dead end of individualism. Long ago Aristotle worried that the hero may be opposed to the citizen and that heroic assertion may threaten justice. The modern formulation might be that the urge to fame can become a threat when it too consciously replaces any other goal of personal or public good. In past ages audiences were often more interested in what we would call failure than in obvious or immediate success. Secular failure was called sainthood in the Middle Ages. From the Renaissance onward, the voices for fame have tended to be positive, although there have always been questioners.

[...]

Since the eighteenth century, the imagery of fame has been more connected with social mobility than with inherited position, and with social transcendence as an assurance of social survival. From Moll Flanders to Ernest Hemingway, success in industrial society seemed to require a self-armoring code to protect the aspiring self. But the nineteenth-century emphasis on self-making and social mobility has disappeared and now it is not the social order so much as an individual's own emotional problems that are conquered, until they can burst forth again under the auspices of *People* magazine. The psychologization of public language (with its assumption of priority over all other sorts of explanation) has made self-monitoring (as Franklin called it), together with the willingness to expose oneself publicly, part of the definition of fame. A "personal" interview these days is therefore more likely to stress a victory over alcoholism or personal tragedy than it is to sketch a Lincolnesque rise from poverty. One wonders how Hemingway's life and death might have been different if he had the resources of the celebrity interview available for insulation and thereby purgation of the pressure of his public image. But some things must happen before others are possible. Hemingway's inability to withstand his own celebrity lies behind Norman Mailer's premeditated effort to create a shielding public persona behind which he can remain free, just as it does behind the ostentatious evasions of publicity carried on by J. D. Salinger and Thomas Pynchon.

The consumer culture and the fame culture are inseparable at the point where anyone of aspiration feels compelled to present himself or herself in the familiar terms by which others are bought or sold by the world. The numerous artistic suicides and quickened dyings in the decades after the Second World War may mark the last stand of a belief that artistic value is opposed to popular approval and of an inability to face that celebrity if it arrived. By the 1960s the development of modern personal identity, with its rapid flickering through a variety of public and private roles, was being brought up to date by a sophisticated media awareness of product consumption, dependent on incessant channel switching and an easy acceptance of costume and irony. The last great shift in the history of fame was in the wake of the Second World War, and I cannot see that anything very new has happened since, only an increase of the volume, with an added detachment about the process. Of course, individuals still loudly proclaim their desire to be recognized. But there is a decadent flavor to the enterprise now, as if all moves were so well known that no one really cares. The complex interaction of aspiration and achievement that weighed so heavily on Hemingway, Pavese, and Plath could become the cliché response of a thousand interviews of the traveling celebrity.

[. . .]

Modern society, with its web of communications and its increasing number of people, is on the way to obliterating the old moral distinction between acting and being that has been used to attack theater since the seventeenth century. Individuals still believe that they can become prominent for the purity of their 'real' natures, apart from the way those natures are perceived by others. But often they are then swept up in an ongoing drama that they refuse to understand enabled their self-presentation in the first place.

[. . .]

The desire for fame is a culturally adaptive trait by which the individual retailors traditional standards of distinctive personal nature into a costume by which he can succeed before his chosen audience. In the present profusion of biography and psychohistory, who can doubt that everyone's public personality and private character can be traced back to some precedent or another. Every individual case can be excavated to prove a general cause. But what is unique about every individual is the way those influences have been brought together. They allow us to tell stories to ourselves and to others of who we are. No nature is original except in its creative connecting. What we call character, that which distinguishes us from each other, is less to be found in the stories themselves than in the way we have put them together. To understand the myriad influences on our desire to be recognized and by that understanding to achieve some distance and a useful irony has been the purpose of this book. By understanding the history of fame we will be better able to escape the urges it incites and the sense of emptiness that supposedly only fame can fill. Then perhaps fame might evolve again, and the frenzy of renown be pruned of its excesses so that its energies can cause more vigorous growth.

Producing Fame: 'Because *I'm* Worth It'

Section Four

5 010015 030942 >

Introduction
Sean Redmond and Su Holmes

Barry King notes that 'from the perspective of the audience ... stars appear as finished products of semiotic labour' (1992: 3). When it comes to the contemporary media context, this argument demands a degree of reappraisal. Consider the now ubiquitous media desire to capture the celebrity 'unkempt and unready' – looking dishevelled and dribbling after a drunk night out, or snapped sporting sweat patches or spots (Holmes, 2005). The fabrication process, or the process of *constructing* the celebrity self, has increasingly become part of the celebrity text itself. Yet in relation to the focus of this section, King's comment raises an important point. However much we may be invited 'behind-the-scenes' of celebrity production and image construction (Gamson, 1994), there remains a larger drive toward concealing the labour that produces the phenomenon, and for some time, academic work seemed to replicate this structure, rendering the work of producing fame invisible. Although there have been signs of change, with both film studies (see McDonald, 2000), and media and cultural studies (see Turner et al., 2000) investigating this terrain, Turner suggests that much research 'has focused on analysis of the celebrity as text – but such approaches have underestimated the importance of understanding how these spectacles got there in the first place' (2004: 136). Dyer's work (1998, 1987) certainly foregrounded how stars were produced: they are ultimately made for profit and are commodities which are then clearly used to sell further commodities (Dyer, 1987). But Dyer also distinguished between different approaches to stardom – stardom as a phenomenon of production and stardom as a phenomenon of consumption. As critics such as McDonald (2000) and Barker (2003) have outlined, the emphasis fell predominantly within the second sphere.

The production and circulation of celebrity is the work of complex and multi-faceted industries, the growth and expansion of which has increased exponentially in the last few decades. As explored by certain authors in this section, investigating this context is crucial to understanding the systematic manufacture of celebrity. But the essays here also occupy a set of broader relations with ideas of production, promotion, economics and ownership. Section Four includes essays which consider the work of the promotions and publicity industries in producing celebrity. Hollywood cinema's relations with the fashion industry, the function of celebrity within business cultures (the celebrity CEO), the issue of who 'owns' celebrity (from the perspective of legal regulation and celebrity privacy), to the commodification of literary celebrity.

To investigate the system which produces celebrity has political implications. The textual construction of celebrity perpetually operates through a rhetoric of 'really' (what is this person *'really'* like?) (Dyer, 1987: 2), but to ask about the pragmatic frameworks which work to support this process is no simple task. Representing a context which (for us), is associated with leisure, entertainment and consumption, images of 'work' here are negotiated in complex ways, whether we are referring to the work of producing the celebrity, or the labour involving in *being* a celebrity. That is not to suggest that the audience is naïve in this respect, particularly when the visibility of the publicity machine, and a heightened awareness of the commercial structures of celebrity, have become so integral to its general circulation (Gamson, 1994). But like much of the discourse surrounding celebrity, the visibility of the production process is required to negotiate a complex dialectic based around the withholding and 'exposing' of knowledge.

As with the use of the term celebrity, or discussions of the history of fame, reflecting on these economic dimensions is not an objective act: consider the popular dismissal of a celebrity because they are 'simply manufactured'. This perhaps partly accounts for the suspicion of economic explanations in earlier scholarly work, given that it was attempting to negotiate the academic legitimacy of star studies. This suspicion was also a reaction to the perceived problems with classical Marxism – the rejection of the economic determinist argument in which the economic was seen to dictate the 'super-structure' of society, where dominant ideologies are housed and maintained (see Storey, 2001). In media and cultural studies in particular, this split equally speaks to a much wider debate about the extent to which economic and cultural concerns are successfully *reconciled* (even though Marx's original paradigm emphasized the inter-dependent relations between the economic and the cultural, and between production and consumption (Marx and Engels, 1974)).

But whichever perspective is taken (and the authors in this section explore a range of different concerns through a range of different perspectives), the point is not that celebrities can be reduced to an economic function, only that we need to pay attention to how they perform both economic and cultural functions simultaneously. As Turner, Bonner and Marshall outline, this combination of commercial and cultural functions is often negotiated in a contradictory tension:

> **Celebrities are brand names as well as cultural icons or identities; they operate as marketing tools as well as sites where the agency of the audience is clearly evident; and they represent the achievement of individualism – the triumph of the human and the familiar – as well as its commodfication and commercialisation. (2000: 13)**

The task of this section in particular is to keep these different investments – the cultural, the symbolic and the economic – in play.

The essays in this section all work from the premise that 'images have to be made' (Dyer, 1987: 4). Graeme Turner's 'The Economy of Celebrity' offers an introduction to the ways in which the celebrity-as-commodity might be conceived and how it is deployed by the entertainment industries. Turner is careful to emphasize that this 'system' should not be seen as monolithic and homogenous: it is comprised of a multitude of over-lapping industries (which vary across national borders), while it is also organised around the conflicting objectives of the parties involved. While celebrity producers aim to maximize the exchange-value of the celebrity-as-commodity, the personal objective of the celebrity may be to construct a successful career through the commercial circulation of their identity. As Turner notes, this highlights how celebrities do not function as commodities in the traditional sense of a standardized product. There may be an effort to rationalize the system, but it also claims to produce a product that is individuated, negotiating the difference and 'uniqueness' of a celebrity in relation to others in the market. Focusing principally on the American context, Turner then moves on to explore the work of cultural intermediaries (Bourdieu, 1984) – such as agents, managers and publicists – in the production of celebrity. This is particularly important given that, while their activities might *appear* to be increasingly visible in the media sphere, much can still remain hidden from view.

While Turner is interested in the idea of a celebrity as a commodity per se, Rebecca L. Epstein focuses on a particular site in which stars are articulated through discourses of consumerism. Following Charles Eckert's seminal article 'The Carole Lombard in Macy's window' (1990), film historians have emphasized how the cinema screen is analogous to a shop window, promoting not simply the stars and a particular consumer lifestyle, but a whole array of consumer products. In her essay 'Sharon Stone in a Gap Turtleneck', Epstein asks, given the shifts in the 'Hollywood studio system, fashion industry and American consumer culture since the 1940s, how do we assess the relationship between film audiences and successful actresses . . . in the 1990s?' In conjunction with changes in star representation which have functioned to deplete the 'auratic' status of the star, Epstein points to broader shifts in the relations between the star and fashion industries. The use of mass market items has resulted 'in the absence of actresses conveying a uniquely personal, let alone personalized style', while at the same time, popular looks are often linked to the origin of the designer ('Gweneth Paltrow in Gucci'), rather than the particular individuality of the star.

Turner's essay emphasizes the often conflicting set of interests which structure the relations between celebrities, celebrity producers and the media, and Philip Drake's 'Who owns celebrity? Privacy, publicity and the legal regulation of celebrity images', explores what has become an increasingly newsworthy aspect of this struggle: the regulation of celebrity privacy. Drake approaches this from the perspective of celebrity as a form of intellectual property and examines the *legal* discourses which regulate the field. Drake suggests that examining the concept of celebrity power through these frameworks enables a consideration of how the circulation of celebrity 'depends on a wider set of social and legislative structures that are territorially and culturally specific'. Indeed, drawing upon high-profile cases which include the model Naomi Campbell and Catherine Zeta-Jones/Michael Douglas, Drake aims to bring out the differences between these structures in the United Kingdom and the United States. As he observes, until recently, English courts have been more cautious about assigning property and privacy rights to the famous when compared to the United States, where 'celebrity rights of privacy and publicity are more vigorously upheld'. This suggests how legal discourses are also deeply shaped by *cultural* values, and the legal regulation of the celebrity image is as much a part of the cultural construction of celebrity as wider media coverage.

In her 'Celebrity CEOS and the cultural economy of tabloid intimacy', Jo Littler focuses on a further area neglected in the study of celebrity, but one which cuts to the heart of 'the business' in another way. As Littler observes, the role of business leaders as celebrities is rarely discussed, and there is something of a tradition which sees their celebrity as *respectable* compared to the apparently 'frothy field of entertainment' (e.g. see Lowenthal, 1961). This leaves the celebrity status of the CEO – and the power relations through which it operates – as what Littler conceives as an 'unproblematic norm'. She examines this power in the context of two key CEO case studies: Dov Charney from *American Apparel*, and the United Kingdom's Alan Sugar (who hosted the UK version of *The Apprentice*). Littler situates these images in the context of key shifts in contemporary promotional practices and business cultures, ranging from the emphasis on PR, branding and the development of 'through the line' publicity – inserting the CEO celebrity into the 'intimate' *tabloid* rhetoric of wider media/ celebrity coverage – to the transition to 1990s modes of ' "soft capitalist" corporate profit-seeking' in which celebrity CEOs can 'foreground "bottom-up" modes of power (often manifest through "unusual", offbeat or "cool" business practices)'. But as Littler concludes, this can function to reinscribe traditional power inequalities in new ways, in that 'turning the despised figure of the "fat cat" into a media-friendly "cool cat" is predominantly a way to encourage customer intimacy, increase promotion and offset the charge of CEO greed'.

Finally, in her essay 'From the Altar to the Market-Place and Back Again: Understanding Literary Celebrity', Wenche Ommundsen addresses what has become a key debate in the study of celebrity: whether famous individuals, from Reality TV, literary authors, political figures to serial killers, are now all 'products' of the same economic and discursive regime – the same structures of celebrity circulation (Turner, 2004: 8). Ommundsen addresses this in relation to the phenomenon of literary celebrity, and questions the conventional tendency to polarize the contamination of 'high' culture ('visions of poor but "pure" writers starving in proverbial garrets still inform constructions of the author'), with the structures of 'low' or popular culture (celebrity). Ommundsen emphasizes how claims to cultural distinction function as marketing brands *in* themselves, while she also traces how these discourses have deep roots in literary history. The essay argues that the economics of contemporary publishing and the competition for sales in global/local markets indeed places a premium on the branding of the author and the exchange value of their celebrity status. But in examining the relationship between the economic construction of literary celebrity and the cultural climate of its consumption, Ommundsen makes clear that we should also negotiate a space for its 'distinct brand of fame'.

16 The Economy of Celebrity

Graeme Turner

A celebrity is a person whose name has attention-getting, interest-rivetting, and profit-generating value.

(Rein, Kotler and Stoller, *High Visibility*, 1997, p. 15)

[...]

The celebrity-commodity

Celebrities are developed to make money. Their names and images are used to market films, CDs, magazines, newspapers, television programmes – even the evening news. Media entrepreneurs want celebrities involved with their projects because they believe this will help them attract audiences. Film producers use stars as a means of attracting investment to their projects, marketers use celebrity endorsements as a means of profiling and branding their products, television programmes feature guest appearances from celebrities to build their audiences and sports promoters use celebrity athletes to attract media attention and increase the size of the gate. Celebrity also makes money for the individual concerned, of course. It does this in two ways. While they are cultural workers and are paid for their labour, celebrities are also 'property' (Dyer, 1986: 5): that is, they are a financial asset to those who stand to gain from their commercialisation – networks, record companies, producers, agents, managers and finally the celebrities themselves. The celebrity can develop their public persona as a commercial asset and their career choices, in principle, should be devoted to that objective. As the asset appreciates – as the celebrity's fame spreads – so does its earning capacity.

The development of the celebrity's public profile, then, is a serious business and it is usually placed in the hands of a third party – most often a manager (although in some markets the division of labour may vary so that theatrical agents or network publicists take on this role). Ideally, this third party has a long-term interest in the celebrity's commercial success. After all, their own income is linked to their effective management (and protection) of the celebrity's personal and commercial interests.

In practice, though, it may not always be that simple. Occasionally, the agent or manager may find that they have a compelling but short-term interest in maximising the current returns from their celebrity-commodity: when the celebrity becomes a particularly 'hot' property, for instance. Further, certain sections of the sports and entertainment industries do not normally offer strong prospects of longevity (popular music, would be one), and so anyone handling a celebrity in such a field has to make a judgement about their long term prospects before deciding what kind of strategy to pursue. In general, the third party – whether a manager, an agent, or a network publicist – will have a number of celebrities on their books. This not only varies and spreads their investment, and thus their commercial risk, but it also reflects their particular need to protect themselves against the fact that they do not have complete control over their investment. Unlike factory-built products, celebrities have minds of their own and the capacity for independent action.

From the celebrity's point of view, their personal objective is most likely to be the construction of a viable career through the astute distribution and regulation of the sales of their celebrity-commodity (Turner, Bonner and Marshall, 2000: 13). Celebrity is typically short-lived and so for this to occur, celebrities need advice about how to market themselves – much in the way a manufacturing business will use specialists to help them develop a marketing plan, a system for modifying and improving the product and a strategy for building and maintaining consumer loyalty (Gamson, 1994: 58). While this will involve acknowledging that their commodified status must generate some personal costs along the way, the aim is to trade as a celebrity-commodity in order to produce benefits for the individual. This, in turn, involves the careful choice of strategies that increase the value of this commodity to the industry and to third party intermediaries, without sacrificing those aspects of the celebrity's existence they see as important to their personal happiness.[1]

The web of conflicting interests embedded in this situation has been no impediment to its expansion. The marketing of, and the markets for, celebrity have increased dramatically over the last few decades. The key to this process may lie in how inter-dependent these competing interests have become, as the structures of celebrity and the media industries today co-exist in 'a kind of twisted symbiosis' (Giles, 2000: 26). The celebrity may well deplore the level of public interest their private lives excite when this public interest results in an exposé in *The National Enquirer* or the *Daily Mail*. However, this same level of interest can also attract people to see their next film or their next live appearance. That expression of interest, in turn, provides them with the power to elicit an adulatory photo feature in *Hello!* or to demand approval of the writer assigned to prepare a profile on them for *Vanity Fair* – all of which go towards enhancing the cultural capital invested in their public image. For the magazine editors concerned, these photos and that feature will sell magazines. The public demand for material on A-list celebrities means that the media (particularly the magazines) must assiduously maintain access to them; the price for this – once the celebrity achieves a certain level of fame – may be to accede to whatever conditions the celebrity proposes.[2] Conversely, since the celebrity in turn will always need the visibility the media can provide, it is in their interests to be as cooperative as possible to maintain a continuing relationship. As a result, they will provide images free of charge to the magazines, they will appear at publicity events to promote this year's new television series, they will do the round of talk shows to promote their next tour and so on.

In a similar network of coordinated but competing interests, the film producer will contract the star to advertise and promote their film as well as perform in it. This is to maximise the visibility and appeal of the film so that it makes a profit for the production company. While they may desire that outcome as well, the star's personal interests here are slightly different. The star promotes their latest work as a means of enhancing their commercial value in general and so it is possible that they will be reluctant to closely tie this publicity to the particular performance vehicle. Gamson suggests that 'the performer who wants to increase her marketability as a celebrity persona', may be 'resistant to the link to work' (that is, the film they are publicising), preferring to promote their personality alone (1994: 84). As Barry King has pointed out, the film actor has little choice but to commodify themselves in this way. There are not enough parts to go around and very little money is paid to those who are not in high demand. As a result, says King, 'competition for parts, *given the operation of naturalistic conventions*, lead to an emphasis on what is unique to the actor, displacing emphasis from what an actor can do *qua* actor onto what the actor *qua* person or biographical entity is' (King, 1991: 178). The construction of a star persona may result in some 'loss of autonomy' (ibid.: 180) in terms of the constraints on their off-screen life and their professional choices, but this is regarded as a reasonable trade-off for increased market power within the industry. A similar pattern can be seen elsewhere. In her account of the rock music industry, Deena Weinstein explains why there is a focus there too upon the individual rather than 'the work': 'If record companies can get listeners to fall in love with the person rather than the song, there's a better chance fans will buy the next album – and concert ticket, T-shirt, video, book and poster' (1999: 65). Joe Moran's account of changes in literary publishing notes the recent expansion of forms of publicity that concentrate on the author (talk shows, feature articles and so on) as well as the increasing investment in celebrity authors for publisher-generated projects (biographies by stars such as Joan Collins or Martina Navratilova). Promoting authors as personalities is a symptom of the integration of literary production into the entertainment industry (2000: 41).

While most parts of the celebrity industry would probably prefer to operate like more conventional manufacturing industries – producing a standardised product in the way a factory production-line might – the whole structure of celebrity is built on the construction of the individuated personality. In practice, the individual star has a highly identifiable, even iconic, physical image, a specific history for the circulation of this image, and accrues psychological and semiotic depth over time (De Cordova, 1990: 9). The interests of the individual seeking celebrity are overwhelmingly in favour of pursuing that kind of specificity. However, in the media and entertainment industries' version of the ideal world, their interests would be better served if they could be guaranteed a steady supply of less specific, more formulaic, interchangeable celebrity-commodities. These would not mature as capital assets and thus increase production costs, and the market value of any one identity would be not much different to any other. While the studios of the classic Hollywood era probably offer the best example of this principle in practice, it is not surprising to find that sectors of the contemporary media have organised themselves to produce celebrities along these lines.

Certain teenage stars of television soap operas, for instance, enjoy a high level of visibility in the US, the UK and Australia (among other locations), but in many cases find that once they leave the serial they are unable to find other work. They are easily replaced and quickly forgotten. In the research conducted for *Fame Games* (Turner, Bonner and Marshall, 2000), my co-authors and I found that a number of the former stars of Australian soap operas such as *Neighbours* and *Home* and *Away* had left the industry because they simply had no credibility as an actor once they had left their original roles. Their celebrity was built on their exposure in a particular, low-prestige vehicle and maximised through an industrial structure that vigorously exploited cross-media and multi-platform promotions. (In the case of the most successful teen soap operas in Australia, the television network that commissioned the production owned the only national television guide magazine, as well as most of the market leaders in the women's magazine sector. Soap stars were routinely featured on their covers as well as in features across this sector.) Once they left the series, however, they were easily replaced on all these platforms by the next cast of fresh young faces. These were examples of Rojek's 'celetoid', moving from maximum visibility in television and magazines to complete obscurity within a matter of weeks. The trend towards reality TV programmes such as *Big Brother* is another example of a format designed to produce a reliable supply of interchangeable celebrities for the television audience. It is very difficult in both these instances for the individual actor or 'housemate' to develop the level of control required to maintain a relationship with the audience that is independent of the programme – that is, a relationship that is not managed by the production company or the network.

The production companies are aware of this situation, but largely find no ethical problem with it: in most cases, the persons concerned might be considered lucky to last as long as they do. Those who do find it a little uncomfortable are the agents, managers and publicists who have become integrated into the celebrity's life and who have to some extent identified with the long term objective of their survival as a public figure. For these people, the interests of the industry and those of the individual come into conflict in ways that create practical, strategic dilemmas. To what extent do they encourage the young soap star to unburden themselves of intimate personal information in an interview, for instance, knowing that this could haunt them for the rest of their career? Similarly, to what extent do they support the celebrity's intention of providing revealing photographs as a way of heightening their short term visibility when the agents know that these could well limit their charge's career options down the track? The metaphor of 'celebrity-commodity' that we have been using contains within it the contradictions the industry deals with every day: the fact that commercial interests may well run contrary to the personal interests of the celebrity.

This is even more of a concern when we look at the effect of media interest in the 'accidental celebrity' – the person in the news – such as Princess Diana's former butler, Paul Burrell. As a result of the court case in which he was involved, he became a celebrity-commodity for a very short time and he seems to have been advised to cash in as fully and as quickly as possible. In Burrell's case, this meant selling his story to one mass circulation newspaper for a large sum (despite having earlier claimed he would never try to make money out of his association with Diana). Those newspapers who did not win the auction for his story were free to attack him and the paper that did – by ridiculing Burrell, undermining his credibility, seeking new information to embarrass him and challenging the details of his story and so on. As the subsequent physical attacks on Burrell's home demonstrate, the acceptance of celebrity-commodity status can carry quite severe personal consequences. It involves a framework of behaviour over which the individual will have virtually no control. In our research for

Fame Games (2000), Frances Bonner, David Marshall and I examined the media representation of one such individual – Stuart Diver, the lone survivor of a catastrophic landslide in the Australian snowfields. The only way such a person could control their media representation was by fully engaging with the celebrity industries that produce it: by hiring a manager and surrendering control of the situation to a media professional who would entirely commercialise all media access. Apparently, Stuart Diver regarded this as an ethically objectionable thing to do (it could appear to be an attempt to cash in on the misfortunes of others), but he was persuaded that this was the only realistic course available to him. And it worked. The provision of exclusive access to one media organisation terminated the interest of the others; they did not want to publicise a competitor's property and in this case they were not interested in turning on a figure who had become a hero to the public.

Once achieved, of course, celebrity can spin-off into many related sub-industries through endorsements, merchandising and so on. Individuals can become brands in their own right, with enormous commercial potential. McDonald and Andrews report that one year after signing Michael Jordan for Gatorade's 'Be like Mike' promotion, Gatorade's annual revenues had increased from $681 million to over $1 billion (2001: 20). Increasingly, the worldwide marketing of such figures as Michael Jordan are serving to expand America's penetration into global markets, especially in film, television and video. In sport, though, this is a relatively recent development.

David Rowe (1995) argues that before the 1970s there was nothing chic or fashionable about sport or sports stars. However, a shift in the cultural and economic location of sport resulted in the increased marketing of sports stars as commodities. The increasing sophistication of televised sport has enhanced their visibility and their cultural purchase. Further, the cultural and industrial convergence of sport and fashion is a particularly interesting development that seems to have exercised an exceptionally strong influence on the role of the sports star. Whannel (2002) describes how functional sporting attire like the tracksuit and the sports shoe, have become stylised fashion items as the mainstream fashion industry borrows from sports styles. More important, perhaps, is the growth of what Whannel describes as 'fitness chic': the extraordinary rise in the popularity of fitness clubs and the 'exercise boom' over the 1990s (2002: 129–32). The level of market penetration achieved by sports goods brands using these stars can be seen in the ubiquity of sports brands in department stores and clothing shops today. Where once we might have seen a range of commercial logos on the t-shirts on sale in mainstream fashion outlets, today the market is dominated by designer names and sportsgood logos – Nike, Puma, Adidas, Reebok and so on. All of these developments have generated a relatively new intensity to the media's focus on the appearance, style and personality of the sports star in their behaviour off the track. As a result, sports people too are 'celebrated and exploited':

> **It is their labour and performance that is minutely scrutinized and whose skills are bought and sold in the sporting marketplace, their bodies which are punished, manipulated and invaded in the quest for greater efficiency, and their images moulded and displayed to sell and promote goods and services. (Whannel, 2002: 113)**

According to Rein et al., sports stars can now expect to earn two-thirds of their annual salary through product endorsements of various kinds – ranging from the tools of their trade (sports shoes, tennis raquets, etc.) to food lines (yoghurt, breakfast cereals) and fashion items (clothing, sunglasses and so on). Hence, Andre Agassi might gross $11 million a year, with only one-tenth coming from his on-court performances and the rest coming from endorsements (Nike, Canon), licenses (a new line of exercise equipment), personal appearances and investments (a chain of restaurants called the Official All Star Cafe) (Rein et al., 1997: 53).

The final point to note about the celebrity-commodity is the close relationship between celebrity and the consumption of commodities. We have already seen how David Marshall's work maps the function celebrity performs in linking ideologies of individualism, consumerism and democratic capitalism. De Cordova's history of film stardom discusses the way that film stars operated as a means of promoting the values of consumerism during the 1920s and 1930s. Drawing on Larry May's research, he argues that the ideological work to be accomplished there was to negotiate the tensions between 'Victorian ideals and consumer ideals' as part of the process of the commod-ification of everyday life. Film stars were a good place for this negotiation to occur. They were not excessively privileged in terms of their social power, they came largely from ordinary socio-economic backgrounds and their success was, 'easily ascribed to democratic aspirations. In conspicuously displaying that success through material possessions, the star vividly demonstrated the idea that satisfaction was not to be found in work but in one's activities away from work – in consumption and leisure' (De Cordova, 1990: 108). The demonstration continues today, when celebrities promote their latest venture in a leisure location – by the hotel pool, at home, in a restaurant, or on the golf course. The consumerist values they work to legitimate are also fundamental to the commercial interests of the media outlets. As Conboy says in relation to the news media's use of celebrity, 'one of the attractions of celebrity news is that it allows the people as readers to be addressed and articulated in terms of consumerist values which are inextricably linked to the newspapers' economic agenda' (2002: 150). Stories routinely present the celebrity as a model of consumption practice and aspiration for the reader. The usual ambiguities appear, of course. While these stories can represent the commodity consumption of the celebrity as spectacular and exorbitant, they can also use their consumer behaviour as a means of constructing their every-dayness, their similarity to 'us'.

The celebrity industries

In this section, I want to outline some of the structures of the celebrity industry, beginning with the function of the third parties mentioned earlier: the agents, managers and publicists. That might seem a rudimentary way to begin, but it is information that rarely finds its way into analysis of the production of celebrity, or of the wealth of texts this production process employs. This is especially damaging in this particular instance because the celebrity industries actively mask their own activities. By presenting publicity as news, by claiming to tell us what their charges 'are really like', by managing the production of 'candid' photo opportunities and so on, the celebrity industries work hard to naturalise their professional practices – or else to submerge their professional practices beneath those of another profession, such as journalism. As a result, what these industries do is not easy to distinguish and therefore their importance is not easy to assess. Currently, there are very few studies available that approach the topic from this angle – to analyse this industry in the way you might want to analyse the film industry or the television production industry. Joshua Gamson's *Claims to Fame* (1994), Marshall's *Celebrity and Power* (1997) and Rein et al.'s *High Visibility* (1997) are probably the most useful and recent books dealing with the American industry and the work of Frances Bonner, David Marshall and myself in *Fame Games* (2000) provides an account of a much smaller and less organised industry. This section of the chapter will draw on these works extensively.

Let us start with what Rein et al. call the 'structure of the celebrity industry'. I should point out that their book deals solely with the American industry and responds to an expansion of the techniques of celebrity marketing into politics, business, academia and religion that is certainly more developed there than in any other country. There will be variations from the model they outline – and I will deal with this later in the chapter – but it is useful to focus on America as it has the most developed version of the celebrity industry. Unlike most other accounts, Rein et al. locate the celebrity industry in the centre of an industrial structure. According to their point of view, it is the entertainment and sports industries that are on the fringe of the celebrity industry. Their justification for this point of view lies in the pervasiveness of the techniques of celebrity (marketing, public relations and publicity) across so many sectors of the economy.

As they describe it, the celebrity industry is supported by seven contributing 'sub-industries'. The activity of these sub-industries is not solely dedicated to the celebrity industry, but Rein et al. describe the celebrity industry as coordinating the services the sub-industries provide in order to produce and promote the celebrity. The first industry they nominate, predictably enough, is the *entertainment industry*, incorporating theatre, music halls, dance halls, sports arenas and movie studios. They differentiate these from the *communications industry*, which encompasses newspapers, magazines, radio, television and film. The activities of both the entertainment and communications industries are promoted through the *publicity industry*, which comprises publicists, PR firms, advertising agencies and marketing research firms. The celebrities themselves are handled by the *representation industry*, which includes agents, personal managers and promoters. The production of the celebrity image is coordinated through the *appearance industry*, which includes costumers, cosmeticians, hairstylists and other kinds of image consultants. The professional performance is dealt with by the *coaching industry* – music, dance, speech and modelling teachers. Finally, we have the *endorsement industry* – souvenir manufacturers, clothing manufacturers and games and toys manufacturers among others – and the *legal* and *business services industry*, which provides legal, accounting and investment advice (Rein et al., 1997: 42–58).

We don't need to accept these categories, of course, but they do give us a good overview of the range of cultural intermediaries required to make this system function. It probably leaves out of the picture, though, what Gamson regards as a key industrial element of the celebrity system. While he also acknowledges the roles of 'paid specialists' who 'surround the celebrities to increase and protect their market value', he also points to 'the linked sub-industries' that 'make use of celebrities for their own commercial purposes, simultaneously building and using performers' attention-getting power' (1994: 61). The whole edifice of commercial branding that Naomi Klein has described in *No Logo* (2000) – an edifice which is certainly larger than the 'endorsement industry' but that is fundamentally concerned with the use of celebrity images – is not contained by the structure presented to us in *High Visibility*.[3]

So, while we must acknowledge that the pervasiveness of celebrity affects our ability to neatly describe the structure of the industry that produces it, these categories provide something of a starting point. Gamson (1994) Turner et al. (2000) and Rein et al. (1999) all provide detailed outlines of the practices and processes performed by the specialists in the celebrity industry: the differences between the roles played by agents and managers, the range of duties performed by the publicist and so on. There is no need to duplicate their work here. However, it is worth briefly reviewing the nature of the roles played by, in particular, the key figures within the representation and publicity industries – agents, managers and publicists. There will be some variations, from market to market, so largely what follows is an account of the American model; where the model varies, in the UK and elsewhere, this will be flagged as we go along.

The role of what was originally called the press agent goes back quite a way, and is described at length in Gabler's biography of Walter Winchell (1995). Appearing around the end of the nineteenth century to exploit the potential for free publicity provided by an expanding print media, they took off as a profession during the 1920s and 1930s. Largely their role then was to locate items in gossip columns such as Winchell's, in return for a fee paid by their client. Widely despised, they constituted 'an unsavoury and forlorn group of men', according to Gabler, but were nevertheless 'the ants that moved the mountain. For without them, there was no celebrity, no gossip, no mass culture, really' (1995: 249). Certainly, it is from their early occupation of the market in celebrity gossip and entertainment industry publicity that laid the ground for subsequent development of the industry from the 1920s to the 1950s. Industrial structures that had developed around theatre and vaudeville were modified to accommodate new means of production and publicity, with the expansion of the print media's coverage of their activities. The theatrical agent's activities crossed over into the film industry as it expanded and the development of television created a demand for network publicists and public relations personnel, as well as a major new outlet for promotional and publicity material. In sport, as we have seen already, the arrival of the agent was much later than in the entertainment industry. 'Sports attorneys' appear in the 1970s to prosecute the interests of the players in gaining access to a fairer share of the revenues from elite sport – particularly those generated by television where the appeal of the individual sports star was of major importance.

The agent in the entertainment industry, in general, is there to find work for their clients, to help negotiate the terms of that work, to provide advice and sometimes developmental coaching and, in certain cases, to arrange publicity for the client. Successful agents have a large number of clients and operate on a percentage cut of the client's fee. Mostly they do not interest themselves in management or 'product development'. Indeed, it is not really in their interests to become too closely identified with a particular client because their value to the industry is as a conduit to many possible performers, not just one. Agents thus tend to have a close relationship with the employers of their clients – the booking agents, casting directors and so on. This can lead to conflicts of interest, where the agent is a little too keen to find someone for the casting agency and pushes their client into an inappropriate commitment. In sports, the agent tends to have a slightly different role, although in many respects even more conflicted. They tend to operate as the middle man in the whole enterprise, 'handling economic relations between individual sports stars, sports organisations, sponsors, advertisers, and television companies' (Rowe, 1995: 112). This is similar to the role played in other sectors by the personal manager.

The manager typically has a smaller number of clients and plays a much larger strategic role in developing the clients' careers. The management service they provide is extraordinarily comprehensive, organising their clients' whole lives: 'answering their mail, investing their money, buying real estate, planning their schedules, placing their children in schools, even hiring the gardener and firing the maid' (Rein et al., 1997: 46). In some cases, both in the American studies and in the work we completed in Australia, the power of the manager developed to the point where they, too, had a media profile equivalent to that of most celebrities. Impresario managers with their own entrepreneurial projects tend to emerge from this kind of system: Michael Ovitz in the US, Max Clifford in the UK and Harry M. Miller in Australia are examples of this.

Public relations is an industry barely a century old and the bearer of a slightly compromised reputation. This wasn't always the case. Indeed, initially, public relations provided a more respectable name for the press agent as well as the rationale for a change in the function of these operatives: the need for positive publicity gradually became a corporate issue, not just a problem for the entertainment industries. These days, public relations touches most facets of commercial and public life: managing corporate relations with the public, providing advice to politicians about how to build their public image, or designing a government public information campaign. In many quarters, this has lent public relations a reputation for massaging the truth through the media; among the reasons for this has been the tendency for businesses or politicians caught in an embarrassing situation to deal with it by commissioning a public relations company. Public relations or PR is frequently used as the generic term to describe, perjoratively, the operation of publicity, media management and 'spin' – even though the actual activities are likely to be carried out by promotions personnel or publicity officers. In the celebrity industry, public relations operatives may be employed by organisations with continuing interests to protect – studios, networks, production companies and so on – but they tend not to get involved in the day-to-day operation of publicity and promotion. To some extent, this is a hierarchical distinction: although publicity is a sub-section of public relations, many in PR look down on the crudely commercial work required by publicity and promotion. From another point of view, however, it simply recognises the greater industrial importance of the publicist to the celebrity and media industries.

Publicists may be hired by the celebrity, by their management, by a specialist publicity or public relations firm or by the production unit, network or promoter involved with the celebrity's current project. They stand between the celebrity and the public, almost literally, in that their job is to manage all communications between them. They write the press releases and secure their placement; they stage-manage the photo opportunity that will feature at the end of the evening news and orchestrate any personal appearances the celebrity performs; they negotiate with magazine editors about how their client will be represented in a photo shoot and a feature article; they will vet the questions asked by journalists and television interviewers, and sit with their client while the interview takes place to ensure that it follows the established rules of engagement. They will deal with the press when their client misbehaves and attracts negative publicity – hoping to cash in on their ongoing relationship with the press to minimise any fall-out. The publicist's function is to control, coordinate and if necessary massage that information and those images of the celebrity, which are circulated to the public. This can involve frustrating the desires of the celebrity they represent, as well as those of the media outlets expecting to have their demands satisfied. The successful publicist's value lies in their ability to do all this while maintaining effective relationships with those on both sides of the transaction. This is possible because what I am describing as controlling, can also be seen as enabling: while they exercise a powerful influence on what kind of transaction actually takes place, they are also the mechanism that organises it and thus enables it to happen at all.

As remarked upon earlier, the key to the structure of the industry is the especially close pattern of economic interdependencies that bind the celebrity and their representatives (agents, managers, publicists, PR people), to the entertainment industries and to the entertainment and news media. The most obvious connections are corporate: such as, when we find that *Time* magazine is featuring a story on an actor who is currently appearing in a film produced by Warner Bros. But there are others: strong social, cultural and professional networks see individuals move easily from one side of the industrial divide to the other – reporters become press officers, journalists become public relations advisers and so on. These networks are supported by a transactional pattern that will see a front page story traded for exclusive access so that both the star and the media outlet achieve their professional goals. These interdependencies are, in my view, deliberately mystified so that the processes through which they work – how a news story on a celebrity finds its way to the front page for instance – are not visible. This serves two sets of interests: those of the publicist, who wants the items published to appear as news rather than as advertising because it will be more credible; and those of the journalist, who does not wish their readers to know that the item under their byline was not the product of the practice of journalism. Neither of these positions is particularly ethically secure and so they are not maintained without tension. They accompany what seems to be a constant battle for power.

Publicity, news and power

[...]

As a commercial enterprise, the celebrity industry must serve competing industrial interests while, as a cultural production, satisfying radically contradictory demands from consumers. As a result, the celebrity industry may be organised but it is not particularly coherent. Much of what it does, obsessively, it does on a hunch. In his research for *Fame Games* (Turner, Bonner and Marshall, 2000), David Marshall talked to a television network executive who, during the 1980s, had the job of protecting *Neighbours* stars Jason Donovan and Kylie Minogue from the news of their romantic relationship becoming public. This was a major task for the network publicity people for a period of four years. The reason for this was the firmly held assumption that the *Neighbours* audience figures would be negatively affected if the truth was published. There was never any research conducted to test this assumption, but it operated with the power of fact in the network's strategy for years. This highlights an important point that Joshua Gamson makes. One of the reasons for the publicity industries' excessive anxiety about media management and control is the lack of knowledge about what will actually succeed in the marketplace, about what audiences actually want. While the television industry will closely watch its ratings and sometimes the TVQ scores, and while film producers routinely test their films before preview audiences, the industrial system that is focused on producing and marketing the celebrity actually pays very little attention to the audience. Instead it is taken for granted that audience interest is reflected in a high level of public visibility – hence the obsession with media coverage:

> [p]ublicists use the *perception* of audience interest as a signal to industry buyers that their client has a reliable market. They do so by bypassing audiences, using the more controllable media coverage as a proxy for audience interest...[T]he working assumption is that media institutions are in touch with and reflect audience interest. As long as that assumption is maintained by entertainment industry buyers, publicity workers can operate without requiring more knowledge about audiences. (Gamson, 1994: 111)

There is an operational strategy, then, for considering the audience's interest but this strategy does little more than simply play back to publicists the effects of their own labour. Publicists would rarely conduct audience research on their celebrity's marketability. Little wonder that one of the talkshow producers Gamson interviews about the basis upon which he decides the line-up of guests on his show admits that, on the whole, 'we don't know shit' about audiences (ibid.: 115).

Gary Whannel also points out that despite the amount of time invested in controlling media visibility, there is a point where media events build up a momentum of their own. At such points, the celebrity industry too becomes an onlooker, as what he calls 'the vortex of publicity' exceeds the capacity of the economy of production:

> The growth in the range of media outlets, and the vastly increased speed of circulation of information have combined to create a phenomenon of a 'vortex' effect, which I term here 'vortextuality'. The various media constantly feed off each other and, in an era of electronic and digital information exchange, the speed at which this happens can be very rapid. Certain major super-events come to dominate the headlines to such an extent that it becomes temporarily difficult for columnists or commentators to discuss anything else. (2002: 206)

The instance he cites is of course the death of Princess Diana, which created a, 'short-term compression of the media agenda in which other topics either disappear or have to be connected to the vortextual event' (ibid.: 206).

Given the conflict of interests structured into the industry, the gaps in its understanding of the context in which it is operating and the capacity for media coverage to become an event with a momentum of its own, it is not surprising that there are certain limits to the power of the celebrity industry. At times there is little it can do to extricate itself from a situation, or to determine how it will play out. When that happens, the same media who have grudgingly honoured their deals with the devil of PR are only too happy to write a feature for the *Los Angeles Times* or the *Guardian* about the operation of 'spin' and its threat to the public's right to know.

Notes

1. Richard Dyer's *Heavenly Bodies* (1986) provides us with three case studies of stars who rebelled against their commodification and whose personal lives were forfeited as a result of their loss of control over the circulation and definition of their image.
2. As David Giles (2001) points out in relation to the music press, the magazine's readers' 'loyalty lies less with the publication than with a single band or artist', and so the music journalist's relationship with the stars is 'permanently on a knife-edge' p. 137.
3. It is hard to find a category, too, for more diverse and obscure activities, such as the celebrity tracking services (for $3000 a year you can receive tracking reports on your favourite celebrity's whereabouts), the directories of personal image consultants marketed to everyday people as well as to celebrities, celebrity look-alike agencies, and the new career category of 'celebrity assistants'.

References

Conboy, M. (2002) *The Press and Popular Culture*, London: Sage.

De Cordova, R. (1990) *Picture Personalities: The Emergence of the Star System in America*, Urbana and Chicago: University of Illinois Press.

Dyer, R. (1986) *Heavenly Bodies: Film Stars and Society*, London: BFI Macmillan.

Gabler, N. (1995) *Walter Winchell: Gossip, Power and the Culture of Celebrity*, London: Picador.

Gamson, J. (1994) *Claims to Fame: Celebrity in Contemporary America*, Berkeley, California: University of California Press.

Giles, D. (2000) *Illusions of Immortality: A Psychology of Fame and Celebrity*, London: Macmillan.

Herman, E.S. and McChesney, R.W. (1997) *The Global Media: The New Missionaries of Corporate Capitalism*, London and Washington: Cassell.

King, B. (1991) 'Articulating Stardom' in C. Gledhill (ed.) *Stardom: Industry of Desire*, London and New York: Routledge, pp. 167–182.

Klein, N. (2001) *No Logo*, London: Flamingo.

Marshall, P.D. (1997) *Celebrity and Power: Fame in Contemporary Culture*, Minneapolis and London: University of Minnesota Press.

McDonald, M.G. and Andrews, D.L. (2001) 'Michael Jordan: Corporate Sport and Postmodern Celebrityhood' in D.L. Andrews and S.J. Jackson (eds) *Sports Stars: The Cultural Politics of Sporting Celebrity*, London and New York: Routledge, pp. 20–35.

McDonald, P. (2000) *The Star System: Hollywood's Production of Popular Identities*, London: Wallflower.

Moran, J. (2000) *Star Authors: Literary Celebrity in America*, London: Pluto Press.

Rein, I., Kotler, P. and Stoller, M. (1997) *High Visibility: The Making and Marketing of Professionals into Celebrities*, Lincolnwood, Ill: NTC Business Books.

Rowe, D. (1995) *Popular Cultures: Rock Music, Sport and the Politics of Pleasure*, London: Sage.

Turner, G., Bonner, F. and Marshall, P.D. (2000) *Fame Games: The Production of Celebrity in Australia*, Melbourne: Cambridge University Press.

Weinstein, D. (1999) 'Art Versus Commerce: Deconstructing a (Useful) Romantic Illusion' in K. Kelly and E. McDonnell (eds) *Stars Don't Stand Still in the Sky: Music and Myth*, London: Routledge, pp. 56–71.

Whannel, G. (2002) *Media Sports Stars: Masculinities and Moralities*, London and New York: Routledge.

17

Sharon Stone in a Gap Turtleneck

Rebecca L. Epstein

> *To be indiscriminate, haphazardly thrown together, trapped in the current "hip" uniform is the affliction of a modern Hollywood in search of its style.*
>
> (Patty Fox, *Star Style: Hollywood Legends as Fashion Icons*, 1995)[1]

In 1978, Charles Eckert's "The Carole Lombard in Macy's Window" revealed the birth of the interaction among Hollywood, merchandising, and American women's consumer practices. With an especially keen eye toward correlating clothing manufacturing with studios' cinematic and promotional productions, Eckert saw film audiences in the first half of this century, and women in particular, as psychologically manipulated into consumerism through the fantasies of film. The showcasing of products in films and "star endorsement" selling techniques, according to Eckert, both cultivated and exploited an emotional materialism based on a dream world of Hollywood narratives and American consumerist ideology and identity.[2]

Given major transformations of the Hollywood studio system, the fashion industry, and American consumer culture since the 1940s, how do we assess the relationship between film audiences and successful actresses relative to popular fashion in the late 1990s? Integral to the history of the public consumption of celebrity-associated products has been the merchandising of female film star "looks"; Joan Crawford's square-shouldered suits and Marilyn Monroe's hourglass glitter matched in fashion popularity Audrey Hepburn's streamlined feminine elegance and Diane Keaton's masculine and millinery frump. But I believe that recent decades have reversed the roles of the Hollywood film actress (as clothing style arbiter) and the female movie spectator (as clothing style consumer). Although certain costumes within films may still inspire female fashions (such as the fad embrace of leg warmers and ripped sweatshirts following the release of *Flashdance* in 1983), Keaton, in fact, with her "Annie Hall" look, appears to have been the last in a line of Hollywood actresses whose eponymous on- and offscreen style filtered down into the mass marketplace. (Indeed, a 1996 issue of *W*, a high-gloss, high-fashion magazine, indicated this stall in Hollywood stars' ability to influence dress styles when, in an article on the impact of Hollywood film on popular fashion, the most current example was that of Keaton.) So why, given a history of connections between the American film and fashion industries, is an actress most famous for her clothing in the 1970s considered the last star who, "with a combination of personal style and great design," could "send an audience straight from the cinema to the store"?[3]

This essay examines what I believe is the decreasing location of movie audiences as *consumers* of celebrity fashion and their increasing place as *critics* of celebrities' fashion "taste." This change, I argue, repositions the popular actress from a dictator of fashion trends to a consumer of the public's "wears." Ultimately, the most acute evidence of this thesis lies in popular critiques of celebrity fashions: from best- and worst-dressed lists to the fashion reporting in supermarket tabloids to the copious celebrity costume coverage at film-industry-related awards shows. Here, female film stars are the target of my investigation due to the persistent commodification of fashion as a feminine interest and the ideological embeddedness in American Culture of women, more than men, as objects of display. And because I seek an understanding of a present moment in American culture through a range of phenomena, this chapter begins with a historical overview followed by a contemporary analysis. In this way I aim to reveal an evolving continuum of intersections of the film and fashion industries through their most visible link: the fashionable Hollywood female star.

Dressing the scene: Film fashion icons from Swanson to Keaton

The relationship of American film to fashion vis-à-vis consumerism goes back to Hollywood's silent era. Cecil B. DeMille, director of films renowned for their material excesses (including the first filmed shopping spree) also introduced audiences to Gloria Swanson, his "clothes horse" diva, whose luxurious costumes brought the conspicuous consumption of fashion into filmgoers' view. Known for her elongating, draped column dress styles to give the illusion of height to her four foot, eleven inch frame, Swanson's glamour on screen playing society woman roles translated to her offscreen persona. Indeed, her stardom was in part both created and strengthened by public knowledge of the actress's own unique and abundant wardrobe.[4] Swanson's and other silent stars' visual appeal was only forwarded by the period's fan magazines, which, as Mary Ann Doane has noted, "linked female obsession with stars, glamour, gossip and fashion."[5] More pointedly, the film frame in this period became, according to Doane, a "Bazinian window to the world" in which objects were fetishized and femininity becomes entwined with conspicuous consumption and decoration. In 1932, Mae West then stepped into Swanson's showcase and became one of the next major film fashion idols with the release of *Night after Night*. Already a success on the stage, West's formidable full figure and wry, ribald performance style greatly contrasted with the delicacy of Swanson's body and character type, yet she too gained much renown for displaying herself in opulent dress; her (ultimately controversial) sex appeal sparkled eminently from her signature beaded, form-fitting gowns.[6]

Both Swanson and West styled themselves, codifying their public images through their personal wardrobe tastes. However, with the bloom of the studio system in the 1930s and the flowering in kind of sound and studio wardrobe departments, the female film star relative to her fashion image underwent its first major shift. Now, instead of actresses supplying their own costumes as they had often during the silent era, studios began "fashioning" their stars, dressing them to suit the cinematic spectacles of what became the "Golden Age" of Hollywood.[7] Professional costume designers now outfitted actresses to project glamour and feminine material indulgence while, across the lot, in-house publicity machines actively promoted potential shining stars. Although the majority of Hollywood film actresses during this period swam in an imposed sartorial sea of satin and organza, a few did emerge to proffer distinctive "looks" on- and offscreen. Most notably: reclusive Greta Garbo became known for her figure-concealing high necklines and face-shielding hats; sexually mysterious Marlene Dietrich found fame with her gam-glorifying skirts as well as her masculine shirt-pant ensembles; and Joan Crawford brought square-shouldered styles to the fashion front with the help of Gilbert Adrian, MGM's chief costume designer, who "materialized" Crawford's typically arch characters and persona through sharp, shaped suits.[8]

[. . .]

The confluence of cultural and economic forces shaping the relationship of film costume and popular fashion trends during Hollywood's Golden Age is the story, as Eckert has asserted, of studio marketing techniques exploiting consumer and social practices through the cultural embrace of film. Most notably, "cinema shops" in department stores, the increasing employment of film stars in advertisements for personal products, and the continued glamorization of stars and their lives through fan magazines and gossip in national presses kept Hollywood actresses and their apparel in full view, tempting consumers to emulate stars' manufactured style.

[. . .]

With the end of the war came new phases on the film, fashion, and culture fronts. In particular, 1947 marked the beginning of the decline of the studio system enabled by corporate divestiture and the infiltration of television into the mass sphere, Christian Dior's attempt at revitalizing the Parisian fashion trade through his wasp-waist "New Look" for women, and the movement in the United States toward subur-banization. Combined, these factors set the looks of film stars who fashioned the 1950s. Doris Day, for instance, and her wholesome, milky-white complexion and girl-next-door characters sprang to life on the screen with the help of a full skirt and fully enhanced (but also *fully covered*) bosom inspired by Dior's choice silhouette.

In the early 1960s, however new fashion icons began challenging the reign of studio imperialism over star fashion successes. The burgeoning youth culture proved an especially formidable fashion force, changing the face of popular taste through the fine and performing arts. In addition, celebrity discourse became laden with greater complexity and irony. Twiggy, a stick-thin teenage English model, and Jackie Kennedy, America's first lady, were only two women in this "style-obsessed era" who claimed status as fashion icons without Hollywood's help.[9] And yet, with actress Audrey Hepburn, Hollywood contributed to the climate as well, offering up what became one of its most enduring images of female fashionability. Hepburn began achieving recognition as a film actress in the 1950s, but her costuming, which combined gamine, tomboy charm with understated elegance, created a "look" that carried into the following decade and "figured" even more in the future. Elizabeth Wilson has noted that Hepburn, due to her working relationship with Paris couture designer Hubert de Givenchy, assisted the bringing of haute couture to the masses. To be sure, the combination of mobility, simplicity, and respectable pedigree that Givenchy's minimalist clothes, in addition to Hepburn's sprightly roles, afforded the actress was integral to her look's successful embrace and replication by the public.[10]

Following Hepburn, the field of new and enduring film fashion plates remained barren for more than ten years, until Diane Keaton appeared in 1977 as Annie Hall in the film of the same name. Keaton came, however, after an important occurrence in cinema-inspired style when, in 1967, Theadora Van Runkle's costume designs for *Bonnie and Clyde* caused an explosion of 1930s retro styles in women's popular fashion.[11] Faye Dunaway received praise as the fabulously fashioned "Bonnie" in long, flared "midi" skirts (which noticeably contrasted with the contemporaneous miniskirt craze), but it is crtical to note that in each of her follow-up roles, the actress wore differently styled habiliments that failed to set any major fashion trends. Dunaway in *Bonnie and Clyde*, then, marked an important shift from actress-based to character-based influences on popular female fashion. "Whereas previous film-inspired fashions tended to conflate the actress's personal style with her many characters' dress, now famously copied "looks" were being generated by an isolated character; in this case, the public's wardrobe emulation was of "Bonnie," not Faye. So when Keaton's renowned "Annie Hall look" of loose-fitting menswear and brow-skimming hats skyrocketed in 1970s fashion consciousness, although in part reminiscent of the Golden Age-styled successes as well as the feminist strides of slacks-wearing Dietrich and both Hepburns, Keaton's look *was not* the product and marketing tool of a film studio. In addition, it *was* named for her character. And this despite the public's knowledge that Keaton's was a primarily autobiographical performance in a role opposite the film's author and her former paramour, Woody Allen.[12] Because Keaton (who over time has deviated little from her desexualized layering for either on- or offscreen appearances) is the last film actress to effect an enduring signature look, how do we assess this move from actress-based to character-based fashion trends? Moreover, what is the role of the film star as possible fashion icon in the 1990s, and how does her audience receive and define her attempts, if any, at her own "look"?

The changing room: The 1960s and celebrity style chaos

[. . .]

As Valerie Carnes has noted, 1960 marked the beginning of the reign of new fashion icons who embodied a "pop iconology of youth, kinkiness and fun."[13] In the interest of "sheer surface shimmer," fashion and other popular presses and entertainment media showcased "real girls, Swingers, Gamines, Ingenues, Kooks, Chicerinos, Littlegirls, JetSetters, SurferChicks, Hippie Girls, Beautiful Creatures, Free Souls . . . all impeccably packaged, pretty, kinky, kooky, and young."[14] Up to this time, fashion style choice typically signified the wearer's socioeconomic class. Now, however, popular dress also widely codified diverse "lifestyles" and indicated the wearer's sociopolitical values. A generation of young designers from England who benefited from their country's postwar push of secondary education included former art students such as Mary Quant, who turned fashion into a symbol of an internationally rebellious youth culture.[15] Significantly, Quant's own critical success with her geometrical and girlish designs at lower than couture prices also reflected the attention of the international world of fashion as it moved away from the wealthy and elite consumer and toward the middle-income fashion follower.

[...]

In this environment, professional fashion models, too, were becoming style setters, inserted into popular culture through the magazine trade and the work of "reality-based" photographers such as William Klein, who took fashion shoots out of the studio and into the urban scene. Red-haired model Suzy Parker had gained national prominence and envy in the 1950s, but the media and artistic hyperexposure of models such as Twiggy, Jean Shrimpton, and Cheryl Tiegs increased both the visibility and the respectability of fashion models as dress personalities.[16]

By 1969, the decade's changed social sensibilities had been fully incorporated into the fashion trade. With mass clothing production at new heights and "radical chic" altering dress styles of the American public, designers such as American Calvin Klein were turning "street fashions," mostly dominated by denim into a best-selling craze. In 1973, the Levi-Strauss Company even received a citation calling its blue jeans the single most important contribution to worldwide fashion.[17] Haute couture was responding to this "bottom-up" trend (if you will) by succumbing to a largely pret-a-porter industry; Pierre Cardin, Courrèges, Gucci, Pucci, and Hermes were some of the designers in the United States and abroad creating ready-to-wear, more practical styles for active, if moneyed, women. In addition, many American couturiers were realizing how to compete with the Parisian trade—as celebrities of their own creation(s). "Big personality" designers such as Bill Blass and Oscar de la Renta now actively effected their own name fame, ingratiating themselves and their designs with wealthy clients before inundating mass-marketing and merchandising outlets with apparel bearing their "designer" logos and signatures.[18] Middle-class women who once followed fashion through film stars were now looking for "looks" from a down-scaling fashion industry, "branding" themselves with clothing from self-promoting designers hoping to tap a large middle-income demographic.

[...]

In a 1970 interview, Edith Head, once chief costume designer for Paramount Studios and by this time a winner of seven Academy Awards for her work, perceived a major difference between young female stars of the late sixties and early seventies and their forebears. Most notable was the younger women's failure to affect "trademark" fashion or unique, personal style. Unlike Mae West or Joan Crawford, who "established something which was a definite person," contemporary actresses (such as Jane Fonda, Ali MacGraw, and Katharine Ross) were no longer "clotheshorses, they don't depend on the glamour image." According to Head, the signature star look was giving way to the paradoxically conformist nonconformism of "doing one's own thing as part of the Now scene." Head characterized these women as distancing themselves from the privileges of personal designers and glamorous Hollywood personas, which contrasted with the "plain modern pictures" studios were churning out and the counter-cultural age of which these women were a part. Theirs was an "anti star image, anti glamour, anti the whole fantasy of early Hollywood." Head bemoaned "the new look, an image of now," in an era of budget cutting and reorganized studios in which "wardrobe people will go out and buy a dress or suit instead of having it tailor made. It is another generation of thinking...and I hate it." Asked if these young stars were at all influencing the public's fashion sense or style, Head answered emphatically, "No. They like to be amusing ... and do whatever is the current fad."[19]

What do you think? Popular critiques of celebrity fashion

Head's comments indicate that by the late 1960s, actresses were giving up their roles as style arbiters, tempering their "elite" status as stars due to industrial and cultural concerns. Meanwhile, journalists also were actively biting at Hollywood fashion pretension. Significantly, the 1960s marked the beginnings of tabloid newspapers such as the *National Enquirer* and the *Star*; part idol makers, part idol breakers, theirs was a "new kind of celebrity reporting" originating in Eugenia Sheppard's gossip column in the *New York Herald Tribune* and "perfected," in fact, by the writers of the fashion trade magazine *Women's Wear Daily*. As Banner notes, this journalism combined "insouciance with a willingness to shock" and was increasingly iconoclastic in its exposure of the good, the bad, and the ugly of public personalities in a consumer culture. Included in the reporting was attention to celebrities' dress:

> **Fashion now emerged as a significant variable in celebrity reporting. Not only were the personal doings of designers deemed newsworthy, but a designer attribution was also given to dresses worn to parties and other social events. The attribution functioned as a validation for women's taste, but it also served as an advertisement for the importance of consumerism in their lives.[20]**

Most illustrative of this burgeoning criticism of stars' styles, in 1960 Richard Blackwell, a moderately successful American couturier, began writing an annual, nationally syndicated column listing the best- and worst-dressed women of Hollywood. Fully expecting "'The List' to last a season at the very most," Blackwell's exposure of screen stars' refined but also tacky taste found an amazed but amused audience, whom Blackwell believed to be "people relieved that someone had the nerve to say out loud what, in truth, they had been thinking for years."[21]

Blackwell's column was, in fact, the latest entry in a history of celebrity fashion critiques. The practice extends back to the nineteenth century, when European theater critics catering to the elite would comment on both the performances and the performers' costumes. By the 1920s, published fashion critiques took on a different form when a group of Parisian designers started a "best-dressed list" for which they polled only each other to decide the "most elegant" among their clients, most of whom were royalty, society women, and women working in the fashion industry. This annual list was published internationally in news-papers. The *New York Times*, in an effort to defuse charges of elitism, assured its readers that the women on the list "must do more than invest the sum of $50,000 with the Paris dressmaking trade. She must have brains, poise and vivacity."[22] The list was adopted by American couturiers in 1940 after the war temporarily halted the Paris industry, followed by fashion publicist Eleanore

Lambert, who created a list based on ballots cast by a range of celebrities, fashion editors, and designers. Regardless of the judges, however, the list tended to include the same women each year, and in 1959 it was finally retired due to its predictability and tedium. *Women's Wear Daily*, revamped in 1960 from a trade paper to a "gossipy, opinionated, often vicious but always readable source of [fashion] information," carved the next niche for rating celebrity style. The newly arrogant publication, under the direction of publishing scion John Fairchild, had become, in fact, "a kind of society gossip sheet" especially renowned for employing superlative categories to adulate rich people considered to be "in" (the "Impeccables," the "Goddesses," the "Cat Pack").[23]

That same year, when Blackwell began offering his opinions and self-proclaimed expertise in a nationally syndicated newspaper column by adding a "worst-dressed" component to a "best-dressed" list, however, he effectively changed the look of looking at "looks." In fact, Blackwell's "best" list has held decreasing interest for followers as the author has become famous for his annual gibes at the public figures he believes should "know" how to dress well. "The List has always stressed celebrities," Blackwell asserts, "because these people have no excuse."[24] Assuming that moneyed people have access to "the best of everything," Blackwell uses his worst-dressed list to argue that if his subjects do not know the trappings of "good taste," they should heed the advice of someone who does. For Blackwell, that authority is himself—and, by implication, his column's readers.

Blackwell's first celebrity fashion critiques, written to "comment on current trends, poke fun at pomposity, ridicule arrogance, and point the finger at the ones who deserve it most," came when film audiences were beginning to feel the effects of the Hollywood studio system's being restructured in the wake of television and a changing leisure landscape.[25] The elimination of in-house costumers and the bulk of Golden Age star-making apparatuses seemed as never before to turn the success of a star over to his or her audience. Indeed, the recognition that both celebrity journalism and audience preferences could "make" a star more than studio publicity departments may have also led audiences to sense their entitlement to "make over" the stars in the audiences' own desired images. With Hollywood in search of a new identity, a major generational and social rebellion at hand, and the "domestication" of film stars as many began appearing in television programs and made-for-TV movies, actresses were no longer in a position to dictate the day's popular fashions.

So, as television came to stem the film industry in the 1950s and early 1960s, and with women's time, in particular, allotted to activities around the home, there came a relationship between viewers and their small-screen stars that was different from that between viewers and big-screen stars.

[. . .]

Moreover, the audience embrace of television performers' appearance, just as it evolved with film stars, is directed toward the characters, not the actors; when Jennifer Aniston, playing the part of "Rachel" on the highly watched mid-1990s NBC sitcom *Friends*, launched a revolution in soft coiffures, her hairstyle was requested in salons and referred to across the country as the "Rachel," not the "Jennifer."

Film studio costume designers' roles as image makers also began to fade as television grew in appeal and acceptance. No longer the leading entertainment industry, film studios folded their expensive wardrobe departments and producers began hiring freelance costumers. Today, these "stylists" work in television studios as well, and they are acknowledged in popular magazines and awards ceremonies as the Svengalis of both film and television stars, despite their regular reliance on off-the-rack, store-bought clothing. Ultimately, the public recognition of stylists' skills, coupled with the accessible, mass-market items they employ, results in an absence of actresses conveying a uniquely personal, let alone persona*lized*, style.

[…]

Help me with this, will you? The star-designer relationship

The question as to whether we will ever have another style setter "like a Joan Crawford" is provoked by changes in the film, fashion, and entertainment industries, as well as celebrity exposure. After all, how many of today's films' fans know the names of *any* of the *many* stylists who dress their favorite stars? In great contrast to earlier periods in film costume history, when Adrian and Head, along with studio-era costumers Travis Banton, Orry-Kelly, Walter Plunkett, and Irene Sharaff were renowned for their talents of the eye as well as needle and thread, more recent audiences are likely to know a costume's name only when a noted fashion designer crosses industries, bringing patterns and pinking shears to designing dress for film. Such designers' moments have included Giorgio Armani for *American Gigolo* (1980) and *Sabrina* (1995) and Jean-Paul Gaultier for *The Cook, the Thief, His Wife & Her Lover* (1989), *City of Lost Children* (1995), and *The Fifth Element* (1997).

The integration of couture with popular cinema was, in fact, attempted in 1931 when Gloria Swanson brought Coco Chanel to Hollywood to infuse films with Chanel's classic cuts. But the difference in designing for film (film costume must be of a color, pattern, and shape that "read" well, and several versions must exist to suit different camera angles), coupled with Swanson's temper, sent Chanel back a year later to Paris, where her talents were more readily welcomed and displayed. The couture gap was not bridged again until Givenchy began designing for Audrey Hepburn—the two names becoming inseparable. The recent employment of couture designers as costume designers, however, has failed to revitalize glamour on the screen. This may be due in part to the public recognition of fashion designers as celebrities and, in turn, the de-exoticizing of design styles prior to their reaching the big screen. A 1995 attempt to "bring back" Hollywood glamour in film demonstrated the significance of fashion's overfamiliarity. For a remake of *Sabrina* (1954), originally starring Audrey Hepburn in costumes by Edith Head and Givenchy, Julia Ormond, an actress with a few disparate roles behind her, played the lead role in dresses by the widely known Armani. Without a predetermined sense on the part of the audience of Ormond and Armani as an image-making team, the two had separate impacts on the film, the vivacity of the costumes distinct from the performance of the actress. Both Ormond and Armani had been successful in their respective but increasingly intercompetitive industries, but their combination in this effort proved disorienting and overly contrived. In fact, with all the hype surrounding the remake's ambitions, a feared result occurred: irrespective of the film's other deficiencies, all the attention to and expectations of the costumes led the clothes to overshadow, or "wear," the character. As Gaines has asserted, "[Golden Age] star designing effects the synthesis between character and actress." But here, such a synthesis failed to take place; Armani's eagerly anticipated costumes bore no relation to Ormond's prior fashion image (such as it was), nor did they harmonize her with her character.[26]

Rather than costuming actresses for their craft, in the 1990s designers have formed relationships with stars relative to stars' public—rather than screen—appearances. Nowhere is this more apparent than at the Academy Awards ("The Oscars of Fashion," wrote one journalist),[27] where the details of which actress is wearing what designer give a nod to both the star and the name on the label she wears. And with each new awards show on the circuit comes more discussion of celebrities' fashions—and a heightened risk of their donning duplicate gowns.[28] Significantly, this "embarrassing" result of clothing design massification and designer worship has led to a simultaneous swing back to custom costume days: with designers and stars crowding the same spotlight, many seek press distinction by working in "exclusive" relationships.

[...]

Au courant: Sharon Stone in a gap turtleneck

In 1996, Sharon Stone, an "A list" Hollywood actress who came to fame through what she was wearing (or, perhaps more to point, the underwear she was not wearing) in *Basic Instinct* (1992), waltzed down Oscar's red carpet in a black ensemble. Upon being asked, Stone announced to the world that her apparel for the evening, despite her having her choice among several designer gowns, was thrown together at the last minute from items she already had in her closet. Her jacket was Armani, her skirt "old," and her black mock turtleneck, she said with a smile, was from the midpriced international chain store the Gap.

Stone's self-proclaimed love of high fashion and her recognition as an "A-list" movie star have kept her on the public catwalk since her notorious appearance in *Basic Instinct*. Indeed, Stone has not only appeared in product advertisements, like many of her celebrity cohorts, but she has also appeared on runways as a model in top designers' haute couture shows.[29] Stone, although typically brazen and firm with the press, is adulated and admired by the tabloids' fashion journalists, arguably the most difficult media makers to please. She is, in fact, consistently praised in tabloid fashion spreads— her Gap turtleneck appearance was one of her many moments of scandal-sheet splendor. Combining the simple elegance of Audrey Hepburn and the assertive attitude of Mae West and Madonna, Stone's aesthetic and personal style have translated well to the mass movie and merchandise market-place. Using fashion to her advantage, Stone has negotiated the tensions of late-nineties Hollywood female stardom: irrespective of her movies and the roles she plays in them, she remains in public discourse simultaneously glamorous, precious, attractive, practical, and tough. That she is celebrated for her taste in clothing, adoring couture but still daring to wear an item so completely geographically, economically, and aesthetically accessible (and Gap scrambled to fill stores with the past-season item following her wearing of it), bears testimony to the skewed paradigm of the contemporary fashionable female film star. Stone is popular not necessarily because of her acting ability, but because she is as much a model for a fashionable film star as she is a film star fashion model. As a result, *W* unabashedly pronounced her "Sharon Stone: Fashion Icon," her sometimes diminished presence on the silver screen balanced by her increased appearance in couture apparel on both designers' and public show runways. Not since Madonna has an actress from the late twentieth century achieved such consistent attention to her dress, her wardrobe profoundly capturing and endearing her to her audience.[30]

Stone, like her contemporary screen sisters, dons numerous designers' fashions. One designer she has particularly favored over the past few years, however, is Vera Wang. Wang, an Asian American designer, worked behind the scenes for *Vogue* for eighteen years before opening a shop to sell her own dress designs. Interestingly, Wang's public recognition prior to that her film celebrity clientele provided was through her bridal gowns and, most famously, her costumes for figure skater Nancy Kerrigan, the 1994 Olympic Silver Medalist. All eyes were on Kerrigan, and, naturally, what she wore, when she competed while recovering from an assault in which her U.S. Olympics teammate Tonya Harding had been implicated. So it was through an internationally televised ice show, a sport of spectacle for mass, primarily female, audiences and defined in the United States by middle-income participants, that Wang found herself catapulted into the conversation of mainstreamed high fashion. Suiting Morin's composite, Wang's dresses are beloved for their lack of ostentation despite luxurious fabrics and figure-refined forms, and actresses show up at functions in Wang designs both custom and non.[31] After the sixties' and seventies' bottom-up "radical chic" and eighties' top-down "excessory chic," the look of the nineties is "simple chic," and Wang's clothes "fit" perfectly.[32] Wang has been so popular with the public that she was named "1996 Designer of the Year" on E! network's *Joan Rivers' Fashion Review*. She was also the "Oscar fashion correspondent" in 1997 for the syndicated television celebrity news show *Entertainment Tonight*.

It's a wrap: How to "look" now

During the 1950s, Edith Head was one of several "experts" on fashion who dispensed everyday dressing advice to average American women. In addition to her film work, she published several books and hosted a radio show to "prescribe" solutions for common figure flaws and dressing woes, often invoking the names of actresses she had dressed with similar figure and style problems. The promise was to increase women's knowledge of how to create their own signature "look" on par with their favorite, and allegedly equally imperfect, actresses.

[...]

Since then, an array of media have offered the masses advice on how to dress and how to *judge* Hollywood actresses relative to popular fashion. Leisure "sights"—film, television, music video, print publications, and fashion runways—have allowed popular fashion to evolve simultaneously from many different sources. The results are innumerable available looks, suited for different lifestyles, economic means, and body types. Indeed, when *In Style*, an offshoot of *People Weekly* covering "Celebrity + Beauty + Lifestyle + Fashion," ran a cover in October 1996 that asked, "Who's got the look?"

the mystery was solved through a feature-by-feature list of the "best" physical attributes and clothing items of different film actresses. The breakdown of woman-centered commodities in the 1940s films of which Doane has spoken finds its contemporary placement in the fissuring instruction of how to look now, the piece-by-piece puzzling and purchasing of the best look for "the everywoman." That Elizabeth Hurley, a model attempting a film career, sat as the *In Style* issue's cover model (and did again for a special issue called "The Look" in fall 1999) further illustrates a late-1990s symbiosis of the American popular film and fashion industries.

Similarly, the redefinition of popular looks as being designer—not star—induced allows *In Style* to group celebrities according to what they are wearing: Halle Berry in the Missoni look; Gwyneth Paltrow in the Gucci look; Angela Bassett in the Escada look. Just as Christian Dior leapt to fame with his New Look in 1947, designers are being revealed in public consciousness as having "looks" of their own—styles ultimately brought to the public eye through their various celebrity clients. Thus emulators copy the designer's look, not that of the actress. As I have shown, this trajectory of film-actress-based to film-character-based, and then film-character-based to film-audience-based fashion trends derives from a complex network of cultural influences. Any signature "look" of an actress has become the celebrated "look" of a fashion designer or, just as likely, the "look" the audience "looks upon" as appropriate.[33]

The contemporary moment is one eager for Hollywood glamour but wary of its worth. Sharon Stone's applause for simplicity speaks to a delicate balance: to be praised, female film stars' manner of dress must meet certain criteria of aesthetic beauty and glitz while still suggesting an eye toward economy. Stone might have been even more materially familiar by wearing a T-shirt and leggings to the Oscars, but she would have then disappointed celebrity watchers such as Blackwell, who still seek a hint of Morin's "exquisite extravagance." In this way, Stone personifies how the role of the costume designer in manufacturing a "star image" has been subsumed by the fashion industry, mass merchandising, and the leveling of style through the "cheap copy." And in this as well we can contextualize Patty Fox's statement that opens this chapter. What *is* the popular look of Hollywood actresses today? By analyzing contemporary representations of popular actresses in popular discourse, the phenomenon of "reinvention," the migration between movie actress and runway model, and actress-related clothing merchandising for mass—often lower economic—markets, my reading of "Mr. Blackwell's Worst-Dressed List" and other modern celebrity fashion critiques reveals a complex but certain evolution in signature star styling. Indeed, if nothing else, the superior amount of media coverage of actresses' dress at each year's Academy Awards ceremony—from network and cable television shows to the popular press—suggests the relevance of reexamining Eckert's model of the film star "fashioned" for her mainstream audience; in other words, how the success of the Carole Lombard in Macy's window gave way to the public's delight in Sharon Stone in a Gap turtleneck.

Notes

I am grateful to Peter Wollen, Chon Noriega, Lyn Delliquadri, Irwin Epstein, Susan Reinhardt, and David Desser for their incomparable support of this project.

1. Patty Fox, *Star Style: Hollywood Legends as Fashion Icons* (Santa Monica, Calif.: Angel City, 1995), vii.
2. Charles Eckert, "The Carole Lombard in Macy's Window," *Quarterly Review of Film Studies* 3, no. 1 (1978): 1–23.
3. Janet Ozzard, "Fashion Flashback: Both On and Off the Screen Hollywood's Celebrities Often Set the Style," *W*, May 1996, n.p.
4. For more on Swanson's wardrobe, see Fox, *Star Style*, 10–19.
5. Mary Ann Doane, *The Desire to Desire: The Woman's Film of the 1940s* (Bloomington: Indiana University Press, 1987), 26.
6. Claudia Roth Pierpont, "The Strong Woman," *New Yorker*, 11 November 1996, 106ff.
7. For more on costuming during this era and shifts into the next, see Jane Gaines, "Costume and Narrative: How Dress Tells the Woman's Story," in *Fabrications: Costume and the Female Body*, ed. Jane Gaines and Charlotte Herzog (New York: Routledge, 1990), 180–228.
8. For more on each of these stars, see Fox, *Star Style*. Also, photographer and journalist Cecil Beaton, who was romantically involved with Garbo, offers a charming account of her dressing style sense in Cecil Beaton, *The Glass of Fashion* (Garden City, N.Y.: Doubleday, 1954), 235–39.
9. Valerie Carnes, "Icons of Popular Fashion," in *Icons of America*, ed. Ray B. Browne and Marshall Fishwick (Bowling Green, Ohio: Popular Press, 1978), 231.
10. Elizabeth Wilson, "Audrey Hepburn: Fashion, Film and the 50s," in *Women and Film: A Sight and Sound Reader*, ed. Pam Cook and Philip Dodd (Philadelphia: Temple University Press, 1993), 40.
11. Brigid Keenan, *The Women We Wanted to Look Like* (London: Macmillan, 1977), 88; Alan Cartnal, "Bonnie, Clyde Style Creator Concentrates on Elegant Look," *Los Angeles Times*, 1 April 1970, 4.
12. See Rex Reed, *Travolta to Keaton* (New York: William Morrow, 1979), 217–22.
13. Carnes, "Icons of Popular Fashion," 229.
14. Ibid., 231.
15. For an overview of 1960s fashion, including Quant, see Nicholas Drake, ed., *The Sixties: A Decade in Vogue* (Englewood Cliffs, N.J.: Prentice Hall, 1988).
16. Lois W. Banner, *American Beauty* (New York: Alfred A. Knopf, 1983), 287.
17. Carnes, "Icons of Popular Fashion," 236. Levi-Strauss also won a Coty American Fashion Critics Award in 1971 for similar reasons. "Fashion Critics Honor Levis," *Los Angeles Times*, 17 June 1971, sec. IV, p. 20.
18. Banner, *American Beauty*, 287.
19. Interview with Edith Head in Mike Steen, *Hollywood Speaks: An Oral History* (New York: G. P. Putnam's Sons, 1974), 247–58.
20. Banner, *American Beauty*, 289.
21. Mr. Blackwell and Vernon Patterson, *Mr. Blackwell's Worst: 30 Years of Fashion Fiascoes* (New York: Pharos, 1991), 3.
22. Keenan, *The Women We Wanted to Look Like*, 11.
23. Sandra Ley, *Fashion for Everyone: The Story of Ready-to-Wear, 1870's–1970's* (New York: Charles Scribner's Sons, 1975), 140–41; Keenan, *The Women We Wanted to Look Like*, 22.
24. Blackwell and Patterson, *30 Years of Fashion Fiascoes*, 4.

25. Blackwell and Patterson, *30 Years of Fashion Fiascoes*, 5.

26. Gaines, "Costume and Narrative," 200.

27. Rebecca Mead, "Don't Hate Them Because They're Beautiful," *New York*, 22 July 1996, 24.

28. "Multiplicity: With So Many Stars Showing Up at So Many Events, Designers Can't Help but Send in the Clones," *People Weekly*, 16 September 1996, 180–85.

29. Louise Farr, "Stone's Clothes Call: She May Be Dying at the Box Office but She Sure Looks Great," *W*, February 1997, 60. On the "humanizing" of couture through the employment of movie stars as models, see Ginsburg and Lockwood, "You Oughta Be in Pictures," 59.

30. Kenneth Battelle, who styled Babe Paley, Jacqueline Onassis, and Marilyn Monroe, was prompted to comment on Sharon Stone's self-determined ever (costume) changing look, stating, "Her life is a role, I guess." Quoted in Platt, "The Untouchables," 137. See also John Lahr, "The Big Picture: Whether Sharon Stone Wins an Oscar for *Casino* or Not, She Should Win One for the Best Role She's Created So Far—That of Sharon Stone," *New Yorker*, 25 March 1997, 72–78. It should be noted as well that the performance for which Stone has received the most critical praise was in *Casino* (1995), a role that allowed her to wear an array of lavish costumes.

31. See, for instance, "The Look of Vera Wang," *In Style*, November 1996, 46–47.

32. *Excessory chic* is my term; it originates with the profligate use of accessories but also the material excesses of fashion of the 1980s; *Simple chic* comes from *In Style's* "What's Hot Now: Secrets of Style '97" issue, January 1997.

33. At press time, Gwyneth Paltrow's "fashion-ability" appears to be particularly reminiscent of Stone's.

18

Who Owns Celebrity?: Privacy, Publicity and the Legal Regulation of Celebrity Images

Philip Drake

Who owns celebrity? Who has the right to circulate and profit from celebrity images and stories? The aim of this chapter is to explore celebrity through the issue of intellectual property rights. Intellectual property refers to the creations of 'the intellect' that have commercial value. For celebrities this includes copyrighted artistic works but also symbols, names and the use of their images. Here I will focus upon 'image rights': the commercial use of an individual's likeness, voice, name or signature. From the perspective of political economy. I will suggest that the allocation, regulation and economic exploitation of image rights are key areas of analysis in understanding contemporary celebrity.

Celebrity and ownership

At first glance the notion of 'owning' celebrity seems almost paradoxical. How can one own an individual as property? Yet an examination of the contractual agreements between celebrities and media companies reveals that their images are continually bought, licensed, marketed and circulated. Decisions about who 'owns' a particular celebrity asset (such as paparazzi photographs) are made daily by newspaper and magazine editors, and subject to regulation by the law courts. However, in order to consider the idea of celebrity as 'property' not necessarily tied to a particular individual body, it is helpful first to take stock of what we actually mean by the term 'celebrity' itself. P. David Marshall, through the lens of political theory, argues that celebrity is a form of 'rationalization' of the social domain. It 'celebrates the potential of the individual and the mass's support of the individual in mass society' (1997: 43). For Marshall, and for Joshua Gamson (1994) and Graeme Turner et al. (2000), a complex co-dependency develops between celebrities and their publics. Celebrity power depends upon audiences and the media's investment in the status and exceptional nature of celebrity. At the same time, celebrities need to regulate and control the ownership of their images to maintain a monopoly power over themselves as individuated brands.

I want to recast this issue somewhat differently here and suggest that celebrity has certain qualities of what economist's term a 'public good'. A public good is a product that gains value within and by its consumption in the public domain (often termed the 'commons') and hence its full value cannot be calculated by the market. Granted, every day the economic value of celebrities is determined *de facto* by contracts with media companies, however their non-tangible symbolic value is less easily calculated. The value of celebrity is more than the labour of an individual, however talented they might be, but also bound up with the meanings invested in them by audiences. If we accept that the social phenomenon of celebrity is, at least in part, a public good, then balancing the freedom of expression of audiences with the personal rights of celebrities becomes quite properly a socio-political as well as economic and legal matter. As we shall see, analysis of intellectual property rights usefully illuminates the division between the rights of celebrities and their publics. It raises important questions over who should be able to own and appropriate celebrity images and how the rights of public expression are balanced with those of privacy.

Examining celebrity as intellectual property: The rights of privacy and publicity

How then are celebrities defined as 'property' in legal terms? Leaving aside copyright (a right available regardless of fame where an individual claims ownership over a work), we can start by analyzing the regulation of celebrity images through the rights of 'privacy' and 'publicity'. These have a long and contested history and their legislation differs considerably across countries (McCarthy, 1987a; Robertson and Nicol, 2002).

A brief history of these rights reveals a number of assumptions about the nature of celebrity. The 'right of privacy' was introduced in the US through a highly influential article written in 1890 by Samuel Warren and Louis Brandeis, where they defined it as 'the right to be let alone'. It is an individual right designed to defend against personal intrusion and, according to Ruth Gavison (1980), it has three elements: secrecy, anonymity and solitude. Initially it would seem that these three elements of privacy are incompatible with the contemporary nature of celebrity, which depends upon public visibility and media circulation. However, defences in celebrity cases invariably define privacy as an 'unwarranted intrusion' into an individual's private life so as to reconcile this apparent contradiction. This has meant that courts have had to attempt to balance the interests of free speech and newsworthiness against the right of privacy.

A number of recent high-profile cases in the UK have been seen where celebrities have complained of intrusion of privacy by the media, most often from 'kiss-and-tell' tabloid stories or the publishing of photographs taken by freelance paparazzi. Celebrity footballers and pop stars, such as David and Victoria Beckham (known in the British tabloid press as 'Posh and Becks') and members of the British monarchy, have regularly attempted to restrict press intrusion into their personal lives. In the UK the privacy situation seems at first glance to be clearly defined: there is no statute in either English or Scottish law called a Privacy Act. Indeed, not only are there no privacy laws, but publicity or personality rights are not recognised in the UK either. Unlike defamation or copyright, for which there is extensive protection, there exists no specific law whereby a newspaper, for example, can be found guilty of intruding into someone's 'privacy'. However, this has led to a stretching of existing legislation in order to accommodate privacy cases, and some recent attempts to establish the concept in English law courts. The lack of an agreed legal definition of privacy in the UK has meant that attempts to invoke this right have had to formulate a definition, with the Calcutt Committee defining it as 'the right of the individual to be protected against intrusion into his personal life or affairs, or those of his family, by direct physical means or by publication of information' (1990: 7).

Although in the UK there is no general law governing the right of privacy, such cases often try to utilize existing common law. This includes the 1998 Data Protection Act and the 1997 Protection from Harassment Act. But the most significant law is the Law of Confidence, which legislates against breaches in trust or the dissemination of information obtained 'in confidence'. This involves establishing whether the information has a confidential nature, and whether there has been unauthorized use of that information to the detriment of the party involved. Geoffrey Robertson and Andrew Nicol define it as 'protection against the disclosure or use of information that is not publicly known, and that has been entrusted in circumstances imposing an obligation not to disclose that information' (2002: 224). Clearly, such a definition lends itself to cases involving alleged intrusion of celebrity private lives, through media making such events public knowledge. Thus, at the very least, it has the potential to regulate the public/private distinction in celebrity media coverage.

In addition to the law of confidence, other voluntary industry regulatory codes exist in the UK. These include the guidelines laid down by the Press Complaints Commission, which discuss the intrusion of privacy, as well as the European Convention on Human Rights (ECHR) and its induction into English law as the 1998 Human Rights Act. Article 8 of the ECHR states that, 'everyone has the right to respect for his private and family life, his home and his correspondence' (cited in Robertson and Nicol, 2002: 298). Cases invoking this Convention have to balance the right to privacy against the need to protect protection of freedom of expression (defined in Article 10 of the ECHR), two rights which often seem to contradict each other in celebrity cases. As we shall see, unlike the US, case-law in the UK has yet to establish a clear set of precedents for dealing with privacy rights. Recent celebrity cases have thus been viewed as significant in attempting to establish a legal precedent.

Celebrity privacy cases in the UK

Cases claiming intrusion of privacy have attempted to invoke it as a human right under the 1998 Human Rights Act, drawn from the ECHR. This has occurred in several legal battles involving celebrities who seek to prevent newspapers or magazines from publishing material about them. Two cases are particularly interesting: *Douglas and Zeta Jones versus Hello!*, discussed in greater detail below, and *Naomi Campbell versus MGN*, owners of UK tabloid newspaper, the *Mirror*.[1]

On 1st February, 2001 the *Mirror* published a picture of supermodel and sometime novelist, singer and actor Naomi Campbell leaving a Narcotics Anonymous meeting in London. On the front page of the paper between two colour photographs was one with the caption below 'Therapy: Naomi outside Meeting' and another with the headline 'Naomi: I am a drug addict'. The articles that were marked 'exclusive' were broadly sympathetic to Campbell and read,

SUPERMODEL Naomi Campbell is attending Narcotic Anonymous meetings in a courageous bid to beat her addiction to drink and drugs. The 30 year-old has been a regular at counselling

> sessions for three months, often attending twice a day. Dressed in jeans and baseball cap, she arrived atone of NA's lunchtime meetings this week. Hours later at a different venue she made a low-key entrance to a women only gathering of recovered addicts.[2]

The article concluded that 'Everyone wishes her well'. However, upon publication of the article, Campbell complained to the newspaper of an invasion of privacy. Their response was to publish a further article on 5th February, this time unsympathetic to her, with a headline proclaiming that 'After years of self-publicity and illegal drug abuse, Naomi Campbell whinges about privacy'.[3] Following further unsympathetic articles, Campbell decided to sue the newspaper, claiming an unwarranted invasion of her privacy. This case was seen by the legal profession as a ground-breaking attempt to establish a privacy law in the UK.

The case of *Campbell v MGN Ltd.* was first heard in March 2002 and Campbell won, although the judge awarded her only £3,500 damages and accused her of misleading the public about her drug addiction. The *Mirror* later appealed this decision and won. Their defence was that Campbell had lied by making a number of public statements saying that she did not use drugs. They then claimed to be exposing hypocrisy by photographing her coming out of the meeting. Campbell subsequently appealed in May 2004 to the House of Lords, who re-instated the original decision by three votes to two. In this judgement they cited Article 8 of the ECHR, breach of confidence, and the Data Protection Act. The Lords indicated that if the newspaper had simply revealed that she was a drug user and thus acting hypocritically then she would have lost. However, it found their revelation of the details of her treatment objectionable and intrusive. In balancing the competing rights found in Articles 8 and 10 of the ECHR, they took issue with the printing of details of the treatment and photograph. In doing so, they upheld Campbell's claim of misuse of private information involving a breach of medical confidence by their publishing details of her addiction treatment. The editor of the *Mirror* at the time, Piers Morgan, viewed this as a celebrity privacy law by stealth, commenting in his inimical tabloid style that 'this is a very good day for lying drug-abusing prima donnas who want to have their cake with the media and the right then to shamelessly guzzle it with their Christal champagne' (Morgan quoted in Purcell, 2004).

It is still unclear whether the Campbell case has established a firm legal precedent in English law. What is notable is that this general privacy test case was one involving a celebrity, and thus it raises the issue of whether rulings over celebrities should be so influential in establishing general legal precedents. We will now turn to another recent legal battle over celebrity image rights, Michael Douglas and Catherine Zeta Jones against the UK celebrity magazine *Hello!*, in order to consider this issue in more detail.

Hello! and two Hollywood movie stars

In 2003 a legal action was brought in the English courts by the Hollywood movie stars and husband and wife, Michael Douglas and Catherine Zeta Jones, along with Northern and Shell (publishers of *OK!*, a UK celebrity magazine) against *Hello!*, another major UK celebrity magazine. After a bidding war between *OK!* and *Hello!* the couple had given the former exclusive rights to cover the couple's wedding at the New York

Plaza Hotel on 18th November 2000 for a payment of £1 million. They retained picture approval and control over publication, and were obliged to implement strict security measures to ensure that other media sources could not obtain access to the wedding. However, a freelance paparazzo evaded the Douglas's security and surreptitiously took photographs of the wedding, then sold the rights to publish them in the UK, France and Spain through an agent to *Hello!*'s Spanish parent company Hola SA (Collins, 2004). Two days later, upon finding out that *Hello!* was about to publish the photographs, *OK!* obtained a High Court injunction to prevent publication. However, this was overturned by the Court of Appeal, and *Hello!* went ahead and published the photographs. As a result, *OK!* was forced to rush their wedding edition into print, with both titles arriving on the news-stands on the same day.

The case was widely reported in the media and it developed a broadly hostile popular press narrative which attacked the couple for complaining about the burden of press intrusion, with many stories arguing that they had deliberated courted publicity by licensing wedding images to *OK!*. Douglas and Zeta Jones therefore decided to sue *Hello!* over publication of six unauthorized photographs taken at the wedding. The couple's complaint was not just that unauthorized photographs were published, but that they were deemed to present them in an inappropriate manner, claiming in court that they were 'devastated' by their publication. Several images were singled out for discussion, including two photographs showing Zeta-Jones eating, one of which she is pictured being fed wedding cake by her husband. The couple said that these photographs were particularly distressing – first, because they were of low quality, and second, because they argued that they made Zeta Jones look gluttonous. These, it was claimed, were potentially damaging issues for Zeta Jones' career as a movie star, and they cited the tabloid headline appearing in the *Sun* on the 24th November 2000 titled 'Catherine Eater Jones.'[4] The *Sun* itself published five of the unauthorized pictures and a small reproduction of the cover of *Hello!* and the following day the *Daily Mail* joined the press frenzy and published four of the unauthorized photographs. In the courtroom Zeta Jones stated, 'I wouldn't want a picture of my husband shoving food down my throat to be photographed. It looks as though all I did that day was eat' (in Higham, 2003b). However, the court also heard that the couple had agreed that the *OK!* pictures would include a photograph of *her* feeding her husband wedding cake (thus reversing the action was deemed by the couple to be acceptable to Douglas' career). In the *Daily Mirror* commentary on the case – by this point running as a daily narrative in the tabloid press – she is reported as distinguishing this as an issue of control and quality, stating that 'one was taken with our knowledge, the other was stolen. It has a hairy arm in the foreground and a flash covering the cake. One is legit. One is stolen' (in Higham, 2003b). This comment points to a distinction between authored and illicit celebrity images, where the only images in the public domain acceptable to the celebrity couple were those that they could control, regulate and licence.

The Douglas-Zeta Jones versus *Hello!* case went to court in February 2003, and thirteen claims were made against *Hello!* These included breach of confidence, invasion of privacy and breach of the Data Protection Act 1998. The first claim was breach of confidence, the law most often cited in UK privacy cases. This involves proving a breach of trust, whereby a trusted party has broken a contractual agreement of confidence. As the wedding of Douglas and Zeta Jones was private, and elaborate security arrangements had been made, they argued that the presence of the photographer was indeed a breach of confidence. In addition the couple had to prove that the publication of the images had been detrimental to them. In the hearing the judge agreed that the photographs had the necessary quality of confidence as the wedding was held to be private. He also held that the claimants had the right to control their portrayal in the media, as this was important to their careers, and that *OK!* was entitled to protect its asset, namely exclusive pictures of the wedding. Having established conditions of confidence, the issue of the third party paparazzo was discussed. Although *Hello!* neither took nor commissioned the pictures, the judge argued that, as they knew that *OK!* had entered into an exclusive £1 million contract with the couple, the evidence was sufficient to 'afflict their conscience'.[5] That is, the exclusivity and conditions of the contract with *Hello!*, the private nature of the event and the surreptitious taking of the photographs were deemed sufficient to indicate a breach of confidence. This judgement therefore rejected the public interest defence usually put in such cases. Again this points to a key public/private distinction being made in law. In reference to the couple's claim for privacy, the judge refused to accept there was an existing law that could be applied, and he considered the protection offered by the law of confidence adequate in this case. However, he also commented that a privacy law may be required, commenting that 'if Parliament does not act soon the less satisfactory course, of the courts creating the law bit by bit at the expense of litigants, and with inevitable delays and uncertainty, will be thrust upon the judiciary.'[6]

Both sides in this case ultimately claimed victory. Douglas and Zeta Jones succeeded only in their claims for breach of confidence, minor breach of the 1998 Data Protection act and in obtaining an injunction to prevent further publication of the unauthorized photos, with the privacy claim failing. The English law courts decided against recognising a personal right of privacy, although commented on an urgent need for it. One important reason for its relative failure (by contrast with the Naomi Campbell case) was that the couple had already entered into a contract to publish photographs of their wedding, hence the law of confidence was invoked to protect their commercial deal rather than their privacy. As we shall now see, this is a key difference in comparing the legal status of celebrity in the UK and the US, where celebrity rights of privacy and publicity are more vigorously upheld.

US publicity rights and celebrity

The relationship between privacy and subsequent publicity rights in the US is a complex one, and it has developed from the engagement between celebrities and commercial interests throughout the twentieth century. Accounts of the US 'right of publicity' trace its development back to the right of privacy. The distinction between the two began to be made by the law courts at the start of the twentieth century, coterminous with the rise of photography as a means of circulating visual images. When applied to non-celebrities the defence of one's image from commercial exploitation might be considered a privacy right. However, this argument was judged to be rather more problematic in the case of celebrities, as through their engagement with publicity seeking activities they were often deemed by courts to have waived a right to privacy (Madow, 1993: 168). It was this problem that led to the introduction of the right of publicity. Put most simply, it can be defined as the right of an individual to control the commercial use of his or her name, likeness and other identifying characteristics as private property. This thereby assigns property rights to celebrity images. As a result companies in the US are prevented from marketing a product with a celebrity's image without their permission, as this would be seen as trading upon their publicity rights.

The way in which publicity rights were derived from the right of privacy is quite revealing of how celebrity has been defined in the US legal system. Although members of the general public could plausibly claim that unwanted publicity was an intrusion of their right of privacy, as noted above, such an argument had been difficult to be made for celebrities whose images were publicly circulated. As celebrities lacked the grounds to complain about unwanted exposure, the legal argument moved from a complaint about invasion of privacy and unwanted publicity to one about *uncompensated* publicity. This shifted the law away from a privacy right towards a property right – the right to control the commercial circulation of celebrity images. Two other important factors for this shift can be identified. First, the right of privacy is an individual right and therefore not descendible, expiring upon death. Second, the right is not assignable to another interest, such as a business.[7] The lack of descendibility obviously meant that the right to control the image of the celebrity was relinquished upon their death and did not extend to their families. The non-assignability of the right of privacy meant that although a celebrity could licence their image to be used for commercial purposes (as did many pre-1950s sports and movie stars), they were unable to enforce this right so as to prevent another commercial interest from also using it. Hence in the first half of the twentieth century celebrities were unable to exclusively capture and licence the monopoly power inherent in their valuable images, or at least unable to prevent others from trading their images.

Significantly, recognition of the right of publicity occurred in the US in the second half of the twentieth century. It was first acknowledged in a ground-breaking case in 1953 between two chewing-gum manufacturers over the exclusive use of the image of a professional baseball player to promote their product.[8] In resolving the dispute, the court ruled that an individual has the right to control the circulation of their image for economic purposes, such as product endorsement. It argued that celebrities should be able to exclusively licence their image for commercial use as otherwise it 'would usually yield them no money unless it could be made the subject of an exclusive grant which barred any other advertiser from using their pictures'.[9] This new intellectual property right was developed by Melville Nimmer (1954) in his seminal article 'The Right of Publicity'. Nimmer, not coincidentally perhaps, was a legal counsel for the Hollywood studio Paramount Pictures, which still had a large cohort of film stars under contract, and he lobbied hard to make the case for the extension and recognition of publicity rights. He did this through appealing to a number of 'common-sense' arguments including one still common in legal defences – that those who achieve celebrity do so through substantial personal investment, skill and effort. However, this 'labour argument' of celebrity, fails to acknowledge the public good aspects of celebrity noted earlier. While most academic writing about contemporary celebrity has moved away from Lockean principles of merited fame towards a greater realisation that celebrities are often manufactured and circulated by the media, these discourses remain prominent in legal discussions involving famous individuals.

In a 1954 article Nimmer explicitly referred to 'the needs of Broadway and Hollywood,' effectively suggesting that celebrities required special consideration in law (1954: 203). His success in lobbying for the right, and that of fellow publicity advocate J. Thomas McCarthy, can now be measured by the fact that the right of publicity is explicitly recognised by common law or statute in at least twenty-eight states, including (most importantly for the entertainment industries) California, New York and Tennessee (Ropske, 1997).[10] Other states implicitly recognize the right through protection against appropriation of name of likeness or unfair competition law, which protects against misappropriation and unfair endorsement. The right of publicity is far more extensive than the laws that protect against false endorsement, being a right that allows celebrities to control who profits from the commercial value of their images. As it is both assignable and descendible, celebrities are able to licence their images and after death these rights are passed on to their families or assignees.

Contesting the terrain of fame

What is at stake in examining these rights? They represent attempts to regulate and control use of celebrity images, and I have suggested that this has potential implications for freedom of expression.[11] What is clear is that the legal frameworks developed to protect the images of celebrities do not offer similar protection to non-public figures. The right of publicity, by its very nature, only applies to those public figures already famous, and who attract publicity, such as celebrities and politicians. At issue here is the distinction between public and private spheres of celebrity, and how the boundary between the two should be policed. As should be clear, my own view is that legislation has been instrumental in defining the extent of celebrity power. From the perspective of political economy, this raises important questions about whether image rights should be allocated to private interests, especially as we have established that the nature and power of celebrities depends upon the public circulation of their images. Michael Madow (1993) offers an insightful dissection of this issue when he argues that the implication of publicity right is also to limit the possibilities of cultural expression. He argues that

> **The power to licence is the power to suppress. When the law gives a celebrity a right of publicity, it does more than funnel additional income her way. It gives her (or her assignee) a substantial measure of power over the production and circulation of meaning and identity in society: power, if she so chooses, to suppress readings or appropriations of her persona that depart from, challenge, or subvert the meaning she prefers; power to deny to others the use of her persona in the construction and communication of alternative or oppositional identities and social relations; power, ultimately, to limit the expressive and communicative opportunities for the rest of us. (Madow, 1993: 146–7)**

Madow unambiguously views the right of publicity as an unwarranted privileging of celebrity property rights over those that consume celebrity images. He suggests that assigning publicity rights to celebrities allows them to control images whose value has been derived by their circulation in the public domain and prevents others from using them. His argument is that assigning publicity rights to stars gives them monopoly power over meanings, in particular the ability to reinforce dominant meanings over oppositional readings. He gives an example of John Wayne greetings cards that were cited in a Bill to introduce a descendible Right of Publicity into New York (1993: 144). One particular card – showing a picture of Wayne wearing a cowboy hat and bright red lipstick, with a caption 'It's such a bitch being butch' – was objected to by Wayne's family. Although the primary complaint was that it 'demeaned' their father's macho heterosexual image, their main legal defence was that they were being deprived of income being made through Wayne's image. The right of publicity, then, has clear implications for the circulation of celebrity images, as the law potentially allows the assignation of rights to dominant or 'preferred' meanings and may legislate against certain kinds of oppositional re-coding.[12]

Roberta Rosenthal Kwall (1997), however, disagrees with Madow and offers a defence of publicity rights, suggesting that there is insufficient evidence to demonstrate social losses arising from the propertizing of celebrity. Furthermore, she argues that the right of publicity works to 'protect the integrity of texts by rejecting fluidity of textual interpretation by the public in favour of the author's interpretation' (Kwall, 1997: 19). In fact this is a similar point to Madow but he views such 'protection' in negative terms, as the right to control the circulation of cultural meanings against the public interest (and we might relate this division to similar debates over the openness of the 'creative commons'). Kwall continues by arguing that 'fame has been democratised' and that celebrity is now potentially open to anyone, regardless of income, sex, class (1997: 21–2). As I have argued, this view has long since been part of the appealing mythology of fame, and celebrity is often very far from democratic or meritocratic.

Conclusion: the private ownership of celebrity?

Through an examination of image rights, this chapter has demonstrated that analysis of the economic and symbolic power of celebrities requires a greater understanding of the part played by the law in legislating, regulating and propertizing celebrity images. The cases discussed demonstrate an important distinction between the legal power that celebrities are able to exert over their images in the UK and the US. English courts have until recently been far more cautious about assigning property and privacy rights to celebrities than in the US, where such rights are often vigorously upheld. A more general point has also been made: assigning rights to celebrities raises questions about the ownership of symbolic and economic capital in contemporary societies, where celebrity culture is so deeply implicated within a system of commodity exchange. Celebrities, and the publicity value that they accumulate, depend both upon their circulation in the media and upon a public that is willing to buy these images and associated products. Who owns and can control their images should rightly be part of public debate.

I have suggested that understanding celebrity as intellectual property links questions of identity and the symbolic capital held by celebrities, to those of ownership and control of public images. Privacy and publicity rulings function to regulate intellectual property rights over images, and recent legal cases pitching the rights of celebrities against the rights of the media have been important in reshaping celebrity power in the latter half of the twentieth century. Celebrities have been able to vigorously defend their rights against more intrusive press interest but such regulation may also limit the freedom of expression available to the public. At the centre is a set of contradictions – never resolved in the courts – namely that the celebrity is founded on public visibility yet celebrities, once famous, often wish to control and regulate their images. Just as Richard Dyer's (1979) early work argued that stars work through issues of cultural identity and self-hood in society, so legal cases involving celebrities dramatize what it means to be famous in the contemporary era. Narratives of fame are not simply played out in media texts, but also through court appearances, legal rulings and the resultant media coverage of them. The law courts become another intertextual site where the meaning of modern celebrity is produced, and celebrity lawyers and public relations gurus (such as the UK's Max Clifford) all operate as part of this publicity system, as do court dramatizations (such as the daily reconstruction of 2005 Michael Jackson trial for Sky/Fox television news).

The mass media is both a producer and consumer of celebrity, voracious in its appetite and glorying in the rise and fall of famous individuals. Examining celebrity power through legal frameworks opens up for consideration how celebrity functions as an economic as well as symbolic commodity and how it depends upon wider social and legislative structures that are territorially and culturally specific. Put another way, celebrity is a nexus of discourses: cultural, legal and economic. The legal system presents a stage upon which the tensions between the public and private spheres of celebrity are played out, and as such can offer some revealing insights into what it means to be famous in the contemporary late capitalist era.

Notes

1. *Naomi Campbell v. Mirror Group Newspapers Ltd.* [2002] EWHC 499 QB and [2004] UKHL 22.
2. Quoted from *Campbell v Mirror Group Newspapers Ltd.* [2004] UKHL 22 All ER (D) 67 (May), (Approved judgement): Judgement 1, para. 2.
3. Ibid. at para. 8.
4. A further article in *The Mirror* on 11th February 2003 lambasted the star for complaining and took a similar punning headline, 'Catherine Bleater Moans'.
5. *Douglas v. Hello! Ltd.* [2003] EWHC 786 (Ch). para. 198.
6. Ibid. para. 229, iii.
7. Ibid. p. 170–71.
8. *Haelan Laboratories, Inc. v. Topps Chewing Gum, Inc.* (1953), 202 F.2d 866 (2d Cir.), cert. denied, 346 U.S. 816.
9. Ibid. at 868.
10. McCarthy explicitly acknowledges his debt to Nimmer in McCarthy (1987b).
11. For further consideration of the cultural consequences of intellectual property right regimes see Edelman (1979), Gaines (1991), Bettig (1996) and Coombe (1998).
12. See Richard Dyer's (1986) analysis of queer re-codings of Judy Garland's star image.

References

Bettig, Ronald (1996) *Copyrighting Culture: The Political Economy of Intellectual Property*, New York: Westview Press.

Collins, Craig (2004) 'Goodbye *Hello!* Drawing a line for the paparazzi', *University of New England Law Journal* 1 (2): 135–44.

Coombe, Rosemary (1998) *The Cultural Life of Intellectual Properties: Authorship, Appropriation, and the Law*, Durham: Duke University Press.

Dyer, Richard (1979) *Stars*, London: BFI Publishing.

Dyer, Richard (1986) *Heavenly Bodies: Film Stars and Society*, Basingstoke: Macmillan.

Edelman, Bernard (1979) *Ownership of the Image*, Trans. Elizabeth Kingdom, London: Routledge and Kegan Paul.

Gamson, Joshua (1994) *Claims to Fame: Celebrity in Contemporary America*, Los Angeles: University of California Press.

Gavison, Ruth (1980) 'Privacy and the limits of law', *Yale Law Journal* 89: 421–71.

Higham, Nick (2003a) 'Zeta court case could make history', 3 February 2005 <http://news.bbc.co.uk/1/hi/entertainment/showbiz/2720543.stm> [accessed 12/05/05].

Higham, Nick (2003b) 'Hollywood at the High Court', 19 February 2005 <http://news.bbc.co.uk/1/hi/entertainment/showbiz/2745907.stm> [accessed 12/05/05].

Kwall, Roberta Rosenthal (1997) 'Fame', *Indiana Law Journal* 73.1 <http://ssrn.com/abstract=846306> [accessed 12/05/05].

Madow, Michael (1993) 'Private ownership of public image: popular culture and publicity rights', *California Law Review* 81. 125 <http://cyber.law.harvard.edu/IPCoop/93mado1.html> [accessed 12/05/05].

Marshall, P. David (1997) *Celebrity and Power: Fame in Contemporary Culture*, Minneapolis: University of Minnesota Press.

McCarthy, J. Thomas (1987a) *The Rights of Publicity and Privacy*, New York: Boardman.

McCarthy, J. Thomas (1987b) 'Melville B. Nimmer and the right of publicity: a tribute', *UCLA Law Review*, June–August 1987: 1703–12.

Nimmer, Melville B. (1954) 'The right of publicity', *Law and Contemporary Problems* 19: 203–23.

Purcell, Steve (2004) 'A good day for lying drug-abusing models', *The Mirror* 6 May 2004.

Report of the committee on privacy and related matters, Chairman David Calcutt QC, 1990, Cmnd. 1102, London: HMSO.

Robertson, Geoffrey and Nicol, Andrew (2002) *Media Law*, London: Penguin.

Ropske, Gary (1997) 'Celebrity status and the right of publicity', *New York Law Journal* 31.

Turner, Graeme, Bonner, Francis and Marshall, P. David (2000) *Fame Games: The Production of Celebrity in Australia*, Cambridge: Cambridge University Press.

Warren, Samuel D. and Brandeis, Louis (1890) 'The right to privacy', *Harvard Law Review* 4.5: 193–216.

19

Celebrity CEOs and the Cultural Economy of Tabloid Intimacy

Jo Littler

Scenes from the recent media coverage of two CEOs:

One: An advert for Britain's first branch of the clothing store American Apparel graces the back of London's *Time Out*. American Apparel markets itself as 'sweatshop-free', as all its LA-based workers get more than the minimum wage. The ad features a grainy, amateur-style photo of the company's CEO, Dov Charney, standing with his back to the camera, his bare butt poking below a t-shirt. 'This September' the ad proposes, 'Come see what we're doing at our community store and gallery'. Clearly, American Apparel wants to be seen as doing *more* than paying decent wages. The ad is part of a wider campaign: other include Charney and an unnamed woman lying in bed, gazing languidly at the camera, and female American Apparel employees in provocatively 'everyday' poses. They also follow a feature in the American glossy women's magazine *Jane*, in which journalist Claudine Ko describes how Charney masturbates in front of her during the interview. This scene tends to be mentioned in most subsequent media interviews.[1]

Two: The front page of May 2nd 2005's *Daily Mail* announces 'Exclusive new series; ALAN SUGAR – My guide to help YOU become a success'. Inside, prominent businessman Sir Alan gazes – unsmiling, bearded and pinstriped – at the camera. The double-page spread features extracts from his new book, *The Apprentice*, a tie-in to BBC2's 'surprise hit of the season'. Based on a US format starring Donald Trump, the reality show follows 12 hopefuls as – by demonstrating their superior entrepreneurial acumen, marketing savvy and corporate promise – they vie to become Sugar's apprentice for an annual salary of £100,000. Over in the *Mirror*, Sugar can be found dispensing financial advice in his regular column, whilst his thoughts on the TV programme appear in the news pages. As with his large number of broadsheet and tabloid interviews, Sir Alan mentions his working-class background and the importance of hunger and hard work if you're going to make it to 'the top'.[2]

In their very different ways, Sir Alan Sugar and Dov Charney are both 'celebrity CEOs'. The function of such famous Chief Executive Officers (CEOs) are, in Hamish Pringle's words, to act as 'walking talking brand stories that provide their companies with a compelling narrative drive' (Pringle, 2004: 72). In this respect, Sugar and Charney are but two in a long string of business leaders whose persona has been deployed in order to augment a company brand image. This is not in itself a new phenomenon, and a number of familiar figures will probably spring to mind, from

Gordon Selfridge to Henry Ford, from Victor Kiam to Richard Branson to Anita Roddick and beyond.[3]

At the same time, the functions they have and the positions they occupy seem to be particularly and interestingly of their moment. Sir Alan Sugar's pinstriped persona is fairly traditional; but the main reason for his celebrity status – his key role in a reality TV series – is less so. Dov Charney is not the first corporate leader to have a sexually salacious image; but to foreground this in an ironic fashion in an advertising campaign and to launch a sophisticated, high-profile PR strategy around it seems to imbue his persona with a more contemporary feel.

In this article, I suggest that it might well be fruitful to analyze the figure of the celebrity CEO by bringing it into contact with work from the field of media and cultural studies on celebrity, a field which has both a rapidly expanding present and a sizeable past (e.g., Austin and Barker, 2003; Dyer, 2003, 1998; Gamson, 2000; Gledhill, 1991; Holmes, 2005; Littler, 2003; Marshall, 1997; Rojek, 2001; Turner, 2004). In the context of media and cultural studies, what stands out is that celebrity business leaders are simply not discussed very much. Indeed, in early accounts of the cultural industries, they often function as the pole against which the expansion of 'celebrity' – meaning celebrities from the frothy field of entertainment – can be measured. To some extent, we might say that they act as 'real' celebrity's repressed double.

The CEO in celebrity context

Leo Lowenthal's seminal 1944 Frankfurt School study 'The Triumph of Mass Idols', for example, charted the rise of entertainment celebrity since the beginning of the century through a content analysis of prominent figures in magazines and newspapers. Lowenthal concluded that a shift had taken place from 'idols of production' to 'idols of consumption':

> When we turn to our present day sample we face an assortment of people which is both qualitatively and quantitatively removed from the standards of the past. Only two decades ago people from the realm of entertainment played a very negligible role in the biographical material. They form now, numerically, the first group. [...] The proportion of people from political life and from business and professions, both representing the 'serious side', has declined from 74 to 45 percent of the total. (Lowenthal, 1984: 207–8)

In contrast, in the early stage of the study, Lowenthal observes that most prominent figures in magazines and newspapers:

> are idols of production, [in] that they stem from the productive life, from industry, business and the natural sciences, There is not a single hero from the world of sports and the few artists and entertainers either do not belong to the sphere of cheap or mass entertainment or represent a serious attitude toward their art. (Lowenthal, 1984: 206)

In Lowenthal's account, business figures, like political figures, become what these mass idols are pitted *against*. The idols of production featured in this media, who were 'representing the "serious side" ' of public life, had declined from 74 to 45 percent', and instead, for Lowenthal, the pages of these magazines and newspapers were being flooded with terrifying idols from the world of cheap entertainment.

The investments Lowenthal's writing betrays – an anxiety towards the possible power of the lower classes, towards pleasure and women – no longer appear so hidden in the wake of cultural studies' extended engagement, in the intervening years, with the writings of the Frankfurt School. Lowenthal's framing of a 'dreamlife of the masses', in which distracting consumption is female, and important, powerful production is male, and in which 'serious' culture is defined against the apparently frivolous delusions of lower class consumers, today stand in stark relief against the backdrop of the long legacy of critiques of such arguments (Bowlby, 1985; Husseyn, 1986; Storey, 1994).

Yet what is interesting here is that Lowenthal's account not only betrays anxiety towards feminized mass consumption, and valorizes 'serious' middle-class culture against 'base' lower class culture, but also normalizes the category of business celebrity as somehow *allowed* and *respectable*. Business celebrities are not the distracting figures of mass entertainment; they are somehow not 'real' celebrities, not the real false idols. The categorizations made by Lowenthal, in other words, not only betray an anxiety towards feminized mass consumption; they also normalize the category of business celebrities, like other political and 'professional' celebrities, as serious and legitimate. In the rush to decry the feminized dreamworld of consumption, there is also a strange seed at the heart of a Marxist text: a problematic implied validation of capitalist business leaders.

This is also interesting in terms of how it indicates a kind of *ur*-history for thinking about celebrity CEOs in the context of media and cultural studies. For dividing celebrities up into frivolous entertainment celebrities versus 'serious' figures was to continue in mid-century critical and cultural analysis. Even the more sociologically oriented C. Wright Mills, for example, in his 1956 work *The Power Elite*, reproduced this binary to argue that institutional and showbusiness celebrity forms were becoming increasing indistinguishable (Mills, 1959: 91). Drawing on similar terminology, Francesco Alberoni (1972) focused upon the category of the 'especially remarkable' world of idols and divas which, he suggested, constituted a 'powerless elite'. A tradition was in place in critical writing on celebrity in which celebrities were being defined as the opposite of figures with serious institutional power. The productive, serious business figure, as part of a broader category of institutional celebrity, was to become the unconscious standard according to which entertainment-based celebrity could be judged frivolous.[4]

A lack of interest in cultural and media studies in how business production stylizes itself might be described, to adapt Mica Nava's usage of the phrase, as a kind of 'disavowal'. Nava (1996) writes of how the historical lack of serious attention to feminized spheres of consumption was part of the same disavowal which came to shape the very theoretical tools inherited by media and cultural studies. Clearly there are some pretty crucial differences here, namely that corporate CEOs are hardly a disenfranchised and oppressed minority. But there is a parallel in the *lack* of analytical attention (as well as their interconnected inheritance). Indeed, on a broader level, we might say that this legacy directly inheres in some of the current attacks on cultural studies, particularly Thomas Frank's bitter attacks on the discipline for not paying attention to the role of business cultures in shaping cultural discourse (Frank, 2001: 276–306). More positively, this legacy of 'disavowal' also relates to some of the interests being developed in the burgeoning work adjacent to cultural studies, such as the nascent interest in cultural economy (Amin and Thrift, 2004; du Gay and Pryke, 2002).

From my own disciplinary standpoint it therefore seems potentially fruitful to use the tools of media and cultural studies to analyze the role of contemporary CEOs. It seems to me that they should not be left alone as an unproblematic norm, but rather their various forms of power, including their media image, should be better understood and interrogated. This issue might be approached in a number of ways, and I want to suggest here that it might be beneficial to situate recent manifestations of the figure of the celebrity CEO in relation to both current tendencies in media culture and the particular cultural-economic context of which they are part. In what follows, drawing on the personae of Alan Sugar and Dov Charney, I attempt to sketch some shared key tendencies in the construction of media cultures and the corporate interests of the celebrity CEO, by drawing on business commentaries alongside traditions and tools from media and cultural studies.

Contemporary CEOs, 'tabloid culture' and cross-promotion

How might we begin to conceptualize the nature of the relationship between current modes of media and celebrity CEOs? One fairly obvious point is that celebrity CEOs are chief executive officers whose profiles extend *beyond* the financial or business sectors of the media. Their dissemination through a broader field of media culture is inherent to their very definition, and their imbrication within entertainment and showbusiness is present from the outset. The two examples of contemporary celebrity CEOs I began with, throw this point into some relief. Charney's image as an entertaining and ironic hustler is used as a hook for feature articles and to directly advertise American Apparel's brand; Sugar's persona as gruff guru is used as a basis for columns and interviews. Their location *within* and *across* a range of media sites and genres works – together with the particular kinds of identity and white masculinity they represent (both louche and 'hard') – to construct their celebrity status.

We could think about this issue of the extended profile in the context of a post-Fordist promotional climate in which corporations have extended their pursuit of new forms of promotion beyond the demarcated boundaries of advertising – enlarging and recon-figuring the realms of public relations and branding in the process. To make this point is not to argue that there was some halcyon, pre-commercial era prior to the present. Rather, it is to recognize not only the increased significance of branding, and the breadth of its role across media forms, but also the reconfiguring of the promotional industries, in which a greater premium is placed on below-and through-the-line publicity and on the continual process of accruing added value through new forms of cross-media coverage (Brierley, 1995; Dyson, 2000; Lury, 2004). Simply put, a very cheap and high profile route via which American Apparel can generate publicity (such as the major interview in *Jane*, which generated a skein of internet discussion and numerous follow-up features), is through the managed flamboyancy of its CEO (Morford, 2005; Sauer, 2005).

Using Dov Charney for promotion and generating a tabloidesque story around his image, then, provides the company with a culturally extensive, through-the-line reach. Such cross-media appearances might also usefully be understood in relation to the concept of 'tabloid culture'.[5] Writers such as John Langer and Kevin Glynn have encouraged us to think about how attributes traditionally ascribed to the 'tabloid' – particularly entertaining forms of news, and human interest stories with strong elements of sensationalism and intimacy – occupy a wider variety of media sites, and a broader cultural field, than the study of tabloid newspapers alone (Glynn, 2000; Langer, 2000). As Glynn puts it, whereas tabloid media 'prefers heightened emotionality' and sometimes 'makes heavy use of campy irony, parody and broad humour', official journalism 'stresses, among other things, objectivism and a proper distance – critical and emotional – from its subjects' (Glynn, 2000: 7).

Whilst the parameters of the term 'tabloid culture' raises as many questions as answers, it also opens up new possibilities for thinking about the changing roles of celebrity CEOs, in particular the forms of social and cultural mobility they are often required to demonstrate. For the media profile of celebrity CEOs crosses genres both in terms of media sites *and* in terms of discursive/symbolic registers. Sir Alan Sugar, for example, has featured in both tabloid and broadsheet newspapers (being interviewed in *The Observer* as well as *The Express*). Similarly, Dov Charney becomes newsworthy because his persona crosses media registers and forms. His 'respectable' figure as a CEO is used to generate sensational stories and salacious images which clearly draw on tabloid conventions. In other words, the persona constructed around Charney is one through which high, middle and lowbrow cultures are blended, enabling the extraction of tabloidesque elements in 'artistic' advertising codes for its middle-class target market. The publicity around him, in these terms, both draws on conventional distinctions around 'tabloid culture' and indicates something of the extent of its contemporary breadth.

Contemporary celebrity CEOs can therefore accrue a fairly expansive media profile by inhabiting a cross-section of media discourses, some of which include or draw from imagery which is intimately or sensationally tabloidesque. Both routes lead to gaining the appearance of social fluidity, providing the celebrity CEO with a reach which is crucial in today's ostensibly 'meritocratic' culture and society (Littler, 2004). To explore this issue further, and to pursue the questions of power it raises, we can turn to the changing dynamics of celebrity in contemporary business culture.

The corporate bottom line: from fat cats to cool cats

If placing celebrity CEOs in the broader context of tabloid culture and post-Fordist cross-promotion is one way of understanding how they accrue their power, another is to locate them in the context of changing corporate cultures. In business commentaries, the widespread emergence of CEO superheroes is often connected to the 'new populism' of 1980s business culture in the Reaganite US and the Thatcherite UK. The restructuring of finance capital at this time meant that whilst the provisions of the welfare state and the Fordist deal were being shrunk, regulations on business trading were redefined to encourage entrepreneurialism and the rise of 'investor capitalism' (Castells, 1996; Brenner, 1998). As Constance L. Hays puts it in her history of the leaders of Coca-Cola company, during the 1980s:

> [a]n information industry burst forth to spread and share information about the business world. If you were a broker, you had to confront a suddenly more aware clientele, and at cocktail parties people talked about their stocks and their rates of return the way they had once talked about pennant races and vacation plans. CEOs who posted superb results lost their facelessness and became celebrities, their photographs featured on the covers of magazines and their names dropped on talk shows. It was a startling shift, for them and for the public. (Hays, 2005: 146–7)

The American business academic Rakesh Khurana argues that it was to a large extent this increased role and visibility for investors which spawned the lionization of superstar CEOs (Khurana, 2002). By the 1990s, one Burston-Marsteller survey found that 95% of respondents had become influenced in stock selection by the CEO's profile, as 'personalising a company, concept or creation was often the only way to nail it down' (Haigh, 2004: 97–8). And so CEOs became celebrities both within and beyond the expanding realm of business media. As Hays puts it, they 'lost their facelessness and became celebrities'. The celebrity as 'face', as Jeremy Gilbert has recently argued, revisiting Deleuze and Guattari's work on faciality, can be located in the long history of capitalism and Western modes of individualism as both its effect and symptom (Gilbert, 2004). To adopt these terms, the celebrity/face as both territorialized locus of power and despotic figure might be perceived as achieving a kind of apogee in the figure of the celebrity CEO, which had come to acquire dizzier heights of media recognition in the 1980s.

However, whilst the dominant image of corporate leaders and workers in the 1980s was one of brashly thrusting up the corporate ladder, the 1990s also came to be identified with alternative models of maximizing profit. 'Soft capitalism' sought to harness interpersonal relationships, cultural bonds alongside informality, emotion and 'creativity' in order to produce economic success (Heelas, 2002; Ray and Sayer, 1999). Nikolas Rose has persuasively traced the slow evolution of this process from the 1970s, when organisations began to become more interested in how an 'emotional, more primitive side of human nature' could be utilised to generate both an increase in workers' self-governance and productivity (Rose, 1999: 114–16). From the 1990s the informality of soft capitalism and the cultural turn could be witnessed across a wide spectrum of workplace contexts in varying levels of intensity, from dress-down Fridays and office parties, through to the collectivist hedonism of dot.com entrepreneurs, and advertising agencies like St Lukes, where employees worked together in informal environments and creative ways for private profit. Or, to put it in televisual terms: from the occasional, officially-sanctioned carnivalesque moments in *The Office* to the torturously insistent informality of *Nathan Barley*.[6] The 'top-down' model of conspicuous authoritarian hierarchies became distinctly old school, and in its place scores of management books discussed how to harness worker consensus and potential from the ground up. Business writer James Surowiecki comments that this spawned 'one of the deep paradoxes of the 1990s' in that 'even as companies paid greater attention to the virtues of decentralisation and the importance of bottom-up mechanisms, they also treated their CEOs as superheroes' (Surowiecki, 2004: 216).

I would suggest that many celebrity CEOs seem to offer a means of reconciling this paradox, by intertwining the twin imperatives of being a 'corporate superhero' with the bottom-up mechanisms symptomatic of the cultural turn. Or, to put it in more graphic terms, many contemporary celebrity CEOs are trying to turn 'fat cats' into 'cool cats' by employing or appropriating discourses of bottom-up power and flaunting them across an expanded range of media contexts.

Such a process has become important because, by the end of the 1990s, dislike of 'fat cats' grew alongside CEO salaries, which had expanded from an average of 50 times their average worker's pay in the 1970s to close to 500 times by the early 2000s in the US (Castells, 1998: 130; Haigh, 2004: 11; Ertuk *et al*, 2005: 54). As John Kenneth Galbraith pithily put it, 'nothing in my lifetime or yours has happened more completely than the loss of confidence in corporate leadership' (Terkel, 2005: 88). By far the fastest loss of confidence occurred in what Haigh calls the 'days of rage' of the 1990s and early 2000s, when anger became registered in protests against CEO pay increases: in the UK in 1994/5, for example, protestors paraded a squealing pig at British Gas's AGM in reference to chairman Cedric Brown awarding himself a 75% pay hike (Haigh, 2004). It was also registered through a more widespread general dissatisfaction with the conduct of CEOs who had 'rigged the books to enrich themselves in the short term', thereby contributing to the collapse of companies including Enron and WorldCom (Hoopes, 2003: xxix). In the US, Jeffery Skilling became known as 'the most despised CEO of his generation' due to his role in Enron's 2001 collapse (Haigh, 2004: 91; 7).

It is in relation to this context that contemporary celebrity CEOs attempt to marry discourses of heroism with those of bottom-up power through both an expanded media field and the broader context of 'tabloid culture'. There are various ways such 'bottom-up' mechanisms' can be articulated to celebrity CEO heroism, with different political implications.

Entrepreneurial meritocracy, customer intimacy . . . and power to the people?

Sir Alan Sugar's persona articulates the celebrity CEO and 'bottom-up power' by enacting the very contemporary neoliberal parable of entrepreneurial meritocracy: a framework which illustrates the possibilities of social mobility whilst creating new forms of inequality. In the first BBC 2 series, *The Apprentice*, Sugar is presented as providing grassroots 'empowerment' by 'giving something back' to the community, a phrase he repeated in many media interviews surrounding the series (Webb, 2005). His image as a white 'working-class boy made good' dramatizes this idea. Like the winner of *The Apprentice* Tim Campbell – who repeatedly spoke of winning for his mother who didn't want him to end up as another black male statistic – Sugar's persona suggests that anyone, from *any* background, can rise to be successful by destroying the competition if only they show the right qualities combined with hard graft.[7]

Sugar's persona illustrates how a sense of social mobility has become integral to contemporary capitalism, but is used in turn to create new stratifications of social division and self-worth. For instance, as Christopher Holmes Smith has written in a different context, discussing hip-hop moguls, the hip-hop mogul 'needs the spectacle of the more impoverished masses for they have given him the raw material, the literal human canvas, for which, and upon which, his ascent can be made emblematic' (Holmes Smith, 2003: 85). Sugar's success is similarly predicated on the existence of 'failures' who remain poor. In this way *The Apprentice* can promote the notion of class mobility, and reflect the more widespread nature of anti-racist discourse, whilst sustaining and reinscribing inequalities of power and wealth.

The cross-media coverage also resulted in a 'brand extension' for Sugar beyond his companies. Well-known on the sports pages as the owner of Tottenham Hotspur Football Club, and in a business context as the CEO of Amstrad, the TV exposure and accumulative media publicity surrounding *The Apprentice* carried Sugar's persona into far wider realms of celebrity. As one journalist put it:

> Before *The Apprentice* came on the telly, I had heard of Alan Sugar, but if I had been asked what he was famous for, and my life had depended on the answer, I would have ventured: "Football?" And then very much dried up. Now, thanks to BBC2, I know that Sugar is the boss of a £700m global empire and so impressive that a bunch of business people have given up jobs (allegedly) to try out for a year-long posting at Sugar Towers. (Wilson, 2005)

Already no. 24 in the *Sunday Times'* 'Rich List', Sugar had no particular need to generate more publicity for his company, and the TV programme did not make him as much money as his 'regular work' (Hutton, 2005). What Sugar's newfound celebrity primarily provided was the opportunity for wider public recognition beyond the business sector.

We might make a connection here to Carol Duncan's work analysing art galleries and museums as 'donor memorials', or sites where corporate capital has often historically attempted to legitimate itself. She argues that, historically, business leaders have often donated money in order to use these sites to rid their personal and company name of unsavoury connotations, channelling the fortunes acquired on the backs of other people's labour into memorials for themselves in the process. In doing so, Duncan argues, they refashion their image into that of caring philanthropists providing services for the community (Duncan, 1995: 72–101). *The Apprentice*, we might say, is an analogous form of 'donor memorial' in an updated media context: a way of ensuring images and memories of Sugar as a pragmatic philanthropist reach a larger public. Sugar's 'benevolent' image was augmented by the reality show format, which has tended to dramatize myths of social mobility (Biressi and Nunn, 2005: 144–55), and by the framing of the series as 'educational' as well as entertaining, with frequent references circulating to how the programme helped fulfill the BBC's public service remit (*The Times* 2005).

Equally, however, the attempted marriage of a CEO superhero with 'bottom-up empowerment' can work by evoking the corporate cultural turn's emphasis on informality. The American Apparel advert with which I opened, featuring the company's semi-naked boss, Dov Charney, is clearly trying to tell us that this brand and company is having a good time. We're flamboyantly informal, it intimates; we're sexual, we're fun, we're irreverent. We're *cheeky*. Relevant CEO precursors to Charney's studied informality include the flamboyant Chrysler CEO Lee Iacocca and Richard Branson (who, like his brand, Virgin, portrayed being young and casual as 'revolutionary'). Both celebrity CEOs were facilitated by the decline of corporate deference which accelerated in the 1990s, paving the way for Charney's even more sensationally intimate image.

Such intimacy also relates to how the mantra of post-Fordist corporations, 'know thy consumer', bred a desire, in the words of one marketing bible, to 'get up close and personal' with the consumer (Grant, 2000). As another business book, *Customer Intimacy*, put it, '[t]he largest source of growth, advantage and profit resides in the design and development of intimacy with customers' (Wiersema, 1998: 5–6). For American Apparel to use an image of their CEO showing his butt, to bring the bedroom into the boardroom, is in its wider context part of the broader post-1990s corporate emphasis on using 'bottom-up mechanisms' to reach a consumer base shaped through the decline of deference. Dov Charney takes customer intimacy and casual dressing down to its logical conclusion: he strips off.

Last, however, some CEOs might be seen to embody the attempted marriage between 'bottom-up power' in another, somewhat different way, by being associated with marketing-led shifts to pay workers a 'living wage'. Dov Charney and Anita Roddick, CEO of the Body Shop, are both good examples here, and as it is a key selling point for both their companies it to some extent explains the ease with which they generate coverage. As one business manual remarks with evident wonder, at one point Roddick herself generated so much publicity that the Body Shop didn't actually need to advertise (Kotler, 2005: 14). At the same time, the politics of their organisations are fraught with contradictions. For example, they promote fair trade but don't participate in international fair trade standards; they popularize 'decent' wages (paying significantly above the average rate for types of labour that is routinely grossly exploited), but their companies are not co-operatives; and American Apparel, at least, has resisted attempts to organise unions (Littler and Moor, 2005). In this sense, there is an echo of the double-edged emergence of the managerial discourse of 'bottom up power' in 1930s America. As James Hoopes writes, this emerged, together with departments of 'human relations', out of broader social demands to improve working conditions and democratic participation and simultaneously, as a means to foreclose radical working class calls for a more thorough egalitarian economic and political restructuring (Hoopes, 2003: 97–8). The politics of Charney and Roddick's organisations are similarly double-edged, slipping between 'soft capitalist' paradigms and projecting their sense of progressive democratic possibility. They indicate that even in the most 'power-sharing' variants of the collision between celebrity CEOs and the discourse of 'bottom-up power', the celebrity CEO retains its function as a means to accommodate and not eradicate inequalities through soft capitalism.

Conclusion

In thinking about how we might interrogate the subject Leo Lowenthal both buried and left open all those years ago, I've been sketching two possible ways of understanding the media lives of contemporary celebrity CEOs. First, the celebrity CEO offers a means for a corporation to gain maximum exposure for little cost. This relates to contemporary promotional culture's emphasis on PR, branding and developing 'through the line' publicity. Using 'tabloid culture' is a key way for CEOs to gain celebrity power in a society which now likes to think of itself as meritocratic. Second, in the context of management and business philosophy, the transition from 1980s thrusting entrepreneurialism to 1990s modes of 'soft capitalist' corporate profit-seeking has created a context in which celebrity CEOs are often conspicuous because they foreground 'bottom-up' modes of power (often manifest through 'unusual', offbeat or 'cool' business practices). Contemporary celebrity CEOs can be seen to be using an expanded media field and the widening realms of 'tabloid culture' to attempt to articulate discourses of heroism with those of bottom-up power. Turning the despised figure of the 'fat cat' into a media-friendly 'cool cat' is predominantly a way to encourage customer intimacy, increase promotion and offset the charge of CEO greed.

Recent studies in cultural economy can open up further ways of thinking about contemporary culture, and I have drawn on a variety of such studies here. Yet I am also troubled by how they can sometimes appear to merely offer a descriptive positivism and evacuate or be devoid of an engagement with question of power. I would like to conclude by emphasizing the importance of linking approaches to cultural economy with questions of power which have been so formative to cultural studies, and to which I am also clearly indebted (see for example Hall *et al*, 1978; Grossberg *et al*, 1992; McRobbie, 2005). In these terms, we can not only think about how the celebrity CEO Alan Sugar becomes a brand through the interrelationship between a wide variety of media formats and company positions; we can also consider how this is connected to a broader and specifically neoliberal cultural-economic discourse of meritocracy. It can be viewed as part of a larger cultural economy, can be connected to the processes which appear to, as Christopher Holmes Smith outlines in relation to hip-hop moguls, build emancipation whilst perpetuating inequalities.

For instance, Sugar's celebrity CEO persona needs to be related to the expansion of 'City Academy' schools which specialize in teaching business skills, cost twice as much as regular state schools, and guarantee a profit for the businesses they have been contracted out to. As is increasingly apparent, such schools have not delivered better grades and have better statistics on progression merely because anti-social students are expelled to nearby state schools which mop up the excluded students (Smithers, 2005). The role of CEOs like Sugar in teaching that corporate competitiveness is emancipatory is part of the same discursive formation of entrepreneurial meritocracy.

At the same time, it is clearly important to stress the range of forms the celebrity CEO might take and connections it might make. Dov Charney's actions continue to reinscribe inequalities between Latina/os and white North Americans and between heterosexual men and women, but they also intersect with a wider movement to pay living wages. If noticing such contradictions illuminates both contemporary complexities and the stealthy perpetuation of social injustice, it might also attempt to beckon towards areas where what Raymond Williams called 'resources of hope' might exist, even where there appear to be slim pickings (Williams, 1988). In the process of connecting to others, the stories of celebrity CEOs might have unexpected effects: Alan Sugar's encouragement of the disenfranchised may result in other actions than that of serving to reinforce late capitalist individualism.

However, at the same time, this should not blind us to the key discourse currently in circulation, which insists that celebrity CEOs need to explicitly demonstrate their support for a 'meritocracy' to augment their heroic personae. We should also not forget that they do so in the service of corporate profit. We live in a moment when there is an unprecedented number of CEOs in the US cabinet, when the George W. Bush administration is 'more a CEOcracy than theocracy'; as Gideon Haigh puts it, 'seldom in history can a caste have been rewarded so richly' (Haigh, 2004: 10–11). If a new 'bottom line' is that celebrity CEOs currently need to demonstrate some elements of tabloid intimacy in order to win their visibility and status, they are predominantly doing so by bolstering corporate power and reinscribing an underclass in distinctively contemporary ways.

Acknowledgements

Thanks to Anita Biressi, Heather Nunn and Henrik Ornebring for the 'Tabloid Culture and Media Spectacle' symposium at Roehampton University in May 2005, which considerably helped me develop my ideas on this subject. Many thanks also to Charlotte Adcock, Nick Couldry, Jeremy Gilbert, Liz Moor and the editors of this volume for their suggestions and support.

Notes

1. *Time Out*, 25 August 2004; Ko 2004; adverts can be viewed at www.americanapparel.net [accessed July 2005].
2. *Daily Mail*, 2 May 2005: *The Apprentice*, BBC 2, BBC/Talkback Thames, 2005; Sugar, 2005; Alan Sugar, 'A Spoonful of Sugar' is a regular column in *The Mirror*.
3. Many such lists appear in business magazine articles; e.g. Benezra and Gilbert, 2002.
4. Whilst Lowenthal divides business figures away from the 'mass entertainment' celebrities of media and showbusiness, the very act of describing the *inclusion* of business leaders in media coverage at all, whilst decrying the media interest in novelty entrepreneurs, demonstrates that such categories could not, even then, be divided so rigidly.
5. I am indebted to the 'Tabloid culture and media spectacle' symposium at Roehampton University, 21 May 2005, for encouraging me to think about the broader concept of 'tabloid culture'.
6. Both comedy dramas, *The Office* was based in a conventionally formal and hierarchical Slough office, whereas *Nathan Barley* was a satire of groovy young new cultural intermediaries.
7. Interestingly, there were conflicting opinions within the business sector over the series. Many disliked its outdated image of corporate life, particularly its presentation of business as 'bloodthirsty', arguing that it should have stressed the importance of teamwork (Kwan Yuk, 2005: 5). In other words, for many in the business world the programme had not gleaned all the lessons of the corporate cultural turn, and the transition to soft capitalism: its modes of profit-seeking were not 'bottom-up' enough.

References

Alberoni, Francesco (1972) 'The powerless elite: theory and sociological research on the phenomena of the stars' in Dennis McQuail (ed) *Sociology of Mass Communication*, Harmondsworth: Penguin, 75–98.

Amin, Ash and Nigel Thrift (2004) (eds) *The Cultural Economy Reader*, Oxford: Blackwell.

Austin, Thomas and Martin Barker (2003) *Contemporary Hollywood Stardom*, London: Hodder Arnold.

Benezra, Karen and Jennifer Gilbert (2002) 'The CEO as brand', http://www.chiefexecutive.net/depts/marketing/174.htm [accessed July 2005].

Biressi, Anita and Heather Nunn (2005) *Reality TV*, London: Wallflower Press.

Bowlby, Rachel (1985) *Just Looking: Consumer Culture in Dreiser, Gissing and Zola*, London: Methuen.

Brenner, Robert (1998) *The Economics of Global Turbulence: A Special Report on the World Economy, 1950–98*; special issue of *New Left Review*, 229.

Brierley, Sean (1995) *The Advertising Handbook*, London: Routledge.

Callon, Michel (1998) (ed) *The Laws of the Market*, Oxford: Blackwell.

Callon, Michel, Cecile Meadel and Volona Rabeharisoa (2002) 'The economy of qualities' in Ash Amin and Nigel Thrift (2002) (eds) *The Cultural Economy Reader*, Blackwell: Oxford, 58–79.

Castells, Manuel (1996) *The Rise of the Network Society*, Oxford: Blackwell.

Castells, Manuel (1998) *End of Millennium*, Oxford: Blackwell.

du Gay, Paul and Michael Pryke (2002) (eds) *Cultural Economy*, Sage: London.

Duncan, Carol (1995) 'Something eternal: the donor memorial' in Carol Duncan, *Civilizing Rituals*, London: Routledge, 72–101.

Dyer, Richard (1998) *Stars*, New edition; London: British Film Institute.

Dyer, Richard (2003) *Heavenly Bodies: Film Stars and Society*, second edition, London: Routledge.

Dyson, Lynda (2000) 'Marketing through the media: image management, branding strategies and the media' *The British Journalism Review*, 11 (3): 61–7.

Ertuk, Ismail, Julie Froud, Sukhdev Johal and Karel Williams (2005) 'Pay for corporate performance or pay as social division?' *Competition and Change*, 9 (1): 54.

Frank, Thomas (2001) *One Market Under God: Extreme Capitalism, Market Populism and the End of Economic Democracy*, London: Seeker and Warburg.

Gamson, Joshua (2000) *Claims to Fame*, Berkeley: University of California Press.

Gilbert, Jeremy (2004) 'Small faces: the tyranny of celebrity in post-Oedipal culture' in Jo Littler (ed) *Mediactive 2: Celebrity*, London: Lawrence and Wishart, 86–109.

Gledhill, Christine (1991) *Stardom: Industry of Desire*, London: Routledge.

Glynn, Kevin (2000) *Tabloid Culture: Trash Taste, Popular Power, and the Transformation of American Television*, Durham: Duke University Press.

Grant, John (2000) *The New Marketing Manifesto: The 12 Rules for Building Successful Brands in the 21st Century*, London: Texere.

Grossberg, Lawrence, Cary Nelson and Paula Treichler (1992) (eds) *Cultural Studies*, London: Routledge.

Guthey, Eric (2005) 'Management studies, cultural criticism and American dreams' *Journal of Management Studies*, 42 (2): 451–66.

Haigh, Gideon (2004) *Bad Company: The Strange Cult of the CEO*, London: Aurum Press.

Hall, Stuart, Charles Critcher, Tony Jefferson, John Clarke, Brian Robert (1978) (eds) *Policing the Crisis*, London: Palgrave.

Hays, Constance L. (2005) *Pop: Truth and Power at the Coca-Cola Company*, London: Arrow.

Heelas, Paul (2002) 'Work, ethics, soft capitalism and the 'turn to life' in du Gay, P. and M. Pryke (eds) *Cultural Economy*, London: Sage, 78–96.

Holmes, Su (2005) 'Off-guard, unkempt, unready? Deconstructing contemporary celebrity in *Heat* magazine' *Continuum*, 19 (1): 21–38.

Hoopes, James (2003) *False Prophets: The Gurus Who Created Modern Management and Why Their Ideas Are Bad for Business*, Cambridge, MA: Perseus.

Hutton, Will (2005) 'Firing, but not on all cylinders' *The Observer*, 8 May, http://media.guardian.co.uk/broadcast/comment/0,,1479026,00.html [accessed June 2005].

Huyssen, Andreas (1986) *After the Great Divide: Modernism, Mass Culture and Postmodernism*, London: MacMillan.

Khurana, Rakesh (2002) *Searching for a Corporate Saviour: The Irrational Quest for Charismatic CEOs*, Princeton, NJ: Princeton University Press.

Ko, Claudine (2004) 'Meet your new boss' *Jane*, June/July: 136–41.

Kotler, Phillip and Nancy Lee (2005) *Corporate Social Responsibility: Doing the Most Good for Your Company and Your Cause*, New Jersey: John Wiley and Sons.

Kwan Yuk, Pan (2005) ' "Apprentice" gets business leaders fired up', *Financial Times*, 5 May: 5.

Langer, John (1997) *Tabloid Television*, London: Routledge.

Littler, Jo (2003) (ed) *Mediactive 2: Celebrity*, London: Lawrence and Wishart.

Littler, Jo (2004) 'Celebrity and "meritocracy"' *Soundings*, 26: 118–30.

Littler, Jo (2005) 'Beyond the boycott: anti-consumerism, cultural change and the limits of reflexivity' *Cultural Studies*, 19 (2): 227–52.

Littler, Jo and Liz Moor (2005) 'Fourth worlds and neo-Fordism: American apparel and the cultural economy of consumer anxiety', forthcoming, based on paper given at *Culture and Social Change: Disciplinary Exchanges*, University of Manchester 11–13 July.

Lowenthal, Leo (1984) 'The triumph of mass idols' in *Literature and Mass Culture*, New Brunswick: Transaction Books, 203–35.

Lury, Celia (2004) *Brands: The Logos of the Global Economy*, London: Routledge.

Marshall, P. David (1997) *Celebrity and Power*, Minneapolis, MN: University of Minnesota Press.

McRobbie, Angela (2005) *The Uses of Cultural Studies*, London: Sage.

Mills, C. Wright (1959) *The Power Elite*, New York: Oxford University Press.

Morford, Mark (2005) 'Porn stars in My Underwear' *SF Gate*, June 24 http://sfgate.com [accessed July 2005].

Nava, Mica (1996) 'Modernity's disavowal: women, the city and the department store' in Mica Nava and Alan O'Shea (eds) *Modern Times*, London: Routledge, 38–76.

Pringle, Hamish (2004) *Celebrity Sells*, London: John Wiley and Sons.

Ray, Larry and Andrew Sayer (1999) (eds) *Culture and Economy after the Cultural Turn*, London: Sage.

Regine, Birute and Roger Lewin (2000) 'Leading at the edge: how leaders influence complex systems' *Emergence*, 2 (2): 5–23.

Rojek, Chris (2001) *Celebrity*, London: Reaction Books.

Rose, Nikolas (1999) *Governing the Soul*, Second edition, London: Free Association Books.

Sauer, Abram (2005) 'American Apparel: All Sweaty', http://www.brandchannel.com. [accessed June 2005].

'Sitcoms have both feet in the grave' *The Times*, 13 July 2005, http://www.timesonline. co.uk/article/0,,2–1691818,00.html [accessed July 2005].

Smith, Christopher Holmes (2003) '"I don't like to dream about getting paid": representations of social mobility and the emergence of the hip-hop Mogul' *Social Text*, 21(4), Winter: 69–97.

Smithers, Rebecca (2005) 'Researchers raise more doubts on city academies' *The Guardian*, 30 June, http://education.guardian.co.uk/newschools/story/0,,1517962, 00.html [accessed July 2005].

Storey, John (1994) (ed) *Cultural Theory and Popular Culture*, London: Prentice Hall.

Sugar, Sir Alan (2005) *The Apprentice: How to Get Hired not Fired*, BBC Books.

Surowiecki, James (2004) *The Wisdom of Crowds*, London: Little, Brown.

Terkel, Studs (2005) *Hope Dies Last: Making a Difference in an Indifferent World*, London: Granta.

Tuner, Graeme (2004) *Understanding Celebrity*, London: Sage.

Webb, Tim (2005) 'The interview: Alan Sugar', *Independent on Sunday*, 13 February.

Wiersema, Fred (1998) *Customer Intimacy: Pick Your Partners, Shape Your Culture, Win Together*, London: Harper Collins.

Williams, Raymond (1988) *Resources of Hope*, London: Verso.

Wilson, Emily (2005) 'It's a dirty business' *The Guardian*, 1 April, http://www. guardian.co.uk/women/story/0,,1449759,00.html [accessed June 2005].

20 | From the Altar to the Market-Place and Back Again: Understanding Literary Celebrity[1]

Wenche Ommundsen

For over two weeks in April 2004, the Melbourne *Age* carried daily instalments of the latest sex scandal surrounding soccer super-star David Beckham: revelations of affairs with a former employee as well as with an Australian model; the reaction of his equally famous wife, Victoria; the views of a great many 'close' associates of the various parties; and speculations by celebrity-watchers. One day, however, the Beckham spot was given over to another story: 'Rushdie Takes Bride No. 4 in Hindi Wedding'. The main point of interest here was the rumour that the actress bride, Padma Lakshmi, would defy Hindi tradition by wearing a white sari. These rumours turned out to be unfounded, as 'the girl from south India bowed to 5000 years of tradition and dressed in dazzling purple' (*The Age* 2000: 7). There was a photo of the couple, both dressed in cream, and an acknowledgement of their age difference (of 25 years). The Rushdie affair was mentioned in a humorous aside: 'At one point, Rushdie knelt – a posture that even the late Ayatollah Khomeini was unable to achieve with his 1989 fatwa after the publication of *The Satanic Verses*' (*The Age* 2000: 7).

Apart from a more conservative hairstyle, there was not much to distinguish the literary from the sport celebrity: the focus was on the glamorous wife, clothing and on marital or extra-marital sexual exploits. Rushdie's literary career only got a brief mention when he was identified as the '56-year-old Booker prize-winning groom', but then, David Beckham's ventures on the soccer field rarely figured either. The conclusions one might draw from such stories are, first, that celebrity culture now has become so ubiquitous that it has invaded those parts of the public sphere normally concerned with matters of a higher cultural order. Second, it seems to suggest that once someone has reached celebrity status, they are, as Daniel Boorstin (1961) put it, famous for simply being famous, and their professional achievements are eclipsed by the usual topics of celebrity gossip – personal appearance, lifestyle sexual relations and anything that can be construed as scandal. But the generic discourse of celebrity is only one aspect of the complex phenomenon that is contemporary literary fame. As a *literary* super-star, Rushdie at the same time exemplifies the relatively recent phenomenon of the global brand and much older tensions between high cultural capital, the marketplace and the popular public sphere which, as I will argue here, are central characteristics of literature as a cultural category.

From Booker glory to target of religious persecution, from a conspicuously private and secret life to a public celebrity wedding, Salman Rushdie has provided 'good copy' for the media for over two decades. His claims to fame span a large cultural register, from global politics to domestic soap opera. The Rushdie story is unique – not even the most unscrupulous of publicists nor the most desperate of starlets could have invented the fatwa. But as an illustration of the workings of celebrity, it provides the perfect mix of personal 'aura', exceptional circumstances and considerable media attention, setting in motion an industry which, once under way, provides the fuel for its own perpetuation.

Media coverage of the various stages of Rushdie's career has been predominantly sympathetic. He was the non-European migrant who won over and entered the literary establishment, the victim of fundamentalist religious fanatics and the champion of freedom of expression. But there have been dissenting voices, and not only from opponents of religious or political liberalism: Rushdie has been taken to task for being too overtly political in his writing, as well as for using his position to gain access to the media. More recently, his more conventional celebrity status has been regarded as somehow inappropriate for a writer of serious literary fiction. A writer, it is implied, has no business courting celebrity: in order to serve the cause of literature he must maintain a position separate from the grubby practices of politics or commercialized culture. Visions of poor but 'pure' writers starving in proverbial garrets still inform constructions of the author, thus aligning celebrity squarely with mass markets, popular entertainment and the lowering of cultural standards. In this paper I argue for a different view. The notion of the author as cultural hero unsullied by the manipulations of commercial or popular culture, though seemingly in stark opposition to common ideas of celebrity, in fact works in conjunction with them to produce a distinct brand of fame.

Indeed, if one effect of the contemporary public sphere has been to weaken the difference between types of fame, and to bring into the category of 'celebrity' individuals, professions and fields of achievement previously untouched by the operations of popular culture, another has been to encourage greater levels of cultural panic about loss of distinction. This in turn produces greater efforts to shore up one's credentials, and one's particular cultural 'brand'. This anxiety is central to literature as a field of cultural production. Literature, or print culture, has predominately been regarded as the domain of the educated middle classes, associated with regimes of taste and modes of consumption equated with 'quality' cultural experiences. According to this conception, it has much to lose through contact with the practices of popular culture: high moral ground, social distinction and intellectual credibility.

Setting out his system of distinction between different kinds of value, Pierre Bourdieu remarks on the 'deep ambivalence' affecting artists and other representatives of high cultural capital as they face the need to market their products in terms of *real* or monetary value (1984: 229). But the problem with the cultural capital/real capital distinction, however, is that it tends to overlook the capacity of the cultural marketplace to capitalize *on* the distinction itself, to incorporate it into its commercial practices and to create niche markets which translate cultural capital into real profit. Within the regime of differential commercial value, the literary celebrity as commodity depends on his or her ability to be 'branded' according to an apparently less commercialized value system and offered as an alternative to other types of celebrity.

The uneasy co-existence of cultural and commercial systems of value is not a unique product of late-capitalist commodity culture. John Frow traces these debates to Balzac's *Lost Illusions* (Frow 2002: 143–4); Marysa Demoor, editor of *Marketing the Author: Authorial Personae, Narrative Selves and Self-Fashioning, 1880–1930*, argues that similar tensions marked the literary scene of late nineteenth century Britain, when the rise of a mass readership was accompanied by 'a growing unease and a sense of doom on the part of the previously privileged, highly educated classes' (Demoor 2004: 2). Charles Dickens, James Joyce and Virginia Woolf all engaged in careful manipulation of their public self-image to accommodate competing regimes of literary value. By the turn of the twentieth century the celebrity author was already an established marketing tool, and early techniques for the fabrication of celebrity were essentially the same as those in use today – personal interviews, photographs in private settings, autobiographical and confessional writing. The implication, writes Demoor, was that in authorship 'identity had become proleptic, containing the promise of the work to come' (Demoor 2004: 4, 15). The image of the author as 'proleptic personality' has survived in much the same form into contemporary culture; what has changed is the nature of the literary market, along with the public sphere in which such images circulate.

The globalization of the publishing industry, along with the incorporation of publishing into large media conglomerates, has resulted in increased competition, both within the literary market and between this market and the market for other cultural products (see Turner et al. 2000). Australia provides an excellent example in this regard. As a relatively small and remote part of the vast English-speaking literary world, it has been acutely exposed to the challenges of the global literary industry. Small publishers have disappeared or have been taken over by multinationals. Fiscal protection for national cultural production is reduced, and the book trade is flooded with international titles at prices with which local products cannot compete. More new books are published than ever before, but the 'shelf life' for new titles is getting shorter (shorter than that of yoghurt, according to industry wisdom), and marketing budgets smaller, except for books that are expected to become best sellers. Non-fiction titles outsell fiction and other literary genres and the profit margin for literary texts is small, sometimes even non-existent (publishers often cross-subsidize in order to produce literary texts). The space devoted to book reviews in the press and other media has shrunk and at the same time broadened its focus to include reviews of popular and non-literary genres.

Marketing the author in this economic and cultural climate has become at the same time more difficult and more urgent. With too much competition, and too little time for the text to create its own audience, promotional tours, media profiles and festival appearances are the only means of drawing public attention to an author and to her/his work. Against the preferences of many writers, their job description now comes with an obligation to be put in the public eye, and to subject themselves to the promotional practices of the celebrity industry (see Turner et al. 2000). For many writers, the strain is considerable: from a sedentary life at their writing desk to the media circuit, from quiet contemplation to public performance. Some refuse, and may find themselves without a publisher. Some are poor performers, and could be overlooked for more marketable authors when they seek publication for another title. Most accept it as part of the literary life and become competent performers; some put their literary gifts to good use by producing authorial selves as intriguing as any fiction. But the performance of authorship also calls for qualities other than literary skills, including good looks, an interesting or 'unusual' life, a 'ready-made' public profile, the ability to fit into a category of writing for which a market is already established ('grunge' or 'roots' literature, children's books featuring magic and wizardry). And like commodity culture in general, and the celebrity industry in particular, literary celebrity creates its own hierarchies in which global brands are ranked higher than local names. Furthermore, literary prizes (from the Nobel and the Booker to national and local prizes) are used as crude tools for organizing the ladder of fame. As a result, publishers, bookshops and literary festivals will promote 'big' international names ahead of all others, and local writers are left to serve the function of warm-up artists or support cast. Similarly, the literary sections of the media will publish profiles of visiting stars with the result that less column space is devoted to book reviews on work by home-grown literary talent.

The globalization of literary production, and of literary fame, pose particular challenges to an art form traditionally associated with notions of national identity and cultural heritage. Turner et al. suggest that today, the best way for an Australian writer to be recognized, even in Australia, is for her or him to have received notice overseas: a contract with an overseas publisher, short-listing (or long-listing) for an overseas literary prize and favourable reviews (2000: 55). The consequence, it is frequently argued, is that writers will abandon topics that are culturally specific and instead 'go universal' in their quest for fame and fortune. And there will be lamentations for the loss of national or local culture, fears that it will be swamped by an undifferentiated global brand – the literary variety of coca-colonization, the 'McMasterpiece'. Against this pessimistic outlook, others point to writers (Salman Rushdie being a prime example), who have received global recognition for works dealing with cultural contexts that are not only local but also unfamiliar to the majority of their readership. Literature may have gone global, but the global has also gone in search of the local, in a complex operation which echoes the famous paradox of globalization: that its most successful manifestation is the anti-globalization campaign.

***

It is a frequently noted irony that the celebrity author gained prominence at the same time as the 'death of the author' was proclaimed with great authority from within academic literary criticism (Barthes 1977). This apparent paradox, often rehearsed in order to mock either theoretically inclined criticism *or* celebrity culture, warrants further scrutiny. It is important to remember that Roland Barthes' 'author' was only ever an ideological construct, a metaphor for the perceived 'centre' of textual authority, a critical tool for limiting the play of the signifier and the text's capacity for meaning. Michel Foucault, in his almost equally famous examination of the role of the author (Foucault 1977), argues that Barthes' gesture merely displaces the centre of authority, creating another metaphor which sustains the notion of transcendental origins:

> **In granting a primordial status to writing, do we not, in effect, simply reinscribe in transcendental terms the theological affirmation of its sacred origin or a critical belief in its creative nature?**
>
> **...**
>
> **This conception of *écriture* sustains the privileges of the author through the safeguard of the a priori; the play of representations that formed a particular image of the author is extended within a gray neutrality. (Foucault 1977: 120)**

Proposing instead a focus on the author as *function*, Foucault shifts the attention to the social, cultural and discursive contexts in which notions of authorship are played out. The author-function, he insists, is 'not universal or constant' but culturally specific; and rather than the simple and spontaneous attribution of a discourse to an individual, it is the product of a 'complex operation whose purpose is to construct the rational entity we call an author' (1977: 125). Authors, though constructed as individuals, are in fact 'projections, in terms always more or less psychological, of our way of handling texts' (1977: 127). His proposal for a different form of investigation is of particular pertinence to the study of literary celebrity:

> **Perhaps the time has come to study not only the expressive value and formal transformations of discourse, but its mode of existence: the modifications and variations, within any culture, of modes of circulation, valorization, attribution, and appropriation. Partially at the expense of themes and concepts that an author places in his work, the 'author-function' could also reveal the manner in which discourse is articulated on the basis of social relations. (1977: 137)**

The author, in Foucault's construction, becomes a direct function of literature as a field of cultural production: its modes of circulation, its status. The contemporary author, it follows, is a projection of the paradoxes that are central to our society's construction of cultural value.

High culture today, as John Frow has argued, must be regarded as 'a *pocket* within commodity culture' (1995: 86), but it is a pocket within which commodity culture itself is the cause of a great deal of anxiety. In *Star Authors*, an examination of literary celebrity in America, Joe Moran cites examples of anxious academic criticism according to which 'the turning of contemporary authors into public curiosities serves them up as part of the meaningless ephemera of consumerism' (2000: 3). Such complaints, Moran notes, 'tap into general anxieties in postmodern mediatized culture about the replacement of the "real" with surface image, and the subsequent blurring of boundaries between reality and fiction, public and private, high and low culture' (2000: 3). It is an anxiety based on the myth of a putative golden age in which such boundaries were absolute and could not be breached. However, as Moran goes on to argue, such a narrative can be challenged from two perspectives. First, by a more complex and sympathetic reading of the phenomenon of celebrity in popular culture, and second, by a recognition that literary celebrity:

> **is not simply an adjunct of mainstream celebrity, but an elaborate system of representations in its own right, produced and circulated across a wide variety of media. Rather than being a straightforward effect of the commodification of culture, it raises significant questions about the relationship between literature and the marketplace, and between 'high', 'low' and 'middlebrow' culture in contemporary America. (Moran 2000: 4)**

Anxiety over the commodification of literature, while certainly intensified in recent years, is not exclusive to the postmodern age. In 'Literature as Regime', John Frow (2002) argues that it may be fundamental to the way literature is produced as a cultural category. Examining Balzac's *Lost Illusions*, 'the first major European text to explore in a detailed and systematic way the commodity production of books' (2002: 143), he observes the tension between 'two contradictory structures of value', the high-minded, apparently autonomous literary realm and 'the corrupt world of journalism and the book trade to which it nevertheless belongs' (2002: 143). Writers, like their textual products, find themselves involved in the competing economies of 'crass commercialism' and 'high art', produced as celebrities according to both popular/commercial and high culture models, even when these models exist in a seemingly paradoxical relation to one another. What Bourdieu calls the 'charismatic illusion' of high cultural capital can only be produced in opposition to other kinds of celebrity, by concealing the workings of the literary marketplace (see Moran 2000: 4–5). It thus becomes possible for public literary culture to adopt a rhetoric of authenticity and artistic autonomy at the same time as this culture itself stands accused of partaking in the postmodern fabrication of surfaces, simulacra and commodities, precisely the kind of effects high art culture professes to despise.

Caught between the competing regimes of value which inform the literary enterprise, writers are variously produced according to what John Frow has referred to as 'the aesthetics of the signature' and 'the aesthetics of the brand' (Frow 2002). The aesthetics of the signature, with its attendant notions of origin, authenticity, ownership and copyright, depends for its effect on the concept of the unique creator, and so on romantic ideas of authorship; the aesthetics of the brand functions more like a trademark or corporate signature, associated with advertising and product differentiation; both are part of consumer culture, bound up with processes of commodification. Moreover, a convergence between the two ('the mass-marketing of high-cultural rarity and the aestheticization (rarefication) of certain forms of popular or commercial culture' (Frow 2002: 70)) is currently under way, with the effect 'that it is no longer possible in good faith to oppose an "authentic" aesthetic of the signature to a "commercialized aesthetics of the brand' (Frow 2002: 71). Celebrity writers are 'branded' in ways not incommensurate with the marketing of consumer goods at the same time as branded consumer items are 'personalized' to produce a 'signature effect.'

Celebrity, or rather the processes of celebrification, are curiously circular in nature, making it hard to distinguish cause from effect. Once imbricated in the discourse of celebrity, writers become cultural functions, subjected to (or subjecting themselves to – they're not all innocent bystanders) practices, meanings and manipulations acted out in the public life of literature (the media, the internet, prize ceremonies, festivals, the publishing and marketing industries) and manifesting as figures of intense scrutiny, projections of various forms of desire. There is a preference for personality over writing, along with a tendency to confuse art and life, and to see writers as seamless extensions of their texts. There is a strong emphasis on performance and an intense investment in the body of the writer, in their sexual exploits and preferences and in the details of their daily lives. There is also desire to recreate the writer as national icon, as representative or spokesperson for particular cultural groups, or even to elevate her or him to the position of spiritual guru. There is a desire for intimacy, constructing the author as kindred spirit, confidant or best friend. There is the aura associated with celebrity worship in general – but there is more.

***

At Adelaide Writers' Week in 1994, at the end of a book launch session, a member of the audience stood up and asked the writer, Rosie Scott, to 'tell us about yourself.'

There was an embarrassed silence and Scott finally asked what she wanted to know. The woman hesitated, and finally blurted out: 'Tell us what we want to know.' I am not quite sure what this rather clumsy request really meant: 'Tell us that which we want to know' or 'Tell us what it is we want to know.' In either case, the power bestowed on the author by this seemingly innocent question is considerable. What is the nature, what are the limits, of the author's knowledge? Is she the custodian of meaning, not just that of texts, not just of her own life, but *our* meaning as well? Can she unlock the mystery of our lives?

Ten years later, Jeanette Winterson entertained the 2004 Writers' Week audience with a spirited defence of poetry, at the same time mocking the tendency to fetishize writing and authors, treating them as the 'spiritual equivalent of fast food' or as quick-fix solutions to all the ills of the modern world. Poetry, she said, becomes 'a spiritual wonderbra', and she had been made to feel like 'a home-help encyclopaedia'. 'You can't put yourself on a spiritual Atkins diet!' she warned, nevertheless succeeding in arguing that the art of poetry was precisely the kind of diet needed to counteract the profit-driven, warmongering, spiritually and culturally deprived world of the present day. Her witty (though mixed) metaphors were received with great hilarity, her faultless performance (learnt, she admitted, through her early training as a fundamentalist evangelist) demonstrating that it is possible for the author to have it both ways: to court the audience's veneration and to mock it too.

The celebrity author, as figured in these stories, is more than a pale echo of Hollywood stars, rock musicians or sporting legends. The aura attached to authorship, and to the living or dead writer as its embodiment, has a history dating back at least to the turn of the nineteenth century, when the Romantic poets celebrated the image of the artist as creative genius and cultural hero. The vision of the author-as-genius survives in various guises in contemporary literary culture, reflected in biographies, author profiles and promotional practices, inspiring organizers as well as audiences at writers' festivals and (dare one say it) informing most critical and pedagogical practice, in spite of much protestation to the contrary from the literary academy. With the elevation of the author to unique visionary, endowed with faculties of imagination and powers of creation superior to those allocated to ordinary mortals, come roles for literature variously echoed in public literary discourse today: as source of spiritual and moral as well as aesthetic enlightenment, as instrument for social and cultural healing, as repository for values of an almost other-worldly order, as defence against, and consolation for, the shortcomings of ordinary lives in the real world.

These roles are by no means identical or consistent, but if I argue that they may be read on a continuum rather than as a history of ruptures, it is because of the features they share, the most important of which is the appeal to a centre of meaning, authority, identity or wisdom organized around the name or person of the author. It may even be argued that the influential twentieth century tradition of anti-author criticism, from T. S. Eliot to Roland Barthes and beyond, worked not so much by removing the author, as by displacing the author-function onto other signifiers of literary authority – impersonality, the 'organic' unity of the text, *écriture*, absence – which somehow always left open an opportunity for the author to slip in through the back door (Foucault 1977: 177, see also Williamson 1989). If the author is always a cultural function – textual effect, projection, product of desire – the elevation of this function to object of high cultural value will, inevitably it seems, construct a unified psychological and/or biological site as its focus. The cult of literature is always, in some sense, the cult of the author. And while the author/text nexus has been endlessly complicated within academic criticism, public literary culture makes the transition with much less regard for theoretical niceties. The projection of the text onto the author, and the idea of the author as text, are encapsulated in an advertisement for the 2000 Melbourne Writers' Festival in which the word becomes flesh and flesh word in a seamless circular movement: 'You've read their words. Now read their minds' (see Figure 20.1).

Figured as word made flesh, literary celebrity is not necessarily a function of bodily *presence*. As in the case of much analysed celebrity figures like Elvis, Princess Diana and Marilyn Monroe, the (actual) death of the author is not the end of stardom but instead an excellent career move (see Frow 1998: 204). If, as Chris Rojek (see also Section Three) suggests, ' "post-God" celebrity is now one of the mainstays of organizing recognition and belonging in secular society' (2001: 58), shrines to dead writers organize iconographies around discourses that, though secular, operate according to transcendent principles such as genius, national identity, cultural heritage and authenticity. Literary pilgrimages, much like other modes of tourism, are haunted by textual 'ghosts' but at the same time rely heavily on bodies (the once-present body of the author, bodily remains, bodily transformation) for their cultural meanings.

A promotional bookmark for the 'Literature Comes to Life Tours', a Melbourne-based company which organizes guided tours to literary sites in England and Ireland reads: 'You'll be amazed . . . at what a tour like this can do for your life.' What it offers is not just an educational, or even spiritual experience, but a physical, sensual and finally mystical one as well:

Listen for the nightingales in John Keats' garden
Run your fingers over the polished oak of Jane Austen's writing table
Feel the heritage under your feet.

The literary 'experience', it would seem, can somehow be transmitted from the physical surroundings of the dead writer to the live body of the tourist. Similarly, literary 'pub crawls', which are popular in cities like London and Dublin, seem to rely on the capacity of brews like bitter, Guinness or whisky to provide participants, through bodily transformation, with the spiritual knowledge which released the creative well-springs of their cultural heroes.

The more serious tourist guides to Stratford-upon-Avon stress that their sites and stories are only 'traditionally' associated with its most famous son. Even so, tour leaders taking their groups through 'The Birthplace' tend to lower their voices as they approach the 'Birth Room', encouraging their charges to worship in silence at what Henry James in his story 'The Birthplace' ironically refers to as 'the Mecca of the English-speaking race' (1909: 134). In reality, Stratford can best be described as a Shakespeare theme park, a cheerful mish-mash of biography, myth and heritage industry. As a religious experience, it resonates simultaneously with high church seriousness and the postmodern myth making of Disneyland.

***

If, as I have argued in this paper, literary fame conflates a 'generic' celebrity function with historical constructions of literary greatness, or, to put it differently, celebrity as

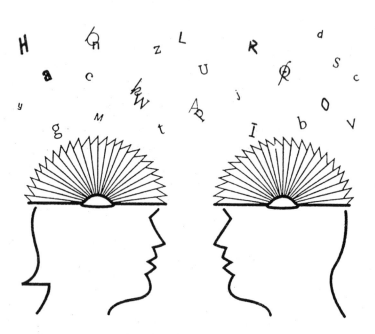

You've read their words.
Now read their minds.

FREE FESTIVAL PROGRAM IN THE AGE SATURDAY 22 JULY.

For a unique insight into how your favourite authors think, don't miss The Age Melbourne Writers' Festival. And for a taste of what's to come, make sure you get the official Festival Program - yours free in The Age on Saturday 22 July. The Festival's a rare chance to rub shoulders with 180 leading authors.

 Meet luminaries like Zadie Smith, Roberta Sykes, and Robert Drewe. And chat with hundreds of like-minded literary devotees.

At the CUB Malthouse, August 25 to September 3.

Seize the day.

The price of every ticket includes a copy of The Age.

Figure 20.1   *Advertisement for the 2000 Melbourne Writer's Festival*

'empty' cultural signifier with fame based on achievement, these discourses are also, paradoxically, evoked as stark opposites, often for the purpose of cultural gate-keeping. In the following (fairly typical) example of literary journalism, the gate-keeping is simultaneously argued along the lines of class, race and gender:

> **The new type of festival visitor now expects a plentiful supply of fairly sophisticated catering with decent wine and good coffee, for which they are willing to pay. Inch by imperceptible inch, the demographic expands beyond passionate lovers of literature to a more general and well cashed-up audience who wants to hear and see the latest Booker winner, the spunky author whose sexy novel was made into a film, the new black chick on the international circuit. (Lurie 2004: 12)**

The *widening* of the audience for literature is here perceived, not as a cause for celebration, but instead as a threat: consumed with 'decent' wine and 'good' coffee, the 'spunky author' and 'new black chick' become embodiments of cultural populism, and the 'cashed-up audience' they attract are denied entry into the privileged demographic of 'passionate lovers of literature.' The cultural anxieties at work in such constructions confound any easy categorization. In terms of class, for example, an 'older' bourgeois demographic of educated, genuine bibliophiles are pitted against a new middle class of 'lifestyle' consumers, victims to literary fashion and thus, it would seem, incapable of literary passion. The question of who 'owns' literature and who, or what, should be excluded from this contested cultural terrain, point to a complex traffic between different regimes of taste and systems of social and cultural distinction with deep roots in literary history.

The antagonism between popular and high culture is real and at the same time profoundly problematic. Literary culture, as I have argued here, derives status from its ability to mark its distance from the practices of popular culture (such as celebrity), but its increasing implication in the global cultural marketplace has made this distance difficult to sustain. The complexity of such cultural traffic is in evidence in the most recent Salman Rushdie story carried by the Melbourne *Age*.

'Mrs Rushdie does New York' reads the title of an article in a fashion supplement of the paper (Trebay 2005: 11). The focus is on Padma Lakshmi, described as a 'former model, cooking show host and celebrity spouse', who 'has seemed to appear at all places and all times during fashion week', looking fabulous and wearing the most prestigious brands of clothing and jewellery. The tongue-in-cheek tone of the article presents a rather unflattering portrait of Mrs Rushdie as a 'semi-celebrated hustler' with an uncanny knack for getting noticed. In the photo accompanying the article, the autho is in the background, looking at his beautiful wife with a rather enigmatic smile (pride, amusement, bemused detachment?). The point of the story, it would seem, is to distinguish Padma from the other would-be celebrities who populate the fashion circuit: while she has 'celebrity bona fides' as 'a burgeoning brand married to a global brand', her competitors in the celebrity stakes are laughed off: 'You were on a desert island for six weeks eating rats, you got voted off, and now you want a front-row seat?' Rushdie himself, while hardly mentioned in the article, is there in the background, propping up his wife's celebrity status, lending her the legitimacy she cannot claim in her own right. Even in the fashion world, it seems, it is not enough to be beautiful, well dressed and well known, and Padma Lakshmi's distinction is the cultural aura bestowed on her by her famous husband.

The author-function underpinning such celebrity stories has, on the surface, little to do with the ideal of the cultural hero worshipped from a respectful distance, or with other established models for literary greatness. The gentle mockery aimed at Padma Lakshmi in her quest for media attention is, implicitly, extended to her husband as well. But the paradoxical attitude of simultaneous mockery and respect says at least as much about celebrity culture as it does about Rushdie himself: it is an industry, and a discourse, given to self-loathing, to deflating the very notion of celebrity in the process of establishing it. Against the construction of the celebrity writer as incongruity, the accidental victim of the relentless progress of commodity culture, it becomes possible to see high-art 'bona fides' celebrity as a cultural necessity. Positioned somewhere in the background, smiling (or frowning) at the extravagant goings-on of the media circus, mocked but also revered by a cultural system which doubts its own credentials, the writer (along with other members of the 'meritocracy' of high-art fame), still figures as a yardstick against which other claims to fame are measured. In a world where fame can be empty or merited, earned, borrowed, reflected or accidental, it is perhaps still Mr Rushdie who has the last laugh.

Note

1. This paper is based on research carried out for the 'Australian Literature and Public Culture' project, funded by the Australian Research Council. It is indebted to my research partners, David McCooey and Michael Meehan, and to our research assistants Maria Takolander, Rebecca Vaughan and David Sornig. A number of illustrations given in this paper reflect the specifically Australian focus of its empirical research, though most, we argue, are indicative of trends in public literary culture world-wide.

References

Barthes, Roland (1977) *Image, Music, Text*, trans. Stephen Heath, Glasgow: Fontana/Collins.

Baudrillard, Jean (1994) *Simulacra and Simulation*, trans. Sheila F. Glaser, Ann Arbor, MI: University of Michigan Press.

Boorstin, Daniel (1971) *The Image: A Guide to Pseudo-Events in America*, New York: Atheneum. Originally published as *The Image or What Happened to the American Dream?* (1961).

Bourdieu, Pierre (1984) *Distinction: A Social Critique of the Judgement of Taste*, trans. Richard Nice, Cambridge, MA: Harvard University Press.

Demoor, Marysa (ed.) (2004) *Marketing the Author: Authorial Personae, Narrative Selves and Self-Fashioning, 1880–1930*, Basingstoke: Palgrave Macmillan.

During, Simon (2000) 'Literary Subjectivity', *Ariel* 31(1–2): 33–50.

Foucault, Michel (1977) *Language, Counter-Memory, Practice*, Donald F. Bouchard (ed.), Ithaca, NY: Cornell University Press.

Frow, John (1995) *Cultural Studies and Cultural Value*, Oxford: Clarendon Press.

—— (1998) 'Is Elvis a God? Cult, culture, questions of method', *International Journal of Cultural Studies* 1(2): 197–210.

—— (2002) 'Literature as regime (meditations on an emergence)', in Elizabeth Beaumont Bissell (ed.), *The Question of Literature: The Place of the Literary in Contemporary Culture*, Manchester: Manchester University Press, 142–55.

—— (2002) 'Signature and brand', in Jim Collins (ed.), *High-Pop: Making Culture into Popular Entertainment*, Oxford: Blackwell, 56–74.

Habermas, Jürgen (1991) *The Structural Transformation of the Public Sphere: An Inquiry into a Category of Bourgeois Society*, trans. Thomas Burger, Cambridge, MA: MIT Press.

James, Henry (1909) *The Novels and Tales of Henry James*, vol. XVII, New York: Charles Scribner's Sons.

Leff, Leonard J. (1997) *Hemingway and His Conspirators: Hollywood, Scribners and the Making of American Celebrity Culture*, Lanham and Oxford: Rowman & Littlefield Publishers.

Lurie, Caroline (2004) 'Festival, Inc.', *Australian Author* 36(2): 8–12.

Marshall, P. David (1997) *Celebrity and Power: Fame in Contemporary Culture*, Minneapolis and London: University of Minnesota Press.

McKee, Alan (2005) *The Public Sphere: An Introduction*, Cambridge: Cambridge University Press.

Moran, Joe (2000) *Star Authors: Literary Celebrity in America*, London: Pluto Press.

Rojek, Chris (2001) *Celebrity*, London: Reaktion Books.

'Rushdie takes bride no. 4 in Hindi wedding', *The Age*, 20 April 2004: 7.

Trebay, Guy 'Mrs Rushdie does New York', *The Age*, A3, 11 February 2005: 11.

Turner, Graeme (2004) *Understanding Celebrity*, London: Sage.

Turner, Graeme et al. (2000) *Fame Games: The Production of Celebrity in Australia*, Cambridge: Cambridge University Press.

Williamson, Dugald (1989) *Authorship and Criticism*, Sydney: Local Consumption Press.

Wordsworth, William (1950) *Poetical Works*, London: Oxford University Press.

Made in Culture: Star and Celebrity Representations

Introduction
Sean Redmond and Su Holmes

If there is one approach that has largely – but not exclusively – dominated the field of star and celebrity analysis then it is the approach of employing close textual analysis to explore the ideological meaning of a star or celebrity image. Stars are imagined to be representations, 'made up' in media culture, multi-faceted in terms of 'what they consist of' (Dyer, 1987: 2), how they signify, and they are historical and political in terms of how they relate to complex issues, conflicts and contradictions that emerge in the social world at any one time. As Richard Dyer very usefully postulates,

> A star image consists both of what we normally refer to as his or her 'image', made up of screen roles and obviously stage-managed public appearances, and also of images of the manufacture of that 'image' and of the real person who is the site or occasion of it... Much of what makes them interesting is how they articulate aspects of living in contemporary society...'. (1987: 8)

Of course, issues of identity and reception are critical to the analysis of star and celebrity representations. An image is only meaningful if people or fans are 'hailed' by it; can identify with it; can see themselves in (to) or against it, in some personal, existential or pleasurable way. Star and celebrity images are complex sign systems that involve meaning generation, identification (and estrangement) in what might be described as a 'cultural circuit' or dynamic exchange of production, ideological and consumption elements (Hall, 1997). Stars and celebrities are products of culture in that they have a political relationship with the social world: they are the very constituents out of which culture is made. They are also decidedly 'personal' in the way that they articulate what it means to be an individual to another 'individual', or fan, in what is configured to be a one-to-one 'intimate' relationship (Redmond, 2006: 36–42).

Representation and ideology are complex and often contested concepts. Representation can be argued to be mimetic, reflective or realist, with an 'image' merely a product of what is already in the real world, in a causal process of one-to-one correspondence. Representation can be argued to be 'author' based, or the outcome of a media producer's hand or general alchemy. In film studies, for example, early auteur theory can be said to be an example of this approach to representation since it was argued that a film's unique artistic vision was the result of the singular creativity of the film director controlling or shaping the filmmaking process. Finally, representation can be argued to be social construction, a political 'language' that operates as a system of power-saturated signs (Barthes, 1972); it can be seen as a 'discursive formation' that says all that there can be about an idea, praxis, or social relationship (Foucault, 1991); or as set or framed within a 'dominant ideology' that renders power inequalities invisible, natural or 'just' (Hall, 1997). It is the latter approach that has almost exclusively concerned the work of academics in this field. Representation is a language, it involves myth making and power struggles, and it has a relationship with social reality in the sense that it is informed by the real, is the 'real', and shapes one's understanding of the real.

Conflict is central to an understanding of representation and ideology. It can be argued that no one representation is secure or fixed. Rather, it can be porous, fluid or leaky, allowing differing interpretations about its meaning(s) and multiple (possibly counter) identifications to emerge (see Section Six and the argument that fans can and do appropriate star and celebrity images). Similarly, ideology can be understood to be multiple in form and marked by contest and division, where the battle for the supremacy of one ideology against another is constantly fought in the metaphorical battlefields of media and 'everyday' culture. As Richard Dyer argues,

> **Our society is characterised by divisions of class and gender, and, secondarily but not reducible to them, by divisions between races and sexual, cultural, religious and other minorities/majorities. Within these divisions ... sense is made out of the world, collectively but also differently. That is to say, all ideologies are rooted in the life activity of given social groups within a given particular society, but that any group may produce several contradictory inflections of its ideology. In any society – and therefore in the ideas and representations of any society – one can always discern contradictions of two orders: *between* the ideologies of the various groups in conflict (potential or actual) and *within* each of these ideologies. (1998: 2)**

Star and celebrity representations are there to be *read*, unpacked, or 'deconstructed' so that the ideology that burns dimly within them is actually revealed to be a burning bright light that draws attraction, commands attention, and shapes people's way of thinking and of being. In reading a star or celebrity image one is hoping to get to the political matters of class, gender, race and sexuality that circulate in and through the public and private persona of the star or celebrity; one is hoping to make a case for arguing that they either support and/or undermine the dominant ideology of society at the time. When one reads a star or celebrity image one is attempting to suggest that they have something to say about the world they/we live in, and the power relationships that exist there. Textual analysis, then, needs to be supported by media, contextual and historical specificity. The language of stardom and celebrity, as Section Three has demonstrated, finds new forms of expression, new ways of dealing with social issues, but this 'language' is always rooted in the culture from which it is enunciated.

In 'The Face of Garbo', the opening essay to this section, Roland Barthes employs his groundbreaking form of semiotic analysis to make sense of the Garbo persona. Historically speaking, this is one of the first times that semiotics has been used to read a star or celebrity persona. Its importance, however, is not just signified by the extent to which it heralds a new way of dealing with star and celebrity images. Barthes' beautifully poetic, flawlessly written 'homage' to Garbo also champions a new way of writing about stars, from the personal and the intimate. In a romantic sense, without this essay Richard Dyer may not have ended *Stars* (first published in 1979) in the way that he did, telling us how much in love he is with Montgomery Clift. In this essay, Barthes uses the image of Greta Garbo in *Queen Christina* (Rouben Mamoulian, 1933) to explore the way an asexual beauty is made an unattainable ideal, present (in Garbo's iconic face) but simultaneously absent – too ideal, too removed from earthly possibility. Garbo's face essentializes desire and identification; it 'offered to one's gaze a sort of Platonic Idea of the human creature .... The name given to her, *the Divine*, probably aimed to convey less a superlative state of beauty than the essence of her corporeal person, descended from a heaven where all things are formed and perfected in the clearest light'. Barthes goes on to make a historically specific point about Garbo in terms of what he argues is the passing auratic or essential magic of cinema. For Barthes, Garbo's face is defined in terms of its universal aura, made possible by the super-iconic nature of the close-up in film, but Audrey Hepburn's face, for instance, signifies 'because of its peculiar thematics (woman as child, woman as kitten)', in an age where the pleasure of film has itself been transformed by familiarity.

In 'The Whiteness of Stars: the Absent/Present Paradox of Kate Winslet', Sean Redmond suggests that star theory, stardom and idealized forms of whiteness have a special ideological relationship with one another. Borrowing Roland Barthes' (1982) concept of the 'photo effect' and his semiotic approach to image analysis, Redmond contends that when idealized whiteness and star image 'come together as conjoining signifying systems, an extraordinarily powerful representation emerges that ontologically privileges and secures (for the white race) this form of whiteness, or white stardom, as the highest ideal available to humankind'. Nonetheless, Redmond also contends that this relationship is built on a potentially destructive paradox that renders the idealized white star a death-like absence. To illustrate his argument, Redmond looks at the star image of Kate Winslet who he argues, 'critically plays out the tensions of idealized white embodiment in and through her unruly (less than 'ideal') white body ... so that the oppressions and repressions of what it means to be an ideal white woman today are laid bare'.

It can be argued that when fame and ethnicity coalesce together in the 'body' of a star, a supercharged representation emerges which says something profound about ethnic identity. This is something that Mary C. Beltran discusses in 'The Hollywood Latina Body as a Site of Social Struggle: Media Constructions of Stardom and Jennifer Lopez's "Cross-over Butt"'. In this essay, Beltran explores 'the complex and interwoven dynamics in the Jennifer Lopez star discourse through 1998, with specific attention on Lopez's body in this construction'. Lopez emerges as cross-over star whose 'backside' carries racial and gender connotations that need to be assessed in terms of whether they either confirm the dominant ideology of the exotic and hyper-sexual woman of off-white race, or empower the off-white star with qualities that energize her difference to the 'dull-dish of white culture' (hooks, 1992: p. 21). Beltran's essay offers a historical dimension both to the question of Lopez's ethnic corporeality and to the representation of Latino stars and performers in general. She contends that in the late 1990s 'cross-over stardom' is rendered highly visible by the promotion, marketing and publicity machines of a range of USA media industries. This she contrasts with previous, heavily sexualized media discourses on Latino identity, arguing that, 'residues of these narratives persist in contemporary culture in representations of Latinas as exotic, sexual, and available, and as much more in touch with their bodies and motivated by physical and sexual pleasure than white women'. Beltran concludes that in the case of Lopez her self-reflexive ownership of her 'butt' posed 'a challenge to standards of beauty simply by unapologetically being herself'.

Historically speaking, one can argue that the 'traditional' entry point for ideological analysis in film and media studies is through the vestiges and traces of class politics. In fact, Marxist analysis of almost any description takes social class to be the primary vehicle for the transmission of dominant ideology. With the rise of new social movements, and a corresponding interest in the politics of race, gender and sexuality, this approach became largely unfashionable. Identity and representation were seen to be wrapped up in multiple and shifting notions of the self, with social class no longer identified as a primary determinant of power relations. Lisa Holderman's essay, 'The Osbournes: A Class Narrative', can be argued to be a timely and necessary return to the position of centring class politics as the force that shapes the meaning and reception of the star and celebrity image. Holderman suggests that *The Osbournes* mediates issues of social class by juxtaposing the notion of 'anyone can achieve success' with the (in this context) seemingly contradictory myth of 'money can't buy you happiness'. In apparently offering viewers both positions, the series plays 'a role in sustaining social class order' since one is constantly offered the 'reality' that success is there for anyone to grasp, as long as you work hard enough to get it, and that wealth (if one doesn't by chance get access to it) isn't all that it is signified to be. Holderman goes on to argue that reality television programmes are 'ideal channels for disseminating myths as they purportedly represent "real life" instead of the "fiction" of situation comedies and dramas'. The *Osbournes*, Holderman concludes, 'serves as a warning that wealth and success have significant drawbacks and allows viewers to reconcile their current social-class positioning by feeling better about the fact that they have not and (may never) achieve the level of wealth or success they desire'.

If the analysis of social class has a long tradition in film and media analysis, then the attention to digital aesthetics and the cyber star is (obviously) relatively new. In 'Mobile Identities, Digital Stars and Post-cinematic selves', Mary Flanagan attempts to consider the implications for theoretical approaches to stardom in terms of the gendered and simulated body of cyber/game stars such as Lara Croft and Ariel (from Ultravixen). Taking a historical approach to star and celebrity theory, Flanagan argues that, 'the cinematic star as a culturally produced body has evolved into a digital star system in which signifiers, identities and bodies themselves are called into question. More than the indulgence of looking in at these stars within filmic worlds, we now embrace the very real pleasures of controlling these desired bodies'. In relation to Lara Croft, Flanagan suggests that digital technology has created an embodied 'excess of information and sexuality' that allows the 'development of an intricate subject/object relationship' well beyond the desire and attraction found in the classical star system. (In this respect, it is worth considering Flanagan's argument in relation to the work of deCordova, found in Section Three, since she makes much of the fact that digital stars do not have on- and off-screen personae). However, while the shape of these desiring fantasies remains patriarchal, 'it is through the recognition, representation and the redefinition of this body, and the understanding of the shaping of the subject within the digital star system that our position as users and our technologically produced, multiple subjectivities can be understood'.

21 | The Face of Garbo

Roland Barthes

Garbo still belongs to that moment in cinema when capturing the human face still plunged audiences into the deepest ecstasy, when one literally lost oneself in a human image as one would in a philter, when the face represented a kind of absolute state of the flesh, which could be neither reached nor renounced. A few years earlier the face of Valentino was causing suicides; that of Garbo still partakes of the same rule of Courtly Love, where the flesh gives rise to mystical feelings of perdition.

It is indeed an admirable face-object. In *Queen Christina*, a film which has again been shown in Paris in the last few years, the make-up has the snowy thickness of a mask: it is not a painted face, but one set in plaster, protected by the surface of the colour, not by its lineaments. Amid all this snow at once fragile and compact, the eyes alone, black like strange soft flesh, but not in the least expressive, are two faintly tremulous wounds. In spite of its extreme beauty, this face, not drawn but sculpted in something smooth and friable, that is, at once perfect and ephemeral, comes to resemble the flour-white complexion of Charlie Chaplin, the dark vegetation of his eyes, his totem-like countenance.

Now the temptation of the absolute mask (the mask of antiquity, for instance) perhaps implies less the theme of the secret (as is the case with Italian half mask) than that of an archetype of the human face. Garbo offered to one's gaze a sort of Platonic Idea of the human creature, which explains why her face is almost sexually undefined, without however leaving one in doubt. It is true that this film (in which Queen Christina is by turns a woman and a young cavalier) lends itself to this lack of differentiation; but Garbo does not perform in it any feat of transvestism; she is always herself, and carries without pretence, under her crown or her wide-brimmed hats, the same snowy solitary face. The name given to her, *the Divine*, probably aimed to convey less a superlative state of beauty than the essence of her corporeal person, descended from a heaven where all things are formed and perfected in the clearest light. She herself knew this: how many actresses have consented to let the crowd see the ominous maturing of their beauty. Not she, however; the essence was not to be degraded, her face was not to have any reality except that of its perfection, which was intellectual even more than formal. The Essence became gradually obscured, progressively veiled with dark glasses, broad hats and exiles: but it never deteriorated.

And yet, in this deified face, something sharper than a mask is looming: a kind of voluntary and therefore human relation between the curve of the nostrils and the arch of the eyebrows; a rare, individual function relating two regions of the face. A mask is but a sum of lines; a face, on the contrary, is above all their thematic harmony. Garbo's face represents this fragile moment when the cinema is about to draw an existential from an essential beauty, when the archetype leans towards the fascination of mortal faces, when the clarity of the flesh as essence yields its place to a lyricism of Woman.

Viewed as a transition the face of Garbo reconciles two iconographic ages, it assures the passage from awe to charm. As is well known, we are today at the other pole of this evolution: the face of Audrey Hepburn, for instance, is individualized, not only because of its peculiar thematics (woman as child, woman as kitten) but also because of her person, of an almost unique specification of the face, which has nothing of the essence left in it, but is constituted by an infinite complexity of morphological functions. As a language, Garbo's singularity was of the order of the concept, that of Audrey Hepburn is of the order of the substance. The face of Garbo is an Idea, that of Hepburn, an Event.

22 The Whiteness of Stars: Looking at Kate Winslet's Unruly White Body

Sean Redmond

Introduction

I have a minor confession to make. I am not even sure that I like Kate Winslet or that I get much pleasure from watching the films in which she stars. When she appears on the front cover of glossy magazines, or talks about herself in confessional-style interviews, I recoil a little, put off by a range of identificatory and representational issues. Winslet seems so typically English; so typically middle-class; and so very white. In fact, she *is* dead boring to watch, read about and listen to. And yet I am also attracted to her, I can't help but invest a little of my self in the 'person' she claims to be, or in the screen performances she gives. Winslet is at the same time so balls-y and unruly: she self-critically and self-reflexively draws attention to her class position, her wayward femininity and to the mechanics of stardom itself. She has celebrated being 'large' and she seems to rally against the privileges that her fame brings her. Nonetheless, it is finally her problematic embodiment of whiteness that I think draws me to her. And it was, at least initially, through her that I could begin to make sense of the close correlation that scholars such as Richard Dyer (1997) have argued exists between stardom and certain forms of idealized whiteness.

In this essay, I want to explore the ideological and mythic function of stars in relation to whiteness and the particular 'star image' of Kate Winslet. It will be my contention that star theory, stardom and whiteness have a special relationship with one another, connected by the mythic trope that stars and whiteness are simultaneously extraordinary and ordinary, present and absent phenomena. In fact, I want to suggest that when the signifying systems of *idealized* whiteness and stardom come together an *extraordinarily* powerful representation emerges that ontologically privileges and secures this form of whiteness (white 'stardom') as the highest ideal available to man/woman.

However, in this essay I also want to look at the key idea that individual stars come to stand (in) for the ideological tensions of an era. Winslet, I will argue, is a star who critically plays out the tensions of idealized white embodiment in and through her unruly white body and 'fighting feminine spirit' so that the oppressions and repressions of what it means to be an ideal white woman (white female star) are laid bare. However, the symbolic power of Winslet's whiteness, finally, is that it goes unnoticed as a racial signifier at all – thus confirming her racial superiority. Winslet may be an unruly white star, but she ultimately exalts in being at its absent/present centre.

The myth of whiteness

As Dyer (1998) argues, stars perpetuate the myth of individualism, on the one hand, by functioning as exemplary ('extraordinary') individuals whose success is down to the 'something special' they possess – the camera loves them, and they sparkle on the screen. On the other hand, and paradoxically (or so it would seem), stars function as ordinary individuals, as representations of everyman and everywoman, whose success is attributed to hard work, effort, some luck, but almost entirely to *merit*. In short, what is suggested is that it is possible for one and all to get a share of the glitter, the fame, the wealth, if only one works long and hard enough to get (at) it. That not everyone who tries to 'make it' actually does, is of course down to the paradoxical or contradictory notion that it takes something extra special, real charisma, to become a star. The ideological sleight of hand keeps one working, producing, consuming, in the (in part mistaken) belief that success will come one's way. And if it does not, then, it is one's own essential fault, the bad luck of nature, and not a capitalist star system that can only ever reward the few.

But the success myth also works in another way, forging a more explicit relationship with capitalist production and consumption. As Dyer observes, summarizing Barry King's work,

> The myth of success also suggests that success is worth having – in the form of conspicuous consumption ... stars imply that not only success but also *money* is worth having, that the stars 'are models of rapid social mobility through salary'. What they earn ... gives them access to the world of good living, to that part of the elite that C. Wright Mills in *The Power Elite* calls 'cafe society'. Thus, argues King, the stars as successes can be seen as affirming 'in fantasised form' wage earning, selling one's labour on the market, as a worthwhile goal in life'. (1998: 42–43)

This success myth is also racially encoded, since it articulates or gives 'truth' to the imagined representational differences or 'qualities' that exist between racial groups. The star success myth posits that stars have a particularly close connection with the 'extraordinary' and the heavenly precisely because they are naturally more spiritual, naturally closer to the heavens, precisely because they are made out of natural light. Stars glow; they emit light and sunshine like no other human beings on earth. The star success myth posits that stars are made in God's enlightened image, are, at least in a metaphorical sense, God's ideal (ized) and favoured children: the beautiful and the pure ones. In fact, some star images are as close to the Western pictorial idealization of Jesus Christ as one can get. Warner E. Sallman's mass-reproduced twentieth-century painting of Jesus, *Head of Christ*, 'consistently depicted Christ with flowing, wavy, fair hair and light complexion' (Dyer, 1997: 68) and one can see such iconicity reproduced, for example, in the promotional stills of a young Robert Redford or Leonardo di Caprio. In short, the star success myth locates the highest qualities of stardom *in* idealized forms of whiteness, so that they become *synonymous* with one another.

This is especially true in relation to white female stars, where the qualities of idealized whiteness – light, purity, and transcendence – seem to exude from their very pores. Here, the 'non-physical, spiritual, indeed ethereal qualities' of the 'white woman as angel' (Dyer, 1997: 127) becomes transposed, or indexically grafted, onto the female star so that whiteness and stardom conjoin to produce a truly extraordinary and highly desirable representation that appears to-be-not-of/out-of-this-world. Here, in this coalescing sign system, the idealized white female star floats between being the ultimate object of desire and a subject who nonetheless remains above and beyond sexual desirability. *She* is 'embodied' in a state of being/not being, as someone who *miraculously* descends from the heavens with her virginity, purity intact.

Idealized white stars in general, then, are made in, and come from, heaven, and this trope can be found stitched into and across nearly all forms of star intertextual relay (fanzines, posters, poster art, biography, trailers, reviews, etc.). One only has to think of Lillian Gish, Mary Pickford, Paul Newman, Robert Redford, Brad Pitt, Julie Andrews, Gwyneth Palthrow, Cameron Diaz and Princess Diana to see how central whiteness was/is to their star images. However, this *ontological truth* works in a more pervasive way in terms of identity politics more generally, since it suggests that white people are, or can more readily be, light/spirit, especially in relation to black people whose physical embodiment roots them to earth or to the libidinal forces of nature that come *from below*. When they do emerge, black stars, at least historically, are often implicitly connected to these racial forces so that they become racialized emblems. Dyer defines Paul Robeson's star image as 'understood primarily through his racial identity, through attempts to see and, especially, hear him as the very essence of the Negro folk .... Robeson's body was the nobility of the black race' (1987: Introduction).

However, not everyone who is white can access such iconic forms of perfection. This is because white people have to be imagined as 'ordinary' (everyday) people too if their failure to enter the 'hall of fame' is going to be attributed to their own short-comings, rather than to social and political inequality. The potential ideological tension here is displaced by suggesting that some white people (often the whitest of white, visually and morally speaking) are more extraordinary than others (white trash people, for example). In the pantheon of white idealization, social class, gender, age, nationality and personal attributes, including skin tone, hair colour, face, physique and 'rarefied and magnified emotions' (Ellis, 1982: 307) are all called upon to justify this extraordinary white versus ordinary white dichotomy.

Extraordinary, idealized white stars, then, can/do also have a degree of difference or 'colour' about them that sets them outside the spectrum of 'sunshine' and blondeness. In fact, in terms of idealized English female stardom/femininity, for example, the trope of red/dark, long hair, rosy full cheeks, translucent blue-white skin, polite manners, becomes the ultimate embodiment of white beauty and spirituality. Both Deborah Kerr and, as I shall argue, Kate Winslet, work in this way, with Winslet's star image in some respects 'mirroring' Kerr's, at least early on in her career.

However, another complexity emerges because national identity is often shored up through imagining the idealized white star as a product of nation and nationhood. For example, the white female star is brought back down to earth, so-to-speak, to embody the core values of the country she finds herself representing. This is how the blonde Norwegian Sonie Henjie became a key signifier of American renewal in the post-Depression era (Negra, 2001), and how Princess Diana embodied the purity, nobility and lineage of English Royalty in a 1980s Britain 'haunted' by immigration, race riots, urban collapse and a loss of the British Empire (Davies, 2001).

The photo-effect of whiteness

John Ellis's (1982) use of Roland Barthes's 'photo-effect' as a metaphor for the extraordinary/ordinary, presence/absence paradox of the star is extremely useful in understanding how whiteness functions as a living paradox. For Barthes and Ellis, photography and cinema produce a vision regime where things, objects, people are simultaneously present, there before us in the image or frame, but also absent, formerly there, or as Ellis puts it, 'this is was' (1982: 97). But film stars, in Ellis's conception, metaphorically echo the photo-effect in a particularly profound way. According to Ellis stars are *present* in the ordinary world, since they do everyday things and act, think, work, play like everybody else. They are in this sense mere mortals who have had to work hard to get where they are. However, stars are also simultaneously *absent* from the drudgery of the ordinary world, since they live glamorous, marvellous lives that one can only dream about. They are in the real/imaginary end of the spectrum, purely heaven sent.

It seems clear that whiteness also metaphorically echoes this photo-effect. White people are (so very) ordinary human beings, concretely present in everyday life. White people are people's next door neighbours, work colleagues, club members, hobbyists, etc. The symbolism of whiteness is also found in the everyday world, in the wedding dress, the doctor's uniform and in the 'signs' of health and hygiene, for example, establishing whiteness as indexical, or rather iconic, of purity and scientific/medical achievement. In fact so absolutely present and mundane is whiteness that its ordinariness means it actually goes unnoticed as a racial signifier at all. One's next-door neighbours are without 'colour' unless the colour is Other than white. White symbols have nothing to do with the white race, only the human race. So, even this ordinary whiteness is at the same an absence because it disappears from view. It becomes an invisible presence that only ever really leaves a trace, an imprint or an echo of itself on the power structures and symbols of the world. *Whiteness is a photograph of itself.*

And yet, to return to the present/absent paradox one final time: for whiteness to be an extraordinary, idealized subject position, and an ideal subject position that has be striven for, worked at, a high degree of cultural and material visibility is absolutely necessary. And since idealized whiteness nonetheless has to try to remain above and beyond race, stardom becomes one of the vehicles through which this is transmitted, negotiated and inflected; because it is through stardom that whiteness appears most vividly as the highest ideal available to man/woman. It is through stardom that idealized white people are given god-like status and racial superiority, or rather *racial exteriority, for all time.* It is through stardom that light, purity, transcendence, and the notion of divine origins are given their ultimate symbolic weight. The higher privileges of whiteness as they manifest in the idealized white star are made into the facts of nature and the Law of God, as if their superior, or rather exterior, status as fact is as authentic as the glowing star photograph itself/of themselves. But there are still clearly a number of tensions working here – tensions that again point to the way that whiteness *is* labour, social construction and performance, and is also a potential tyranny or type of non-life or 'death' sentence to those who (come to) possess its idealized form, in white stardom.

The life and death of white stardom

The extraordinary/ordinary paradox and present/absent effect which is at the heart of white stardom, draws attention to the constructed nature of both whiteness and stardom, and reveals them to be fantasy mechanisms that attempt to work in terms of racial superiority/exteriority and capitalist production and consumption. When whiteness reveals itself to be a living paradox between its extraordinary (idealized) and ordinary (everyday) forms, what is also being recognized is its exploitative, mythical and performative nature. By having to bring whiteness into cultural visibility, into a concrete form of idealized subjectivity – here in the form of the glowing, ethereal white star – one is also revealing, or drawing attention to, the amount of labour (construction) one actually has to put in to achieve it (because, in this ideological sleight of hand, everyone (white) *is* and *is not* ordinary in the first place). But one can toil one's whole life to get at the success trappings and higher status that idealized whiteness/stardom brings and get nowhere near it. No amount of body work, cosmetics, dieting, hair dye and fashion accessories can actually guarantee the symbolic and material success that idealized white stardom brings. One may always remain *special* in relation to ordinary people of 'colour' but one exists at a lower order of status and privilege to the wonderful creatures that one has spent one's life trying to imitate. In fact, because these idealized white stars are imagined to be so (racially) exterior, such exteriority points to the impossibility of ever reaching it.

But imitation or performance is also central here to the way whiteness 'outs' itself as a racial category 'made up' in culture. Because when one reaches for idealized whiteness; when one acts out the representation of what it is to be a white star, to *become* a white star; when one *sees* or bears witness to the representation of idealized whiteness in and through the images and intertextual relays of the idealized white star (captured in glow, halo light, and glitter) one is demonstrating how whiteness, or this form of idealized whiteness, *is* social construction and not an *a priori*, naturally powerful, exterior subject position at all. When idealized whiteness shines it can be seen to be the result of the work of mise-en-scene and the star's own hard and intensive labour and not the work of God in whose image they are supposedly made. White stardom becomes not God's Law but *White Law*. However, that is not to say that these performances do not still hold real representational and ideological power – they absolutely do – but the fissure that results from the play of whiteness potentially opens it up to contestation and critique.

This contestation or critique or *auto-destruction* also generates, perhaps more powerfully, from *within* this form of idealized whiteness. This is because the qualities and constraints of/on being an idealized white star are so paradoxical and contradictory. On the one hand, it is all to do with absence, abstinence, repression, purity and perfection. Idealized white stars are supposedly above and beyond their own (and everybody else's) sexual desires, greed, and vices. They are 'holy' vessels, embodiments of all that is good and virtuous about (super) human kind. They are *supericons* to whose higher values one is meant to aspire. On the other hand, idealized white stars are the ultimate images or symbols of desirability; they are all about presence, expression and idealized reproduction. Their mere corporeality embodies sexual and racial perfection even if they are not meant to be fully charged sexual and racial beings. In Richard Dyer's (1987) reading of Monroe we see this oscillation at work: she is 'the ultimate embodiment of the desirable woman' but is 'nevertheless not an image of the danger of sex'. Monroe is the 'ultimate white playmate' and yet her innocence and naiveté suggests that this is beyond her, or rather, that she is beyond this.

Idealized white stars, then, have the weight of expectation, the imprint of dominant white ideology, on their shoulders. And yet this imprint is always unsteady, always in flux, always at war, struggling to win consent within/across the performance of the embodied idealized white star as much as wider society itself. This is because idealized white stars are mere mortals (they come from ordinary stock) and so the performance requires them to deny, suppress and repress a great number of those earthly desires, needs and wants that would mark them out as less than holy, as less than idealized white, as *really* white: needs, wants, desires that nonetheless burn brightly within them. In a brief list of ideals, one can see how limiting, potentially lifeless, it must be to be an idealized white star. Idealized white stars have to be heterosexual rather than bi-sexual or homosexual; monogamous rather than polygamous; glamorous but not excessively so; expensive but not 'cheap': bronzed but not brown/dark; muscle but not flab; thin/slender and never fat; muscular but not too masculine; (natural) light but not neon; reproductive but not sexual; desirable but not available; available but pure. When, or if, white stars are or 'become', any of these competing opposites, they can and do suffer a major fall from grace.

Idealized white stars regularly suffer a fall from grace because the experience of living this 'holy' life is potentially death-like, an impossible combination of absence and presence, interior and exterior, transcendence and controlled corporeality. The ideological and physical work they have to do to appear as idealized white icons leaves them without *real* lives to lead. No matter how much material and symbolic success they are granted for this performance, it cannot always compensate for the contradictory lives that they are asked to live. In fact, the health and fitness regimes, beautification, excessive moral constraints, all have the potential to leave the idealized white star feeling *lifeless*.

But this must also be as much a lack of life for the adoring fans who want more life to/in their fantasy white figures. The pleasure of the star revolves around concrete desire: a desire of/for something extraordinary but culturally concrete: a gorgeous face, a beautiful body, the rooted and projected promise, possibility, of great sex with the fantasy figure (Stacey, 1994). Idealized white stars who are too saintly, too pure, too exterior, become too unattainable, too much of 'not of/from this world' for adoring fans to get a proper hold of/on. As such, in the tyranny of all this self-control and repression, in the collapse of identification between fan and star, idealized white stars often resist and rebel against their own star image and subject position, or *just are* embodied star images who are 'made up' to wrestle with the contradictions of their idealization, so that fans can, in the end, identify, interpellate, and ultimately bring greenback back to the cinema machine. In terms of idealized white female stars this is often projected in and through their unruly white bodies.

It is this very struggle between *letting go* (being allowed to let go) of one's idealized whiteness, by being unruly, fully embodied, desirable and available, and being positioned, or positioning oneself, in its arguably repressive mechanisms, through purity, absence, denial, and transcendence, that I now want to explore in relation to the star image of Kate Winslet. Winslet (nicknamed the 'English Rose') seems to be the contemporary exemplar case study for exploring the material evidence for, and the contradictions and contestations of, idealized white stardom. This is because hers is a stardom that not only pitches spirit against body, extraordinary against ordinary, presence against absence, arguably in an attempt to undermine them, but is one that collapses spirit into the body and body into the spirit, to reclaim for her a desired/ desirable corporeality against the threat of negation that idealized white stardom would bring.

I shall begin by briefly considering Winslet in terms of how she seems to play with the extraordinary/ordinary dichotomy of her white status. On the one hand she appears as the extraordinary idealized white female star, the glamorous, radiant, ethereal, English Rose. On the other hand, she appears to be so very ordinary, so very down to earth, with flaws, bodily and behavioural imperfections, and everyday desires and stresses that contradict the exterior values attached to the English Rose persona. In fact, at times, 'early' Winslet appears to be not just 'ordinary' white, but also anti-stardom and anti-glamour. She seems potentially anti-female 'ideal-white' – in the way that her contradictory public persona, and her fat/thin body, upset such star, racial, national and gender idealizations. And yet then again, 'later' Winslet appears as the epitome of light, glamour and transcendence – a supercharged 'blonde' who lights up the world as only extraordinary, ultimately exterior white stars can.

One of the reasons for the potency of Winslet's representational flux is because of the different types of films that she appears in: film being, as Dyer argues, the 'primary' text that star images emerge in (1998). I want to contend that there is a 'Heritage Winslet', a persona found and built upon in the English heritage pictures and literary adaptations of the mid-1990s, including *Sense and Sensibility* (Lee, 1996); a Hollywood 'Titanic' Winslet, which glamorizes and in part more fully liberates, the repressions of the 'Heritage' persona; and an 'indie' Winslet, where a rebellious, more explicitly unruly Winslet emerges, apparent in such films as *Hideous Kinky* (Mackinnon, 1998) and *Holy Smoke* (Campion, 1999). It is at these different sites, with their correspondingly different publicity machines, where we see the meaning of her white stardom shift and contradict. The remainder of this essay focuses on the early moments of the Winslet persona.

Heavenly Winslet

One only has to go back to the gossip magazines, commercial film magazines and tabloid press, in the UK, Europe and America, to see how Winslet was being groomed as a polysemic star whose class and nationality-inflected idealized whiteness would be a key feature of her international appeal. Winslet was to be understood as a *quality* English actress – as someone whose performance could move people to *tears*. Winslet was also to be understood as the embodiment of all the core values and visuals of the *fetching* and *charming* upper-class English Rose figure – a soft, delicate and noble white English Lady. And yet Winslet was also to be understood as someone who had, as we will see more concretely below, the potential to be a truly celestial and international star figure, with a heavenly white face that spoke above and beyond national borders. Winslet was literally to be a *Heavenly Creature*; a moniker picked up in numerous fan-dedicated websites to her, itself a play on the title of her first full-length feature. Finally, and this is where the paradox again emerges, Winslet was also to be understood as someone who was also a good degree less than all this finery and purity. Winslet was in the end just the 'ordinary' girl that one could very well live next door to, and with multiple imperfections to boot.

In all these inflections, though, idealized whiteness appears as a marker of her identity and star meaning, but disappears as subjectivity at all, either through displacement (Englishness, class, gender) or essentialism, where Winslet is not considered to be racial, but just an ordinary or extraordinary girl with huge 'natural' talent. Nonetheless, one only has to *read* Winslet's 'performance' in these texts to see that she was, to a degree, compliant or active, in promoting or grooming this oscillation, an active and dynamic oscillation, then, that allowed her be a fluid white star from the outset – present and absent, celestial and 'common', national and exterior, *just like* the metaphorical photo-effect of whiteness itself.

One can immediately begin to see the tensions of this particularized extraordinary/ordinary paradox of her white stardom operating the moment she was 'introduced' to the public in 1996/1997, before, during and after the release of *Sense and Sensibility*. Named as one of '10 new stars we predict will brighten up the year' (*Newsweek*, January 1996), the feature continues,

Drama Queen
KATE WINSLET JUST ADORES Emma Thompson – good God, she's absolutely one of her greatest friends! Last night her 'Sense and Sensibility' sister banged on her hotel room door while holding a glass of red wine and shouting, "Let me in, you cow, and give me a bloody cigarette" Brilliant!

It is in this headline pun, strap-line and brief paragraph, that one sees the importance of light to stardom, the beginning of a star image being manufactured, and a central part of the representational framework that Winslet will come to be understood in, emerging. Written in a mock 'luvvy' style, with affected 'speech', this immediately connects Winslet to an English acting dynasty, and in turn, the connotations of quality and performing ability/nobility that the English (the Thompsons) are admired for (in the UK but especially in America). Winslet, we read, keeps only the best of acting company. Winslet, in fact, *comes from* the best of acting stock – her parents were both *stage* actors. But Winslet is also being connected to English heritage cinema, to quality drama and 'high-art' literary adaptations. Again, this positioning begins to locate her as a quality English actress, as someone who can play or embody the English female ideal, the English Rose figure, found in such heritage films. Of course, Winslet can only do this because she is being imagined to be an 'authentic' English Rose in her *real life*. Winslet is, at least for the Americans, then, being identified as 'English heritage' personified. She *is* the *Drama Queen*. She *is* the ideal English white woman with class, breeding and lineage.

In short, in the prose here, the nature of Winslet's extraordinariness is located in the context of superior or 'exterior' acting/performance; the extraordinary (almost *royal* assented) nature of English heritage cinema and literature; and in Winslet's ability to *really* be the quintessential (supericonic) white English female ideal, rather than to general (more 'vulgar'?) notions of glamour, charisma or overt sex appeal – although, a post-*Titanic* Winslet will become, to a degree, all these things also, in what will be a part reversal of her star image.

However, Winslet is also being made to seem so very ordinary here; so very natural, just like any or every (white) woman, in fact. Winslet drinks, gets drunk, curses, smokes, gets locked out of her hotel room, and as the feature later reveals, blurts out on set that her 'knickers have gone up my arse!' Winslet is funny, friendly, matey, girl-y, imperfect, just like the (white) girl/boy next door in *any country*. As such, her ordinariness is also a force that de-nationalizes her so that 'anyone', 'anywhere' can consume her, can identify with her. But Winslet is also, in one sense, clearly being imagined as so very anti-glamour. It as if glamour (gloss) in this context is somehow less special than the natural light or aura that emits from all this real English acting history, ancestry and literary lineage that she is being connected to.

But also already, finally, Winslet is being imagined/imaged to have an unruly or at least materially 'present' body: red wine not white wine or water passes her lips; there is the ingestion of tobacco; and her own corporeal body draws underwear inwards, upwards. Winslet is not the super thin white woman of modern, popular media imagination in this representation, nor is she the passive, English Rose Lady. Winslet likes to live, eat and drink, just like any real white woman in fact. She is not, in this moment of articulation, then, an idealized white English Rose at all, but every (white) woman with everyday vices. In this play, again, between extraordinary/ordinary, presence/absence, spirit/body, English Rose/girl next door, we see the contradictions and paradoxes of whiteness and stardom talking place, in mutually supportive structures of meaning.

Winslet's early star image emerges in and through the heritage film, a term taken from Andrew Higson (1995) and Clare Monk (1995) amongst others, and which applies to a group of 'backward looking', and white 'nostalgic' films that began to emerge in the 1980s. This is an emergence which, on one level, works to establish and to symbolically privilege Winslet as an idealized 'English Rose', the personification or embodiment of idealized white English femininity, but which on another level works to (deliberately) undermine such a 'constraining' or 'death-like' representation: as an unruly performer, Winslet brings a critique or a rejection of such passive, controlled and 'absent' femininity to the heritage text.

But Winslet brings this rupturing force to the heritage film that is already filled with contestation and critique. This is because, as John Hill suggests (1999), gender, class and sexual conflicts are at the (implied) core of many of the heritage narratives, and as such, there are already present a number of potentially highly subversive narrative ingredients. Such narrative tensions, especially around desire and constraint, are visually played out in and through what Claire Monk (1995) refers to as the excessive, and emotionally charged mise-en-scene – a mise-en-scene that draws attention way from the desirable/desiring nature of the woman, and which metaphorically stands-in for the body-that-is-sexually charged but denied its detonation. In my understanding of the conflicts that circulate in these texts, it is idealized whiteness that is at the core of many of these contests and it is in and through Winslet that I want to explore the way (her) idealized female whiteness is seemingly scorned and savaged. The case study I want to look at to do this is *Sense and Sensibility*.

Heritage Winslet

The character Winslet plays in *Sense and Sensibility*, Marianne, is initially presented as a translucent figure. The first shot of her in the film is in medium close-up, as she mournfully plays the piano. Bright, 'natural' light strikes her face, her neck, and because she is wearing little make-up, and her hair is a vibrant copper-red colour, she appears almost transparent, as if her white skin is indeed paper-thin. Her appearance, in fact, is just like a delicate English Rose figure, at 'home' in a sumptuous mansion-size music room. But there is also a degree of 'death' in this static shot, with very little character emotion being expressed. While Marianne is literally in mourning after the death of her Father, the blue, chalky form of her white skin here creates the impression that she is herself close to being a female corpse. The melancholy piano solo confirms the lack of life here as it is embodied in Marianne. In essence, in terms of Marianne's role in the film, this is an apt metaphor or filmic foreshadow: the constraints on/of her white femininity are killing her and this is what she will resist, a resistance that will be played out in the mind/body, present/absent dichotomy.

We quickly learn that Marianne is headstrong, independent, unconventionally daring and deeply passionate. She says to her mother (Margaret) that her sister Elinor's suitor is not right for her because he is too polite, and that 'to love is to burn, to be on fire ... to die for love ... what can be more glorious'. And yet for the most part, early on in the film, Marianne plays out these emotions in her *head* and in the 'classics' that she reads. She is petulant but she is also kept under strict control, under restricting corset and full dress, so that her voluptuous body is (partly) hidden, and her corporeal desires are all but denied to her. One powerful way that the terror of this constraint is played out is through the dining/food scenes.

Marianne simply does not eat. At the lavishly prepared dining table, familial and romantic contexts always seem to conspire to make her at her most repressed and this manifests itself in her not eating, as if eating food would be an outward sign of desire, a marker of flesh and body, something she/the ideal white woman is not supposed to possess. For example, in the first dining sequence in the film, Marianne is distraught at the behaviour of the new matriarchal 'owner' of her Father's house; but she sits totally silent, hardly moving and in the whole sequence doesn't attempt to eat any of the food before her. In short, her anger and resentment is channelled through the 'white female' expected behaviour of absence, of self-denial, of not eating.

The not eating seems to be an enforced activity in these films – an activity or performance that is literally and metaphorically killing the women, turning them into simulacra of female corpses, without life, body and desire. Marianne is clearly not happy when she is *not eating*; the absence of food makes her *visibly* upset. Marianne clearly wants life in her body: she wants to eat (to fall in love, to fuck) but the demands of/on idealized female whiteness cannot allow it. Marianne (Winslet) is also clearly not thin, not slender, but full-bodied. Marianne does or will eat, of that we can be certain. *We only have to look at her.*

Of course, this is where the emerging star image of Winslet comes into play. The story of her body size and weight is scripted throughout her career. She has championed the philosophy that women can (should) be big and beautiful and, until recently, she has resisted the media onslaught for her to be ideally thin. So, having Winslet as

Marianne not eating adds an extra semantic or semiotic dimension to the representation. We know Winslet likes to eat. We know that Winslet is herself also wrestling with the repressions put on her extra-textually by the promotional mechanics of a star system that is trying to groom her as a quaint, spiritual English Rose figure, with her purity, innocence, morality, *thinness* championed as core values. Winslet's own articulations in this promotional work, in contrast, reveal an actress who wants to work outside, or subvert this persona: they reveal an actress whose independent spirit and unruly body will not be constrained within the parameters of idealized whiteness.

Marianne will be no English Rose. She repeatedly resists, if not by eating, and not just through 'free spirit', but through unashamed and wanton desire for Willoughby. This is best illustrated in their wild carriage ride through the village, with Marianne screaming out in near orgasmic pleasure. The romantic fiction/poetry they read together; the open, 'public' affection they show one another; and the barrage of passionate letters that she sends him when he has moved away, are all traits of unruly behaviour for the ideal white woman. Marianne comes alive at this point in the film, and it is the pulse of this behaviour that seems to carry the representational weight in the film.

The more unruly Marianne becomes, the less white she literally appears to be. The more blood, life, in her veins, the more unruly the body, and the more immoral the behaviour. The further away Marianne moves away from idealized whiteness, the greater an object of corporeal desire she becomes. Marianne rejects this form of English Rose femininity for something much more like (white) life itself and the audience are asked to identify, with her, be more attracted to her the further she moves away from this repressive 'exterior' ideal.

Marianne can do this 'movement away' convincingly because it is Winslet who is playing Marianne, and she brings this dichotomy and resistance to the part. This then, on the surface at least, seems highly transgressive. In what becomes a supra-articulating critique, idealized whiteness, in the form of the English Rose, is being rejected and undermined by Marianne, the star Winslet, and the heritage aesthetic. However, one can argue that the rejection of this type of ideal whiteness is one that will ultimately allow the star Winslet to be truly stellar – a borderless supericon. Once Winslet throws off, throws away, her nation-specific white identity, she can/will be an ultimate extraordinary/ordinary white star with international appeal above and beyond the specific constraints of the English Rose ideal found in this film.

Of course, there is a price to pay, a degree of moral retribution for Marianne/Winslet daring to be more than this idealized white, English Rose figure. Willoughby cheats on Marianne, and abandons her for money, and the film ends with her marrying the man whom she had earlier spurned for Willoughby, and therefore probably does not love. However, this man (the Colonel) is himself a transgressive figure, who as a younger man had wanted to marry someone outside his class but was unable to; and so her unruly freedoms are, it is suggested, largely safe with him. Similarly, one could argue that there is eventually a degree of moral retribution for Winslet also, forced to become the slender ideal of modern media imagination in her most recent public incarnation, after years of jibes and commentary about her 'fat' body. However, to return to a point which is worth reiteration, the empowered oscillation between fat/thin, red/blonde, and so on, may in the end confirm Winslet's exterior status as the ultimate white star who can make herself up as she pleases. Not retribution, then, for Winslet, but divine revelation, for an always absent/present star.

In summary, one can begin to argue that Winslet is generally a rather 'problematic fit' in terms of the meaning of her white stardom. Regardless of timeline or film form, Winslet is a troubling, transgressively cohering force in her films: a transgression that bleeds over from the range of extra-textual texts that reveal her to be an unruly woman, especially in terms of her body size/weight, and her independent mind. Across these media texts, across a great number of her films, Winslet constantly subverts what it means to be an English Rose, an ideal white woman, and an idealized white star. Winslet is on one level a transgressive white-fantasy figure who, through her unruly body, and aggressive 'feminized' roles, resists absence for presence, spirit for body, fat for thin, empowerment for docility.

Nonetheless, on another level, Winslet's shifting and contradictory form of white stardom may after all serve to shore it up as an exterior form of subjectivity. The superhuman qualities of her white stardom: extraordinary, ordinary, heritage-esque, independent, promiscuous, 'English Rose', 'blonde bombshell', unruly, fat, thin, and so on make it an *unearthly* corporeality that cannot be named as white at all. The meaning of Winslet continues to float as if she herself possesses the qualities of an extraordinary angel.

References

Davies, Jude (2001) *Diana: a Cultural History*, London, Palgrave.

Dyer, Richard (1987) *Heavenly Bodies: Film Stars and Society*, London, Palgrave.

—— (1997) *White*, London, Routledge.

—— (1998) *Stars*: New Edition, London, BFI.

Ellis, John (1982) *Visible Fictions*, London, Routledge.

Higson, Andrew (1995) *Waving the Flag: Constructing a National Cinema in Britain*, Oxford, Clarendon Press.

Hill, John (1999) *British Cinema in the 1980s*, Oxford, Clarendon Press.

Monk, Clare (1995) 'Sexuality and the Heritage', *Sight and Sound*, October 1995, 34.

Negra, Diane (2001) *Off-White Hollywood: American Culture and Ethnic Female Stardom*, London, Routledge.

23

The Hollywood Latina Body as Site of Social Struggle: Media Constructions of Stardom and Jennifer Lopez's "Cross-over Butt"

Mary C. Beltrán

It was the *Entertainment Weekly* photographs that clinched it. When actress Jennifer Lopez graced the October 9, 1998 *Entertainment Weekly* cover and headlined that week's cover story on entertainment industry "divas," the cover and inside photos were unusual, even as far as cheesecake photos go. The cover photograph consisted of Lopez wearing only a pair of black tights and a satisfied smile and posed with her back to the camera, a pure fetishization of her posterior. The photo inside was in the same vein, covering two pages and set up like a centerfold; Lopez's rear end filled a good deal of the right-hand page. The headline superimposed on top, "From here to DIVANITY," reiterated that Lopez had arrived as a celebrated, or at least heavily hyped Hollywood body. This media text was just one artifact of the overall publicity surrounding Puerto Rican actress Jennifer Lopez during late 1998 that focused on her prodigious backside and her expressed satisfaction with it, publicity which begs exploration of the complex interplay of ethnicity and stardom in the media construction of the so-called "crossover" of Latino and Latina film stars who become popular with mainstream audiences...

In October and November 1998, dozens of newspapers, entertainment magazines, and entertainment-oriented television programs around the country and the world reported the "news" of Jennifer Lopez's large and well-rounded buttocks and lack of desire to change her body to conform to Hollywood ideals, a discourse that appeared at best ambivalent with respect to her rising power in the Hollywood scene. To provide a thumbnail overview of the media coverage, multitudes of newspaper columnists, many adding their own commentary to the discourse, wrote about the aforementioned *Entertainment Weekly* story and photos and what they described as the new, public obsession with Lopez's rear end. Christopher Goodwin writing for the Style section of London's *Sunday Times*, for example, praised "Jennifer Lopez's bottom, her backside, her butt, her rear, her rump, her posterior, her gorgeously proud buttocks, her truly magnificent, outstanding booty" (6). And television notables were not to be left out of the fray. Jay Leno, after waxing poetic on the virtues of the Jennifer Posterior, twirled Lopez when she came on to the stage of his late-night talk show so that his live television audiences could get an eyeful. *Saturday Night Live* even spoofed Lopez when guest host Lucy Lawless portrayed her with a gargantuan rear end and ego in a skit during an October 1998 episode ("A & E").

The public obsession with Jennifer Lopez's backside during this period merits analysis as a dominant aspect of the star discourse that has positioned Lopez as a crossover figure. Minimal research bears out that Lopez currently is the most powerful Latina actress in Hollywood aside from Cameron Diaz ("Star Power® '99"), at a time when there still is a paucity of Latina actresses even considered for speaking roles in films. This is an accomplishment not to be taken lightly. As Richard Dyer asserts, star images serve as definers of power and identity for a society (1986). Non-white stars have particular salience in this regard, given that social and racial hierarchies are both reflected in and reinforced by a nation's system of stardom. The construction of Lopez's stardom and apparent bicultural appeal to both Latino and non-Latino audiences thus deserves closer scholarly scrutiny as a case study both of the media construction of Latino "crossover" celebrity and of the social climate of the star system in general with respect to racial and social hegemony.

To consider audience reception in this exploration reveals an even greater complexity in regard to the construction and marketing of Jennifer Lopez-as-star in late 1998. In relation to Latino/Latina audience reception, it's not apparent that this undue attention to Lopez's body was necessarily a matter of compromise. As Linda Delgado reminds us, Latinas in the U.S. don't necessarily buy into white American cultural standards that pose that women should strive to be model-thin. Although young, acculturated Latinas increasingly internalize conflicting ideals, traditional Latino cultures often tend to consider women most beautiful with some weight on their bones, which connotes health, inner peace, and success. So from the perspective of Latino audiences, for Lopez, as a Puerto Rican with a short, curvy body, to declare beautiful and unashamedly her well-endowed posterior during this time period could be viewed as nothing less than positive – a revolutionary act with respect to Anglo beauty ideals generally reflected and perpetuated through media images...

With this focus in mind, I explore here the complex and interwoven dynamics in the Jennifer Lopez star discourse through 1998, with specific attention to the over-whelming emphasis on Lopez's body in this construction. I pose the following questions for guidance: can connections be found between this highly body-oriented publicity and Lopez as a Latina or as a so-called crossover success? Does "crossover" necessarily involve containment; must it ultimately be a hegemonic process that keeps non-white stars in their place? Was this the case for Jennifer Lopez? Or could her publicity more accurately be viewed as a stretching of the status quo or of an increasingly multicultural media mainstream?...

In this discussion, I begin by briefly reconstructing the chronology of the roles and publicity that resulted in the Jennifer Lopez star image at the end of 1998. Following this summary I explore questions of the "politics of representation" in the case of Latino crossover in the scholarship on Latino stardom and non-white celebrity in general (Valdivia 247), and of Jennifer Lopez's body-oriented publicity in particular in the literature on social systems of bodily representation and ethnicity. Finally, I'll focus on the areas where these fields of scholarship meet in a final summary of the implications of the body fixation in the publicity surrounding Lopez-as-celebrity during her liminal, crossover stage.

The construction of Jennifer Lopez as star

What exactly is crossover, or crossover stardom? With respect to film stars it often is used, particularly by the entertainment news media, to refer to non-white performers who succeed in becoming popular with white audiences. Given this definition, Jennifer Lopez can be seen as a promising case study of both of the phenomenon of crossover and of its roots within the general popular culture.

According to interviews, Jennifer Lopez had a middle-class upbringing in the Bronx, the daughter of a kindergarten teacher and a businessman. Lopez acted in her first film role at the age of 16, in a small part in a film that was not widely released, *My Little Girl* (1986), but she became a blip on the entertainment publicity radar in 1990, when she won out over 2000 hopefuls to become a "Fly Girl" dancer on Fox Television's Afrocentric comedy series *In Living Color*. Her exposure on *In Living Color*, which aired from 1990 through 1994, led to further roles on television and in such films as *Mi Familia/My Family* (1995) and *Money Train* (1995). All of this culminated in Lopez snagging the star-making role of slain Tejano singer Selena Quintanilla Perez in the Gregory Nava-helmed film *Selena*, which was released in March 1997.

The body-focused publicity actually began at this time, when Lopez engaged in publicity for *Selena*. Much of Lopez's publicity for the film, especially in the Spanish-language and English-language Latino-oriented media, focused on the fact that she didn't use any padding to play the bottom-heavy singer who often wore body-hugging costumes on stage. True to the role, Lopez looks decidedly zaftig as Selena, as is evidenced in publicity stills for the film (*Jennifer Lopez Gallery*). The discussion of Lopez's body often was initiated by Lopez herself in the Spanish-language media, perhaps to woo and convince Latino audiences that she, as a Puerto Rican, could (literally) embody the role of Mexican-American Selena. Frances Negrón-Mutaner describes how Jennifer Lopez's appearances on Spanish language-talk shows often would progress during this period:

> As in other talk shows during the promotion of Selena, there came a moment during the interview when the question had to be posed to Jennifer Lopez: "Todo eso es tuyo?" (Is that body for real?) In other words, is that big butt yours or is it prosthetic? ... Jennifer Lopez smiled as if she had been waiting a long time for this moment. She stood up, gave a 360 degree turn, patted her butt, and triumphantly sat down. "Todo es mio." It's all mine. (186).

Negrón-Mutaner's interpretation of Lopez's "need to speak" about her rear end during much of the *Selena* publicity is that Lopez was claiming power not previously ascribed to Latina role models in the media through declaring and in fact bodily demonstrating her pride in the size of her rear to the public. While I agree with Negrón-Mutaner's analysis in relation to the Latino-oriented media, I feel this interpretation does not carry over neatly to Lopez's publicity in the English-language media. Throughout the *Selena* publicity in the Spanish-language media, discussion of Lopez's curves took a wholesome tack and was paired with visual images of the girl-next-door variety; along these lines, the above-mentioned *People en Español* article is accompanied by a front-view photo of Lopez wearing a fairly demure outfit and expression. This was a far cry from the almost raunchy sexiness that pervades much of the late 1998 Jennifer Lopez star discourse in the English-language media, as is discussed further below. The differing construction of Jennifer Lopez in the Spanish and English-language media markets points to a potentially "different sexual and cultural energy in *gringolandia*" when it comes to Latina icons, as Negrón Mutaner points out (192).

The publicity for Jennifer Lopez in the English-language media immediately following her big splash as Selena was low key, and none of the films she appeared in that were released during this period were especially successful. The Spanish-language and Latino-oriented English-language media did not forget Lopez, however. She was often discussed in Latino-oriented popular magazines and on Spanish language television talk shows; Lopez also graced the cover of the popular bilingual women's magazine, *Latina*, a vision of understated elegance in a satin dress and hair pulled back, school marm fashion, in February 1998.

Simultaneously, Jennifer Lopez made several moves that rekindled the discussion of her body in the mainstream media. In an interview for *Movieline*'s cover story in February 1998 (notably, the magazine's annual "Sex" issue), Lopez candidly discussed, seemingly without prompting, her curvy body and its uniqueness among the ranks of Hollywood actresses. Asked what nickname she might like to be called by the press, she declared:

> The first thing that came to my head was the 'Butt' Girl because that separates me from everyone else. I love my body. I really, really dig my curves. It's all me and men love it. Some guys like skinny girls, but they're missing out. When a dress is on a woman, it shouldn't look like it's on a coat hanger.... My husband calls it 'La Guitarra,' like the shape of a guitar, which I love because that was always my ideal woman growing up. So call me the 'Guitar Girl'! (Rebello 93)

Lopez also participated in other choices in her presentation during this period that contributed to the 1998 "butt obsession." At awards shows in the early months of 1998. Lopez appeared in skin-tight, slinky dresses that decidedly made her back and rump a focal point. These dresses garnered attention for Lopez and for her posterior in the media reviews of the events, as several newspaper and magazine articles and their accompanying photographs of Lopez demonstrate. The reactions of the entertainment news media ranged from that of one Golden Globes reviewer, who blasted Lopez for wearing a dress that was "two sizes too small" (cited by news anchor Susan Campos on the NBC news show, *Saturday Today*), to media reports, most especially by male media professionals, that pointedly trumpeted Lopez's beauty and style in these butt-emphasizing outfits. As one reviewer declared, "Best dressed [at the Oscars]: Jennifer Lopez. OK, so this is a man's perspective" (Saunders 38A).

Which brings us to the time period of my most intense scrutiny, the rise of the fixation on Lopez's body in late 1998. The release of *Out of Sight* apparently served to add more fuel to Lopez's increasingly sexy star image in the entertainment media. While the role of Karen Cisco in *Out of Sight* was seen by critics as having substance as well as style, much of the film's success centered on Lopez and George Clooney's acclaimed on-screen sexual chemistry. The *Out of Sight* reviews, which appeared in tandem with the U.S. release of the film in late June 1998, appear to have prompted the second major wave of body-oriented focus in the Jennifer Lopez star construction. Even while the reviews themselves focused predominantly on the film, several reviewers made mention of Lopez's sexy body and/or general sexiness in *Out of Sight*, describing her as, among other things, "scandalously sensual" (Kemp 16) and a "smoldering femme fatale" (Matthews B3) who wielded "Hispanic pocket dynamism" (Curtis 26) and "sexily slinky powers" (Hornaday 1E).

It was at this time that the greatest amount of publicity to date on Lopez in the English-language media appeared, most likely to publicize the film and generate buzz around Lopez as a rising global star property. Her debut as a singer and video artist was to follow only months later. At this time Lopez's star image as an outspoken, sexy, and confident vamp solidified, with the focus on Lopez's body very much a part of this construction. Lopez appeared at the *Out of Sight* premiere in a dress that "caused a near riot," according to Jeryl Brunner of *In Style* magazine (184). Lopez also willingly spoke about her body, at times seemingly without prompting, in interviews that appeared in popular magazines and newspapers and on television talk shows, through-out the weeks following the film's domestic and international releases. In illustration, all but one of the feature stories on Lopez that appeared during this period make mention of her body.

Subsequently, the publicity born from this period admires, obsesses on, and ruminates on Lopez's butt. The *Tonight Show With Jay Leno* twirl mentioned above took place shortly after *Out of Sight's* release, in September 1998. This was followed by the infamous, topless *Entertainment Weekly* photos and cover story. Almost simultaneously, in the October 1998 issue of *Premiere*, "Jennifer Lopez's ass" was declared the "feminine asset" currently In in Hollywood circles, replacing "Sharon Stone's crotch" (42). And on October 5, 1998, *Time*, a magazine known for its emphasis on hard news, published a brief interview with Lopez, using the teaser "Jennifer Lopez discusses her derriere" in its table of contents to entice readers. Fully one-third of the one-column interview with writer Joel Stein was about rear ends and specifically about that of Lopez.

In reaction to all of this publicity, other media organizations apparently scrambled to run their own Lopez "booty story" or tidbit. In October and November 1998, numerous newspaper columnists wrote about the media coverage by other sources and what they described as a new national and international obsession with Lopez's rear end, or they simply re-ran excerpts of stories to that effect that had been released to the news wires. The end result was that the publicity focused on the publicity, and so continuously re-circulated it. *¡Qué loco!* With the entire frenzy in mind, it's not surprising that Lopez was spoofed later in the month, on the October 17 episode of *Saturday Night Live*.

It also is notable that direct mention of Lopez's ethnicity appears to have been downplayed in the English-language press during this period, while it unsurprisingly was emphasized in the Spanish language press, as it had been during the past publicity for *Selena*. Discussion of Lopez's childhood in mainstream media articles emphasized her upbringing in the Bronx, as opposed to her Puerto Rican heritage. This likely may have been a deliberate construction on the part of Lopez's publicists to sell her as a rising A-list "actress who is Latin – not a Latin actress as in one who just does Latin roles," as Lopez told reporter Sarah Gristwood regarding her status in Hollywood (4). Of course, as is generally the case when it comes to celebrity publicity, the behind-the-scenes intentions and strategies of Lopez's management and of Lopez herself remain an unknown component of this picture...

Crossover and the "white gaze"

In his work on star discourse and whiteness, Dyer asserts that star images tend to assume a public that has traditionally been constructed as white. In his analysis of the star image of Paul Robeson, the foremost African American actor and singer from the 1920s through the 1940s with respect to reception by white audiences, Richard Dyer discusses how Robeson's blackness had to be negotiated in his image in order for the actor-singer to establish and maintain crossover appeal with white audiences. This was accomplished, Dyer asserts, through the inscription of white, stereotypical notions of "blackness" in Robeson's star discourse aimed at white audiences, involving, among other things, an emphasis on fetishized notions of the black male body and Robeson's portrayal of African American heroes with a prominent profile among the white mainstream, such as Othello (1986). Both strategies, interestingly, have parallels in Jennifer Lopez's star construction, considering Lopez's breakthrough role in *Selena* and the fixation on her body in her publicity. In the case of Robeson, through this inscription of white notions of blackness, the potentially transgressive element of his race was "deactivated," according to Dyer (1986: 115)...I would argue that the phenomenon of deactivation described by Dyer...was an aspect of the obsession with Jennifer Lopez's body and ascription of such traits as a "fiery" nature to Lopez in her 1998 star discourse, though deactivation was only one aspect of the complex and contradictory dynamics at work.

As cultural critic Coco Fusco asserts, one function of contradictory representations of cultural difference in a society is to express questions of identity as a culture's borders shift and change. From this perspective, non-white or "crossover" star images can be seen as giving voice to the schisms of American confusion around identity in a time of rapidly changing ethnic demographics, culture and social mores. As other scholars interpret the contradictory nature of the media representations of non-white celebrities, these representations also function to simultaneously celebrate and objectify difference, a process they deem necessary in order to make such images palatable from the predominantly white mainstream. This dynamic, the inclusion of elements that echo cultural stereotypes and nullify potentially transgressive elements of difference in the construction of non-white representations and/or star images, is described alternately by scholars as containment, "deactivation" (Dyer 1986), or "neutralization" (hooks 1992). It can be extrapolated from this scholarship that for Latino/a film actors, as for other people of color working in front of the camera, there is a fine line between crossover success and exploitation that only serves to reinforce racial hegemony.

Alberto Sandoval-Sanchez, in his study of Latino participation and representation in American theater, describes this dynamic as a constant conflict between "Latinization," or commodification and appropriation of aspects of Latin cultures without a broadening of notions of American culture in general, and "Latinidad," which is produced through Latino agency and active participation in the production of popular culture forms and may result in increasingly hybrid cultural forms (15). The example of Jennifer Lopez-as-star is an excellent one to illustrate the tension between "Latinization" and

"Latinidad" in contemporary media representations and particularly with respect to Latino and Latina star publicity.

The broader social context: systems of the body and beauty

As the work of such scholars as Marcel Mauss, Claude Levi-Strauss, and Susan Douglas documents, the body is an especially loaded symbol in the overall structure of representation that serves to organize society. Racial hierarchies have existed in this country for centuries, with bodily and facial characteristics historically utilized to ascribe individuals with mental characteristics such as intelligence, morality and self-control and accordingly to a position within social hierarchies of the American imaginary. The position of Latinos within these hierarchies has long been unclear, however, as historian Antonia Castañeda and anthropologist Martha Menchaca...discuss, Mexican Americans have been categorized within the U.S., particularly after the signing of the Treaty of Guadalupe Hidalgo, based on skin color, facial features, body type, and social class; lighter skinned Mexican Americans with European features and wealth were considered "Spanish" or "white" and accorded the social status of whites, while darker skinned and Indian-featured Mexican Americans were ascribed traits of and oppressed as "colored" or "Indian."

Similarly to African Americans, Mexicans and Mexican Americans deemed "colored" historically have been viewed as more "bodily" than whites. According to Castañeda, "both stereotypes [of "white" and "colored" Mexicanas] revolved around sexual definitions of women's virtue and morality...The elite Californianas were deemed European and superior while the majority of Mexican women were viewed as Indian and inferior" with respect to the potential for sexual domination (225)...This history provides a useful context from which to come to a greater understanding of the emphasis on the body in the media constructions of contemporary Latina stars; it becomes evident that the mass media continues the process of inscription and reinforcement of social norms in its representations of the body, and particularly of women's bodies.

The historical exoticization and sexualization of the non-white body is especially notable, in fact, in relation to constructions of non-white women. One aspect of colonialism and slavery in this country involved the construction of black women as "amoral Jezebels who could never truly be raped," as Bordo points out (9)... Representations of the black female as having "inviting" bodies with overly exaggerated genitalia and rear ends were prevalent, contributing to notions of black women as fair game for sexual conquest. Sartje Bartmann, also referred to in the literature as Sarah Bartmann, a South African woman with a large posterior who was dubbed the "Hottentot Venus," served as an extreme illustration of this colonizing dynamic, as Susan Bordo and Patricia Hill Collins document. Bartmann was exhibited in a cage and at fashionable parties in London and Paris during the eighteenth century as a scientific specimen, an illustration of the hypersexual black female... This image of Sartje Bartmann calls to mind the image of Jennifer Lopez in the *Entertainment Weekly* "centerfold" photo. It would appear that Jennifer Lopez is displayed as "presenting" to her public. This can be construed in a variety of ways, certainly as illustrative of an exploitative element in Lopez's 1998 publicity.

While Bordo indirectly poses that Hispanic women are not depicted in as severely constraining a fashion as African American women, given that black women were historically constructed as property in the realm of slavery, Latinas deemed non-white were at times represented in a similar fashion. Because of the colonization by Europeans of North American land that was formerly Mexico and of Latin American countries, Latinas historically have been enslaved, raped, and otherwise constructed similarly through narratives of colonization as available and accessible sex objects. These constructions subsequently became emblems that came to represent Latinas as a whole to many European-descended Americans. Residues of these narratives persist in contemporary popular culture in representations of Latinas as exotic, sexual, and available, and as more in touch with their bodies and motivated by physical and sexual pleasure than white women. In the case of Jennifer Lopez, it also is helpful to consider, as Negrón-Mutaner posits, representations of the Puerto Rican female body in particular, as they tend to include the notion of large, rounded rear ends in direct relation to Puerto Ricans' Afro-Caribbean roots.

These standards continue to impact on systems of stardom in Hollywood film. With respect to body ideals in particular, Susan Bordo describes the contemporary system of body image in the U.S., perpetuated through the mass media, and particularly the star system, as encouraging women to achieve the "slender body" at all costs, equating such a body with the qualities of discipline, self-control, and success. According to Bordo, fat, or even curves, are associated with powerlessness, both actual and perceived, and lack of self-control. From this perspective, a curvy, non-slender Latina such as Jennifer Lopez in 1998 can be viewed as either deficient or as threatening, a symbol of dangerous female appetite and desire. Media representations of the Latina body thus form a symbolic battleground upon which the ambivalent place of Latinos and Latinas in U.S. society is acted out.

Although a heavier range of weights is acceptable and even considered desirable among many Latinas, as is posited by Emily Bradly Massara, younger, more acculturated Latinas are most likely to internalize media-driven images and to find their own bodies wanting. Linda Delgado speaks of this cultural dissonance experienced by many young Latinas in the U.S. Given that the typical Latina has a body type that is vastly different from the average fashion model, I would venture that many young Latinas have more than their share of struggles with social norms of beauty and ugliness. This assertion goes beyond what may initially seem to be an oversentimentalized position; for Latinas and other women of color, American ideals of beauty can have a real impact on their day-to-day lives and livelihood. Because with cultural ideals of appearance and particularly of "beauty" come associations with social status and power. As scholars such as Richard Dyer (1997), Susan Bordo, and Wendy Chapkis assert, social status, privilege, love, and even goodness are most often associated with white-appearing bodies in contemporary media representations, while oppression and negative traits tend to be associated with bodies that are of non-white ethnic appearance. Given these connections, it is possible to view Jennifer Lopez not as another victim constructed in a still-racist society as an ethnic sexual object (although there are no doubt elements of this dynamic in the representations of Lopez in late 1998), but as empowered and empowering through asserting qualities such as intelligence, assertiveness, and power, while also proudly displaying her non-normative body and declaring it beautiful.

Summary

The Jennifer Lopez publicity in her "crossover" period of late 1998, ultimately, demonstrates complex and contradictory discourses and social dynamics at work simultaneously in her evolving star construction... Aspects of the Lopez star image appear to be indicative of containment or "deactivation" of the threat of her celebrity to hegemonic American social norms, as is discussed above. Non-white media celebrity arguably doesn't necessarily translate into the absence of racial hegemony for the individual celebrated; being positioned as "crossover" celebrity may always include an ultimate compromise and forfeit of at least some amount of agency ... The end result is that, crossover celebrities, while potentially offering a challenge to the status quo, also often serve a contradictory function as "homogenizing" role models of the social order, as Susan Bordo has pointed out... From this perspective, Lopez can be considered a modern-day Hottentot Venus with respect to this publicity, kin to other non-white film actresses who have been constructed similarly before her.

Despite such genuine elements of containment in the Jennifer Lopez star discourse in her liminal period in Hollywood, this body-obsessed publicity also was a sign.... of Lopez's role and social power as an active agent in the star-making process and of most importantly of changing cultural standards within the mainstream media as a whole. The commentary by journalists who explored the significance of the obsession with Lopez's body lends confirmation to this interpretation. For while J. Freedom du Lac, writing for the *Sacramento Bee*, ventured wrongly that the Lopez might be no more than the "flavor of the month" in 1998 (12), Donna Britt, a syndicated columnist at the *Washington Post*, and Christopher Goodwin of the (London) *Sunday Times* defended the notion that Lopez's publicity was in fact indicative of larger changes in the cultural landscape. Britt and Goodwin discussed the obsession in relation to what they described as an increasingly diverse society and related changing norms of beauty, as well as an entertainment media that increasingly understood the need to reach out to Latino movie-goers. Britt aptly encapsulated Lopez's role in this evolution in her playful description of Lopez as having "a big ole cross-over butt" (Tempo 1).

Given that Lopez's "cross-over butt" and general appearance repeatedly was described in the print and broadcast entertainment news media in positive terms as beautiful as well as merely sexy, it does appear that Lopez posed a challenge to standards of beauty simply by unapologetically being herself...

Lopez also appeared to have the upper hand, or to at least be content with, this focus on her body in her publicity. Far from being uncomfortable, she appeared to leap at opportunities to express her body and (to a lesser extent) ethnic pride. She continuously stated that she felt no need to change her body in order to attain success as a Hollywood actress. "I don't know what it is with everyone," Lopez said in *The Straits Times*. "I guess I'm a little hippy. Latinas and black women have a certain body type. We're curvy. It's in the history books. I didn't start a revolution. But I don't mind if the big-butted women in the world are a little happier because of a few cameramen's obsession with my behind" (1, L7). Lopez's casual tone in fact belied the power behind her successful utilization of a body-oriented discourse to sell herself as a star, albeit before undergoing the very transformation that she earlier argued was unnecessary. Nevertheless, with respect to her star discourse in late 1998, Jennifer Lopez had the potential to disturb not just notions of appearance but also of the social order.

Works cited

Anaconda. Dir. Luis Llosa. With Jennifer Lopez, Ice Cube, and Jon Voight. Sony Pictures Entertainment, 1997.

ANTZ. Dirs. Eric Darnell, Lawrence Guterman, and Tim Johnson. With Woody Allen, et al. (voice). Dream Works Distribution, 1998.

Bordo, Susan. *Unbearable Weight: Feminism, Western Culture, and the Body*. Berkeley: University of California Press, 1993.

Castañeda, Antonia. "The political economy of nineteenth century stereotypes of Californians." *Between Borders: Essays on Mexicana/Chicana History*. Ed. Adelaida R. Del Castillo. Encino. CA: Floricanto Press, 1990. 113–126.

Chapkis, Wendy. *Beauty Secrets: Women and the Politics of Appearance*. Boston: South End Press, 1986.

Delgado, Linda. "Arroz con Polio vs. Slim Fast." *Reading Women's Lives: An Introduction to Women's Studies*. Eds. Lin Distel, et al. Needham, MA: Simon & Schuster Custom Publishing, 1992. 208–211.

Diawara, Manthia. "Black spectatorship: problems of identification and resistance." *Black American Cinema*. Ed. Manthia Diawara. New York: Routledge, 1993. 211–220.

Douglas, Mary. *Purity and Danger: An Analysis of the Concepts of Pollution and Taboo*. London: Routledge, 1966.

Dyer, Richard. *Heavenly Bodies: Film Stars and Society*. Hampshire, England: MacMillan, 1986.

—— *White*. London: Routledge, 1997.

Fusco, Coco. *English is Broken Here: Notes on Cultural Fusion in the Americas*. New York: New Press, 1995.

Gledhill, Christine. Introduction. *Stardom: Industry of Desire*. Ed. Christine Gledhill. London: Routledge, 1991. xiii–xx.

hooks, bell. *black looks: race and representation*. Boston: South End, 1992.

In Living Color. Dirs. Terri McCoy and Keenen Ivory Wayans. With Keenen Ivory Wayans, et al. 20th Century Fox Television, 1990–94.

Levi-Strauss, Claude. *The Savage Mind*. Chicago: University of Chicago Press, 1966.

Massara, Emily Bradley. *¡Que Gordita! A Study of Weight Among Women in a Puerto Rican Community*. New York: AMS Press, 1989.

Mauss, Marcel. "Techniques of the Body." *Economy and Society* 2:1 (1973): 7–88.

Money Train. Dir. Joseph Ruben. With Wesley Snipes and Woody Harrelson. Columbia Pictures, 1995.

My Family/Mi Familia. Dir. Gregory Nava. With Jimmy Smitts, Edward James Olmos, and Esai Morales. New Line Cinema, 1995.

My Little Girl. Dir. Connie Kaiserman. With Mary Stuart Masterson, James Earl Jones, and Geraldine Page. Black Swan/Merchant-Ivory Productions, 1986.

Negrón-Mutaner, Francis. "Jennifer's Butt." *Aztlán: A Journal of Chicano Studies*. 22.2 (Fall 1997): 181–94.

Out of Sight. Dir. Steven Soderbergh. With George Clooney and Jennifer Lopez. Universal Pictures, 1998.

Pettit, Arthur G. *Images of the Mexican American in Fiction and Film*. College Station: Texas A and M University Press, 1980.

Ríos-Bustamente, Antonio. "Latino participation in the Hollywood film industry, 1911–1945." *Chicanos and Film: Representation and Resistance.* Ed. Chon Noriega. Minneapolis, MN: University of Minnesota Press, 1992. 18–28.

Sandoval-Sánchez, Alberto. *José, Can You See? Latinos On and Off Broadway.* Madison, WI: The University of Wisconsin Press, 1999.

Selena. Dir. Gregory Nava. With Jennifer Lopez and Edward James Olmos. Warner Bros., 1997.

"Star Power® '99." *The Hollywood Reporter Online.* Jan. 1999 and Aug. 2000. <http://www.hollywoodreporter.com>

Woll, Allen. *The Latin American Image in American Film.* Los Angeles, CA: University of California Latin American Center Publications, 1980.

Primary resources cited

"A & E Biography: Sean 'Puffy' combs." *Saturday Night Live.* Exec. Prod. Lorne Michaels. Dir. Beth McCarthy. Perf. Tim Meadows, Lucy Lawless, Darrell Hammond. NBC. KXAN, Austin. Oct. 17, 1998.

**Bardin, B. "Woman of the Year: Jennifer Lopez." *Details* Dec., 1998: 141–145, 199.

Britt, Donna. "It's ethnic America through a rear-view mirror." *Newsday* [New York, NY] 14 Oct. 1998: A41.

Brunner, Jeryl. "Scene + heard/premiere." *In Style* Sept., 1998. 184.

Cover photo, Jennifer Lopez. *Entertainment Weekly* Oct. 9, 1998. Cover.

Cover photo, Jennifer Lopez. *Latina* Feb. 1998. Cover.

Cover photo, Jennifer Lopez. *Movieline* Feb. 1998. Cover.

Curtis, Quentin. "The arts: vision of lowliness." *The Daily Telegraph* [London] Nov. 27, 1998. 26.

du Lac, J. Freedom. "2 minute know it all." *Sacramento Bee.* Oct. 25, 1998: 12.

Goodwin, Christopher. "Bum's the word." *Sunday Times* [London] Sept. 20, 1998, Style sec: 6.

**Gristwood, Sarah. "Features: mouth of the border." *The Guardian* [London] Nov. 20, 1998: 4.

"Hollywoodland: elements of style." *Premiere* Oct. 1998: 40.

Hornaday, Ann. "'Sight' for sore eyes." *The Baltimore Sun* June 26, 1998: 1E.

"Jennifer Lopez." *Internet Movie Database.* Nov. 7, 1998. <http://www.imdb.com>

Jennifer Lopez Gallery. Jan. 1999. <http://member.tripod.com/~alfonso05/index.html>

Kemp, Stuart. "A new view of death." *The Herald* [Glasgow, Scotland] Dec. 3, 1998: 16.

Levins, Harry. "Newsmakers." *St. Louis Post-Dispatch* Oct. 4, 1998: A2.

Matthews, Jack. "The Robber Steals a Marshall's Heart." *Newsday* June 26, 1998: B3.

Pener, Degen. "From here to divanity." *Entertainment Weekly* Oct. 9, 1998: 28–31.

Rebello, Stephen. "The wow." *Movieline* Feb. 1998: 48–53, 90, 93.

**Rodriguez, Rene. "Jennifer Lopez is poised for mainstream success." *Miami Herald* June 26, 1998: F1.

Saturday Today, transcript. NBC. KXAN, Austin. Mar. 21, 1998.

Saunders, Dusty. "Great Moments on Oscar Night." *The Denver Rocky Mountain News* Mar. 24, 1998: 38A.

Stein, Joel. "Q & A: Jennifer Lopez." *Time* Oct. 5, 1998: 97.

Thompson, Bob. "Lopez answers call to stardom/spotlight's on *Out of Sight* star." *The Toronto Sun* July 9, 1998: 68.

Tong, Kelvin. "Curvy? Butt it's in the history books." *The Straits Times* [Singapore] July 9, 1998: Life 1.

The Tonight Show with Jay Leno. Exec. Prod. Debbie Vickers. Dir. Ellen Brooks. Host Jay Leno. NBC. KXAN, Austin. Sept. 1998.

Williams, Jeannie. "Jennifer Lopez: she's proud of her 'bottom line.' " *USA Today* July 2, 1998: 14D.

Wiltz, Teresa. "Booty boon: Jennifer Lopez's backside makes an impression on the nation's cultural landscape." *Chicago Tribune* Oct. 15, 1998: Tempo 1.

** These stories were carried on news wires in excerpted form or in entirety and run again in other news outlets.

24

'Ozzy Worked for Those *Bleeping* Doors with the Crosses on Them': *The Osbournes* as Social Class Narrative[1]

Lisa Holderman

Introduction

In the winter of 2002, *The Osbournes* debuted on MTV, achieving the highest first episode audience ratings in the history of the network. Following the day-to-day lives of rock star Ozzy Osbourne and his family (wife Sharon, daughter Kelly, and son Jack), *The Osbournes* received a tremendous amount of media attention because of the warts-and-all approach to the subject matter. Touted as a reality sit-com, *The Osbournes* has been called 'Rock-'n'-roll fantasy meets take-out-the-trash reality' (Poniewozik 2002: 64) and 'funnier than the Simpsons…freakier than the Munsters…scarier than the Bushes' (Hedegaard 2002: 33). Given Ozzy Osbourne's legendary image as the heavy metal 'premier prince of darkness' (Miller 2002: 24) who bites the heads off bats and who may (or may not) worship Satan, it is no wonder that a record number of viewers tuned in to see the 'reality' of his day-to-day domestic life.

This chapter, however, examines *The Osbournes* in a different light – as an effective hegemonic media-constructed social class narrative. Specifically, this study examines how the *The Osbournes* supports popular, although apparently contradictory, American social-class myths – specifically the myths of the 'American Dream' and 'Money Can't Buy Happiness.' It will be my contention that these mythic narratives play a role in sustaining (the belief in) social class order. I will analyze the first 'season' of the series which comprised of ten episodes, and which aired on MTV America during 2002.

The myths the media tell

The mass media are important cultural storytellers, imparting hegemonic values and beliefs about normative behaviour in the social world. Prevalent myths related to race, gender, sexual orientation and social class are transmitted by the media, yet are conveyed in such varied modes that audiences are often unaware they are told the same ideological stories repeatedly. However, research reveals that narratives of social class and social mobility, among other narratives related to master statuses, are mythicized in the media.

Thomas defines myth as 'any belief in a culture that is so ingrained in and pervasive among members of the society that, for the most part, what the belief asserts goes without question' (1990: 331). She suggests that the media serve an important social-order maintenance function by teaching viewers 'appropriate expectations' based on, among other statuses, their social class (Thomas 1986). Specifically, the prevalent myths that 'anyone can achieve' and 'money can't buy happiness' are perpetuated in the American media by regularly portraying extreme upward mobility along with depictions of wealthy families, or individuals as dissatisfied, discontented, and experiencing more tribulations in their lives than those without great wealth (Thomas & Callahan 1982). These myths play a role in maintaining the social order by keeping less-than-wealthy people viewers satisfied with their less-than-wealthy lives and, paradoxically, giving them something to reach for or attain (accessible, liberal or 'democratic' wealth).

Of course, in order to be effective, these myths must be circulated in concrete narrative forms through cultural institutions including, and perhaps most importantly, the popular media. In order for myths to be operational and accepted by audiences, they must resonate with viewers' values. In fact, some research suggests that working-class viewers, for example, are fairly resistant to television messages when they contradict their values (Butsch, 2001). Studies of social class myths, however, indicate that certain myths are communicated repeatedly, and that these myths do indeed ring true with mass audiences.

Studies of social-class narratives within popular media reveal components of the American Dream myth as the poor and working classes are underrepresented, upper classes are overrepresented, and upward social mobility and success are achieved mainly through individual action (Berk 1977; Bullock, Wyche, & Williams 2001; Butsch 1992; Byers 1987; Desser 1981; Freeman 1992; Gentile & Miller 1961; Giroux 1990; Haggins 1999; Jhally & Lewis 1992; Jordan 1996; Lipsitz 1986; Schor 1998; Signorielli & Kahlenberg 2001; Traube 1992). Moreover, research reveals that narratives of social mobility encourage people to work hard in their quest for upward mobility while, at the same time, such narratives circulate in the same space as other discourses – such as the Money Can't Buy Happiness myth which portrays the wealthy as unhappy (Berk 1977; Gray 1982; Horton 1989; Levy 1991; Thomas 1990). Freeman finds this to be especially true of television comedies:

Television comedies reinforce the myth that the United States is a land of economic opportunity where anyone can become anything through industry and persistence. Paradoxically, the same comedy programs would seem to deter individuals' aspirations for significant mobility and discourage challenges to the current social and economic order. The repair of conflicts and negation of change are necessary for the maintenance or restoration of felicitous social life. (1992: 405)

Jones (1992) supports this thesis and claims that situation comedies serve as a vehicle for 'selling' the American Dream. One might argue that reality television programs, such as *The Osbournes*, are ideal channels for disseminating myths as they purportedly represent 'real life' instead of the 'fiction' of situation comedies and dramas. Shales (2002) explains, how 'more and more the ethic promoted by mass media is grab what you can while you can and hope for the kind of big ridiculous payday that winning "Big Brother 3" or "American Idol" or "Survivor" or, of course, a state or regional lottery-can bring.' Among other reality programs, *The Osbournes* narrative cultivates the American Dream myth by putting forth a popular story of extreme upward social mobility. And yet, at the same time of course, its cross-generic form recalls the classic structure of the television sitcom through familiar spaces, characters, and comedic events. In fact, *The Osbournes* social class narrative seems particularly dominant and yet paradoxical because of its play with, or 'confusion' over, its generic form. Viewers are watching real lives unfold before their eyes yet (mis) recognize the fiction (naturalized or humanized myths) at the centre of the show.

The American Dream: How *The Osbournes* keeps us hopeful

Several articulating ideological themes are interwoven throughout the first season of *The Osbournes* to support the myth that the American Dream is alive, well, and attainable for all. Although achievement of significant upward mobility or the 'American Dream,' in real life repeatedly has been shown to be difficult if not impossible (see, e.g., Gyourko and Linneman 1993), this program clearly portrays that upward social mobility does occur and that wealth and success are worth the effort. Given Ozzy Osbourne's success as a musician and the extreme popularity of the family's reality program, the popular press suggests that the Osbourne family is, in fact, 'an American Dream' (Shales 2002: 23).

An important factor in *The Osbournes* working as an effective hegemonic social class narrative is to allow audiences to pick up on the multiple allusions to Ozzy Osbourne's working class roots. Audiences hear about his meager beginnings while simultaneously viewing the grandeur of his current lifestyle; the two work together to illustrate clearly that upward mobility happens and can/could happen to anyone, regardless of social class background. In a number of episodes viewers hear about Ozzy's aspiration to be a plumber, his recollections of scanty Christmas gifts as a child, and his dislike for ostentatious limousines. However, the final episode of the first season, 'My Dinner with Ozzy', gives viewers a chance to hear Ozzy speak in detail about his working-class background. In addition to revelations of his plebeian history though bits of self-analysis (such as his explanation of why he often does everyday chores), Ozzy illustrates his rise to success by contrasting his current Beverly Hills home with his childhood, wherein his financially disadvantaged parents' top priority was to provide food for their children. The message clearly communicated is that the American Dream is accessible to everyone, including those not born in the United States and especially to those members of the lower social classes who pursue their (sometimes half-realized) 'dreams' to fulfillment. In fact, *The Osbournes* makes it clear that individuals can rise from adversity to a much better state of living. References to Ozzy's incarceration for stealing, his arrest for the attempted murder of his wife, his father's insanity, and battles with dyslexia and Attention Deficit Disorder, suggest upward social mobility is achievable despite *any odds*. The final episode offers audiences a sense of what Ozzy was like when he was his son's age; he explains he was 'drinking massive amounts of booze, smoking pot, doing speed' and biting creatures' heads off. Clearly, the implication is that, in spite of considerable obstacles, Ozzy rose above the myriad hardships he faced to become a very wealthy and successful celebrity. A major part of this success, as advanced by *The Osbournes* narrative, is hard work and sacrifice.

Hard work and sacrifice produce success

Another important factor in the portrayal of the American Dream through *The Osbournes* is the recurrence of the Protestant work ethic, or the idea that success is achieved by self-sacrifice and hard work. This work ethic is evident in several of Ozzy's comments such as his lecture to Jack that he cannot skip school and party late into the night ('can't be all fun and no work, has to be a certain amount of work') and his remark to Sharon that life cannot be 'one never-ending party, it doesn't work that way'. The fourth episode in the first season, however, is unmistakable in its message about social class and the importance of a work ethic in realizing the American Dream.

Entitled 'Won't You Be My Neighbor', this episode follows the battle between the Osbournes and their British next-door neighbors – as initiated by the neighbors' loud music which is played late into the evening. Despite the theatrics, a very clear and critical message emerges from this episode: one must *work* for money and success. Sharon Osbourne is unambiguous in her thoughts on wealth acquisition as she labels the neighbor 'little rich boy' who 'lives off Daddy's and Mummy's money.' In response to the neighbors' barbs regarding the many crosses on the doors of the Osbourne's mansion, Kelly fumes that Ozzy 'wrote that music' and 'worked for those *bleeping* doors with the crosses on them'. Again, the clear ideological message being communicated is that Ozzy worked for and therefore deserves his wealth, while the neighbor, who presumably was born into a wealthy family, does not.

Given that repetition is integral to the construction of myth, it is meaningful that the story of the verbal battle is told over and over again throughout the episode. As Sharon repeatedly recounts the argument to Kelly, to Jack, and to Ozzy, she stresses the point that the neighbor did not *earn* his money. In one recounting, Sharon tells how she chastised the neighbor for living off his parents' money and that he had no response. She later brings up this point again, foregrounding how – despite her critique – the neighbor did not defend his position (by insisting, for example, 'how dare you... I'm a *bleeping* rocket scientist!'). That the producers of *The Osbournes* chose not to edit out these semiotic redundancies is significant. The narrative thread which foregrounds how working for money and success is central to the American Dream, is apparently important enough to show again and again.

'It's good to be the king': Wealth is satisfying

The Osbournes completes the portrayal of the American Dream myth by advancing the notion that wealth is enjoyable and fulfilling. This narrative thread is crucial in promoting the American Dream myth. Believing in the likelihood of upward social mobility and success through hard work and sacrifice are only relevant if the success is unmistakably satisfying and worth the effort. Money, the ultimate goal in the quest for the American Dream, is referred to in a positive manner in every episode of *The Osbournes*. Money is the direct focus of several storylines in the images we see of Sharon's spending habits (and to a lesser extent, Kelly's). Numerous images of Sharon shopping in expensive stores and boutiques and the resulting items being brought home are shown throughout the first season. In one episode, Ozzy describes Sharon as a 'shop-o-holic and spend-o-holic', while in another Sharon tells the camera 'the Virgin Mary told me to go to *Tiffany* and *Cartier*.' In addition, nearly every episode contains offhand remarks which foreground how money is available for use, such as allusions to shopping in expensive stores, purchasing a mink stole, hiring party planners and caterers, or paying a Beverly Hills pet therapist to work with their dogs.

Without a doubt, then, *The Osbournes* portrays a family living in the lap of luxury. The abundant wealth is evident within minutes of the premiere episode, which focuses on the family moving in to their new and mostly renovated Beverly Hills mansion. Throughout the season the viewer gets a sense of the grandeur of the house and its myriad extravagances – such as elaborate technology and media systems, pools, waterfalls, video games, antique furniture, expensive rugs and cars. The family's prosperity, then, is visually and narratively apparent. When Ozzy complains about some things he does to make a living, the director of his music video says 'You? You're a *bleeping* millionaire!' to which Ozzy laughs and replies, 'Well, there is that.'

In addition to luxuries in the home, *The Osbournes* presents numerous images of Ozzy and family enjoying the perks of his hard-earned success in travel and treatment at various music-related events. Stretch limousines, private jets and helicopters, expensive hotels, elaborate meals, personal trainers, hairdressers, and enormous tour busses are unmistakable evidence of an American Dream realized. The program further constructs the magnificence of Ozzy's life by showing him socializing with celebrities and making appearances on popular television programs. Such material and celebrity inflected encounters and events indicate to viewers that the American Dream is more than just a collection of objects and services but a power and status driven existence. Viewers may desire the upward mobility depicted in *The Osbournes* because it will ultimately net or guarantee a life lived at the social centre. When a pretty girl sits on Ozzy's lap for a photograph, he says in no uncertain terms, 'It's good to be the king'. Overall, one of the messages threaded through *The Osbournes* is that wealth and success are satisfying and something for which to strive.

Money can't buy happiness: How *The Osbournes* keep us satisfied with the status quo

Although a great number of storylines in *The Osbournes* create an overall message that the American Dream is achievable and rewarding, a conflicting or opposing myth is just as prevalent. Several themes emerge in the show which create what might be called a counter-myth: that money and success are problematic and do not buy happiness. This myth works to temper the influence of the American Dream myth by showing viewers that upward mobility is possible but may not always be desirable – a myth that is necessary since real material and symbolic wealth and success is limited.

Despite the many images of wealth and luxury on *The Osbournes* much of the show revolves around the family being like any other: doing everyday chores, cleaning up after mischievous pets, dealing with rebellious children and arguing over finances. These five themes work together in *The Osbournes* to suggest that wealthy people have the same problems as those without great wealth. The subtext seems to be that no matter how wealthy one becomes, 'ordinary' and mundane issues still dominate one's life. First, viewers see the family members, usually Ozzy or Sharon, doing unexciting, everyday household chores such as vacuuming, washing dishes, and loading the dishwasher. Although Sharon claims she will never wash or cook again, she often does both throughout the season. Using a humorous musical accompaniment which constructs Ozzy as a downtrodden husband, one lengthy scene focuses on him struggling with the multiple garbage receptacles in the home. In addition, it is especially noteworthy that, except in the case of a catered Thanksgiving dinner, viewers never see any household staff: no cleaning crew, cooks or gardeners. Surely a house of this size requires hired help, yet the show's producers choose to keep them invisible. The resulting image is that of wealthy people doing as much, if not more (given the size of the house), housework than people of less wealth.

Second, multiple episodes portray the tribulations the family faces with their many household pets. With seven dogs and, eventually, two cats, Ozzy claims, 'this is a *bleeping* Dr. Dolittle house here'. After one montage of dogs urinating, defecating, and chewing furniture, the camera pans over to focus on dog excrement on the floor as Ozzy yells, 'I won't pick up another turd – I'm a *bleeping* rock star!' In another scene, Ozzy complains that they 'might as well live in the sewer because the dogs piss everywhere', while Sharon uses Ozzy's personal bathroom towel to mop up the urine. These storylines, along with the failure of the pet therapist to control the dogs, send a clear message that no amount of money will help this family out of their predicament. Third, *The Osbournes* reveal that wealthy people experience family problems and strife. A significant portion of the season focuses on problems related to the children such as their using and losing Ozzy's credit card, making trouble at camp, driving tickets, drinking alcohol, smoking marijuana, Mohawk haircuts, tattoos, false identification for admittance to clubs, staying out late, refusal to attend school and consistent sibling bickering. Finally, after a family meeting in which the children complain about not fitting in at school, Ozzy and Sharon set stricter rules about curfews, school, and drugs.

Fourth, the family members, usually Ozzy and Sharon, often argue about financial matters. Just as money is referred to in a positive manner in every episode of *The Osbournes*, it is also invoked negatively. Ozzy often complains about how much he spent buying and renovating their Beverly Hills home; in one episode, Sharon tells the children that Ozzy 'is pissed because I spent too much money on the house'. In another episode, Ozzy severely chastises Sharon for scheduling him to play back-to-back shows and accuses her of caring only about making money and nothing else. This storyline clearly implies that money, whether due to lack or abundance, can be the source of great conflict. Finally, a host of everyday, commonplace problems are shown throughout the season. These include Ozzy confessing he needs an impotence pill in order to make love, Kelly holding her cat while it has its temperature taken rectally, Ozzy's struggling to operate household technologies, and his stumbling around the yard with a broken foot searching for one of their pets while the other family members ignore his pleas for help. These depictions, among others, illustrate for audiences the sundry minor crises the family encounters on a daily basis.

The above five themes, collectively, narrate a component of the Money Can't Buy Happiness myth: wealthy and successful people experience many of the same unexciting, routine problems that plague the rest of us, mere mortals. Despite the truth or falsity of this notion in reality, *The Osbournes* suggests that no level of affluence or accomplishment allows one to escape from the problems that keep people from truly being happy and carefree.

Wealth breeds trouble

In addition to demonstrating that a wealthy family has to deal with everyday problems, *The Osbournes* also shows the difficulties the family faces *because* they are wealthy. This narrative thread serves as a cautionary mythic tale, which indicates that wealth and success require sacrifice and often makes life complicated and difficult. These troubles are illustrated in *The Osbournes* through three general themes: the advantages people take of the wealthy; the physical and mental toll of the work it takes to achieve wealth and success, and the exclusion, isolation, and ridicule that wealth and success ultimately bring.

Multiple storylines address the experiences the Osbournes have with thieves and moochers. Examples of this include the family's security guard being arrested for robbing their home and multiple images of the children's friends visiting late into the evening, enjoying the many luxuries of the Osbourne mansion. Ozzy complains about the latter by stating. 'I haven't paid all this money for a *bleeping* amusement park'. One friend in particular, a professional skateboarder named Jason Dill, spent so much time at the house that an entire episode revolved around his stay. Though Ozzy claims not to know him, Dill becomes the family's houseguest and is portrayed as a negative character who takes advantage of the family's wealth and causes damage to the Osbourne home.

A second way wealth is equated with difficulty is in the portrayal of the toll taken on Ozzy and Sharon by Ozzy's work as a musician. Many episodes focus on the physical and mental exhaustion caused by Ozzy's touring and other promotional activities. Despite working hard with a personal trainer to prepare, Ozzy is often shown to be fatigued and stressed out; during one visit to New York he complains that he is so tired he 'doesn't know what planet' he is on and is shown having a great deal of difficulty reading a simple promotional spot for a radio station. Sharon verbalizes the problem by telling the camera that the tour is demanding for Ozzy and that 'he can't handle it'. In a later episode, Ozzy sustains an injury to his leg during a show, and this requires him to wear a special boot and to use a cane. Sharon is also shown to work diligently as Ozzy's manager, acting as the organizer and negotiator of his business. Numerous portrayals of Sharon doing business both at home and in the office construct her as a very hard worker, who pays the emotional price of Ozzy's wrath when she makes a decision he does not support.

A final way *The Osbournes* shows the drawbacks of wealth and success is through the portrayal of Ozzy as an object of ridicule, as well as someone who is excluded and isolated from those around him. With the aid of editing and musical enhancement, Ozzy is constructed to be a rather wasted figure, bloated and confused from all the years of drug and alcohol excess, who is often oblivious to his surroundings. Ozzy is shown to be sadly inept and out of control as he falls backward in his chair, walks the dog in the middle of the road while stoned on wine and painkillers, and struggles at length to extract a DVD from its case. Finally, Ozzy explains on multiple occasions that he feels invisible and ignored much of the time. Woven together, these portrayals form a picture of a wealthy, but silly and drug-scarred individual who often feels excluded from the people close to him. Further, it is meaningful that Ozzy (more than the other family members) is shown as the victim of ridicule and isolation as he is the one constructed to have worked to achieve the American Dream.

The mediated stories conveyed in *The Osbournes* about wealthy people experiencing everyday problems and the troubles produced by wealth, operate in concert to create and narrate the Money Can't Buy Happiness myth. This component of the narrative of *The Osbournes* serves as a warning that wealth and success have significant drawbacks. It perhaps allows viewers to reconcile their current social-class positioning by feeling better about the fact that they have not (and may never) achieve the level of wealth or success they desire.

Hegemonic implications of social class and mobility myths

Scharrer explains that 'because they enjoy a currently powerful position in the political and economic structure, media outlets theoretically benefit from preserving the status quo rather than stirring up feelings of discontent among 'lower' classes and the less powerful' (2001: 23). This study supports past research that finds media narratives of social mobility work hegemonically: encouraging people to work hard to achieve upward mobility while concurrently lessening this desire by portraying the wealthy as unhappy. As a media creation, *The Osbournes* tell both hopeful and cautionary tales of wealth, success and upward social mobility. The truth or 'falsity' of these myths in real life is immaterial – what is important are the stories that are created and presented to viewers. Given that 'popular television reflects a desire to simplify terrains of ideological confusion and contradiction within our society' (Press & Strathman 1993: 8), the myths narrated in *The Osbournes* simplify notions of social class and mobility and operate to maintain hegemony. If viewers accept and support these myths, they are, in effect, supporting a status quo that keeps the majority of society working and striving for wealth and success while also accepting their current social-class positioning.

On the one hand, the program conveys that upward social mobility does happen and that wealth is enjoyable and satisfying. *The Osbournes* presents narratives of hope for those looking to achieve the American Dream. The story of Ozzy's rise from the working class to wealthy celebrity via hard work and in spite of many obstacles suggests to audiences that the American Dream is alive and well. On the other hand, *The Osbournes* shows the disadvantages of wealth and mobility by presenting the problems the family faces despite, and often *because* of, their level of wealth and success. This narrative runs parallel to the hopeful tales and narrates that wealthy, successful people are plagued by problems and are often victims of ridicule and isolation. Birmingham (2000) argues that television maintains the status quo by both providing anxiety and offering relief. The dueling myths presented here illustrate this concept: they suggest both a way in and a way out of the struggle for upward mobility.

As stated above, myths are only effective if their content and the manner in which they are transmitted resonate with audiences. Given its incredible popularity, it can be argued that *The Osbournes* speaks its ideological message of desire and compliance in a language that resonates with audiences on some level (Shales 2002). The mythic narratives conveyed by this program work to sustain the social order by keeping the working class, in particular, hopeful and hardworking, while at the same time keeping them complacent and content with their current (lowly and alienated) class positioning.

Note

1. This paper was presented at the Popular Culture Association and American Culture Association Conference, April 16–19, 2003, New Orleans, Louisiana.

References

Berk, Lynn (1977) 'The great middle American dream machine', *Journal of Communication*, 27 (33): 27–31.

Birmingham, Elizabeth (2000) 'Fearing the freak: How talk TV articulates women and class', *Journal of Popular Film and Television*, 28 (3): 133–139.

Bullock, Heather, Wyche, Karen, & Williams, Wendy (2000) 'Media images of the poor', *Journal of Social Issues*, 57 (2): 229–246.

Butsch, Richard (1979) 'Legitimations of class structures in Gone With the Wind', *Qualitative Sociology*, 2: 63–79.

—— (1992) 'Class and gender in four decades of television situation comedy: Plus ça change', *Critical Studies in Mass Communication*, 9: 387–399.

—— (2001) 'Class and audience effects: A history of research on movies, radio, and television', *Journal of Popular Film and Television*, 29 (3): 112–120.

Byers, Thomas (1987) 'Commodity futures: Corporate state and personal style in three recent science-fiction movies', *Science Fiction Studies*, 14 (3): 326–339.

Desser, David (1991) 'Race, space and class: The politics of the SF film from *Metropolis* to *Blade Runner*', in Judith Kerman (ed.), *Retrofitting Blade Runner: Issues in Ridley Scott's Blade Runner and Phillip K. Dick's Do Androids Dream of Electric Sheep?*, Bowling Green, Ohio: Popular Press, pp. 110–123.

Edington, K (1995) 'The Hollywood novel: The American dream, apocalyptic vision', *Literature/Film Quarterly*, 23: 63–67.

Freeman, Lewis (1992) 'Social mobility in television comedies', *Critical Studies in Mass Communication*, 9: 400–406.

Gentile, Frank & Miller, S M (1961) 'Television and social class', *Sociology and Social Research*, 45 (3): 259–264.

Giroux, Henry (1980) 'Norma Rae: Character, culture and class', *Jump Cut*, 22: 1–7.

Gray, Herman (1989) 'Television, black Americans, and the American dream', *Critical Studies in Mass Communication*, 6: 376–386.

Gyourko, Joseph & Linneman, Peter (1993) 'The affordability of the American dream: An examination of the last 30 years', *Journal of Housing Research*, 4: 39–72.

Haggins, Bambi (1999) 'There's no place like home: the American dream, African-American identity, and the situation comedy', *Velvet Light Trap*, 43: 23–36.

Hedegaard, Erik, Fricke, David & Shaw, Lucy 'The Osbournes, America's first family: Funnier than the Simpsons. Freakier than the Munsters. Scarier than the Bushes. Inside the year's hottest TV show', *Rolling Stone*, 9 May 2002: 33–36.

Horton, John (1982) 'Class struggle and the American dream: A Marxist analysis of communication', *Studies in Communications*, 2: 111–141.

Jhally, Sut & Lewis, Justin (1992) *Enlighted racism: Audiences, The Cosby Show and the Myth of the American Dream*, Boulder, CO: Westview.

Jones, Gerard (1992) *Honey, I'm Home! Sitcoms: Selling the American Dream*, New York: St. Martin's.

Jordan, Chris (1996) 'Gender and class mobility in 'Saturday Night Fever' and 'Flashdance', *Journal of Popular Film and Television*, 24 (3): 116–123.

Levy, Emmanuel (1991) 'The American dream of family in film: From decline to comeback', *Journal of Comparative Family Studies*, 22 (2): 187–204.

Lipsitz, George (1986) 'The meaning of memory: Family, class and ethnicity in early network television programs', *Cultural Anthropology*, 1 (4): 355–387.

Miller, Nancy 'American goth: How the Osbournes, a simple, headbanging British family, became our nation's latest reality-TV addiction', *Entertainment Weekly*, 19 April 2002: 24–30.

Poniewozik, James 'Ozzy knows best: *The Osbournes* has a bleeping thing or two to teach the networks about comedy – and decorating with crucifixes', *Time*, 15 April 2002: 64–65.

Scharrer, Erica (2001) 'From wise to foolish: The portrayal of the sitcom father, 1950s–1990s', *Journal of Broadcasting & Electronic Media*, 45: 23–40.

Schor, Juliet (1998) 'Keeping up with the Trumps: How the middle class identifies with the rich', *Washington Monthly*, 30 (7): 34–38.

Shales, Tom (2002) 'Mining the American dream', *Electronic Media*, 21 (33): 21.

—— (2002) 'Essential lessons from "The Osbournes"; I don't think people watch the Osbournes just to laugh at them. I think they now have an emotional investment in this anything-but-typical clan – a zany family that nevertheless celebrates the whole idea of familyness' *Electronic Media*, 21 (48): 23.

Signorielli, Nancy & Kahlenberg, Susan (2001) 'Television's world of work in the nineties', *Journal of Broadcasting & Electronic Media*, 45: 4–22.

Thoman, Elizabeth (1993) 'Media, technology and culture: Re-imagining the American dream', *Bulletin of Science, Technology and Society*, 13 (1): 20–26.

Thomas, Sari (1986) 'Mass media and the social order', in Gary Gumpert & Robert Cathcart (eds), *Inter/Media: Interpersonal Communication in a Media World*, New York: Oxford University Press, pp. 611–627.

—— (1990) "Myths in and about television", in John Downing, Ali Mohammadi & Annabelle Sreberny-Mohammadi (eds), *Questioning the Media: A Critical Introduction*, Newbury Park, CA: Sage, pp. 330–344.

Thomas, Sari & Callahan, Brian (1982) 'Allocating happiness: TV families and social class', *Journal of Communication*, 32 (3): 184–189.

Traube, Elizabeth (1989) 'Secrets of success in postmodern society', *Cultural Anthropology*, 4 (3): 273–300.

Weiss, Richard (1969) *The American Myth of Success: From Horatio Alger to Norman Vincent Peale*, New York: Basic.

25 Mobile Identities, Digital Stars, and Post-Cinematic Selves

Mary Flanagan

Lara Croft, the 3-D star of the action game series *Tomb Raider*, has become the most popular computer game character ever. Created by Core Design in England, Lara's game series *Tomb Raider* (I, II, III, IV: The Last Revalation, and soon to be released *Tomb Raider Chronicles*), distributed by Eidos Interactive, has helped create a new star system in the arena of electronic gaming. Since premiering in 1996, her games have sold over six million copies—some of the best-selling video game titles in history. In the game, players control Lara Croft, a female Indiana Jones-style swashbuckling archaeologist on a global quest to whisk away artifacts from "exotic" locales in epic, colonialist CD ROM adventures. She is the best-known computer generated character in the world and her creation has brought into existence a virtual star system. As the millennial icon, she has been featured on the cover of over eighty magazines with characters such as Bill Gates and America Online CEO Steve Case, and touted as one of the fifty "cyber elite." Lara is more than a character; she is a celebrity. "She's developed a persona," says Keith Boesky of game publisher Eidos Interactive. "She's the first digital character that's really treated like a person."[1] Lara Croft might be compared to a person, but she is much more onscreen. Lara wields amazing physical prowess and multiple firearms. She is capable of any physical activity demanded by the game's incredible situations: back-flipping out of buildings, swimming underwater, punching tigers, round-housing monks, and even biting foes (blood/gore included)—while barely clad in scanty, skintight "explorer" clothing. In addition to her superhuman traits, Lara is precise, rides in great vehicles, and, unless there is user error, never needs a second take.

Inevitably, the comparison has to be made between this new star system and film history's account of stars and star discourse. A review of this material will help us understand how and why the cinematic star as a culturally produced body has evolved into a digital star system in which signifiers, identities, and bodies themselves are called into question. More than the indulgence of looking in at these stars within filmic worlds, we now embrace the very real pleasure of controlling these desired bodies: Lara is at the apex of a system in which looking manifests into doing, into action. The digital star is the location on which fantasies of desire and control are projected; they embody the fears, desires, and excess of our culture in the form of obnoxiously sexualized female stars. The subject, object, audience, director, viewer, participant, creator, and user tangle and double over; these roles blur into a new phenomenon that refuses to take on a shape.

Lara is clearly our first digital star,[2] and the role of information and technology in the construction of the digital star cannot be ignored. Rob Milthorp has pointed out that the lure of the video game fantasy is "that of a vicarious escapist experience that also responds to men's technological passion."[3] Beyond the attraction of technology, however, this essay suggests that it is through the excess of information and sexuality, the absence of the "authentic," and the development of an intricate subject/object relationship that these fantasies have organized into a truly new form of star system "personified" through Lara Croft. Using Lara Croft and other digitally-rendered female images—Kyoko Date, Kiss Dolls, and Ultravixen—as examples, this essay seeks to expose and complicate new manifestations of the coded subject/object positions examined by feminist scholars of popular media for the last twenty years. I will show that "cults of personality" could only develop from the electronic entertainment industry when virtual personalities embodied a marketable, consumable, idealized, and entirely "man-made" female form. It is through the recognition, representation, and redefinition of this body and the understanding of the shaping of the subject within the digital star system that our position as users and our technologically produced, multiple subjectivities can be understood.

Seeing Stars

In his essay "The Emergence of the Star System in America," Richard deCordova distinguishes phases in the development of the classical Hollywood star system. His concepts are useful when comparing the "cults of personality" that developed almost a century before the digital star system. Starting with discourse on legitimate stage acting and comparing it with "performing," (as opposed to acting) for the camera, he describes the differences between a "picture personality" and the "star." There was a marked difference between personalities and stars in the way they related to discourse and products. Popular film magazines included quizzes about the players' names and listed their filmographies; however, actor-centered dialogue was always second to the discourse on the films themselves. deCordova notes, "The picture personality was to be the principal site of product individuation"[4] and by 1907, the star system had evolved, making the name of the star more important than the films in which they starred. The interest in the private lives of screen performers—and the excess of biographical information sold about a performer's personal life—created the star system, and with it a commodification of an actor's biographical data. This focus on an individual actor's life and family may have helped to legitimize the cinema and its practices—as deCordova notes "The private lives of the stars emerged as a new site of knowledge and truth"[5] and, of course, commodity.

The star system evolved as an important component in the development of the information age by blurring distinctions between the personal and the private. Technology-bound, technologically determined, both digital stars and cinema stars were birthed in an environment of spectacle. The star system produced the personality as commodity to be consumed by audiences—a product to be desired, and ultimately, acquired.

Like the arcades of electronic gaming, early cinema was exhibited in predominantly male spaces, but exhibition practices are not the only shared elements between the star systems. The first stars in both films and computer games are females: the marketable names of Florence Lawrence (the first popular screen player at Biograph Studios) and Lara Croft have drawn large audiences. But from the picture personality "Biograph Girl" (Lawrence) to the star "IMP Girl" (Lawrence's name at her next studio) to the "Bit Girl"[6] the representation of biographical excess and overt sexuality changed dramatically. While the "innocent" early film stars gradually evolved into more sexual and objectified stars, Lara Croft and clone characters are immediately coded as sexual objects upon arrival.

Star Sex

Scott Bukatman points out that contemporary culture "eroticizes the technological;"[7] and thus in addition to her appearance, Lara Croft is by virtue of her existence bound to erotic codes and interpretation through the means of her production. A look at the first cinematic sex symbol, Theda Bara, gives historical insight into the design of the sex object screen star. Fox Studios director Frank Powell cast her as a vampire in the film version of *A Fool There Was* (1915). She became Fox's biggest star, appearing in as many as ten feature films per year.[8] Theda Bara's success as a sex symbol stems from her construction as a persona without a fixed personal history. A key factor in her design as a sex symbol was the mystification of her true, "authentic" identity. Though she was almost thirty and obviously had a personal history of her own, Fox studios created a fictional personal history for her with each film role she played. At hundreds of press conferences, Theda Bara acted out these roles, dressing in veils, furs and silks, petting snakes or eating exotic fruits. The media played along with the spectacle and printed as fact obviously jumbled biographies. According to one report, Theda Bara was born under Egypt's pyramids, the daughter of a French actress and an Italian artist.[9] Similarly, Lara Croft's past is also recreated, multiplied, and retold. Her lack of a true history is masked by the excess of life stories created by multiple agencies—Eidos' marketing department, gaming magazines, and countless fan fiction sites. Like Theda Bara, Lara's excessive biographies are filled with impossible fictions.[10] Yet while Theda's histories were concocted to create a media stir for the studio, Lara's past continues to be filled in by fans across the world. Internet sites such as *Lara's Scrapbook* and *Lara's Oasis* fill in details continually. This act of viewer/user/participant generation of these histories is significant as they multiply Lara's "reality" into many fictions which represent multiple realities. While each fan community may have its own version of her story, no one story is considered more or less true than any other. This works in part because of the immensity of the interested group: six or seven million fans can create "regional" narratives of the hero in what ends up being localized oral, written, and pictorial histories—legends.

Lara and Theda are alike in that they both embody excess and spectacle and exist in a duality between the text (the films, games) and in sub-texts and extra-texts. Their personal histories are coded as "exotic," vague, and undecipherable. Their bodies with their assorted histories are fractured into multiple fictions to act as shells for a viewer's desire.

Stars of the cinema share qualities with computer-generated stars; not static or fixed in time and space, they inhabit screen worlds. A star system draws upon the separation between the image and the body, the public and private, the historical, biographical persona and the location of many fictional biographies, between the scripted and the "real," to create a culture of consumption around the "persona." The representation of Lara Croft's body is essential to understand the issues of (dis)embodiment of computer personalities and the particular place of gender in these embodiment relationships. Lara's body is an interesting culmination of numerous western ideals. Box art, press releases, and fans describe her as "icy" and "sexy." She shoots, climbs, and runs with mechanical precision; controlling her body is like driving a fine machine. In addition, Lara Croft has an over-idealized female physique. She is a self-less body created from 540 polygons.[11] With beyond-Barbie statistics (pushing Lara as a pin-up icon, Eidos has claimed her measurements are 88-24-84),[12] Lara is an over-idealized construction of EuroAmerican standards of beauty.[13] Modeled with brown hair and eyes and a deep skin tone, Lara could be one of the few non-white characters within Euro-American-dominated games. However, Lara is perceived most often by her fans as Caucasian.[14] Creator company Eidos provides only a rough sketch of Lara's life, and as a result there should be few elements which remain stable about her biography. But even within the reinterpretations of Lara's history, she is consistently read by fans to come from a position of economic privilege: well-bred, educated, and feminine even as she guns down attackers.

Lara is young and beautiful—and she will always be. Lara will not know physical age. She will, however, be subject to the outdating of her technology. Any digital star's repertoire will consist of a set of obsolete file formats on aged media storage devices. As the body coordinates and texture maps are refined through the years—remapped, refracted, holographed into the technology of the time—her previous incarnations will grow more and more obsolete. However, she will stay eternally young; reborn, more perfect than before, with each technological advance. The experience of a digital star, then, is one of continued present. The technology of the present is the only way to maintain the star. Lara represents the circumstance described by Gilles Deleuze as the process of "becoming." She exists not as an identity but as a site of becoming—winning or losing the game, adventuring, controlling, pleasuring, moving, fighting. In his essay "What is Becoming?" Deleuze describes a state of event-centered being that is a useful way to examine interactive experiences.[15] The characters, landscape, and entire world of *Tomb Raider* are a continuous, data-driven event. "The artificial is always a copy of a copy,"[16] data looping and changing in a viral manner. Lara, as a pure data loop, makes discourse about the concept of the authentic, the "instance," impossible. Thus, the absence of a physical body means the absence of history, the lack of a "real" biography; the data is the entirety of the star. Her female identity further complicates this intersection. Judith Butler argues that the very position of "woman" is a construction within this constant flux as well: "Woman itself is a term in process, a becoming, a constructing that cannot rightfully be said to originate or end."[17]

Set Prototypes

What we see on the screen of a digital star—the body, the gender, the matrix of social and cultural ties—is as much as we get. Or is it? Postmodernism brought us the disintegration of the subject, the fragmented receptor constantly in flux. The boundaries between humans and machines are becoming irretrievably blurred. So too have the boundaries between the subject and object, the voyeur and the object of the gaze, the user/ participant and the avatar representation of that user in a virtual world. The blurring of boundaries that has come to fruition in Lara Croft can be traced through three important evolutionary stages.

Kyoko Date

To begin looking at existing examples of prototypical digital stars and understanding the apparatus, the technological means that have pre-shaped us as subjects, we can examine one of the first internationally known virtual beings, the Japanese character Kyoko Date. Of all prototypical digital personas, Kyoko may be the best known. Called the "Daughter of technology" by some fans,[18] Kyoko Date, or "DK-96" (DK for "Digital Kids") was the first virtual idol. Created by the Japanese entertainment company Hori Productions Inc, Date is a 3-D model consisting of over 40,000 polygons; it is easy to mistake printouts of Date for photographs of human subjects. The production of Date was enormous: ten designers at HoriPro alone worked on her facial features.[19] Kyoko is physically attractive; but she is not solely touted for her sex appeal. According to CNN/fn's news reporter John Lewis, Kyoko "has just that desired mix of purity and lost innocence, she has the cute pout down pat, and she's fashionably slender in all the right places."[20] Kyoko Date was not based on an existing media personality, nor was she created in order to further the media career of a human star. And while Kyoko Date did not erupt from a computer game, toy, television program, or movie, she quickly became an influential media figure through commercials, music videos, and pop songs. HoriPro chose to make its star as "real" as possible using an abundance of "normal" human references. Kyoko Date "grew up" in the suburbs; the "girl-next-door" image behind the media blitz was constructed to make her as human as possible. She is represented as a typical sixteen-year-old entertainer and lives with her parents just outside of Tokyo. Kyoko is said to have one sister, a year younger than herself, and works at her parents' family-run restaurant in Tokyo.

It is important to note that the fame for Kyoko Date was not perennial. Kyoko was the prototype for the digital star system, but her meticulously detailed personalized history created more of a "self" than a digital personality can have.

Kiss Dolls

A big hit in Japan since the early nineteen-nineties and a swelling American phenomenon, KISS games are electronic drag-and-drop paper doll computer games that one plays on the computer. KISS dolls are an interactive strip show with the goal of exposing and eroticizing images of anime characters and barely pubescent girls. Available in the underground software scene,[21] the creation, production, and distribution of KISS are performed by fanatics, technicians and programmers—not corporate pornographic agencies. Newer KISS dolls, dubbed "FKISS," can incorporate limited animation and sound; this movement most often manifests as blinking eyes, animated clothing, giggling sounds, or animated sex toys. The interaction—the user has power over the doll and is able to click and drag items off or onto the body of the doll—compels the user to play. The significance of the animated paper dolls lies in the type of control offered to users and the animations embedded in the files. The user not only controls the female image and visual identity through clothing and hair, but the user can actually act upon this body—shave it, make it wet, and ultimately rape it with objects found in the scene. One animated doll, Sailor Mars, features a young anime-style female figure, about nine-years old, wearing a Japanese school uniform: white top and a grey skirt. When the player clicks on the doll's skirt, the skirt bunches up to expose the girl's underwear, as though the hand of an adult has reached under the skirt to expose her. Similarly, when the player clicks on the girl's shirt, the shirt pops open but stays on the body. Clicking on the underwear results in the underwear bunching down to expose the girl's genitalia. Meanwhile, the drawing stays expressionless, the cartoon child returning the gaze of the player, her eyes, wide and shiny, blinking passively. [...] Thus while Kiss dolls offer virtual, "manipulate-able" striptease shows for the users, this particular doll confronts, albeit passively, the manipulation of the female image directly.

[...]

Unlike other kinds of pornography, the dolls arrive to the user as innocents and it is through interactivity that they are inscribed as erotic. As Zimmerman and Gorfinkel point out, they constitute "a curious double sexuality: at once garishly innocent adolescents and hyper-sexualized porn objects, a complicity of awkward pubescence and demure seduction."[22] Kiss dolls, as anonymous shells upon which users can play out fantasy of control and desire, are "safe" precisely because of their lack of authenticity. Users do not, however, manipulate the girls' bodies (except for the few dolls accompanied by sex toys); rather, users can decide the level of exposure (indecent or otherwise). Kiss dolls incorporate a level of control that is defined by exposure of the body rather than the direct manipulation of it. As anonymous electronic strip shows, they exist in between worlds and experiences as "trading cards of desire." Their lack of history, their spoiled innocence that is completely at the service of the user for the pleasure of the user alone, and their capacity to fulfill the fantasy of the visible by maneuvering the image within interactive technology leads to the fulfillment of user desire.

Ultravixen

Ariel, aka Ultravixen, is the "hypersexy superheroine of the 21st century" in the "world's first Internet Anime Sex Game."[23] Created by Pixis Interactive, purple-haired hero Ariel is billed as the "super-hot sci-fi sex star." The story on the Pixis web site begins with her torture and rape at the hands of a professor. Her powers emerge as the result of the rape. Ariel becomes the Ultravixen, the bearer of the "super climax": an orgasm capable of warping time and space. Her sexual "weapon" is the means of defeating an evil OverLord from the future, who uses a time travel network to acquire girls and enslave them in his maniacal sex machines. The role of the user is to play her "lover" and serve as the operator of these sexual torture devices. Players manipulate the "sex machines" to arouse Ultravixen to the point of orgasm so that she may in turn destroy the machine, and with it, the Overlord.

While the narrative makes the Overlord into a diabolical character because of his rape of women and dominance over the girls using sex machines, the game is designed so that players must duplicate his actions to save the world. The interaction in Ultravixen is a complex set of objectifications: the user controls elements in the game (implements of torture) which in turn gives the user power over the sex object, Ariel. Yet as players we are absolved of any moral guilt as the narrative clearly tells us that Ariel wants to be tortured. She appears in a machine, and the user is told that Ariel desires "pleasure." Ultravixen represents the point at which the gaze is given the power of manipulation, a place where the gaze MUST manifest into sexual control and abuse in order to play and finish the game. Consequently, torture is legitimized and sanctioned by positing the relationship between user, machine, and victim as a consensual act. This "rape and rescue" fantasy is used to justify the subjugation of the disenfranchised female body. Though the portrayal in Ultravixen is abusive and negative, the user does not directly control Ariel—control is mediated through the sex machine. In comparison, even though Lara Croft exists in a game which does not submit her to torture, she is submissive to the direct control of the user.[24]

These three examples show varying degrees of the creation of the digitally-rendered female image's overt sexuality. Each one bears marks of the evolution towards the digital star system. On the surface, Kyoko Date seems to be a digital star: she is a three dimensional artificial character created to sell media work While her name differentiates and sells products, she is created with a grounded, stable history—not created from excess but rather from "satisfactory" spheres of knowledge. She becomes too "realistic" and historically situated to be the site at which we play out fantasies. Kiss Dolls are crude examples of the enactment of anonymous control fantasies. An individual doll's identity is not as important as the power to manipulate the doll, and thus product differentiation relies more on the features of a particular doll set versus the character depicted therein. Ultravixen has little identity and exists for the player's pleasure alone; the only way we relate to her is through manipulation somewhat removed from the game world. These digital prototypes help form the conditions necessary for a star system to develop but are not digital stars unto themselves. The economic, racial, and gender hierarchies embedded in these electronic games "allegorize" the social relationships in our time much like cinema,[25] creating a-historical digital female imagery for the fulfillment of fantasy. Each of these examples offers us a few of the elements which contributed to the construction of the digital star system, yet they do not each bear enough elements to fully launch it.

* * *

Objects subjects

The games above feature prototypical digital stars. A central reason that they could not offer true stardom to their characters is that they did not offer complex subject positioning for players. The ability to feel as though one is shifting viewpoints while manipulating character one identifies with in a variety of ways offers tremendous possibilities for theories about subject/object relationships. The space between experiencing first hand (inside) a virtual character, to controlling the avatar as a separate object is like Deleuze's phantasm: the movement by which the ego opens itself up to surfaces and "liberates" the halted differences contained (such as point of view);[26] the phantasm covers the distance between psychic systems with ease, going from consciousness to the unconscious and vice versa—from the inner to the outer and conversely."[27]

More than an inner and outer dichotomy, we can identify five points of action/ identification/subject positioning within a three-dimensional gaming environment like *Tomb Raider*. First, through the keyboard, players make Lara act. Second, she acts—sometimes on her own accord, through pre-scripted animation, and sometimes as an extension to our influence. Third, as players we act with her or next to her as a friend or companion. Fourth, we act through her/within her in the first person. In other words, we become Lara. Finally, we react to her. For example, players respond to her positions in the game, whether in fear or with mirth. Never before has there been a figure in any media that has become such a unique axis of complex identification with the audience. We move from the first person position—sitting in front of the monitor using the keyboard—to the third person simultaneity of being inside the game worlds with our characters. We are again in first person controlling the gaming experience through the characters—we can actually become them and see the world through their eyes; then with a keystroke, we can move to the third person omniscient perspective in order to control the character like a puppet. Through this network of positions, the boundaries between subject and object, the delineation between various points of view, and the notion of self and other are inextricably intertwined.

Though players physically interact in *Tomb Raider* through keyboard keys, Lara is the means by which the user is extended into the virtual environment. Users have control over her body, true; but users identify with her body in a variety of ways. Of Lara Croft, Herz notes, "In *Tomb Raider*, Lara Croft is the protagonist, the hero. When a boy plays the game, Lara is not the object, as she would have been in older games: she is the game. The boy who plays the game plays it as a woman."[28] Herz, while showing the potential of the technology to experience truly "virtual realities," exposes the cultural confusion about subjectivity in electronic games. Herz's words confuse the manipulation of a female object with the becoming the very object manipulated. But the situation is even more complex, because there are women and girls who do enjoy playing the game. Interviewing a young woman "newbie," Mark Snider includes "At first I was teasing (my dad) about playing *Tomb Raider* because there was a half-naked woman in it," but when she began to play the game, she became a fan. "You don't just feel like you're playing the game, you're going adventuring with Lara Croft."[29] So while Lara is an object to manipulate, she is also a friend or partner. Different players relate to this simultaneity in different ways. The subject/object relationships exemplified by the interactive Lara Croft experience do represent a new model for discovering female or alternative subjectivity, but this model has not been used with feminist content. Through the player/character relationship exemplified by *Tomb Raider*, we may someday be able to have multiple experiences of reality and identify sites at which we can adequately be addressed as subjects. The development of the sheer numbers of points of view may create an alternate subject position that could address the largely excluded female audience. These alternate spaces, exemplified within the postmodern subject position offered in *Tomb Raider*, exposes fissures in which alternate subject positions, or new combinations of subjective positions, will gain footing and representation. Thus (perhaps even *more so* for female players), the multiplication of the subject position offers an opportunity at which new ways of gaming (and more) could develop. True digital stars, that is, stars without need of their own physical body, did not exist until our culture was ready to rethink the body in the context of technology, and until the technology could present this body in a pleasing, "hyperreal" aesthetic. It also took a female digital character in a female body to spark these conventions. These female bodies are not bound by physical, biological traits of race and gender, but rather are bodies which are entirely technologically and culturally determined.[30] The digital star system arose, like cinema's star system, through the development of an intricate subject/object, through an excess of information and sexuality, and alongside the absence of the "authentic," but it is an evolving and changing phenomenon. The current narratives offered on the gaming market, however, work against these possibilities by offering hyper-sexual or victim characters. Even though they suggest that multiple points of view can be destabilizing, right now they remake stereotypical female sex objects. This is popular media's chance for opposition or total dissolution of conventional ideas of the self through the destabilization of the subject, to create selves in the relationship between the user and the narrative through gameplay and interactivity design in electronic media. The incorporation of movement, agency, and multiplicity within virtual worlds have tremendous possibilities for repositioning the subject and opening up narratives to non-stereotyped female roles and helping users find their favorite spot among a spectrum of viewpoints and subject positions.

Notes

Author's note: Near the time this article went to press, advance previews of *Tomb Raider V: Chronicles*, became available. *Tomb Raider V* allows users to x-ray Lara Croft. See <http://www.cubeit.com/ctimes/news/2000/09/news0633d.html>.

1. Mark Snider, "Tomb Raider blasts into Virtual Stardom," *USA Today*, 17 Dec. 1997: 1D.
2. "Girl Trouble," *Next Generation* 4.37, January 1998: 98–102.
3. Rob Milthorp, "Fascination, Masculinity, and Cyberspace," in Mary Anne Moser and Douglas MacLeon, eds., *Immersed in Technology* (Cambridge and London: MIT Press, 1996), 143.
4. Richard DeCordova, "Emergence of the Star System," in Christine Gledhill, ed., *Stardom: Industry of Desire* (London and New York: Routledge, 1991), 24.
5. DeCordova, 26.
6. N'Gail Croal and Janes Hughes, "Lara Croft, the Bit Girl: How a Game Star Become a 90's Icon," *Newsweek*, 10 Nov. 1997, 82.
7. Scott Bukatman, *Terminal Identity* (Durham, N.C.: Duke University Press, 1993), 328.
8. Glen Pringle, *Theda Bara: Silent Star of May 1996*. 1996, 1 July 1998 <http://www.cs.monash.edu.au/~pringle/silent/ssotm/May96/>.
9. Ibid.

10. Bowen H. Greenwood, *Lara Croft's Tales of Beauty and Power*. 1997. 20 July 1999 Ctimes.net: <http://network.ctimes.net/tales>.
11. Croal and Hughes, 82.
12. Croal and Hughes, 82.
13. Snider, 1D.
14. Robert Wheeler, *The Tomb Raider Archive*, 1998 31 July 1999 <http://trarchive.ctimes.net/index.html>.
15. Gilles Deleuze, *The Deleuze Reader*, trans. Constantine V. Boundas (New York: Columbia University Press, 1993), 39–41.
16. Gilles Deleuze, *The Logic of Sense*, trans. Constantine V. Boundas (New York: Columbia University Press, 1990), 265.
17. Judith Butler, *Gender Trouble: Feminism and the Subversion of Identity* (New York and London: Routledge, 1990), 38.
18. Matthew Dumas, *Kyoko Date Website* <http://111.etud.insa-tlse.fr/~mdumas/kyoko.html>.
19. HoriPro, Inc., "Notes on the Development of Virtual Idol DK-96," 31 July 1999 <http://www.dhw.co.jp/horipro/talent/DK96/dev_e.html>.
20. John Lewis, "Virtual Reality Entertainment in Japan," CNNf/n News In Play: Video Transcript, Cable News Network, Inc., 5 Feb. 1997.
21. Kiss Dolls are a huge net phenomenon and can be found at sites such as <http://otakuworld.com>, and *The Blue Page H n'H Times Supplement* - Issues 5 - #11. Ed. Dominatrix. June 1999 <http://www.terra.es/personal/domina/hnhtimes.htm>.
22. E. Zimmerman and E. Gorfinkel, "KISS and Tell," *21C Magazine*, Jan. 1997: 74.
23. Pixis Interactive, "Ultravixen Website," 1997. August 1999 <http:www2.ultravixen.com/choose.html>.
24. Moira Muldoon, "Growing Up in Gameland," 1998, *Salon: 21st The Culture of Technology the Technology of Culture*, July 1998 <http://ww1.salonmagazine.com/21st/feature/1998/06/02featureb.html>.
25. Ella Shohat, "Gender and Culture of Empire: Towards a Feminist Ethnography of the Cinema," *Quarterly Review of Film and Video* 13: 1–3, May-Oct 1991: 45.
26. Deleuze, *The Logic of Sense*, 213.
27. Deleuze, *The Logic of Sense*, 217.
28. Quoted in Gregory Kallenberg, "J.C. Herz: What's in a Game," *Austin-American Statesman:* Austin 360.com. Internet. 10 July 1997 <http://www.austsin360.com/tech/browswer/071097.htm>.
29. Snider, 1D.
30. Anne Balsamo, *Technologies of the Gendered Body* (Durham and London: Duke University Press, 1996), 5.

Consuming Fame/Becoming Famous?: Celebrity and Its Audience

Section Six

Introduction
Sean Redmond and Su Holmes

> [F]ame [is] ... a social process and any explanation of fame must ... include the place of the audience

(McDonald, 1995: 65)

Without consumption, the practices and processes of fame could not exist. Representation, identification and consumption have to exist in articulating frameworks for meaning to enter the social universe. As audiences, we fuel the economic enterprize of celebrity by purchasing the media products in which celebrities appear. The media, and a range of ancillary sites, provide the public stage on which celebrities perform, but for someone to become *known* means that their performance must ultimately meet with an *audience*.

There are many different ways in which audiences interact with celebrity culture – from singing as part of a crowd at a rock concert, logging onto an Internet forum, to reading the headline of someone's newspaper on a bus. These all suggest different modes of consumption and reception. As such, we need to be sensitive to the range of attitudes and investments such relations might encompass, moving across 'special' moments of intense investment and adoration, the more mundane province of scepticism or disinterest, to the (little researched) position of 'anti-fandom' (see Hills, 2003).

Writing originally in 1985,[1] James Donald noted that the relationship between stardom and audiences involved 'the most complex and hotly disputed question in the whole study of stars' (1999: 39). At the time, and speaking from the perspective of film studies, he saw this as closely linked to the paucity of knowledge on the subject, given that issues of spectatorship, audience and reception constituted the foggiest area of star studies. Although an imbalance still remains, the interest in the audience became increasingly important as the field of star/celebrity studies has developed – particularly as energized by the wider interest in audience studies in the 1980s and 1990s. Examining the role of the audience in star/celebrity studies is often to observe its symbiotic relationship with changing paradigms in audience studies (for a detailed discussion of the latter see Brooker and Jermyn, 2002). At different moments in the history of star and celebrity studies, we can variously witness the influence of Marxist paradigms, psychoanalytic and spectatorship theories, empirical audience research, interest in subcultural and/or fan communities and more recently, the impact of new media technologies. This dialogic relationship between star/celebrity and audience studies means that debate has revolved around the relative power of the audience in shaping the processes of meaning making and cultural production.

Pressures for reappraisal here can also come from the external contexts of celebrity culture – changes in the ways it is produced, circulated and consumed. For example, Matt Hills has recently argued that star and celebrity studies have perpetuated a rigid binary between fandom and celebrity, pivoting on the assumption that they represent two different spheres or orders of existence (Hills, 2006). Yet Hills draws attention to how celebrity can operate *within* fan communities, and he explores how 'Big Name Fans' can occupy the position of a 'hybridized fan-celebrity', becoming mediated figures (however niche), within their own subcultures. Hills focuses here on the Internet, which has rapidly become established as a focal point for fan studies. At the same time, the Internet has represented a space for the concept of the 'cyber-celebrity', a form of 'DIY' fame which circumvents some of the economic and technological structures through which celebrity is usually produced and consumed (see also Mary Flanagan's essay in Section 5). Nevertheless, this form of fame can take on some of the same commodified attributes as mainstream celebrity (see Turner, 2004: 65), while it can also replicate the hierarchical structures within which it circulates. For example, an article by Richard McManus on Read/Write Web discussed the difference between A- and C-list bloggers, while at the same time mulling over the pervasive debate about popularity or 'well-knowness' versus 'merit'. As he explains: 'I judge the quality of a weblog by its ideas, but it seems some people equate quality with popularity. Is the "culture of celebrity" that afflicts Western movies, television and radio creeping in to weblogs as well?' (McManus, 2003).

While this particular example might suggest as much similarity as difference from other media contexts, the Internet is part of a broader media landscape which is putting pressure on more traditional concepts of the (mass) audience, edging us closer to the 'new media persona of the "user"' (Marshall, 2004: 11). Furthermore, it also points us towards a culture in which – again questioning the reified concepts of celebrity/audience – the user/viewer/reader is entering the frame media themselves. As Nick Stevenson comments, '*audience members* are now increasingly likely to perceive themselves as potential stars and celebrities, rather than being content to admire others from afar [original emphasis]' (2005: 159). It is impossible to engage with debates over the democratization of celebrity without confronting its implications for conceptualizing the role of the audience. Reality TV has emerged as a particularly visible cultural site in debates about the democratization of modern fame, largely because it recruits its celebrities from the audience (Marshall, 2004: 100). Yet while we *are all audiences* for celebrity culture, we are *not* all celebrities. Several authors have remained sceptical of the emphasis on democratization here (Turner, 2004; Stevenson, 2005; Holmes, 2006), not least of all because celebrity has long since pivoted on this mythic promise as integral to its ideological form. However, if Reality TV has increasingly catered to a desire to have one's social existence validated though the gaze of others (Biressi and Nunn, 2004), it moves us beyond thinking about an affective relationship between *a* star/celebrity and their audience, while further emphasizing how celebrity functions within broader social processes.

Empirical work on audiences dominates this section. This is not because it singularly represents the scope of work in the field (in which a variety of theoretical and methodological frameworks have been brought to bear on the consumption of celebrity). The concept of the audience has been a constant theme throughout many of the essays in this *Reader*, but section Six engages with this topic in more detail, while simultaneously offering a space to explore approaches which the book has not fully covered elsewhere. This section also works from the premise that empirical evidence is a powerful site upon which to explore the identity practices and subjectivities which are shaped by fame.

Jackie Stacey's *Stargazing: Hollywood Cinema and Female Spectatorship* (1994) represents a seminal attempt to investigate the relationships which exist between film stars and their audiences. Stacey's focus was on female stars from Hollywood cinema, and their consumption by female audiences in 1940s and 1950s Britain. Given the patriarchal bias of much spectatorship theory, Stacey was keen to contribute to knowledge about how '*women* look at images of femininity on the cinema screen' (1994: 9). In this excerpt, Stacey examines the later period of the 1950s and how women's relations with stars motivated 'extra-cinematic identificatory practices', bids to transform the self by imitating stars' performance styles, clothes or hairstyles. At the same time, Stacey recognizes the contradictory nature of these practices: they are part of the commercial construction of femininity, while also a site of negotiation and resistance. (Women may have sought to replicate the fashion practices of Hollywood stars, but they did so complexly and variously, far from simply passive consumers within a capitalistic machine). Stacey's research had many important implications for understanding both female film spectatorship, and audience-star relationships. This was not least of all in emphasizing how the latter cannot be generalized: interactions with stars must be approached and understood as historically and geographically specific.

Stacey's *Stargazing* complicated the notion that stars function as the epitome of desirability within a heterosexual economy, with her female respondents suggesting blurred lines between intimacy, desire and identification. The idea that stars and celebrities can function as fluid figures of erotic identification – androgynous, camp, playful, and sexually transgressive – is further foregrounded in a very different context by Yiman Wang's essay. In 'A Star is Dead: Leslie Cheung and the Nostalgia for the Present', Yiman Wang produces a lyrical reading of the Hong Kong film and pop star, Leslie Cheung. The fluidity of meaning and desire which circulates between star and fan can be placed in relation to wider social changes, especially those that, in an age of global consumption patterns, render national borders and boundaries porous. Wang's essay draws on queer theory, and debates about postmodernity and globalization in order to make sense of the continued 'global' appeal of Cheung, whose well-publicized suicide on 1st April, 2003 was met with waves of public mourning. Wang suggests that Cheung's androgyny and sexual ambivalence enabled the star to connect with a range of fans caught up in the flow and flux of global communications and transformations. Cheung come to stand for an 'age that has come to an end', a 'beautiful' certainty in a time of liquid impermanence. The irony here, of course, is that it is through the virtual or hyper-reality of the Internet where worldwide fans come to consume the transnational icon that is Leslie Cheung. Its through his polysemic nature and multi-textual reference points that fans get some of the existential truth that they need and see/feel in the romantic death of their forever young star.

Like Stacey, Catharine Lumby is interested in how gender shapes audience responses to, and identifications with, fame, but within the context of the contemporary media environment. In 'Doing it For Themselves?; Teenage Girls, Sexuality and Fame', Lumby draws on empirical audience research in order to explore the role that fame and celebrity play in the everyday lives of teenage girls. As Lumby points out, teenage girls have been constructed as 'particularly vulnerable to the hype surrounding the fame industry', as hysterical and obsessive devotees to male singers or movie stars. While Lumby questions that such consumption practices were ever 'passive', she also notes that such a perspective – predicated exclusively on female idolization of male stars – is increasingly outmoded. Over 'the the past decade…popular concerns about young women's relationship to fame have been gradually shifting away from concerns about their irrational idealization of predominantly male idols to concerns that they are obsessively fantasizing about becoming famous themselves'. Lumby ranges across responses to Reality TV contestants (principally Sara-Marie from the Australian version of *Big Brother*) to teenage girls' construction of 'cam-girl' sites, examining the 'blurring of the boundaries between fandom and the quest for celebrity'.

But in exploring the extent to which audiences might aspire to fame, we also need to consider how this desire is nurtured and (perhaps most crucially) *naturalized*. Nick Couldry interrogates this within the context of his wider concept of the 'media/ordinary hierarchy', the 'symbolic hierarchy of the media frame' (Couldry, 2000: 44). For Couldry, this hierarchical division, which is constructed by the media, divides the social world into two domains, presenting the media world as not only our privileged access point to social 'reality', but also a 'special' space, a *higher* order which is at the 'centre' of things. One of the key ways in which this hierarchy is played out is around celebrity. As Couldry expands: 'It is "common sense" that the "media world" is somehow better, more intense, than 'ordinary life', and that 'media people' are somehow special' (2000: 45). The first part of the excerpt re-printed here sets out this concept, before leading on to an analysis of how fans discuss the stars from the long-running British soap, *Coronation Street* (1960–, ITV1). Couldry draws upon empirical audience research, as gathered from fans visiting the set of the programme (on a Granada Studios Tour), to explore how audiences negotiate the symbolic hierarchy of the media frame, and the idea of meetings of power For between 'media people' and non-media people.

Note

1. The first version of *The Cinema Book* (London: BFI) edited by Pam Cook was published in 1985.

26 With Stars in Their Eyes: Female Spectators and the Paradoxes of Consumption

Jackie Stacey

This chapter considers the ways in which female spectators related to Hollywood stars through consumption in 1940s and 1950s Britain. In an attempt to challenge some of the work which assumes this relationship to be one of totally successful domination, tying women tightly into positions of subordination, I shall argue for a more 'complex and contradictory' model of the female spectator as consumer. The central concern of this chapter, is how Hollywood stars are connected to the consumption practices of female spectators in the production and reproduction of particular formations of female subjectivity at this time.

Consumption can be a confusing term since it has been used to refer to many different things within sociology, cultural and film studies. Sociological studies have tended to use the term to refer to the purchase and use of commodities, particularly in the domestic sphere; whilst in cultural studies consumption has usually referred to the 'making sense' of cultural texts (generally popular ones) such as adverts, music, television programmes or films which sometimes, but not always, involves commodity purchase. In film studies, where the term consumption has probably been used the least, it has often referred to the place of cinema in consumer culture and the ways in which the film industry promotes the purchase of other commodities. It is this final conceptualisation which I adopt within this chapter.

[...]

The female spectator as consumer: Subjectivity as subjection?

> In our social order, women are 'products' used and exchanged by men. Their status is that of merchandise, 'commodities'..... So women have to remain an 'infrastructure' unrecognized as such by our society and our culture. The use, consumption, and circulation of their sexualized bodies underwrite the organization and reproduction of the social order, in which they have never taken part as 'subjects'.

(Irigaray, 1985: 84)

Women's relationship to commodities has frequently been conceptualised in terms of their being the objects, and not the subjects, of exchange (Doane, 1989a). The analysis of women as commodities of exchange within patriarchal culture, of their 'being' rather than 'having' commodities, has been developed within feminist film theory in terms of the specific processes of objectification, fetishisation and display of the female body as sexual spectacle within Hollywood cinema (Mulvey, 1989).

The simultaneous positioning of women as subjects and objects of consumption took a specific form in relation to female spectatorship and Hollywood cinema in the 1940s. In a rather Foucauldian reading of women's relationship to image consumption, Doane argues that the very discourses through which female subjectivity is constructed tie women in even more tightly forms of subjection. Despite their roles as subjects, Doane argues that:

> the woman's ability to purchase, her subjectivity as a consumer, is qualified by a relation to commodities which is also ultimately subordinated to that intensification of the affective value of sexual relations which underpins a patriarchal society. (Doane, 1989a: 24)

Thus the fact that women are both the objects and subjects of commodity exchange is only *apparently* contradictory. The forms of female subjectivity produced through consumption simultaneously reproduce forms of female subjection within patriarchal culture. Thus Doane concludes:

> The feminine position has come to exemplify the roles of consumer and spectator in their embodiment of a curiously passive desiring subjectivity....In her desire to bring the things of the screen closer, to approximate the bodily image of the star and to possess the space in which she dwells, the female spectator experiences the intensity of the image as lure and exemplifies the perception proper to the consumer. The cinematic image for the woman is both shop window and mirror, the one simply a means of access to the other. The mirror/ window, then, takes on the aspect of *the trap whereby her subjectivity becomes synonymous with her objectification....*The female subject of the consumer look in the cinematic arena becomes, through a series of mediations, the industry's own merchandizing asset. One must ask at this point, 'Whose gaze is ultimately addressed?' and 'Who profits?'. (Doane, 1989a: 31–2; my emphasis)

This reading of the female spectator's relationship to consumption suggests that popular cinema represents the ultimate site of women's subordination. The combination of the spectator/consumer role for women traps them into a hopeless position of passivity in which even their role as subjects in consumer society is ultimately subsumed by the inevitable processes of objectification: commodities are purchased in order to produce the self as object of the male gaze. The female spectator prepares to be 'consumed' herself in the processes of consuming cultural commodities (stars and other products). The cinema might thus be seen as the physical and imaginative space serving the needs both of heterosexual masculine desire and of consumer capitalism.

The problem with such a conclusion, in which women are tied into these mutually reinforcing relations of powerlessness, is that it robs women of any agency in the reproduction of culture, and may even contribute to dominant notions of female passivity. What hope is left for change, for diversity or for resistance in this rather monolithic and functionalist account of female consumption and Hollywood cinema? After all, forms of control and subjection are never fully successful, otherwise none of us would be writing about them.

It is the question of the *inseparability* of subjectivity from objectification that I wish to challenge in the light of my own research. I argue that whilst Doane may have successfully identified the meaning of femininity within cultural production, this is not synonymous with the uses and meanings of commodities to *consumers*. Following existing cultural studies work on consumption I shall suggest that women are subjects, as well as objects of cultural exchange, in ways that are not entirely reducible to subjection (Winship, 1981; Partington, 1990; Nava, 1992).

Studying consumption: From producers to consumers

[…]

My argument concerns the specificity of gendered forms of consumption in relation to Hollywood cinema. Femininity is constructed within a very particular set of paradoxes within discourses of consumption – the feminine subject being the object of cultural consumption. By drawing on female spectators' memories of Hollywood stars in the 1940s and 1950s, this chapter continues the investigation of the meanings of consumption to a particular group of consumers. My research aims to extend and rethink the conclusions of much work on the female cinema spectator as a consumer which approaches the subject at the level of production (Eckert, 1978; Allen, 1980; Doane, 1989a). My aim is not to refute their conclusions completely, since such studies have produced important critiques of the femininity and consumer culture. They have also provided the only available *historical* accounts of the female spectator of Hollywood cinema as consumer; they are thus drawn upon in order to analyse the historical dimensions of Hollywood cinema and consumption. However, in addition to these accounts I shall consider the material I received from respondents in this study which do indeed complicate the picture by highlighting women's active agency in the consumption process. Thus, I shall argue both that female spectators are successfully constructed as consumers by Hollywood cinema *and* that they also used commodities connected with stars in ways that do not conform to the needs of the market (both in its marital and in its economic senses).

Shared investments

An analysis of female spectators' memories of Hollywood stars in 1940s and 1950s Britain demonstrates the significance of the discourse of consumption to the spectator/star relationship. In addition to escapism and identification, consumption appeared frequently in spectators' accounts of their attachments to Hollywood stars at this time. That female spectators and film stars were closely connected through commodity purchase, then, can be established through the study of *both* commodity production and consumption. But the question here is what conclusions can be drawn from such connections. How do female spectators remember the significance of consumption practices and how might their accounts highlight a more contradictory relationship between spectatorship and consumption than that presented by the production studies? Did consumption simply tie women more tightly into forms of subordination, and if so, what is to be made of their pleasure and delight in such cultural practices?

I examine spectators' memories of their consumption practices in terms of the importance of feminine cultural competence. The knowledge and expertise involved in such competence forms the basis of intense bonding with, and emotional, as well as financial, investment in, particular stars. In addition, connections between female spectators are formed through such shared knowledges and the use to which they may be put.

> I favoured Lauren Bacall most of all during the 1940s and 1950s and still have an interest in her.... My colouring was the same as hers, I wore my hair in a similar style and wore the same type of tailored clothes. In the early 1940s... matching shoes, gloves and handbag were a 'must'. I remember Lauren Bacall always kept to this unwritten rule, and I identified with her because of that, they were my 'trademark' for years. It was surprising how quickly fashions from the films caught on. In *To Have and Have Not* Lauren Bacall wore a dogtooth check suit and small round pill-box hat, black gloves and shoes and handbag – I can remember I had one very similar with a tan pill-box... and my hair in a page-boy like hers. The only difference was that she wore hers without a blouse. (Kathleen Lucas)

Here Lauren Bacall is written about within the language of product selection: she was 'favoured' above others. She is also appreciated for her enduring value: 'I still have an interest in her'. In turn, the female spectator, through her identification with the star, becomes a product herself, using the language of commodities to describe what characterised her particular personal style: her 'trademark' was the same as Lauren Bacall's in that they both shared the knowledge that matching shoes, gloves and handbags were a 'must'. Interestingly, the term 'trademark' is set in inverted commas by the respondent, as if to suggest a self-awareness, even irony, about this process of self-commodification: it is inappropriate for a woman to have a trademark, since this usually signifies a commodity, and yet it captures very well that production of self as image that is being described here.

The star is selected because of a recognition of resemblance with the spectator (Lauren Bacall had similar colouring); thus star selection involves female spectators looking for themselves (in every sense) in their star ideals. However, differences are also remembered as significant: the style and pattern of the suit is a mimetic representation, but the colour of the hat is different and Bacall's lack of blouse was obviously striking enough to be remembered. The more sexualised star is significant both in terms of national difference and in terms of the licence of Hollywood stars to present a more sex-ualised image than would have been acceptable for most women in 1940s Britain. Despite this difference, however, there is a strong memory of recognition and similar-ity. Indeed, this particular example suggests the importance of a shared feminine cul-ture during this period based upon knowledge, expertise and 'unwritten rules'. The shared recognition in the conventions of feminine appearance produce the basis for pleasure and appreciation for this female spectator: 'I remember Lauren Bacall always kept to this unwritten rule, and I identified with her because of that'. Consumer taste, linking star and spectator, is based upon the recognition of shared feminine expertise, invisible to the 'outsider' since these rules are felt to be 'unwritten'.

Female spectators remember Hollywood stars through their connection with particular commodities and the ways in which they were worn or displayed. Typically, this association is made in relation to clothes, hairstyles, make-up and cosmetics, and other fashion accessories. It is the commodities associated with physical attractiveness and appearance that are especially remembered in connection with female stars: clothes and accessories in this case, as in most others.

The speed with which the images on the screen become images 'on the streets' is commented upon here: replications of outfits and styles are remembered as taking place swiftly after the viewing of a particular film. Another respondent offers a similar account of purchasing an outfit to copy a star after seeing a particular film:

> and I bought clothes like hers [Doris Day] . . . dresses, soft wool, no sleeves, but short jackets, boxey type little hats, half hats we used to call them and low heeled court shoes to match your outfit, kitten heels they were called . . . as people said I looked like her [Marilyn Monroe]. I even bought a suit after seeing her in *Niagara*. (Patricia Ogden)

The detail of the memory of particular fashions and how stars wore them in films is part of the specificity of feminine cultural competence: the colours, patterns, cut and design of clothes remains a vivid memory some fifty years later. This attests to the significance of this connection for female spectators and demonstrates the intensity of their emotional, as well as financial, investments in such details of personal appearance. Pride in having an eye for detail and the ability to recall it so many years later is expressed in the following example:

> The female stars of my major film going period made a big impact on me. I can see a short clip from a film and know instantly whether I've seen it before or not – and as like or not, be able to add – 'then she moves off down the staircase' or 'the next dress she appears in is white, with puffy net sleeves'. (M. Palin)

The extraordinarily vivid memories here demonstrate the intense emotional investment in Hollywood at this time. This intensity may be because of the heightened emotional investment many young women make in feminine ideals and thus is explicable in terms of life stages. This might also be reinforced by the process of looking back and reminiscing about youthful pleasures and thus be explained in terms of nostalgia. Finally, this intensity could also be due to the feelings of recognition of the significance of Hollywood stars in the lives of respondents, after many years of little external recognition and indeed, in many cases even ridicule for their fandom.

It is worth pausing for a moment to reflect upon the forms of memory used by female spectators here. Iconic memory can be seen here to be connected to the reconstruction of the star image through a knowledge of the details of her appearance. Indeed, iconic memories of female stars, extracted from the narrative action, depend upon detail for their reconstruction of past images. Such knowledge constitutes the shared cultural competence of female spectators and connects them to each other and to their favourite female stars. The centrality of 'being an image' to definitions of femininity is thus manifest in the forms of memory employed here.

What is striking about the two examples given by M. Palin (above) is the way in which the memories selected both, though in different ways, focus on particular icons of femininity. The woman descending the staircase is an image from Hollywood in which female stars are typically displayed to onlookers below, and to cinema spectators, often at moments in the film when their costumes are of crucial significance. This female icon is also significant to another respondent quoted elsewhere who remembered replicating such movement after the film screening: 'Our favourite cinema was the Ritz – with its deep pile carpet and double sweeping staircase. Coming down one always felt like a heroine descending into the ballroom' (Anon). The second image selected to exemplify the endurance of this particular respondent's memory also draws upon a particular feminine iconography: the whiteness of the dress signifies purity and virginity, the puffy sleeves an abundance of material and the net material a semi-transparency to display the female body.

Although these examples do establish a clear link between formations of female subjectivity and processes of self-commodification through consumption, they also demonstrate that this is by no means the only significance of consumption practices to female spectatorship. Within the world of female knowledge and expertise, consumption also importantly involved processes of (mutual) recognition between spectators, and between them and their favourite stars, and a passionate connection to feminine ideals. Thus although the end product of such emotional and financial investments in ideal and self image may be the patriarchal institution of marriage, it is important not to deny the intense pleasure and delight in forms of feminine culture reproduced between female spectators and stars in the process.

'The intimacy which is knowledge'

There are important forms of intimacy involved in these shared feminine identities, between spectator and star ideal, and between female spectators. The recognition of shared knowledge forms the basis for such intimacy between femininities which has tended to be ignored in existing accounts of feminine consumption.

Hollywood stars in the 1940s and 1950s were strongly remembered by female spectators for their connection with fashion, and many stars became favourites because of this association:

> The Doris Day films I used to watch mainly for the clothes – she was always dressed in the latest fashions. (Mrs D. Delves)

> The clothes and the make-up were of great interest. Bear in mind 'teenagers' had not been invented in the late 1940s, so clothes were not on the market for that age group. We seemed to go from school children to grown-ups. The fashion scene was nothing like today's mass market. We had a few outfitters and the chainstores. What was worn on the screen was of importance. (Anon)

> I loved the cool charm of stars such as Deborah Kerr...my childhood dream was to become like her and I used to spend hours shop window gazing and selecting what she would wear. (Judith Ford)

In these statements the role of film stars as fashion models, advertising the latest styles to female spectators, comes across clearly. In the first example, a particular star is appreciated for her up-to-date clothes in her films. The selection of Doris Day in this role occurred frequently amongst respondents: 'Doris Day was a natural star to me, when she did anything it was always 100% – everything about her is perfect, the clothes she wore and everything' (Shirley Thompson). Clothes and fashion are central here to the attainment of feminine ideals: 'clothes and everything' could be read here as clothes are everything; if you can get them right your femininity is established. There is a delight expressed here in the star who always 'got it right' which again exemplifies a shared cultural competence. Consumer taste is thus based upon forms of recognition between women which constitute a shared cultural competence (see Bourdieu, 1984).

The second example highlights the importance of 'what was worn on the screen' in relation to the transition to adult femininity. Hollywood film stars seemed to play a key role in this rather nerve-wracking and treacherous journey, typically full of potential pitfalls and failures. Transition from childhood to adult femininity is signified through the transformation of the body and how it is clothed and presented. Given the centrality of physical appearance to cultural definitions of femininity, the stakes are high in this process of transformation. Film stars, representing cultural ideals of feminine beauty and charm, played a key role in these processes of identity formation. This memory draws attention to the contrast between contemporary consumer markets and those of the 1940s and 1950s. The significance of stars to spectators' knowledge of consumer fashion is reconstructed as particularly focused in the light of the expansion and diversification of fashion markets since that time.

In the final example, the spectator takes on the imaginary position of her favourite star in relation to consumption of female attire. The spectator's own identity is replaced through her imaginary identification with her ideal. This replacement of self with ideal subject position is effected through the fantasy of consumption; thus the spectator and star are linked, not through the purchasing of clothes, but through the gazing and desiring of the female spectator/consumer who imagines her ideal's choice of commodities. Cinema screen and shop window both display their spectacles: respectively, the female star and her imaginary outfits. Hollywood stars are thus linked to other commodities by the desiring female spectator/consumer who fantasises an ideal feminine self-image through imaginary consumption. The desire to clothe your favourite star, to predict her taste and style and to imagine her in the outfit of your choice suggests an intense intimacy between female spectators and stars. Indeed, it further points to a recognition of 'self-in-ideal' in being able to predict what the star would consume.

All three examples point to the personal investments of spectators in particular stars in terms of commodities associated with female appearance. As the final one suggests, this investment may not be financial, but often took the form of fantasy and imagined identities.

But Doris Day wore some beautifully cut clothes in some wonderful colours...this was in the 1940s when I first became aware of Doris Day – 'My Dream Is Yours' – need I say more! (Marie Burgess)

Here the spectator and a favourite star are linked through a common dream in which clothes are the currency of a shared femininity. The language of dreams is used frequently by respondents to describe their longings and desires in relation to

Hollywood stars. The dream metaphor not only suggests the star ideal is unreachable, but also indicates a state of blissful happiness. Here the title of Doris Day's second film, *My Dream Is Yours*, is used as a self-explanatory statement in which the respondent hopes to encapsulate the exchange between spectator and star, an exchange involving particular commodities, in this case 'beautifully cut clothes in some wonderful colours'. Thus spectators are linked to stars through imagined intimacy with the Hollywood ideal; what more intimate than a shared dream?

Star styles

In this section the connection between Hollywood stars and spectators is examined through an analysis of the construction of feminine style. The national differences between American and British femininity are especially significant to the attachment of fans to particular Hollywood stars. Differences of taste are articulated in relation to the meanings of British and American femininity at this time. Conforming to star styles in some cases could be seen as the successful reproduction of ideals of feminine appearance through consumption. This would certainly reiterate the claims made in the production studies of mutually beneficial collaboration between Hollywood and other industries (Eckert 1978; Allen, 1980; and Doane, 1989). In other cases, however, American feminine ideals are clearly remembered as transgressing restrictive British femininity and thus employed as strategies of resistance:

> Joan Crawford looked good in suits with big shoulder pads; Barbara Stanwyck shone in diaphanous creations (it always intrigued me how dressed up they were in ordinary everyday situations). (Marie Burgess)

Many respondents used discourses of fashion to write about their favourite Hollywood stars. Some appreciated the 'fit' between fashion style and star: the semi-transparent nature of the outfit allows the star quality to shine through, for example, in the above statement: 'Barbara Stanwyck shone in diaphonous creations'. Similarly, Joan Crawford's star image as a fierce and powerful woman, rivalled only by Bette Davis, is constructed partly through her more 'masculine' costumes: 'suits with big shoulder pads'. The final comment here suggests a fascination with the incongruity of the narrativised situations and the costumes of Hollywood stars, pointing to a use of films to display women's fashions at the expense of 'realism'.

As well as remembering favourite stars through a variety of different styles of femininity, some respondents associated Hollywood stars with particular items of clothing:

> I'd like to name Deanna Durbin as one of my favourite stars. Her beautiful singing voice, natural personality and sparkling eyes made her films so enjoyable, and one always knew she would wear boleros; in one film she wore six different ones. I still like wearing boleros – so you can see what a lasting effect the clothes we saw on the screen made on us. (Jean Davis, Member of the Deanna Durbin Society)

In this case an item of clothing, the bolero, is remembered as Deanna Durbin's 'trademark'. The spectator takes pleasure in the fulfilment of the expectation that

Deanna Durbin would appear in her films wearing this particular item of clothing. The spectator is connected to one of her favourite stars through her own purchase and wearing of this distinctive clothing sign. Again the enduring quality of these investments in star styles, replicated through commodity consumption, is striking: some forty years later the same item is worn with pleasure.

Some items of clothing were associated with Hollywood generally:

> We copied whatever we could from the stars we saw in the films. We even sent off by post to Malta and Gibraltar for Hollywood Nylons. And we got them by post. (Mary Wilson)

The use of Hollywood as an adjective here connects the cinema to the fashion industry. In particular, 'nylons' were a luxury item in Britain at this time, much sought after and extremely scarce; the connection to America would have been reinforced through the presence of American troops in Britain and their easier access to such products. In addition, nylons signify a specific form of display of the female body: the translucent covering of the leg with a fine material which emphasises smoothness and shapeliness. The display of particular parts of the female body, as I shall go on to discuss, is something which connects female spectators and stars, often a connection cemented through commodity consumption.

The connection between Hollywood and the women's fashion industry is made especially clear in the way that certain products were named after stars, not by the industries, but by the female spectators:

> I had a pair of Carmen Miranda platform shoes with ankle straps. (Vera Barford)

> The earliest film star I remembered was Shirley Temple, because I was the proud owner of a Shirley Temple style dress. (Mrs M. Breach)

Products are thus named after the stars associated with them, and female spectators purchase styles which give them a feeling of connection with their ideal:

> It was fun trying to copy one's favourite stars with their clothes, hats and even make-up, especially the eyebrows. Hats were very much in vogue at that time and shops used to sell models similar to the styles the stars were wearing. I was very much into hats myself and tried in my way (on a low budget) to copy some of them. Naturally I bought a Deanna Durbin model hat and a Rita Hayworth one. (Vera Carter)

Stars are inextricably linked to consumption in these examples in that their commodification extends beyond the cinema and into spectator's purchasing practices of female fashions. Stars are thus commodities within the Hollywood film industry and, in addition, their names become commodities in the fashion industry in Britain as they are used to describe particular styles.

This naming and copying of star styles was remembered in relation to hairstyles, as well as clothes and shoes:

> Now Doris Day.... I was told many times around that I looked like her, so I had my hair cut in a D.A. style....Jane Wyman was a favourite at one stage and I had my hair cut like hers, it was called a tulip.... Now Marilyn Monroe was younger and by this time I had changed my

image, my hair was almost white blonde and longer and I copied her hairstyle, as people said I looked like her. (Patricia Ogden)

Physical resemblance here links the spectator to Hollywood stars and the replication of stars' hairstyles affirms this connection further. Self-image is infinitely transformable, mirroring Hollywood ideals with new colours and styles of hair. Recognition of self in ideal shifts from star to star in an endless chain of commodification. Public recognition is crucial here; it is through other people's recognition of the spectator/star resemblance that this respondent presents her connection to particular stars.

Hairstyles were an important part of the physical transformations which took place in the attempt to become more like one's ideal: whether the more 'masculine' short crop of Doris Day's down-to-earth tomboyishness or the seductive 'peek-a-boo' hairstyle of Veronica Lake:

Doris Day is the greatest and in the 50's she had a haircut called the 'Butch cut' which I had to be like her. (Shirley Thompson)

I think we all liked to identify with our favourite entertainers. Why else did we copy their styles and clothes. During the forties there were thousands of Veronica Lakes walking about. Girls who copied her peek-a-boo hairstyles – long and waved over one eye. (Mrs Patricia Robinson)

Hollywood star styles and fashions are frequently referred to in the British context in terms of representing something different, something better and often something more sophisticated or even risqué. The impact of star styles on women in Britain was so strong that it was recognised as a problem by the state, which introduced safety regulations about women's hairstyles in factories during this period (Braybon and Summerfield, 1987). It also meant frequent conflict or power struggles with authority figures such as parents: 'Girlfriends talked incessantly about stars.... We discussed film star fashions – we were clothes mad. We wanted to dye our hair and copy the stars but we couldn't get permission from our parents' (Anon).

'Dyeing one's hair' clearly represented some kind of act of transgression or rebellion against the codes of respectable femininity in Britain at this time, since dyed hair suggested sexuality, independence and even prostitution. But it was not only sexuality that was seen as threatening, it was also the imitation of images of powerful femininity associated with stars such as Joan Crawford or Bette Davis: 'My father used to say "don't you roll those Bette Davis eyes at me young lady"' (Patricia Ogden).

The conventions of feminine appearance are remembered not only in terms of the reassuring conformity and predictability of Hollywood stars, however, but also in terms of stars breaking with certain fashion codes:

We were quick to notice any change in fashion and whether it had arrived this side of the Atlantic. We were pleased to see younger stars without gloves and hats – we soon copied them. Had it not been wartime we might not have got away with it, because British fashion then was very old-fashioned and rules were rigid. (Kathleen Lucas)

Hollywood stars represented fashions on the screen which were identified by spectators as transgressing restrictive codes of British feminine appearance. Indeed,

Hollywood stars were considered exciting in contrast to images of femininity offered by women in everyday life in Britain:

> I liked the clothes they often wore, we talked about their hair, make-up, figures and dress. I liked stars unlike myself because in my young days they appeared much more attractive. . . . Our mothers were very matronly at quite an early age. (Anon)

The reference to 'matronly' mothers here in opposition to glamorous Hollywood stars reinforces the familiar pervasive cultural dichotomy between motherhood and sexuality. The two main sources of information about femininity in the 1940s and 1950s, kinship and the cinema, are thus understood as being in opposition to each other and further reinforced by stereotypical national difference, American glamour versus British respectability.

The negotiation of idealised Hollywood femininities with mothers led to memories of intense emotional struggles:

> I was fascinated with Shirley Temple . . . she always looked perfect. I loved her curls and as I was about the same age I begged my mother to do my hair like hers with rags or tongs. But I was made to keep my plaits. As for her dresses I was envious of them. However I remember my mother receiving a second-hand dress for me which was very much like the ones she used to wear. I was thrilled and told everyone it was my Shirley Temple dress. (Muriel Breach)

The language used here suggests a strength of feeling in the attempt to copy the star ideal: this respondent felt love, fascination and envy towards her childhood idol, 'begged' her mother to copy Shirley Temple's hairstyle and was 'thrilled' when she had a Shirley Temple dress. These examples from childhood demonstrate the breadth of the impact of Hollywood stars on women in Britain during this period: it was not only regular cinema spectators with purchasing power who were addressed as consumers by Hollywood, but young girls, too, who relied on second-hand clothes for their star-like replications.

As well as being vehicles to encourage female spectators to become consumers, and to improve their appearances, then, Hollywood stars were also contested terrains of competing cultural discourses of femininity. As I have shown, they were central to challenges to what was perceived as restrictive British femininity, be it 'the dowdiness' of women in wartime Britain, the restrictions of factory regulations about hairstyles or the perceived lack of glamour of motherhood. Many respondents had vivid memories of Hollywood stars as representing an alternative to what they perceived to be these constraining forms of British femininity. In the 1950s particularly, when the purchase of fashions and cosmetics increasingly became a possibility for many women in Britain, the reproduction of self-image through consumption was perceived as a way of producing new forms of 'American' feminine identity which were exciting, sexual, pleasurable and in some ways transgressive.

Conclusion: Consuming and producing the self – femininity and commodification in postwar Britain

My argument draws rather different conclusions from those found in the 'production studies' of the relationship between femininity and consumption discussed at the beginning of this chapter (Eckert, 1978; Allen, 1980; Doane, 1989a). When considered in terms of its relationship to the production of consumer commodities, Hollywood cinema has often been seen as the ultimate site of the successful combination of the dominant interests of the marriage and the commodity markets in 1940s and 1950s Britain. The cinema space has been seen as a key site for heterosexual courtship and romance, reinforced by the Hollywood message that happiness for women lay in catching a man and keeping him. It also offered the physical and imaginative space in which captive audiences, surrounded by luxury and abundance, were introduced to new styles and commodities on the screen. Female stars offered spectators ideals of feminine desirability which, through the purchase of certain commodities, they tried to recreate for themselves.

However, as I have shown, the dominant discourses of Hollywood producers are not necessarily equivalent to consumer practices of female spectators in specific contexts. This is not to argue for the supremacy of the consumer as determining her relationship to femininity through commodities, nor to champion the pleasures of consumption as inherently transgressive. Rather, it is to argue for the importance of maintaining a theoretical understanding of the space between dominant discourses of consumption and female spectators' consumer practices in different locations. Whilst the forms of pleasure taken in Hollywood stars are often centrally concerned with appearance and image and involve self-transformation in terms of commodities sold to women to improve their appearance and their bodies, the forms of spectatorship that I have explored in this chapter involve a complex negotiation of subject and object, and of self-image and ideal image. Challenging the rather functionalist model of the relationship between female spectators and consumption found in the production studies discussed earlier, I have offered an account which analyses the very contradictions of the relationships between Hollywood film stars, female spectatorship and consumption practices.

References

Allen, Jeanne (1980) 'The film viewer as consumer', *Quaterly Review of Film Studies* 5, 4: 481–99.

Boutdieu, Pierre (1984) *Distinction: A Social Critique of the Judgement of Taste* (trans. by Richard Nice), London: Routledge & Kegan Paul.

Braybon, Gail and Summerfield, Penny (1987) *Out of the Cage: Women's Experiences in Two world Wars*, London: Pandora.

Doane, Mary Ann (1989a) 'The economy of desire: the commodity form in/of the cinema', *Quaterly Review of Film and Video* 11: 23–33.

Eckert, Charles (1978) 'The Carole Lombard in Macy's window', *Quarterly Review of Film Studies* 3, 1: 1–21.

Irigaray, Luce (1985) *This Sex Which is Not One* (trans. by Catherine Porter with Carolyn Burke), Ithaca, NY: Cornell University Press.

Mulvey, Laura (1975) 'Visual pleasure and narrative cinema', *Screen* 16, 3: 6–18.

—— (1989) *Visual and Other Pleasures*, Basingstoke: Macmillan.

Nava, Mica (1992) *Changing Cultures*, London: Sage.

Partington, Angela (1990) 'Consumption practices as the production and articulation of differences: rethinking working-class femininity in 1950s Britian', unpublished PhD Thesis, University of Birmingham.

Winship, Janice (1981) 'Woman becomes an "individual"– femininity and consumption in women's magazines 1954–69', *Stencilled Occasional Paper* 65, Birmingham: Centre for Contempory Cultural Studies, University of Birmingham.

27 A Star is Dead: A Legend is Born: Practicing Leslie Cheung's Posthumous Fandom

Yiman Wang

Introduction

it may sound like I'm a freak for being sad over a dead celebrity, *but you don't understand – for a lot of us, we grew up listening to his songs … and later watching his movies. He was a legend in hong kong, and in asia – you can sorta tell when* newspapers all over the world reported his death. *almost everyone who grew up in hong kong in the 80s was, at one time or another, a fan of his*

(LiveJournal for eggtart posted April 2, 2003, 10:01 pm, italics mine)

At 18:41 on April 1st, 2003, the day Hong Kong was declared a disaster area, and was quarantined due to the SARS disease, Leslie Cheung Kwok-wing, 'the most widely adored and admired male diva of the late 20th century' (Corliss in Steward and Hawker 2003, back cover), leapt to his death from the twenty-fourth floor of the Mandarin Oriental Hotel on Hong Kong Island. Nicknamed 'Gor Gor' (the elder brother), Cheung was a film/pop star, with a legion of adoring fans across the world. His stellar popularity, and ability to connect with a diverse audience, was in part based upon his androgynous identity and ambivalent or 'queer' sexuality. His unexpected suicide also suggested that the confusion at the centre of his star-being was too much to bear, and his death turned him into a loss irrecoverable – *legend* irreplaceable. Cheung is described as 'Heaven's gift (Wong 2003), a term that invokes discourses of 'magic' and specialness where conceptions of stardom are concerned. This is of course part of the construction of his star image, but his omnipotent and omnipresent power will forever enthrall his admirers, and this is something that I would like to explore in this essay. In particular, I focus on one site that helps to preserve and produce Cheung's (posthumous) celebrity. This is computer technology, something which represents a most recent development in worldwide economics and culture. In studying the star practices which are enacted and mediated in the virtual space, I intend to demonstrate that Cheung's dead celebrity status should be understood as arising from current technological conditions, which in turn mirror local and global cultural politics.

The cultural impact of 'Gor Gor's suicide can not be overestimated. His death triggered 10 youth suicides, or attempted suicides, in Hong Kong and Beijing. This was termed the 'Leslie Cheung phenomenon' by a number of psychiatrists (Cai 2003). The local, national and international media reported on this phenomenon, and coverage extended to his suicide anniversary and to posthumous birthday celebrations. In mainland China and Hong Kong, filmmakers, musicians, and cultural critics commented upon Cheung's legacy as a pop singer-composer, an actor who essayed a wide range of roles, and a transgressive 'entertainment' figure whose gender-bending concert performances were seen as scandalous by the Hong Kong media (yet were adored by his many fans around the world). The continued commemoration of Cheung, however, is particularly interesting as it stretches across identifactory practices and media representations. For example, his fans have gathered in Hong Kong to continue the Leslie legacy through imitative cross-dressing. Taiwan fans donned red heels on the first anniversary of Cheung's death as a way of celebrating his costume at from a 1997 pop concert in which he declared that his love was 'not tolerated by convention'. Cheung's photo albums, songs, concerts and films have also all been re-released. Capital Artists, which signed Cheung in the 1980s, released a special collection, entitled *History – His Story*, including some of Cheung's songs and MTV videos from the 1980s, and his oral autobiography which was recorded by a TV station in 1985. The first book in memory of Cheung was published in mainland China in the same month he committed suicide (Shuang Cheng 2003). By the Spring 2005, nearly ten books and commemorative volumes (in Chinese, English and Japanese) had been published since his death. A multi-media performance entitled 'Eternal Leslie Cheung' (*Yonghen de Zhang Guorong*), starring Leslie look-alike Chen Zhipeng, started touring in China on April 1, 2004. A life-size wax figure depicting Cheung in a traditional Chinese long gown (taken from his image in *Rouge* (Kwan 1987)), was unveiled in Hong Kong's Madame Tussaud's Memorial Hall on 31 March 2004, for the first anniversary of his death. Finally, a number of internet fan sites have emerged which are dedicated to keeping alive the myth and memory of Cheung. In her discussion of the death of Princess Diana, Rosalind Brunt uses Foucault's idea of 'an immense verbosity' or 'the incitement to discourse' to describe the excessive public commentary triggered by the event, which she argued challenged Western taboos around death (Brunt 1999: 22). The 'carnival of media' following Cheung's death can be regarded as precisely a mediated version of such 'immense verbosity' in that, 'everybody could feel entitled to express a view' and 'an excess of analogy' was produced to describe what the dead celebrity was like (Brunt 1999: 22).

One of the central agents/agencies in producing this verbosity is computer technology, especially the internet and multimedia software, the former significantly reshaping remote communication, and the latter offering a new means of media production and exhibition. Indeed, my research on Cheung's celebrity image has been constantly overtaken, stretched, and reshaped by the new information loaded onto the web on a daily basis. My task in this essay is precisely to study the various strategies involved in constructing Cheung's posthumous fandom that played out at transnational and local levels. The term 'posthumous fandom' is meant to highlight Cheung's *increased* charisma after his death. As a dead celebrity, the iconic Cheung acquires a spiritual dimension (the way Diana did, according to Brunt 1999: 36–37). But also, aided by the unparalleled reproductive and re-creative capacities of digital media, such liminal spirituality works to collapse normative binary oppositions, including time and space, the center and the periphery, the straight and the queer, the here/now an the dead/gone. Charisma, as S. N. Eisenstadt argues in his introduction to Max Weber's *Charisma and Institution Building*, becomes especially significant 'when the social order is uncertain, unstable and ambiguous and when the charismatic figure or group offers a value, order or stability to counterpoise this' (Eisenstadt, cited in Dyer 1998: 30–31). As a dead celebrity situated in between omnipresence and absence, Cheung's posthumous charisma interestingly demonstrates how an age of instability calls into being an iconic figure; and how, conversely, the death of a celebrity reconfirms the need to build a collective identity.

Mediating the multiple facets of the Leslie legend

Computer technology has played a prominent role in providing the context for Leslie fandom to take place, while it has also disseminated news of Cheung's suicide, and created his posthumous spectacle. Many of Cheung's fans first learned about his suicide through cell phone conversations or in internet chat rooms, and then went online to check web headline news. Reactions from Cheung's relatives, friends, and colleagues in mainland and Hong Kong were soon posted on the internet. Major Chinese internet portals, such as www.sohu.com, instantly opened special columns dedicated to updating information on Cheung's suicide and its after (a)effects on devoted fans. Leslie Cheung fan sites, such as the first and largest mainland Leslie domain, 'Rongguang wuxian' (or boundless glory of Leslie) (www.lesliecheung.com.cn) received record hits.

In addition to 'news' reporting, the internet facilitated the fan activities of organizing and disseminating commemorative events. It provided an important venue for geographically dispersed fans to gather together in the virtual space. A key example is the first anniversary of Cheung's death – an event entitled 'Always Adoring Leslie Cheung – Nation-wide Leslie Fans Remembering Leslie on April 1' ('Yongyuan chongai' Zhang Guorong – Si Yi quanguo gemi zhuisi zhuti huodong). This event was sponsored by two fan groups, www.lesliecheung.com.cn (Rongguang wuxian) and www.lesliesky.com (Ronghua juedai). It took place between 1–10th April in different locations in mainland China. People could register online by going to the registration link assigned to their province. Those unable to attend in person could meet other Leslie fans in chat room (http://chat.lesliecn.com or http://295839.Bliao.com), which allowed a maximum of 150 people online at the same time. In addition, web broadcasting (mms://lesliecheung.vicp.net:8080) was available during the event. The event allowed fans to 'thoroughly enjoy sharing their tears, songs and memories of Gor Gor with each other,' as one participant observed (Jin 2004).

Not only was there grass root commemoration, as university-sponsored seminars were dedicated to the analytical study of the Leslie legacy. These also took advantage of the internet, using it to store verbal, visual, acoustic, and multi-media information. The series of seminars on Cheung's artistic life held in Hong Kong, for instance, were taped and loaded on the Hong Kong-based 'Gor Gor's' Website, www.leslie-cheung.info, accompanied by transcription in classical Chinese and Japanese. The online bilingual transcripts and the audio-visual clips demonstrated the intention to make the Leslie legacy international, or at least pan-East Asian. Other multi-lingual web sites include Leslie Cheung Cyberworld (http://lesliecheung.cc) (in English and Chinese), and Ju Rong Tang (literally meaning 'The Hall of All Leslie Fans' and implicitly combining Cheung's first name, Rong, and his same-sex lover's last name, Tang) (http://www.leslietong.com). The English website of the Leslie Legacy Association (http://xoomer.virgilio.it/nguidett/) also provides separate web links for Chinese, Korean and Japanese fans. In January 2004, it mobilized enough fan support to successfully campaign for HKFAA (Hong Kong Film Awards Association) and HKTB (Hong Kong Tourism Board) to extend to Cheung the Life Achievement Award and to place his name plaque on Hong Kong's Avenue of Stars, which officially opened on 27th April, 2004.

The virtual re-incarnation of Cheung has become so central to fan identification that an article jokingly describes a new incurable virus, named 'Loving Leslie' (*Ai Rong*). The importance of the computer to the textual construction and circulation of Cheung's image prompted a mainland fan to fictionalize a long humorous conversation between 'a certain fan' and her computer. In the fan vs. computer scenario, the fan complains about the computer's declining performance, including frequent fainting (freeze), heart attack (CPU problem), high blood pressure (mother board overheat), asthma (inadequate hard disk), as well as such smaller problems as wrinkles (unstable screen resolution) and sluggish movement (malfunctioning mouse and keyboard). The computer, on its part, counters the fan's accusations by complaining about its long-term abuse by its owner: the computer maintains that the owner is always online, has many windows running simultaneously, and periodically pours tears and saliva into the keyboard (triggered by emotional responses to Cheung-related reports). Having listed these, the computer concludes that its owner is suffering from the contagious 'Leslie fans syndromes' (*Rongmi zonghe zhen*) and should thus be strictly quarantined (Fan Articles at LCIFC discussion forum 2003).

The centrality of computer-based fandom is further reflected in fans' almost morbid anxiety about losing the new technology. A Leslie fan posted a question posted on 13 March 2003 at www.lesliecheung.com.cn, 'If one day, your computer broke down, your CD or cassette player broke down, all your collection and all things about Leslie were gone, what would you do?'. To preserve his memory, many fans requested that the web site and forum remain open because 'surfing this site is my only motivation in life' ('Zui Ai' (Beloved) 4 May, 2003), or 'at least we would still have memory' ('Shiqu le ni' (Losing You) 2 April, 2003). One fan defiantly announced that: 'This [losing all Cheung-related data] would never happen. I've backed up all my files' ('Piao' (Floating) 6th April, 2003).

Internet technology not only enables access to Cheung, but it also enables fans to learn more about each other. A mainland fan, who had spent years waiting for Leslie news to trickle in from Hong Kong, expressed her excitement when the internet made her aware of the existence of other Leslie fans (Fan article posted at LCIFC discussion forum at 11:27 am on 25 December 2002). This became more important after Cheung's suicide. Thanks to its capacities of transcending physical distance between geographical locations, and metaphysical distance between life and death, computer technology served to link grieving fans, bringing them together as a mourning *community*, thereby generating consoling effects. As one Hong Kong fan wrote:

> Actually, we have never met each other. Yet we have all met Leslie Cheung. I might live at Wong Tai Sin, while you live at Sai Ying Pun. Nevertheless, because of Leslie, we know each other. This, perhaps, is what they call 'collective memory'. (Yun 2004: 92)

Following Baudrillard's (1994) seminal study of simulacra in the postmodern capitalist society, critics have explored how to re-conceptualize identity in the digital world. The virtual space generated by computer technology and new media in the late twentieth and early twenty-first century, hinge upon simulation and simulacra, a state characterized by hyper-reality or the mimicking of real space to provide life-like experiences (especially sensorial stimuli) which are nevertheless carefully programmed to eliminate excessive real-life contingencies. However, this position does not necessarily contradict the argument that digital technology enables easy, seamless transformation of the 'original'. In fact, the two sides combine to constitute the virtual world of simulacra. The virtual space reproduces, extends, expands, redeems *and* fictionalizes the real space that once existed. Because of this, it is particularly important in preserving and reviving Leslie fandom and extending it to a 'dead celebrity' culture. It does so by producing the illusion that the idol does not cease to exist upon his death, but rather becomes omnipresent. For where there is a computer and internet, you can find 'Gor Gor' preserved and re-created at his best.

The imagined, transnational, internet community

An article published two days after Cheung's suicide summarizes the four groups of people most attracted to Cheung, namely, the 1970s generation who are Cheung's staunch supporters; a great many Chinese film cineastes; people who worked with Cheung, and finally those who value *self-assertion* and *freedom* ('Four Groups of People Attracted to Leslie Cheung' 2003). These groups do whereas the first group, the 1970s generation, suggests a collective identity; the last group seems to be based on individualism. This divergence underscores the ambivalent address of Cheung's star image. We may argue that Cheung's posthumous broadly fandom operates on two levels – transnational and local – the first encompassing all those who value self-assertion and freedom, the second referring specifically to the 1970s generation.

A mainland college woman's web posting exemplifies how her real life constantly interrupts the virtual space; or rather, how she actively incorporates real life happenings to enliven Leslie fandom (Fan article posted on 6 November 2003 at LCIFC discussion forum). The writing of the web article, according to the author, was encouraged by her roommates, when her school reopened after SARS came under control. Indeed, her roommates' presence in the writing process was so obvious that she constantly paused her writing to respond to their teasing, which in turn suggested the communal dimension of her own production. At one place, she wrote that she once burst into singing one of Cheung's most well known songs, 'Red' (Hong), the bold lyrics of which instantly shocked her roommates, who now saw her as a lustful girl.[1] At this point, her writing was interrupted by the following joke-ish insert: P.s.: my roommate just saw me writing this. She twitched her lips, as if saying, 'You're airing your dirty laundry! It's enough you are so shameless in our dorm. And you've the guts to show that shameless face on the web!' At a later point, she wrote, 'p.s. my roommates saw me tapping away on the keyboard and asked, 'You've lost enough face recently, and still have some left?' I smiled in my heart and thought, 'Haha my face is long lost, and now I'm losing *your* face on the web!'

In this writing, the fan's virtual space is never isolated or abstracted from the real space, but is rather an intimate part of it. The fan presents herself not as an anonymous alias that constantly metamorphoses into some totally different identity. Rather, she lives and writes as a college student surrounded by roommates and classmates, whose interruption and mocking of her star-worship becomes a form of participating in the writing. Consequently, the virtual space is by no means merely a site of simulacra and identity tourism which, according to Nakamura, is a space where unidentified travelers-surfers play non-committal games by assuming and exploiting stereotypical racial and gender identities (Nakamura 2000: 713–715). Rather, it can be seen as a site for the overflow of real life interactions. It addresses specific needs and interests of individual fans who differ from each other significantly, yet all gather together in Leslie Cheung's virtual space. To take Nakamura's use of 'passing' in a different direction, one may argue that, in this grass root virtual space, everybody desires to be and passes as a Leslie fan by describing how their *embodied* identities enable them to become such.

An important internet venue where international fans come together is LCIFC (Leslie Cheung Internet Fan Club at www.lesliecheung.com). This site features a special 'foreign (non-Chinese) fans' section in its 'fans area.' The posts indicate that non-Chinese fans come from a wide geographical area, including Japan, Indonesia, Korea, France, Sweden, Britain and the United States. These non-Chinese fans especially value the English online forum that helps to remove their linguistic barrier. An American fan who once lived in Hong Kong and became a Leslie fan in Japan wrote:

I think the fact that LCIFC is on the internet makes it a great place for all kinds of people, all kinds of Chinese people, as well as people from many different backgrounds, to come together and share something in common. And, although I understand the problems with using English as the common language, I know I'm not the only one who really appreciates it!!'. (Lori 2000)

The different star practices suggest that Cheung's trans-local fandom is actually enhanced by the fans' ready acknowledgement of their racial, national, geographical and cultural distance from the idol. The fact that they live and embody their real-life identities in the virtual space leads to the question of how they negotiate the gap between their embodied differences (often foreignness) and Cheung's Hong Kong affiliation. In the rest of this section, I highlight three interrelated, yet differing strategies of appropriating Cheung and their ideological implications. The fan comments I cite mostly come from forum.lesliecheung.com.

First, for some of Cheung's fans his Hong Kong ethnicity is effaced; and his cultural, racial otherness is characterized as 'Chinese.' This is suggested by the fact that, despite their wish to learn Chinese in order to bridge the linguistic gap, they do not seem to make any distinction between Cantonese (Cheung's mother tongue) and mandarin Chinese (which Cheung learned while making *Farewell My Concubine* with a mainland director, Chen Kaige). A South Korean fan living in Malaysia, Cheong Im, for instance, believed that she would be able to understand the lyrics of Cheung's songs (mostly in Cantonese) once she mastered mandarin (Cheong 2000). Such a lack of understanding of the heterogeneous make-up of 'Chineseness' has led many fans to see Cheung as a straightforward representative, or a gateway, to Chinese – even Asian – cinema and culture.

For other fans, the linguistic barrier and Chinese/Hong Kong specificity are superseded by Cheung's non-linguistic art. A Japanese fan claimed that his lack of Chinese did not matter, since many of Cheung's movies aired in Japan had English or Japanese subtitles, 'just the same as watching Hollywood movies.' What makes Cheung more attractive than Hollywood stars is that 'he is Asian just as I am' (Aya 2000). Another Japanese fan, Yamashita Mie similarly viewed language barrier as inconsequential, as Cheung's dancing, singing and acting convinced her that his charm needed no language. 'It is my great honor to be born in the same era as such a legend' (Yamashita 2004: 156). The common emphasis here is the shared Asian background, which allows East and Southeast Asian fans to construct a pan-(South)east Asian fandom around Cheung.

Cheung's celebrity appeal becomes further transnationalized when non-Asian fans describe Cheung as a handsome and spunky idol who will make a good 'Chinese boyfriend' (William 2000),[2] the 'epitome of beauty', a great actor (Annabel 2000), and a 'phenomenal artist' (Martino 2002).[3] These fans emphasize Cheung's *individual* qualities and lifestyle, which are seen as essential, universal, and disconnected from his representative value (either of Hong Kong, China or Asia). Yim Chan, a Hong Kong architect who had emigrated to Canada to 'pursue his ideals,' also argues that Cheung posed an uncompromised challenge to any collective identity. For Chan, Cheung's significance lies in the fact that he did *not* represent his time, nor the obsessively money-driven Hong Kong. Rather, his artistic ambitions and idealist personal qualities contradicted the anti-intellectual; anti-art Hong Kong so strongly that he had been constantly rejected and exiled by the city he loved (Chan 2004: 154–155). Lin Chaorong's comments that a superstar like Cheung could not be boxed-in by the TV screen, but must appear as an enlarged image on the big screen to emit his electrifying power (Lin 2003). Chan laments, 'To a great artist like Leslie Cheung, Hong Kong was nothing but a box' (Chan 2004: 154–155). This is epitomized, Chan argues, by one of Cheung's well-known songs, entitled 'I Am What I Am' (Wo jiushi wo). By avoiding a title like 'I Am Chinese,' Chan suggests, Cheung defied categorizations imposed by nationality, religion and tradition (Chan 2004). The opposition posited between the individualist Cheung and commodified Hong Kong makes him a subversive, yet lonely, figure in the Byronic tradition.

The star practices at work here suggest that non-Chinese fans generally understand Cheung's 'charisma' independent of his particularity as a Hong Kong performing artist active from the late 1970s to the early twenty-first century – an important period in Hong Kong history. For these fans, the significance of Cheung's charisma lies in the fact that it emanates from his individual strength, and resists various external interpellations. As Cheung's iconicity gets increasingly globalized, he gradually loses temporal-spatial specificity and acquires universal value. On closer analysis, however, the universalistic discourse is not as innocent as it seems. What is labeled as purely aesthetic is actually positioned against the mainstream as a set of alternative values. This includes his androgynous physical beauty, bold artistic experimentation, and courageous announcement of his same-sex relationship. The apparent depoliticizing discourse thus turns out to be a strategy of re-politicizing him, making him amenable to interests that go against nationalism, yet which contribute to forging alternative social groups. Packaged as an alternative figure, Cheung's political significance can be described as a 'transvaluation of values' (Taylor 2000: 117).

Cheung's legendary death itself contributes significantly to his mythologization and his drastically growing fandom. The 'Hou Rongmi' (or post 1 April Leslie fandom) phenomenon amply testifies to Cheung's heightened posthumous charisma. An increasing number of people are describing themselves as Leslie fans since, or perhaps because of his death. This emphasizes the power of the media which has been instrumental in disseminating Cheung's charisma, even transplanting Cheung's *memory* from the older generation to the younger generation, as some teenage post-April 1 fans note. The role of memory leads me from Cheung's transnational fandom to the more locally based fan community. Indeed, if the transnational internet community seems to include those who appreciate Cheung's individual charisma as the basis for depoliticization and universalization, the local fan community tends to emphasize their *shared memory* of Cheung. The shared memory ultimately leads to a form of collective nostalgia.

Collective nostalgia and glocalization in the new millennium

The nostalgic fan community revels in the uniquely transgressive and global/local star qualities of Cheung. For them he is/was simultaneously avant-garde and passé, too advanced and yet too romantically perfect to be a part of the mundane contemporary world. Cheung's pop concerts are seen to showcase his transgressive and self-reflexive performance style. For example, at his 'Crossing 1997' (Kuayue 97) concert where he declared his long-term gay relationship, he wore red lip stick and red heels, and performed a male-male tango, in addition to singing several songs dedicated to his male lover. At his 'Passion' (Reqing) concert that toured internationally (in mainland China, Japan, Korea, Hong Kong and North America) from 2000 to 2001, he wore a series of costumes designed by French fashion designer, Jean-Paul Gautier. These included a feathered white suite, an Egyptian-style long shirt, a Scotland short skirt, a bright red long coat and a black body-fitting dress. His seductive body postures (such as self caressing and changing clothes in front of the audience) also caused a furor in the Hong Kong media.

Cheung's style and aesthetics were perceived as so bold and subversive that a Hong Kong fan, JoJo, lamented that Cheung's tragedy was prompted by the fact that his beloved audience were never 'ready' for him. The 'perfect gift from heaven' (an analogy of James Wrong, Cheung's good friend and a late Hong Kong veteran lyric writer) was sent to the wrong place at a wrong time (JoJo 2004: 152–153).[4] Contrary to JoJo's pessimistic conception, Li Yinhe, a mainland woman sociologist who studies homosexual subculture in China, saw Cheung as a harbinger of our common future where a binary sex prison will be eliminated and everybody will be free to choose their sexual orientation (Li 2003). Comments on Cheung's avant-garde or modernist spirit, however, are counterbalanced by an opposite discourse that describes Cheung as belonging to a bygone era – as opposed to Hong Kong's contemporary money-driven, throw-away 'show-biz' culture. Attention to Cheung's material and discursive context separates the local nostalgic community from Cheung's transnational internet fandom. Although the nostalgic fans also emphasize Cheung's 'individual star quality', they ultimately see him as a symbol of a bygone era, one that they have collectively experienced *and* lost. Cheung's death has initiated collective melancholia of an epoch among fans in different geopolitical regions of China, especially the 1970s generation. Importantly, the shared past reconstructed by this generation is not removed from reality, but is rather bound up with Hong Kong's prosperity from the 1980s to early 1990s. The focus on Cheung, a Hong Kong mega-star, as the cementing power for the 70s generation of different regions of China, precisely has to do with Hong Kong's increasing importance in technological, economic and cultural domains in the late twentieth century. In other words, Cheung comes to stand for the convergence in technological, economic and cultural developments in Hong Kong, the developments desired in mainland China and Taiwan.

In mainland China, the 1990s witnessed a significant commercial turn that further facilitated the influx of Hong Kong, Taiwan and Japanese pop culture. This phenomenon continued into the late 1990s economic slump in East Asia (Hong Kong included) in late 90s. When Cheung committed suicide in 2003, the war in Iraq was raging; Hong Kong economy was still suffering from the slump, and as discussed, it was to be quarantined due to severe SARS problem. Cheung's death instantly raised new media sensation, which some journalists welcomed as a change to the drone of war reports from Iraq.

The (perceived) close parallel between Cheung's life/career trajectory and the trajectory of local/global economic, cultural and political shifts, makes him a perfect symbol for an age with its dramatic ups and downs. Even though he is often seen as 'too good' to fit into his age, his iconicity helps to consolidate the age and allows the geographically dispersed 1970s generation come to see themselves as part of a shared history. Born in the 1970s and growing up in the 1980s, this generation witnesses economic takeoff in all three geopolitical regions (Hong Kong, mainland and Taiwan). They actively partake in the proliferating pop culture. They are also the first generation of computer users, which enables them to further collapse the geographical and cultural distance between the three regions. In mainland China, for example, when the Westernized Hong Kong popular culture came as a fashion to a country that was still stumbling on the road of 'socialism with Chinese characteristics,'[5] mainland youth eagerly listened to Cheung's and other Hong Kong pop stars songs as a way of becoming modern. This was their response to the state campaign of 'Four Modernization.'[6] Consequently, Leslie Cheung, as an important icon of the Westernized Hong Kong pop culture, became the 'Gor Gor' for every fan growing up in the 1980s mainland – Taiwan as well as Hong Kong.

According to an anonymous mainland fan who had a hard time coming to terms with Cheung's suicide, the whole thing 'feels odd. I've never shed tears for a stranger.

Yet, the thought of him brought tears to my eyes' (quoted in Ren 2003: 88). Similarly, Taiwan fans described Cheung's death as bereavement of part of oneself. Kathy T. wrote, 'His departure took away the memories of our generation .... I know for sure he was inseparably part of my youthful memories' (T. 2004: 123). The 1970s generation's attachment to Cheung was most clearly articulated by a Hong Kong fan, Hong:

> To be born in the 70s Hong Kong was my luck. While other people record their time as year, month, day, hour, minute and second, my time has been marked by Leslie. Whenever I forget what happened in a certain year, month or day, one of Leslie's songs will immediately evoke the picture of the time. Leslie is the clock in my remembrance.

Eva Man (2004), a Hong Kong cultural critic and a post-April 1 Leslie fan, saw Cheung as *emblematic* of the entire Hong Kong population:

> Why his death was such a heavy impact, as if part of myself needs to be reviewed? *Perhaps we share the same era and grew up together.* He shared a lot with us. He is a product of the colony, a very delicate product who understands Western and Eastern cultures. As an artist, *his charm has to do with his self-contradiction, which is also a self-contradiction shared by all Hong Kong people.*

Such collective mourning suggests that Cheung's death was traumatic not only because the 1970s generation lost their life-time idol. The trauma comes from the disruption, even exhaustion, of the meaning of their own lives. An anonymous Leslie fan wrote online after that moment on 1 April:

> our youth was broken! The youthful memory of the Chinese-speaking generation born between 1968 and 1978, aged between 25 to 35 was broken – broken like the metal rail outside the Mandarin Oriental Hotel – by Leslie Cheung's falling body. (Anonymous 2003)

If Cheung's image once made an entire generation and their time comprehensible and meaningful, his demise triggered a sudden awareness of the end of an era (defined in individual as well as collective terms). Consequently, fans from the 1970s generation lost part of their context (so to speak) within which they could make sense of their existence. Paradoxically, it is also because of the traumatic loss and the subsequent collective mourning that the collective history shared by the 1970s generation is *retrospectively* constructed. In other words, the loss becomes potentially productive through the star practice of Lesley Cheung.

Aided by computer technology and new media, Leslie fans engage in proliferating creative star practices at both individual and collective levels. They see themselves as the legitimate agent in spreading and carrying on the Leslie legacy. Borrowing Walter Benjamin's model of 'prehistory' and 'afterlife' in his analysis of the ruins, we may argue that Cheung's death sealed his life and consigned the time he represented to 'prehistory,' whose 'afterlife' depends upon his fans. For Benjamin, the significance of ruins lies precisely in its wreckage and imminent disappearance. Only when freed from its designated uses, or apparent use value, can it be revisited as an allegory that crystallizes the Then and the Now, thus reborn into a new life (Gilloch 1996: 113). Likewise, Cheung's significance as not just an idol, but also what Mo Cheng calls a 'cultural hero', can be recognized only after his death and legend-ization (Mo 2004: 135). That is, his significance surfaces when he becomes a *dead* celebrity. The death of an authoritative figure can free fans to become authors in their own right, which in turn facilitate 'afterlife' and omniscience.

The fact that the Leslie legacy both enables and depends upon fans' creative participation suggests a subtle shift of authorship (if not authority) from the celebrity to the fan. To take over the authorship means to continue Cheung's 'afterlife,' so that their life experiences and self-definition can be defined in a generational frame. Thus, the fan-authorship and the generational nostalgia become mutually constitutive, and both were facilitated by computer technology and new media. These are tools which the 1970s urban generation in mainland Hong Kong and Taiwan have utilized to foreshorten the distance between geopolitical locations, between celebrity and the fan, between the real and the virtual, author and the audience, and most importantly, between life and death.

Conclusion

In this essay, I have studied the legendary Hong Kong pop star-artist, Leslie Cheung's (posthumous) fandom in relation to virtual relationships and identifications energized by computer technology. I have examined two major dimensions of Cheung's fandom: 1) his transnational celebrity appeal and the imagined, transnational, internet fan community; 2) his localized, *generational* appeal and collective nostalgia. The two aspects represent differing emphases in appropriating or 'poaching' (Jenkins 1992) Cheung's charismatic appeal. The first casts him as a lonely *Byronic hero* by depoliticizing and universalizing his individual talent and style (while taking into consideration his linguistic and cultural specificities to a certain degree). The second stresses Cheung's socio-cultural value as a *cultural hero* of the entire 1970s generation located in diverse Chinese-speaking regions (including the diasporic population).

Both fan communities apparently prioritize Cheung's unique star qualities. Nevertheless, closer analysis reveals that such discourses of individualism are ultimately embedded within larger contexts and agendas. As a gay Hong Kong star active in the last two decades of the twentieth century when Hong Kong's economy, politics and culture were constantly spotlighted, Cheung conveniently converged issues such as gender, sexuality, identity and globalism – issues that tend to galvanize critical and popular attention. Moreover. Cheung's legendary suicide and the phenomenal posthumous fandom make him a perfect case for studying celebrity culture in terms of its geographical range and historical significance. Only when we fully understand these underlying material conditions and agendas can we assess the ramifications of Cheung's posthumous fandom as played out simultaneously in local, pan-Chinese, pan-Asian, and transnational arenas.

Notes

1. The line she sang goes, 'making love is not to have a clandestine love affair; or to steal one's heart, you must first have a clandestine affair, just to bring upon yourself a pleasurable charge.'

2. William described him as a 'gweilo' living in Hong Kong. 'Kweilo' is a derogatory Cantonese word referring to a Westerner in the East, often self-mockingly appropriated by the Westerner.
3. Martino described herself as a 'gweilo living in the UK'.
4. The argument that the audience was 'not ready' for Cheung deliberately goes against the fact that his fans unanimously yelled 'Yeah' when Cheung asked 'Are you ready?' before singing 'Red' (Hong) at his *Passion* concert. I shall return to a more detailed description of this moment later.
5. This is Deng Xiaoping's cardinal principle premised on his analysis that China was still at the initial stage of socialism, its main task being developing economy and increasing social resources. This principle was used to justify his economic reform, which was meant to correct ultra-leftism in Mao's China, and reaffirms the socialist bedrock at the same time so as to avoid alienating ultra-leftists.
6. The 'Four Modernization' means modernization of industry, agriculture, science and technology, and national defense. Whereas the socialist state under Deng's regime was actively modernizing itself by absorbing advanced technology, it tended to regard Western (including Hong Kong) culture with suspicion, which led to a variety of strategies ranging from cautious tolerance to strong-willed purgation. As a result, the self-modernization on the part of the 80s youth constantly met frustrations when the government decided things had gone overboard and needed to be contained.

References

Annabel (2000) post on 31 Dec. 2000, available at http://forum.lesliecheung.com [accessed 4 Dec. 2004].

Anonymous (2003) 'The 70s Generation; The End of Our Idol-worshipping Age' (70 niandai de women, ouxiang shidai jiesu le) available at http://fm974.tom.com [accessed on 4 Dec. 2004].

Aya, Shimoe (2000) post on 31 Dec. 2000, available at http://forum.lesliecheung.com [accessed 4 Dec. 2004].

Baudrillard, Jean (1994) Simulacra and Simulation, trans. Sheila Faria Glaser. Ann Arbor, MI: University of Michigan Press.

Bianca (2004) 'Warum/Why?' available at http://february87.de/Warum_Why.htm [accessed on 25 Dec. 2004].

Brunt, Rosalind (1999) 'Princesss Diana: A Sign of the Times', in Jeffrey Richards, Scott Wilson & Linda Woodhead (eds) *Diana, The Making of a Media Saint*. London: I. B. Tauris Publishers, pp. 20–39.

Cai, Fanghua (2003) 'What's the Cost of 'Poeticizing' a Star's Suicide?' (Dui mingxing de 'shiyi zhuipeng' daijia jihe) *Beijing Youth Daily* (Beijing qingnian bao) 8 April 2003, available at http://www.people.com.cn/GB/wenyu/64/130/20030408/965980.html [accessed on 28 Nov. 2004].

Chan, Yim (2004) 'The Life of An Artist', in *The One and the Only...Leslie Cheung*, Hong Kong: City Entertainment, pp. 154–155.

—— (2004) 'I Am What I Am, A Smoke of A Different Hue', available at http://xoomer. virgilio.it/nguidett/yim02.htm [accessed on 6 Dec. 2004].

Chen, Baoyi (2004) 'Remember the One I Don't Want to Forget' (Jizhe buxiang wangji de ren), in *The One and the Only ... Leslie Cheung*, pp. 98–99.

Chen, Jieling (2004) 'reminiscences on Cheung', in *The One and the Only ... Leslie Cheung*.

Chen, Kaige (2004) 'reminiscences on Cheung', in *The One and the Only ... Leslie Cheung*, p. 79.

Cheong, Im (2000) post on 31 Dec. 2000, available at http://forum.lesliecheung.com [accessed 4 Dec. 2004].

Cohan, Alvin (1999) 'The Spatial Diana: The Creation of Mourning Spaces for Diana, Princess of Wales', in Jeffrey Richards, Scott Wilson & Linda Woodhead (eds) *Diana, The Making of a Media Saint*. London: I. B. Tauris Publishers, 163–176.

'The Confession of Post-April 1 Fans' (Hou rongmi zibaishu) (2003), fan article at LCIFC discussion forum, posted at 11:00 am on 30 Aug. 2003, available at http://forum.lesliecheung.com/Forum8/HTML/000055.html [accessed on 25 Nov. 2004].

Cutting Edge (Group) (2000) *Digital Desires: Language, Identity and New Technologies*. London; New York: I.B. Tauris Publishers.

De Hui (2004) 'Ashes of Time – the Leslie Cheung Version' (Dongxie xidu zhi Zhang Guorong ban), in *The One and the Only ... Leslie Cheung*, pp. 142–145.

Dyer, Richard (1998) *Stars*. London: BFI, 1998.

Fan article at LCIFC discussion forum, posted at 11:27 am on 25 Dec. 2002, available at http://forum.lesliecheung.com/Forum8/HTML/000055.html [accessed on 25 Nov. 2004].

Fan article posted at 10:37 pm 28 Jan. 2003, available at http://forum.lesliecheung.com/Forum8/HTML/000055.html [accessed on 25 Nov. 2004].

Fan article at LCIFC discussion forum, posted at 11:19 p.m. on 6 Nov. 2003, available at http://forum.lesliecheung.com/Forum8/HTML/000055.html [accessed on 25 Nov. 2004].

'Four Groups of People Attracted to Leslie Cheung' (Zhang Guorong gandong de sida renqun), *Beijing Evenings* (Beijing wanbao) 3 April 2003, available at http://www.people.com.cn/GB/wenyu/64/129/20030403/962581.html [accessed on 3 April 2003].

France-Presse, Agence 'Leslie Cheung, 46, Pop Singer and Actor, Is Dead', New York Times 2 April 2003.

Gilloch, Graeme (1996) *Myth and Metropolis: Walter Benjamin and the City*. Cambridge: Polity Press.

Hgl (2003) 'Lebewohl, Leslie Cheung' (Farewell Leslie Cheung), *Die Welt* 4 April 2003.

Hong (2004) 'Only You Can Talk about Yesterday with Me' (Zhiyou ni keyi he wo tan zuotian), in *The One and Only ... Leslie Cheung*. Hong Kong: City Entertainment.

Jenkins, Henry (1992) *Textual Poachers: Television Fans and Participatory Culture*. New York: Routledge.

—— (1998) 'The Poachers and the Stormtroopers: Cultural Convergence in the Digital Age' (talk presented at the University of Michigan), in *Red Rock Eater Digest*, available at http://www.strangelove.com/slideshows/articles/The_Poachers_and_the_Stormtroopers.htm [accessed 15 July 2005].

—— (2003) 'Quentin Tarantino's *Star Wars?*: Digital Cinema, Media Convergence, and Participatory Culture' in D. Thorburn & H. Jenkins (eds), *Rethinking Media Change: The Aesthetics of Transition*. Cambridge, MA: MIT Press, pp. 281–312.

Jin (2004) message posted on April 10, 2004, available at http://www.lesliecheung.com.cn/cgi-bin/topic.cgi?forum=1&topic=185&show=30 [accessed 7 Dec. 2004].

JoJo (2004) 'Are You Ready for Leslie Cheung', in *The One and the Only... Leslie Cheung*, Hong Kong: City Entertainment, pp. 152–153.

Jun Jun (2000), available at http://forum.lesliecheung.com/Forum33/HTML/000001.html, [accessed on 24 Nov. 2004].

Kaoru (2004) 'Never Forget Leslie Cheung', in *The One and the Only... Leslie Cheung*. Hong Kong: City Entertainment, pp. 116–117.

Li, Yinhe (2003) 'A Bird that Announces the Commencement of a Wonderful New World' (Qimiao xin shijie de baochun niao), in Shuang Cheng (ed.)

Lin, Chaorong (2003) talk at 'Always Be with Leslie – in Reminiscence of Leslie's Artistic Life Seminar,' chaired by Evan Man on 12 Sept. 2003, available at http://www.leslie-cheung.info [accessed on 15 Dec. 2004].

Lin Peili, 'He Acts by Drawing upon Real Life Sufferings and Sincerity' (Ta yi tongku jinyan zhenqing yanchu), *Asia Weekly*, available at http://www.lesliecheung.cc/memories/asiaweekly/asiaweekly 1.htm [accessed on 01/23/05].

Lin, Xi (2002) 'Always Remember the "First" (Yongyuan jide de diyici), available at http://bbs6.netease.com/ent/readthread.php?forumcode=34&postid=8 [accessed on 18 Jan. 2005].

Lin, Xi & Jimmy Ngai eds. (2003) *Leslie Legacy: His Charm, Charisma and Craft Remembered on Celluloid* (Fengliu wujia, zhuozhuo qihua), Hong Kong.

Lori (2000), available at http://forum.lesliecheung.com/Forum33/HTML/000001.html, [accessed on 24 Nov. 2004].

Man, Eva (2004) presentation at 'Do Not Wanna Leave – in Reminiscence of Leslie Cheung's Artistic Life Seminar', chaired by Lu Weili on April 30 at Hong Kong Baptist U, available at http://www.lesliecheung.info [accessed 15 Nov. 2004].

Martino (2002), post on 6 June 2002, available at http://forum.lesliecheung.com [accessed 4 Dec. 2004].

McDonald, Paul (2003) 'Stars in the Online Universe: Promotion, Nudity, Reverence' in Thomas Austin and Martin Barker eds. Contemporary Hollywood Stardom. London: Arnold; New York: Oxford University Press, 29–44.

Nakamura, Lisa 'Race In/For Cyberspace: Identity Tourism and Racial Passing on the Internet', in David Bell and Barbara M. Kennedy (eds) *The Cybercultures Reader*, London and New York: Routledge, pp. 712–720.

Ren, Er'xi ed. (2003) *Metamorphosing into a Butterfly: A Retrospective Look at Leslie Cheung* (Hua Die: huimou Zhang Guorong), Suzhou: Guwuxuan Publishing House.

Sheila McNamee (1996) 'Parallel Lives: Working on Identity in Virtual Space', in Debra Grodin & Thomas R. Lindlof (eds) *Constructing the self in a mediated world*. Thousand Oaks: Sage Publications.

Shuang Cheng compile (2003) *The Half Life of Gor Gor: A Special Collection in Memory of Leslie Cheung* (Gege de bansheng: Zhang Guorong jinian teji), Shanxi: Shanxi Normal University Press.

Stewart, Clare & Philippa Hawker (eds) (2003) *Leslie Cheung*, Australian Center for the Moving Image ACMI.

T, Kathy (2004) 'Hold You for a Night' (Yiyejian yongyou), in *The One and the Only... Leslie Cheung*. Hong Kong: City Entertainment, pp. 122–123.

Taylor, John A. (2000) *Diana, Self-interest, and British National Identity*. Westport, CT: Praeger Publishers.

William (2000), post on 31 Dec. 2000, available at http://forum.lesliecheung.com [accessed 4 Dec. 2004].

Wong, James (2003) 'Leslie Cheung Is Heaven's Gift to Us' tribute to Leslie Cheung at the latter's funeral, available at http://ent.sina.com.cn/s/h/2003-04-09/1021143597.html [accessed 12 Nov. 2004].

Wood, John ed. (1998) *The Virtual Embodied: Presence/Practice/Technology*. New York: Routledge, 1998.

Xu, Ziyin 'Hong Kong on Sept. 12 – A Complete Record of My Soul's Travel' (Jiuyier Xianggang – Xinling zhi lu quan jilu), available at http://bbs.leslieclub.com/dispbbs.asp?boardid=3&id=16297 [accessed on 12 Nov. 2004].

Yamashita Mie (2004) 'If Only You Could Come Back' (Wei yuan ni nenggou huilai), trans. Maricoqi, in *The One and the Only ... Leslie Cheung*, p. 156.

Yu, Sen-lun 'The Leslie Cheung Legend Lives on', *Taipei Times* 10 April 2003: 16.

Yun (2004) 'When the Unbridled White Cloth Shoes Meet Paris and Pepsi' (Dang buji bai buxie yushang bali kele), in *The One and the Only ... Leslie Cheung*, pp. 92–93.

'Zuisheng mengsi' posted on 31 Oct. 2002 at LCIFC discussion forum, available at http://forum.lesliecheung.com/Forum8/HTML/000055.html [accessed on 25 Nov. 2004].

28 Doing It For Themselves? Teenage Girls, Sexuality and Fame

Catharine Lumby

We waited in the cold all morning. It was a Saturday in early June, only a few days before my fourteenth birthday. An early present – a full-length denim coat to match my denim flares and denim clutch bag – kept out the wind.

Roadies lugged equipment in through the stage door, jeans slung unfashionably low under beer bellies. We tried flirting with them but they had real groupies to contend with, mature women of 16 who'd come all the way from Sydney. We were nice girls and none of us had ever kissed a boy. The groupies hung out with us long enough to flash albums full of actual photos of The Band. Then the roadies spirited them inside for The Sound Check.

Late in the afternoon a coach pulled up and our heroes emerged flanked by security guards. We barely got a glimpse. By then the alleyway was thronged with screaming fans – nine hours for the privilege of breathing the same air. But we were used to waiting. Waiting was how you showed you were a true fan. We didn't just queue for tickets. We slept outside the box office to get front row seats. We counted down the days before a new album was due in the stores. We paced each other's lounge rooms waiting for *Countdown*, Australia's weekly Sunday Top of the Pops counterpart, to begin. We sat patiently by the radio ignoring real boys at parties in the hope the DJ would play our favourite song. We had no VCRs and our tape recorders were crap. So we worked as a team to commit everything our idols did to memory – every performance, every word, every gesture, every facial expression. This waiting, this worship, this imitation, was central to what we understood by fame.

It is not as if female rock stars were unheard of in 1975 – there were precedents. Suzi Quatro enjoyed a brief sojourn on my wall next to David Cassidy the year I started high school. But I certainly never dreamed of donning a leather jump suit, picking up a bass guitar and watching a sea of teenagers pass out at my feet. The idea that ordinary teenage girls – girls who weren't particularly beautiful or talented – should take their own shot at fame was unthinkable. Boys formed garage bands, ordinary boys. The girls hung out in the driveway hoping to catch a lead guitarist in the making. Back in 1970s Newcastle, Australia, when fame knocked for the average teenage girl it was usually a bloke offering a backstage pass in exchange for some backseat head. Not necessarily a bad deal for a chance to party with rock stars and take a sip at what passed for bohemia in a country town.

Through the looking glass

Teen and pre-teen girls have long been depicted as particularly vulnerable to the hype surrounding the fame industry, as liable to scream, faint and morph into an hysterical mob when confronted with a pop idol or a movie star. This is a characterization which is clearly an extension of the broader depiction of female consumers as more emotional, at risk of becoming 'addicted' to forms of consumption, and as in need of protection from mass culture – a phenomenon about which there is a broad body of literature (see Wilson, 1985; Huyssen, 1986; Felski, 1995; Lumby, 1999). It is critical then, to begin any exploration of shifts in the modalities and expression of young girls' relationship to fame, by acknowledging that the traditional female fan experience has never been as passive as some academic and popular commentators have suggested. Sarah Baker, who has done intensive ethnographic research with girls aged eight to eleven, notes that one of the striking aspects of young girls' reactions to pop stars is their physicality. She writes:

> For the girls in my research, bodies were subjected to a rigid and sometimes hidden system of control... The Catholic college the girls attended enforced regulations regarding how the school uniform should be worn, and emphasised, above all, modesty and control. Music therefore became a vehicle for the body's release, especially in its expression through dancing and also through the scream. (Baker, 2003: 20)

She goes on to argue that the screaming, the rushing and the crushing which characterizes crowds of young women confronted with male pop heroes, opens up a public space where pre-teen girls 'make themselves publicly visible (and audible) to the extent that they can be counted as active members of society' (Baker, 2003: 24).

Over the past decade, however, popular concerns about young women's relationship to fame have been gradually shifting away from concerns about their irrational idealization of predominantly male idols to concerns that they are obsessively fantasizing about *becoming* famous themselves. Put simply, the new lament about teen girls is not that they're too passive in the face of the fame industry, but that they're too interactive. Epitomizing this view Australian journalist Diana Bagnall writes in an article on 'girl power':

> What makes girls today so different is not that they're cleverer or prettier or even that they are necessarily more ambitious than girls in previous generations. What's different about girls is that their publicity is so good. And that they believe it. (Bagnall, 2002: 32)

The underlying theme of Bagnall's article is that the 'girl power' ethos is a Trojan horse for a neo-liberal philosophy which young women are adopting at their peril. This is a concern which has also been echoed by some prominent scholarly commentators in the field.

In their book *Young Femininity*, Sinikka Aapola, Marnina Gonick and Anita Harris map two dominant and competing discourses around girls and girlhood in late Western society: one they dub the 'girl power' discourse and the other the 'reviving Ophelia' discourse, after a popular book by American psychologist Mary Pipher (Aapola, Gonick and Harris, 2005). Summarizing the thrust of the now ubiquitous girl power label, the authors note that its usage 'marks a celebration of both the fierce and aggressive potential of girls ... as well as a reconstitution of girl culture as a positive force embracing self-expression through fashion, attitude and a Do It Yourself (DIY) approach to cultural production' (Aapola, Gonick and Harris, 2005: 20). Commenting on this ethos elsewhere, Harris cites Angela McRobbie in support of the notion that the girl power agenda represents a distortion of feminist values by linking them to individualism and consumerism. She writes,

The combination of the imagined capacity of young women as economic agents and their desires to be political agents makes for rich marketing material. Making a difference to one's social and political world and making a choice in the shopping mall have become somewhat blurred experiences for young women. (Harris, 2004: 89)

The term 'girl power' has been dated by numerous authors to the early 1990s and the formation of the US 'Riot Grrrls' movement, which had its roots in punk rock. In the wake of the Riot Grrrls, numerous all-girl bands formed, including the contentious but enormously popular Spice Girls. This mass market global proliferation of the 'girl power' message fuelled claims by both popular and academic commentators that a political movement had been co-opted and ultimately sold out to market forces. Clearly, however, this popularizing of feminism is not a new phenomenon. Feminism was arguably already thoroughly culturally commodified long before 'girl power' came along – the feminist tag has been selling magazines, books and television programmes since the 1970s. Debates about the shape and worth of feminist agendas belong as much to a popular cultural field as any academic or self-consciously political articulations (Lumby, 1997; Driscoll, 2002).

The notion that the meaning and circulation of 'girl power' can, let alone should, be contained by a particular feminist politics, arguably misconstrues the historical realities of the circulation of feminism and denies the pluralism inherent in the term. It is, of course, important to note, as the authors of *Young Femininity* do, that a simplistic neo-liberal appeal to the power of individuals to change their circumstances fails to take account of the structural limitations placed upon individuals because of gender, class, ethnicity, race, sexuality or disability. At the same time, it is critical to avoid accepting, at face value, claims that a neo-liberal style individualism is an everyday driving force in young women's interactions with each other or the wider world. These claims, made without reference to rigorous quantitative and qualitative studies of how girls and young women actually interact with relevant media texts, are ultimately as hollow as marketeers' assertions that young women are suddenly free to 'do it for themselves'. In the following chapter, I want to use the lens of young girls and their relationship to fame, to interrogate how this determinism/agency binarism continues to coagulate around young women in the course of an exploration of what young women themselves are doing and saying about fame in the twenty-first century.

Feeling real

In 2004, a 16 year old Indigenous Australian girl stood at the top of the Sydney Opera House steps and contemplated a sea of screaming fans. The event was the final of the second *Australian Idol* series. Overweight, shy, socially awkward, and known for favouring baggy clothes and a messy room, Casey Donovan was hardly the traditional poster girl for MTV. But she went on to win *Idol* that night, beating her clean-cut boy-band rival to a lucrative recording contract. Her biggest fans – the voting block who delivered her crown – were teenage girls.

Over the past five years, a suite of Reality TV shows with high appeal to teen girls have colonized Western prime-time screens. *Big Brother, Search for a Supermodel, Popstars,* and the various *Idol* series are all programs whose appeal is grounded in the notion that they put 'ordinary' young people on the other side of the screen and they invite the audience to participate in the outcome of the show. At one end of the spectrum they promise a say in the making of and breaking of would-be stars, at the other, they promise a shot at fame.

Su Holmes has noted that these programs 'self-consciously articulate ideologies surrounding the construction of stardom and increasingly – with an emphasis on interactivity – its relationship with the politics of audience response' (Holmes, 2004: 149). The first reality pop program began as a low budget and local production in New Zealand in 1999, before the concept was bought by Australia's Channel 7 network and moved to Australia in 2000. The format was then sold internationally and it spawned related programs such as *Pop Idol* in the UK, *American Idol* in the US, and then *Australian Idol*. In an extension of *Big Brother*'s appeal to the audience as the 'author' of the show (the virtual jury deciding on the ethics of the housemates' behaviour), the reality pop genre directly appeals to the notion that it is the pop audience, not the corporate image makers, who are the rightful arbiters of taste.

In her analysis of *Pop Idol*, Holmes argues that the series takes this invocation of 'audience interactivity, democracy, and popular taste' further by apparently handing control of the development of an extra-televisual text (a pop star and their musical output) to the viewer/voters (Holmes, 2004: 149–50). The relationship between the claims the program makes and the nature of the text's appeal is, of course, more complicated than this. Holmes notes that the show is perpetually trying to manage the contradictory discourses which, on one hand, identify stardom as some kind of inborn, 'natural' quality with 'the discourses of labour, production, and commercial enterprize' (Holmes, 2004: 158). She suggests that it is these very contradictions which make the program 'work' – providing spaces for pleasure and personal investment in the narrative which wouldn't be possible if the programme was framed purely as an 'expose of the fame game. Central to this pleasure is the emphasis on 'ordinary' people displaying real emotions as opposed to simply 'performing'. In this respect, it offers a play between the on and off stage reality which, like reality TV in general, 'places an exaggerated emphasis ... on the concept of the real self' (Holmes, 2004: 160).

Extensive research conducted by Elspeth Probyn and myself into Australian teenage girls and media consumption lends weight to Holmes' reading of *Idol*. In 2001, we began a three year Girl Cultures project over the course of which we interviewed and solicited questionnaires from over 300 young women aged 12–18 who were selected from a demographically representative sample of high schools across the Australian state of New South Wales. When we began our research one of the most popular television stars among young women was a bubbly, size 16 blonde named Sara-Marie, who had a penchant for wearing bunny ears, flannelette pyjamas and drawing attention to the size of her ample bottom with her much-imitated 'bum dance'. Talking with young women, it became increasingly clear that a core element of their enthusiasm for Sara-Marie centred on their perception that she was able to negotiate the relationship between a public and private self. Sara-Marie was perceived as aware that a certain level of performance was involved not only in being a *Big Brother* housemate, but in being female – and she openly played with those performative codes. On one hand, she flirted with the boys in the house and self-consciously entertained her housemates and viewers with her extrovert antics. On the other, she gave the impression of being emotionally honest with her audience and cognisant of the limitations of performance and image for women. The figure teenage girls in our research frequently offered as a counterpoint to Sara-Marie was Jemma, a thinner and more conventionally attractive young woman who the cameras constantly caught anxiously adjusting her attire and applying her lip gloss.

This is a comparison summarized in this exchange between 12 and 13 year old interviewees:

Alice:	And there was Jemma … she didn't once go topless or naked in the shower. She wore clothes. She used to get changed under a sheet and hide in the dorm
Sarah:	Sara-Marie just went in there …
Alice:	She skinny-dipped a couple of days
All (laughing):	Yeah!

It is important to note that, for these girls and others we interviewed, it was Sara-Marie's emotional and physical exhibitionism that guarantees her 'realness'. Indeed, contrary to media critics cited above who argue that such exhibitionism is a demonstration of the way 'ordinary' people are exploited by reality or tabloid formats, young girls again and again cited Sara-Marie's knowing attitude to the presence of cameras as evidence that she was *not* a victim of media manipulation.

The following exchange between Sara-Marie and Gretel Killeen (the host of Australian *Big Brother*) epitomizes the attitude that many focus group participants found so appealing:

Gretel:	How do you feel about sunbaking next to Jemma?
Sara-Marie:	Well, we have the same body – mine's just bigger.

Contrary to the concerns expressed in much popular discourse portraying young women as mindlessly mistaking the heavily edited show as equivalent to everyday reality, it was precisely the young women's awareness of the contrived and performance-oriented nature of *Big Brother* that heightened Sara-Marie's 'reality' value for them. Young women commented on the way she exhibited flagrant self-assurance despite her context (a house filled with cameras) and the stereotypes that shadowed her performance of femininity (she was fat, she was 'slutty', she was sloppy, she was stroppy). In short, our research suggests that Sara-Marie was a refreshing reality check for young women who, rather like the *Big Brother* housemates, feel themselves to be under constant surveillance from a variety of sources – their peer group, men, the popular media, parents, educational authorities, and various 'experts'. A knowing object of knowledge, Sara-Marie revealed herself as more than willing to return those gazes (Lumby, 2003).

Framing Fame

The production of fame, as Graeme Turner, David Marshall and Frances Bonner document in their book *Fame Games*, is now central to contemporary Western culture. It is a massive industry stoked and maintained by an army of publicists, stylists, agents, managers and media producers (Turner, Marshall and Bonner, 2000). But it doesn't follow that there is a consistency to its production or lifespan. Fame seemingly has no necessary relationship with wealth, 'natural' ability, looks, intelligence, family, character or social charisma, although all those characteristics can be useful in acquiring it. Fame is both radically democratic and brutally random. Anybody, it is claimed, can become famous, but there are no sure-fire ways of gaining admission to a club which now offers its members privileges (and obligations) once only bestowed on royalty.

As Graeme Turner notes in his book *Understanding Celebrity*, there is an inherent tension in the construction of celebrity. While celebrity is the product of a commercial process, public interest in a celebrity can (and does) operate at times as if it is completely independent of this process (Turner, 2004: 55). Significantly for the subject under investigation here, Turner uses the Spice Girls as a lens for exploring the productive tensions inherent in this meeting of commercial process and public will. He writes,

> **Tempting though it is to see them as the popular music industry's most elaborate expression of bad faith, I think a significant component of their appeal to their audiences was both their explicit acknowledgment of their commodification and their refusal to allow this to de-legitimise them. (Turner, 2004: 56)**

This is description which might equally be applied directly to many teenage girls themselves. Indeed, young women are arguably ciphers for broader tensions over the relationship between cultural and personal authenticity and conformity to a consumerist society. They frequently surface in both popular and scholarly texts as a kind of social body over which debates about citizenship, agency, globalisation and consumerism are fought. To understand this opposition in simple binary terms, however, is to misrecognize what it produces. As Catherine Driscoll observes: 'Complicity and empowerment are not separable, though neither are they opposed by one being the rectification of the other' (Driscoll, 2002: 280). The Spice Girls, in this light, were really hinge figures in an ongoing but productive debate about the relationship between identities and ideas which, in everyday life, are never as opposed as they seem when they are mapped in abstract terms.

Certainly, there is a growing body of research suggesting that teenage girls themselves are highly pragmatic when it comes to these supposed oppositions between conformity and resistance. This is a knowing and ambivalent relationship which surfaced clearly in the Girl Cultures research around teenage girls' attitudes to fame. On one hand, young women often spoke frankly about what they saw as the potentially damaging effects of women packaging themselves as an image to be consumed by the public but, on the other, they were very aware that fame offers a potential escape from other kinds of surveillance and repression they encounter in their everyday lives as teenage girls.

In a typical exchange, a group of 14 and 15 year olds from a regional co-ed state school talked frankly about the benefits of the celebrity lifestyle:

Vanessa: Money. How you look, and looking how you look, and the clothes and just...
Anne: And boys!
Vanessa: And the thing you get to go to, say if you become a supermodel, you get to go to all these like get-together things. And you know people...
Anne: And travel.
Vanessa: And people would know you.

A very common theme of these discussions about the benefits of the celebrity and/or modelling lifestyle was the freedom it offered young women from the constraints imposed by parents, teachers and other 'protectors', as this discussion of Australian singer Nikki Webster by 14 and 15 year olds from a regional co-ed state school illustrates.

Justine: I hate Nikki Webster... but I'd love to be like her, be like 14, 15.
Paulina: Who?
Justine: Nikki Webster.
Clare: She has a career in singing but that's the only aspect. She can do whatever she wants now.
Justine: Yeah, but being 14, 15 and famous all over the world.
Clare: Not all over the world. They cut her part out of the Olympic Ceremony in America. They couldn't be bothered explaining all this Australian background and everything.

Justine: But she's like a millionaire at 13, 14 whatever it is.
Maggie: But like all her fans are 8 years old.
Justine: Yeah but I would love to be like her, famous.

However, at the same time it is crucial to note that teenage girls are highly aware of the downside of celebrity: an invasive scrutiny of the celebrity's body and their private life. Indeed, any mention of the subject inevitably returned to the question of how such scrutiny apparently resulted in female celebrities developing eating disorders. Here's what a group of 12 and 13 year olds from an inner city single sex, state selective school had to say on the subject:

Eleni: I think a lot of them are way too... skinny, but I don't think everyone should then assume that they're anorexic, because that's like a big assumption to make of someone. I mean Calista Flockhart...
Susanna: My mum, whenever she goes on the TV, she's like, 'Oh she's so thin'.
Eleni: You've got to admit, her baby looks like it's bigger than her. She looks like a lolly-pop, with a big head. Really quite scary... also like Gerri Halliwell... Madame Tussaud's made a wax figure of her, and now they have to keep shaving lumps off her because practically her butt's disappeared, and she's got no chest to speak of anymore, and she used to be really big busted, and everything.

One of the of the unspoken, but enormously refreshing, aspects of doing research with teenage girls is the (re)discovery of how brutal they can be in their assessment of others, as well as themselves. Teenage girls certainly suck up a lot of the popular culture which is so obviously targeted at them. But as consumers, there is nothing simple or passive about them. Fickle, emotional, frank, and frequently scathing about blatant attempts to manipulate them, they wear their ambivalence about the centrality of image on their sleeves.

Returning the gaze

Kate is an 18 year old Australian girl who lives in the formerly-industrial town of Newcastle. In 2005, Newcastle bears very little resemblance to the culturally isolated and socially conservative working class hub my friends and I fantasised about escaping from. No longer centred around the steel industry and the dockyards, Newcastle has become a tourist centre and increasingly an extension of Australia's largest city, Sydney, which is now a two hour commute away. In the 1970s, the majority of Australian girls left high school at the age of 16. Today, 80 per cent stay on until Year 12 and almost one fifth go on to complete a university degree. Kate is studying for a Bachelor of Science at Newcastle University. Her website is called Fangirl (www.freewebs.com/kateuncut/) and according to her bio:

> I'm a uni bludger by day and a supermarket bitch by night...i love to travel. i like to act, dance & sing – though am not particulary [sic] talented at any one of them. i love to wait for hours in anticipation before concerts & then scream my lungs out when the music finally starts to play. obviously i'm into the internet, i've had many websites over the years. i started on expage with/ozcool, when i was in yr7.

Biographical info on Kate's home page is immediately followed by a list of individuals, groups and shows she's a fan of. It is a promiscuous array ranging across male and female pop singers and groups from the past and present (Elton John appears alongside Christina Aguilera), footballers, celebrities (Paris Hilton), books (*Bridget Jones' Diary*) and television shows (*MASH, Queer Eye for the Straight Guy*). It is a list which is as much an exhibition of self as a declaration of fandom.

Kate's site is decorated with pictures of herself in poses which run the gamut from cute to overtly sexual. Like many other cam-girls, she maintains a journal detailing her daily life and thoughts, as well as offering visitors an opportunity to email her, write in her guestbook and engage in a two-way video conference. The tone of Kate's diary entries echoes her photos, whether flirtatious, emotional and quotidian. Her posts combine effusive declarations of fandom with effervescent narcissism. In a typical entry describing a night out at a pop concert reads:

> last night was the Shannon Noll & Zinc concert. it was freakin' awesome! i LOVE zinc like i can't even tell ya, those guys are so totally cute and talented....i got a photo with the guys...i cant even tell ya how much it meant when Adam told me he remembered me! that totally made my fangirly day....and daryl (shannon's keyboardist who is coincidentally human nature's keyboardist) pointed at me, waved and smiled.

Kate's journal – which combines video, stills and text – epitomizes the blurring of the boundaries between fandom and the quest for celebrity. Her reference to famous individuals and shows are peppered with real and imagined encounters in which the spotlight is on her.

Kate's site is just one of many thousand such websites across the globe on which young girls and young women are embarking on DIY fame ventures using newly domesticated media technologies to produce and distribute their own images online and invite virtual voyeurs into their lives. The cam-girl phenomenon, as it is known, comprehends a very broad array of genres and formats – from simple websites set up by girls to display pictures of them dancing with friends, holidaying and dressing up, through self-consciously sexual and confessional amateur sites, to commercial porn sites trading on the 'amateur' cam-girl tag. Some sites blur the boundaries between the amateur and the professional by soliciting gifts and cash for intimate photographs (often by providing 'wish lists' on Amazon.com or similar sites, or by making money by directing traffic to porn sites).

Much of the popular response to the advent of the cam-girl has been to portray the girls as naive and unaware of the dangers they are courting. Yet as Salon journalist Katharine Mieszkowski noted in one of the first investigations of the trend, the ethics of the wish list is hotly debated by cam-girls themselves. 'Are you a 'cam-whore' if you put a wish-list? If you don't show your tits, does that mean you're not 'whoring for hits'? What if you put up a wish-list, but don't show skin?' (Mieszkowski, 2001). On one hand, the sites can be viewed as exemplifying what Graeme Turner has described in his analysis of them as the classic cultural studies bind, of balancing determination and agency (Turner, 2004: 66). But on the other, they might equally be seen as sites in which this opposition is actively and actually being unpacked. In the same way that the young women interviewed for the GirlCultures identified with a *Big Brother* housemate because she exemplified the impossibility of either accepting surveillance (in all its guises) or entirely disavowing it, initial research into cam-girl sites suggests that a similarly productive ambivalence is fuelling the evolution of the genre.

Susan Hopkins writes that:

> **If we are moving toward a society of image logic, then girls and women may be positively advantaged in this new media age. After, all it seems the most powerful icons of contemporary culture built their careers not on any 'true' 'authentic' talented self, but on their successful management of media images and illusions. (Hopkins, 2002: 10)**

This is a line of argument which suggests that the historical training in maintaining and performing image which defines femininity is finally moving to the centre of cultural and economic power.

It is important, however, to avoid homogenizing the motives teenage girls might have for creating and maintaining websites which invite others to view aspects of their lives and selves. And it would be trite to overstate the parallels between the conventional production of fame via the production of a public self and the multiplicity of genres and practices which make up the cam-girl websites. Perhaps a less strained way of understanding the role these websites play in reconfiguring the relationship young girls have to fame is to see them as spaces in which they can openly explore anxieties and desires which have always underwritten fandom. Certainly, there is a growing body of research which shows that, at the very least, young women are using websites as a way of negotiating and exploring the relationship between a private and a public self. Jacqueline Reid-Walsh and Claudia Mitchell propose that by:

> [C]onstructing a personal Web site, a girl can obtain a virtual 'room of one's own', no matter how cramped her physical living conditions may be. Thus, analogous to their physical rooms, we consider these Web sites to be semiprivate places of creativity and sociality...[original emphasis] (Reid-Walsh and Mitchell, 2004: 174)

As the authors note, the idea of that girls' 'bedroom culture' constitutes a distinct cultural form dates back to Angela McRobbie and Jenny Garber's much cited article 'Girls and Subculture' (McRobbie and Garber, 1991). Using Foucault's concept of heterotopia, they argue that girl's websites can be understood via the lens of Foucault's discussion of the fifth principle of heterotopia: they are spaces which appear to invite an intimacy which they do not ultimately deliver to the visitor. They conclude that teen girls' home pages occupy a contradictory space, 'a *private* space that exists in an openly public domain [original emphasis]' (Reid-Walsh and Mitchell, 2004: 181).

This toying with the boundaries between private and public – this play with the performance of self – is something which underpins much teen girl fan behaviour. In her study of Spice Girls fans aged between 10 and 17, Bettina Friztsche observes how the girls performed their fandom through an imitation of their idols and notes that this mimesis involves something more than passive reproduction. The Spice Girls, she argues, allow their fans to 'try out' different ways of being 'girl' and having power (Fritzsche, 2004: 157). Her point is not reducible to the (banal) observation that the Spice Girls offer five different female stereotypes to play with. What Friztsche is reminding us, is that mimesis has always been at the heart of the romantic and sexual fantasies young women have projected on to male stars. That it is the play between an on and off stage reality – a play with the performance of self – which has always been at the heart of young women's fascination with fame. Many of the rituals accompanying fandom are, after all, rituals which involve young women in transforming themselves and transporting themselves to an imaginary space where the ordinary proscriptions about how young women are to behave, dress and express themselves physically and sexually don't apply. Dressing up, staying out late, dancing without inhibition, directing openly sexual comments towards their idols, leaving behind all the injunctions about lady-like behaviour – all these practices are part of the ecstasy of fandom, part of why it can be such a literally transporting and transforming experience for young women.

Yes means yes

In adult life, I renewed my friendship with one of the teenage girls I used to hang around stage doors with. Sue, who was one of my closest early teen friends, was always unafraid of the gendered moral judgements cast on girls who were openly sexual. She was unique in many ways. She made her own clothes and refused to follow fashion. She talked back to boys who put her down. She experimented in ways that were available to boys, but girls were punished for. Sue didn't just admire local rock stars – she had sex with one of them and laughed about how bad he was afterwards.

I have a vivid memory of Sue and I sitting up late one night sewing. We were making toy rabbits to give to our favourite members of a popular rock band called Rabbit. We were anticipating a concert they were giving on their return to Newcastle after some national success. Frustrated by my complete lack of sewing prowess, I complained to Sue that I'd never be able to make a stuffed animal appealing enough to win the admiration of my idol – a gaunt bass guitarist named Jim. Sue, characteristically, burst out laughing. Didn't I know that making the rabbits was a ruse, she asked? Did I really think that the way to Jim's heart lay through a pile of stitched felt? The point of the rabbits was to convince our parents that our relationship to the local rock stars was domestic, romantic and puerile. For her part, Sue was planning to get laid again. She wanted to learn more about what she liked and didn't like about men, but most importantly she wanted to escape the scrutiny of parents and teachers long enough to explore her own sense of self. She told me in detail about sexual feelings and practices – she was the first person who ever talked like that to me. And the excuse for sharing this information was always a discussion of pop star we liked.

I was a lot less adventurous than Sue as a teenage girl. But I do clearly remember that the genuinely erotic dimension of fandom related to a fantasy of escape. It was a virtual space for reinventing the self, for exploring sexuality, for playing with and laughing about the state of being female. And my memories of those intense times with Sue, when were just 14, are as powerful as the memory of standing endlessly in line, waiting and weathering the cold.

References

Aapola, Sinikka, Gonick, Marnina and Harris, Anita (2005) *Young Femininity*, Basingstoke and New York: Palgrave Macmillan.

Bagnall, Diana (2002) 'The Girl Power Myth', *The Bulletin*, 17 July, 2002: 32–35.

Bettina Fritzsche (2004) "Spicy Strategies: Pop Feminist and Other Empowerments in Girl Culture", *All About The Girl*, ed. Anita Harris, Routledge, New York and London: 155–162.

Driscoll, Catherine (1999) 'Girl Culture, Revenge and Global Capitalism: Cybergirls, Riot Grrls, Spice Girls', *Australian Feminist Studies*, vol. 14, no. 29: 173–192.

Driscoll, Catherine (2002) *Girls*, Columbia University Press: New York.

Felski, Rita (1995) *The Gender of Modernity*, Harvard University Press, MA: Cambridge Mass.

Harris, Anita (2004) *Future Girl: Young Women in the Twenty-First Century*, Routledge: London and New York.

Hartley, John and Lumby, Catharine (2003) 'Working Girls or Drop Dead Gorgeous? Young Girls in Fashion and News', *Youth Cultures: Texts. Images and Identities*, Praeger: Wesport, Conn. and London: 47–68.

Holmes, Su (2004) 'Reality Goes Pop!' Reality TV, Popular Music, and Narratives of Stardom in *Pop Idol'*, *Television and New Media*, vol. 5, no. 2, May: 147–172.

Hopkins, Susan (2002) *Girl Heroes: The New Force in Popular Culture*, Pluto Press: Sydney.

Huyssen, Andreas (1986) 'Mass Culture as Woman', *After the Great Divide: Modernism, Mass Culture and Postmodernism*, Indiana University Press: Bloomington.

Lumby, Catharine (1997) *Bad Girls: The Media, Sex and Feminism,* Allen and Unwin: Sydney.

Lumby, Catharine (1999) *Gotcha: Life in a Tabloid World,* Allen and Unwin: Sydney.

McRobbie, Angela and Garber, Jenny (1991) 'Girls and Subcultures', *Feminism and Youth Culture: From Jackie to Just Seventeen,* Cambridge, MA: Unwin.

Mieszkowski, Katharine (2001) 'Candy From Strangers', *Salon.com,* August 13.

Reid-Walsh, Jacqueline and Mitchell, Claudia (2004), 'girls' Web Sites: A Virtual "Room Of One's Own"?', *All About The Girl,* ed. Anita Harris, New York and London: Routledge, 173–182.

Turner, Graeme (2004) *Understanding Celebrity,* Sage: London.

Turner, Graeme, Marshall, P. David and Bonner, Frances (2000) *Fame Games: The Production of Celebrity in Australia,* Cambridge University Press: Melbourne.

Wilson, Elizabeth (1985) *Adorned in Dream: Fashion and Modernity,* Virago: London.

Media Power: Some Hidden Dimensions

Nick Couldry

[. . .]

In my account of the symbolic hierarchy of the media frame, I will speak of the distinction between 'media world' and 'ordinary world'. 'Media world' (used in inverted commas) here denotes a *constructed* term within this binary opposition, which may variously be mapped onto media institutions, the 'worlds' implied by media fictions, and so on. 'Ordinary world' denotes the other term within that binary opposition. There is no 'ordinary world', and no 'media world', only one social world of which the division between 'media' and 'ordinary' 'worlds' is a product.

[. . .]

It is 'common sense' that the 'media world' is somehow better, more intense, than 'ordinary life', and that 'media people' are somehow special. This is not based either on fact or on a cultural universal, but rather is a form of unconsciousness ultimately derived from a particular concentration of symbolic power. The media sphere itself is *not* different in kind from the world in which viewers live; it is a part of the same world dedicated to mediating it. Yet, through the naturalised hierarchy between the constructed terms 'media world' and 'ordinary world', this division of the social world is generally reproduced as legitimate.

Many forms of social distinction overlap in the single term 'ordinary', which makes analysing actual examples of the media/ordinary distinction particularly complex. The word 'ordinary' is, as Raymond Williams (1983: 225–7) noted, ambiguous, covering both what is shared by everyone ('the regular, the customary') and what is ranked lower in a hierarchy. Affirming 'the ordinary' (as shared) can have remarkable resonances, not least in Williams' own work (1989), but the term's usage also crosses many hierarchical divisions. In any particular case ('ordinary life', 'ordinary world', 'ordinary people'), more than one distinction may overlap: the basic distinction of (1) 'ordinary' versus 'out of the ordinary', but also (2) 'ordinary' versus 'abnormal' (in a pejorative sense), (3) 'ordinary person' versus any 'important' or powerful person (in relation to politics, royalty, the police, and so on), and (4) 'ordinary' (domestic) life versus the (implicitly more important) world of the public sphere.

The symbolic division of the world

What does the media/ordinary division involve in practice? First, it symbolically categorises *people*. It implies that the type of person who is 'in the media' is different in kind from the person who is not (Snow, 1983: 151–2; Altheide and Snow, 1979: 43–4). Put the other way round, 'ordinary people' are not expected to be the same as 'media people': certainly they are not expected to have the skills or characteristics which being in the media is assumed to involve. Indeed, 'ordinary people' are not expected to be 'in' the media at all, but only to appear 'on' the media in certain limited circumstances. When 'real people' (non-media people) do appear on television, they are often ' "employed" to be ordinary' (Root, 1986: 97). A game-show producer quoted by Root precisely reproduced the media/ordinary hierarchy: 'I wouldn't pick someone to be a contestant who would attempt to be a star. I want nice ordinary people who just come along for a bit of fun: some of them are so ordinary they are surprised to be chosen' (ibid.: 98). Alternatively, in news coverage, 'ordinary people' appear as agents only if they have done something 'especially remarkable' (Langer, 1998: 48). When they do so, they indirectly confirm the usual distance of 'ordinary people' from media attention, even as they appear to challenge it. Importantly, it is not only the language of media texts themselves that confirms this division. Applying Foucauldian terminology, the whole 'discourse' of television, for example – not merely its texts, but its institutional arrangements and hierarchies, and the way both television people and their audiences talk – produces the regular 'subject-position' (cf. Fairclough, 1989: 39) of the viewer (*not* a media producer) who is 'ordinary'. Here, for example, is an excerpt from Granada Television's bid document to run a major new current affairs programme, leaked to the *Guardian's* Media Section. It describes the options for human interest stories as follows:

> profiles could involve a celebrity . . . alternatively, it could be a politician . . . Or we could even focus on an ordinary person in an extraordinary situation, e.g. a day in the life of a Lottery jackpot winner, or the parents caring for a teenage daughter with CJD . . . (*Guardian*, 18 January 1999, Media Section)

From this highly arbitrary perspective, viewers are simply 'ordinary people who watch television'.

I am not, of course, claiming here that broadcasting discourse in Britain has remained unchanged since its original, explicitly hierarchical form (represented by Lord Reith's BBC in the 1920s). There have been significant changes, and changes are still continuing. But I am claiming that hierarchy remains in media discourse in various forms. There are, incidentally, overlaps with other areas of cultural production, for example music. As two fans said about meeting the pop stars they followed: 'you think of them as being wonderful people . . . everything that everybody ordinary isn't' (quoted, Vermorel and Vermorel, 1985: 175). The difference between 'fans' and 'stars' here also is registered as a difference in kind.

Second, the media/ordinary distinction implies a difference in kind between *worlds:* between the 'world' of the media (everything involved in it: stories, studios, work practices) and the 'world' of 'ordinary life'. The 'media world' is 'larger-than-life' (Altheide and Snow, 1979: 20–1; Snow, 1983: 21–2), the 'ordinary world' is automatically mundane. As with Durkheim's sacred/profane distinction, this is not so much a distinction based on detailed comparison, but an absolute distinction that divides the world up in advance. As Cecelia Tichi has put it: 'to be transposed onto television *is* to be elevated out of the banal realm of the off-screen and repositioned in the privileged on-screen world' (1991: 140, added emphasis). Yet paradoxically media institutions, as an essential part of their function, must also seek to represent the world of the everyday. The paradox does not undermine the symbolic division; they run alongside each other. As one man said, when I asked him what type of place *Coronation Street* was: 'just everyday sort of living, well larger than life type of thing'. Alternatively, media coverage may make everyday life seem strange. As one participant in MTV's 'living soap' called *The Real World* put it: 'you feel everything you do is imbued with significance because there is a camera crew there pointing a lens in your face'.

Third, following on directly from the second point, the media/ordinary distinction involves a *boundary* between separate 'worlds', which it is automatically significant to cross or approach. Patricia Priest's important work on US talk show participants (1995, 1996) vividly brings out the sense that to appear on television is 'to "step[] in" to a valued place' (1996: 81). Any entry to the 'media world' can be similarly described, as in the marketing of tourist locations: 'Step Inside the World of Television', 'Break into the World of Broadcasting'. There may also be wider resonances of crossing such a significant boundary: thus one game show participant quoted by Root (1986: 112) said appearing on television made her feel 'almost like royalty'. It follows, more generally, that appearing in the media normally comprises a form of prestige or cultural capital.

Meeting Stars

Meeting the *Coronation Street* cast is one way the Street set's authenticity is staged. Such meetings, therefore, have an 'evidential' role, as well as offering participation in the fictional space of the programme. They can also be understood as real negotiations of the power relations between 'media people' and non-media people.

Stars are essential to the economics of soap production and most other areas of cultural production. Soap stars are promoted not only through the storylines themselves but through a host of secondary productions: newspaper reports about plot developments and the cast's lives, television magazines (such as *Inside Soap* and the 'official' magazines for particular soaps, *Coronation Street* and *Brookside*), celebrity magazines (*Hello* and *OK*), star autobiographies. Soap stars make promotional appearances all over Britain (opening shops, playing in charity football matches). *Coronation Street* stars, once established, are central also to the economy of GST [Granada Studios Tour] itself. Its shops sell countless souvenirs tied to characters. The possibility of meeting or seeing a Street star has been part of what GST markets. While the scheduled star 'walkabouts' ended in 1995 (as the cast's workload increased), special appearances are often guaranteed for coach tours, the cost included in the tour price (source: informal discussions with guides). Some holiday breaks include 'Nights with the Stars': special evenings of entertainment by Street stars outside GST's normal opening hours. In any case, since GST is situated next to the Granada Television Studios, people hope to see the cast as they walk to or from the filming studios. Coach operators tell their passengers good times to spot them. Every weekday lunchtime people gather at the railings behind the Street set, waiting for stars to appear. Occasionally, promotional events involving Street stars occur on the set: the handing over of a cheque to a charity (Fieldnotes), even a photo-opportunity involving the Labour Party leader (not yet Prime Minister) Tony Blair, drinking beer with the cast outside the Rovers Return in August 1996, which I witnessed! The 'stars' theme is repeated frequently around the site: on the Backstage Tour, you walk up the 'Stairway to the Stars' and visit astrologer Russell Grant's 'Reach for the Stars' (pun intended). The possibility that you might see a star is, in any case, implicit in the idea of any 'Studios' tour. Many people mentioned contact with stars as important (fourteen cases) or expected (six cases).

How are we to understand people's talk about meeting members of the cast? It is too easy to dismiss them simply as forms of 'para-social' involvement: (Horton and Wohl, 1956). I found only two cases where people referred to media stars as 'friends', although perhaps people were reluctant to admit such emotional investment to me face to face. It is more productive to understand these meetings as negotiations of power.

'We're worse than them fans'

Meetings with Street stars generally do not involve an intense emotional investment with the *star* (judging by the interview and letter material); instead they have a generic, abstract quality. I asked some people on site, who had said they wanted to meet a cast member, if it mattered who they met. Of those who gave a definite answer (N = 38), a majority (twenty-four) had no particular preference. Those who did, generally referred to a character or character type, not an actor or actress. As Glenys put it, 'You don't go to see the actress Helen Worth, you go to see [the character] Gail Platt'. Even Michael, who came closest to regarding the Street cast as individual celebrities, spoke of them in character: 'I was delighted to meet Vera [the fictional name] (...) I think she is the [most] famous landlady [i.e. pub licensee] in the world.' As often noted, television 'celebrities' are less likely than film stars to have detailed star profiles outside of the programmes in which they perform (Ellis, 1982: 106–7; Marshall, 1997: 122–31; Reeves, 1988: 155–9).

Some people were defensive about being seen as a fan who mistook fiction for reality: 'I wouldn't be so daft... as if anybody died to send them a wreath.' While there are no doubt pathological forms of living in a mediated society, the more interesting general question is how particular positions and actions within the media frame get constructed as pathological.

This process of pathologisation was certainly reflected in visitors' comments. They generally avoided presenting themselves to me as a fan of the cast rather than of the programme. More interestingly, while some people gathered to see cast members, many others quite deliberately did not and walked past. This was not simply lack of interest. Some of the keenest fans I interviewed said they never waited in the crowd (Barbara, John, Peter). Perhaps those with the most active interest in the programme felt this 'passive' activity beneath them. However, the low status of acknowledging the cast's status so explicitly was reflected in others' language as well:

NC: Would you like to meet a member of the cast...?
Woman: ...we're not that *way-out minded* are we? No.

Man: (...) No, I don't think I'd be all that bothered one way or the other (...) I don't think I'd *scurry off to skawp* at them or something like that [laughs]. [added emphasis]

Man: I mean when you go round there to the railings, where everybody's looking over as they come in, you know, what it reminds you of really, they're a load of *monkeys at the zoo* [wife laughs], and we're all paying our money to stand there and *gawk* at them [laughs]. [added emphasis]

Even those who did wait for the stars might distance themselves from the others standing there:

A woman in her 60s says to another elderly woman who she is with: 'What are you waiting for? For the stars?' The other replies: 'We could wait all day. We're worse than them fans.' (Fieldnotes)

The same pathologisation could be imagined from the point of view of the stars themselves: 'if you're pestered by people, it can be a real bind', 'they'd get mobbed', 'they'd be robbed'.

'Actually meeting them'

When people talked about an actual or imagined meeting with a member of the *Coronation Street* cast, they described themselves or others as 'freezing', standing with mouth wide open, eyes staring, not knowing what to say. In other words, they acknowledged the extraordinary nature of the contact being made. The extraordinariness lies not in the detailed content of the meeting, but simply the *fact* of it. Just as what matters most about being on the Street is simply 'being there', so meeting a star above all means making contact with the world in which stars move. So, when people talked about their meeting, instead of mentioning details about what the star said, or how (s)he looked or dressed, most comments revolved around whether the star was or was not willing to talk. Positively, stars could be 'lovely to talk to', have 'all the time in the world', be 'friendly', 'a gentleman', 'approachable', 'natural', 'patient with fans'. Negatively, they might be 'grumpy', not like to be touched, avoid people, not acknowledge them, or be rude. In each case, it is the quality of contact that is emphasised; it is through such contact that the symbolic boundary between 'ordinary' and 'media' 'worlds' is, temporarily, crossed.

The specialness of such a contact was reflected in another way. Since not all stars might be approachable, or people anticipated being tongue-tied when they met them, some preferred to make contact at a distance. Standing in the crowd and waiting for the stars was one way of doing this, provided it involved being seen by the stars (at least collectively), as Debbie's comment makes clear:

Seeing the stars coming over for their lunch, that was brilliant! (...) But I mean they didn't...bother...well, not coming over, but sort of like acknowledging us or anything like that (...) one of them was really grumpy (...) and that's really put me off him now.

Even a look from the star would be an acknowledgement of contact and therefore significant (cf. Gamson, 1994: 132). The most common form of distant 'contact' imagined was seeing the stars as they walked among the crowd on site (there were scheduled 'walkabouts' most days until 1996 and, when I interviewed people, many still thought this practice continued). This way, risks of embarrassment from direct engagement were minimised (cf. Goffman, 1972 on minimising risks), yet the contact seemed natural. The importance of 'natural' contact is worth exploring further.

When stars appeared, or were imagined to appear, they are usually doing something not staged, but routine and natural: 'walking amongst us', 'walking around', 'knocking about', 'floating', 'strolling', 'ambling', 'wandering around', 'we may see them around' (Fieldnotes). The star should be behaving in an ordinary, relaxed way but, crucially, *in the same space* that the visitors themselves occupy. In fact, since 'walking around' is precisely what visitors do most of the time at GST, the star is simply imagined doing what everyone else does. But it is precisely this 'ordinariness' that is a sign of the extraordinary. As Michael Billig comments on people's accounts of meeting royalty, if royalty are encountered doing 'ordinary' things, this is treated as a 'discovery' that they are 'ordinary *"after all"'* (Billig, 1992: 78, added emphasis). But it is precisely the fact that their ordinariness is a 'discovery', which confirms that royalty, in reality, is not ordinary at all. So too with the stars. A related point about stars' presence is that meetings with them should be spontaneous: this is another way of saying that these meetings' authenticity should be successfully 'staged' in MacCannell's sense. Their staging should not be too obvious. No one suggested meeting a star in an artificial setting, even though in earlier years stars had made staged appearances on the Backstage Tour. That, one woman suggested, was not a real meeting. John is explicit on the importance of spontaneity:

> I've never actually looked for them [the stars] . . . And again I don't think I'd want to because the spontaneity of seeing (. . .) [Seeing] Chloe Newsome [a CS actress in 1996], it was so unexpected and because no one else had seen her and because she was going into the studio and I actually saw her doing it.

An appearance of spontaneity is important, even if you know that a star appearance has been planned: 'we knew we were going to meet two, but we didn't know who and we didn't know how, when or what you see. So she just turned up' (Julie). As Billig comments on meetings with royalty: 'the preference was for the informal, chance meeting' (1992: 75). Such 'natural', apparently spontaneous contact, even if indirect, is special because it confirms that the space you are in (doing nothing special) *is* the space where the Street stars themselves 'ordinarily' are. What matters is making real contact with the media world. A spontaneous, chance meeting allows you to feel the contact is real. A meeting too obviously staged does not.

In all this, it is the generic quality of the 'contact', rather than any personal relationship with a particular star, that is important. Yet it would be wrong to overlook the powerful personal significance that this generic contact can have. Here John describes meeting Bill Roache (who has played 'Ken Barlow', since the series' first episode):

> I was just wandering around and the door opened (. . .) and William Roache came out. And nobody had noticed at all (. . .) it was on a Sunday and he'd been doing the outdoor shots, and Tracey [his daughter in CS] was in hospital, it was that time. And he walked, and I looked at him, and I said, 'Hello', and he said, 'Hello there', and I said, 'Can I take a photograph?'

'Of course you can, take as many as you want.' And still as I was speaking to him, nobody'd noticed, and there was nobody with him, and he wandered around, and I'd taken three photographs, and nobody's looking (...) [and then] everyone just made a beeline for him. And he stood there for an hour, not an exaggeration, because I was there the whole time.

This moment, as he tells it, has a strange intimacy: John and the star at first seem abstracted from the public space and yet, in spite of the extraordinary situation, John is 'still speaking', still making contact. For a moment which (by watching others as they came up) he prolonged into an hour, John remained in the same space as the star ('I was there the whole time'). Consider also this extract from an interview with a middle-aged woman and her elderly mother (I was silent during this dialogue):

Mother: ... I just wish I could have met a star (...) Or if I'd have gone round a studio.
Daughter: It'd be nice if somebody came up the Street and wandered around, one an hour, one an hour, a different one every hour.
Mother: Oh, it would've been lovely.
Daughter: Just to see different people, probably not to talk to them, just to see them, walking up the Street, or around wherever we've been, yeah.
Mother: Yeah, it would've been lovely.
Daughter: Just to see one.

All the themes of this section are condensed here: the generic nature of the contact ('just to see them', 'just to see one'), the preference for keeping a distance ('probably not to talk to them'), the importance of spontaneity and ordinariness ('wandered around'), and above all the intrinsic importance of connecting two spaces, two 'worlds': the importance of feeling that 'they' have been 'around wherever we've been'.

The significance of meeting stars, then, as with being on the set, is explained by the overall framework I have been developing: both are contacts across the differential implicit in the symbolic hierarchy of the media frame.

Bibliography

Altheide, David and Robert Snow (1979) *Media Logic*, Beverly Hills: Sage.

Babington, Bruce (2001) (ed.) *British Stars and Stardom: From Alma Taylor to Sean Connery*, Manchester: MUP.

Barker, Martin (2003) 'Introduction', in Thomas Austin and Martin Barker (eds), *Contemporary Hollywood Stardom*, London: Arnold, pp. 1–24.

Billing, Michael (1992) *Talking of the Royal Family*, London: Routledge.

Biressi, Anita and Heather Nunn (2004) 'The especially remarkable: celebrity and social mobility in Reality TV', *Mediactive* (2): 44–58.

Boorstin, Daniel (1971) *The Image: A Guide to Pseudo-Events in America*, New York: Atheneum. Originally published as *The Image or What Happened to the American Dream?* (1961).

Bourdieu, Pierre (1984) *Distinction*, trans. R. Nice, London: Routledge.

Braudy, Leo (1986) *The Frenzy of the Renown: Fame and Its History*, Oxford: Oxford University Press.

Brooker, Will and Deborah Jermyn (2002) (eds), *The Audience Studies Reader*, London: Routledge.

Couldry, Nick (2000) *The Place of Media Power: Pilgrims and Witnesses of the Media Age*, London: Routledge.

deCordova, Richard (1990) *Picture Personalities: The Emergence of the Star System in America*, Urbana and Chicago: University of Illinois Press.

Donald, James (1999) 'Stars' in Pam Cook and Mieke Bernink (eds), *The Cinema Book*, London: BFI, pp. 33–39.

Durkheim, Emile (1915) *The Elementary Forms of Religious Life*, New York: Free Press.

Dyer, Richard (1998) *Stars*, (second edition), London: BFI.

—— (1987) *Heavenly Bodies: Film Stars and Society*, London: BFI.

Eckert, Charles (1990) 'The Carole Lombard in Macy's Window', in Jane Gaines and Charlotte Herzog (eds), *Fabrications: Costume and the Female Body*, London: Routledge, pp. 100–122.

Ellis, John (1982) *Visible Fictions: Cinema: Television, Video*, London: Routledge.

—— (1992) *Visible Fictions: Cinema, Television: Video*, London: Routledge.

Evans, Jessica (2005) 'Chapter one: celebrity, media and history', in Jessica Evans and David Hesmondhalgh (eds), *Understanding Media: Inside Celebrity*, Berkshire: Open University Press, pp. 12–55.

Fairclough, Norman (1989) *Language and Power*, London: Longman.

Foucault, Michel (1970) *The Order of Things: An Archeology of the Human Sciences*, New York: Vintage Books.

Gamson, Joshua (1994) *Claims to Fame: Celebrity in Contemporary America*, Berkely, CA: University of California Press.

Geraghty, Christine (2000) 'Re-examining stardom: questions of texts, bodies and performance', in Christine Gledhill and Linda Williams (eds), *Reinventing Film Studies*, London: Arnold, pp. 183–201.

Gledhill, Christine (1991) (ed.), *Stardom: Industry of Desire*, London: Routledge.

Goffman, Erving (1972) 'Where The Action Is' in *Interaction Ritual*, London: Allen Lane.

Gramsci, Antonio (1998) 'Hegemony, intellectuals, and the state', in John Storey (ed.), *Cultural Theory and Popular Culture*, Hemel Hempstead: Prentice Hall. pp. 206–219.

Hall, Stuart, (1997) *Representation: Cultural Representations and Signifying Practices*, London: Sage.

Hills, Matt (2003) 'Putting away childish things: jar jar binks and the "virtual star" as an object of fan loathing', in Thomas Austin and Martin Barker (eds), *Contemporary Hollywood Stardom*, London: Arnold, pp. 74–89.

—— (2005) '"Off guard, unkempt, unready?": deconstructing contemporary celebrity in *heat* magazine', *Continuum: Journal of Media and Cultural Studies* 19 (1): 21–38.

—— (2006) 'Not just another powerless elite? When media fans become subcultural celebrities', in Su Holmes and Sean Redmond (eds), *Framing Celebrity: New Directions in Celebrity Culture*, London: Routledge.

—— (2006) '"Starring … Dyer?"': Re-visiting Star Studies and Contemporary Celebrity Culture', *Westminster Papers in Communication and Culture* 2 (2): 6–21.

Holmes, Su and Sean Redmond (2006) (eds), *Framing Celebrity: New Directions in Celebrity Culture*, London: Routledge.

Horton, Donald and R. Richard Wohl (1956) 'Mass communications and para-social interaction: observations on intimacy at a distance', *Journal of Psychiatry*, 19(3): 215–229.

King, Barry (1992) 'Stardom and symbolic degeneracy: television and the transformation of the stars as public symbols', *Semiotica*, 92 (1–2): 1–47.

Langer, John (1998) *Tabloid Television: Popular Journalism and the 'Other News'*, London: Routledge.

Lowenthal, Leo (1961) 'The triumph of mass idols', in Lowenthal, *Literature, Popular Culture and Society*, California: Pacific Books, pp. 109–140.

Marshall, P. David (1997) *Celebrity and Power: Fame in Contemporary Culture*, Minnesota: University of Minnesota Press.

—— (2004) *New Media Cultures*, London: Arnold.

Marx, Karl and Frederick Engels (1974) *The German Ideology*, edited and introduced by C.J Arthur, London: Lawrence and Wishart.

McDonald, Paul (1995) 'I'm Winning on a Star: The extraordinary ordinary world of *Stars in their Eyes*', *Critical Survey* 7 (1): 59–66.

—— (2000) *The Star System: Hollywood's Production of Popular Identities*, London: Wallflower.

McManus, Richard (2003) 'Culture of Celebrity and Weblogs', *Read/Write Web*, 26 October, 2003, found at http://www.readwriteweb.com/2003/10/26.html [accessed 17 September, 2005].

Mishra, Vijay (2001) *Bollywood Cinema: Temples of Desire*, London: Routledge.

Priest, Patricia (1995) *Public Intimacies: Talk Show Participants and Tell-All TV*, Cresskill, NJ: Hampton Press.

—— (1996) '"Gilt by Association": talk show participants' televisually enhanced status and self-esteem', in Debra Grodin and Thomas Lindlof (eds), *Constructing the Self in a Mediated World*, London: Sage.

Reeves, Jimmie (1988) 'Television stardom: a ritual of social typification and individualization', in James Carey (ed.), *Media, Myths and Narratives: Television and the Press*, Newbury Park: Sage.

Rein, Irving, Philip Kotler and Martin Stoller (1997) *High Visibility: The Making and Marketing of Professionals into Celebrities*, Lincolnwood: NTC Business Books.

Rojek, Chris (2001) *Celebrity*, London: Reaktion Books.

Root, Jane (1986) *Open The Box*, London: Comedia.

Snow, Robert (1983) *Creating Media Culture*, Beverly Hills: Sage.

Spigel, Lynn (2001) *Welcome to the Dreamhouse: Popular Media and Postwar Suburbs*, Durham and London: Duke University Press.

Stacey, Jackie (1994) *Stargazing: Hollywood Cinema and Female Spectatorship*, London: Routledge.

Stevenson, Nick (2005) 'Audiences and celebrity', in Jessica Evans and David Hesmondhalgh (eds), *Understanding Media: Inside Celebrity*, Berkshire: Open University Press, pp. 135–172.

Storey, John (2001) *An Introductory Guide to Cultural Theory and Popular Culture* Hemel Hempstead: Harvester Wheatsheaf.

Tichi, Cecelia (1991) *Electronic Hearth: Creating an American Television Culture*, New York: Oxford University Press.

Tolson, Andrew (1996) *Mediations: Text and Discourse*, London: Arnold.

Turner, Graeme, Frances Bonner and P. David Marshall (2000) *Fame Games: The Production of Celebrity in Australia*, Cambridge, Cambridge University Press.

Vermorel, Fred and Julie Vermorel (1985) *Starlust: The Secret Life of Fans*, London: W.H. Allen.

Vincendau, Ginette (2000) (ed.), *Stars and Stardom in French Cinema*, London: Continuum.

Willis, Paul (2005) (ed.), *Stardom: Hollywood and Beyond*, Manchester: MUP.

Index